TWELFTH INTERNATIONAL CONVENTION

OF THE

YOUNG PEOPLE'S SOCIETIES

OF

CHRISTIAN ENDEAVOR

MONTREAL, P. Q., JULY 5-9, 1893.

First Fruits Press
Wilmore, Kentucky
c2015

First Fruits Press
The Academic Open Press of Asbury Theological Seminary
204 N. Lexington Ave., Wilmore, KY 40390
859-858-2236
first.fruits@asburyseminary.edu
asbury.to/firstfruits

REV. FRANCIS E. CLARK, D.D.
President United Society of Christian Endeavor

2

TWELFTH INTERNATIONAL CONVENTION

OF THE

YOUNG PEOPLE'S SOCIETIES

OF

CHRISTIAN ENDEAVOR.

MONTREAL, P. Q., JULY 5-9, 1893.

THOSE who were present at the Tenth International Christian Endeavor Convention, held in Minneapolis in 1891, were deeply impressed with the eagerness of the Canadian delegates to secure the convention within their borders for 1892, and many sympathized with them in their disappointment when it was announced that the convention would be held in New York, — a disappointment partly allayed by the announcement that Montreal had been decided upon for the convention of 1893. Such was the enthusiasm of the Canadian delegates on this occasion that it was confidently predicted that when the convention should meet in Montreal it would receive a rarely cordial welcome. This prediction was amply fulfilled. Long before the month of July arrived, circulars of information were being sent repeatedly to all parts of the country, indicating a state of preparedness on the part of the Committee of '93 which augured great things for the coming convention. Every possible arrangement for the comfort and convenience of the delegates was made, and the work of the committee as a whole and of the several sub-committees received unqualified praise.

The incoming delegations were met by scouts from the reception committee at some distance from the city, giving ample time for "billeting" and answering questions. A novel device adopted by the committee this year was the wearing, by every member of the reception committee, of a white yachting cap, thus readily distinguishing the members of the committee even in the midst of a large crowd. There were the usual scenes of interest at the railroad depots and steamboat wharves as the hosts of delegates arrived. The arrangements were so admirable, however, that everything connected with the preliminaries of the convention went smoothly and satisfactorily.

Reasoning from the attendance at the New York convention, the committee had planned upon taking care of at least 23,000 visitors. Owing to various causes, however, chief among which were the severe financial stringency prevailing throughout the United States and the failure to secure reduced railroad rates from the South and West on account of the World's Fair, the attendance was considerably less, the registry showing at the close of the convention a total attendance of 16,500. This, however, considering the circumstances, was a remarkably good showing, and stamped the convention as the largest yet held, with the exception of that at New York, which was altogether phenomenal.

A novel feature of the convention this year was the division of the audience into two great assemblies for most of the sessions, holding simultaneous meetings with programs of equal merit. One place of meeting was the government Drill Hall or "Salle d'Exercise," an immense stone building used as military headquarters, arranged to seat 9,000 people, and providing besides numerous committee rooms. The interior of this building was profusely and elegantly decorated with flags and festoons of bunting, the Union Jack and the Stars and Stripes being everywhere conspicuously interwoven. The platform at one end of the building was still further decorated with Christian Endeavor emblems and a huge pyramid of potted plants and flowers. The whole interior effect was rich and beautiful. The other place of meeting was a large tent on the Champ de Mars, or parade ground, on the other side of the street from the Drill Hall. This was arranged with chairs to seat about 9,000 people ; and while the conditions for speaking and hearing were naturally not so favorable as in the hall, it proved an acceptable audience room, and its capacity was tested more than once.

No souvenir program was issued this year, although mementoes of Montreal and of the convention were to be had in great number. The United Society, however, furnished every delegate with a handsomely prepared pamphlet of some sixty pages, containing, besides the program complete, a large number of selected Christian Endeavor hymns, Scripture selections, etc. The Committee of '93 also gave to every delegate an excellent map of the city and a convention badge, the latter consisting of a maple leaf in white metal with "C. E." raised from an enameled background and backed by a red or blue ribbon.

PRELIMINARY SERVICES.

WEDNESDAY EVENING.

A new arrangement of the convention program was adopted this year. Instead of the sessions beginning on Thursday afternoon, as heretofore, preliminary services were arranged to be held in several of the churches on Wednesday evening. A large proportion of the delegations arrived in season to participate in these services, which were all of great interest.

St. James Methodist Church.

In this edifice, the largest and handsomest of all the Protestant churches in Montreal, a large audience gathered at the evening hour of service, crowding the spacious auditorium to the doors.

Rev. T. S. McWilliams, of Montreal, presided. After a brief, but inspiring, song service, prayer was offered by Rev. J. H. Dixon and Bishop B. W. Arnett of Vicksburg, Miss. Mr. McWilliams followed with a few verses from the Scriptures, after which he introduced Rev. J. W. Chapman, D.D., the well-known evangelist, as the speaker for the evening. Dr. Chapman's address was as follows :—

Receiving the Holy Ghost for Power.

Address of Rev. J. W. Chapman, D.D.

TEXT : Have ye received the Holy Ghost since ye believed ?—*Acts 19: 2.*

This is not at all a question of regeneration. It is a question of the life more abundant; of deep abiding peace, and of power with God and men. It touches not so much the Father nor the Son; it brings you face to face with the third person of the blessed Trinity, the Holy Ghost. There is no question which could be better put to us than the one Paul asked of the Corinthian church members, as he met them in Ephesus,—"Have ye received the Holy Ghost since ye believed?" There may be life without the answer—there certainly cannot be power. There is a woful amount of ignorance concerning the Holy Ghost. We do not seem to be impressed with his personality. We not infrequently use an impersonal pronoun in our petitions and remarks in referring to him, when the fact is, he shares with God, the Father, and the Son the honor and power of the Godhead. The successful Christian everywhere is the one who honors him and makes room for his entrance and control over his entire being.

What a change there would be in our Christian living and in our Christian experience did we but have a definite testimony concerning this one question. One of my friends in New York City has given up a high social position and all selfish interests that she may work among the fallen women of the metropolis. She has opened the "Door of Hope" for every one who would apply for admission. One evening, leaving her home, she took a pink rose, saying she would give it to the vilest woman she should meet in her wanderings. In a Mulberry Street dive she found her subject, a young girl with face bruised and bleeding, eyes bloodshot, clad in rags, and surrounded by a band of New York's worst characters; the vilest profanity was proceeding out of her mouth. My friend pushed her way through the crowd and put the pink rose in her hand, with the request that if she ever needed a friend, she would call upon her. The girl received the gift with a sneer. My friend passed on about her work, but with a prayer that God might touch her heart. Some days afterward she found her sitting in the entry of the "Door of Hope," looking even more wretched than when her eyes first beheld her. Her first thought was to send her away, thinking that she was too low to be saved. Her second thought was, "What would the Master do if he were here in my stead?" and then with a great rush of love, because she beheld a soul for whom Christ died, she stooped and took the sin-stained face in her hands and kissed it twice. The touch of love broke the girl's heart. She fell upon her knees in the entry, and then and there gave herself to God. She became transformed—almost transfigured. She went up and down the streets of New York City, into the lowest haunts of sin, herself a missionary and evangelist to her fallen sisters. Wherever she went she carried the light of heaven. Whenever she spoke it was with the power of God. A few months later she lay in her coffin at the ": Door of Hope." Hundreds flocked to look at the face, which was like an angel's, and went away to thank God that she had not lived in vain. With a record of only a short Christian experience, my friend writes me that more than a hundred souls had been converted through her ministry. This change was all wrought because first of all she received the Son of God as her personal Saviour, and then that she threw open every door of her nature for the indwelling of the Holy Ghost. The change was great, but not greater than would be witnessed in the life of any child of God who would make an unconditional surrender to the spirit of God bidding him at any cost, at any sacrifice, to come in and abide with him.

It is very encouraging to know that we do not need to pray for the spirit of God as if he were afar off. In one sense the hymn is wrong where we say, "Come, Holy Spirit, heavenly dove," for he is here, and is but waiting to completely fill us. There is a beautiful figure in the Old Testament which some one has used with great blessing. In the days of the flood Noah opened the window of the ark, and the little dove flew forth, and finding no place to rest the sole of its foot it came back again to the outstretched hand. The second time he opened the window the dove flew forth, and finding an olive branch bore it back to the hand of Noah. The third time he opened the window of the ark, the dove flew hither and thither, and finding a resting-place for the sole of its foot, it came back no more forever. The dove is always a figure representing the Holy Spirit. He came first in the Old Testament, touching Abraham and Moses, and Isaiah and others, but does not seem to abide permanently; he came again when Jesus Christ was crucified, and plucking the olive branch from the cross he made his way back to God, saying, "Peace hath been made in the death of the Son." He came the third time at Pentecost, with a rushing sound as of a mighty wind, filling all the place where the people sat, resting upon them with cloven tongues like as of fire. He has never gone back since the day of Pentecost. He is here, waiting to fill us if we but fulfil the conditions.

For many years in my Christian experience I was somewhat troubled by the fact that I could not tell just the day and the hour in which I was converted. It has ceased to trouble me now; first, because I should know I were living in this world even if I did not know my birthday, and secondly, because there is something far better than knowing just the time you were converted, and that is, a definite experience concerning the receiving fully of the Holy Ghost. It is a very serious question in my mind whether any one can have a full experience of power until, first of all, he has had definite experience concerning the receiving of the Holy Ghost. Have you had this?

There are some things which might be suggested which may make the way plainer for us all. There must be a deep longing for his coming, even as we longed for salvation through Jesus Christ. When we are satisfied with nothing else, when we long for nothing more, I believe he will come in and fill us, and the result will be power.

Sometimes we find people longing for such an experience in order that they may have peace or blessedness. Not infrequently ministers cry out for him that they may have more power in preaching. I am convinced that he will never fill us so long as these are the first thoughts. Bid him come in that he may have power over yourself first, and you are on the way to enlarging blessings. Let him come in that he may drive out everything contrary to the will of God, and you will find yourself very shortly in a full possession of his power. There is another suggestion which must not be overlooked; namely, there must be a full surrender. He can never fill the heart that is only partially given up. Every door of the nature, every impulse of the will, every affection of the heart must be surrendered to him. Then we may expect him.

The Rev. F. B. Meyer has made two helpful suggestions just here. If you cannot at once reach this position, then come before him and say, "Lord, I am willing to be made willing about everything," and "if you cannot give up everything for God, then say, 'I will let thee take everything.'" Then another suggestion is this, we must receive him by faith. The foundation for it is in Galatians, iii: 14, "That you might receive the promise of the spirit through faith." I am convinced that if one fulfils the conditions, he has a perfect right to stand before God, claiming the promise of the Holy Spirit with a faith which may be utterly devoid of emotion, just as one has the right to claim the free gift of salvation when he has surrendered his will unto God.

Why have we not received the Holy Ghost? It may be because we have disobeyed some clear command. Mr. Meyer well says: "If one has broken one of God's commands, or has been a disobedient child, he can never be filled with the power of God, neither can he claim his blessings, until he goes back to the place where he made the mistake, and makes it right with his God."

It may be because we have not confessed our sins. The trouble with us is not so much that we sin, but rather that when we sin, we do not immediately confess it before God. The abiding of an unforgiven sin in the heart of the Christian will absolutely prevent the infilling of the Holy Ghost. It may be because we have too little communion with God in his word. When one of my friends was presiding at a great convention in the city of Washington, a number of years ago, in the midst of the deliberations a number of Indian chiefs, who had been conferring with the President, came into the convention. They looked about with interest. At last an old chief, through an interpreter, rose and spoke. He said, "What is the secret of all his happiness? Our men do not look like yours; their faces are sad, their hearts heavy. Our women are not like yours. Our children are growing up in ignorance. Our homes are miserable. Tell us, if you can, what the medicine is which we must take." Then Gen. O.O. Howard, with his empty coat sleeve, his arm being left on the battle field, sprang forward, and lifting up the Bible in one hand, cried out, "Mr. Speaker, tell him that this is the good medicine." And it is quite true; it is the medicine which will cure the world's sickness; it is the medicine which will fill you with a new life, purging your heart from all that is evil, making your heart free from all that is sinful, making your heart throb with new impulses, emotions, and desires. Your trouble may be here.

Not very long ago a woman died in London. Only a few years ago she was utterly unknown, but at her funeral a great concourse of people passed through the great church to look upon her face. There were representatives of royalty, lords and ladies, people of high degree. Then the poorer people came. Finally there came one woman carrying a little babe on one arm and holding another child by the hand. She reached the casket, put the baby down and was just bending over to kiss the glass that covered the sweet face when the guard exclaimed, "Move on, move on." Stopping for a moment and looking at him, she lifted up her hand and shouted out until every one in the church heard her, "I will not move on. This woman saved my boy and I have a right to look." It was Mrs. Booth who was resting in her coffin. One of the grandest women of all God's family; she has been transformed by the Holy Ghost, and thus become a winner of souls. So may we all be.

Out in the hill country of Scotland a shepherd counted his flock and found that three sheep were missing. Going to the kennel where the shepherd dog was resting with her young, he pointed to the wilderness and said, "Three sheep are missing, go." The dog looked for a moment at her young and then at her master, and was lost in the night. She was gone an hour, then came back bruised by the thorns and beaten by the wolves, but she had the two sheep that were lost. The shepherd counted his flock once more, finding one still missing. He stood again at the kennel door where the mother was resting with her little ones. Pointing to the wilderness once more, he said, "Go." With a look of mute despair, first at her little ones, then into his face, she rose up and was lost in the darkness. Two hours passed and then three, then she came back bruised, bleeding, almost dying, but she had the one sheep that was lost. The shepherd picked it up, wrapped it in his shepherd's plaid and turned away to his fold, while the dog staggered back to her young, entered the kennel door and fell dead.

When I read it, I said, Oh, that a dumb beast of the field with no thought of God, no hope of eternity, no prospects of hearing the Master say " Well done, well done," should be so faithful to its master's command, while we sit with folded arms, as our Master with his pierced palm is pointing to the wilderness, saying, " The thousands are lost, go, go." If we were but filled with the Spirit of God we would hear his cry: " Have you received the Holy Ghost since you believed ? "

Erskine Presbyterian Church.

Another great throng gathered in this edifice, attracted by the announcement that Rev. T. L. Cuyler, D.D., was to be the speaker. The pulpit platform was tastefully decorated with flowers.

Rev. S. P. Rose, D.D., of Montreal, presided. First the audience joined in singing the old hymn, " Coronation." Dr. Rose then read from the eleventh chapter of Luke, after which Rev. Dr. Barbour, principal of the Congregational College of Montreal, led in prayer. " At the Cross " was then sung, followed by prayer by Rev. J. Mowat, pastor of the church. Dr. Rose then introduced Rev. Dr. Theodore L. Cuyler, of Brooklyn, who was given an enthusiastic welcome. Dr. Cuyler spoke as follows : —

The Prayer That Has Power.

Address of Rev. T. L. Cuyler, D.D.

I am happy to look into all these eyes tonight. All hail to the " Young Guard " in the noble army of the glorious Captain of our salvation ! We are facing each other now; we are grasping each other's hands. This is all well and right; but there is something infinitely better, and that is to face God and to lay hold of his everlasting arm.

The first word for the opening of this convention is — pray ! The second word is pray !! The third word is pray !!! and all through these days and nights to " pray without ceasing." All of God's mighty men and women have been mighty in prayer. When Martin Luther was in the mid-volley of his terrific fight with the " man of sin," he used to say, " I cannot get on without three hours a day in prayer." John Welsh of Scotland often leaped out of bed at midnight and wrapped a plaid about him and wrestled with the Lord until the breaking of the day. Charles G. Finney's grip on God gave him a tremendous grip on sinners' hearts. The greatest preacher of our times — Spurgeon — had, pre-eminently, the " gift of the knees." The noblest man whom the American Republic has produced — Abraham Lincoln — once said, " I have been driven many times to my knees by the overwhelming conviction that I had nowhere else to go. My own wisdom and that of all around me seemed insufficient for the day." Oh, for the spirit of prayer to descend mightily upon this convention of Endeavorers; that, like the first gathering of the disciples in that Jerusalem chamber, it may have a baptism of power, and continue, with one accord, in supplication to God !

But what is prayer? Has every prayer power with God? Let us get clear ideas on this point at the start. Prayer is not mere noise. Last year they tried, in Texas, to bring down rain by explosions of gunpowder; but it was of no avail; and the combined clamor of thousands of voices here might bring no shower of blessings. Many people regard prayer as a rehearsal of a set form of solemn words, learned by rote from the Bible, or from a liturgy or elsewhere.

Millions of so-called prayers have risen no higher in character and purpose than that. They were only from the throat outward. Genuine prevailing prayer is an earnest soul's direct converse with God. Phillips Brooks condensed it into four words, — a " true wish sent Godward." By it a contrite soul confesses sin and seeks pardon; by it a needy soul tells its wants; by it a devout God-loving soul pours forth its praises; and by means of it precious blessings are brought down from heaven.

The richest blessing that prayer can bring to us is to bring us into closer communion with God and into completer agreement with God. A man stands in the bow of a boat and pulls on a rope attached to the wharf. His pull does not move the wharf, but it does move the boat toward the shore. So when you and I attach the line of our faith to the Everlasting Throne, we don't expect to move the Throne, but to draw ourselves closer to it. When we get into closer fellowship with our loving Lord, and fuller harmony with him, then we receive what our hearts most desire.

(1) This is the first characteristic of the prayer that has power. I will give you Bible proof of that; there it is,— " Delight thyself in the Lord, and he shall give thee the asking of thy heart." A great deal of so-called prayer is born of selfishness, and tries to dictate to God. But none of his promises are unconditional, and we have no such spiritual assets standing to our credit that we have any right to fill up our checks and demand payment. The indispensable requisite of right asking is to have a right feeling toward God. When any soul delights in seeing God reign, and to let God have his own way, then its desires will be so purified from the dregs of selfishness that they may be fearlessly poured out before God. The desires of God and the desires of a sincere Christly soul will agree. God loves to give to us when we love to let him have his way. We are then seeking not our own glory but his; we find our happiness in the chime of our own desires with the will of God. A capital illustration of the difference between right and wrong desires is furnished in the biographies of James and John. These two fisherman-disciples came to our Lord and Saviour and said to him, " Master, we would that thou shouldst do for us whatsoever we shall desire." Then they bolt out the astonishing desire that Christ would put one of them on his right hand and the other on his left hand when he should set up his imperial government at Jerusalem! They were as selfish office-seekers as any that pester our President yonder in Washington. Their dream was of twelve thrones, and of their two in the middle of them. Jesus tells them plainly that it is not a crown or a throne, but a cup of suffering, that was preparing for them; are they ready for that? As long as these two ambitious disciples were self-seeking, Jesus would not grant them the desires of their hearts.

Now if you will look on a few years later, you will find these very two men making the strongest declarations as to the power of prayer. They have become so renewed by the Holy Spirit, and are so consecrated to Christ, that they begin to have pure and unselfish desires. James declares that " If any one of us lack wisdom we must ask of God, who giveth liberally." And then — as if he remembered what an awfully selfish prayer he had once offered — he says, " Ye ask, and ye receive not, because ye ask amiss that ye may consume it on your own pleasures." The other disciple (beloved John) exclaims, " Whatsoever we ask, we shall receive from him, because we keep his commandments to do what is pleasing in his sight." Just as soon as those two Christians found their supreme happiness in pleasing Christ, they received the desires of their hearts. The first characteristic of prevailing prayer is that we offer it in the right spirit, and from the right motive. If any of you hunger and thirst that Jesus Christ may be glorified here by this convention, your petition will have power with God.

(2) The second trait of the prayer that has power is that it aims at a mark, and the offerer knows what he is after. When any of you go into a store you do not ask for everything on the shelves, but you just name the article you want and the salesman hands it down to you. There is an enormous amount of pointless and prayerless praying done; it starts after nothing and ends nowhere.

A good test of your prayer is for you to ask yourself after it is over, "There, did I ask God for any particular blessing? Did I tell him just what I want?" The prevailing prayers mentioned in the Bible were short and sharp; they were aimed at a mark. The penitent publican cries, "God be merciful to me a sinner!" Sinking Peter calls out to Christ, "Lord, save me!" The poor centurion entreats the Saviour, "Come down ere my child dies!" All these men knew what they wanted. Old Rowland Hill used to say, "I like short, ejaculatory prayer; it reaches heaven before the devil can get a shot at it."

(3) The third essential of successful prayer is that it is offered in the name of Christ. "Whatsoever ye shall ask in my name, that will I do, that the Father may be glorified in the Son." Christ elsewhere tells us that he is the "door," and that no man cometh to the Father except by him. True prayer is not besieging a reluctant God behind a barred gateway; it is really taking hold of the Divine willingness. To him that knocketh it shall be opened. Sometimes it is for our spiritual good that there be some delay in opening the door. The Syro-Phœnician woman discovered that; her faith grew stronger every moment that she was kept waiting. This is a part of our discipline. Faith must learn the lesson of submission, and this does not mean a tame, lazy submission to evils which we can ourselves roll out of the way, but an entire acquiescence in God's withholdings as well as in his bestowals. Mercies grow sweeter if there have been some trials of faith in the pleading for them. A dear friend of mine found the conversion of a beloved child was all the more precious because both had been brought closer to Christ in seeking the blessing. Those easily discouraged Christians who pull the door-bell and then run away have really no claim to enter. Nor will the door open to any of us who try to smuggle in our favorite sins with us. There is prodigious power in the knock of faith, even though it be the gentle tap of a little child.

(4) Fourthly, the prayer that has power with God must be a pre-paid prayer. If we, in the States, expect a letter to reach Canada, we pre-pay it; if we do not value it enough to put a two-cent stamp on it, the document will go to the dead-letter office. There is a dead-prayer office, and I fear that thousands of well-worded petitions are buried up there. Valuable things cost something, and divine blessings are no exception. All God's promises have their conditions: we must comply with the conditions or we cannot expect the blessing. No Canadian farmer is such an idiot as to found his expectation of a crop of wheat on God's general promise of seed-time and harvest when he has not ploughed a rod of ground or sowed a kernel of grain. In prayer we must do our part if we expect God to do his part. Yes, we must do our part toward answering our own prayers.

At a missionary convention a venerated minister was called upon to offer prayer. He halted, and began to fumble in his pocket. "Father A—, they want you to pray," whispered somebody in his ear. "Yes, yes," replied the wise old man, "but I cannot pray until I have given something." That old saint prepaid his prayer. For the Christian churches in these days to offer the petition, "thy kingdom come!" and then actually expend more money in jewelry and cigars than for all their enterprises of foreign missions, looks very much like a solemn farce. As far as the Lord's people are willing to prepay their prayers for the conversion of the world in solid cash and hard, self-denying work, just so far will their prayers have power.

God has no blessings for stingy pockets. What is true of pecuniary sacrifice is equally true of personal efforts. Often when I listen to "requests for prayer" for the conversion of a husband, or a son, or a Sabbath-school scholar, I say to myself, "How much is that person doing for the conversion of that husband, or child or scholar?" The Christian wife who does her utmost to make her every-day religion attractive to her unconverted husband prepays her petition to God. She works with the Holy Spirit. A noble woman in my church was instrumental in the conversion of her whole big Bible class; she prepaid her prayer for them by loving personal efforts for their salvation. God demands that we prove our faith by our works. Much of the pious prattle in church prayer meetings and Christian Endeavor meetings comes to nothing, because the person who utters the empty words is not working himself! He asks the Almighty to do what he will not lift a lazy finger to bring about. Christian Endeavorers, how much are you endeavoring to secure the answer to your prayer? Oh, I fear that it will be an awful thing to meet some of our own prayers at the Day of Judgment! Out of our own mouths they will condemn us! Genuine, self-denying, effective, prevailing prayer is always prepaid. The offerer of it is willing to make any sacrifice to secure the blessings sought for. In short, every prayer may be said to be prepaid for whose fulfilment we are glad to co-operate with the Holy Spirit, cost what it may.

Dr. Cuyler gave some striking illustrations of the power of prayer, and said that answer to prayer covered all providential history as thickly as bright-eyed daisies covered the western prairies. He described a wonderful prayer which Mr. Spurgeon had made on the last evening that he ever spent with him in his London home; and he closed with a fervent appeal for a united call upon God to pour down a glorious blessing on this convention.

St. Matthews Presbyterian Church.

Rev. W. R. Cruikshank, the pastor of the church, presided. First there came the inevitable and always delightful song service. Rev. Mr. McIntosh, of Yarmouth, N. S., read the Scripture lesson, and Rev. Thomas Hall offered prayer. The church choir then rendered very beautifully the anthem, "Jehovah's Praise," after which Rev. J. Z. Tyler, D.D., of Cleveland, Ohio, was introduced as the speaker of the evening.

Some Pressing Needs, and How To Supply Them.

Address of Rev. J. Z. Tyler, D.D.

TEXT: And of the children of Issachar, men that had understanding of the times, to know what Israel ought to do; the heads of them were two hundred, and all their brethren were at their commandment.—*1 Chron. 12 : 32.*

It was a crisis in Israel. Saul was dead, and Jonathan, his son. Abner had failed to perpetuate Saul's dynasty, and had deserted to David. Ishbosheth, Saul's son and successor, had been slain. The eyes of all Israel were turning to David, the hero of the harp and the sling, who had been the king over Judah and Benjamin. It was the time of the gathering of the tribes to Hebron, to turn the kingdom of Saul over to David, according to the word of the Lord. Of Judah that bare shield and spear there were 6,800, ready armed to war; of Simeon there were 7,100, mighty men of valor; of the tribe of Levi there were 4,600, with Jehoida as their leader; of Benjamin, the kindred of Saul, who had hitherto kept the ward of the house of Saul, there were 3,000; Ephraim sent 20,000 mighty men of valor, famous throughout the house of their fathers; of the half tribe of Manasseh there were 18,000, who had personally pledged themselves to the movement to make David king; Zebulon had 50,000 crack soldiers; Naphtali, and Dan, and Asher, and Reuben, and Gad, and Issachar joined to swell the numbers to more than 300,000. What a mighty Christian Endeavor convention was that! It is in the midst of the description of this great gathering that the words of the text occur: "Men that had understanding of the times, to know what Israel ought to do." They were in touch with their times, and had insight into the Divine purpose. They knew that it was a period of change, of progress, of revolution. They had such a clear and comprehensive insight into the meaning of all this, they were in such accord with the Divine will, and were gifted with such practical judgment, that they knew what Israel ought to do. They adjusted themselves to the changed conditions.

And is it not a truth which should always be recognized, that the times determine in large part what Israel ought to do? The hand of time turning the kaleidoscope causes each generation to present a new and strange aspect. New elements enter and the old ones are shifted. New conditions present themselves, new theories are advanced, new problems demand solution, new foes enter the field or the old ones adopt new tactics. The battles fought by our fathers are not the battles we are to fight. The future will have its Waterloos and its Gettysburgs, but they will not be fought on the fields already historic. What Israel ought to do today is to be determined by the conditions which prevail today. Yet, let us not conclude that the church is to be a weather-cock, changing with every wind that blows. It is marked by the Changeless. Like its head, it is the same, yesterday and today. The same Christ, the same spirit, the same Father over all and in all. It has the same Gospel message for all men, under all circumstances and for all time. The faith once by inspiration delivered to the saints was delivered for all, and he who preaches any other gospel than that proclaimed by the Apostles rests under a divine anathema. Yet this changeless Gospel has infinite adaption to the varied and varying needs of men. The church has apostolic precedent for becoming all things to all men, if by all means it may save them.

The most casual observer is impressed with the thought that we live in stirring times. Changes are taking place with startling rapidity. A decade now means more of change than some centuries. There is a breaking with the past. Dynasties perish; thrones change. Much that past generations have cherished is being thrown overboard. The spirit of unrest is working mightily in the heart of humanity, and society in every part is like the troubled sea. Fundamental matters are subjects of debate, and things which our fathers regarded as settled are now treated as open questions. Creeds are being revised, and the Bible itself is being taken apart and examined with keenest scrutiny. Many who have broken with the past are now drifting on an uncertain sea, without chart or compass or guiding star. With me the impression is almost daily deepening that we are approaching a crisis involving alike the political, social, and religious interests of the race. We seem to be on the eve of changes radical and world-wide, marking the transition from one age to another. The rush of events is like the rush of maddened waters pouring themselves through the channel of a narrow Niagara from one lake into another, and we are now tossing on the rapids above the great cataract.

With this conviction there comes of necessity the conviction that there has never been a time in the history of the church when her ministries were more needed. It is no time for idleness, for indifference, for worldliness. It is a time to draw very near to God and to bow very humbly before him. The Divine hand swings open the door, inviting every believing soul to larger usefulness and to a closer union with the thought and word of God. It is the great day of opportunity for Israel. May the Spirit guide me as I endeavor to indicate some of our needs in view of our times.

First, it seems to me, we need a larger understanding of Christ's purposes. His purpose is not simply to save the individual soul by bringing it into right relation to God, but to save human society by bringing man into right relation to man. Human institutions need saving. Righteousness is not meant to be simply the law of the individual, but is meant to be the law of the nations. For we may easily conceive of men being, as concerns themselves, strictly Christian, excellent and exemplary members of the church, and yet the institutions with which they are connected, and through which their influence is largely exerted, possessing not one particle of the spirit of Christ and subject in no measure to the Gospel of which He is the author. Self-interest is the basis and rule in the business of this world. Its general enterprises rest upon a purely pagan basis. The golden rule, the teachings of the Sermon on the Mount, are admired, but are not practically applied. There seems to prevail an opinion that they were not meant to be applied in the practical affairs of life.

Now, in opposition to this narrow view of the purpose of Christ there is need, —yea, our times make an imperative demand upon the church—that it take the larger view of the great and gracious sweep of Christ's purpose. While the conversion of individuals must stand first, it must not be regarded as exhausting the ultimate purpose of the Gospel of Christ. This is a sociological element of the Gospel which needs to have tremendous emphasis. There are wide-spread wrongs which need to be righted, injustice needs to be exorcised by the spirit of Christ, and human brotherhood, which lies at the basis of the Gospel, needs to stand as the basis of human society. This is one of the needs of our times.

In the second place, we need a deeper insight into the meaning of the cross. It is not meant to be a device by which we may sin and yet in some mechanical way be saved, but is meant to change the whole spirit and purpose of our lives, and to make us saviors of others. He who is truly saved must become a savior. To be saved does not mean to enter into some ark and thus be rescued from some external element which endangers, but it means that the spirit of the cross shall so enter into us that sin shall be cast out. If any man have not the spirit of Christ, we are told by an apostle, he is none of his. It was a sad and significant manifestation of the feeling which prevails, at least in some sections of society, when, not long ago, in a labor convention, the name of Christ was applauded and the mention of the church greeted with hisses. And yet the church should be dominated by the spirit of Christ. The mind that was in him should be in us. A Christian is Christ continued. Read the opening verses in the second chapter of Philippians. Behold the manifestation therein displayed of the mind that was in Christ. The dying need of the church today is that it be possessed by the same spirit. There is need of self-denial and cross-bearing now as much as at any previous time in the history of the church. There are Calvarys and Gethsemanes today, and we shall find them along the path of service, if so be the Spirit is in us.

There is need, in the third place, of a clearer faith in the supernatural. We are not needing so much to learn of the natural law in the spiritual world as of the spiritual law in the natural world. Loss of faith in the supernatural produces spiritual paralysis. It stifles the voice of prayer. It robs us of courage. It chills our enthusiasm and quenches all high and holy aspiration. If prayer reaches no ear and brings no answer, but, like a health-lift, be only a good exercise, then will we cease to pray. The faith that made the first believers victorious over the world was a faith in an ever-present Christ. He went before them and worked with them. From the day his spirit armed them for service, they maintained an unchanging attitude of triumph. They attacked the world as those who were victors from the outset. They saw the unseen and wrought the impossible. They walked in a divine fellowship, and worked with a divine enthusiasm and power. In the materialistic tendencies of our times, in these times when the universe is being interpreted as under the administration of blind force, and we are asked to eliminate the miraculous from the Bible, there is need of a renewal of faith in the Divine presence and power. "Without me," said Christ, "ye can do nothing." Let us not quench the Spirit. A Christ-filled church must be a Christ-working church.

The fourth need of our times is a more intimate, open and practical fellowship among believers. We should be one in such a way that the world may see it and be led to believe in Christ. The times of our text furnish an excellent illustration of what Israel ought to do today. Israel for centuries had, with temporary exceptions, existed only as tribes; but there came the time when they were to be more closely united. Of that time we read in the history of the crowning of David. Those who had understanding of the times to know what Israel ought to do led the tribes together at Hebron, that David might be anointed king over all, and a new period of prosperity was inaugurated. It is one of the gratifying signs of our times that spiritual Israel is coming into a more manifest union under King David's greater son. To my mind it is daily becoming clearer that the movement which has brought us together is led on of God. Its spirit and its methods seem to be peculiarly called for by our times and adapted to its needs. We are living at a crisis. The changes which are taking place are of profound significance.

We are living, we are dwelling.
 In a grand and awful time ;
In an age on ages telling
 To be living is sublime.

Worlds are changing, Heaven beholding,
 Thou hast but an hour to fight ;
Now the emblazoned cross unfolding,
 On, right onward, for the right.

On, let all the soul within you
 For the truth's sake go abroad ;
Strike, let every nerve and sinew
 Tell on ages, tell for God.

Douglas Methodist Church.

Rev. E. M. Hill, of Montreal, presided and conducted the opening praise service. Prayer was offered by Rev. Mr. Gunn, of Cowansville, and Professor Shaw.

Miss Hollingshead sang "Jerusalem" with fine effect. Mr. Hill then introduced Rev. Dr. W. H. McMillan, of Allegheny City, Pa., as the speaker of the evening.

Conditions of Receiving the Holy Spirit.

Address of Rev. W. H. McMillan, D.D.

Christian Friends : — I come tonight to speak to you concerning one of the greatest mysteries of the Gospel, the indwelling of the Holy Spirit in the hearts of the Lord's people. It is the greatest of all our privileges; it brings us face to face with one of the most majestic truths which the Gospel reveals, and therefore, before I attempt to speak on this subject, may I ask you to join with me in a moment of silent prayer, that the Lord may help me to speak and help you all to hear his Word of Truth. [*The congregation bowed their heads in silent prayer.*]

When our Lord had completed his earthly ministry, and was about to ascend to his throne on high, he gave to his disciples the great commission, "Go ye into all the world and make disciples of all nations." And this commission, given first of all to the eleven apostles, has been extended to all his disciples throughout the world until the end of time. "As the Father hath sent me into the world, even so send I you. These are the words of the Master, spoken not to a few officers in his church only, but to every one of his followers. "Ye are the light of the world; ye are the salt of the earth," are words spoken, too, not to a few but to all. According to the measure of his ability, every servant of Christ is responsible for carrying the Gospel of the Son of God to those who have it not. You remember the inspired apostle Paul likens the church to a human body, of which Christ is the head, and says, "The whole body fitly joined together and compacted by that which every joint supplieth, according to the effectual working in the measure of every part, maketh increase of the body unto the edifying of itself in love." There we are taught concerning the church of Christ that it is to be extended by the effectual working of every part; and the work which the servants of Christ are called upon to do is nothing less than the salvation of lost men. Paul, in speaking to the Ephesians, says: "You hath he quickened who were dead in trespasses and sins." There he applies to them a designation which was not peculiar to those Ephesian Christians, but is the condition of every man and woman until changed by the life-giving power of the Spirit of God. The Scripture also says, " If any man be in Christ, he is a new creature. Old things have passed away; behold, all things are new." "Verily, verily, I say unto you, ye must be born again." That which men need, therefore, for their salvation is resurrection from spiritual death. It is a new creation; it is a new birth. The work, therefore, upon which your Master has sent you, each one, is nothing less than that. You remember the prophet Ezekiel was shown the valley of dry bones, and was asked, "Can these bones live?" And it is a similar question which every servant of Christ has to answer for himself at this day. The Lord did not show his prophet of old a number of people enfeebled, having life though that life were impaired, but he showed him a valley of dry bones, and said, "Can these live?" And so the people of the world, to whom the servants of Christ go to bring them this Gospel of salvation, are not those who have any spiritual life, but those who are "*dead* in trespasses and sins." And the work you are called upon to do is nothing less than to give them life. If this work were to be accomplished without obstacles in the way, it would be great enough, it would rise beyond our comprehension; but it is generally in the face of the mightiest obstacles. "We wrestle not against flesh and blood, but against principalities, against powers, against spiritual wickedness in high places, against the rulers of the darkness of this world." This mighty work of the Master that he has given us to do must be done in the face of these oppositions.

Now, when we undertake any common enterprise in life, we count the cost. We measure our resources over against the object to be attained, and try to decide if we are able to accomplish it; we estimate our own resources, and we compute the expense likely to be involved, and we ask ourselves the question, "Have I the resources at command to accomplish this?" If it is something that involves putting forth physical strength, we look at the burden, we estimate our ability, and decide whether it is possible to lift it. As we look into the face of the duties we have to do, — bringing life to those that are dead, — and then think of our own ability, the question arises, "Are we able for these things?" Or rather, are we not constrained to cry out, "Who is sufficient for these things?" Is not this the manner in which our Christian duty presents itself to our thought? When we consider what our Master has given us to do, the obstacles in the way, our inability for the task laid upon us, it seems to me that the question which I have suggested to occupy our thought for a little time tonight is intensely practical: How shall we accomplish the duties which our Master has given us to do?

What is the secret of Christian efficiency? We have not to go far for the answer to this question out of the Divine Word: "Ye shall receive power, after that the Holy Ghost is come upon you." "Not by might nor by power, but by my Spirit, saith the Lord;" that is, not by human ability, but by divine ability is this work to be done. The question for us, then, to solve is, What are the conditions upon which we may receive that power of the Holy Spirit in us, which alone is sufficient to qualify us for the work which the Master has given us to do?

I think these conditions may be summed up in two words: separation, consecration; separation from all that is evil, and consecration to our Lord. We have these words of Scripture concerning the duty of separation from the world: "Come out from among them and be ye separate, saith the Lord; and touch not the unclean thing, and I will receive you, and will be a Father unto you, and ye shall be my sons and daughters, saith the Lord Almighty." We must come out then from the world, which is in opposition to God, which is unclean in his sight, and take our stand on the Lord's side in a life of separation from the world. Then he will receive us and give us his blessing.

You remember what the Scripture says about that heroic moral surgery which we must practise upon our sinful natures, if we would receive the blessing of God and his indwelling presence: "If thy right hand offend thee, cut it off, and cast it from thee. If thy right eye offend, pluck it out and cast it from thee." The Scripture also says, "If any man would come after me, let him deny himself and take my his cross and follow me." The case is put still stronger in these words: "If any man cometh after me and hate not his father and mother and wife and children, yea, and his own life also, he cannot be my disciple." You know what that means. Not that we should positively hate those dear ones, for the love of Christ only makes every other true love the purer and stronger, but it means that our love for Jesus should be so supreme that all other affections shall seem but hatred in comparison, and that none of these human loves shall, if they would, come between us and the love of the Master.

These are the declarations of the Divine Word concerning the necessity of separation from evil, if we would receive the Holy Spirit. You remember that the Philistines once captured the Ark of God, and placed it in the temple of their idol and left it there, and behold, on the morrow, the idol had fallen prostrate before the Ark of God, and his hands and head were broken off on the threshold! When the Ark of God came in, Dagon had to fall. It is equally true with this spiritual temple of our Lord; if the Holy Ghost is to come in, *the world must go out.* We cannot serve God and mammon. You observe that this Divine teaching shows us that the Lord will make no compromises with sin. It is not enough to surrender some sins, or most of our sins. One sin indulged in is enough to exclude the presence of the Divine Spirit. One act of disobedience on the part of the hosts of Israel brought them defeat in the presence of their enemies. We must be willing to make an entire surrender of sin, and give ourselves to the Lord.

That we may understand more accurately the sins to be surrendered, let us take that inspired classification of sins given in the Word of God: "Love not the world, neither the things that are in the world, for if any man love the world, the love of the Father is not in him. For all that is in the world, the lust of the flesh and the lust of the eyes and the vainglory of life, is not of the Father but is of the world." "The lust of the flesh" — the Scripture tells us about that, and how we must surrender it, if the Holy Spirit is to make his habitation in our hearts.

"He that raised up Christ from the dead shall also quicken your mortal bodies by his spirit that dwelleth in you." So, then, we are not debtors to the flesh, to live after the flesh, "For if ye live after the flesh, ye shall die, but if ye through the Spirit do mortify the deeds of the body, ye shall live." This shows us what we are to do with this fleshly nature of ours. There are desires of our bodies which are holy and right, but all sinful desires must be crucified, if we are to receive this blessing which we crave. If we are to be in-dwelt by the Spirit of God, we must be lifted immensely above the fleshly life, in whatever form.

The next class of sins is the "*lust* of the *eyes.*" I think this means that habit of life which looks upon the things of this world as the best things. Those are guilty of indulging in this lust who are looking, not at the things which are unseen and eternal, but at the things which are seen and temporal—looking at all this " glare and glitter and tinsel of time," and forgetting those things which neither fade nor die, "in the light of that region sublime." It is feasting our eyes upon the things of the present, rather than looking beyond this to the life that is to come.

"The lust of the flesh, the lust of the eyes, and the *pride* of *life.*" This is another name, I think, for ambition. It is seeking the world's applause; thinking more of what men think of us than of what God thinks of us. And as long as it is true that I am caring more for the opinion of my fellowmen than I am for the approbation of God, I cannot be filled with his Holy Spirit. I am guilty of the vainglory of life. That desire for the approbation of men brings with it another sin which we know to be very common in our own experience, and from our observation of others, namely, quenching the Spirit within us through fear of criticism. Who does not know that the fear of men is sealing many a lip that ought to be speaking for the Master, and tying many hands which ought to be busy in his service? They ask the question, "What will people say if I enter upon this life of holy consecration in the service of the Master?" What will they—that terrible *they* — what will *they* say? That fear of the criticism of men is holding back and holding down very many of the servants of Christ. And if we analyze that feeling, what do we find it to be but this vainglory of life which must be cast out that the Holy Spirit of God may come in? It is our desire for the approbation of men which makes us fear their criticism. But the true disciple of the Master looks so intensely into His blessed face that he almost forgets the world around him, and he is so desirous of that Master's approbation that he cares but little what men may think of his acts. You remember how it was with the apostle Paul: "It is a small thing for me to be judged of you, or of man's judgment." He was thinking of his Master. And when this vainglory of life is cast out, when the pride of our hearts has been surrendered and the Holy Spirit of consecration to Christ has come in, then that fear of man that brings a snare will have gone.

Once in a series of revival meetings where the Spirit of God was present in his mighty power, which we long for so much, a beautiful young woman, modest and timid, who, before the coming of that Divine Spirit into her heart, could have been induced by no consideration to have opened her mouth to speak to the great congregation, arose in her place in the choir and delivered one of the most powerful addresses to the impenitent that was ever given in that sanctuary, and never thought of fear. The Holy Spirit had carried her upward beyond the thought of man's judgment into the very presence of God.

Now, then, these are some of the things that must be surrendered,—the lust of the flesh, the lust of the eyes, and the pride of life. These must be given up before the Spirit of God can enter our hearts. This is not to say that we must be made perfectly whole before the Spirit will come to us. If that were the condition, no one could receive him. But it means this, I think: that we must be willing and desirous that every sin should go. We should be ready to present to our Divine Master a clean temple, or one that we are willing he should make clean. The trouble with us is, is it not, that when we pray for the coming of the Divine Spirit. we do so with a mental reservation? We are not willing to be entirely separated from sin. There are some sins which we cherish, there are some duties which we are not willing to do, and the surrender is not complete. An Achan is cherished in the camp and Israel still suffers defeat. The surrender of sin which the Lord asks of us is willingness to take out that offending right eye just as soon as we discover it is an offence to us; willingness to cut off that offending right hand, whatever the pain, when we discover that it is an offence to the Lord; willingness for any sacrifice of our desires. our inclinations, or our habits for the Master's sake. It means simply this: That the old man, our sinful nature, "the evil that is in us," as the Apostle Paul describes it, has been nailed to the cross and is being crucified. That old nature will die hard, but it is nailed to the cross, and it is dying. It may die with pain, as it will, but it is dying; it may die slowly, but it is *dying*— because of the holy purposes of our will. We have surrendered our sins and we have nailed the evil that is in us to the cross, and are " crucifying the affections and the lusts of the flesh." That is the surrender which is the condition of our receiving the Spirit of God.

We have said that there is, over against this spirit of separation from sin, the duty of dedication to the Lord. We take ourselves away from all that is evil, and give ourselves unreservedly to the Divine Master. And this involves, I think, three things: unquestioning belief, complete surrender of will, and controlling affection for the Master. Unquestioning belief —"If any man cometh unto God, he must believe that he is. and that he is the rewarder of them who diligently seek him." Have we that unquestioning belief in Jesus Christ? As we think of him tonight, are we looking across nearly nineteen centuries to an historic character of the olden time, or are we thinking of Jesus as the friend who walks with us through these days? As we read the Bible, do we see there printed words which by our intellectual conviction we are persuaded are the words of truth, or do we hear in those words the voice of the living Christ speaking to our hearts?

There is a speculative faith and there is a living faith. Speculative faith is in the head, and is cold and dead and fruitless. Living faith is in the heart, and is the power and potency of a new life. Have we that living faith in Jesus Christ which brings to us what old Doctor Mason designated as "that delightful recumbency of soul that rests on him." That delightful *resting* in Christ! *Resting* in his wisdom to guide us! What a safe guide our Master is! There is no mistaking the way when he leads on. All questions solved by his divine wisdom; looking up to his face and asking, "What wilt thou have me to do?"; trusting his divine wisdom to show us *what* we shall do and *how* we shall do it; letting him answer every question for us, and *trusting* his *strength*.

You remember when Joshua was entering upon the conquest of the promised land, there were before him those walled cities, defended in some instances by giants; all of them defended by strong garrisons, determined to hold their habitations against the coming invaders. Joshua knew the forces he had to encounter, and he looked round about upon a vast host of unorganized followers, ill fitted for the conquest of a land so strongly fortified. Doubtless the heart of the brave man was filled with many a misgiving as he thought of the duties before him. In a dream that night he saw standing before him an angel, with a drawn sword in his hand. How his heart trembled until he asked the meaning: "Art thou come for peace or for war?" And the answer was: "As the captain of the Lord's host am I come forth." That removed all his doubt and fear. Henceforth, as Joshua led the host, he would see that angelic leader going before in every battle, wielding a sword with more than human might, hewing for him a path to certain victory.

Does our faith look to that same captain of the Lord's host leading on to victory? Are we not too often looking at human agencies, at social influences, at the power of learning, at the power of money, and all these subordinate agencies? Each have their place of importance, but are we not too often forgetful of that divine power which is able to take the smallest and feeblest instrument and make it accomplish the grandest results? Has he not "chosen the weak things to confound the mighty, that no flesh might glory in his presence?" Have we faith in the divine power of our Leader which can make our weakness mighty through God?

Again, does our faith in Christ take hold of his *unchanging faithfulness?* God is the same yesterday, today, and forever. We take up our Bible and read of the passage of the Israelites through the Red Sea; we think of them with Pharoah's army behind and the rolling sea before them, and no possible escape, and we see God coming down and parting the waves to make a dry path for his people. We see Peter attempting to walk the sea, and beginning to sink, crying for help; and the Divine hand is immediately put forth to save him from death. We hear Solomon asking God for wisdom, and God gave him a wisdom which has made his name a synonym for the greatest and best in human attainment the world over. And now we know that the God who came to his people at the Red Sea, the same Master who helped Peter, the same Lord who helped Solomon, will in like manner help us. He is the same yesterday, today and forever.

Now, have we this unquestioning faith in our Divine Lord, in his Word, in his wisdom, in his faithfulness?

And this surrender to the Lord means also another thing. It means unquestioning obedience. Not long ago we studied in our international Sabbath-school lessons, the story of Esther, one of the most magnificent characters which the Bible describes.

There is the noble queen arrayed in her royal apparel, with the crown of an empire on her brow, and surrounded by all the beauty and luxury of an eastern palace. But a great duty confronts her, and to do it she must face not only the possibility but the probability of death within the next hour. Will she do it? Yes. You hear from her queenly lips the holy resolve, "I will go in unto the king and speak for my people, and if I perish, I perish." That is the ring of the true metal; that is the spirit of true Christian Endeavor, unquestioning and prompt obedience to the call of duty, whatever dangers or obstacles may lie in the way.

Christian Endeavorers, have we that spirit of surrender to Christ? Why have we not the spirit of entire surrender that Paul had when he said, " Lord, what wilt thou have me to do?'" and I will do it. When we make our pledges in our consecration meetings, is there not sometimes a mental reservation that we will make a complete surrender to the Lord, provided he does not lay upon us too severe duties or call for too great sacrifices? As if the Master was unkind and we could not trust him! I remember a writer on this subject puts it in this way: Here is a mother. She has a boy that she loves as a mother only loves. Now, suppose that boy comes up to her and says, " Mother, I will promise to do everything that you want me to do; I will obey in everything, if I can." Hear that mother say, " Aha, I have him now! He has promised me that, and I will test him. I will give him this that he dislikes, and I will lay a heavy burden upon him. He has promised to do whatever I tell him to do, and I will tell him hard things to do." Would she? No; you know she would not. And how is it with our blessed Master? Have we not been thinking of him as I have supposed that impossible mother would do? When we say to him that we will do " whatsoever thou wouldst like to have me do," let there be no reservation, and then when the instrument is given up to the Lord to be his alone, will he not take it?

Now, Christian Endeavorers, here is this weary, waiting world; there are souls around about you in the homes, perhaps, from which you have come, who are living without God and without hope in the world. You know that your mission as the servants of Christ requires your testimony, and you labor for their salvation. " Ye are the light of the world, the salt of the earth." There is no other way of God's appointment by which those lost ones are to be saved but by the instrumentality of his people. We saw at the beginning that this is a work no less than the bringing of life to those that are dead. This is nothing less than a divine work. We can do nothing without the Spirit. You have just been singing, " Throw Out the Life Line." No arm but that of God can throw out the life line so as to reach the perishing. There will be no soul rescued from those dark waves except as the Spirit of God comes into your words and into your efforts for the accomplishment of the result.

What are the conditions, then, upon which you and I can have the Holy Spirit of God abiding in us, and working by us? Entire surrender of all sin, and entire dedication to his service. Give to him a clean temple and he will come in and fill it with his glory, and he will use your instrumentality, though it may be feeble and nothing in itself, and fill it with divine power for the accomplishment of the greatest things for God.

I think last year the report was that over a hundred thousand of the associate members had been brought into the fold of Christ by the activity of the active members. If all the Christian Endeavorers in this convention and all throughout this country and the world were filled with the Spirit of God, as we may be filled — how many hundreds of thousands would be reported next year?

Let us tonight open the door to the Divine Spirit and say, " Come in," and say to all evil and sin, " Go." Though it may be like the cutting off the right hand, or the plucking out the right eye, let us say to the sin, " Go," and to the Holy Spirit, " Come."

American Presbyterian Church.

Rev. W. B. Hinson, pastor of the Olivet Baptist Church of Montreal, presided, and gave the preliminary exercises into the hands of the audience. First a brief prayer would be offered, then a verse of some familiar hymn sung, then another prayer, and so on for half an hour. It was a typical Christian Endeavor prayer meeting, except that Dr. Farrar gave all the testimony. Promptly at 8.15 the chairman introduced Rev. Dr. H. C. Farrar, of Albany, N. Y., who spoke as follows : —

Individual Consecration.

Address by Rev. h. C. Farrar, D.D.

I am to speak to you tonight concerning Individual Consecration. The theme is opportune; it belongs to this hour, to this congregation, to this convention. It belongs to us, because we have been called into the kingdom of our Lord Jesus Christ, not for our pleasure but for his service, so that every one of us should be able to say, with that man who followed Jesus most closely, "I am not my own; I am bought with a price; *therefore* —" but you are familiar with your Bibles, and I will quote no more.

I do not come to you with this question, "For *what* do you mean to live?" That is low, base, sordid; it has to do with things; it brings confusion, trouble; it is full of emulation, strife, bitterness, and it results in nothing satisfactory. I come to you with the greater question, "For *whom* do you mean to live?" The very moment I put that question, it makes God the centre and you a factor in the problem of life. It makes you a force and a power as he shall call you, because the moment you grasp that thought, it lifts, it broadens, it intensifies. You cannot ask it without there being a response, if you are loyal to yourself, and it will be a man's deepest failure if he fails to be loyal to himself. No man can ask that question, "For whom shall I live?" unless it thrusts him out.

My subject — individual consecration — has at least this thought for me tonight,— individualism. It is just here that Christianity puts its emphasis. God deals with men, not in masses but as individuals. "One by one," says the prophet Isaiah; and that is the way that God deals with men today — one by one. We also are called to deal with men in the same manner. The progress of the human race has been along these two lines: the development of the individual and the organization of society; and it is according as these two principles have obtained in the world's history that we have had the civilization of the past ages. That civilization has been prominent in which the idea of the individual or the organization has been dominant. A low form of civilization and a low form of organization produces the savage. A low form of civilization and a little higher form of organization produces the barbarian. With the individual sacrificed to the organization you have the civilization of old Egypt and Assyria and India and China. With the organization subordinated to the individual you have the strangely brilliant and strangely brief civilization of Greece. Christianity, however, is teaching us to lay emphasis on both the development of the individual and the organization of society. The individual today counts the highest; the organization is an afterthought, and comes in only relatively. The individual is first and foremost. And God ever deals with the individual directly. He never operates through secondary causes, where he can get at the primary. God talks with men today as much as he ever did in the history of the world. He reveals himself to men today, in the closet, in the cloister, at home, in the desert, on the streets, in the busy marts of trade, just as much as he ever did. Whatever God has done through the history of the old Hebrew race, that he is doing with the American people today.

So, then, we have not only the thought of the individual developed, but we have the thought of the organization — home, church, society, state. Never was the home so pure, so noble, so grand. I have been delighted, as I have looked at these women and seen here and there a white ribbon. Think of the fact that there are in this North American continent of ours 500,000 consecrated women belonging to the Women's Christian Temperance Union. It is Eve trying to build again her lost Eden, gathering her motherly, wifely, sisterly, friendly sympathies around her loved ones, to protect, to build, to develop. Hence the *home* in America has reached its high-water mark in the world's history. There were never so many people in the world's history that have land on which to plant a home. There were never so many people that own their own homes as there are on this continent today. And it is one of the glories of our country that if we can get a man to build a house and plant a home and own it for the most part, we have that man's sympathy with every organization — home, church, society, and state. The more homes we plant, the more we develop not only the idea of the individual but of the church, because the home is God's holiest institution on this earth. The church and state and school are afterthoughts, but the home is first. Adam and Eve in the garden of Eden in their purity — there is your home idea, there is the organization idea, there is the individual idea.

Individualism is the spirit of the age. You see it everywhere. You see it in business, you see it in the great corporations. Everywhere you find the individual spirit to be the predominant spirit of today, and Christianity puts its emphasis here. It was Andrew that called Peter; it was Philip that called Nathaniel; it was the Earl of Shaftsbury's old nurse that laid her molding hand on that boy (and all the reforms that England has witnessed in the past fifty years, some great Englishman has said, came out of the Earl of Shaltsbury's brain and heart), and this servant woman made the Earl of Shaftsbury, by reading, by praying, by talking with him, by loving and lifting him. God's Spirit operates through the individual touch on the individual heart.

This law of individualism operates as did the rod of Moses when he struck the rock at Horeb and forthwith there flowed out that which had been hidden away, for the refreshment of the thousands gathered there. It operates on individuals as Columbus's discovery of America opened up to Europe a new world. When an individual catches this spirit of individualism and pushes this thought out on its legitimate lines, then God helps and blesses.

Organization is good, but it is too often a danger. There is sometimes danger in a great church — the danger of too many silent partners. There is power in a little mission church where each individual feels responsibility,— the power of a larger sociability, a larger geniality, a more hearty and enthusiastic consecration to the work in hand. Gideon's three hundred men felt each his own personality: each felt. "The. battle depends on me," and his right arm was made powerful for victory. When God can get men to individualize themselves, then he says, "Go to, I will help those men." That is law and grace.

Now, this individualism becomes *one-idea*ism. Somebody has said that one-ideaism is a terrific idea. Paul was never worth anything to this world until he got hold of that great thought that he had crystalized into his being, "This one thing I do." Then did he just sharpen his soul, spirit, and body to a single point, and God diamondized that point and took hold of him and etched the great thoughts of his living gospel on the age. For Paul's epistles, exclusive of the four-fold life of Jesus Christ, have done more for this world than almost any other one thing that has ever been wrought in it. The man that follows the crowd isn't worth the snap of your finger. The man that cannot decide, and is carried withersoever outside forces direct, is no better than a piece of pewter that you can twist around your fingers. The man of individual thought and individual purpose is like Bessemer steel — one of the grandest inventions, by the way, of the nineteenth century. I can put Bessemer steel into a relationship by which it will spring back and forth a million times and then be ready for another million, and then for another million. The man that is thoroughly individualized and is conscious of his individuality is immovably centered, and one can say, like David, "My heart is fixed, O God, my heart is fixed."

Individualism is concentration. The mind is like light, air, water: diffused, it is powerless; concentered, it is almost omnipotent. If I could concentrate all the rays of the sun, I could burn this world to a crisp in five minutes. If I could compress the air, I could blast the Andes and the Rockies in one second so that you could hardly find a fragment. If I could gather the steam that rises insensibly from off the vast waters and apply it, I could drive all the machinery of this earth that goes on land or on water multiplied by the thousand. So with the mind or spirit: if it shall centre itself in Christ, if it shall sharpen and bring its thoughts and influences and sympathies to bear on a given line to a given work, there is nothing that it shall not be able to do. The great apostle has said, "I can do all things through Christ which strengtheneth me."

I do not forget that my theme is *individual consecration.* Consecration is a human word; sanctification is a divine word. Consecration belongs to us; it befits us in all the moods and tenses of our active and passive lives. It is that word that relates the human to the Divine. The idea of consecration is that there is a recognized difference between God and mammon, between right and wrong; and a man, in consecrating himself, offers himself for the right and for God. Every service, every right thought; every pure motive, every inspiration of soul, is the product of a conscious voluntary consecration. It may be done quickly; it matters not. It is there, and it cannot be otherwise than there. Consecration is simply yielding to God, hearing his call, following his leadership, and stepping out into full relationship with him. Oh, how full the Old Testament is of consecration! We sometimes think that consecration is a New Testament word. Not at all. Every time that God appeared in the old world it was to make a new consecration. I will give you an instance: " Moses, take thy shoes from off thy feet; for the ground whereon thou standest is holy." And this was a call to Moses, and to Israel, and to the world. Every time that God appears to you, it is for a purpose, and that purpose is consecration and concentration. It is nothing else; and the very moment that you renew your consecration, then will come your new mission. Not all of it, nor yet all of it at once, for God is an economist. He never wastes words on a man. He never avalanches grace on a soul. He will never give a second blessing until you have used your first, and used it all and well. God never puts a storage battery into a man's soul and supplies him with grace for the next half decade. Not at all. He will give you blessings according to your need, and no further. So is the sword of the Spirit; the sword of the Spirit is that, and that only to you which you can handle. It is not your Bible. The fact that I have a Bible in my house is nothing; but the very fact that I turn something of it into my brain and spirit and can use it, — that is the length and sharpness of my sword, no longer, no sharper. Some people have no sword at all, nothing but a handle; therefore are they worsted in every encounter.

The New Testament is full of this idea of consecration. The Lord Jesus Christ came into this world on a consecrated mission. At twelve years of age he recognized his mission. Later on he yielded to it, and all through his life, as he said, " I sanctify myself." Consecrated hearts and consecrated brains are God's chosen instruments. God always prefers to work through the best instrumentalities. He is of necessity compelled to use many dull instruments, because he has used us; but God loves to use clean and sharp instruments. Yonder is a carpenter. When he gets hold of a nice tool that is clean and sharp, and in perfect order, it is a luxury for him to do his work. It is a luxury for God to use a consecrated man or woman. Oh, how God wants all the members of the Christian Endeavor organization to be consecrated young men and young women! God could revolutionize this world morally and spiritually in this generation, if every one of us would step to the front and say with emphasis, " Here am I; use me."

Now, if we turn very slowly the pages of history, we shall find those pages packed with illustrations of the thought I am giving you tonight. The great thoughts that have swayed the ages and lifted them to loftier heights were, without a single exception, born of individual brains and individual hearts. You know that every invention, every discovery, that is of any great value to the race, God has whispered only to his believing ones. God never whispered his secrets to an atheist or an infidel or a doubter. Go back into the world of discovery and invention; the men who have invented and discovered and unfolded and brought out great things for the progress of the race have been men that believed. God uses believers. No army delivered the Hebrew nation from Egyptian slavery ; one called and consecrated man did it — Moses. No senate raised Israel to a first-class national power, but one single consecrated young man did it — David. No school of divines translated the Bible and gave it to us in its English wording, but one consecrated man did it — John Wycliffe. No royal court discovered America; one earnest, believing, consecrated man did it — Columbus. No parliament saved England from abuse of royal authority, but one earnest man, crystallizing in himself the convictions and plans and thoughts of his age, did it—Oliver Cromwell. No confederacy rescued Scotland from the grip of the throne that was perverting her; but one consecrated man did it—John Knox. History is packed with such illustrations. Life never means anything to any boy or girl until they are consecrated to God. No one of us ever fills the niche that we are divinely called to fill except through this personal consecration.

.The mightiest thought that comes to us from all sides is that of work. God is the greatest of workers. He is not an infinite quiescence. He is the most active being in the universe of thought or being. Man, true to himself and true to his divine Maker, must be active. When God made Adam and put him in Eden, he gave him something to do in his primitive condition: "Go, dress the vineyard and take care of it." The work law is universal for every man. No man is excusable. There are no passes over this royal road. There are no favorites, no exceptions. "To every man his work." When Christ came into the world he said, "I must work." "Ah, but," you say, "I am not a church member." It doesn't make any difference whether you are a church member or not; "Go work in my vineyard" is God's order to you, and you have got to do it, or suffer the eternal results. "But I am not a Christian," you say. It doesn't make any difference whether you are a Christian or not; "Go work in my vineyard" is the divine order, "But I am perplexed about my creed." It doesn't make any difference. If you are perplexed over a creed, you have given predominance to your reason and not to your faith.

There is nothing that will cure doubt so quickly as a little activity. There is nothing that will cure dyspepsia like a good handsaw and half a cord of wood. This work law is individual — not some work, not a work (that doubtless is true), but *my* work. Every man's personal work is a part of the divine plan. What, do you say that I am tinctured with predestinarianism? I don't know what that big word means. I have just to say to you that facts are stubborn things; they confront us wherever we go, the world over. Gather up the whole history of the race: the males and females born into this world are almost exactly alike. Is that an accident? Not at all. I do not live in a world of accidents. Yonder is a man born with a musician's talent; there is a poet; there is an orator; there is a mechanic; there is a farmer. So it is; God mixes men's brains and God gives men talent and women talent, and he never makes any two people alike and no two people can be alike. Among the grasses or tr es, or these beautiful flowers and ferns, no two are alike. God has put great variety, and yet unity, in this world. Every man fills his own niche: I cannot fill yours, you cannot fill mine. Mr. Baer could have telegraphed to four hundred men in the Society of Christian Endeavor who might have made a better speech to-night than it lies in my power to make; but there is no man in all God's universe who could make my speech or do my work. You are called to do a work in the world; no one else can do it. Therefore you are doing yourself the highest injustice when you excuse yourself from service, from prayer, from visiting, from working in the Sunday school, from developing any department of your church work. You are doing yourself a great injury. I did not order the time of my birth into this age; I did not order that I should be born of Christian parentage; I did not order that I should be rocked in a Christian cradle. God ordered all these things for me; and when I came into the world I found a loving father and mother and a Christian cradle and a Christian lullaby, and as I grew up I found the Sunday school ready for me and the church ready for me, and the schools ready for me, and society ready for me, — everything. God furnishes these things. Now it is my business to step in and work as a loyal, obedient child, if I am to win his approval at his right hand, — my crown, the everlasting glory that God proposes to give the obedient and that I shall sigh for if I have it not.

Hence God says, "Behold, I set before you an open door" — *the open door of opportunity*. Did you ever turn to your Webster to see what the word "opportunity" means? You have heard it from preachers, from parents, from teachers, from moralizers on all sides until it may be that your ear is pained with the repetition of the word. *Ob* and *porto* — you Latinists have caught it already — "before the port." Yonder, outside of the harbor, is a richly laden vessel, with choice cargo, waiting the permit to come in and trade. Outside of every one of us are untold opportunities — riches in character, mental, moral and spiritual — which you and I have only to go out and take hold of and forthwith we shall begin to trade and grow. It does seem to me that God was never so anxious to make the people of this country rich and great and good and wise and powerful as he is to-day. Everywhere the doors are wide open; everywhere around us the fields are white to the harvest; everywhere are beckoning hands from Macedonian Kingdoms, calling us to come over and help them. The boys and the girls that are growing up hungry of mind and heart, without God and without his grace, are appealing to us — oh, what appeals little boys and little girls make! And we parents and teachers are so dull and so selfish that we do not heed their appeals, and they go hungry because we do not feed them; they turn away and feed on the husks of the world, and are dissatisfied.

Pardon me — the church of God is a great stumbling-block to boys and girls today, because we do not understand the boy nature and the girl nature, and reach out and get hold of them while they are young. I am so thankful that at nearly every communion service I receive boys and girls into my church, seven, eight, nine, and ten years of age. I am coming to understand, as a great many other Christian people are, that we can get a larger number and a better class of Christians through child-culture, than we can by the old lasso method. You understand me. I mean this: here are boys and girls from sixteen to twenty years old — wild, out on the prairies of life — all about us. We jump on our ecclesiastical steeds and go out and try to get these sharp, keen young men and women into our fold. And they beat us — they beat me as a clergyman, and I cannot get them. I don't know how it may be with you pastors, but I have turned away from any attempt to win a man over twenty-five years of age, except by all manner of kindness, and I turn my energies into my Sunday school. The primary department in our Sunday schools is the most important department in the entire church of God. We are gathering four-fifths of our membership out of the Sunday school. The Sunday school is the permanent revival field of the church of God today, and if I had a thousand increments of power, I would turn nine hundred and ninety-nine of them into my Sunday school. There is the hope of the church. I don't preach to a great many unconverted people, but I know that in my Sunday school, nearly one-half, from the primary department up, are unsaved. There is my field. I am in my Sunday school. It is our biggest field of opportunity for Christ.

Do you think I am off my subject? Not at all. Consecration — toil, service, sacrifice — reaching out for the people! Here is a white field and its doors are wide open. Do not wait to be organized. Go out and pick up your boys and girls and bring them in. They are out in the highways and by the hedges.

Oh, that the Christian Endeavor organization were wise! I sometimes think, brothers and sisters, that God has called our Dr. Clark just as surely to create this organization as he ever called any man in this world to do any special work. Do you know that our Sunday schools, including pupils from the age of twelve up to twenty-five, have been losing fifty percent for the past twenty-five and thirty years? That is the average loss to the churches today out of the Sunday school, — one-half, from twelve to twenty-five years, for causes which I will not stop to discuss. Now, here is where the Christian Endeavor Society comes in with its Junior work, drawing in the boys and girls, leading them into the associate department and then graduating them from that into the department of activity; and by the blessing of God, we shall save, at least, twenty-five of that fifty percent.

Opportunity! Did you ever read the first chapter of Joshua? Do you remember that God says to Joshua, "Every place that the soul of your foot shall tread upon, that I will give you," — no more, no less. And then God proceeds with great bold outlines to mark out Israel's dominions. Solomon, in his greatest glory, never occupied more than about one-third of that great territory. I wonder if that is true of us here tonight — that you and I are only about one-third of what we ought to be, in morality, in intellectuality, in spirituality, in consecration? Oh, the opportunities for gathering knowledge and rendering service in all departments of our church work are enough to call us into the highest activity!

The burning question of North America today — I do not forget that I stand on Canadian soil — is not the blending of the Union Jack and the Stars and Stripes, or whether the United States shall come up and you annex us, or we shall annex you. The burning question of the North American continent today is the education and elevation of the present generation! We cannot serve the past nor the future. We can only serve the present generation. Ah, but, you say, that is a great undertaking. Look at the factors: God's Christ, God's Spirit, God's Word, God's church, God's people, in their individuality and entirety. A consecrated people; a man, a reed; a saved man, an oak. A consecrated man will echo with Paul, "I can do all things through Christ which strengtheneth me." In our late war, in an important campaign, the general commanding the forces sent a despatch back to General Grant and said to him, "I have lost my connections; how can I make them?" Grant's reply quickly came, "Push to the front!" Oh, there are people in the church who have lost their connection with the Divine Spirit! I say to you here, before God, "Push to the front, and you shall make them; you shall break your way through to a larger and a better life!" With our blessings and opportunities and emoluments, we ought to live better lives than our mothers and fathers did. We ought to share a Pentecost. Pentecosts are expensive things. It is so much easier to get a revivalist and pass in our check. But a Pentecost takes days of united church pleading — business suspended, visits adjourned, the last book unread, the last magazine untouched; days of prayer and meditation and consecration. Then you have a Pentecost in which souls are born. But Pentecosts are such costly things, we rarely have them because we can't afford to.

The future is overworked. There are thousands of young men and women who are going to do something by and by, later on, farther out. Alfred De Vigney, that great French poet who died a few years ago, wrote poetry that charmed the nation. He once said to his intimate friends, "I am going to write the great poem of my life. I think I have gathered material enough, and it will be one of the greatest epics of the world's history." His friends urged him to begin at once. He said, "I will begin it tomorrow." Tomorrows came and passed into todays and yesterdays. They urged him to begin. "Tomorrow," he said, "I will begin." Two or three years ago he died in the city of Paris with his great poem unfinished. And some of us are going to do something for God, and we are twenty, twenty-five, thirty, thirty-five years of age, and yet we are all the while "going to do." I like that dear old man's religion who said that he spelled it with four letters: "d-o-n-e." When a duty comes to you, do it, and it is done. There are so many who are going to do their duty. That is not Christianity. Christianity is obedience — at the very moment. Do you know that opportunities never circle like hawks, but fly straight-winged, from eternity to eternity. They fly right by you; and if you are quick, alert, thoughtful, consecrated, you will grasp them and turn them into character, into power, and so out into deeds to make the world blessed. So many let the opportunity go by, and sigh and sigh for it to come back! It never will.

A few years ago I saw a man in the Louvre who taught me a lesson. I had been in the day before and had marked a dozen royal paintings that I wanted to study. I came in very early, as soon as the gallery was open, and there before me, in the middle of the large room, over against one of the paintings that I had marked in my thought and in my catalogue, stood a man with his easel and his brush hard at work copying that painting. I went up to him; he did not observe me at all. I went around him; he did not lift his eye. Others passed and repassed; he did not notice them at all. I said to one of the guards, "Who is that man?" "He is a painter," was the reply. "I see that," I said, "but who is he?" "He is the foremost painter of Italy. He has been commissioned by the pope to come here, and the French government has given him permission to copy that picture." It was small, only four inches wide by perhaps six or seven inches long, but it was a great painting. There was before me Italy's present greatest painter, commissioned by the pope of Rome to paint one of the finest paintings that hung in the Louvre gallery, by the permission of the French government, and he did n't care anything for me or for the other visitors. He was absorbed; he had only one thought: To copy that picture on his canvas and make it live. I watched him, and I received the biggest lesson that the Louvre could give me. This I thought, That man is consecrated; that man is absorbed; he has but one thing on hand. I ought to be like that man. God has planted me in a vineyard. I was born in a Christian land; I have been reared under Christian influences, and I ask myself oftentimes, "What have I done? What am I doing? Am I altogether consecrated to God?" I tell you, my brethren, that that day I went out of the Louvre a thoughtful man. That incident has never gone from me. I see that man painting, with no eye for visitors or anything around him—one work!

Do not sigh for opportunities. They are right at your hand; they are in every hour and event that come to you. Listen! "Moses, what have you in your hand?" "Lord, I have only a shepherd's crook that I have carried for twenty years and that I cut on Horeb." "It is enough. Moses, take that shepherd's crook, go down into Egypt, and lead my people forth victoriously." "Shamgar, what have you in your hand?" "I have only an ox-goad with which I am driving my ox team to hasten them up in my plowing, so that I can get the grain in." "Shamgar, go use that ox-goad as I shall bid you:" and he turned it end for end and with that little ox-goad he slew 600 of the Philistines, the enemies of God's people." "David, what have you in your hand?" "Only my little shepherd's sling with which I have practised so many years in flinging stones at a mark." "It is enough. Go use it;" and away he ran, picking up five smooth pebbles out of the brook. Putting one of them into his sling, he flung it, and the giant fell, and forthwith he brought in his head as a trophy. "Dorcas, what have you in your hand?" "I have only a little needle, and with it I am sewing garments for some of these boys and girls in this part of Palestine and keeping them from the cold and helping these poor mothers in their home work." "It is enough. Use it;" and she used it so much that she was a necessity to the early church, and God had to come down in a vision and tell Peter to resurrect that woman from death and give her back to her helpful work for a dozen years. "Francis Ridley Havergal, what have you?" "Lord, I am gifted with a little power of expressing my thought in verse." "Go on. It is enough;" and there is not a hymn book in all America, worth having in our churches, that has not one or more of the beautiful hymns of that royal poetess.

A celebrated pianist once said, "If I neglect my piano for one day, I sense it; for two days, my friends sense it; for three days the audience sense it." Ah, friends, that little time of prayer, when by ourselves we go and kneel down and look up in the face of our divine Lord and catch the enthusiasm of his love and the inspiring of his grace—that is what is vitally needed in our work. Did you ever read Sir Wilkie Collins's "Moonstone"? Do you remember that yonder in India there was an idol that had a very choice gem? By some means this gem was stolen, and when the priests found that it was gone, they said, as they knelt before the idol, "We will go out, and we will search, and we will never rest—and we will never come back—unless we find it." Do you remember how Wilkie Collins goes on with that marvelous story, full of stimulating thought of its kind, and tells how those priests wandered here and there in disguise, suffering poverty and trouble, until by and by, after years and years of search and sacrifice, they found it and bore it back to the idol? Brother, there is a gem that the adversary has stolen away from the diadem of your Redeemer's crown, and who shall go and search for it? O Redeemer, send me.

One of the greatest of chemists, Sir Humphrey Davy, complimented one day upon his great achievements in his department, was asked, "What was the greatest discovery you ever made?" "The greatest discovery I ever made was Michael Faraday." I sometimes think that if we have been toiling for the Master, up yonder there will be surprises for us, and somebody will touch us on the shoulder and say, "I was in your class; I saw your faithfulness in going to church, I heard you testify. I watched your life, and it is through your example that I am here in heaven." Oh, that God would give us the power so to work that we may have many, many surprises in heaven of people who have been won to Jesus through our example!

Let me give you a little incident out of my own life. About a year ago I was going over into a certain portion of my parish, and I saw ahead of me a little fellow who was making the welkin ring with his great cries. I saw, dodging around the corner, a larger boy, and I connected that boy's flight with this boy's crying, and it made one. I came up to him on the sidewalk, and he was yelling unmercifully. "Oh," said I to him, as I threw my arm around his neck, "don't cry any more. Never mind. He has gone away. I saw him go around the corner. He wont touch you." He looked up at me and put his sleeve up and wiped his face. "There," said I, "I wouldn't cry any more." "But he hurt me." "Never mind. Don't feel bad over this thing. If you get an opportunity don't pay him back. No, no, that is n't right." I talked to him just as I would talk to one of my own boys; and when I got to the corner where I had to leave him, I said to him, "God bless you, my boy. Now kneel down when you get home and pray for that boy and ask God to make you a good man. I hope he will make a minister of you." He looked at me with eyes and mouth wide open. "Good-bye," he said, and I left him. The incident passed out of my mind, I had no further thought of what I had done, when, about eight weeks afterward, as I was passing that way again, walking rapidly to see a sick person, I noticed a woman crossing the street diagonally and hurrying toward me. "Is this Mr. Farrar, the pastor of Trinity Methodist church?" she said. "I am," I replied. "Do you remember a few weeks ago talking to a little boy crying on the street?" "Yes, I now remember it; what of it?" "I don't know" — and then the tears began to come — "I don't know what is the matter with my boy. He is a different boy. It used to be hard work for me to get him to pray. Now he goes off ofttimes alone to pray, and he prays, ' O God, bless that man that spoke to me so kindly, and O God, if it please you, make of me a minister.'" Now that little fellow attends a Baptist Sunday school.

You don't know, brother, whom you are touching. You don't understand the relation which you sustain to your fellow-men. By a word, by an act, by a gift, by an example, by something that God has given you, if you will give it back to him and let his touch be on it, you shall lay these thoughts and feelings and sympathies on your fellow-men, and they will result in wondrous blessings. Did you ever hear of the legend of Solomon? Let me give it to you and with it close. There came two bright, beautiful, powerful angels into the presence of King Solomon as he sat on his throne arrayed in his royal robes; and they said to him, "The fame of your wisdom has reached to heaven, and we are come down to see if what is reported be true." Instantly they picked up Solomon and his throne and transported him far out into the desert over by a vast ledge of rocks. There they placed his throne and said, "We propose to give you a specimen of our skill, and you must decide which of us is greatest." One of them drew from a scabbard at his side, hitherto unnoticed, a sword. and. stepping up to this ledge of rock, carved right and left, and in an incredibly short time had carved the form of a man, beautiful, perfect. Solomon instinctively rose from his throne, and was about to pronounce judgment in his favor, but he resumed his seat and waited for the other. The other stepped to the statue and with his finger touched it; and lo! it became a living being. Solomon arose and fell before the face of him who touched the statue, and said, "To you is the meed of praise given." And He who touched the statue was the Angel of the Covenant. Beloved, God has carved out every boy and every girl. It is our mission, as Christian men and women, to be so instinct with divine power that, as we touch these living images, we shall somehow give them the divine anointing. God always works through instrumentalities. God always uses men to save men. God always uses opportunities and circumstances and conditions, with individuals back of them, to touch some others.

You are come to this convention praying that you may be endued with spiritual power. It depends upon you whether you will or not — whether or not you will go back to your society of Christian endeavor in your quiet and orderly village, without any of the excitements of a large city and an enthusiastic convention,'and drop back again into your circle and do your best work, O brother, don't go back the same man that you were. Sister, go not back the same woman that you were. Go back better, stronger, diviner; go back empowered of God! God has brought you here; it is your opportunity. Seize it. Take advantage of every thought, and by every circumstance draw near to the Master; and I pray that on your soul may be shed such a light, into it come such a warmth, around about you be such a girding of divine power, that you shall go back to your Sunday-school class, to your day-school teaching, to your pulpit, to your shop, to your old home, even to your humdrum life, with a new purpose and a new plan, by the grace of God: "I will touch somebody into life, if God will only help me." *He will, if you will!*

THURSDAY MORNING.

Ideal weather was vouchsafed to the convention for its opening day. The delegates (most of them) were early astir, and at half-past six o'clock prayer meetings were held at the five rallying points included in the previous evening's services, — St. James, St. Matthews, Erskine Presbyterian, Douglas Methodist, and American Presbyterian churches. All the meetings were largely attended and proved helpful.

DRILL HALL.

The hour for the opening session was fixed at 9.45 o'clock, but long before that time the delegates began assembling at the hall. Generous applause greeted the several state delegations as they came marching in with their state or local banners. The California delegates were especially welcomed, as they made known their purpose thus early to capture the convention for 1895. When the hall was about half full, somebody started the hymn, "At the Cross." It was taken up at once with full volume. Director Lindsay and cornetist Burleigh mounted the platform and joined in, and the old-time convention enthusiasm was immediately apparent. Hymn followed hymn, the Park Sisters of New York, two young lady cornetists, joining their forces to those already on the platform. It was grandly inspiring.

At ten o'clock the great hall was nearly full, and for the opening hymn "Coronation" was sung, the audience rising. Pres. F. E. Clark, whose appearance upon the platform had been greeted with warm applause, then asked that the first spoken words of the convention might be the words of Scripture and gave out the twenty-third Psalm, all joining in the recitation. Rev. Fred C. Klein, of the Methodist Protestant Mission of Japan, then invoked the divine blessing.

At the conclusion of the prayer, Director Lindsay started the hymn, "Blest be the Tie that Binds," the audience joining fervently.

The organization of the convention was then effected. Rev. H. W.

Gleason, of Minneapolis, was appointed scribe, and the president was empowered to nominate the necessary committees.

The hymn "What a Wonderful Saviour" was then sung, after which Dr. Clark introduced the first speaker of the morning, as follows: —

DR. CLARK: My friends, you know that we have never desired any other motto than that which was chosen so many years ago at the beginning of the Christian Endeavor movement, "For Christ and the Church." It expresses our belief and our aspiration. It is altogether fitting that the one who should speak to us first this morning, to welcome us from all parts of the world, should be the representative of the churches of Montreal. I am very glad that the one who speaks is such a thoroughly earnest Christian Endeavorer, to whom we are indebted in so many ways for work that has been done here in Montreal. The Rev. J. MacGillivray will bring the greetings of the city pastors. [*Loud applause.*]

Address of Rev. J. MacGillivray.

Welcome to Canada, Dr. Clark!

Fellow Endeavorers: — I deemed it fitting to give President Clark a good old-fashioned hand-shake welcome to his native land. [*Applause.*] He has been touring, as you know, round the world, but like a true patriot he at last comes back to Canada, the land of his birth. It was like him, too, that the first time he brought his great family away from home it was to show them his native province. Well, we are right glad to have you all.

And, to be frank with you, we are glad you did not come last year; because you are a better band of Endeavorers this year. [*Laughter.*] Don't misunderstand me; I mean you are older, and to Christian Endeavorers that always means one year better, one year's growth in grace, one year's added spiritual power. We wanted you, therefore, and we were bound to have you this year, although stupendous difficulties faced the brave Committee of '93. Yes, I say brave, for few of us know their plucky, herculean labor that cleared the way for this great convention. [*Loud applause.*]

If extreme measures had to be adopted, we knew we could accommodate the great bulk of you denominationally. For example, we could camp the Congregationalists on our royal mount [*applause*], where they could have absolute independence [*laughter*]; the Baptists we could "boat" on the mighty St. Lawrence [*laughter*]; the Presbyterians, we feel sure our brethren of the Roman Catholic faith would house in their many fine churches, where they could gladly give them all the "confession" they might desire [*laughter*]; and the Methodists — well, we could let them run about in the city and start a revival meeting wherever they liked. [*Applause.*]

But we are glad such a system of separation was unnecessary. We want to think of you and to see you as one united host.

We were greatly assisted in welcoming you. Citizens of every race and creed were eager to have you come. Our grand old river never ran clearer and swifter, and did you observe how, as you floated on his great bosom and neared our city, he became more eager to welcome you, and shot you, as it were, the more rapidly into the arms of our hospitality? [*Applause.*] Nature lent her kindly hand, and decked out our royal city in her queenliest robes. Every July leaf that quivers on Mount Royal whispers welcome to the young summer hearts before me. Why, our very stones (and we have a goodly number of them) would cry out, did we not join nature's choir and sing the hosannas of your welcome.

Again, our past civic history — two hundred and fifty years of it — spurred us on to maintain the renown of our past hospitality. Every race that peopled this island was famed for the cordiality of their good cheer,— the Indian, the French, the British. We are told that when Jacques Cartier, the discoverer of Canada, landed not far from this very spot, he visited the Indian village of Hochelaga, where he and his men were most cordially entertained, and on his departure it is gravely reported that the squaws kissed them all good-bye.

Whether we can come up to this high degree of hospitality [*laughter*] it is not for me to say, as it would not be fair to bind my brother pastors' wives to entertain you in this unique and delicate fashion; but in any case I can assure you that they have already greeted you all with the "holy kiss" of fellowship and cordial welcome. [*Applause.*]

I wish that the pastors' words of greeting could reach you all, but if our words reach not your ears, your every eye can reach this cap [Reception Committee cap.] Well, if you do not see the sign of this practical character of our welcome on the head of every brother pastor, it is because he is engaged in other forms of active labor. For this is only one form, and a small type, of the earnest, practical, work-a-day welcome the pastors of this city give you. The truth is, that while we in Canada are quite ready to mount up on wings as the eagles, we believe in a whole-souled annexation in Christian Endeavor between the eagles and the beavers [*applause*], uniting the uplifting, soaring qualities of the one with the plodding persistency of the other. Or, if annexation is not possible, then let us all be eagles at convention seasons, and all be beavers when we go back to our several spheres of labor. [*Loud applause.*]

But permit me to mention another fact to be united with this practical one as the best evidence we can give of the sincerity of our welcome. It is this: While our Ministers of State are fighting over slippery questions of international law, the ministers of this city have settled all denominational questions by uniting in an upper room for weeks in earnest, united prayer for an outpouring of God's spirit. [*Applause.*] We are, therefore, as pastors, in the happy position of being able to extend to you a banner welcome shot through and through with the golden threads of work and prayer.

This is the Twelfth International Convention. You come to our midst in your twelfth year. We especially welcome you because you come to us in the spirit of the boy Jesus. He is in your midst; in your person. He in his twelfth year has come up to this Jerusalem, and we, the pastors, like the doctors of the temple, are only too glad to sit at your feet, and listen to your fresh thoughts and eager questions. We need you much. We need the stimulation of your fresh enthusiasm. We would feel the buoyancy of your hopes. We want to keep step with your vigor and zeal. We would look on the world now and again with your open, clear eyes, and catch a full breath of the fresh morning air in which you live. Stay with us a week, stay longer if you will, and we will be your disciples, and will gladly take a post-graduate course in your class-room. For in the routine of our work as pastors we are apt to get into ruts, and we feel you can lift us out of them. We are apt to think that only eyes of age and experience can see how the world is to be saved, but you persuade us that the "first open look of young eyes on the condition of the world is one of the principal regenerative forces of humanity."

We love you for this spirit, and we welcome you in our midst; but let me add that we love you the more, we welcome you the more, because, like your Master, the boy Jesus, after quickening our spirits you go back to your several homes and are subject to your parents in the Faith — your pastors and local church officers of your several congregations. [*Applause.*] No higher testimony of your loyalty to your own church and pastor can be given than this, and you are worthy to receive it. The spirit of your Lord is proof against your being spoiled by conventions, or being carried away by one enthusiasm. The opposite is the truth.

Your wider fellowship with God's people, the sweet oneness of your spirits here, send you back home broader in heart, clearer in faith, and consequently a mightier spiritual factor in your own church. You are not of those who boast of belonging to a church that has "not the tiniest creedlet," but of those who have convictions, dogmas, or creeds — call them what we may — that buttress faith and duty. Yet I believe I speak the mind of my brother pastors when I declare that we welcome you most of all because of the Christly spirit you exhibit in fellowship, in unity, in love. You show us pastors the limbus into which to throw non-essentials in faith and doctrine. You present to us a telling object lesson of how to live in the spirit of our Lord's prayer for unity. It is high time we should catch your spirit, especially in view of the whole heathen world massed and in easy approach of our Gospel artillery. It is thrillingly inspiring to look into your faces, to confer with you, and to know that you are one in Christ Jesus, redeemed by the same Lord, thrilled by the same spirit.

Just one word more. You delegates who have come from afar, from Europe, Australia, from China, India, and the isles of the sea, we would give you a special welcome. We would not leave you in the suburbs of our hospitality — we would take you to our hearts. We would regard you as the Benjamin of Father Clark's family, the youngest and well-beloved member, and are prepared to give you the finest silver of our welcome, five changes of raiment, and a mess of fish larger than for the rest. We admire the youthful zeal that bridged sea land. We know, too, you are the Aarons and the Hurs, that held up the hands of your pastor. We remember that among you are the Joshuas who fight in the misty valleys of heathenism — the missionaries of the cross. May your stay in our midst make your hands stronger, and send you back home inspired to fight and conquer on many a battle-field of Rephidim. [*Applause.*]

I have been deeply, undeservedly honored, in giving this greeting in behalf of my brother pastors — as true-hearted, whole-hearted a band of pastors as can be found in any city, unflinchingly loyal to truth, alert to read the signs of the times, wise to encourage and guide every spiritual movement, and sympathetic and confidential with young Christian hearts. In behalf of such pastors it is a delight to say once more, Welcome, President Clark, and welcome, every one. [*Prolonged applause.*]

The convention then joined in singing "This Blest Endeavor Band." During the preceding address it was noticed that a fine-looking gentleman, wearing a heavy gold chain about his shoulders, came and took his seat upon the platform. Dr. Clark introduced him to the audience as follows : —

DR. CLARK : One sight I have seen in all lands during the past year. Most of the countries which we visited varied in their characteristics and in their mode of welcome, but almost everywhere we saw two flags blended. We saw them in Australia, in Japan, in India, in Turkey, over and over again in Great Britain, — the two flags which are most prominent in this room, the Union Jack and the Stars and Stripes. [*Cheers and loud applause.*] It is most appropriate that we should have, at this time, a word from the highest civic authority of Montreal. We, as Christian Endeavers, are good citizens because we are Christians. We must be good citizens, if we live up to our profession ; and I am glad that this morning the Mayor of Montreal will extend the greetings of the city to us. [*Enthusiastic applause.*]

As the mayor stepped to the front of the platform, he was greeted with an ovation such as even a Christian Endeavor convention seldom witnesses. When the enthusiasm had subsided, he spoke as follows : —

Address of Mayor Desjardins.

Ladies and Gentlemen : — I do not know really whether I am to welcome you or to receive a welcome, such has been the kindness of your reception. I do not know whether my first expression should be an expression of thanks for your kindness, or an expression of the cordial and sincere welcome with which the population of Montreal receive you amongst them today. [*Applause.*] When I say the population, I do not make any exception ; the whole population is greeting you today.

And there is a fact which will come from this convention, a fact which will speak very highly for the Christian spirit with which on this continent we may agree to disagree. [*Applause.*] Every one of you knows that I am a Roman

Catholic, yet I am here to tell you that while the population of Montreal is in great measure a Roman Catholic population, still there are none who will extend to you a more cordial welcome than the whole population of Montreal, irrespective of creed or nationality. [*Loud Applause*]

I think, after all, ladies and gentlemen, that we can find ground wide enough upon which we can walk together. You come here and you teach us what is Christian charity and what union can do. Well, we think we believe in that ourselves. There is a fact which I think must have struck you forcibly since you arrived here — a fact in which we take great pride — and that is this: we have not yet allowed the chimneys of our manufactories to go above the spires of our churches. [*Applause.*] We believe in industry and progress and commerce; but we do not believe, as you do not, — and in that respect we are in accord with you, — that the whole goal of life is industry or commerce, or merely the physical well-being of humanity. When you look at the top of one of our chimneys, you will see a cloud which prevents you from seeing above, but when you look at the spire of a church, that gentle finger pointing toward heaven, you feel, as we do, that we have something more — that we have another destiny which Providence has prepared for us. So amongst Christians there is now a great feeling that the old strifes must be laid aside, and that other occupations must engage our minds. The great battle now is not between creed and creed, but between believers and those who do not believe [*prolonged applause*], between those who go to church and worship their God, and those who have made the earth the ultimate end of their ruling ambition. I think this great convention is to show that on this continent, where progress, where science, where activity and pushing enterprise have shown themselves developed to the utmost degree, we can find men and women by thousands and by hundreds of thousands believing that they must not rest the whole of their ambition on things worldly, but that they must look above and beyond.

Well, ladies and gentlemen, in that, and in the expression of opinion that I am just uttering, you will find the reason why the population of Montreal is so happy to greet you and to welcome you amongst them. We feel that the days that you will pass amongst us will not be useless days, but that a strong and permanent impression will remain which will reach the minds of our own young people, and tell them what they must do, if they want to follow the good example that you have come to set them.

I will not detain you any longer. You know that, for the time being, I have the honor to be the first magistrate of Montreal. As such, when I heard that a great army was going to invade Montreal, I felt a little uneasy [*laughter*] — an invasion by so many thousands. I was trying to remember some historical facts which would give me an instance of that kind. Would it be an invasion of the Romans, or a meeting of the Romans and the Sabines, or would it be something else? But when I saw the army and the gentle way in which it was managed, composed of so many young ladies and so large a number of gentlemen, I felt greatly reassured on that point, although I am not so sure now about that annexation question which was brought up here. [*Laughter and applause.*] You see, we have always been endeavoring to fight against political annexation; but there is another kind of annexation, and speaking for myself, I have felt that we have always been very weak in that line. That annexation in detail has been going on between the two countries pretty freely, to the great advantage of those who were led in that way and to the benefit of the two countries which have gained by that social intercourse those friendly feelings which will stand always above any political question, and which will, I am sure, for a long time prevent any serious difficulty between us, and will make of these two peoples, not two distant or foreign peoples, but two populations whose traditions, whose aspirations, and whose Christian feelings are the same.

Ladies and gentlemen, I thank you for your kind attention. I wish that not only your attendance at the hall, but your visit in Montreal may be as happy, as charming, as attractive as it can be, so that when you return home, and when in the course of years you think of certain villages and cities, a good remembrance will be kept of Montreal. [*Enthusiastic applause.*]

VIEW OF MONTREAL FROM MOUNT ROYAL.

Notwithstanding the noticeable French accent of the mayor, his address was well appreciated, and at its close the audience tendered him another " Chautauqua salute," with the waving of thousands of handkerchiefs. Then followed a striking incident. Director Lindsay started the English national anthem, " God save the Queen," the audience joining in with enthusiasm. At the third verse he drew forth an English flag and beat time with it, the audience waving their handkerchiefs in response. Then he immediately started the hymn " America " (the same tune),— " My Country, 't is of thee," — which was sung with magnificent effect. Again at the third verse he drew forth an American flag, and again the audience responded enthusiastically with their handkerchiefs, giving three rousing cheers as they resumed their seats.

Dr. CLARK : It is manifestly impossible to receive delegates from all those societies and organizations from which we would like to hear and who would like to send delegates to us. You can see why : we should have time for nothing else. But at this time of welcome and greeting it is most appropriate that one should bring greeting and welcome from that organization which is the elder brother of the Christian Endeavor Society, the Young Men's Christian Association, and the representative of that association will, in some sense I am sure, speak for young men the world over, — General Secretary Budge, of Montreal. [*Loud applause.*]

Address of Secretary Budge.

Mr. Chairman, Ladies and Gentlemen : — On behalf of the Board of Directors of the Young Men's Christian Association of Montreal, and on behalf of the young men who comprise its membership, and, may I not say, on behalf of the Christian young men of this city, I bid you a hearty welcome. It is most appropriate that this, the oldest Young Men's Christian Association on the continent of America, should welcome you, because I understand that your organization was first suggested by the Young Men's Christian Association, and is an application of its methods of work to the needs of the individual churches.

They tell me that your organization is but little more than twelve years old, and yet it has reached a membership on this continent of a million and a half. What an army of hearts God has touched! Think of a million and a half of young people with the power of the Holy Spirit resting upon them. Imagine the result of a million and a half of young people committed to personal effort on behalf of their companions. And what glorious promise have we for the future of God's kingdom, with a million and a half of young people, true to the Church, true to the Word of God, true to the Son of God! May we not expect to see the overthrow, or, at least, the power of those giants broken, which at present threaten the welfare of this fair land? I refer to the giant of *drink* [*applause*], the giant of Sabbath desecration, the giant of immorality, the giant of covetousness, the giant of political corruption. [*Applause.*]

Let me point to two dangers of the present day: the depending upon organizations as a remedy for existing evils; and the dependence upon the power which comes from the enthusiasm of members. The bringing of young people into living union with Jesus Christ and into the fold of the church is a supernatural work and requires supernatural power. Organization, however perfect, or enthusiasm, however absorbing, cannot take the place of the Holy Spirit needed for this work. But what may our eyes see in the next ten years in the ushering in of God's Kingdom, and the hastening of his Son, if the million and a half are daily asking and receiving this supernatural power for effective service? The need of today is to harvest souls, for the fields are white. Aggressive effort is called for by the church today as never before. Personal work on behalf of your fellow is the unoccupied field. The cry still rings out, How can I except some man should guide me ? "

May this convention prepare this mighty army of consecrated young people to push the war into the enemy's land, under the power and direction of the Holy Spirit. May cloven tongues, as of fire, rest upon each member, and may the aggressive work for which this organization stands be begun in this old city, so that thousands of lives may bless God through all eternity for your coming. [*Loud applause.*]

Two verses of "Onward, Christian Soldiers" were then sung, after which Dr. Clark introduced the next speaker as follows : —

DR CLARK : The question was asked in Bible times once, I remember, " What shall be done unto the man whom the king delighteth to honor ? " We are going to ask some such question this morning, but we will not answer it in the same way in which it was answered of old. I will ask you: What shall be done unto the man, the chairman of the Committee of '93, whom this convention delighteth to honor? [*Response: "Hear him."* We will hear him. That is right; and I will introduce to you Mr. A. A. Ayer. As he comes forward, will you not rise and give him the Chautauqua salute ? He deserves it, and so do his companions. [*Applause.*]

The audience rose and greeted Mr. Ayer with a very hearty salute, followed by three cheers for the Committee of '93.

Address of Mr. A. A. Ayer.

Fellow Endeavorers : — With that peculiar joy which belongs to those who have planned and worked, we this day, on behalf of the citizens and the '93 Committee, welcome you to the commercial metropolis of Canada, the city of Montreal. We are so bound to you by kindred ties and feelings that neither political lines nor divisions, nor land nor sea, nor race nor tongue, nor any other created thing can separate us from you. [*Applause.*] "Blest be the tie that binds our hearts in Christian love."

On March 7, 1863, as the Danish princess, with ceremony of state, sailed up the Thames to meet the one she was to wed, Albert, the future king of England, children on the banks of the river sang an ode prepared by Tennyson : —

> "For Saxon, or Dane, or Norman we,
> Teuton, or Celt, or whatever we be,
> We are each all Dane in our welcome of thee,
> Alexandra ! "

So to-day,

> Presbyterian, Baptist, or Methodist we,
> Congregationalist, Anglican, whatever we be,
> We are each all Christian in our welcome to thee,
> Convention of '93. [*Loud applause.*]

The city press and pulpit, both Catholic and Protestant, have expressed their pleasure at your coming. The buildings we now occupy were granted by the Government of the country, and the tenting grounds opposite were granted by the city. The Mayor, the Board of Aldermen, and other civic officers have helped us prepare to give you this welcome. [*Applause.*] The churches of this city are united, as you have heard from their representative; the Christian young men of the city have welcomed you through their much-esteemed secretary; and most heartily does the '93 Committee join with these in expressing our good will, good words, and great joy. From the far and golden Pacific, from the rugged mountain states, from the sunny South, the adjacent East, and the great West of the United States. as well as from the nations across the deep sea, you have come, — and we are all here with one accord in one place. Every British regiment has two flags, one regimental, the other national. The flag of the regiment is less important on grand rallies than the great emblem of national unity. To-day we present our united grand Christian flag, "One in Christ Jesus."

I do not think there are seven happier men in this building than the seven who compose the active chairmen of our '93 Committee. Each has tried to make his department the best, and each has succeeded. [*Laughter.*] So, if there be any success, give these young men the praise, and introduce yourselves to them by name, through the Montreal souvenir number. If you have crossed the Atlantic on the modern monster steamers on a pleasant passage (whatever may be said of stormy times), you have learned that the quickest way to pick out the captain from the other officers is to seek the officer who apparently is doing nothing. [*Laughter.*] I have not been an overworked man. We have had no storms, but make no mistake, we have had plenty of difficulties and hard work. But what are difficulties? To a business man they are only stepping-stones to success [*applause*]; to a Christian, only a call to look for help to him who (as my pastor, Hinson, says) could build across the Red Sea a wall of water, and replace the same much easier than human hand could build and demolish a wall of stones. Our various committees have been enthusiastic, because they loved the work; love made the labor light, and this day is their reward; for one look into your faces, one feeling of the enthusiasm your presence brings, affords us ample recompense for any part we have taken in this great convention. [*Applause.*]

Well — Come. It is " well " that you have "come" [*laughter*] — well, for Christ's sake. It is as true today as in the days when the woman touched the hem of his garment,

> "The multitudes throng thee."

> "What means this eager, anxious throng,
> These wondrous gatherings day by day —
> What means this strange commotion, pray?
> Jesus of Nazareth passeth by."

You expect to hear about him from those who in their souls have seen him, and whose inmost hearts have been communing with him, and so you have come — come for Christ's sake. It is well you have come for this country's sake. You who have come from the South will find a people whose laws, habits, and feelings are akin to your own, and where the differences even in language and customs do not vary more than between south and north, or east and west in your own country. I hope this visit will correct wrong impressions, and reveal to you that there is not so much difference between a Canadian and an American; and that at least, we Christian Endeavorers are one, and whether we live in this far North or in the sunny South, we have a common love for the things that are holy, good, and true, and abominate evil in all its ways.

In my boyhood days, there came into a beautiful Canadian village (a facsimile of so many that nestle among the New England hills) two men from Boston, who had a great desire to see what Canada was like. After dining at the neat little hotel, they came out on the front verandah, and as I was passing asked, "Boy, how far is it from here to Canada?" [*Laughter.*] It took them some time to find out why I was such a stupid boy, and then some time to convince them that they were really across the Canadian border. You have passed that imaginary line, easier found on maps than on the roadside; you have come down the river, or you have crossed the bridge and have hardly perceived it, yet here you are, safe within our city, and in Canada. No doubt we have our peculiarities. We sometimes have snow and ice — as white as silver, and as unstable. [*Laughter and loud applause.*] Have you seen our snow? Did you bring your furs? I once said to a Southerner that Richmond was the hottest place I have ever visited. He replied, "Montreal is the hottest place I have ever been in." I do not know who was right. Have you heard of our fish? Have you heard of our fish stories? We can't match Dr. Henson; we wont try.

For our sake, as individuals, it is well you have come. You are Endeavorers. You live, you think, you act. You are alive. Past generations have had too many Christians akin to the famous father, of whom his son said that he might be a Christian, but he had never seen him working at it.

Some people never find anything to do, so they never do anything (buried talents). Others (they are Endeavorers) seek something. " He who seeks shall find," so they are always doing something (five and ten talents).

You stand for truth and righteousness as taught in the Bible, and you do well. " Be ye doers of the Word, and not hearers only." There is much talk about business morality and good principles. Good principles are not sufficient; spiritual vitality is necessary to keep business life straight. The business morality of the world needs to be put on a higher plane. The world needs to understand that true prosperity consists in something higher than the accumulation of dollars and cents. [*Applause*.] Herein is a field of work for Endeavorers. Some one says the minister must preach it, the church must teach it. True, but the world may neglect the preacher and may neglect the church, but every day the world must and does see the Christian's life. "Ye are living epistles (walking advertisements), known and read of all men." This convention is a great, mighty, pulsating, live epistle, which thousands in this city who never read the Bible will take knowledge of.

We welcome you to our city, therefore, and may you teach this lesson as you walk our streets, and as you stay in our homes, humble though they may be. We welcome you for the enthusiasm this great meeting will create. There is little use in this world for the man who has no interest in his work, but he who has a true interest in that which he is doing will soon generate enthusiasm. Others will know it, will catch the inspiration, and be better in the sphere they occupy. You cannot buy enthusiasm with dollars and cents, and yet it moves the world and makes things go. You have brought enthusiasm with you, you will leave enthusiasm behind you, and yet, you will take with you more enthusiasm than you brought. As iron sharpeneth iron, so doth a man the countenance of his friends, and we are all, if not " Quakers," at least " Friends." Enthusiasm is like the steam in the boiler which must find some escape : when rightly directed, even through one speaker, it will warm many hearts. When properly turned on, it will set many Endeavorers systematically working, and the sound thereof will be pleasant in the ears of the Great Architect and Engineer.

Welcome, thrice welcome, because you oppose evil in all its phases, forms, and forces. The leaders of evil are marshalling their hosts and attempting to rule the world. It is high time that the pastors (the so-called clergy) should not be left alone to cope with those evils. Therefore, we heartily welcome the hosts of Endeavorers, and ask that they be upheld and helped by all good citizens. You know we are called straight-laced and too particular. Men say, " We want none of this restraint, " and " We will not have this Man, Christ, reign over us. " We are not straightened, not restrained, not ruled. Our Lord and Master is love, and we rejoice and love his service. But there are some who do not so walk, and we trust this Christian Endeavor movement will place the line of difference between the true believer and the make-believer so plain, that he who runs may read. The devil's agents are growing bolder. What means the black heading in the Sunday newspaper? " The Sunday was made for Palestine and not Chicago. " [*Loud applause.*] As a business man — as an employer of labor — I protest against all attempts to thus destroy law and order, and to deprive men of their God-given rights. [*Renewed applause.*] I believe in the wisdom of the God who made this earth — this universe — and gave us a place in it. Woe be to the man or people who shall lightly treat his orders. Christian Endeavorers want no Sunday newspaper, — one of the curses of this day [*applause*], — no open places of amusement on Sunday and no turning aside in any direction from the commands of God. These gatherings are worth all they cost, for the enthusiasm generated and the backbone created.

I met a man the other day who said that he was exchanging the boilers in his large manufactory for new ones that would stand 70 pounds of steam pressure to the square inch. I don't know how weak his old boilers were, but as I know of a similar concern that was throwing out boilers that stood 90 pounds pressure, and was putting in new ones that would stand 140 pounds, I rubbed my eyes to make sure that I was living in the year 1893, and not in the days of my boyhood. Who says that Christians have not the moral force today that man had 200 or 300 years ago? Do they mean to tell me that in these days of steam power and electricity, when more and stronger work is needed, and when the genius of man proves itself equal to the advancing yearly needs, — that in moral power and Christian vigor mankind is standing still? Let the men who once thought a convention of 1,000 people a great affair say so. But, fellow-Endeavorers, we do not believe it. There is Christian enthusiasm and backbone sufficient in this building, at this hour, to match all the Christian heroes who lived for a whole generation three centuries ago. [*Applause.*]

I must not forget to give a special welcome to the ladies, the young women who have done so much for this great society, and whose efforts for God and the church the Christian Endeavor movement so heartily appreciates. The world and the church need the devout Marys, the domesticated Marthas, the sewing Dorcases, and the teaching Priscillas, — all Endeavorers, — whose gentle hands and true hearts help much in all phases of life.

When I was scarcely four years of age, I — without permission — went with an older boy across a small river near the old farmhouse. We crossed on a log, small and dangerous. My mother soon missed me, and finding the direction in which I had gone, she hurried down to the river-side just in time to see me coming back, — just in time to see me fall in the river. I caught hold of a branch. My mother ran out on the log — and how the frail woman managed to reach down and take a firm hold of me, I never could understand — but it seems to me that to this very day I hear her voice calling me by name, and saying to me calmly and firmly, "My son, let go." I knew the voice I had learned to obey. I heeded the call, and was soon safe at home.

Fellow-Endeavorers, many a time since our childhood have we wandered away, crossing dangerous places. "Our feet have well-nigh slipped," but our watchful Father rescued us. The marching orders from the Great Captain of Christian Endeavorers are clear and distinct; we do well to take heed thereto, so that when the time comes for us to cross the river to the promised land, we may hear his voice, feel his strong arm, and easily let go of our hold of this world. In that day may each of us be able to say, "I have fought my way through, I have finished the work which thou gavest me to do." [*Loud applause.*]

After singing the hymn "Bringing in the Sheaves," Dr. Clark announced the following committees for the transaction of the business of the convention : —

Committee on Resolutions. — Rev. H. B. Grose, Chicago, Ill.; Mr. C. L· Stevens, Ypsilanti, Mich.; Rev. M. Rhodes, D. D., St. Louis, Mo.; Rev. D. J. Burrell, D. D., N. Y.; Rev. P. S. Henson, D. D., Chicago, Ill.; Rev. F. M. Gardner, East Boston, Mass.

Business Committee. — Secretary, John Willis Baer, Boston, Mass.; Mr. Rolla V. Watt, San Francisco, Cal.; Mr. J. Newman Hall, Belfast, Ireland; Mr. F. E. Curtis, Orlando, Fla.; Rev. J. K. Fowler, D. D., Cedar Rapids, Ia.; Mr. W. H. Chapman, Montreal, Que.; Mr. Chas. F. Mills, Springfield, Ill.

Registration Committee. — Mr. A. R. Grafton, Montreal, Que.; Miss Jeannette Prince, Spencer, Mass.; Mr. William Palmer, Buffalo, N. Y.; Mr. V. Richard Foss, Portland, Maine; Mr. W. H. McClain, St. Louis, Mo.; Rev. George Brown, Montgomery, Ala.; Mr. W. L. Noell, Huntingdon, Tenn.

Committee on Nominations for Convention Vice-Presidents. — Rev. W. O. Carrier, Wausau, Wis.; Mr. W. S. Gillespie, Philadelphia, Pa.: Miss J. Kennedy, Winnipeg, Man., Miss Lucille Twyefort, Paris, France; Rev. Geo. F. Rutledge, Norfolk, Va.; Mr. F. S. French, Ogden, Utah; Mr. Wm. S. Leslie, Toronto, Ont.

During the preceding addresses the great hall was nine-tenths full. Dr. Clark called attention to the fact that this was the largest audience at the opening session of any convention, with possibly the exception of New York.

DR. CLARK: Now, who shall respond to these cordial greetings? That is always a question which comes before the program committee. If that question had been put to this audience of Christian Endeavorers from all over the country, I think we should have had an answer. Of course it was impossible to put the question, but I know how you would have answered it. Multitudes of you would have said, "Dr. Henson, Dr. Henson!" [*Applause.*] Well, your unspoken wish has been gratified, and Dr. Henson is to respond, on behalf of the trustees of the United Society of Christian Endeavor, and the delegates present, to these cordial greetings. [*Loud applause.*]

Response to Addresses of Welcome.

By Rev. P. S. Henson, D.D.

Mr. President, Brethren and Friends, Citizens of Montreal: — It is with exceeding embarrassment that I undertake the office that has been assigned me. And well may I feel it as I look about me at the many high dignitaries of church and state, and confronting only just now your magnificent mayor — and I notice, with the discretion that becomes him, that the "prudent man, forseeing the evil, hath hid himself" [*laughter, the mayor had just retired*] — would that you could lend him to us in Chicago for just four months! [*tremendous applause*], I have been profoundly impressed by the presence of so many men of continental and cosmopolitan reputation; and surveying this vast assembly, the like of which has seldom been gathered under one roof, I have felt very much like a colored brother who came to my church some years ago for a collection. We gave him a collection; it was generous. It was emptied upon the table in the prayer-meeting room. He surveyed it with eyes glistening with tears. His heart was evidently full. I thought it would be a relief to have him express himself, and so I asked him to offer the closing prayer. He began by saying, "O Lord, have mercy on thy poor unworthy colored servant and teach him how to behave himself, for he never was in such good company before." [*Laughter*]. I can sympathize with him. [*Laughter and applause.*]

In common with my fellow-laborers, I have listened with exceeding satisfaction to the right royal welcome — and I may use those words appropriately, for we are now in her majesty's dominions — which has been given us. I would that I could make fitting response. And yet there seems to be a sort of incongruity — an anachronism, if I may venture to say so — in the selection by this army of youthful Christian Endeavorers of a gray-beard to be their spokesman. I am sure the selection has not been made on account of any supposed superior ability of the present trespasser upon your patience. I suspect the choice has been made from two other good and sufficient reasons. And first of all, this : One of the distinguishing characteristics of Christian Endeavor, and Christian Endeavorers, the wide world over, is their determination to do deference to their seniors. [*Applause.*] And this is extraordinary in the proud, pretentious, conceited, iconoclastic age to which we belong; for in the chariot of modern progress, at least on the other side of the line, the older folks occupy a back seat while Young America sits on the box and holds the reins and cracks the whip, and his driving is like that of Jehu, the son of Nimshi. But Christian Endeavorers do honor to age, and so do honor to themselves. Another reason, I suspect, was in the minds of those who made this choice : they had found the fountain of pepetual youth. They believe that those who are fired with the enthusiasm of Christian Endeavor will never grow old, though they live a thousand years. [*Applause.*] They believe that their youth will be renewed like the eagle's, that they will still bring forth fruit in old age and be fat and flourishing ; and therefore they have selected the most magnificent specimens of the blessed old boys in all the country and put them on the platform [*laughter*], and have put forward the best preserved — not to say the handsomest — of them all to be their spokesman. [*Laughter.*] I am proud and happy to be their orator,— at least I should be proud and happy, if I was not so scared! [*Laughter.*] Proud any man might well be.

You may remember that Daniel Webster,— a name that is a household word wherever the English tongue is spoken, — in a magnificent burst of patriotic fervor said a long time ago, "The day will come when the proudest exclamation of man will be, 'I am an American.'" I do not expect our cousins across the sea or our brothers here across the St. Lawrence and the lakes will quite be disposed to echo that sentiment. I do not believe, indeed, that that time will ever come. I do believe, however, that the time will come, yea, has come already, when the proudest exclamation of man will be and is, "Thank God, I am a Christian." [*Loud applause.*] And I take it that the highest style of Christian is a loyal Christian Endeavorer. They say that "a touch of nature makes the whole world kin;" yea, rather and better, a touch of grace makes the whole world kin. [*Applause.*] The water separates us, at least most of the way along the border; but blood is thicker than water, and we are bound together by the blood of the Lamb. [*Applause.*] Two flags, many flags, and yet one flag the world over for Christian Endeavorers. Father Clark has just been around the world. He is a sort of "*avant courier.*" There is a bond that binds the whole race, in so far as it hath been touched by grace. When we were boys, in the lecture-room or in the laboratory, we used to join hands and form a circle, and those who came at the ends of the circle touched each a Leyden jar charged with subtle electric fluid, and instantly there was a flash and a thrill that passed through all that circling group. Christian Endeavorers around the whole world join hands, and then as they approach, they touch the cross of Calvary and there is the thrill of a common love, the touch of a common life, that all feel at once. "Blest be the tie that binds."

Yonder, on the shores of Lake Michigan, is a city that has risen like some marvelous phantom out of the bog, — a "White City," the astonishment of the world. There is a great exhibition in Chicago today. But, friends, there is a more magnificent exhibition here on the banks of the St. Lawrence [*applause*], a sublimer spectacle for men and angels. I have sometimes thought, since the smirching of that "White City" by the perfidy of local directors, that the angels do not care much about it, except the fallen ones. But I suspect that all the angels of God hover with delighted interest over this magnificent concourse of Christian people whose hearts all beat as one. "*Quam fluctus diversi, quam mare conjuncti*" — that is about all the Latin I can remember, and I thought this would be a good occasion to get it off. [*Laughter.*]

We have gathered as a Young People's Society of Christian Endeavor. I beg you to consider the meaning of these words. First of all, it is a *society.* The Lord meant that we should live in society. I beg you to notice that heaven is not a prairie; it is a city, and that means compacted and consolidated society. It means the closest contact of high and holy intelligence. God saw that it was not good for man to be alone. God meant that we should live together and work together, that we should be banded together for the highest and noblest purpose. The very birds go in flocks, the cattle in droves. the fishes in schools. The very flowers bloom in beautiful array and the raindrops come down in companies, and blend and glow on the bright pavilion before the sun. The very stars are gathered in constellations. God meant that we should be banded together in society. This is a society, the noblest that ever was organized. Just as soon as the disciples became disciples, they came together; being let loose, they went to their own company, like homing pigeons. I do not believe you can keep a true Christian man or woman outside the pale of a Christian society [*applause*], and I do not believe, when this life is over, that it will be necessary for the angels to come and carry a real Christian to the paradise of God. I think it is likely they will come because they want to, because they enjoy that sort of service, but it is not necessary that they should come. Here is a swaying balloon, struggling to be free. One cord after another is cut, and when the last is severed, upward it springs to its native element and vanishes out of sight. A Christian has something in him that lifts him, something that struggles to be free. " Rise, my soul," — that is the way he sings,— "and stretch thy wings, thy better portion trace." And when the earthly ties are cut, upward he springs by spiritual gravitation toward his native place and the blest society of the church in heaven,—and this Christian Endeavor Society comes the nearest to it of anything I have seen here below.

This is also a *young people's* society. Birds of a feather are bound to flock together. I glory in old saints—those fathers to whom I do deference; but I remember the beloved disciple wrote to the young men because they were strong, " Old men for counsel, young men for war." And, brethren, this is war. I remember how, on the other side of the border, in 1861, when there was the tap of the drum and the shriek of the fife and the unfurling of the flag and the call for men to go to the front, — I remember how the boys jumped over the counters or dropped their pens and followed the flag to the tented field and were transformed into magnificent soldiers. That was in '61. In '81 there was the tap of the drum again, there was the call for volunteers. " Father Endeavor" Clark summoned the hosts of young people from the roller-skating rinks [*applause*] and from all the frivolities and follies on which they were sliding to the very mouth of the pit. The trumpet called, and soldiers sprang up as though they had heard the whistle of Roderic Dhu. It was not the whistle of any mortal man; it was the inspiration of Almighty God, the call of the Divine Spirit to the young people of this land and of all lands, to be marshalled for the mighty conflict that is to shake the world with the last thunders of celestial revolution.

It is a young people's society. What shall we do with our young people? I remember the experience of a boy of mine when we lived in Philadelphia. He was a little fellow, and I got him a hoop and he trundled it on the street. By and by he came back with the fragments of the hoop; the policeman had said it was " Contrary to an ordinance." I got him a velocipede, and he went careering away on the velocipede. By and by he came back with the velocipede in disgrace; the policeman had said, " Contrary to an ordinance." I said, " I tell you what I will do; I will get you a base ball and a bat, and out in some vacant lot you and the boys can have some sport." I sent him forth with joy; he came back with grief [*laughter*], the tears in his eyes, and minus ball and bat. The policeman had said, '' Contrary to the ordinance," and had confiscated the implements and taken them home to his own small boy. [*Laughter.*] My boy struck an attitude. Putting his arms akimbo, the tears rolling down his cheeks, he said, " Papa, what can a boy do? " I said, " My son, let's go to Chicago." [*Laughter.*] Now we do as we like. [*Laughter and applause.*] The question was among our churches, What shall we do with our young people? " What can a boy do? " What can a girl do? Thank God, the Christian Endeavor Society has answered that question. .[*Applause.*] People are beginning to find out, — here in Montreal, last year in New York, in St. Louis, all over the country and all over the world, — what young blood can do when it is enthused and fired with the love of Jesus Christ.

Again, this is a young people's society of *endeavor*. That is very modest, is n't it—beautiful and modest? They do not say, of achievement; they do not boast; it is not a society that professes to have achieved anything; it is a society that endeavors That is all the Lord requires. The great apostle to the Gentiles was the foremost Christian Endeavorer of his times. Listen: " Forgetting the things that are behind, and reaching forth to those that are before, I press." etc. "*I press;*" I am not responsible for results; I am simply responsible for my humble endeavor. It is for God to do; it is for me to endeavor. Oh, the sweet surprises of the beautiful hereafter, when the Lord shall array before his people all the transcendent results of their lives and shall say, " You did this; you did that; you did that." And as the panorama sweeps before them in beatific vision, they say, " Lord, when? Lord, when? "

And this is not only a society of endeavor, but of *Christian* endeavor, and that is the only sort of endeavor that is really good for anything. Longfellow, you remember, had a young hero that was an endeavorer,—the youth that in the twilight passed, climbing the Alps. I used to know that poem, " Excelsior," but I do not undertake to repeat it in such a presence. I do remember, however, how he wound up. That always gave me a chill. [*Laughter.*]

> " A traveller, by the faithful hound,
> Half buried in the snow was found."

There was his flag,—poor, little, snow-clad flag,—" Excelsior;" but the hand was stiff, and the lips were dumb, and the flag was all coated with ice. You never saw a Christian Endeavorer in such a plight as that. [*Laughter.*] Why, he would melt out in an avalanche. The Christian Endeavorer is the only endeavorer that is sure to get there [*applause*] every time. He does not perish half way up the mountain; he conquers. " Whatsoever he doeth shall prosper." Christian Endeavor, therefore, is sure of its results.

And Christain Endeavor is rooted in Christian conviction. Let me underscore this and emphasize it, that " C. E." stands for Christian conviction. Talk about bigots—who is a bigot? A bigot is a man that holds on to something, he doesn't know what, and holds on to something, he does n't know why. ".What do you believe?" "Why, what the church believes." "And what does the church believe?" "Why, what I believe." [*Laughter.*] "And what do you both believe?" "We both believe the same thing." [*Laughter.*] There is your bigot. But I honor the man who has the grip of an honest conviction. These Christian Endeavorers are not bigots, and they are not what we call "liberals"—people who give away what does not belong to them. [*Laughter.*] That is liberality with a vengeance. They give away the Lord's truth and sacrifice it. The most illiberal people on this earth are those who have outgrown all the sects and have become so big that it takes a whole establishment for one of them. Save me from a liberal, falsely so-called. These young people are not bigots, and they are not liberals in any such sense of the word. Let me say to you that fruitage depends upon rootage. I never knew a man who amounted to anything that did not have rooted convictions. " He shall be like a tree planted by the rivers of water "—*rooted* by the rivers of water. The Psalmist must have been describing a Baptist. [*Laughter.*] Be loyal to your denomination. I believe in a true-blue Presbyterian [*" hear, hear "*]; I believe in a blood-red Methodist [*" amen "*]; I believe in a deep-water Baptist; I believe in a man who believes in what he believes in and yet is willing to learn. " In things essential, unity; in things non-essential, liberty ; in all things, charity." That is the motto of Christian Endeavorers the world over.

Yet I must be frank, Father Clark, and say that I do not believe in denominationalism a bit. I believe we have got to get over it. I wont say which way we will get over it, but we have got to get over it. There are some people who comfort themselves with the thought that these denominations are all good because they reach different classes Here is a church of an æsthetic turn of mind, and it reaches the rich and fashionable and cultured; here is a church with a different kind of service, and it reaches the poor and forsaken away down there in the slums. Do you know, I do not believe in a church for the rich and a church for the poor. " The rich and the poor meet together; the Lord is the maker of them all." [*Applause.*] There are those who comfort themselves with that " rainbow figure." That " rainbow figure " makes me tired. [*Laughter.*] They say, " Here are the Presbyterians ; they have one ray, and the Baptists have another, and the Methodists have another, and so on; and when they are all gathered together, they make a beautiful rainbow of blended hues and prismatic colors." Now, I don't believe that the Presbyterians have any business to get away with the blue ray and keep it all to themselves, or the Methodists to get away with the red ray and keep it all to themselves, or the Baptists—I am not sure what their ray is, but it is water-color,—green, perhaps. [*Laughter.*] I don't believe we have any business to parcel out the rays of divine truth. " Who are these before the throne?" " These are they that have washed their robes and made them white "—*white*, that is the combination of all the rest blended into one. [*Applause.*] There is none of your " Dolly Varden " business in heaven, and there ought not to be on earth. I tell you, brethren, the world is coming to a crisis, as sure as you live. No thoughtful man can sweep the whole horizen around without being profoundly persuaded that the world is nearing a great crisis. What do we see politically? All Europe is in a ferment. The steam is hissing at the rivets of all the boilers in Europe. The Kaiser is trying to hold down the safety-valve. The monarchs of Europe are trembling on their thrones. There are great convulsions today in Paris; the streets are barricaded; there is rioting and bloodshed. Capital and labor are contesting, hand to hand and foot to foot; their hot breath is on each other's cheek; they are in a death grapple. What is to be the end of it? Theologically, we are all adrift. The forces of evil are massing for the destruction of the sanctity of the Sabbath, for the demolition of the institution of marriage, for the overthrow of faith in that old Book on which this Society of Christian Endeavor is founded. We have got to come together. The forces of evil are massing and so must we. We must get into line and learn to keep step; we must form a Macedonian phalanx. We must leave out of sight the little things about which we have been contending. Do you know that if soldiers keep step when they are crossing a bridge, they will break it down, if it be an ordinary structure? They have to break step, or they will break down the bridge. Now, let us keep step and break down the bridge. And do you know, brethren, when the bridge breaks down, where you will all go to? [*Laughter.*] I beg pardon for that denominational allusion. [*Renewed laughter.*]

Brethren, we are beginning to utilize the forces of nature as never before. We are tapping the rock-bound earth, and the gas is spouting and the fiery flambeaux flame out upon the midnight air. We are tapping the earth and getting out the oil, and there are great gushing wells. And there is the subtle electric fluid that swings its splendors over our cities and drives our cars apace. We are getting at the latent resources of the earth. Do you know what we are doing at Niagara? We Americans and Canadians have a common interest there. Many a man, standing and looking into that awful abyss at Niagara, has had the feeling of that old countryman who said, "What an awful waste of water power!" But it is not being wasted so much as it was. They have constructed channels and turbine wheels, and now, by transmitted power, cities far away are to be illuminated. So, as we have looked abroad on Christendom, we have thought of the waste of power. " Awake, O Zion, put on thy strength, O Jerusalem," thy latent strength, thy unused strength, O Niagara of spiritual power! And I seem, in this Christian Endeavor convention, to hear the thunder of the Lord's Niagara that is being harnessed up to do service, and cities afar are to blaze with the electric light of the Gospel and whole continents to be kindled with a new glory. God speed the day! I believe we are nearing it. I believe the time is coming, like unto that epoch in Switzerland's history when the invaders crept through the mountain defiles and no gallant Switzer appeared anywhere in sight, until at last there was a cry which rang out in the clear blue air as if it came from heaven, "In the name of the Father, the Son and the Holy Ghost, let go, let go!" The Switzers, up there among the everlasting crags, held mighty masses of stone in leash, and at the command of their leader they let go, and down the avalanche came with a roar of thunder and buried the enemy. Its seems to me I can hear already the thunder of the Lord's guns advancing to the last attack, the last charge, and I fancy that these Christian Endeavorers are come together for that great fight. May the Christian Endeavor banner wave in triumph on every hilltop, on every mountain, and in every valley, until all the world shall shout, " Hallelujah! Hallelujah! The Lord God omnipotent reigneth!" [*Long and enthusiastic applause.*]

During the closing portion of Dr. Henson's address the booming of cannon on the parade ground was heard, making the speaker's reference to the "thunder of the Lord's guns" very effective. Dr. Clark announced that this was the **wedding day of** Prince George and Princess May, an announcement which was received with cheers, and that the event was being celebrated in this way. As an appropriate proceeding he called on Bishop Arnett to offer prayer, invoking God's blessing on the future king and queen of England.

Bishop Arnett offered a fervent prayer, at the close of which the doxology was sung and the benediction pronounced by the bishop.

THURSDAY AFTERNOON.

DRILL HALL.

The entire afternoon session in the Drill Hall was devoted to the Junior Christian Endeavor Society. Mrs. Alice May Scudder of Jersey City, N. J., presided.

The service began at 2.15 o'clock with a fifteen minutes' praise service, at the close of which the audience united with Mrs. Scudder in repeating the 23rd Psalm. A hymn was sung, followed by prayer by Rev. Geo. H. Tyndall, of New York.

MRS. SCUDDER : We are here this afternoon to consider the past, present, and future of our Junior Endeavor work. If we glance back nine years, we shall find but one Junior Endeavor society in all this vast land. It is a noticeable fact that the West always knows a good thing when it sees it, and it was a Western church which was the pioneer in this Junior Endeavor work. In the city of Tabor, Iowa, Rev. J. W. Cowan was the first Junior Endeavor leader, and we shall now have the very great pleasure of hearing him speak on the past of our Junior Endeavor work. [*Applause.*]

The First Junior Society : Its Origin and Its Growth.

Address of Rev. J. W. Cowan.

There are three questions, as I suppose, which this address is expected to answer concerning Junior Endeavor: First, How and where did it originate? Second, By what means has it grown from the first beginnings to its present magnitude, and third, What, on the whole, has it amounted to anyhow? The first of these questions is easily answered. In the extreme south-western corner of Iowa, perched upon prairie hilltops from which you may look over into the State of Nebraska, and almost into the State of Missouri also, there is a little college town, in which, ten years ago, there was but a single church, within whose spacious walls professor and student, mechanic and farmer, for miles around, gathered and worshipped together week by week. It was here, so Secretary Baer says, that Junior Endeavor was born.

It came about in this way. When, ten years ago, a new pastor came to the church, he found the students of the colleges and nearly all the other young Christians of the place working in the College Y. M. C. A. and Y. W. C. A., and so well were these organizations doing their work that there seemed no occasion for any other agency among the young people. This is why no Y. P. S. C. E. was organized. But the children were not so adequately cared for. A devoted teacher in the public schools was doing much for them, gathering them weekly into a kind of Bible training-class, and giving them much helpful instruction, but she herself felt the need of something more — some means of training them in Christian testimony and Christian work. It was then that the suggestion came, Why not form them into an Endeavor society? Now in this there was nothing original, you will understand. We Juniors don't like to have you talk as if we were gotten up as a kind of after invention, and on a different plan from the rest of you. We simply said, Endeavor is good; why shouldn't it be good for us? and we took it and tried it and found it good, and so here we are, regular, " Simon-pure " Endeavorers of the original sort, derived of the true apostolic succession straight from Father Clark, as much as any of you. And we would have adopted the suggestion at once, and Junior Endeavor would have been several months older than it is, but for the wise caution of one trusted adviser, whose relation to the children's work and his experience and character gave him the right to be consulted. He objected. " What," he said, " saddle a pledge like that upon the tender conscience of a child twelve years old ! Why, it is more than you ought to ask of a grown person. And then you are going to have a monthly experience meeting, and teach these little things to be religious parrots, professing impossible experiences in cant phrases borrowed from their elders, and you will make a lot of little spiritual prigs and pharisees out of children hardly old enough to spell ' ab.' No, no, it will never do. I would rather have my children out on the streets playing marbles for keeps, than to have them in such a meeting being drilled into an insincere and artificial religiosity like that." Our good friend did not use just those words — he was too considerate and courteous for that — but that was the purport of his objections. However, after some months these objections were partially overcome, and we had his modified approval of the plan. Accordingly, at the close of school hours on the afternoon of March 27, 1884, the Christian teacher gathered in her room the ten youngest members of our church, and one boy, a scholar in the school and a member of a church elsewhere. A constitution, including the pledge in its iron-clad form, was read to them, the plan was explained in full, and then we waited for their decision. It was not given hastily. After full deliberation, and many questions asked, we said, " Now we will take a vote, and in order that you may vote with entire freedom we will vote by ballot. Those in favor will write yes, those opposed write no. When the ballots were counted it was found that ten had written " Yes," and only one " No." And as his then teacher said recently, the boy who voted " No " that day has been voting " No " to everything Christian ever since. Then the constitution, including the pledge, was signed by the ten, and we went out at the close of the hour, a full-fledged Endeavor society.

And it is not merely as men and women, but as workers, that the Christians of the next generation are to be better for having been Junior Endeavorers at the start. What a splendid column of workers already trained is constantly passing from the Junior ranks over into the older societies — trained, too, as they never could have been, if they had waited to be trained in the Y. P. S. C. E. Were you not asking the professor of music the other day at what age he would prefer to begin with his pupil on the piano? And what did he say? At eighteen or twenty or twenty-five? By no means. He said, If my pupil is to be really a fine pianist I must begin with him while he is yet a child — about as soon, in fact, as he is able to sit on a piano stool. And are the spiritual muscles and tendons so much less susceptible than the physical, and so much less swiftly developing into form and permanency, that they can be neglected through all the plastic years of childhood, and no priceless advantage be lost ? Before the child sings, he thinks. Long before he begins to ask about chords and melodies, he begins to question about God. The religious nature is often ripe while as yet the body is in all the greenness and callowness of unformed youth. Train the muscles later on if you will. But if you would train the soul you must take it at the start. And since the grand aim of Christian Endeavor is to train Christian workers, it seems to me that the grand mission of Christian Endeavor is to the children.

And we Juniors believe that the Endeavor idea belongs to us, not by a sort of adaptation, which brings us within the Endeavor circle by grace of the courtesy of our elders. It belongs to us primarily, rather than to you older ones. Among the children, even more than among the young people, is the natural field for Endeavor activity. And what, after nine years' experience, has become of the fears with which we started out? Where are the little prigs and pharisees which were going to be manufactured? Where are the precocious professions, the spiritual egotism, and all the unpleasant results which were so lugubriously prophesied? I call my fellow-workers in Junior Endeavor to witness that there is nowhere to be found a more refreshing exhibition of childlike simplicity in religion than may be seen any day in the average Junior prayer meeting. I only wish that the absence of artificiality were half as conspicuous in our grown-up prayer meetings. Such straightforwardness in testimony and prayer, such touching little confessions of temptation and penitence, such artless statements, and yet artlessly profound, of child philosophy and child theology — why you can't find it anywhere else as you find it in the Junior meeting. And this is just what we ought to have expected. It is the repressed growth which becomes artificial. It is the plant that is put under a bushel or down in the cellar which develops itself in sickly and yellow and unnatural forms. If you would have it natural and healthy and exuberant, then give it liberty and sunlight, and let it sport itself to its heart's content in the putting forth of leaf and blossom and clinging tendrils of hope and faith. So a child religion which is repressed and hindered in its unfolding — coldly frowned upon in its first timid expressions of itself, and bidden let itself be seen, not heard — this will be the artificial growth. If you would have it natural, then give it air and room for expansion, and encouragement to put itself forth freely in all proper expressions and activities.

That is what Junior Endeavor seeks to do. It is an incarnation of the Saviour's bidding, "Suffer the little children, and forbid them not, to come unto me." And for one I can testify that not only have I seen all and more than I expected in the religious development of the Juniors, but I have seen an unexpected sturdiness and constancy in standing by their Endeavor principles in daily life. Our own little society very soon found that there were temptations to be met. In our public schools were found certain Tobiahs and Sanballats, who set themselves to hinder the work. One form of their opposition was the starting of children's parties at every hour of the Endeavor meeting, to which, of course, every young Endeavorer was invariably invited. Did they go? Not once. Not one of them. They said, "Here is our pledge, and we must stand by it." And stand by it they did, with the result that very soon the parties were given up or changed to another time in the week, and the party-goers became Endeavorer-goers, instead of the contrary. If any of the older societies can show a more faithful keeping of the pledge, or a more intelligent or consistent adherence to Endeavor principles concerning things wrong and things doubtful, than can be seen among the Juniors, then they surely deserve great praise. [*Applause.*]

MRS. SCUDDER: Only an hour with the children, cheerfully and pleasantly given; yet seed was sown in that hour which shall bring forth fruit in heaven. It is only we who are in close touch with Junior workers who realize how many magnificent men and women are leaders of our Junior societies. When I was in Chicago I saw a great machine which could cut, reap, gather, and bind grain in the twinkling of an eye. Down in Missouri we have a great Junior Endeavor reaper, one who has gathered many children into the fold and who will show you how much is being gathered throughout the country. We shall now listen to the Roll Call of the Junior superintendents of the societies in the different states of our Union and the provinces, conducted by Miss Kate H. Haus, of St. Louis.

Roll Call of Junior Superintendents.

Conducted by Miss Kate H. Haus.

MISS HAUS: Now, my Endeavor friends, please find seats and clear the aisles. [*Loud applause on account of the speaker's splendid voice.*] Another thing, to those who are state Junior superintendents: Please make your remarks short, spicy, and to the point. We haven't much time to waste, and we don't propose to waste what little we have. Now, although we have crossed over the boundary line, as far as national lines are concerned, we are still at home in Christian Endeavor work. [*Applause.*] But we are going over the boundary line to hear from the city of Washington in the District of Columbia, — Mr. P. S. Foster.

MR. FOSTER: I come from a union not very large for numbers, but for quality — oh, my! On the 17th of November, 1892, we organized a Junior union. I was consulted about it, as president of the district union, and I said we would try it although we had not many societies. We organized with fourteen societies and 425 members. The first day of July we had 33 societies with 1,200 members. [*Applause.*] This shows the effect of union work; and I am here today to recommend that where you have only two societies, organize a Junior union. [*Applause.*]

MISS HAUS: Now we will hear from California, that golden garden state,— and they have made a garden of it in Junior Christian Endeavor work.

MISS NASON: California sends greeting to this grand convention. We are looking forward to welcoming you all in '95. [*Applause.*] We feel that we have done a good work this past year. Only in 1892 was our first superintendent of Junior work elected. We have now ten superintendents, and have organized in 31 counties. We have 170 societies with a membership of 5,148, — a gain of 21 counties, 140 societies and 4,388 members. We have thus gained 535 percent in the past year. We organized our first city union in San Diego just in time to send greeting to your last great convention. We have now organized five city Junior unions and two county unions, and we feel encouraged in our work. [*Applause.*]

MISS HAUS: Now we are going to hear from Connecticut.

MRS. E. C. SMITH: I come with greetings from Connecticut. " Be of good courage, and he shall strengthen your heart, all ye that hope in the Lord." I want to say that we organized a Junior union in Bridgeport in 1891, and from that two other unions have been organized. We now number 106 societies, with a membership of 5,360. We believe in the babies entering the "cradle roll" at one month old. We believe in the intermediate society which takes the Juniors after they leave the Junior society and cares for them until they enter the senior society. We believe also in the parents being interested in the children. We believe in mission work, and that the Juniors are to take an interest in this work. [*Applause.*]

MISS HAUS: Now we are going down to the gas region, way over there in Illinois, and hear what the wind has blown to us along the line of Junior work from that direction.

MR. THOMAS WAINWRIGHT: Last July we went to New York with 266 Junior Christian Endeavor societies. We march to Montreal today with 433 societies, and with 16,847 members under fifteen years of age [*Applause.*] Sixty-two of our societies report raising altogether $1,131.77 in less than twelve months. These 62 societies have given to home missions during the past twelve months, $280.36; to foreign missions, $322.12; to the home churches, $519.29. [*Applause.*]

MISS HAUS: I am very glad that they have such a strong wind over there in Illinois, and I hope it will be strong enough to blow to the gates of that Fair on Sunday.]*Applause*] The representative of the Hoosier state, Indiana, is not here today, but they have sent us word that they have 204 Hoosier societies.

We will now hear from the state of New York, that thinks it is big enough to enclose the whole world. [*Laughter.*]

MISS SANFORD: Our Junior superintendent is not here, but I am glad to say that the last year of Christian Endeavor work in the state of New York among the Juniors has been marked by growth, organization, consecration, and advancement all along the line.

MISS HAUS: We will now go down to "Little Rhody." She may be small as a state, but she is pretty big along the line of Junior work.

MISS JENNIE P. FRASER: About a year ago we had only four societies; now we have thirty. That is a gain of over 600 percent. You must not judge us according to size, for we cannot compete with other states; but we do mean to have a good quality of boys and girls marching forward every day. We have just organized the Providence Junior union, and we hope to draw in all the other societies around Providence. We have covered about half the territory of the state in a year, and we hope to have all our boys and girls enlisted under the Junior Endeavor banner. [*Applause.*]

MISS HAUS: Now we will go down to Tennessee.

MR. J. R. McCOLL: Tennessee has 64 Junior societies, 44 of which have been organized within the past year. The total membership is 2,200. We are trying now to get hold of the Sunday-school superintendents of the state, for we think that in them we have the best friends for organization work.

MISS HAUS: Now we will come over the line for a little while and hear from Ontario.

MR. C. J. ATKINSON: The premier province has increased in Junior societies during the last nine months 100 percent only, but we have only got started; we have three months left. When we hear of 600 percent gain I am sure it will spur us on. We have nearly all the evangelical denominations represented in Junior work, and we also have a Junior society in a large industrial school for boys, a school to which incorrigibles are committed. Our society is very flourishing there. It seems as if the Junior society was just the thing for that institution. I hope that by another year we may be able to report a Junior society wherever there is a young people's society.

MISS HAUS: Now we are going over to Missouri — it is n't "misery" any longer, as they used to call our state because we did n't get the World's Fair. Missouri is a great state for breweries, and we are brewing a long line of Junior societies. We have 152 societies, with an active membership of 3,507, and they are active — every last one of them. We have had 97 unite with the church this year, and we have given $200 to foreign missions and $232 to home missions. We will next hear from Nebraska.

MRS. NEEDHAM: Since last October the Junior work has increased from 52 societies to 125, and from a membership of 1,000 to 2,500. Our motto is, "Nebraska for Christ."

MISS HAUS: Next we will hear from Manitoba.

REV. MR. ERQUHART: I am not the delegated representative of Manitoba, but finding there was no other representative of the territory here, I thought it would not be right for you to go away thinking that we are behind in this matter. We are aggressive all along the lines of Christian Endeavor work. We do not take a secondary position to any new country on the face of the globe. We not only held the banner last year, as you know, but we are making aggressive work along the line of Junior Endeavor work. I am sorry we have not a full report to give you. Next year we will bring one which will enable you all to know where we stand. [*Applause.*]

MISS HAUS: We will hear from Minnesota next.

A DELEGATE: Sixty new societies have been organized since Feb. 1, and the work is going on. Our Juniors are earnest and faithful workers.

MISS HAUS: It used to be the rule that the children were never allowed to speak, but we have advanced so far that here is a senior who asks permission to speak for Maine.

MR. FOSS: Down in Maine we raise Yankees, and rocks, and prohibition, and

Christian Endeavorers. [*Applause.*] The first prohibitory law ever enacted was in the state of Maine. The first society of Christian Endeavor ever organized was in the state of Maine. We have 100 Junior Endeavor societies. We cannot get along without this, the most important department of Christian Endeavor work. We are doing all we can along the line, and we want to recommend it to our brothers and sisters all over the continent.

MISS HAUS: Prohibition is a fine thing when it doesn't prohibit Junior societies in your churches. Now we shall hear from Iowa, the cradle of Junior Endeavor.

MR. GEO. H. PARKER: I am sorry that our Junior superintendent is not here to-day. I do not know much about our numbers outside of Des Moines. We have ten societies in that city and they are going to form a city union in September. We expect to go to Cleveland with at least a gain of 200 percent in Des Moines, and we expect more than that in the rest of the state.

MISS HAUS: Next we will hear from the Keystone State, — Pennsylvania.

MR. W. S. FERGUSON. We are working today to free the Keystone State from all corruption and impurity by bringing the children to a knowledge of the love of God as it is in Jesus Christ. We have this year brought 1,804 of our Junior members into the church. We have a membership of 15,800 Juniors. We are working upon this line; that if we can bring the boys of Pennsylvania who are twelve years of age under the influence of religion, in the next twenty years the officers governing the state of Pennsylvania will be Christian men. [*Applause.*]

MISS HAUS: Now we will hear from New Jersey.

MR. WILLIAMS: The superintendent of the state is not here today, but I am interested with her in one society, and I will speak for that in particular. Our Juniors are very active; they enjoy their work and they do a great deal in helping the older ones and carrying on Christian work that the older Endeavorers cannot always reach.

MISS HAUS: Kentucky will now be heard from.

MR. W. S. WALLER: Junior work in Kentucky has increased 100 percent during the past year.

MISS HAUS: We will now hear from across the sea — from Japan, represented by Mr. Klein.

REV. F. R. KLEIN: The first Junior society organized in the empire of Japan was formed in the Methodist Protestant mission, in the city of Okayama, about the middle of last December. I am sorry that I cannot tell you the number of Junior societies now in the empire. As to our own work in Japan,— we have labored there for eight years,— I am prepared to say, after some thought, that I do not know of any single agency in our work more calculated to bring the young of that land to a knowledge of Christ than the Junior Endeavor Society. [*Applause.*] I do not think I would exchange the Junior society work for any other particular work in our mission. Mrs. Kosimi, educated in an American college, is the superintendent. She has 2,500 children that she gives Christian training to weekly, though not as in these and other Christian lands. The children of our church people cannot receive that training at their own homes which is received in Christian homes here. [*Applause.*]

MISS HAUS: This is the last of our Junior reports. I want to say just this in closing, to you who have no Junior societies in your city or state or province. How in the world do you expect to meet such terrible wrongs as we have over there in Chicago, with that World's Fair open on Sunday, if you do not train the children aright? The reason why that Fair is open on Sunday is because the children were not trained aright years ago, and they were given over to the control and the training of Satan. And now, dear friends, let us go home and take these children from Satan's control, and train them up " For Christ and the Church," so that they shall form a mighty army, and so that the history of this grand country of ours shall never be blotted as it is with Sabbath-breaking, in the years to come. And may we older Endeavorers be able to stand before God's throne, not empty-handed, but with our heads bowed with the weight of jewels of these young souls that we have brought to Christ — jewels so many that in the ages of eternity we shall never be able to count them. Go home and go to work for the children, [*Loud applause.*]

After the singing of "Bringing in the Sheaves," Dr. Wayland Hoyt, of Minneapolis, was introduced, and spoke as follows : —

The Possibilities of the Junior Society.

Address of Rev. Wayland Hoyt, D.D.

It is the great art gallery at Dresden. Pictures almost innumerable, far-famed, precious, glow upon the walls. The master-pieces of the master-workers in form and color are accumulated there — of Carlo Dolce, Paul Veronese, of Corregio, of Titian, of Rubens, of Rembrandt, of many more esteemed the peers of these. If it be such a day as the one on which I visited it, the gallery is thronged, and the noises of a multitude are around you. People are moving through the halls, pointing out to each other the beauties and the excellences of this picture and of that, talking and laughing.

But come with me to a small room curtained from the larger gallery. The room is full, for in this place is enshrined the heart and paragon of the entire exhibition. And will you notice — I am sure you cannot miss marking it and being yourself immediately subjected to the imperious spell — the hush which falls on every one. Speech has ceased ; what movements there are are subdued and chastened, and only for sight at better angle. Every eye is reverently held by the one picture — Raphæl's Madonna di San Sisto, perhaps the most supreme picture that ever looked from canvas. And what is the picture? Barring the few accessories which a little fringe it, it is the picture only of the Virgin Mother and the Holy Child. But as you stand there gazing, the homaging hush compels you. You can see and feel it all — the sword which is to pierce her heart, the love in Him which is to culminate upon the cross.

You cannot help it. You willingly put the sceptre into the child's hand, and let Him sway you. And will you just now notice — it is the picture of a CHILD which makes the knees of your soul bend. Ah, how that picture hallows childhood.

That is a significant and far-reaching truth to which a strong thinker has given speech, — "I find a child in no religion but in the religion of Jesus. Mahommed seemed to know nothing about a child. The heathen seemed to know nothing about children in their mythology. Their gods were not born children. They were never clothed with the sympathies of children. They never threw themselves into the sociabilities of children. They were gods of terror, gods of passion, gods of lust, gods of might; but they were never gods of helplessness a span long. Oh, no. That would not have been natural ; that would not have been divine, in their conception. And hence they make no provision for children. But the great, elemental fact of Christianity is the Holy CHILD Jesus. Born of a woman, born under the law, in total helplessness physically, laid in a manger, cared for by no man. But the child of the Everlasting Father, and the Prince of Peace. So that the Gospel of Jesus is the only religion on earth that makes provision for a child, and is the only religion in which a child is laid as the basis, and foundation of its faith."

And so Christian Endeavor, on the Junior and Child side of it, on this side of its caring for and nurturing the boys and girls, is in closest chime and contact with that religion which has for its foundation a little child.

And I am to speak to you of the possibilities of Junior Christian Endeavor.

Consider, then. — the Possibility Strategic of Junior Christian Endeavor. It is the vale of Chamounix. Directly before you towers the stupendous and snowy crest of Mt. Blanc. Rightly Coleridge sings of it,

" Hast thou a charm to stay the morning star
In his steep course ? So long he seems to pause
On thy bald, awful head, O Sovereign Blanc !"

Yes, Mt. Blanc is Sovereign ! All things thereabouts must adjust themselves to him; not he to them. The marshalling of the companion mountains, the courses of the glaciers, the trend of the valley, the sort and winding of the roads, the footways — all these must get direction from the monarch mountain; must do as he says, not as they say.

As immovable, invincible, compelling, are the words of our Lord and Saviour Jesus Christ. Here is one of them, — " Verily, verily, I say unto you, ye must be born again." As stands that sovereign mountain, grappling with its rocky roots, the earth's centre, piercing with its topmost height the utmost blue, which no earthquake can shatter down, which no most plunging tempest can cause to quiver; before the heart of every one of us stands thus this word of Christ, solemnly saying its changeless charge, — " Ye must be born again."

A perpetual note and test of life is growth. The destiny and doom of life is — that it must grow. But growth is not increasing, simply; it is fixation. One does not only grow, one grows into. And as the growth goes on, the direction into which the growth goes on becomes more firmly fastened. You remember Tennyson's marvelous analysis and portraiture of a child's growth

" The baby new to earth and sky,
    What time his tender palm is prest
Against the circle of the breast,
    Has never though that ' This is I.'

" But as he grows he gathers much,
    And learns the use of ' I ' and ' me,'
And finds ' I am not what I see,
    And other than the things I touch.'

" So rounds he to a separate mind
    From whence clear memory can begin,
And through the frame that binds him in
    His isolation grows defined."

And so he must go on growing. And he must grow morally as well. And he must grow into somewhat morally. And growth is fixation. I confess to you that there is to me a brooding solemnity over a company of boys and girls. For I cannot help saying to myself concerning them, Grow they must; and grow into somewhat they must; and growth in this direction or that is more and more fixation in this direction or that.

And so the vitalest of questions is, Whither are they growing? In what direction are they fixing themselves?

" Yon stream, whose sources once,
    Turned by a pebble's edge,
Is Athabasca, rolling toward the sun,
    Through the cleft mountains' edge.

" The slender stream had strayed,
    But for the slanting stone,
To evening's ocean, mid the tangled braid,
    Of foam-flecked Oregon.

" So from the heights of will,
    Life's parting stream descends ;
And, as a moment turns its slender rill,
    The widening torrent bends.

" From the same cradle-side,
    From the same mother's knee ;
One to long darkness and the frozen tide,
    One to the crystal sea."

And surely, if you are to turn that stream, the place to do it is not where its waters have gathered, directed and rushing current, but back there at that slanting stone.

I believe in the conversion of children. I believe that upon them — and likeliest upon them — the birth from above may fall. I believe that, quickest of all, the little child will adjust itself to this demand of the Lord Jesus for the new birth. More than that. I believe that so easily may a little child be moulded, so facile is a little child to a rightly directing touch, that a child may even unconsciously meet this demand of the Lord Jesus and almost from earliest consciousness, yielding its childhood to Christ as Lord and Master, grow up in Christ. Rightly asks another, "What authority have you from the Scriptures to tell your child, or by any sign to show him, that you do not expect him truly to love, and obey God until he has spent whole years in hatred and wrong?" Nay, seek to turn the child Godward at the earliest moment, and so forestall and prevent the years of indurating wrong. [*Applause.*]

Nor would I in the least make obstacle to such little Christian children's uniting with the church, or at all deny them her fullest, and most welcoming communion. [*Applause.*]

Back here in the earliest years is the strategic opportunity. Not only can you here win most easily to Christ, but also how much of evil growth from Christ can you prevent.

Save only a Christian mother's bosom, there is no place more crowded with strategic possibility than a Junior society of Christian Endeavor, where the boys and girls are gathered — even the smallest of them — that they may be led to accept that Christ who himself became a little child, and so may start on the glorious process of growing up into Him in all things which is the head, even Christ.

There was to be a Sunday-school concert at which a little child of eight was going to recite. Her mother had taught her. The night came. The little thing was all a-tremble. She could scarcely speak. She began, "Jesus said," — she could not remember. She girded herself and tried again — "Jesus said, suffer " — again she failed and waited. Gathering herself once more, and with supreme effort she burst out, "Suffer little children — and, don't anybody stop them, for he wants them all to come." And no truer truth was ever said by lips mature. He does want them all to come. And the best, and likeliest time to win their coming is in the earliest years. The Junior Society of Christian Endeavor is the place of possibility most auspicious and strategic.

Consider, next, the possibility of training of the Junior Christian Endeavor Society.

His eye was failing, his hands were trembling. Age has set its shackles on him. To younger hands the unfinished picture must be resigned. " I commission thee, my son," said the aged artist, " to do thy best on this work." And the young man hesitated, thinking the duty was too vast for him. But still kept sounding the injunction, " Do thy best; do thy best." And then with prayer for help, and with high purpose in his heart, the young man began. And as he wrought his hand grew steady; his conception cleared; each stroke became a master stroke. At last before the finished picture, with teaful exultation, the aged artist gave over into the worthy hand of Leonardo da Vinci, who had done his best, the duty from which his own hand was failing. But the untrained hand of the young Leonardo da Vinci could have done but a poor and pitiable best. When the trained hand does its best, its best amounts to something.

I read it, — this last summer, — that beautiful and hopeful legend set into the pedestal of the bust of John Wesley in Westminister Abby, — " God buries the workers, but he carries on the work."

Yes; but always through workers. And as never before the cry of the church is for trained workers. Trained workers — there is always room and use for them, where a herd of bungling workers is but a hindrance.

And what Christian, as he forecasts the future, and marks the thronging and marshalling opposition, — Romanism, with its false and subtle front professing adjustment with the new age, but necessarily, since, as itself declares, it is unchangeable and infallable, with the old, hard, cruel, spiritual and political tyranny at its heart, a false and blatant science with its negation of God; the vain show of a glittering and wealth-loving worldliness; an encroaching so-called Biblical criticism, which would turn the vereties of Revelation into a cunning and deftly foisted priest-code and pitiable romance; all the anarchic, God-defying tendencies with which the time is full; the sanctities of Sabbaths trampled under foot by a World's Fair, the management of which ought to stand in history as almost the most gigantic example of unfaith history can make a record of [*applause*],— what maturer Christian beholding such thing, and things like them, must not be thankful that Christian Endeavor is at the training of the immediately coming generation for personal service; must not be even more thankful that Junior Christian Endeavor is laying its hand upon the boys and girls, who are of the next succeeding generation, that beginning with them earlier, that generation may be the better trained.

Personal service—the particular service of each special Christian for his Lord; so that the number of borderers, and laggards, and idlers, and those who are saying, "Somebody else will do it," shall be cut down; and the number vastly swelled who shall gladly answer to the call for individual service, and that service, trained service—that is now, and in the future must be more even, the great needs,—personal service, trained to appreciate the value of personal influence. Out in the Western wilds a Sunday-school missionary was trying to organize a Sunday school in a log school-house. Going through the clearing he met a little boy, and asking him to sit with him on a log, gave the boy a picture-card, and said, "We are going to have a nice school and we want all the boys to be in it; you'll come and join us tonight, won't you?" "No," said the boy. Then the missionary took out a picture-paper, and putting his arm tenderly round the boy and telling him about the picture-papers and books which were to be had at the Sunday school, said confidently, "You'll come and get some of these papers and books, won't you?" "No," blurted out the boy. But the missionary could sing sweetly; he would try music; so he sang some verses of "I have a Father in the promised land," and then said heartily, "There, we are going to have such singing as that in the Sunday school; won't you come and hear it, and learn to sing for yourself?" "No," resolutely replied the boy. Had he met the inaccessible boy? He arose to go. "Say," called out the boy, "are you going to be there?" "Yes, I expect to be there tonight," said the missionary. "Then I 'll come," responded the boy. [*Laughter.*] And the boy was there and the school was started. That is what we need—a trained appreciation of personal influence.

Personal service— trained to the use of God's word. After all, what is mightier than the word of God, treasured by the memory and flushed with the hues of a personal experience?

Personal service— trained to prayer. In our non-liturgical churches, the prayer meeting is our liturgy. What we need is multitudes of Christians who shall gladly and audibly take part in it.

Personal service—trained to speech for Jesus. Oh, the Christian with lips open for fashion, fun, business, but padlocked toward speech for Jesus!

Personal service — trained toward giving for Jesus.

There was a man once listening to a morning sermon for some Christian enterprise. He would give a dime, he said to himself. The sermon went on. He would give a quarter, he said to himself. The sermon went on. He would give a dollar. he said to himself. The sermon ended. The offering box approached. He seized his pocket-book, and emptying nearly the whole of it into the offering-box, exclaimed, "Now, squirm, old natur." [*Laughter.*] That was better than not giving. But we want men and women so trained and principled in giving that long since the old nature has learned it is no use to "squirm."

And now the Junior Christian Endeavor is laying hold of the boys and girls and training them along just such lines as these and to such noble ends. Imagine, if you can, and thank God for its possibility of training.

Also, consider the possibility (economic) of Junior Christian Endeavor. Said Justin Martyr, "There are some of us eighty years old who were made disciples to Christ in our childhood." What a saving for Jesus Christ — such long lives dedicated to him! And that is what Junior Christian Endeavor is doing,— seeking to present whole lives for the use of our Lord and Saviour.

Also consider the possibility of service for ourselves in Junior Christian Endeavor. Washington Irving tells somewhere of a man who determined that he would jump over a great mountain rather than walk over it. So he took a run of three miles to gather impetus. And when he had reached the mountain he could only sit down and rest, and so had to walk over it, step by step, at last.

Thus, too often, we gather ourselves, in plan, desire, emotion, for some huge and even impossible service, and with our energies all spent, refuse to step into the daily opportunities of service, opening along the path of our common living. But the boys and girls are all around us. We need neither jump nor climb some jagged mountain front to find them and to win them. What seems lowliest is often loftiest. He that is greatest among you, let him be your minister, said the Master. Looking, a little even, at its possibilities, there is no taller or larger service than to win, and train, and hold, for Jesus Christ, the boys and girls by the controlling and beneficently shaping hand of Junior Christian Endeavor. [*Applause.*]

At the close of Dr. Hoyt's address the audience joined in singing "A Christian Band from Far and Near," after which Mrs. Scudder introduced Rev. H. N. Kinney, of Winsted, Ct., as the leader of the Free Parliament.

Junior Methods of Work.

Free Parliament.   Conducted by Rev. H. N. Kinney.

Mr. KINNEY: I ask your attention to the Scriptures as recorded in Proverbs the 30th chapter. I think you will see from this that the Bible recognizes that even older people can learn something from little people. The words of Agur are:

> "There be four things which are little upon the earth,
> But they are exceeding wise:
> The ants are a people not strong,
> Yet they provide their meat in the summer;
> The conies are but a feeble folk,
> Yet make they their houses in the rocks;
> The locusts have no king,
> Yet go they forth all of them by bands;
> The lizard taketh hold with her hands,
> Yet is she in kings' palaces."

All of which four references seem to me to mean, in a certain sense, the Junior Endeavor Society.

To a Yankee visitor the most impressive paraphernalia in the British Parliament is the speaker's mace and the wool-sack. For our Parliament today we have no mace, so I propose a pepper-box, and in place of the wool-sack a bushel basket.

1. The pepper-box. A Y. P. S. C. E. parliament shakes the pepper-box of facts from the floor over the omelette of oratory from the platform. The audience, especially Junior workers, are now free to exude Junior Endeavor information at every pore. The eccentric Lord Timothy Dexter, of Newburyport, wrote a book in which he put no punctuation marks, except that at the end of the book he printed several solid pages of hyphens, asterisks, exclamation points and periods. He said his readers could pepper and salt to suit.

The audience can now pepper away. Use red pepper, please, — concentrated, — and shoot quick. Sixty-three speakers in sixty-minutes was the record at the Parliament at St. Louis, one hundred in sixty minutes at Minneapolis; but at a recent convention in Connecticut I heard fifty-two genuine Juniors speak in eight minutes. At this rate in our twenty minutes today we should hear from one hundred and fifty speakers.

2. The bushel basket. A barber of my acquaintance in the hills of New Hampshire went fox-hunting for the first time and did not shoot quick. When those who followed the fox came up, the only explanation he could offer was, his eyes sticking out of his head, "That fox's tail — that fox's tail was as big as a bushel basket!" Though the tale you have to tell of excellent Junior Endeavor methods seems as large to you as a bushel basket, tell it quickly.

Take the bushel basket, however, as your model of Junior or senior Endeavor speech in parliament or prayer meeting : first, It is a "round unvarnished tale." Second, Though a bushel basket has depth, it has no length. Third, The mouth of a bushel basket is wide open. Fourth, You can put a good deal into a bushel basket. Fifth, A bushel basket always has something you can take hold of and carry it home with you. Sixth, The Bible says if you have a candle, you should not put it under a bushel, but in a candlestick, where it will give light to all that are within the house.

Now we desire to fill up our bushel basket this afternoon with clams from Rhode Island, and wooden nutmegs from Connecticut, and little wee bears from California, and suckers from Illinois, and small alligators from Florida, and shad from the Hudson River. Some one now please tell us something about Junior Endeavor work, from Maine to California.

A DELEGATE : Minnesota is going ahead in Junior work. Some of us are trying to start a Baby Christian Endeavor Society.

Mr. KINNEY : There are already two Baby Christian Endeavor societies in existence. "C. E." now stands for "Cradle Endeavor."

"The North Congregational church, Bridgeport, Ct., has a Baby roll of 30 members, and Park Street church has another Baby roll of 60 members."

"A New York Junior society, with 91 members, finds it profitable to invite the parents to the meetings."

"The Juniors of Lamberton, N. J., go to the regular church prayer meeting once a month."

"A society at New Brighton, Staten Island, gives systematically to missions."

"A society of 40 members at Kingston, N. Y., elects a new president every three months. The members take turns leading."

"The Cumberland Presbyterian church at Vincennes, Ind., has a society of 55 members. In that society the children are drilled from six years old up to fifteen; we have some as young as three years old. They carry on their regular prayer meeting and learn to pray just as in the senior society. They have their own sociables, and make contributions for every church enterprise."

"Out of a San Francisco society of 91 members, 33 active, 20 united with the church last year."

"A Pennsylvania church lately received eighteen members from the Junior society."

"A West Virginia church received fifteen."

"A Boston society has four flower committees visiting the hospitals."

"A Philadelphia society distributed 9,300 papers — good literature — in two months."

"Whenever you speak for Junior Endeavor, ask for pledges. At a meeting in Pennsylvania recently I asked for pledges from those present that they would go home and form Junior societies. As a result six societies were formed."

"The Pearl St. society in Hartford, Ct., gained 26 members in six months. They teach the seniors how to take part in meeting."

"A New York society of 100 members is larger than the senior society. At a recent public meeting they led the Seniors in participation."

"A society of 40 members in Versailles, Ky., is educating a child in China, has started a building fund for a new parsonage, and bought a clock for the church."

"The society of the Williston church, Portland, Me., numbers 60 members. Several have united with the church and constitute the best trained workers in the church."

"A Chicago society supports a day school in India."

"A Sunday-school prayer meeting in Philadelphia is led by the Juniors."

"The Riverside Presbyterian society of Chicago is composed almost entirely of boys. They all attend the senior society, and all take part."

Mr. Kinney here asked all who were Junior superintendents in the audience to stand up. About 300 stood up.

"A society in Ontario was the means of starting 20 other societies."

"An Iowa society is supporting a young girl on missionary ground."

MR. KINNEY: I want to say a word in closing of what all the societies are doing. I am not very fond, as a minister, of clearing up my backyard. In the spring there is a lot of debris left over from the winter, old roots have to be grubbed up, etc. Last spring I built a bonfire or smudge in my backyard. When I built it there was not a child in sight, but the moment there was the first sign of flame, six little fellows appeared on the scene wanting to assist, and by the time the flame had leaped up ten feet there were 40 small boys in that yard. I said to them, "Now, boys, that fire is a grand fire, but it will go out unless there are some roots or branches or debris put upon it." The result was that I did n't do any work all that afternoon. [*Laughter.*] Those Juniors took hold and piled up all the old sticks and begged permission to lug away the rocks. Every pastor who has built a bonfire in his heart and has brought down fire from heaven and started a Junior Endeavor society, has had things cleared up around his church. Dear brother, if you have n't a Junior Endeavor society, build a bonfire with fire from on high. [*Applause.*]

Two more verses were then sung of "A Christian Band," after which Mrs. Scudder introduced Mrs. F. E. Clark, who was received with the Chautauqua salute, the audience rising.

Junior Christian Endeavor in Foreign Lands.

Address of Mrs. F. E. Clark.

The subject that has been given to me this afternoon is a very large one. The most I can hope to do with it is to give you little glimpses of Junior Endeavor here and there, in the hope that this may give you a desire to know more about your little brothers and sisters in other lands, and that as you learn more about them your Christian Endeavor will grow world-wide in its sympathies and effects.

So many little faces come up before me this afternoon, in all colors and shades of color, black faces and white faces, brown faces and yellow faces, rosy faces and pale faces, some of them bright and happy, and some of them such sad little faces that it would bring the tears to your eyes to look at them. How can I choose among them or how can I know which ones would most interest you? I wish I could show you all the pictures that linger in my memory today; of Christian Endeavor in many colors, and of bright colored pictures with the Christian Endeavor left out, perhaps for want of help that we might give; of the happy little children in Samoa with their brown skins polished with cocoanut oil till they shone like varnished mahogany; of the rosy-faced English children in Australia; of the bright-eyed Juniors in Japan, and the queer little Chinamen with their funny queues pieced out with red or purple strings, and their quaint Chinese costume; of the beautiful black-eyed boys and girls in Ceylon, and those pretty "symphonies in brown" in India; of the audacious little Arabs begging for "backsheesh" in Egypt and Syria; of the boys in the red fezes in the old city of Tarsus, where Paul was born, and the dear little children in the Kindergarten in Kaisarieh; of the sweet Spanish maidens in San Sebastian, and the earnest Endeavorers in Paris; and, last of all, those boys and girls in Old England who were so interested in Christian Endeavor across the waters, and who sent to their friends in Montreal such a rousing British cheer that it rings in my ears yet, and I think you might almost have heard it over here.

Can you see all these bright little brothers and sweet little sisters of yours across the waters, as they send you their greetings and salaams this afternoon, and ask, through me, for your love, your sympathy and your prayers?

I wonder what you would think if you could hear that little nine-year old girl crying in Lucknow. Poor little brown-faced lassie! Her sobs and cries were so loud that they reached across the street and into our room in the mission bungalow. As we went out on the veranda and looked across the street, and saw the crowd assembled, and heard their drums and horns and cymbals making a noise rather than music, as we saw them lead away the sobbing little lassie while the poor mother stood crying in the doorway, our hearts were deeply touched though we could not understand it at all. When we asked what was the trouble we were told that the little maiden was married and they were taking her to her husband's home and she did not want to go. She wanted to stay with her mother. She is only nine years old, and now she must be shut up in a house for the rest of her life. Perhaps she has been allowed to go to school till now, but she cannot go again, for it would not be proper now that she is married. She must go to her husband's house; she must be obedient to her mother-in-law, who may be kind to her or who may be unkind, as she pleases. She will have to learn to cook her husband's food, and after he has eaten she may cook her own. She may amuse herself by looking at her jewelry, and trying on her earrings, and her nose jewels and her bracelets. She must pass the slow hours away as well as she can inside the walls of her home, for she will not go out very often. This is all life has to offer her. No wonder she cries. Poor little brown-faced lassie of Lucknow! Let us hope that some kind missionary lady will gain entrance to that zenana, and that in her secluded home she may learn something of the love of Jesus, and perhaps may even learn to read his words for herself, and thus may find comfort for the weary hours before her. This is only one little girl of the many thousands in India who are looking to us today for help. Shall we not give it? I could show you many sad pictures, but let me show you one bright one before we leave India. Come with me to Madura and look into one of the school buildings there. It is a long, low stone building with broad shady verandas. There is very little furniture to be seen, but the bright, happy brown faces make the room look so pleasant that we do not care whether it is furnished or not, for here are twenty or thirty children sitting on the floor singing a hymn. They are singing in the Tamil language the old hymn that so many children have sung in our own land, "I am so glad that our Father in Heaven tells of his love in the book he has given." This is the Junior Endeavor society of the Madura Girls' School. One of the girls from the older societies is their leader; her brown face and her bare brown arms and feet contrast very prettily with the white cloth which makes such a becoming costume. The little girls wear gay costumes of red or yellow or green, but all very gracefully draped, and their earrings and nose jewels and bracelets and anklets and necklaces add another touch of color to the picture. Through the open doorway we catch pretty glimpses of cocoanut trees and palm trees with bright colored parrots flitting through the branches. The whole picture is a very attractive one and our eyes love to dwell upon it, but the meeting is beginning and we must pay attention. One after another the children rise in their places and say a few words in the Tamil language. Of course we cannot understand them, but Miss Noyes tells that each one is repeating some verse of Scripture that she likes and telling why she likes it and how it has helped her. Then their leader reads a few verses from the Bible and explains it to them and they all bow their heads in prayer; and very reverend the

JUNIOR SOCIETY OF CHRISTIAN ENDEAVOR, MADANAPALLE, INDIA.

childish voices sound as they offer their brief petitions. Then their happy voices ring out again as they join in the song " Tell me the old, old story of Jesus and his love." Then with closed eyes and bowed heads they repeat together the Lord's prayer, and the meeting closes. Who would have thought of finding a real live Christian Endeavor society right here in the heart of heathenism, here in this old city of Madura, not far from the greatest heathen temple in the world? These little girls are very much in earnest in their endeavor and their committees are actively at work. They wear the Christian Endeavor badge, too, and though it is one of their own manufacture it is very pretty. They have not much money at their command; but they have nimble fingers, and with blue and gold beads and a bit of wire they have fashioned a very pretty " C. E., " and they wear it just as proudly as the children in America wear their silver ones.

But we must not linger so long in India. Let me show you one or two pictures in Japan. Come with me to the temple of the 33,000 gods in Kioto. See these people at the door who want to sell us some counterfeit cash. These coins look very much like the genuine ones, but they are a little thinner, and we can buy twenty of them for a cent instead of ten. But why should we buy counterfeit money, we ask. Because it looks so much like the genuine that the gods will not know the difference, and they will credit us for twice as much money as we have really given. We can cheat the gods and get more blessings for our money, they say. And now see those forlorn little beggars coming to meet us. Poor little dirty, ragged, starving boys, living near a whole temple full of gods, knowing little about them and caring less, shivering under their miserable rags, begging, lying, stealing, getting a living as best they can! Is it not pitiful? Poor little lads, is this all that heathenism can do for you? Of what use are all these 33,000 gods in the temple if they can do no more? But let us turn to a brighter picture and see what Christianity has done for some children in Japan. Come with me to Okayama and look at some happy boys and girls there. Here is another heathen temple, but how different from the first. The gods have been moved to a small, inner room, where an old priest goes in once a day and goes through the service in the heathen manner. But he has this little room all to himself; there seem to be no other worshippers, and the large outer room has been hired by an earnest Japanese Christian, and is used for an orphanage. Let us look in for a minute and see the contrast. Instead of 33,000 hideous idols, here are 150 bright, happy children, sitting on the floor in Japanese fashion, the boys on one side and the girls on the other. The boys are singing at the top of their voices "Onward Christian Soldiers," and they sing it as though they meant it. As their song dies away the girls begin, " Jesus loves me, this I know, for the Bible tells me so." Then the boys of the school band rise in their places and give us a stirring Japanese national air. As we look about in the other rooms and see the various trades that are being taught, we realize that these children, when they are old enough to leave the orphanage, will be self-supporting, self-respecting young Christians. There is a flourishing Junior Christian Endeavor society here, too, and these boys and rls are learning to be faithful Christian workers.

These are only two pictures of child-life in Japan. I could give you many more if there were time. I could show you much that has been accomplished. I could tell you of much more that might be done if there were more workers and more money. There is a large heathen temple called the Hongwangi temple, now being built in Kioto. The wood carvings are very fine, and it will be, when finished, one of the largest and one of the most beautiful temples in Japan. As we walked through it one day, in company with some missionary friends, we all agreed that it would be just the place for the great International Christian Endeavor Convention to be held in Japan in the year 19—, well, we did not quite decide upon the year. Perhaps it depends partly upon us to determine when in Japan our help is needed?

I wish I could show you some of the children in China. You would like to have seen that pretty Chinese maiden in that Buddhist temple in Canton, whose tiny little feet, encased in small slippers no larger than a baby's, were of very little use to her. Though she could not walk alone, and had to be led by the hand, and though every step seemed to give her pain, yet she seemed to be pleased to be in the fashion, and took what comfort she could in thinking she was dressed in the latest Chinese style. She burned her incense and bowed down before the idols and worshipped in her own way with as much reverence as many of her fashionable sisters in other lands. I suppose she has never heard of a better way, and, perhaps, never will, until more of her sisters in Christian lands wake up to a sense of their sisterhood and their responsibility. There is a Chinese Christian Endeavor society in Foochow, which is called the "Drum and Rouse Up Society." I think, perhaps, that might be a good name for our missionary committees to take upon themselves, for I am sure we all need to be roused up to a realization of what we owe to our brothers and sisters in eastern lands. I would like to show you that bright little Junior society in Shanghai. They are just average Chinese boys taken from the day schools. Most of them came from heathen homes, knowing nothing about the true God and knowing very little on any subject. Not very promising material for a Christian Endeavor society, you would say. But there was one missionary who had faith to believe that those Chinese boys would like to hear about their Saviour, and that when they knew about him they would love him, so she invited them to her house and formed a Junior Endeavor society. She did not let them sign the pledge at first, for she knew they could not understand it, but she called it by that name from the very beginning, for that was what she meant to make it as soon as possible. Every week she held a little meeting with them, telling them of the love of Jesus, and praying with and for them. She read the Christian Endeavor pledge to them, and explained it sentence by sentence, word by word, till at last, after several months, she felt that some of them understood it and would like to sign it and keep it. Now she has a flourishing Junior society, and I hope that the boys and girls in Christian America are as much in earnest in keeping their pledge as those little Chinamen in Shanghai. The missionaries told me that there was a very noticeable difference in the behavior of those boys, not in church, but in school and on the street and in their homes, since they became Christian Endeavorers, a good proof that their endeavor is genuine.

I wish I had time to tell you of the bright little Junior society in the girls' school at Adabazar, for there are still a few societies left in Turkey. One day on the "Alaska," as we were sailing across the Atlantic on our homeward voyage, I took a little package from my pocket. It was marked "From the Juniors of Adabazar, to be opened on shipboard." I opened it and found what looked like a little package of homœopathic powders, labelled "For Seasickness." When I opened them I found some beautiful Bible verses that would certainly help any one to bear that malady, if they did not wholly prevent it. I have had many remedies for seasickness offered me during the last year, but these little maidens in Asia Minor were the first ones to offer me just that kind of help, and I think their remedy proved far more effective than any other I have tried. I shall never forget those little Endeavorers in Adabazar, though I have not time to tell you about them; and though they talked in Turkish and I in English, yet I think we understood each other very well. I should like to tell you of that little Junior society of missionary children in Talas, with their twelve-year old president, and their ten-year old secretary, and the eight-year old missionary committee, and the five-year old boy who is the music committee, and who takes great pleasure in choosing the hymns, and the sweet little three-year old girl who is "the sunshine committee" and who carries a little gleam of sunshine with her wherever she goes.

If I could show you those pretty little Spanish sisters of yours in San Sabastian, who greeted us with songs when we arrived and showered us with rose leaves when we came away, I am sure you would want to stretch out a helping hand to them. In this Columbian year you would remember how much Spain did for us in giving us Columbus, and you would want to repay a part of the debt by giving to these daughters of Spain a large building and better rooms and more opportunities for a Christian education.

I should like to tell you about the earnest little workers in Australia. I remember one Junior society there that gave, last year, nearly a hundred and fifty dollars to missions, and that is only a sample of the energy and zeal that little society was putting into its work in every direction. And that one society is only a sample of many more in Australia. I think we might learn many lessons in Christian Endeavor from these enthusiastic little workers in the land of the Southern Cross.

I should like to tell you of the two or three Junior societies that I saw in England, for Junior Endeavor is just beginning there, but I am beginning to realize that while it has taken us eleven months to go around the world, it would take at least eleven years to tell all we have seen.

In all these countries and in many others that we could not visit, there are boys and girls, and young men and young women who have promised as we have promised, that all their lives they "will try to do whatever He would like to have them do," and I have sometimes thought that many of them are trying harder than we are. As I have seen these earnest Endeavorers in all lands, I have felt that there is a Christian Endeavor chain reaching all around the world, and that each one of us is a link in that chain. But the separate links are of little use unless they are bound firmly together. Let us make this Christian Endeavor chain as strong as possible, keeping our own links bright and firm and trying always to keep all the links closely bound together. And let us never forget that "Love is the little golden chain that bindeth up the trust." Though this chain has links in many colors, yet the black ones and brown ones are very strong, I think, and the yellow ones may be pure gold. And I am glad to think that there are so many little links in the chain, for we cannot do without them, and I hope the day is coming when there will be as many little links as large ones. Shall it not be our aim to make this Christian Endeavor chain longer and stronger every year?

Let us then in spirit today clasp hands with our brothers and sisters in Christian Endeavor all the world around, beginning right here in Montreal and stretching out across our own continent to the Pacific shores, reaching out to the little brown hands in Tasmania, not omitting the yellow hands in China and Japan, or the brown ones in India, including in our grasp many hands of all sizes and shades of color in Egypt and Syria and Turkey and Germany and Spain and France and England, till at last the circle is complete at Montreal again.

As we think of all these Endeavorers in other lands, let us always remember that

> " We work together, if far apart,
> Loyal and strong is each loving heart,
> One is our Master, Christ, the Lord,
> And we catch the sound of His guiding word,
> We will follow on where he leads the way,
> Till we stand together in perfect day." [*Loud applause.*]

At the close of Mrs. Clark's address, which was listened to with great interest, various announcements were made, after which the audience joined in singing the hymn, "God be with you," closing with the Mizpah benediction.

THE TENT.

The first session of the convention in the tent had for its general topic, " Soul Winning." About 5,000 of the delegates were present. Rev. Wm. Patterson of Toronto, Ont., presided, and after a short prayer and praise service the first speaker, Rev. Rufus W. Miller, of Hummelstown, Pa., was introduced. His address was as follows : —

Special Work for Young Men.

Address of Rev. Rufus W. Miller.

Never was there such an effort put forth in behalf of the young men as now; never were the young men themselves so active in work for their fellow young men as now; never was the Church of Christ so alive to aggressive endeavors for reaching the men as now; yet the need of the hour is more skilfully directed, more earnest, manly, special work for young men.

The majority of men are not in the church. The columns of great city dailies are filled with the discussion of the question, " Why don't men go to church ? " In every religious mixed assembly, the women far outnumber the men. The largest proportion of non church-goers — those not Christian — is found among the young men between the ages of sixteen and forty, and they constitute one-sixth of the population. Some estimate that 65 out of every hundred young men never attend church at all. The fact is the young man is conspicuous by his absence from church. On the other hand, the world's temples are all filled. The saloon, billiard-hall, concert room and other worse places are supported almost entirely by young men. In this " age of lodges " city and country teem with secular orders, clubs and societies, whose tendency is to draw their members away from religious influences and to unfit them for Christian work.

The church must meet the changed conditions of modern life and the new phases of our aggressive civilization. The family is no longer the sole channel through which the church can reach the world. Concentration of population and enormous industrial developments tend to make man more and more solitary. The worker of today (though surrounded by thousands) is as lonely in his work as an exile in a Russian mine. The exacting duties of factory work and of the great stores give no time for fellowship or social recreations. Even in agriculture, agreeable companionship no longer lightens the heat and burden of the day. The long line of merry hay-makers is superseded by the solitary man directing a machine. The young man no longer lives in the family of the master during his apprenticeship. At an early age he is emancipated from parental control and deprived of the inestimable advantages of well-ordered family life. Thousands of young men are on the move. A great army are commercial travellers. There is an annual exodus from country to city of hundreds upon hundreds, and a multitude know no home life beyond the artificialities of the boarding-house. These strangers to home and proper social life stand in special need of personal touch and sympathy. There are, too, the peculiar dangers and temptations of young men in the formative and crucial period of their lives,—their unbounded energy, keen imagination, love of pleasure, craving for companionship, untried principles and untrained wills, make them peculiarly objects of solicitude.

Four hurtful influences may be said to control the modern man's actions: (1) Absorbing devotion to business, leaving little strength of mind or body for religion. The age spells God with an " L," making the Deity, "gold"; (2) The bold, malignant attacks of infidelity, caricaturing the Bible and holy living; (3) The breaking down of the regard for the Sabbath, including Sunday trains and newspapers; (4) Evil lives, sinful habits, false moral standards, a wrong business, or wrong business methods. These come with exceptional force upon the young men.

Another cogent reason for this special work is found in the fact that in every department of religious philanthropic work. preaching alone excepted, the ministering women are first and foremost. We are living in the golden age of woman's work; for this let there be rejoicing. Witness the many lines of distinctive work for women in the church activities of today: The Women's Missionary Societies. the Ladies' Aid Societies, Dorcas Associations, King's Daughters, the W. C. T. U., etc. This emphasis upon women's work calls for a like emphasis upon men's work. It is high time to call to the Baraks to go to the front with the Deborahs. The men must not be allowed to be active in everything but religion. Lift up the perfect man — Christ — and men will not only be drawn, but manly operation and co-operation will be called forth.

It goes without saying that this special work must be done by the young men themselves, and by the young men associated together as young men. The Hon. John Wanamaker has well said, speaking of the Men's Brotherhood in Bethany Presbyterian church, Philadelphia: "Their activity as soul-winners has been one of the most encouraging things in the thirty-five years of Bethany's history. A distinctive work in any church of men for men is one of the best things that any church can undertake, in my opinion." Work for young men by young men is in accord with a fundamental principle of human nature. The young man's social nature craves the companionship of his fellows. He is susceptible, most of all, to the influences for good or ill from young men of his age, tastes and work in life. The peculiar work to be done to reach him can best be done by his fellows. The young men are clannish, are gregarious, and herd in kind. The numerous secular orders, clubs, lodges, societies, composed as they are exclusively of men, testify to the power of this clannish feeling. And the Young Men's Christian Association, as a united enterprise of the church, is a marked illustration of successful work by men for men. [*Applause.*]

Now, this kind of work can be done still more effectively by securing the co-operation of the young men in the Christian Endeavor Society, which works from the congregation as a centre, and which brings its fruits home to the church. And you will please understand that it is by request that I present a tried method of work along this line.

The plan is simply this: to incorporate the fundamental features of the Brotherhood of Andrew and Philip — a young men's organization in the local church — into the Christian Endeavor Society by the formation of a Brotherhood Committee. This is a combination that for the sake of co-operation and simplicity is especially desirable in small churches.

This Brotherhood Committee differs from other committees in that its number is larger and is made up of volunteer young men, who pledge themselves to the two rules of the Brotherhood of Andrew and Philip. The rules are, the Rule of Prayer, — to pray daily for the spread of Christ's kingdom among young men and for God's blessing upon the labors of the Brotherhood (or Brotherhood Committee); the Rule of Service, — to make an earnest effort each week to bring at least one young man within hearing of the Gospel of Jesus Christ as set forth in the services of the church young people's prayer meetings and young men's Bible classes. These are simple definite obligations, which any Christian young man can assume and fulfil, and yet they aid the most advanced worker, for they are capable of endless development and outreach in Christian work. The great matter is to reduce work for Christ to such a system as that for all and for each there is a plan; or, as Sydney Smith would have said, a hole fitted for every peg, whatever its size or shape. Beginnings are confessedly difficult, and none more so than in the doing of spiritual work; now, by challenging our young men with these two rules, they soon learn for themselves to do Christian work freely and intelligently. These rules of prayer and service become the A, B, C, of the Christian worker's training. They give a man a definite starting-point. They teach the truth, — if you want to grow, — G-o R-ight O-n, W-orking. [*Applause.*]

There is a vast deal of special work for young men in this Brotherhood Committee.

Work among commercial travellers, ushering, invitation work on the streets and at the hotels, visitation of the sick; and in institutional churches the management of the gymnasium, the reading-room, the formation of cycle and athletic clubs, etc. What a grand work if our young men in our church services and other meetings would act as "The Welcomers," as they are called in the Pleasant Sunday Afternoon Men's Bible Classes found in many places in England. Their instructions are to shake hands with everybody all around, to find their places and to make them feel that they are at home. And if throughout the land the Brotherhood Committees in country churches would promptly notify similar committees in city churches of the intending removal of young men from their neighborhood; and in turn they would at once affectionately look after the strange young man, what multitudes might be saved. Oh, the dangers of transition! The first ten days are fatal, if the young man is not kept from that society which is naturally offered to him, and to which in his ignorance of the blandishments of refined vice he is naturally drawn.

We sometimes wait until a man is clean gone to the devil, and then we pity him and try to help him, and we wonder at his cold treatment of our offers. Some time ago one of our criminals was hanged. As his vile life was near its end, Christian people tried in vain to tell him of a Saviour's love. He answered their solicitude with blasphemy, saying that if they had found any good in Christ, they had heretofore kept it pretty carefully from him; and he finally dismissed them angrily with the statement that if it was true, it was too late to be true for him; and that if they had shown him one hundredth part of the attention before he began his career of infamy, which they had shown him as he was about to finish it on the gallows, he might have been a decent man. Think, friends, of those who, unbefriended, feel the forces of moral chaos contending in them. The lonliness of a man drifting out and out to sea on the pathless ocean and no help in sight is the loneliness of these men often, so far as moral help is concerned. It is piteous to see passion and sin tightening about a young man with noble impulses in his heart, and to hear him in despair, crying, "Oh, no one wants to know me, nobody cares for my soul." In times past, in some places and in some congregations, it has been nobody's business in particular to look after the strange young man. It is always somebody's business, in the name of Satan, to try and ruin the young man; let it be the business of this Brotherhood Committee, in the name of Christ, to try to save him.

The Brotherhood Committee can also be a connecting link between the work of the Young Men's Christian Association and the local congregation, in that it can bring the young men reached through the association under the influence of the divinely instituted means of grace in the church.

Brotherhood work gives a direct and specific training in soul-winning, and thus prepares first-class church officers. It steers many a man directly into the holy office of the Christian ministry. Fifteen of our chapters at the last convention reported twenty-six men studying for the ministry as a direct result of Brotherhood work.

This Brotherhood Committee, adapting the principles of the Brotherhood of Andrew and Philip in doing its special work, sustains a direct relation to the pastor. They are pledged to do the work he assigns them, and they act for him whenever possible.

It was once said by a lad who was going to war that his sword was too short for him. His parent said: "You can add a step to it, my son." If the minister stands for the sword of the congregation in doing aggressive work to win and conquer the strange young man, it is plain that in most cases to succeed he must add a step by means of the Christian man, who is already between the young man and the pastor, but who, too often, stays the path of the sword, simply because he is allowed to be spiritually idle or at least indolent in relation to his fellow young man.

For after all, the great work to be done is personal work. It is the application of man to man, and life to life. The Rule of Service forms the habit of making at least one conscious and conscientious effort of word or deed in behalf of some one young man each week. This means sharp shooting, taking aim. It means fishing with hook and line, catching fish one by one. The Brotherhood Committee finds its work for each member in his week-day life and work. Just where you are you may serve God and bless your fellowmen. You may be a manufacturer, a merchant, a mechanic, a clerk, a man of leisure, a student. The Rule of Service bids you remember God wants you to serve him just where you are. All great works are done by serving God with what we have in hand. We sympathize with Jethro's herdsman — a lonely stranger owning nothing, not even one of the lambs that he watched. He had nothing but his shepherd's rod, cut out of the thicket, the mere stick with which he guided the sheep. Any day he might throw it away and cut a better one. And God said " What is in thy hand? With this rod, with this stick thou shalt save Israel!" And so it proved. Young man, you may have a poor opportunity, a lonely station, only a single talent, but all God asks us to do is to be faithful and earnest. The Scriptures emphasize the power of personal influence in touching individuals. St. Paul constantly changing his place of living, moving among large bodies of people, never overlooked individuals. In his speech to the elders of Ephesus he could challenge them to bear witness that he had taught not only publicly, but from house to house, and had warned every one night and day with tears. Like his Master he was moved by the sight of a multitude, and gladly sought opportunity to tell the Gospel story to many. Like his Master he was quite as ready also to preach to the small company of women, of whom Lydia was one, at the riverside, or to the soldier to whom he was chained in the Roman prison. The Gospels are largely taken up with conversations between Christ and individuals. He bestowed as much care and pains in setting forth the nature of his kingdom to individuals as He did when he was speaking to great multitudes. He even put himself in the way of individuals. He styled himself the good shepherd, who called all his sheep by name. The lost one concerned him more than the ninety and nine safely in the fold. We can truly say " Individuals " was on his heart as the watchword of his ministry. When will we learn that the most important work is that which attracts the least observation, the quiet work of personal influence done in the seclusion of the family, in the presence of the little Sunday-school class, in the few words spoken over the counter or in the store, in private conversation with a neighbor, or in loving care of a little child, a waif it may be, from the streets.

The most important special work for a young man is the daily personal endeavor to influence the man nearest him. Andrew goes and lays hold of the man nearest him and the one he loves best. But too often, that is just what we fail to do. There was a great man in the last generation who used to be greatly sought after, whose conversation was the brilliancy of every dinner table, but his wife used to say that he hung his fiddle as he entered his own door. The home or the small circle of friends among whom we move is where we are to live and speak for Christ. First of all, there, if anywhere, we are to testify for him. If the problem of the non-attendance of the men is to be solved, it must be by the personal work of Christian men. So long as we keep ourselves shut up in our churches, so long as we put our largest amount of reliance in the ministers preaching in the pulpit, things will go from bad to worse. There is no substitute for the personal work of Christian men, who have found Christ for themselves. Great multitudes are inspiring, but it is better for us to be occupied with the units of which they are composed. We may pray for a hundred souls or a thousand, but they must be saved one at a time.

And this special work, which is so old as to be apostolic and scriptural, must be done, let it be emphasized, by the young men. For upon the young men rests the work of the church, as of the nation and the world. The solvent of many of the great problems of today is found in this "personal-work idea" as it lays hold of the Christian young man, and as through him the next man is reached.

We are at the dawning of great changes, perhaps of a social and religious revolution. Monopolies and class laws must be blotted out, and enactments at once democratic and Christian written over them. The despotic dominance of dogma and mere profession in religion must give way to the fairer rule of conscience and heart.

Pharisaism, priestism, bigotry and hypocrisy must be cast out and trodden under foot of men, and social and religious conventionalism and shams, as dead as they are weighty, must be buried out of sight. And you, young men, must do it. The old will not. Improvement for them is in the past. The spontaneous conservatism of middle age resists progress; only death and youth prevent stagnation in this world of ours. On you, young man, God and the ages cast the tasks of the times. As Moses sent young men to spy out the land of Canaan, as Christ called young men into the circle of his chief messengers, and as the Anointed One — the Christ — was a young man, so now heaven's choice fixes upon you. Accept the call and play the man.

Consecrating your life to a life of prayer and service you will come to apprehend more clearly your personal responsibility, both for your own religious convictions and for the salvation of others. An ever-burning consciousness of our personal responsibility and the high privilege of being Christ's representatives will give us a holy, constant enthusiasm in personal soul-winning. At a dinner given by a few friends of Daniel Webster, when he was secretary of state, he was asked, " What is the most important thought that ever occupied your mind? " The great statesman considered a little while, and passing his hand across his face, answered, " The most important thought that ever occupied my mind was that of my personal responsibility to Almighty God." [*Applause.*] And after speaking in the most solemn manner on this subject for twenty minutes he arose and silently left the room. The great apostle has said, " We must all be made manifest before the judgment-seat of Christ; that each one may receive the things done in the body, according to what he hath done, whether it be good or bad."

" We are personally responsible to do all we can for all within reach of our influence."

Another message for the men of this era comes to us from afar,— out of that storm which tossed the great ships of war before Samoa. In one supreme moment of agony it seemed as if the flagship " Trenton " must strike the coral reef and perish with her precious freight of four hundred and fifty souls. The steam had given out and the vessel, a mere plaything in the storm, seemed to be driving hopelessly to destruction, when her commander, as a last resort, and forlorn hope, ordered the whole crew into the port rigging, that the compact mass of humanity might serve as a sail, and at the same time throw the whole weight on the storm side, in stern defiance of the tempest. The daring manoeuvre was successful. The stars and stripes were run to the gaff. The band on deck played the " Star Spangled Banner." The men, who still clung as sails to the shrouds, lifted their voices in a mighty cheer, and when the sport of the wind drove the " Trenton " against the " Vandalia " the crew in her rigging sprang adeck of the flagship and were saved. For, when the flagship struck at last, it was on a friendly shore, rather than the ragged reef, and from her deck were taken not only her own complement, but those of the sister ship, who, in her peril, she had not failed to rescue. This, O men, is your work in the emergency of the church. Run up the pennant of the cross. Have all voices join in the chorus of praises to God. And then, O men, mount to the rigging with all the weight of your manhood to catch the breezes of God's grace, and rescue the perishing in the Master's name. [*Applause.*]

Next on the program was an open meeting, conducted by Mr. J. Howard Breed, of Philadelphia, Pa.

How To Reach Young Men.

Open Meeting. Conducted by Mr. J. Howard Breed.

MR. BREED: In taking charge of this meeting, I want to say that this audience is composed of two distinct parts,— the talking part and the hearing part. A sailor once said that he liked the Episcopal church best because he had a chance to talk back. The audience will like this part because they have a chance to talk back; but please remember that each one has but a little time.

Question : — Is it an advantage to have a Brotherhood Committee, or to organize a Brotherhood of Andrew and Philip as a separate organization?

The responses from all over the house seemed to favor a Brotherhood Committee in the Y. P. S. C. E., and that through this committee they could get certain work done that they could not get done in any other way among the young men. The following suggestions were made : —

"The Central Presbyterian society of Erie, Pa., have a committee in that society to visit the hotels during the week, leave an invitation to come to church services, and watch in the corridors of the church for the young men and welcome them. This comes in along the line of Brotherhood work, and it is working successfully. We also give a card indicating a desire to become acquainted with the members."

"New York City African M. E. society: We have out-door meetings. We go out and gather in the wanderers, and then walk back to our church, where we have prayer meetings. And then we have two members of this band of brothers go out in the highways and gather in friends and bring them into the church. I am one of those men, and have been for twelve years." [*Applause.*]·

"Have a special committee of young men, and let them go in and out in the congregation. They will get the young men if they want them, and if they don't want them, they won't get them."

"First Presbyterian, New Haven, Conn.: We have several young men in our society who take particular care to meet every young man that comes into the church, and if we meet them anywhere near the church we invite them into the society. This plan has worked very successfully."

"The Congregational society of Utica, New York, has three men whose duty it is to go into the slums of the city, and only men can do this work."

A delegate from Vermont thought that the ladies should join in the work of receiving and welcoming strangers.

An Ohio delegate thought that the best way to reach the country young men when they go to the city is to give to them the hand of fellowship.

"First Presbyterian church, Florida: We have got to get down to individual work. Committee work does n't amount to a row of pins. What you must do is to get down to the individual." [*Applause.*]

An Illinois delegate asked the following question : "Do you think it wise to use printed matter in approaching men on the street?"

MR. BREED: It is wise to use printed matter on the street sometimes, and sometimes it is not wise, and a man who tries to use it has got to have a great deal of common sense. Nobody can say it is never useful, and nobody dare say it is always useful.

A delegate from Montreal spoke of the necessity of reaching the boys, and of looking out for the Juniors.

The Open Meeting was followed by the song "Stand up, stand up for Jesus," which was heartily joined in by the congregation. Mr. Patterson then introduced Rev. F. D. Power, D.D., of Washington, D. C., as the next speaker.

Evangelistic Methods of Church Work.

Address of Rev. F. D. Power, D.D

Christian Endeavor means work for souls. The Christian Endeavor Society must be a soul-winning as well as a soul-keeping force, to accept all its privileges. In religion the greatest thing is to save souls, and as this was Christ's work and this is the work of the church, it is the work of the Christian Endeavor Society, which is "For Christ and the Church." "Go," said Christ. Christians are goers. They are not to stand and wait for men to come; they must move toward them, get among them, bear to them the gifts of the Gospel. "Go ye," said the Master. The work is general. There are to be no stay-at-homes; no silent partners; no privileged order in the matter of delivering the message. Whether with or without age, learning, script, priestly ordination, skill of tongue, or power of worldly influence, Christ's people must go; too many souls are too needy, the delights of the King's service are too full and real with those who have them, that any should be denied the privilege of extending the sovereignty and enlarging the territory of the King. All are goers, and the limits of this going are "all the world" and to "every creature."

What shall be the methods? Take with me a study of one of the miracles of Jesus — one of the few miracles recorded by all four evangelists. He has been near Capernaum teaching, and multitudes have thronged him. He has had no leisure even so much as to eat. He needs rest, and taking the twelve, he crosses the head of the lake, and lands in a quiet glen, closed in by hills, six miles from Capernaum, but the people follow along the shore, and as his boat touches the retired and desolate spot, he beholds the slopes alive with the multitude. Out of all the villages they had come, bearing their sick, and are waiting for him; and passing through the crowds he heals and comforts, and ascending the hillside speaks to the gathered crowds of the kingdom of God. The day passes, and still the people linger. The sun goes down behind the western hills, and the disciples become anxious and ask that the people be sent away. But to their astonishment Jesus commands, "Give ye them to eat." They must not go hungry. Impossible! They have five loaves of common barley bread and two small fishes, while two hundred pennyworth would not give a mouthful apiece to so great a number. "Make them to sit down," is the short reply to their cry of helplessness. It is Nisan, the month of flowers. The vernal rains are over. The soft, rich green grass clothes the hills. The disciples divide the vast multitudes into companies of fifties and hundreds, reminding Peter long after, from the bright colors of their Oriental dresses, of the flower beds of a great garden. Then lifting up his eyes to heaven, the Master breaks bread and distributes to the disciples, and they to the multitude and all are filled.

How shall we distribute the bread of life? 1. As the disciples to the five thousand, take one at a time. The disciples were all engaged in the work of distribution, and every hungry man was waited upon personally with his portion. The food, though supernaturally given, is borne through ordinary channels to the people, and the apparently inadequate resources are made sufficient by divine grace. How shall we reach the masses is the question. The church presents a sorry picture often, sitting down and reaching, reaching, never rising and going forth, but reaching and crying, "How shall we reach the masses?" I answer, Through the masses, individual reaching individual, every man his man. The early Christians scattered abroad went everywhere preaching the Word. All were busy, each had his task. We are not to understand that every one had a pulpit and a set sermon and thirty minutes' time, but into houses, fields, shops, market-places, the Gospel was carried. The Scriptures emphasize man not the mass. The little captive maid of Israel led Naaman to the prophet; Andrew found his own brother Simon and brought him to Jesus; and Philip found Nathaniel and said, "Come and see." Jesus preached to one woman at the well, and to one member of the Sanhedrim. Philip was divinely commanded to join himself to the chariot of one man as he journeyed, and preached Jesus to his solitary auditor till he won him. Ananias is sent to one man to instruct him and two disciples lay hold of another and teach him the way of the Lord more perfectly. There is joy in heaven over one sinner that repenteth. Let every one win one. Get hold of the individual and you get hold of the masses. How is it with the church today? We trust to the committee. The machine is expected to conquer the world. The church gathers itself into comfortable quarters and says, "Here we are, the feast is spread, you may come." Or it expects the one poor fellow in the pulpit unaided to bring them in. It forgets the word of the Master to his servants, "Go out and compel them to come in." The majority, like Betty's husband when the bear came, who fled to the garret and drew up the ladder after him, and left Betty to fight the beast alone, are ready to cry at every stroke of the tongs, "Go it, Betty! Hit him again, Betty!" and when Bruin is dead, come down rubbing their hands gleefully, and exclaiming, "We did it well. Betty, didn't we do it well?" [*Applause.*] Want of individuality is the most dangerous sign of our modern civilization. It is true in politics, it is true in religion. It is the most crippling influence in the modern church. There must be organization, but it should be like that of an army, every man in the ranks; every individual force making itself felt in the movement of the whole. The unit must be recognized. The hungry multitude is fed by individual waiters. The one house, the one person, must be sought after as the patient fisherman fishes for the one fish, as the skilful politician looks after the one voter. Every man to his man. The church must not reach out merely one pair of hands from the pulpit, but Briarius-like stretch forth a hundred through her members. Distinction between clergy and laity is not apostolic. To every man there must be his work. The fruit must be picked by hand, and hand-picked fruit is always the best. If we are ever to succeed in reaching our great centres of population, we must have pastors that are willing to spend and be spent to get to the people, and churches that understand the value of the individual soul and the measure of individual obligation in winning it. [*Applause.*]

2. As in the case of the miracle, the bread must be direct from the Master. These thousands fed with food fresh from the hands of the Son of God are filled and satisfied. If people come asking bread and we give them a stone, they will not be likely to come again to our tables. The alienation of the masses from the church is too often alienation, not from the Gospel, but from human substitutes for the Gospel. The story is told of a certain king who gave a series of feasts and bade men to them day after day. His servants received supplies from him, and were commissioned to invite the people and serve them. But by-and-by the people ceased coming. The great mass cared not for his banquet. The king made inquiry, and found the food that was provided did not satisfy them. He visited the tables and saw that the food was not that which his storehouses furnished. "Whence came these dishes?" he demanded of his servants. "My oxen and my fatlings were killed, but this is hard meat, the meat of cattle lean and starved. This bread is of chaff, and not of the finest of the wheat. This water was not drawn from my wells." And they answered, "O king, we thought the people would be surfeited with marrow and fatness, and so we gave them bones, old bones, on which to try their teeth. We thought they would weary of the best bread, and so we prepared bread of husks and of bran. We thought they would lose taste for the pure water of your springs, and so we drew from our own cisterns. We thought these things more suited to the times." Then the king knew why the people came not to his banquets. His servants had failed to serve the good meat, and had chopped up odds and ends and tainted bits — a hash of their own invention — and the people were turned against it. Then said the king, "Clear my tables; cast out this rubbish to the dogs, take away these gewgaws, bring on my royal bounties." And it was done, and the people thronged again his banqueting hall, and were glad. [*Applause.*]

Is not the parable true? Have not men spread the King's table with sawdust and slops and gimcracks and every false thing in place of the plain old Gospel dishes that feed the hungry? [*Applause.*] Has not "Christ and him crucified" been put aside for discourses on evolution, agnosticism, higher criticism, everything save the eternal truth that conquered Samaria and Corinth and Ephesus and Rome? Is not the bread too often from other hands than Christ's, and without the Divine grace that multiplied the loaves on the shores of the Galilean lake? Is not the same sweet, plain, old-fashioned Gospel that the common people heard gladly from the lips that spake as never man spake, and which among the villages and hills and forests has subdued its thousands and hundreds of thousands, the Gospel that is needed by kings in their palaces, mammon worshippers on their Wall Streets, and the disinherited in their slums? It is so. Human nature is the same from boodler to bootblack, from president to pauper. It calls for the same regeneration, it hungers for the same peace.

Don't labor to make big speeches; take reverently the bread broken by the hands of the Master and feed men. [*Applause.*]

3. As in the distribution of the loaves and fishes, the Gospel must be given to all the people. No doubt there were prominent Jews in that great assembly, men of wealth and rank and culture, as well as the lowliest of the lowly; but the Master divides them up without distinction into companies, and has all treated alike. What is our plan? We draw lines between classes. We seek A people, not THE people. We aim to make proselytes to our denominations; and each separate school would rival every other in getting the largest number of " rich neighbors " to its feast, while the poor and maimed and halt and blind are left to shift for themselves. [*Applause.*] Hence the tendency in city churches to pride and covetousness and to become exclusive social clubs in the West End. In our city of Cleveland, ten wards, containing a population of 54,000, have half the church members, while the other half is distributed in thirty wards with four times the population. That is, the percentage of church membership is four times greater in the wealthy wards than in those that are poor. In New York, below Fourteenth Street, is one weak church to every six thousand inhabitants. Above Fourteenth, where the wealthy reside, is one strong church to every three thousand.

Protestant establishments, at least, follow the wealth of the city, move out of the poor districts, and the Gospel becomes a vestibuled Pullman palace car, limited express, extra fare, every-man-owning-his seat; and once a year [*applause*], possibly, the priest and Levite of this system solemnly go from Jericho up to Jerusalem to a convention to consider the best methods of reaching the masses [*applause*], while only the good Samaritan, whom they despise, is left to do the work which they are neglecting. James writes an epistle to these church establishments which would profitably bear an annual reading. [*Applause.*]

Now this state of things must be changed. The church must stay among the people. St. Paul's, in London, is in the midst of the din of business, as is Trinity in New York. St. Peter's, in Rome, is surrounded by dark and filthy streets, as is St. Stephen's in Vienna. Rich and poor meet together in Old World cathedrals, Mohammedan mosques and heathen temples, where, costly and magnificent as are the shrines, floors are bare and seats are uncushioned. Let our churches be free. Let them be furnished plainly. Let people be welcomed from cellars and garrets and alleys as cordially as from Fifth Avenue and brown stone fronts. Let the publican and the harlot and every sin-sick, lost soul feel " This is my Father's house," and let every disciple be busy to minister to them of the bread blessed and given to the master for this purpose. And we shall hear no more of the estrangement of the masses from the church. Christ is not confined up in the West End. He is down here in the midst of the multitude.

4. Finally, as with the disciples in the distribution to the five thousand, we must be united in this service.

> " The parish priest of austerity
> Climbed up in a high church steeple
>   To be nearer God,
> So that he might hand
> His word down to his people.
>   And in sermon script
> He daily wrote
> What he thought was sent from heaven,
>   And he dropt this down
> On his people's heads,
> Two times one day in seven.
>   In his age God said :
> ' Come down and die,'
> And he called from out the steeple
>   ' Where art thou, Lord?'
> And the Lord replied,
>   ' Down here among my people.' " [*Applause.*]

What is the greatest barrier to the evangelization of the world? The crime of division among the people of God, the sin and selfishness of sectarianism.

Christians in every town are divided into a dozen feeble sects, struggling often not so much against sin as against each other. Millions are wickedly wasted in the furtherance of party claims; the mind of the Master is unfulfilled, the integrity of the faith is threatened; the poor and needy cry for the bread of life; the forces of Satan are massed in the great centres of population, and we sit down and indulge our petty jealousies and strifes, and let the great tide of evil sweep on and over us. Fancy the disciples at the time of the miracle falling into a row among themselves over some question as to the character of these miraculously multiplied loaves, or the methods of distribution, or the philosophy of their operation in appeasing the hunger of these Jews, while the people went away disgusted and unfed, and you have a picture of the Church of Christ in our modern times. If a secular army were to undertake the reduction of New York or Chicago or Montreal, it would have a method of attack, and would combine for one common purpose. Can the Church of Christ today expect to conquer strongholds for Christ without plan, without unity, by a species of guerilla warfare, aimed mostly at its own? Let the children of light learn a lesson from the children of this world. Let the church come together in Christian sympathy and co-operation, and move as one man against the hosts of evil. Let the disciples go as a body at the bidding of their Lord, bearing the food provided by heaven to the hungry thousands at their doors, and the problem of reaching unsaved humanity will be solved. Let Christian Endeavorers remember, every soul for another soul, every one dispensing the bread from the Master's hand, all seeking the people and all the people, and all going forth as one body for Christ, and the world must be evangelized. [*Great applause.*]

After another hymn, Mr. Patterson announced that, as a kind of postscript to the discussion, the delegates were now to be asked the question, "What is your society doing?" the open meeting to be conducted by Mr. P. S. Foster of Washington, D. C.

What Evangelistic Work Is Your Society Doing?

Open Meeting. Conducted by Mr. P. S. Foster.

Mr. Foster began by reading a few verses from the tenth chapter of Matthew, after which he spoke as follows:—

MR. FOSTER: I read these verses to draw your attention to the Master in sending out the disciples upon their missionary work. In the last verse of the last chapter of Matthew we have this: "Go ye, therefore, into all the world and make disciples of all nations, baptizing them in the name of the Father and of the Son and of the Holy Spirit, and lo, I am with you alway.' To whom is this? Is it directly to our brothers, the ministers on the platform? Do you think it was directed simply to the 70 disciples, or is it yours and mine? So many of us are satisfied, as brother Power has said, to sit in a Pullman palace car down here, and ride comfortably and undisturbed, but I want to tell you that the sooner we have the realization of the personal responsibility of this soul-saving work, the sooner these two things will occur: the one will be that of our trying to do the Master's work which should be done, and the other that deep devotion to Jesus Christ and love for his service. Work will then come to you as it has never come before. "What Evangelistic Work is your society doing?" You notice it says *society*. The society represents what you and I are doing as individuals. Now, how many societies here have a special committee for "city missions," "soul saving," — or whatever you may choose to call it — work in your society? If you have, tell us what that committee is doing.

A score of delegates at once sprang upon their chairs in various parts of the tent, and tried to catch the eye of the leader. The first to be heard from was the Second Disciples church, of New York City.

"This Christian Endeavor society did evangelistic work by dividing the district into blocks, and the members of the committee visited every house in these blocks. This did not prove very successful, on account of the large foreign population in those districts; nevertheless, they propose to continue the work in the fall, and feel confident of bringing some souls into the kingdom."

"A Congregational church in Connecticut has a Christian Endeavor society that conducts evangelistic meetings in the country districts, and has been winning souls for Jesus Christ right straight along."

"An A. M. E. church of Brooklyn has a committee connected with the Christian Endeavor society, which has, within a very short time, brought half a dozen young men to Christ, and has driven out of business one pool-room and one liquor saloon." [*Great applause.*]

MR. FOSTER : We have two churches in Washington which have been successful along this very line. One has practically driven out of a certain section, known as "Hell's bottom," in the city of Washington, nearly every disreputable saloon in that locality. Another one, brother Power's church in Washington, has done a great deal of this soul-saving work.

"A Congregational church in Vermont has a society that sends out three or four of its members every Sunday, to hold meetings in the outside districts, and also has a committee of young ladies to call on the sick, carry flowers, read to them, etc."

"A Methodist church of Utica, New York, has a band of young men to promote the work of temperance in their midst. They also have a rescuer, who takes care of those who are degraded."

"The First Church of the Disciples in Philadelphia has a committee that is doing mission work in the slums of the city, and has organized a mission which is to be maintained by the Christian Endeavor society."

"The Cumberland Presbyterian church, of Cincinnati, has a committee of young men in their Christian Endeavor society, whose work it is to conduct open-air services at one of the market houses, gathering together from two to three hundred people every Sabbath afternoon. This plan was found to work very successfuly. The young men and women of this society go out into the tenement houses with invitations to attend church services."

MR. FOSTER : I will ask this whole audience how many Christian people, and Christian Endeavorers especially, have personally tried, in all of their days since becoming Christians, to help a single soul to Jesus Christ by personal button-holing? How many of you? [*Many hands were raised all over the tent.*] How many tried to do it in the last week? [*Quite a large number of hands were raised.*] The Word of God says, "Freely ye have received, freely give." Let us not depend upon our own strength to do this work, but lean on Jesus. If we go in our own strength, it will all come to naught. Jesus said, "I do not these things of myself but of the father."

"A society in Utica, New York. took a census of the number of young men who were in the twenty-five churches of that city, and found that there were 2,300. Then they took a census of twenty-five of their saloons, and found that there were 4,500 in the saloons. From that hour they made up their minds that one of the things that Christian Endeavor wanted to do was to fire a solid shot at the saloons, which they consider the greatest power that has to do with drawing young men away from evangelizing influences."

In Salem, Mass., last fall several Christian Endeavor societies united and appointed a temperance committee, and entered upon a campaign for no license. This season Salem is a no-license city, and they have made it one of the cleanest cities in the state of Massachusetts. [*Applause.*]

The hymn, "All Hail the Coming King" was then sung, and the benediction pronounced.

THURSDAY EVENING.

DRILL HALL.

As was to be expected, the evening program drew out an audience which completely filled the immense Drill Hall. The delegates gathered early, and found much to interest them before the time for beginning the meeting. The song service was grandly inspiring.

Rev. Dr. Teunis S. Hamlin presided and opened the exercises by calling upon the audience to join with him in repeating the 100th Psalm. Rev. Canon J. B. Richardson, of London, Ont., representing the Church of England in Canada, a newly elected member of the Board of Trustees, then offered prayer. Two hymns were sung, "As Pants the Hart" and "Send Showers of Blessing," after which Dr. Hamlin made the following announcement :—

DR. HAMLIN: One of the very interesting things about our Christian Endeavor convention is that it has come to be a thing that all the cities in the country large enough to hold it desire to have with them. We never have to go around begging for invitations, but the trustees are always embarrassed with a superabundance of riches, and the only question for us to decide is where we can go to the best interests, first, of the convention, and then of the place where the convention shall meet. It is the custom, as you know, to decide two years in advance where we will go. Last year the decision was made and announced that we should go to Cleveland. Last year and the year before and again this year we have been honored with very cordial invitations from that marvelous city of the Rocky Mountains [*applause*] which has had its representatives before the trustees year after year, asking us that we should go there. We very highly appreciate that invitation and have the very best opinion possible of what Denver and Colorado and all that great region would do for a Christian Endeavor convention. There are certain conditions that must be complied with in order to make the convention a success. One of them is that there shall be a suitable place of meeting, a hall or halls large enough and well enough equipped to accommodate the crowd. Another condition is that there shall be hotel accommodations and accommodations in private houses sufficient for this vast multitude. Another, and a very prime condition is that the railroad rates shall be such that those who want to go may be able to pay them. When an invitation came to us from the Pacific slope this was the great question, Whether the railroads of the country were anxious enough to have this convention travel over them to make rates that would justify us in going to the Pacific. That matter has been before the trustees yesterday and today; and I am honored and privileged to say that, if these conditions shall be met, we have unanimously voted that the convention of '95 shall be held in San Francisco.

Instantly, upon this announcement, there was great cheering, particularly by the California delegates, who rose in their seats and shouted out their state "call" again and again.

Showers of yellow ribbons bearing the legend, "California '95" were thrown into the air, while the audience applauded. The California delegates then sang the popular Junior Christian Endeavor hymn, "There is Sunshine in my Soul Today," which was likewise appreciated by the audience, who caught up the hymn and sang it heartily.

After the enthusiasm had somewhat subsided, Dr. Hamlin introduced the next speaker, as follows : —

DR. HAMLIN : There is one man to whom the eyes of all of us are constantly turning with gratitude, respect, and love, whom we acknowledge joyfully, not simply as the originator and founder of the Christian Endeavor idea and society, but as its constant friend and champion and promoter, who inspires all our hearts and whom we loyally recognize as our leader. There is not one among us, I am sure, who has not followed him during these last ten or eleven months from land to land and across sea after sea with earnest prayer, and there is not one of us who does not wish tonight, when he comes before us to deliver his annual address, to give him such an enthusiastic and unmistakable welcome as shall assure him of our undying love. I count it a very great honor and pleasure to have the privilege of presenting to this great audience one whom we all know so well that the sight of his face is a joy to us all, one in whose modesty and humility, in the midst of unparalleled success and almost if not quite unequalled affection from all parts of the world, we rejoice, and for which we give the credit to his Lord and ours. We shall listen to him tonight, as always, with the greatest delight and the greatest profit. I am very happy to introduce to you now our honored president, whom you will rise and receive standing. [*Three hearty cheers, and a prolonged Chautauqua salute.*]

World-Wide Christian Endeavor.

Annual Address of President Francis E. Clark.

Fellow Endeavorers [*renewed applause*]: — An old saying which contains more truth than poetry has recently been applied with much force to the Christian Endeavor movement,— a saying to the effect that every new and successful organization must pass through three stages of development,— the " pooh-pooh stage," the " bow-wow stage," and the " hear-hear stage."

The society early passed through the " pooh-pooh stage," and survived it. Men sneered at it as a hothouse for the forcing of premature spiritual vegetables, sometimes changing the figure by calling it a " wishy-washy flood of youthful gush." They gave it two years to live, and then five, and then ten, and now twenty. But time has answered these prophets, whom arguments could not reach ; and they have for the most part ceased to sneer.

Then the " bow-wow stage " was reached, and in basso profundo the critics said, " This is a dangerous movement, outside of the church." When pointed to our pledge and our motto as inculcating the quintessence of loyalty to the church, their growl changed its note, but still it was an unmistakable growl. " The society is a little church within the church," they would say ; and in high-sounding Latin they proclaimed it an *imperium in imperio*.

When again these well-intentioned but mistaken critics were proved to be in the wrong, — by time, not by argument, for argument has so little influence compared with time,— some of them joined the ranks of the encouraging " hear-hear " army, who through evil report and good report have proclaimed their faith in our principles and our plans.

Another section of these critics paid the Society the compliment of imitating it word for word, and with these plagiarized copies undertook to supplant the original. However, these attempts to supplant the Society have happily failed ; but from still others, who heretofore have been critical or indifferent, has lately come the shrill response, " Adopt my reform ; " " Promote my scheme ; " " Grind my axe," " and your Society may yet do some good."

So the " hear-hear stage " may be said to have ushered in two other developments, the imitative and the " grind-my-axe " stage.

In some respects this last is perhaps the most dangerous of all ; but with God's good grace, which has brought the movement through sneers and growls to popularity and success, we believe it will survive this danger, too.

It has been said more than once during the past year by these critics that the Christian Endeavor Society must have a new mission, a crusade of its own, or else it was doomed to extinction. " Let it devote the energies of a million and a half of young people," they have said, " exclusively to *our* reform for only ten years, and the world will be regenerated."

Many of these friends who are thus clamoring for " a new crusade " have not grasped the first principles of Christian Endeavor. They would use the Society simply as a convenience, as an advertising medium, to promote their schemes. They would pad the constitution, and tinker the pledge, in the interests of their particular notions. In the opinion of some of these good people,— and they are not diffident about expressing it,— the Society has done nothing worth speaking of ano will do nothing until it bestrides and rides their particular hobby.

Now, with all due deference to these friends who would usher in this fourth stage of the development of the movement, let me ask a few questions.

Is it nothing, O advocate of a new crusade, is it nothing that the Society has created or revived and rejuvenated twenty-six thousand young people's prayer meetings? [*Applause.*]

Is it nothing that it has poured the warm life-blood of its youthful enthusiasm into thousands of week-night church prayer meetings?

Is it nothing that it has comforted and strengthened pastors in all their work, as myriads of them are ready to testify? [*Applause.*]

Is it nothing that for a multitude of young people it has solved the question of worldly amusements, not by preaching against these amusements, or by passing laws against them, but by the higher legislation of substitution, of overcoming evil with good?

Is it nothing that thousands of Sunday schools have been enlarged through the efforts of the Sunday-school committee?

Is it nothing that tens of thousands of young strangers have been made to feel at home by the Calling committee?

Is it nothing that a multitude of churches have been made bright with God's hand-painted pictures, the flowers, and that an equal multitude of hospitals have afterward glowed with their radiance, the beautiful radiance that follows the footsteps of the Flower and Sunshine committees?

Is it nothing that missionary meetings have been multiplied, that hundreds have given *themselves* to proclaim the good tidings, and that at least a hundred thousand dollars were given last year by the Christian Endeavor societies, in addition to what would otherwise have been given, through the agency of Missionary committees, and through the regular denominational boards? [*Applause.*]

Is it, above all, nothing that through the efforts of the Lookout and allied committees, and of faithful helpers in every society, scores of thousands of our associate members came into the evangelical churches, and came in, not to be drones, but to be working Christians?

I recount these things, not to boast, but simply that we may remind the good people who do not understand our purpose and methods, and who are crying out for a new crusade, that we *have* found our mission, and that mission is, to promote in every way the spiritual life of young people; that we *are* waging our crusade, and that crusade is, the upbuilding in all ways of the Church of Christ [*applause*]; that the only axe that we have to sharpen is not theirs, but the one that our own individual church lays on the grindstone; that we will keep on in the same way in which we have begun, giving all our allegiance, all our powers, all our endeavors, to CHRIST AND THE CHURCH with which we are connected. [*Applause.*]

It will be a sorry day for the Society when it loses its first love, when it is untrue to its first principles, or when it seeks to substitute for the quiet, unobtrusive, spiritual work that it has to perform for its own church a more showy and noisy Endeavor, which leaves souls unsaved and the work of the church undone. Thank God, I can see no signs in any part of the world that our societies are yielding to these blandishments, that they are losing their spirituality, or holding to their prime purpose with less tenacity than of old.

The world does not stand in need of another temperance society, or another missionary organization, or another anti-opium guild, or another society for the prevention of cruelty to animals and children. There are splendid organizations (God bless them all) that are the appropriate channels for all these reforms and philanthropies; it is the mission of the Young People's Society of Christian Endeavor to put spiritual life-blood into these and every good cause by quickening the conscience, training the intellect, stimulating the activities, enlarging the sympathies, promoting the generosity, of young people under the direction of, and in conformity to, the will of the churches with which they are connected.

Every moral and philanthropic reform, as well as the churches, would lose vastly more than any one would gain, should the energies of these societies be diverted, as some advocate, from these normal channels, and turned for one or ten years to the accomplishment of some one reform.

Nevertheless, while I feel most strongly the necessity of holding to the fundamental principles for which the name "Christian Endeavor" has come to stand, I also sympathize most strongly with those whose watchword is ever onward and forward and upward, and who are always crying out for larger and better things; who, while holding to the principles involved in the pledge and the lookout committee and the consecration meeting, would ever apply the spiritual strength gained through these means to all the needs of mankind.

I sympathize, too, with those who would have *definite* purposes, according to the demands of the times, to occupy our accumulating energies.

Let me go so far as to suggest two or three "larger things" for the year to come, which, I believe, may well occupy the thoughts, the prayers, the energies, of all Endeavorers.

1. One of these advance steps that we may take is the cultivation of a larger and more intelligent spirit of patriotism and of good citizenship. [*Applause.*]

How shall this be done? By all joining, as a society, some one political party? Not unless we know of some party that embraces all the saints and none of the rascals [*laughter*]; one that is always right and never wrong. But whether you are a Democrat or a Republican, a Third-party man or a Populist, a Liberal or a Conservative, a Blue or a Grit, it can be done by bringing your vote and your influence — for your influence, fair Endeavorers, is often as powerful as your brother's vote — to the supreme test of the Christian Endeavor pledge. [*Applause.*]

You have promised in that "to do whatever He would like to have you do;" then *vote* as He would like to have you vote. [*Loud applause.*] Then you will not knowingly vote for a bad man or a bad measure; and, if need be, you will sacrifice your party rather than your principles.

When politicians realize that men with principles are watching their nominations, they will not dare to put up a bad man for your suffrage [*applause*], for they will realize what so many of the secular papers expressed last summer, after that wonderful Convention in New York City, that there is a new moral force in this country that must be reckoned with. Go to the primaries of your party, and take your Christian Endeavor pledge with you. Go to the caucus; get into the legislature; stand for Congress or for Parliament; but, when you get there, for God and your church and your country, do what *He* would like to have you do. [*Loud applause.*]

So, in humbler ways, let your influence be felt for every right cause. I am glad, for one, of the stand that Endeavorers have taken for the Christian and the American Sabbath. I believe that the course of the Society on this question has set an example that we may wisely follow in the future.

We have proved, for one thing, that we are not boycotters, whatever ill-natured people may say. There is a suspicion of lawlessness in that word borrowed from the bogs of old Ireland. It is not our word, nor does it express our attitude. We protested and petitioned; we did everything that we could as individuals and societies to save the nation from the threatened disgrace; and now we, each one for himself, without judging others, will decide what *He* would have us do in regard to going to the Exposition, or staying away from it.

Let it be understood that there is no power or wish in the Endeavor Society to compel uniformity, or to force the conscience of its members in regard to the World's Fair or any other subject.

This Convention can pass no votes or resolutions that are binding upon individuals or societies,—nor can any State or local union,—but it can and should lead us in this and every such matter more fully to recognize our individual responsibility as citizens as well as Christian men and women. Some phase of this very important subject of good citizenship viewed from the Christian standpoint may well occupy our attention at more than one of our society prayer meetings, and at more than one local-union gathering of the year to come. How may we become better citizens? How may we be truer patriots? Let us give to these questions a worthy answer.

2. Another important enlargement for the year to come is an enlargement and more practical exemplification of the missionary spirit. [*Applause.*]

I may as well confess it now and here—one great object of my long journey of nearly forty thousand miles across land and sea, a journey that has been no summer-holiday trip, has been to make, if possible, more concrete the demands of your brothers and sisters in all lands, to kindle your missionary zeal into a larger and brighter blaze, and to increase many-fold your gifts to missions. If this might be the result, I should feel that the journey had not been a mile too long. [*Applause.*]

As I speak to you, I can, in imagination, see myriads of heathen hands held out to you for your Christ, for your Bible, for your civilization. From the crowded house-boats of the Canton River; from the thronging wretchedness of the narrow streets of Shanghai; from the eager millions of Japan, who are deciding between Christ and Buddha and materialistic infidelity, for whom, as a nation, some think that the great decision will practically be made before men date their letters, January 1, 1900; from the dry, baked plains of Southern India; from the jungles of northern India; from wretched, Mohammedan-cursed Egypt, Syria, and Turkey; from sunny Italy; from awakening Spain; from the pleasant land of France—from all comes the cry of unconscious need and want.

If the needs of the one little province of Macedonia could appeal so loudly to the apostle of old, in what thunder tones should all these countries speak to you, Christian Endeavorers!

I would bring you their message; I would interpret their cry, "Come over and help us; come over and help us." If you cannot go, you can send. *You must go or send.* [*Applause.*] Money is as much needed as men and women, perhaps more, just now, for the recent great missionary revival has touched the hearts of consecrated young people more than it has touched the pocketbook of the average Christian.

May it not be the glad mission of the Christian Endeavor Society to introduce a new era of benevolence, not to perpetuate the grudging dole that has been wrung from tight fists in the past, a meagre offering that will never evangelize the world, but to bring in an era of proportionate and systematic giving as God hath prospered us? [*Applause.*]

Who will join me this year in a pledge of proportionate giving of at least one-tenth of what God may give us? Do you want a larger mission, Christian Endeavorers? Do you want a new crusade? Here it is. Could anything be larger? It reaches to the ends of the world. It embraces every nation and people and kindred and tribe. It means salvation, *yours* as well as theirs. It means the filling of our missionary treasuries; for we will always give, as we have done, through our own wisely directed denominational channels. It means that no worthy cause at home or abroad will suffer. In time, as we grow more numerous and richer, it will mean thousands where now there are hundreds, and millions where now are given thousands. It means obedience to our Lord's last command. It means that the twentieth century, yes, that this little remnant that is left of the old nineteenth, will usher in the glad era of an evangelized world which has heard in its remotest corners the gospel message. [*Loud applause.*]

This mission is large enough for you. This is one of the things He would like to have you do. Who will enlist himself and secure recruits for this crusade of a revival of proportionate and systematic beneficence?

3. One more definite, tangible, all-important purpose I would present to Endeavorers for the coming year,—an enlargement and cementing of our inter-denominational, international fellowship. [*Applause.*] Could there be a more appropriate year for this than when, for the first time, our Convention is held in a sister country, outside the limit of the United States. [*Applause.*] The lines of this fellowship have been laid down. Can any one who is not wilfully blind misunderstand them? Can any one who is not a bigoted sectarian object to them? Ours is a spiritual union. It seeks no organic unity. It demands no uniformity of creed or polity. It sneers at no conscientious difference of opinion. It insists, first of all, on the uttermost loyalty of each society to its own church and denomination. It is a union in service; there is the "Endeavor;" it is a union of spirit and fidelity to the one Master; there is the "Christian." It is expressed by our name "Christian Endeavor," which is the only guarantee of our principles, the only outward and visible token of inward and spiritual union.

This has, indeed, been an auspicious year for our world-wide fellowship.

I bring you, my friends, the greetings from your fellow-Endeavorers in all lands. I rejoice to be the personal bearer of personal greetings from personal friends to personal friends. [*Applause.*]

From warm-hearted, generous Australians, who speak our common mother tongue, I bring greetings.

The first vessel that I saw in Australian waters was a steam launch bearing two pennants, the Stars and Stripes from one masthead and the Y. P. S. C. E. flag from the other. [*Loud applause.*] That flag waved for you; that international greeting was for you, rather than merely for the messengers that were to bear it to you. At every railway station where we stopped, I saw hundreds of Endeavorers with badges and banners, and fluttering handkerchiefs in their hands, and hearty cheers on their lips. Those greetings and those cheers were for you.

In Sydney and Melbourne, in Adelaide and Brisbane, in Ballarat and Geelong, and in many other places, I saw buildings, the largest that could be obtained, crowded to the very utmost; and over and over again the thoughts of these generous hearts turned to you here in Montreal, and sent by me their love and most affectionate greetings. [*Applause.*]

As we sailed away from Brisbane, after speaking to more that seventy audiences of Endeavorers during six busy and happy weeks in that vast island continent, the last sound that greeted our ears was the same song that we heard floating from the San Francisco docks, "God be with you till we meet again." That song was for you as well as for us who heard it.

I bring you greetings from the Christian Endeavorers of Japan; from Yokohama and Tokyo, from Kyoto and Kobe, from Nagoya and Osaka and Okayama. In all these cities and many others are young hearts linked to yours by the supreme tie of Christian service. From the Endeavor society of the stately Christian university, the Doshisha of Kyoto, and alike from the humble society of little orphan boys that holds its meetings in the regenerated Buddhist temple of Okayama, I bring you greeting.

China's Endeavorers greet you to-day. From the society of the South Gate Church of Shanghai, where the Juniors meet in another old heathen temple, from the printer's society of the mission press of Shanghai, from the "Drum-and-Rouse-up" Endeavor societies of Foochow,—their literal translation of "Christian Endeavor" in Foochow Chinese,—from the Christian girls and boys of Canton, where Mr. Fulton works, I am the bearer of good tidings. [*Applause.*]

India's Endeavorers greet you. They speak many tongues,—Tamil and Telugu and Bengalee and Hindi and Hindoostanee and Marathi; but in all these tongues they tell of one purpose, of one pledge, of one motto, of one fellowship.

Syrian and Turkish Endeavorers greet you. They are persecuted and hindered ; their name, even, is under the ban ; and their meetings are broken up and their organization in many places forbidden by tyrannical rulers ; but their hearts are not chilled, nor their purpose cooled, nor their love to Christ subdued, nor their fellowship with you sundered by the persecutions that they endure.

Black-eyed Spanish Endeavorers greet you. The land from which Columbus sailed is linked by another tie, the tie of Christian Endeavor, in this anniversary year, to the land that Columbus discovered.

French Endeavorers greet you. Worldly Paris is not so worldly that nine active, spiritually minded Endeavor societies cannot flourish there as well as in Philadelphia or Toronto.

English, Scotch, and Irish Endeavorers greet you. Within a year our societies have increased from less than three hundred to nearly seven hundred in the United Kingdom. [*Applause.*] Seventy societies are found within the limits of London. Strong Endeavor local unions exist in Glasgow, Manchester, Birmingham, Chester, Liverpool, Swansea in Wales, and half a score of other places ; and everywhere I went I saw the C. E. badge joining together in loving embrace the Union Jack and the Stars and Stripes [*loud applause*], just as it always does in Canada and the United States ; and thousands of earnest young people in all parts of the United Kingdom, by rising and clapping and cheering as British audiences know how to cheer, have sent by me to you their message of good fellowship and love.

One of the divisions of the Methodist denomination in Great Britain has just led the way by adopting and approving Christian Endeavor, pure and simple, as its young people's organization. [*Applause.*] And this leads me to say that interdenominationally, in all parts of the world, as well as internationally, has our cause advanced during the year past as never before. I regret to say that in my own land alone, of all the lands that I have visited, in one or two sections of the Christian church is Christian Endeavor still looked upon as an alien interloper, and our fellowship is discouraged, if not forbidden.

But this shadow need not drive away the sunshine of the greetings that I bring to you from many lands and many languages. Nor need it obscure the great principle that I verily believe God would have us stand for,—the principle of international and interdenominational spiritual fellowship. [*Applause.*]

Let us follow the pointing of God's finger. The events of the year show us God's will. He has spoken of this fellowship in a score of different languages. He has spoken from nearly twenty different countries, and through good men in more than twenty different sects, bidding Christian Endeavor a hearty welcome.

Here is still, perhaps, our greatest mission. Enlarge your unions : multiply your societies ; enlarge your boundaries ; not for the sake of the societies, not for the mere sake of Christian Endeavor, but for the brotherhood and Christian fellowship that they represent. In the name of Christian brotherhood the world around ; in the name of the fatherhood of God ; in the name of Christianity hitherto torn and rent by sectarian jealousies ; in the name of heathen peoples, distracted by names and creeds whose deeper bonds of union they hitherto have not been able to understand ; in the name of the Master, and as an answer to his prayer that " they all may be one," make of your different Endeavor links a strong girdle that shall bind Christian hearts together, not by a uniform creed or ritual, but by pledged loyalty to Christ, and pledged service for Christ. [*Applause.*] Until this largest possible fellowship is reached, that fellowship which this year has so marvelously increased, let us still keep for our yearly motto our Lord's own words, making them more and more concrete in the actual life of the world of Christian young people, " One is your Master, even Christ ; and all ye are brethren."

Dr. Clark's address was followed by long-continued applause and the waving of flags and handkerchiefs. Director Lindsay started the hymn " Blest be the Tie," which was sung enthusiastically.

While the doors were being opened for a few minutes another hymn was sung, after which Dr. Hamlin introduced Miss Hollingshead, one of the leading vocalists of the city, who had kindly consented to favor the audience with a solo. Miss Hollingshead ascended the director's platform and sang, with accompaniment of piano and organ, "The Holy City," by Stephen Adams. Her voice, a rich and pure soprano, easily filled the great hall, and the song was rendered with such fine effect that the audience went wild with enthusiasm. In response to the persistent demand, Miss Hollingshead sang Sullivan's "Lost Chord" as an encore very beautifully, and the audience expressed their pleasure by the Chautauqua salute.

It was announced that the tent opposite was full to overflowing, and as a great crowd continued to enter the hall two more hymns were sung in splendid style.

DR. HAMLIN: There is something about the enthusiasm of such a convention as this which carries every one away. He must have a cold nature indeed who is not stirred by it. They say they have more enthusiasm out on the Pacific coast than we have on the Atlantic and in the region of the St. Lawrence, but I don't know about that. We have seen that they can make a great deal of noise. [*Laughter.*] They say they can fulfil any conditions that we impose, no matter how hard they are. But I think that right here and now there is a degree of enthusiasm and earnestness that stirs us all to the depths. I know that you are all enthusiastic for every one of our officers. No society or organization on earth was ever more fortunate in its officers than we are. [*Applause.*] We all know Dr. Clark and what he can do. Then there is a little man up there in Boston by the name of William Shaw. Did you ever hear of him? [*Loud applause.*] He doesn't say a great deal, but he does a great deal. He keeps the wheels of this great work moving to an extent that very few of us realize. Stand up, Mr. Shaw, and let us look at you. [*Mr. Shaw was greeted with generous applause and the Chautauqua salute.*]

They think we are going to have a better time in California in '95 than we had in New York last year. I don't know about that. We had a great time in New York last year, but there was one man we all missed.

> "One blast upon his bugle horn,
> Is worth a thousand men." [*Laughter.*]

We are going to have such a blast now, and I am sure you all rejoice with me and thank God that our dear General Secretary, — so wise, so faithful, so patient, so consecrated to his work, — is well and with us again. Let us show Mr. Baer how glad we are by the way we receive him.

This was the signal for another demonstration. The audience rose and greeted Mr. Baer with the Chautauqua salute, followed by three rousing cheers. Mr. Baer, who had just come in from reading his report at the tent meeting, then spoke as follows : —

Annual Report of John Willis Baer, General Secretary.

We have come together for the twelfth annual international and interdenominational gathering of a great providential movement among young Christians, in the evangelical churches of the world.

Twelve years ago the first society was organized in the Williston church, Portland, Me. Today there are thousands of societies, and every society, if really entitled to the name Christian Endeavor, emphasizes in its constitution, certain distinctive principles, which, under God's guidance, have made the Christian Endeavor movement what it is today.

Can one man, however privileged, give you a report of what has been accomplished in one year by thousands of societies, especially when those societies declare, first and foremost, personal devotion to our divine Lord and Saviour Jesus Christ; adhere to the covenant obligation embodied in the prayer-meeting pledge, without which there can be no true society of Christian Endeavor; believe in constant religious training for all kinds of service involved in the various committees, which are, equally with the prayer meeting, essential to a society of Christian Endeavor; are strenuously loyal to their own, *their own* churches and denominations, of which each society is a subordinate part, like the Sunday school; are also having increasing confidence in the inter-, *inter-*, INTER-denominational spiritual fellowship [*applause*] through which we hope, not for organic unity, but to fulfil our Lord's prayer "that they all may be one," thus in every way, by the loyalty expressed in the pledge, and in every other principle, showing in theory and in practice that the Christian Endeavor Society is as loyal a *denominational* society as any in existence, as well as a broad and fraternal *interdenominational* society? When we grasp these facts, is it to be wondered that the question is asked, " Can one man give a report of a year 's work?" No, No! No!!

This convention closes a year of unexampled prosperity for Christian Endeavor. Quiet, steady work filled with the Spirit of Christ has accomplished much.

We might dwell, if time would permit, upon the widening of our interests and international fellowship as we have followed President Clark around the world; and now having an acquaintance none the less real, though distant, with Endeavorers in the islands of the Pacific, in Australia, Japan, China, India, Africa, Syria, Turkey, Spain, France, England, we can strike hands in a Mizpah circle that belts the globe.

The favor gained in all evangelical denominations, save *one*, never has been so marked as during the last twelve months. Our attitude toward denominational movements is becoming understood and appreciated; and now as never before we may see that the closest denominational oversight is easily compatible with the widest Christian Endeavor fellowship, meeting it here, as we do, in Canada, where this feeling has the fullest recognition and expression in the Epworth Leagues of Christian Endeavor of the Methodist Church of Canada. [*Applause.*]

Systematic benevolence has been more earnestly advocated than ever, and more widely practised. Proportionate giving to God has found new converts, and hundreds have made their covenant with God, thereby giving not less than *one-tenth* of their income to him and his work.

If we were to report fully the unprecedented missionary year just closed, we could speak of thousands of dollars given to the various denominational mission boards; new missionaries supported; churches built at home and abroad; city missions that have received fresh life.

Mention could be made of missionary extension courses; local-union missionary work; many denominational Christian Endeavor missionary conferences; the appointment of especial missionary secretaries for the young people's work by the denominational boards. More and more it is plainly to be seen that the Christian Endeavor Society is a mighty missionary and evangelistic force. [*Applause.*]

Time would have to be given, were it possible, to an advance step, the Senior Society of Christian Endeavor, quite a number of which have already been formed; to the Floating Societies of Christian Endeavor, of which there are now twenty-one; to work among the life-saving stations; the formation and growth of the Travellers' Union of Christian Endeavor; the society among the policemen, "New York City's finest; " the societies in army and navy, and among the unfortunate inmates of prisons and houses of correction. [*Applause.*]

There have been forward steps in practical religious work, such as temperance mass-meetings; war waged against the cause of intemperance and the sale and manufacture of intoxicating beverages of all kinds [*loud applause*]; special evangelistic meetings; definite personal work among associate members; of work and interest in the Sunday-school, the midweek prayer meeting, and the Sunday evening service; and last named, but not least of all, *open hostility to every plan for destroying in any way the sanctity of the Sabbath day, illustrated, very emphatically, by the united desire to exert an influence upon the Directors of the Columbian Exposition that would prompt them to close their gates on Sundays.* [*Loud applause.*]

I want also to mention the management of the many bright local church papers; of the growth, for their worth's sake, of state, territorial, provincial, and local-union papers, and, especially, of one of the most important factors in the promotion of Christian Endeavor, the work of the secular and religious press, particularly the denominational and interdenominational religious press.

The good-literature committees have been doing a good work in extending the circulation of their denominational religious papers. The gospel can be preached with printer's ink most effectively in these days, and your own church paper contains not only denominational news and matters of denominational interest, but the gospel concerning the advancement of the kingdom of God in all parts of the earth. I take occasion at this time to urge the claims of the whole religious press upon our young people.

But I must stop, for I might go on for some time to come, reporting the results of the past year. I can only take time to tell you that the printing department of the United Society has prospered, largely through the good business management of our agent, Mr. William Shaw. [*Applause.*] Mention is made of this, as it is often asked how so large a work as that accomplished be the United Society of Christian Endeavor can be carried on without asking thy societies for a penny to pay expenses from one year's end to the other, while at the same time the only source of income is from the sale of the badges and literature, and the printing done for local societies. The answer is that everything is conducted in the most economical way, and that very much service is rendered to the societies "free gratis for nothing." [*Laughter.*] We do not know of any organization to which so much time and labor is gratuitously and gladly given. Let me again emphasize the fact that the United Society levies no taxes of any kind, and receives no contributions from local societies. It asks for no material support, but craves your prayers that it may be an instrument in God's hands to promote an earnest, Christian life among the young people, to increase their mutual acquaintance, and to make them more useful in their service "for Christ and the Church." [*Applause.*]

Now without further delay let me give you some figures. If your state, territory, or province ought to be credited with more societies, it is no fault of mine. The societies have not enrolled, and consequently have not been counted. I know that there are many hundreds of societies in existence that have never enrolled. The banners might have belonged to your state, to your province, to your territory, had you enrolled your society. Enroll, *enroll*, and be counted, and let me announce the fact at Cleveland next year. I cannot take your time to name each state, territory, and province, but will content myself with mentioning the five leaders among the states and provinces. The official enrolment is as follows: New York state still leads, with 2,985 societies. Pennsylvania is a good second, with 2,628; Illinois, third, with 1,822; Ohio, fourth, with 1,766; and Iowa, fifth, with 1,186. Massachusetts and Indiana are not far behind, however.

Here in Canada all loyal to the Union Jack, as are we from the States to the Stars and Stripes, we find 1,882 societies. Ontario leads, with 1,072 societies; Nova Scotia has 393; Quebec, 135; Manitoba, 94; and New Brunswick, 89; and so on, through the Dominion.

The growth in the Southland has been encouraging. Right royally are the societies thriving in the "sunny South." Maryland, Tennessee, and Texas each have over 200 societies; and Georgia, Florida, West Virginia, and Arkansas each have over 100, with Virginia and South and North Carolina not very far behind.

THE MONTREAL COMMITTEE OF '93.

1   Mr. A. A. Ayer, Chairman   5.   Mr. Robert Greig, Treasurer.
2. Mr. H. A. Barnard, Music Committee   6.   Rev. S. P. Rose, D.D., Representative of the Local Unions.
3   Mr. A. R. Grafton, Hall Committee.   7.   Mr. H. B. Ames, Press Committee.
4   Mr. Arthur F. Bell, Reception Committee.   8.   Mr. Geo. R. Lighthall, Hotel Committee and Secretary.

But we must now turn our attention to our brothers and sisters in foreign lands and across the seas. If we think our growth has been remarkable, what can we say of the history of the movement in England with over 600 societies, Australia over 525; India, 71; Turkey, poor persecuted Turkey, still has 41 societies; New Zealand, 39; Japan, 34; Madagascar, 32; Scotland, 30; Mexico, our neighbors, 22; West Indies, 19; Africa, 15; China, 14; Ireland, 10; France, 9; Samoa, 9; Sandwich Islands, 6; Bermuda, 3; Brazil, 2; Persia, 2; and Chile, Columbia, Norway, and Spain, each 1. In all, more than a thousand societies in foreign lands, making a grand total enrolment for the wide, wide world of 26,284 local societies, with a membership of 1,577,040. [*Applause.*]

The net gain in local societies is the largest ever made in the history of the movement. *Net* gain, I say, for every Christian Endeavor society that has become an Epworth League — and hundreds have changed each year for the last three years — has been stricken from the lists.

The net gain in number of local societies in 1882 was 6; 1883, 49; 1884, 100; 1885, 97; 1886, 597; 1887, 1,464; 1888, 2,565; 1889, 2,793; 1890, 3,341; 1891, 5,261; 1892, 4,806; and 5,276 is the forward step this last year. In other words, more societies have been organized since our New York convention than were organized during *seven* years of the Society's early history.

You will be interested to know that the Model Constitution has been translated, and is printed in the following languages: English, German, Swedish, Norwegian, French, Danish, Dutch, Spanish, Chinese, Japanese, Tamil, Telugu, Hindi, Hindoostanee, Bengalee, Marathi, Arabic, Turkish, Bulgarian, Armenian, and modern Greek.

At St. Louis, three years ago, a badge-banner, made up of badges from hundreds of societies, was displayed amidst much enthusiasm. According to a suggestion made by a representative from Minnesota, it was decided to place that banner for one year in the custody of the state, territory, or province that should show the greatest *proportionate* increase in its number of local societies during the year. Oklahoma carried that banner away from Minneapolis, brought it to New York, and turned it over to Manitoba, where Christian Endeavor, like its wheat, is graded No. 1, hard. Manitoba brings her banner, after a year's possession, to Montreal. and this year will please present it to New Mexico.

You will remember that at St. Louis it was also decided that another badge-banner should be made and given at Minneapolis to the state, territory, or province that should show the greatest *absolute* gain in one year. Pennsylvania captured that banner. She, too, last year, relinquished her possession, and turned the banner over to Ontario. Ontario, after holding the banner this last year, will please return it to the Keystone State [*great cheers from Pennsylvania*], as Pennsylvania has even a better record than ever, having gained 799 societies this past year.

But there are other banners to be assigned this evening.

In March, 1884, the first Junior society of Christian Endeavor was organized in Tabor, Ia., by Rev. J. W. Cowan. And today there are hundreds of city unions of Junior societies, some of which are large in numbers. No branch of Christian Endeavor has a larger promise of usefulness. In every way are the Juniors being heard from. No convention programme, be it local, state, or international, is complete unless generous provisions are made for the Juniors and their work.

Two years ago 855 societies had reported. This year great progress has been made. Junior superintendents of state, territorial, and provincial unions, and of local societies, your work has been wonderfully blessed of God.

Notwithstanding it is particularly difficult to gather statistics from Junior societies, we have actually enrolled today 4,136 Junior societies. [*Applause.*] Illinois has, from the start, stood first, last year carrying away the banner for the largest number of Juniors. Illinois has brought her banner to Montreal, and can return with it, for she now has 433 regularly reported societies on my lists. New York is not very far behind, and is second, with 403; Pennsylvania next, with 395; Massachusetts has 234, and Ohio 219.

Two other Junior badge-banners have been provided. One will be given to the state, territory, or province showing the largest *proportionate* increase, and it is secured by the District of Columbia.

The other banner will be given for the greatest *absolute* gain in Junior societies, and goes to the Empire State, New York, the gain being 189 societies. Make way, I say, for the Junior movement; it bids fair to rival any of the streams of Christian Endeavor that are making glad the city of our God.

The Christian Endeavor "local-union" idea is assuming larger and better proportions every month. It contains so much of the blessed idea of inter-denominational fellowship, and its possibilities in the way of inspiration and fraternity are so large, that it is evidently an institution that has come to stay. Many of these unions are doing practical work through their missionary, executive, correspondence, lookout, press, and visiting committees. More and more are these Christian Endeavor unions becoming evangelistic forces. In passing I want to mention some of the largest Christian Endeavor city unions, — those that according to my enrolment have more than one hundred local societies banded together. The figures named include the *Juniors*. Philadelphia, the largest, is composed of 337 societies; Chicago is next, with 326; New York has 151; Cleveland has 129; Brooklyn, 122; Baltimore, 106; St. Louis, 105; and Boston, 101. The two largest city unions in Canada are the Toronto Union, with 75, and Montreal, with 44.

If any one thing has been made clear by the history of these twelve years, it is God's design to bring the young people of all evangelical denominations together, not for the sake of denouncing denominations or decrying creeds, but, in a common fellowship that respects differences and believes in diversity. The fears of those who thought the Society would destroy all distinctive beliefs, and demolish the principles for which the fathers suffered persecution, have been largely allayed, for it has come to be acknowledged that the Society makes every young person more loyal to his own denomination, at the same time that it makes him more generous toward others.

Thirty evangelical denominations are represented in our fellowship.

Not counting the denominations outside of America, the denominational representation is as follows: The Presbyterians still lead, with 5,411 societies [*cheers*]; the Congregationalists have 4,882; the Baptists, 2,910; the Disciples of Christ and Christians, 2,142. The Methodist Episcopal denomination has stood fourth, but, for reasons too well known to be referred to again, has now taken fifth place, with 1,585. I have doubts if all Christian Endeavor societies that have been changed to Epworth Leagues have advised me, though I have taken especial pains to inquire. There may be but 1,200 Christian Endeavor societies left in the Methodist Episcopal church. I have recently heard from nearly that number. Many of these, as all Methodist Christian Endeavor societies should, have enrolled as affiliated chapters of the Epworth League, thereby showing their sympathy with the action of their General Conference. This has been done without giving up their Christian Endeavor name and its interdenominational fellowship. [*Applause.*] The Methodists of Canada are sixth, with 823, including 557 Epworth Leagues of Christian Endeavor. The 266 Christian Endeavor societies in the Methodist church of Canada would do well to become Epworth Leagues of Christian Endeavor ["*Hear, hear*"], making that their denominational name for their regiment in the Christian Endeavor army. The Presbyterians of Canada have 760 societies: the Methodist Protestant have 708 societies, and so on through the very long list.

Now for the best of it all, the very best. I have been speaking a good deal about the growth of local societies, local, state, territorial, and provincial unions, the forward movement denominationally, etc., and have not referred to our individual members. The importance of individualism is made manifest more and more in our work and in many ways. We do not forget *our* part and *our* work in this warfare. We believe in co-operation, and we also believe in individualism, and emphasize it prominently by accepting for ourselves individually definite pledged service. You will agree with me, of course, that the growth of the local societies "is marvelous in our eyes," but what can we say when we number the additions to our churches from this rapidly increasing international and interdenominational host? Listen. At St. Louis it was reported that 70,000 had joined the churches from our societies; at Minneapolis it was 82,500, and last year at New York "Praise God from whom all blessings flow" was sung when it was known that 120,000 of our members had become church-members. Another year, what would it bring forth?

How many souls could be won to the Lord Jesus' Christ in the coming year? Thousands consecrated their energy to that end at the New York convention in its closing hours; thousands more have stood in our conventions all over the world, pledging themselves under God's guidance to lead one soul to him. How richly has God answered our prayers!

Hand to hand, effective personal work has been done, "trusting in the Lord Jesus Christ for strength." We find that during the last year more than 158,000 of our members have become church-members. [*Loud applause.*] How much or how little our own individual work or that of the Society has influenced this blessed result, we know not; sufficiently happy and thankful are we to know that these additions, to the number of so many thousands, have come from our membership.

The past year's history has been the most notable, the growth unprecedented, and to know that, better than all that, 158,000 have joined our churches, is to proclaim in the best possible way our motto, "For Christ and the Church."

You rejoice in this. Well you may. God grant we may with modest and teachable spirits take up the greater work before us in the coming year. Let us have a genuine revival, a true religious revival. As some one has said, "That does not mean fuller emotion merely; it means ability and readiness to do more, and that can only be revealed by larger self-denial." God grant it. We now number 1,577,040. Think of it! 1,577,040 individuals banded together for service. Our responsibilities are equal in number to our opportunities. What shall another year bring forth? God will answer in his good time. May he give us the strength and grace needed for another year's campaign under the leadership of our Saviour King, Jesus Christ.

Mr. Baer's report was followed by great applause and the waving of handkerchiefs. The hymn "For Christ and the Church" was then sung, after which came the presentation of banners, conducted by Mr. Baer.

Presentation of Banners.

First came the presentation of the banner for the largest absolute gain in societies.

MR. BAER: Ontario carried this banner across the imaginary line between the United States and Canada last year. They cannot have it any longer. We are going to have Mr. E. A. Hardy, secretary of the Ontario union, hand this banner over, with the happiest speech and the best grace he can, under the circumstances, to the president of the Pennsylvania state union, the Rev. Charles Roads. [*Applause.*]

MR. HARDY: It was a pleasure for Ontario last year to take away this banner. It has been our pleasure to send it all through that thriving province during the past year. But there are other duties in the world besides those of pleasure. There are duties of saying good-bye, sometimes. [*Laughter.*] Our president said last year that the Yankees would never look upon it again, except to take a momentary glance at it, but his prophecy has not been fulfilled. Though the duty which devolves upon me is a melancholy one, it is sweetened by one or two thoughts. In the first place, we people are not very great for show, anyhow [*laughter*], so we let the great republic to the south of us have that pleasure for the next year. The other thought, — perhaps a better one, — is that Pennsylvania has fairly and squarely beaten us clean out of sight, and so for that reason we hand this banner over to the president of the Pennsylvania union. It has been an incentive to us, and we know it will be to them. [*Applause.*]

REV. CHAS. ROADS [*receiving the banner in the midst of cheers*]: The first reason which my brother gives for presenting this banner to Pennsylvania will hardly do, because, of all people in the world, the descendants of William Penn care the least for show. So that we do not receive this banner because we love show, but because we love to prove to the world that though the descendants of William Penn are plain and sometimes called slow, when they get on the scent they follow it to the death, and when they set themselves to win any victory, the rest of the world will have to do their utmost to get even within sight. [*Laughter and applause.*] We will take this banner back, having won it by 799 societies. We will bring it to the next convention with over a thousand new societies organized "For Christ and the Church." [*Cheers from Pennsylvania.*] If a thousand do not keep the banner, we will make it any number that is necessary to hold the banner in the Keystone State from now on, until God shall do things for Christian Endeavor that none of us now dream of. [*Applause.*]

Here the Pennsylvania delegation rose and sang, amid the laughter and cheers of the audience,

" Home again, home again,
From Ontario.
And oh, it fills my heart with joy
To have it home once more."

Next came the presentation of two Junior banners.

MR. BAER: The other two banners have been presented in the tent, but there are two Junior banners to be presented here. I am glad to make this presentation, because they are now starting out on their journey from Montreal. I am one who is most deeply interested in the work of the Junior Society of Christian Endeavor, and there are a good many people here who know why I should probably be more interested than some others. But I want to say to you that the boys and girls are being won for the Lord Jesus Christ, and they are coming into our churches early. And now, older boys and girls, young men and young women, old men and old women with young hearts, let us take into our minds and on our hearts the fact that in almost every church there is a band that can be gathered together of these boys and girls who can become soldiers for the Lord Jesus Christ quite as easily at the age of six as they can at the age of sixteen. I believe that from the bottom of my heart. [*Applause.*] This banner which we have arranged, and which is to be given for the largest proportionate increase in Junior societies, goes to the District of Columbia; and I am glad to say that with Mr. P. S. Foster, the president of the District of Columbia union, will stand one of the Juniors of Washington, Miss Rachel Mothershead, who will take this banner to Washington and place it in the keeping of the Junior societies for one year. [*Applause, as the little girl came forward and received the banner and hung it over the platform railing.*]

MR. FOSTER: When Mr. Baer expressed surprise a few moments ago as to where this banner was going, he did not know us. We only started this Junior union, as was said this afternoon, on the 14th day of November last, and we have increased wonderfully as the result of union work. I once heard of a little dialogue between a Quaker and a Methodist. When the latter asked the former who he was, he replied, "I am a Quaker." The Methodist responded, "And I am an earthquaker." [*Laughter.*] That is what we of the District of Columbia mean to be for Christian Endeavor—earthquakers—during the next year, and we hope we may be able to keep this banner, although our territory is very small. Some one has said, "What we are should thunder out so loud that we cannot hear what we say." This thunders out what we are. I have no more to say. [*Laughter and applause.*]

Here ensued another demonstration. The Washington delegation rose and sang " Marching on for Christ our Captain," the audience responding with the handkerchief salute.

MR. BAER: I was down at Washington not a great while ago, and I read in a copy of the Washington Post this incident: It is said that they run very slow trains down South, and on one of these trains was a very brisk man from Massachusetts, who, trying to be smart, asked the conductor as they were going along, "Conductor, have you any objections to my stepping off this train for a while?" "No," said the conductor, "what do you want to get off for?" "I would like to see which way we are going." [*Laughter.*] The Empire State does not want you to step out of this convention to see how they are going. They are going straight along for banners, and I want to say that Pennsylvania wants to look out for that other banner. The Empire State now takes this banner, and Rev. Henry W. Sherwood, the beloved president of that union, will receive it. [*Applause.*]

REV. MR. SHERWOOD: About one year ago the Empire State began to wake up to the importance of the Junior work. We are beginning to get very much awake; but when we get thoroughly awake, from Long Island to Lake Erie, look out! Mr. Secretary, it gives me special pleasure to bear this banner home to New York, because I am not obliged to take it away from anybody to get it, and nobody will feel bad to let it go. I receive this banner reverently and gladly, in the name of Him who took a little child and set him in the midst of his disciples. I receive it in the name of those churches whose lambs are being gathered and fed. I receive it in the name of those Christian workers who lovingly and patiently and prayerfully have been gathering the children about them, and teaching them the truths of the Master and instilling his spirit into their hearts. I receive it in the name of the thousands of bright-eyed, ruddy-cheeked boys and girls, healthy in body and growing in grace, who are already organized in Junior Endeavor societies. I receive it, also, in the name of the hundreds of thousands of boys and girls from New York to Buffalo who are not yet organized but who are yet to be taught the truths of Christ. I receive it, also, in the name of that blessed spirit which is going abroad into all Christendom and suffers the little children to come to Christ, and not only does not forbid them, but goes out seeking them, prayerfully and earnestly, and bringing them about his feet. I receive it also as a token of that brighter, better, cleaner future in the Empire State which shall lead finally to the regeneration of our great metropolis itself. I receive it, also, admiring its beauty, and shall weave into its folds our Empire State motto, and I will wave it in the name of Christian "Excelsior." Christian Endeavor delegates from the state of New York, rise and receive this banner with your salute. [*New York delegates scattered all over the hall rose and saluted the banner.*] Now be careful that we do not have to part with it too soon.

This closed the evening's program, and the audience was dismissed, after singing the doxology, by the benediction pronounced by Rev. Dr. M. Rhodes, of St. Louis.

THE TENT.

In the tent the delegates occupied the time before the hour of service singing familiar hymns, under the leadership of Mr. W. A. Coates, of Montreal. Mr. W. J. Van Patten then called the assembly to order and gave out the hymn " Sun of My Soul."

MR. VAN PATTEN: It is my pleasant duty to introduce to you this evening one who needs no introduction, for I know that every member of every Christian Endeavor society all over this broad continent feels a personal acquaintanceship and a personal friendship for our general secretary. But I wish to bear a word of personal testimony, for perhaps more often than any of you I see him in his office in Boston, and I want to say how much we all appreciate the devoted work he is doing, the loyalty he is showing to that work, and the genuine merit of what he does. And so you will rejoice with me that we have this year our general secretary with us to make his report, as he was not able to be last year. So, dear friends, we will have tonight an official report which will differ from the usual official report in most places. You know we expect those to be dry, but the reports that have come to us from year to year from the officials of the Christian Endeavor organization have not that defect, for always they bring to us something that is uplifting, something that is stimulating, something to make us thank God for this movement and for its growth and prosperity. And so, tonight, will come to us the most important, perhaps, and the most enjoyable of all we shall have in this convention, — the report of the grand progress that has been made in the year past and the prospect for the coming year. It is now my pleasure to introduce to you our good friend General Secretary Baer.

Secretary Baer was accorded an ovation as he stepped forward to deliver his address, which was the same as that reported in the Drill Hall proceedings, and was received with equal enthusiasm. When the announcement was made that during the past year more than 158,000 from the ranks of the Christian Endeavor Society had become church members, there was much cheering on the part of the audience, and then all joined in singing spontaneously, " Praise God from Whom all Blessings Flow." At the conclusion of the report the audience sang, " All Hail the Power of Jesus' Name."

The presentation of banners then followed, conducted by Mr. William Shaw, Treasurer of the United Society.

Presentation of Banners.

MR. SHAW: The first banner we shall have the pleasure of presenting, we sha'-n't have the pleasure of presenting for some time, for it is somewhere in the express office. There are lots of things that I have been trying to get for the last few days; they are down in the Custom House, and I have found that that imaginary line is not such an imaginary line, after all. [*Laughter and applause.*] It is a tremendously large line and a strong line, and it is a line I could not break. Well, one of our banners is on the way here, the gentleman who is going to present the banner is here, and I am going to present him. I have great pleasure in introducing to you the Rev. Alexander Urquhart, of Manitoba, who will have the great pleasure of presenting the banner that was given to Manitoba last year to New Mexico tonight, and I hope he will be very happy in making his presentation speech to you.

MR. URQUHART: It has been said that Manitoba can usually make herself heard on great public questions. I am not sure whether I shall be able to make myself heard on this great occasion or not. I think I hear some one in the audience asking the question, " Where is Manitoba ? " Well, I am not surprised that you should ask such a question. We only rescued it from the buffalo a few years ago, but we hope to reap today from that small province, and small part of that great territory, if the present prospects are realized, 25,000,000 bushels of the world's choicest wheat, to send over, — perhaps, in part, to give delicacies and delicious feasts, — to many who are present here tonight from various parts of the world. [*Applause.*]

The special object for which I have been introduced to the audience this evening is that of handing back the banner won last year by our young province to New Mexico, which has so nobly won it for the present year. We all have observed, in listening to the Annual Report just read, that Ontario also had to give up her banner. So you see we feel, as true Canadians, that we do not like to act too long the selfish part, and so, having tasted of the good things that have come to us, and which we have enjoyed to the full, we wish to pass them around and let others share alike the joy and blessing which we have had. [*Applause.*]

It is, therefore, with great delight and pleasure that informally, — since, as you have heard, this banner is on its way, or perhaps now in the express office, so that formally we cannot present it, — we hand this banner over to New Mexico; and we trust that, if permitted to meet together on a similar occasion next year, we shall hear of New Mexico having the pleasure of handing it over to some other state, province, or territory, so that it shall pass around. Then you will notice one feature in this connection: Ontario is handing over her banner across the line whence it came; Manitoba is also handing over her banner across the line whence it came, proving that we believe in reciprocity. [*Great applause and laughter.*] Also, in the presentation of this banner, I am permitted to illustrate one of the fundamental principles of Christian Endeavor, namely, that we live the life of faith, and I hand it over in faith to New Mexico, [*Laughter and applause.*]

We, in that remote part of the Canadian Northwest, are seeking to plant Endeavor societies in every nook and corner of that great and growing land, establishing that country on a solid basis of Gospel principles, so that from ocean to ocean, over this fair Canada of ours, the song of praise and thanksgiving shall ascend unto our king and Lord; so that when that great assembly and gathering of all kindreds and peoples and nations shall take place, and when we shall hear the glad welcome from the Captain of the mighty host thus beckoning us on to receive us into his everlasting habitation, we shall join the mighty host of God that is being thus increased year after year through this unparalleled and mighty movement for God. That one and all may seek thus to aid it, and that we may all meet above, is our earnest prayer and wish from the far province of the West. [*Loud applause and cheers.*]

MR. SHAW: You will have to take a great many things on faith tonight. You must imagine that now there stands before you a young woman from New Mexico, who was to have been here to receive this banner, but is unavoidably absent. By mistake she got into the Drill Hall, and we cannot get her out, and so I am here. [*Applause and laughter.*] I want to give you a text now, which is this: "The things that are seen are temporal, but the things that are not seen are eternal." [*Laughter.*]

Miss Hall of New Mexico appeared in the tent at this moment, and was introduced to the audience by Secretary Baer, and given the Chautauqua salute.

MR. SHAW: Now I have another very pleasant duty to perform. I wonder how many of you have read about Uncle Tom. A great many, I presume. Well, we have an Uncle Tom in Christian Endeavor, and he lives in the city of Chicago. You know Chicago has the reputation of getting all that she can and then holding on to it. [*Laughter and applause.*] And so we are not suprised that, since the state of Illinois took the Junior banner a year ago they should bring it up here tonight just for the satisfaction of saying, "Now look at it, for it is the last time you will see it this year." Illinois has still the largest number of Junior societies in our Christian Endeavor fellowship; and the man, who, I believe, above all men, deserves the credit for this is Mr. Thomas Wainwright, the president of the Junior Union of Chicago. I have great pleasure in introducing him to you. He will present the banner, and receive it, and carry it back to Chicago. [*Laughter and applause.*]

MR. WAINWRIGHT: It is with great pleasure and satisfaction that I take this banner back to the state of Illinois. As you have heard, we have a larger number of Junior Christian Endeavor societies than any other state, province, or territory, and we intend to keep up to that record. But, my dear friends, we are not working just simply to hold that banner; it is my heart's desire that the state of Illinois shall be the banner Junior state in soul-winning and conversion [*applause*], and intensely alive to every good work for our dear Master. I firmly believe that it is noble in God's sight for us to excel each other in love and devotion. If you want to take this from Illinois, you have got to sit up nights and hustle. [*Great laughter and applause.*]

The hymn "Hear us, O Saviour, while we Pray" was then sung, closing the banner presentation exercises.

MR. VAN PATTEN: The nineteenth century is said by Dr. Strong, the author of that well-known book, "Our Country," in a new book that he has just published, to have been a century of preparation. To me it is one of the most inspiring thoughts that the work of our Young People's Societies of Christian Endeavor is a work of preparation of strong young Christian manhood and womanhood for the work of their adult years as Christians. If in the nineteenth century all the great advance in science, in education, in religion, is but a preparation for what Dr. Strong says is the coming century of achievement, how great will be the glories of that coming century? And if the work of our Young People's Societies of Christian Endeavor in these passing years and decades is but a work of preparation of this generation for the greater achievements of the coming generations, how great and inspiring is the thought of what we are now doing!

I think that one of the grandest thoughts of all that can come to the heart of our beloved president, Dr. Clark, is that his work in the last years has been this work of preparation. He has been on this wonderful trip around the world, going on in this way of preparation, looking over this broad field, considering its wants, considering what further can be done to bring forward the work of Christ's kingdom in these far-off lands; so he comes to us tonight to tell us something of this wider field, to let us know more fully what part we have to do in the work that is going on.

We rejoice with great rejoicing that our Heavenly Father has so abundantly poured out his blessing upon him and his in these past months, that without danger and without illness these months have passed, until once more he is with us, and now he will again speak to us. Let us receive him right royally. It gives me great pleasure to introduce to you our beloved President, Rev. Francis E. Clark, D. D.

President Clark was in fact received "right royally" with cheers and the Chautauqua salute. His address, which was the same as that previously delivered in the Drill Hall, was received with marked demonstrations of enthusiasm. The immense tent was packed with an audience of over 9,000 people, and thousands were gathered on the outside, listening attentively. It was estimated that nearly 20,000 people were present at the services, in the Drill Hall and Tent.

The meeting closed with the hymn "What a Wonderful Saviour," and the benediction was pronounced by Rev. J. F. Cowan, of Pittsburg, Pa.

FRIDAY MORNING.

Friday was a warm day, though at no time was the heat seriously uncomfortable. The host of delegates who attended the five early morning prayer meetings enjoyed the coolest portion of the day. The meetings were all intensely spiritual and helpful.

DRILL HALL.

The general topic for the morning session in the Drill Hall was " The Four Essentials of a Christian Endeavor Society." There was the usual praise service to begin with, and at ten o'clock President Clark called the audience to order. First came the beatitudes, recited in unison ; then Rev. Mr. Wilkinson, of Chicago, led in prayer ; then the hymn " Coronation " was sung.

Dr. Clark announced the first address of the morning to be upon the vital element of the Christian Endeavor Society — the pledge — and introduced as the speaker Mr. Herbert L. Gale, of Worcester, Mass., Secretary of the Y. M. C. A.

The Pledge.

Address of Mr. Herbert L. Gale.

The pledge is the backbone, the cornerstone, of this great organization. Without it, as has been said so many times, there is no such thing as a Christian Endeavor society. Upon our conception of and fidelity to the pledge will depend the strength or weakness of every local society ; and as the strength of the majority of the local societies is, so will be the strength of the great organization as a whole. The great danger confronting the organization today is the laxity with which the pledge is being kept, and the feeling rife in so many societies, that the pledge binding men and women to definite and positive work is in itself logically wrong. Let us first put ourselves right as regards the principles which call the pledge into existence, for if the principle upon which the pledge idea is founded is wrong, all argument in its favor is in vain. If it is merely a human instrument, it ought to have very little weight; but if it is a living principle, recognized by both God and man, then the importance of it becomes at once apparent.

In the first place, let us take man's view of it. No nation has ever existed in any age without first of all laying the foundation, which is the constitution — the pledge or covenant. Without this it would be but a mob without a guide, a ship without a rudder. No man is compelled to sign it, but once having put his name to the paper, he is bound to keep it; any violation of it is subject to severe penalty. We find no fault with pledging ourselves to country or to nation. We love our country, and are willing to give it the best we have. Take the armies of England and America, except in great crises, everything is voluntary. If the interests of the nation demand protection, she appeals to her loyal sons, and they willingly give all they have, even their lives; not because they are compelled to, but because they love their country. Take the business life of any nation, and business men could not do business for a single hour without the pledge.

> " Man to man is so unjust,
> We hardly know in whom to trust."

On account of the frailty of human nature, we demand a pledge in even the smallest transaction. We demand it freely of our best friends, and we give it willingly. Take the family relations. No true home has been established without the most sacred and binding pledge. If there is a time when a pledge seems superfluous, it is when a true man and a true woman stand up together,

loving each other, and are called upon before God and living witnesses to give
the most solemn and binding pledge and have it recorded; and yet there is no
true man who would think of taking the truest woman that ever lived, unless
she was willing to give him her pledge — not a general pledge, but definite,
very definite in regard to particular things. Husband and wife are willing to do
anything because of their love, one to the other. They do not pledge in order
that they may love, but because they love they give the pledge. Look into any
department of life, and you will be astonished to see how everything is based
upon a pledge, business firm with business firm, nation with nation.

But this is all human. Let us look upon God's side and to his dealings with his
chosen people, and you will be surprised, as I was the more I studied it, to see what
a prominent place the pledge held. God shows the importance of taking a positive stand on one side or the other; and as his chosen people gave to him their
pledge, he in return voluntarily gave to them his pledge in regard to the details
of life. God might have spoken and it would have been done, for he cannot
lie. But no; to Abraham, to Isaac, to Jacob, to Moses, and all along the ages,
he gave to them a pledge, written by his servants, sometimes on parchment,
sometimes on stone, and once he himself took his pen and dipped it into a
mixture of all the colors, and he put that everlasting pledge upon the sky for us
all. [*Applause.*] Look at the old Book, and from Genesis to Revelation you
will find it filled with the pledge of Almighty God to men. Think of him as he
pledged to us the Saviour; and although it took thousands of years for him to
fulfil it, yet in the minutest detail God honored the sacred pledge. There is no
doubt that God honors a definite pledge for all time.

Now to the practical work of the hour. Probably nine-tenths of this audience
are professing Christians, and therefore must believe in a pledge. No more
solemn or binding covenant is ever made than when we vow our allegiance to
Christ and the church. We do here literally give ourselves to him, body and
soul. We lay ourselves on the altar, never to be taken back. We are no
longer our own; we are separated from the world by a voluntary act, and are
received by God. Our citizenship now is yonder in heaven.

Now, as to the Christian Endeavor pledge. We have been speaking of
pledges in general, but now we will speak of this one in particular. We are not
called upon to again give ourselves to God; this we have done once for all, now
and forever; but to pledge ourselves to a definite and positive work, not as we
have already done in a general way, but in some particular form. If the Young
Men's Christian Association has learned anything, it is the importance of
definite pledge work; and every year for the past twenty-five years they have
made the pledge stronger, more binding, and put in many more of them. The
last pledge that the Association has made is the pledge for definite, delegated,
personal work. I would not give a cent for any society without this definite
pledge work. [*Applause.*]

Now, my brother, if I have been honest in my first pledge to the work, I will
willingly and gladly take the second. The cry of every true child of God is,
"Lord, what wilt thou have me to do?" The watchwords of success in any
department of life are positiveness, definiteness, and earnestness. He who starts
out to do business in a general way will meet with failure. He who enters
college and does not pledge himself to a definite line of work, finds himself in
the great ocean of knowledge, drifting from place to place without any port in
which to anchor. Brother, as we are called upon to be definite and positive
in everything else, let us be more definite in our work for Christ and the church.
I am not speaking to you alone, but I trust that by your firm conviction upon
this subject you may present it to your different societies, and show them that
it is not only right, but a duty we owe to God and man. And then, after we
have taken the pledge, let us feel our responsibility. God spoke through
Solomon and said to us, "When thou vowest a vow unto God, defer not to pay
it, for he hath no pleasure in fools; pay that which thou hast vowed. Better
is it that thou shouldst not vow that that thou shouldst vow and not pay."

My brother, God needs today men and women of conviction; God needs
today men and women who are definite; God needs men and women who are

terribly in earnest. It may keep some of them back; they may falter and say, "I cannot go with you, for you make the standard so high." Let them stay back. Don't bring the standard down to them, but bring them up to the standard. [*Loud applause.*] The cry of God today is not for more men but for better men. God is not for quantity but for quality. [*Applause.*] Ten true men will accomplish more in the service of God than one thousand nominal Christians. It is because of the weakness of character in those who profess to be the followers of Jesus Christ that the condition of the world is what it is today. It is because of inactivity and indefiniteness that the great majority of men and women have never heard the Gospel of Jesus Christ. Out of the 1,500,000,000 in this world, two out of three have never heard the name of the Son of God. Out of the 60,000,000 in America, 40,000,000 are out of the pale of the church. Out of the 13,000,000 young men under thirty years of age in the United States and Canada, only 1,000,000 belong to the church and 8,000,000 practically never darken her doors. We have more young men in the United States today with the stamp of criminal upon their brow, who have been incarcerated at some time in jails or prisons, than all the young men in all the churches. More than a million young men today, under thirty-five years of age, walk up and down through the streets of America with the stamp of criminals upon their faces. John Knox said: "Give me twelve men and I will move Scotland; but the men must be men who will say, 'Give me Scotland, or I die.'" John Wesley said: "Give me twenty men and I will move the world; but they must be men on fire for God." God gave Knox twelve men, and Scotland is feeling the effect of it today. God gave Wesley the twenty men for whom he called, and the whole world has been made to feel his power and is feeling it now. [*Applause.*] With such a body of men and women, what could not be done? When they said to India's officers, "Upon a certain day thou shalt take a census," they were ready, every man to do his definite line of work. Within twelve hours after the order was given to take the census, every man, woman and child's name was put upon the book. When they asked the officer how long it would take to send the message to the entire world, he said he could do it in eighteen months. There is not a city in the United States of America but what, if the Christian men and women in it were in earnest and each would do his definite work, could tell the story to every man, woman and child within twenty-four hours. Yet eighteen hundred years have passed away since the command was given, "Go ye into all the world," — that was the general command; "and preach the Gospel to every creature," — that was a definite command. And there was something more definite than that — "beginning at Jerusalem." God honors a definite pledge.

Now, dear brother, much will depend upon our conviction in this matter. Do we believe in it? Are we willing to take the pledge and try to lead others to take it also? I never was more impressed in my life than when, in the city where I lived, after my most wonderful conversion, when God had opened my eyes and showed me the wonderful reality of a Christian life, I saw the need of definite, downright consecration. I had spoken in our church of this until the King's Daughters asked me if I wouldn't speak to them more definitely on what I meant, and I said, "Yes, I will." We met, and when I presented to them what I meant, every one, with one exception, said, No: they had consecrated themselves in general but not in particular. When God through his Word and through me showed them what ought to be done, they were not willing to do it. But God's Spirit was with us that night, and we stayed until nearly 12 o'clock. One after another took the stand on the side of definite consecration, and when just before 12 o'clock I asked them to kneel with me and take the final vow, with one exception everybody knelt. This was the prayer: "Where thou leadest, I will follow. It may lead me to suffer, it may lead me to death; but where thou leadest, I will follow!" [*Loud applause.*] Heretofore their lives had been a failure, mixed up in this and that, with no definite purpose and no definite results; but when they remembered the responsibility that rested upon them, they said, "Lord, as thou hast given thy life for me, I will give mine definitely to thee." From that place those girls went, and they are accomplishing today in that city what nobody, in my opinion, ever accomplished before.

England calls to her loyal sons and says, " We need you for definite work," and the loyal sons rise gladly, and throw themselves into the army to fight for the Queen. Although it may mean the burning suns of India, it matters not; they are willing to follow the flag. America said, " On to Richmond ! " and many a son gladly gave his life and fought under the Stars and Stripes to preserve the Union. [*Great applause.*]

God calls upon us to do definite and positive work among the millions in yon heathen country and the millions in our own land, and can we refuse to go? No, forward let us go! " Where thou leadest, I will follow!" It may mean death, it may mean hardship; but never mind. God helping me, " Where thou leadest, I will follow ! " [*Prolonged applause.*]

At the close of Mr. Gale's address Dr. Clark announced the next topic to be " The Committee Work," to be presented in the form of a Free Parliament, led by Mr. E. A. Hardy, of Lindsay, Ont.

The Committee Work.

Free Parliament. Conducted by Mr. E. A. Hardy.

MR. HARDY: Last year it took a Baptist to lead the parliament; this year it will take another Baptist all his time. Now we are to have a free parliament here this morning, of which I am to be speaker and you are to be members. I feel that it is fortunate for you that a parliamentary speaker differs from an ordinary speaker, in that he doesn't speak; he lets others have a chance. I am going to let you all have a chance. I want you all to take advantage of it. I suppose you may have noticed that some of the people down this way speak French occasionally. Just go back to your school days, and remember that parliament comes from *parler*, and you will see how appropriate it is that we are holding a free parliament in this city where you can "parlez vous" committee work for a little while. [*Laughter.*] I believe that our subject, "Committee Work," is one of the most important subjects in Christian Endeavor. Committee work is the outward expression of the inward life. "Out of the abundance of the heart the mouth speaketh," and, we may reverently add, the man worketh. I wish I had time and power this morning to deal with the relation of soul life and culture to committee work, but I believe with all my heart that consecration, real and true, is absolutely essential to the real success of our committee work. That committee work which is based on Paul's foundation, "The love of Christ constraineth me," I am ready to vouch for; but that committee work which is done through love or fear of pastor or president, through desire to outshine another person or even another committee, through love of our church without the higher motive of love for Jesus Christ, I am often afraid of. Let us dig as deep as Paul for our foundations, and then the work we build will be as lasting as eternity.

But this is to be a free parliament. Two years ago 67 people took part in the free parliament; last year over 100 took part. Can't we beat that this morning and break the records? Let us see. Will all those in this hall who have served on a committee in their society during the past year rise for a moment? [*Nearly all the convention stood up.*] That will do; be seated. Now, Mr. Chairman, I hold that we have beaten the record, for 8,000 people have taken part in one minute. [*Laughter and applause.*] We will now talk over the lookout, prayer-meeting, missionary committees, in the order named. We want testimony freely on the work of these standard committees. Let your speeches be wonderfully brief and pointed. In just one sentence for each speech, tell us what your committee has done in the past year. Write your speech and memorize it if that will help you to be brief.

Responses came promptly from the audience. The following were among the statements made : —

LOOKOUT COMMITTEE.

" Twenty-seven new members brought in the past six months, and each one was examined before a committee and the pledge explained to him." " Takes charge of the prayer meeting preceding consecration meeting and makes the most of it." " Began with a society of seven members, and now have over forty, and are still growing." " Made twelve hundred calls during the year." " Brought 30 persons into the society, and held a special consecration service for each one." " Brought 42 members into the society in six months, and gave $100 toward supporting and educating Armenian boys."

PRAYER-MEETING COMMITTEE.

" Keep a note-book with a blank space for every Sunday, where they put down the thoughts gathered at that meeting." " Meet every night before the meeting begins, to assist the leader in every possible way they can." " To assist timid leaders, have blank programs printed and filled out from beginning to end before the meeting, and by this means the most timid in the society can lead with the most perfect ease." " Holds a session of fifteen minutes before the regular meeting, and invites others who would like to come." " Makes a member of the prayer-meeting committee responsible for each meeting during the month, so that if anything happens to the leader, they always have a leader." " Co-operates with the pastor in connection with the midweek prayer meeting."

MISSIONARY COMMITTEE.

"In connection with other work have, for the last six months been taking care of a colored woman who cannot work." " Secures a missionary to speak to them every six weeks, and has adopted the plan of giving two cents a week for foreign missions. It is also their work to provide books for a missionary library." " Supports a Bible reader." " Sent their state treasurer as a foreign missionary, and also sent out two young men for the ministry." " Holds missionary meetings once a month, and holds prayer meetings before these missionary meetings. This committee has organized eight societies." " Gives to each member a box in which they are to put two cents a week for home missions, and two cents a week for foreign missions. A young lady from Paris, France, said that the most important work of their missionary committee was to get students from colleges and art schools to come to their meetings.

MR. HARDY: I hope we will take these lessons to heart, and remember that real committee work must come out of love for Christ.

The Hymn " O glad and glorious Gospel " was then sung, after which Dr. Clark introduced Rev. E. K. Young, D.D., of New Britain, Conn., who spoke on " The Consecration Meeting."

The Consecration Meeting.

Address of Rev. E. K. Young, D.D.

The consecration hour is to the Christian the season of realized nearness to God. Thought is centred upon him. Energy is directed toward him. Devout search has found him. Appropriating faith reveals his presence. It is the supreme hour of a Christian life, for it is the hour of entire self-surrender and unquestioning trust. It is borne in upon the consciousness then, as at no other stage of developing experience, that strength does not come by struggling, victory is not achieved by violent contention, and God is not found by an impatient eagerness that keeps the soul in unresting pursuit. In the quietness of submission, in the attitude of voluntary captivity, in unreserved compliance with the divine will when the "spirit of highest heroism before man stands as a little child before the face of God," there is realization such as never came to the soul in the strain of pursuit and the incessant struggle for possession. It is the marvelous paradox of our religion that strength lies in weakness. Surrender is the condition of conquest. Submission is mastership. Abasement is exaltation. Emergence from the consecration hour is into continuing fellowship with Christ and conscious nearness to God. The altar has sanctified the gift, surrendered selfhood has brought induement of superhuman power. God is henceforth a revealed presence. It is then that the doctrine of the divine indwelling passes into blissful experience. The dimly apprehended truth that the Creator dwells with his creatures brightens into a clear and comforting realization. God fills the whole sphere of being. He is the element in which we live, the inspiration of all we do. We are walled in by his love, sheltered in his care and protected by his grace. The consciousness that he abides with us brings down upon our lives the strength that is infinite and puts into our endeavors the courage and patience that prophesy victory.

In the light of this definition of the word and this apprehension of the act, we find an explanation of some things that have sorely puzzled us. We can easily interpret careers that move our admiration and excite our wonder when we trace their beginnings to this fountain head. The consecration hour was the Gethsemane of every life that spent itself in useful service to God, or yielded itself to martyrdom for his cause. "Thy will be done," was the prelude of every career that God has honored. Resignation to the divine will preceded and prepared the way for the descending spirit, and the illumination that came when the agony of struggle ended in the triumph of submission sent its light along the whole path of future service. St. Paul was in the fulness of this devotement when he declared it to be his life policy, "to know nothing among men save Jesus Christ and Him crucified," and put the divine will in the foreground of all his ministry. John Knox was out of the region of doubt and plainly "seeing him who is invisible" when he denounced corruption in Queen Mary's Court and roused the conscience of Scotland with his fearless preaching. John Wesley had surrendered his will to God and was living in gracious nearness to him, when he laid aside the preferments of the church and carried the gospel of free grace into the slums of England. Henry Martyn came from a season of consecration to his missionary labors. The cultured scholar who has turned his rare accomplishments into service for the outcast and degraded; the daughter of wealth endowed with the choicest qualities of heart and mind, who has exchanged the luxurious home for the noisome wards of the hospital and the offices of lowliest charity; the men or women who in any sphere of life walk their daily round of duty with serene spirit and unfaltering step, all came into their lives of sacrifice and service through the gateway of consecration. Controversy ended there. Doubt vanished there. Vague questioning gave place to steadfast confidence. The courage and composure that marked their after lives had their springs in that crisis hour. Faith was confirmed, power came, God revealed himself when dropping all resistance and yielding without reserve they looked up into the face of the Father and said, "Thy will be done."

Am I giving undue prominence to this service? Is it too much to say that in this great society of ours the consecration meeting holds the central place? [*Applause.*] I was enjoined to be practical in my remarks. If by that injunction it was meant that I should indicate the modes and methods of the consecration service, the best order to observe, length of time to occupy, the most efficient way of directing the machinery, then I am disappointing expectation. It has not seemed to me that there was great need of instruction along these lines. In the hour set apart for introspection and selfdevotement and communion with God, formality of procedure is not the essential thing. It is not desirable that the machinery should be seen or heard. The precision of operation should be as far as possible concealed. The one purpose dominating all others, is to realize the presence of God and feel the influence of his spirit. This is the practical result to be secured by this meeting, and its fruits will be manifest in the more effective work of the committees, in the sweeter fellowship of the social gatherings and in the cheerfulness that glows in all departments of service. As I conceive it, the consecration meeting is the arsenal of our society where every member must go for equipment. The Lookout Committee, our picket guard, finds here new reasons for diligence, fresh courage for duty, holier enthusiasm for its distinctive branch of service. There is danger that this peculiar line of work shall become irksome and these important outposts be left unguarded through listlessness on the part of those to whom this special service is entrusted. This danger suggests a need, for which our spiritual arsenal makes rich and abundant provision, the need of a deeper consciousness of the far-reaching importance of this work.

Under the illumination of the consecration hour, the sense of obligation is deepened, the path of duty brightens, and the delicate and difficult duties of that important committee are discharged with a fidelity inspired by the presence of him " whose they are and whom they serve." The Social Committee will have its work better defined and its religious aspect more distinctly portrayed under the spiritual enlightenment of the consecration hour. The social forces have never had full play in the life of the church. Its means of grace have never included, to the degree that they might and ought, these inherent elements of human nature. From childhood to the tomb the heart craves companionship. Society in some form is a feature of every kind and grade of civilization. It is the part of wisdom for the church to recognize this craving and make provision for it. But it is manifestly unwise to turn the social tides into secular channels, and answer this demand for society by introducing the frivolous pastimes and dissipating pleasures of the world. [*Applause.*] The social hour is an opportunity that the Social Committee should promptly seize, an opportunity to carry the Gospel into the festal hour and lay the joyful emotions under tribute to Christ. Everything connected with it should be suggestive of the bright side of life, nothing sombre, nothing gloomy, one unbroken melody from opening to close. It is an occasion for preaching the gospel of gladness and impressing young hearts with the fact that religion places no harmless pastime under ban and seals no fountains of genuine pleasure. But it should never degenerate into an hour of frivolity. It should be carefully guarded against the intrusion of that class of amusements that, whether intrinsically sinful or otherwise, have been demonstrated by the sure test of experience and observation to be harmful in tendency and hurtful in their influence upon life and character. It is the province of the Social Committee to determine the nature of these festal occasions, and in its hands lies the power to so direct them that every one shall be a season of chaste and elevating pleasure. No department of our organization covers a more productive field of influence, and no committee has greater need of the inspiration and guidance that comes from the consecration service. The prayer meeting will be marked by greater fervor, missionary zeal intensified, the sacred obligation of the pledge more deeply impressed, and activity on all lines of endeavor increased by every consecration meeting that God transforms into a pentecostal season.

This is the one meeting of all others that should be in the hands of the pastor. No other brings him into such close contact with the young people of his church. No other affords such favorable opportunity to teach helpful lessons and impart truths that will root themselves in the soil of permanent conviction. He is nearer to them there than he can come in any other service. His words of counsel will fall upon listening hearts; his admonitions will be kindly received, his instructions will be eagerly accepted, and his appeals will stir the languid consciences and evoke a sympathetic response. He is in friendly touch with every beating heart before him. His hand is upon the secret springs of life. He is in the sanctuary of their confidence; it is his time and place to deal honestly and faithfully with them, to chide with tenderness, to encourage with cheerful words, to point out the snares and pitfalls that lie across the paths of unfaithfulness, to lead the wayward feet through gateways of repentance back to forgiveness and God, and show the trusting spirit the way to the still waters of a better experience. No pastor can wisely relinquish the high privilege of such an hour. He is the divinely commissioned leader of the consecration meeting, and in that atmosphere of sympathy and revelation and honest heart-searching, with the unconscious tact of love, he can direct its ministrations to far better results than would be possible by any other hand. I would much more willingly commit the weekly prayer meeting to one of my official brethren than transfer the leadership of this delightful service to other hands. I know the young convert will be there, needing instruction and willing to receive it. I am certain to meet the young man whose first flush of Christian experience has passed into the nebula of doubt and discouragement, who will be there, eager to have his doubts removed and ready for the enlightenment of the Spirit. The young lady whose zeal has abated and whose first ardent love for the Master has grown cold will bring a heavy heart to that meeting, and wait at its altars for some power to lift the burden and turn the life energies back again into the paths of joyful service. I esteem it the highest privilege of my ministry to be there myself, in the midst of these questionings and longings and faltering hopes and confessions, and put the precious promises of the Word over against these burdening doubts and fears and lead their young lives into a new experience of the Father's love. [*Applause.*] All the conditions of that meeting are favorable for pastoral counsel. The seed falls upon prepared soil. There is desire and longing and expectancy awakened by consciousness of need and intensified by the influence of the Holy Spirit. There is an outreaching of the soul for instruction, that grasps with eager credulity the teachings the leader brings. The road to the convictions is cleared of all obstruction. It is the hour when the mind is tractable, the heart impressible, the spirit hungering and thirsting, and every door open to welcome the truth. The pastor has the flower of his congregation in easy range and his words find ready access to hearts around which doubt has not yet built its barricades, nor worldliness its impassable barriers. He can ill afford to lose that chance to impart lessons that will be remembered to the end of life, and weave into convictions the righteousness of the Gospel. The consecration meeting is the pastor's golden opportunity.

Again I say the consecration meeting is the arsenal of our Society, in which is stored the power that moves its machinery, the wisdom that guides its plans, the energy that vitalizes its forms and the life that throbs in all its vast organism. Every time we enter into the stillness and solemnity of its holy precincts, we are in the presence chamber of the King, to be freshly anointed with his grace and newly equipped with the enrichments of his Spirit. Conspicuously in every place of meeting should be displayed the injunction of St. Paul, "Yield yourselves unto God." By its side his sublime paradox, "When I am weak, then am I strong," and over all the inspiring assurance of the prophet, "They that wait upon the Lord shall renew their strength; they shall mount up with wings as eagles; they shall run and not be weary, and they shall walk and not faint." [*Applause.*]

After the singing of a hymn, Dr. Clark introduced Mr. R. W. Dillon, of Toronto, as the speaker upon the next topic — " Christian Endeavor Fellowship : Its Limitations and Possibilities."

Christian Endeavor Fellowship.

Address of Mr. R. W. Dillon.

Dear Fellow Endeavorers : — In the serried ranks of Christian Endeavor I am not a veteran, browned and scarred with the holy toil; I am only a humble soldier. But I have a profound conviction in the necessity for and the importance of united, aggressive, Christian work for Christ and the Church. You who are marshalled here on this, one of God's own Review Days, stand most of you in the "golden gateways of the dawn." You are rich in resolve, in courage, in strength, in opportunity. You stand here with your loins girded, ready to go down into the battle and through storm and stress fight manfully on till it pleases God to call you home. To me it is not only a duty but a privilege and an inspiration to witness for Christ before you, and to remind you that you are his reserve force, whom he must call to face the music of the guns, when those who carry the flag today have fallen asleep. Because of these things, and because I know there is no Christian Endeavorer who can live in this busy, throbbing, thinking world, and not be thrilled through and through with a quenchless desire and ceaseless determination to utilize all its forces and activities, and to use them as levers to lift mankind upwards to truth and God, that I venture to speak to you now touching the onward march of the kingdom of Christ, under the suggestive title of " Christian Endeavor Fellowship: Its Limitations and Possibilities."

O, fellow-soldiers of Christ, have you considered the march of the centuries? Know you not that it is almost high noon in the history of the world today? In spite of ever-increasing materialistic agencies, with their tendency to reduce all things to a gospel of "grind," in spite of the vast social unrest, which, marching to the iron feet of change, vibrates around the world, — in spite of all these, there are sunny outlooks in life which might make the pessimist pause and send the old blood dancing merrily through the veins of chilled and despairing old age. But the sunniest outlook of them all is the one open to our view this morning, as we stand upon the mountain of facts accomplished by Christian Endeavor and survey the things that remain. And, as a focus for your vision, take this one thought along: that this century, which began with a blood-thirsty and obstinate declaration of the rights of man as evinced in the French Revolution, is ending with a peaceful and willing acknowledgment of the rights of God, as manifested in the Christian Endeavor movement. [*Applause.*]

As regards the necessity for fellowship, all that I need say is that while the fundamental gifts of the religious life can be received by the individual, the highest gifts can only be received in fellowship. In nature, everywhere, there is a co-perfecting of all the kingdoms of life, and the higher you ascend in the scale, the more pronounced is the principle of co-perfection and interdependence. In the spiritual world the analogy is even closer, for as we grow in a knowledge of God, we grow also in the understanding of the saying, " I am my brother's keeper."

Christian Endeavor fellowship for the individual is found in his local society, which ought to be as a family, where each sacrifices himself for his brother's good. Thus has it been a wonderful spiritual benediction to the individual, and has been the messenger of God to many a lonely life, transfiguring its circumscribed, care-encumbered life into a living testimony to the truth of Christ's evangel, and filling it with an infinite passion for souls. Christian Endeavor, while it holds high communion with the transfigured Master on the mountain top, does not seek to build there any abiding tabernacle, but hastens down to fling the splendor caught from heaven upon the weary multitude below.

Christian Endeavor fellowship for the societies is accomplished through unions — local, county, and state. I wish to say it emphatically — say it as a Methodist, say it as one whose privilege it has been to aid in the formation of Epworth Leagues of Christian Endeavor, say it as a fundamental axiom that needs no defence, — that Christian Endeavor Unions should be composed of Christian Endeavor societies alone. [*Applause.*] This is a vital limitation. The basis of Christian Endeavor fellowship is loyalty to and belief in Jesus Christ. We often substitute assent to theological propositions for loyal devotion to the Lord Jesus, and intellectual agreement with theological systems for enthusiastic obedience to the Saviour of men, thus degrading faith into a logical process, and the trust that overcomes the world into a miserable superstition. The essentials of Christianity are for all evangelical churches the same; beliefs, opinions, creeds outside of these, are changing words, whose meaning changes with the years — they can be no basis for Christian Endeavor Union or Christian co-operation of any kind. This must be found in common work for Christ. [*Applause.*] Often as I pondered its meaning it seemed to me that never poet's dream or prophet's utterance was more "Utopian" than that saying of Christ's, "that they all may be one." I believe, sirs, that Christian Endeavorers will make that saying a living reality. [*Applause.*] The young people of this generation, who have met together in Christian Endeavor Union fellowship, when they bear the burdens of their fathers in the high places of the church, will not forget the lessons that are now being learned, but will use them to solve the problem of a visible and spiritual church union. [*Applause.*] This is why in Canadian Methodism we have stood loyally by the Christian Endeavor movement. We covet for ourselves the widest interdenominational fellowship compatible with denominational loyalty; and such an ideal we have reached in the Epworth League of Christian Endeavor. We pray that our brethren across the "line" may attain unto like perfection. [*Applause.*]

Just here comes an important limitation: our fellowship must not be used to cut our societies loose from denominational control. Every church has the right to demand that its young people's societies be in harmony with its teaching and laws. [*Applause.*] I hope that at the Methodist rally steps will be taken to adopt one common title for Methodist societies everywhere — a title at once denominational and fraternal — the Epworth League of Christian Endeavor. This would bring about the union of the various Methodist bodies within the next twenty-five years (as suggested by Dr. Carroll in his admirable article in the *Independent*). When every denomination has formally adopted the Christian Endeavor movement, there will have to be a limitation as to conventions. Our societies cannot endure a heavy financial burden; it is not right that they should. We would have to adopt some plan whereby denominational conventions could be held one year and the International the next, probably on a federated basis.

Now, to come back to the main subject, there are certain things which are not within the province of the Christian Endeavor Union. We are soldiers of that kingdom which cometh not with observation — the kingdom of Christ. It is the embodiment of all those ideas and principles which are dear to the hearts of men — its fruits are righteousness, joy, love, peace. Anything that is foreign to this, is outside the scope of a Christian Endeavor Union. But our unions are not substitutes for individual responsibilities, or for the work of our local societies, or for our church duties. All the old responsibilities that belonged to us before we entered Christian Endeavor fellowship belong to us after, only they have become a deeper reality; for we have had a truer vision of Christ. Our unions then must not trespass on the rights or assume the work of the society or the denomination. We must not countenance anything because it seems good in itself; we must not lend ourselves to any man's dictation, or we shall become the "happy hunting-grounds for cranks," who "like the little rift within the lute, they soon will make the music mute." [*Applause.*] We must not forget that our power is the Spirit of God working through consecrated hearts and enlightened minds, and that while we are in the real, the only apostolic succession of truth and righteousness, with a diocese as wide as the walls of heaven; we have to be just to each other in our union fellowships and not encroach on the duties of others, nor evade those that seem to belong of right to a Christian Endeavor Union.

Inasmuch as personal regeneration is the highway, not only to any moral reform, but also to the general progress of humanity, what are the possibilities that lie within a Christian Endeavor Union, composed of men and women regenerated by the Spirit of Christ? The possibilities of Christian Endeavor fellowship — it seems to me that they are too grand to be qualified by any adjective within the range of human comprehension. As I sat in my study and pondered over these, there seemed to unroll before me the procession of the coming years.. Silently as the stars that whirl in space, noiselessly as the power of gravitation that binds the spheres together, there was established the new heavens and the new earth,· wherein dwelleth righteousness, and for one brief moment I had seen realized the thought of God.

The union meetings for fellowship and inspiration,—we all know what a benediction they have been; these should be held every month for spiritual intercourse and profit,—conducted in various ways, as local circumstances seem to demand. If you take a piece of fluor-spar and heat it to intense redness, it emits the beautiful light we call fluorescence; the heat enables the molecules to exert their long latent powers of vibration and produce the unsuspected light; so the love of God, acting on our hearts as we have met in fellowship, has thrown new light on life and enabled us to see hidden needs, unsuspected responsibilities, and undreampt-of privileges. Thus, we have learnt that the work for the coming twentieth century will be to establish, not a church but the kingdom of heaven on earth, and that the true wealth of this kingdom is its citizens.

Our local unions must then care for these citizens of the kingdom as they move from place to place. There must be a Correspondence Committee, with a live, energetic secretary, who will give immediate notice to all concerned of removals and arrivals. The sheep need shepherding, some so easily go astray when they have not the surroundings of the home life to hearten them. Many a Christian has been lost because he has kept his religion in his trunk. As our fellow-Endeavorers come from the sweet country hillside and the old bush farm, into our great cities, where the smoke of men's passions is forever rising, like a mantle of darkness, between them and heaven's light, how they hunger for the friendly touch of a human hand, the kindly cheer of a human voice! I know something of the loneliness of a crowd. The last time I was in this city, I walked its streets a stranger in a strange land. The infinite pathos of those few weeks of sojourn I shall never forget. They taught me, whenever possible, to open my house to the stranger within the gate.

Oh, friends, we must look after these, our brethren; our Correspondence Committee need never be idle. They must be ready to surround with Christian influences any for whom their services are asked. What more pitiable sight than a woman-child alone in a great city that has no time to think of her, no glance to give her, no ear to lend to her sob! It becomes the old, old story too soon, of love, trust, desertion, and then,—the mad delirium of a suicide's grave. This is no imaginary fable; it is only a sketch of the short, sad stories which the streets of any great city cover up, and, like its dust, as little noticed. Death comes and brushes such dust away, but it gathers again on the morrow. Fellow-Endeavorers, there is ample work for your unions here.

No union should be without a Lookout Committee, whose business it should be to advance the cause of Christian Endeavor by the establishment of new societies wherever practicable — to introduce new societies into the union, and to present the desirability of Christian Endeavor societies to all pastors. In short, it must be the general-committee for the propagation of the Christian Endeavor movement.

The possibilities of these committees will develop in their working; this is the law of life. God himself seems to create nothing perfect at the beginning of its destiny. He puts the seed of a possible perfection within and leaves it to rise by the path of an unresting movement into an expanding breadth and sublimity of life.

Every Christian is the measure and definition of Christ to his fellows. According to the way he appropriates and utilizes Christ from day to day, so does he see and know Christ and get his power to represent him. This is equally true of a Christian Endeavor union. Hence to my thought there is one committee that is absolutely indispensable to every union :—a "Good-Citizen" Committee.

The state is as much God's as the Church. [*Applause.*] We must stand for God and his ideas in all the departments of life and labor at and for the state till it is made the effective instrument for the establishment of God. It is ours to establish the supremacy of the law of conscience, enlightened and inspired by Christ in every department of human life, and so exalt the whole idea of patriotism into a Christian principle. A nation cannot be made moral by statute, but Christian Endeavor unions should create a healthy moral tone, and demand the application of the laws of God to the lives of men. The exposure and the prevention of wrong is the business of every Christian Endeavor union. Through its "Good-Citizen" Committee it must unite the members of the various churches in a holy crusade against every moral evil.

No crueller fate can befall any nation than that its social progress should be effected by men opposed to its churches and religion. It is this which will make religion hated, God unreal, and scepticism well-nigh universal. The only place for the Church of the Lord Jesus is first in all self-denying reforms, first in all unselfish service in the van of every battle with iniquity, and first in everything that prevents the waste of manhood, diminishes vice, promotes national well-being and saves the bodies and the souls of men. This is not the work of any one section of the church but of the church as a whole, through some corporate union, such as Christian Endeavor affords.

Therefore, I maintain, it is the business of every Christian Endeavor union to try to stop the circulation of foul literature, to be vigilant in the defence of the oppressed, to punish the traffickers in harlotry and to aid in the annihilation of strong drink [*applause*], for these are the elementary tasks in the building of the kingdom of God.

I believe that the Good-Citizen Committee must create a healthy moral opinion that shall declare that no moral leper shall legislate for Christian people, declare that that which is morally wrong cannot be politically right, declare an equal punishment for impurity for men and women alike, declare a ceaseless crusade against profligacy and gambling and every kind of vice, and thus build up the "new world of the nobler life."

Let no one here think that I am going outside of the sphere of a spiritual society — there are no social problems that are not spiritual at heart. Defeated energies and ruined lives, starving children and crushed old age, bitter despairs breeding weakness and wickedness, keen miseries that make darkness more welcome than light and the grave the only gospel of rest, — are these not the things of the spirit?

You may say these things are only my ideas, — I care not. Ideas are the mightiest forces of this world, whose power is measured by their truth. Let an idea, born of truth and bright with purity, enter into men's hearts, and, quiet as the sunbeam but irresistible as the lightning, it will accomplish the desired end. It was only an idea that struck like a spark in the mind of Wycliffe, it took fire in the heart of Huss, and in the torch of Luther set all Europe aflame. An idea, springing up in the mind of Wilberforce, stepped upon opposition, overcame difficulties, and achieved the grandest triumph of any age in knocking the fetters from the bleeding limbs of a million slaves. Only an idea, emerging yonder in an obscure corner of the Roman Empire, spread over the face of society like a new creation, trampled down oppression, closed temples, hushed oracles, gave smiles to the widow and songs to the orphan, until it supplanted the pagan civilization by the Christian. [*Applause.*]

The only Christian idea that has deepened and broadened in its influence through all the Christian centuries in the strongest thinkers and the purest minds has been that the ideal Christian spirit, with its moral reality, inflexible truthfulness, and spiritual purity, should be the one great motive, animating and bringing into its confines all our manhood.

Oh, fellow-Endeavorers, knit together by the bonds of Christ, in societies and unions, every country under heaven needs new enthusiasms, burning aspirations, noble examples; everywhere there are Augean stables of trade and politics to be cleansed; there are false ideals of life to be shamed; a loose morality to be expelled. In your midst there is growing up a lessening sense of the sacredness of the marriage tie, an increasing disregard for the sanctities of the Sabbath. Here is your reasonable service. Devote your fellowships and your unions and all their forces to God for this end. It is not wealth, nor learning, nor lineage, that can make our unions powerful, but the Christ-like mind in the lives of its people, coupled with the omnipotence of combined and tireless activity. Act with the courage and the spirit-honesty of men lit up with the spirit of Christ. Do it not from duty, for that is to be your own master, sovereign of your own will; do it from love, having surrendered to the mastership of Christ; and then, O soldier of Christ, you shall understand that this is the victory that overcometh even your faith. [*Applause.*]

Some years ago I witnessed a review of the British army. When the sun rose on that Easter morning, it rose on as brilliant a spectacle as the eye could desire or the earth could furnish. Royalty was there. The scions of England's noblest and haughtiest families were there, in the pomp of their retinue and the pride of their wealth. Martial music, such as sets the blood dancing madly through the veins and stirs the heart to deeds of manliest daring, was there.

And anon, with banners streaming and bagpipes playing " Scots wha hae wi Wallace bled," the men of the Black Watch, sturdy, stalwart Scottish High-landers, men, who with dinted claymore and heroic slogan had earned on many a hard-fought field the right to be considered England's premier regiment, came marching on. Following these came the Household Brigade on gaily caparisoned horses, the brigadiers themselves glittering in silver and gold, with their waxen silky moustaches and their dainty delicate smiles seemingly better fitted to adorn a ball-room than a battle-field, had not Inkerman and Waterloo attested the bravery of these spoilt children of fortune. Then amid clanking of spurs and clashing of steel, garlanded in green and wreathed in shamrock rode the Royal Irish Dragoons, men who would ride into battle with a tear but meet death with a smile, — men from whose ranks England's greatest generals have come. Behind these there were the Welsh Fusiliers filled with the vigor of their moun-tain air, and proud of the fact that never on any battle-field had they been known to yield. Then how pride deepened into thoughtfulness, as we saw following these, dusky and silent native Indian troops turbanned and swarthy, reminding us that England still keeps watch and ward at the gates of the East. And so they kept marching on, those regiments, till in that mixed and serried mass there was no form or division of arms unrepresented. How cheer after cheer went up as we gazed upon that thin red line, which safeguarded England's honor and defended England's homes. No one there but felt amidst that inspiring scene that he could be true, true till death, to England's Queen, and that it was his proudest boast to be a loyal subject of the Empress Queen. Today I behold another army review, the plain of whose conquest is the wide earth and whose onlookers are God and his angels. Not with sound of trumpet or noise of drum, or clash of cymbals do they assemble — its regiments are always on service and on guard. Nor are they always marshalled into regiments or grouped into armies, for some of their most effective fighting is done on lonely outposts and alone. Not through flaming sword or sounding cannon do they conquer, but through the irresistible might of a loving human heart and through the cross of Christ.

Soldiers of Christ are we, whose mission it is to give not death but life, and who when earthly victory seems impossible accept even defeat and death as a benediction from God. Every soldier is a recruiting sergeant, and every enemy overcome is a warrior gained.

Soldiers of Christ you are here, are you not? Lift your flag a little higher, let the world see where you stand, and then fight loyally on until having gone to inquire in his temple you behold the King in his beauty as you enter into your rest in the land of life. [*Loud and prolonged applause*]

The audience then joined in singing the favorite hymn, " At the Cross."

DR. CLARK : What is the reason, do you suppose, that so many silver-tongued orators come from the state of Colorado? Is their any connection between the mines and the orators? [*Laughter.*] Anyway, we are sure that, whether silver is fluctuating or not, the tongues of these orators never falter. You will hear one of them this morning, the Rev. Kerr B. Tupper, D.D., pastor of the First Baptist church of Denver, who speaks on "The Christian Endeavor Society a Typical Church Institution." [*Great applause.*]

The Christian Endeavor Society a Typical Church Institution.

Address of Rev. Kerr B. Tupper, D.D.

"What a wide-awake body of young people," one of these pastors said to me a little while ago when you were listening to my Canadian friend; and the remark brought to my mind a story which I read a short time ago in a Presbyterian journal. Some time ago, as the story goes, an Episcopal rector, in making his rounds through his parish, came to a home where there was a little boy who had a kitten which he wished to sell. With an eye to business as well as religion, he came into the room where the mother and rector were talking and made a plea for the purchase. "Well, how much do you ask for the kitten, my boy," said the rector. "Only fifteen cents, sir." "Why do you want to sell it to me, an Episcopalian?" "Because, sir, it is an Episcopalian kitten." The Episcopalian recognized the compliment to his church, but said he didn't feel he could make the purchase. A short time afterward a Presbyterian minister came in, and there was the same boy, the same cat, and the same eye for business. He made the same plea for ministerial purchase. "Well, my boy, how much do you ask for your kitten?" said the minister. "Only twenty-five cents, sir." "Why do you want me, a Presbyterian clergyman, to buy it?" "Well, sir, it is a Presbyterian kitten." "O Willy," said the mother, who heard the conversation, "how was it that just a few weeks ago you offered this same kitten to an Episcopalian for fifteen cents, and now you want twenty-five?" "That is all right, mother; it has got its eyes open now." [*Great laughter and applause.*] Now, what was said about that Presbyterian cat may be said about the young people of the Presbyterian societies, because they have the honor of having the largest number of Christian Endeavor societies of all Christian denominations. [*Loud applause.*] You have your eyes open to a sense of the responsibility that rests upon you as servants of God, for we young people have a mighty part in advancing the kingdom of our Lord and Saviour, Jesus Christ.

My subject this hour, as already announced, is "The Young People's Society of Christian Endeavor, a Typical Church Institution of our Century"— typical, because representative and illustrative of three fundamental elements in the activity and success of modern Christianity. And may the great head of the church and of Christian Endeavorers, our common Lord, sanctify to us this simple, sympathetic discussion. With the recognition of the fact that the Church of Jesus Christ has had in every age of its history some special phase of thought and activity, some peculiar mission of reform, if I were called upon to characterize Christianity in our nineteenth century of enlightment and progress I should designate its prominent, preponderating aspect as clearly three-fold: first, the church at work; second, the church unitedly at work; third, the church unitedly at work, in a unique way, for the elevation and salvation of that class among us, who, in the coming generation, are to be the strongest pillars in our national structure, namely, the youth of our day. Indeed, this is a distinguishing, differentiating feature of our age. I do not overlook our day as one of art and science, of philosophy and literature, of invention and discovery, of railways and steamships, of telegraphy and telephony, of banks and commerce, but far above each and all of these merely material and mental achievements stand out and up, in magnificent proportions, the moral and spiritual triumphs of the Church of Christ in these notable and glorious directions: consecrated energy on the part of God's people, and enthusiastic effort among God's people for saving our strong young men and noble young women. Just as in the past the world has had its Stone Age, its Golden Age, its Dark Age, its Age of Chivalry, so today the church is passing through this age of triple glory. And the Y. P. S. C. E., if I interpret aright its origin and genius, its influence and end, emphasizes and illustrates just these features of modern Christianity. [*Applause.*] To every thinking, candid mind that has examined into this newest offspring of our common Christianity, it must appear that its heaven-born aim and God-inspired purpose have always and everywhere looked forward 'and pressed forward to those three things: a consecrated church, a united church, and a church by which and for which and in which to save our youth. To have come in contact with Christian Endeavor and not to be convinced of this is like visiting Westminster Abbey and passing by unnoticed the beautiful chapel of Henry VII.— the choicest, most attractive piece of architecture in all that hallowed spot. Let us analyze for a brief time, amid the solemn, sacred scenes of this glorious hour, this trinity of inspiration and aspiration. In the first place, I regard and pronounce the Y. P. S. C. E. a typical Christian institution of our nineteenth century, because it so deeply emphasizes and so largely realizes the Church of Christ at work — not so much the church in creed as the church in deed. This aspect of Christianity suits our age. We live in an age of outward activity, of practical benevolence, of utilitarian tendencies. Here we are, unlike all our predecessors. The sturdy old Roman craved a display of wondrous power and imperial sway. The refined, scholarly Greek delighted to lose himself in the labyrinths of abstruse metaphysics. The ancient, ritualistic Hebrew made it a part of his religion to bow down before hoary rites and flaming robes and significant symbols and sacred sacrifices. Not so we today. We live in the stern age of facts — an age that honors no custom, no ceremony, no institution, no person, that is not practical. Longfellow shapes his Psalm of Life to the characteristic American idea when he says:

> " Not enjoyment and not sorrow
> Is our destined end and way ;
> But to live that each tomorrow
> Finds us farther on our way "'

Now, it seems to me that in these days God has instituted and blessed the organization under whose glad auspices we meet in this convention, as a special agency to place foremost the practical aspect of Christianity. The very name of our Society indicates this, — " Christian Endeavor." Its holy mission proclaims this: " For Christ and the Church." Its multitudinous organizations declare this: now some 25,000 in number. Its mighty and gloriously increasing membership reveals this: now more than 1,500,000. These things stand for plan, purpose, persistency, progress, power. Christian Endeavor means something distinct, definite, decided, dutiful. [*Applause.*] To the young people enlisted in this progressive wing of King Immanuel's army, " the church is no mere ark in which the few elect may take refuge and placidly float over perishing millions to their haven of rest; no mere ferry-boat to bear idle passengers from the shores of time to the shores of eternity; no mere school where delighted pupils sit at the feet of their master; no mere place of worship even where sleepy souls sit and sigh and sing their souls away." None of these loose, lazy conceptions of Christian life and duty does our society encourage; but on the other hand, teaches that the church is a place for industry, training, growth, enlargement, organization — a place established by the Almighty God for saving men, and that, too, in the highest and broadest and noblest sense of that big word, save — saving them from sin and saving them to service; saving them in body, mind and spirit; saving them to family, church and nation; saving them in time and saving them in eternity. Oh, can there be a grander, diviner mission than this! — " to be a husbandman sent forth by the Lord of the harvest; to be a builder erecting God's Church on a sure foundation; to go out proclaiming a Saviour's inimitable life and illimitable love; and all this sacred embassy under the energizing authority of Him who said, " Lo, I am with you alway even unto the end of the world." Oh, men and women, brothers and sisters, we need more institutions like the Y. P. S. C. E. to declare to the Church of God that religion's reality and power are to be tested, not by the depth of emotion nor by the height of enthusiasm, nor by the degree of moral finery, nor by the connection with the church, nor by soundness of theological conceptions and utterances; but by the value and efficiency of personal, practical, progressive Christian work. The church needs "not more men but more man; not more Christians, but more Christian " [*applause*]; a higher idea of what it is to bear Christ's name and wear Christ's yoke and honor Christ's cause; more women like Elizabeth Fry, humbly but truthfully saying, " I believe I have seldom awakened from sleep, in sickness or in health, by day or by night, without my first thought being this: How may I best serve my Sovereign and Saviour;" more men like Arndt, of whom it was said, "His writings are good, his speech better, his life best of all;" more Christians who can say with a body of earthly disciples, "We do not speak great things, we do them; more of God's children hearkening to the call of honest Kingsley:

> " Do noble things, not dream them all day long,
> And thus make life, death, and the vast forever,
> One grand sweet song."

and replying to this uplifting sentiment:

> " I count that thing to be grandly true
> That a noble deed is a step toward God,
> Lifting the soul from the common sod
> To a purer air and fairer view."

Secondly, I esteem the Y. P. S. C. E. a typical nineteenth-century Christian institution, because it believes, not only in the church at work, but also in the church unitedly at work — not, as Dr. Boardman would put it, not so much the church organized as the church organic; not so much the church local as the church universal; not so much the church divisible as the church indivisible; not so much the church mortal as the church immortal; not so much constructed by man as the church born of God. I am not one of those who believe that there will ever come a time on our planet when there will be organic union between the different Christian denominations. It was false conception of a united church that rendered Père Hyacinthe's visit to America some years ago a dismal failure. He delivered strong speeches. He made a host of friends. He created genuine admiration for his spirit and purpose, and yet the good man failed because his plea was based upon the impractical theory that Protestantism and Romanism should die simultaneously, be buried on the same day, in the same grave, and out of their "dead selves," as Tennyson would express it, there should spring a universal Christian church, all branches of which should present the same liturgical service, the same ecclesiastical government, the same canonical hours, and even the same architectural form. The idea is chimerical, impracticable. Men differ too widely, in birth, in endowment, in education, in environment, in providential callings, to make this theory work. The universal law of God is diversity in unity, multiform variety amid beautiful harmony. And yet, with the widest differences in minor points, the Christian world, true to the great fundamental principles of the Gospel, may realize the prayer of the Master, " That they all may be one "— not one in organic union, for that is not the union of Father and Son, who are distinct personalities, but one in union of heart and purpose, a union spiritual, intimate, indissoluble, eternal. And the Y. P. S. C. E. not insignificantly undenominational, but essentially interdenominational [*applause*], is becoming a mighty factor, under God's guidance, I heartily believe, to bring about a heartier union among the members of Christ's universal church. Like the Y. M. C. A., it is drawing in close and beautiful co-operation the various organized branches of the church, and blending their respective abilities into one grand force. Such a convention as this means that this consummation devoutly to be wished is year by year becoming more and more an occasion of joy. Differ we may speculatively, but never shall we differ essentially so long as we agree upon this: absolute fidelity to the Scriptures as the very word of God and absolute fidelity to the Saviour as the very Son of

God. We cast away all man-made creeds, whether Athanasian or Augsburg, Nicene or Westminster, when we kneel at the feet of the once buried but now risen and exalted Christ and lovingly, adoringly exclaim in the one great belief of our enraptured souls, "My Lord, my God." And this service of united adoration and consecration Christian Endeavor has always rejoiced in, conscientiously and courageously, amid all variations of theological thought and all the controversies of theological schools, singing in its majestic movements for the glory of God and the salvation of man, the beautiful song of united brotherhood :

> "Like a mighty army
>   Moves the Church of God ;
> Brothers, we are treading
>   Where the saints have trod ;
> We are not divided,
>   All one body we,
> One in hope and doctrine,
>   One in charity." [*Applause.*]

Third, and last, I consider the Y. P. S. C. E., a typical Christian institution of our day, because it advocates, not only the church unitedly at work, but also the church unitedly at work for youth.

"Each human being," writes a noted American author, "is permitted by his Creator to pass through a form of golden age, which, according as it is shaped and developed, leads to glory or gloom. We call this period, "The flower of youth" or "The flower of manhood." Just as the plant has its blooming period, so man passes from the weak condition of infancy up into the magnificent bloom of youth, which opens before him marvelous opportunities and magnificent possibilities. Beautifully declares sweet-souled Frederick W. Robertson, "There is a moment in every true life — to some it comes very early — when the old routine of duty is not large enough ; when the parental roof appears too low, because the Infinite above is arching over the soul; when the old formulas in creeds, catechisms and articles seem to be narrow, and they must either be thrown aside or else transformed into living, breathing realities; when the earthly father's authority is being superseded by the claim of the Father in heaven. That is a lonely, lonely moment when the young soul first feels God — when this earth is recognized as "An awful place, yea, the very gate of heaven" — then the dream ladder is seen planted against the skies, and we wake, and the dream haunts us, a sublime reality. Now, the Church of God, through the Y. P. S. C. E., seeks to seize and mould and develop the soul at this critical, formative period. It recalls what men have done in early youth — David a king at thirty-one years of age, Solomon at eighteen, Alexander at twenty, Charlemagne and Charles V., each twenty-seven ; at twenty-seven Calvin the greatest religious author of Europe, and Luther the most renowned reformer of Europe, and Napoleon the most successful general of Europe ; aye, more, at thirty-three years the young Judean peasant, yet Son of the Highest, laying aside his work, a perfect model of perfect excellency, on which the scrutinizing criticism of eighteen hundred years has failed to find a single flaw to mar the beauty of its infinite excellence. Ah, when these and other illustrations of youth's illimitable possibilities and opportunities rise before the church, is it any wonder that its sympathy is excited and its enthusiasm kindled, and that it prayerfully stops, in the midst of all its multiplied and multiform enterprises, to crystallize that sympathy and enthusiasm in a special department of work for the education of our young men and women, not so much in outward lore and worldly knowledge, as in spiritual aptitude and heavenly culture, not for this life pre-eminently as for life beyond that awaits the emancipated spirit ; to teach them that the fear of Jehovah is the beginning of wisdom, and soul-culture the highest attainments; to cultivate in them that character which with the years grows broader in its outreachings after human happiness, and higher in its upreachings after divine glory ; to make them to know that there may be the manly form and manly intellect, and yet the crowning glory of manly dignity and worth is wanting if the soul lacks those high, transcendent virtues which are at once "the garment

of its beauty and the girdle of its strength;" to teach them so to cultivate the
spirit that from day to day and from year to year that spirit shall thrill with the
music of the everlasting principle:

> "I live for those that love me,
>   For those that know me true;
> For the heaven that bends above me
>   And waits my coming too,
> For the cause that needs assistance,
> For the wrongs that need resistance,
> For the future in the distance,
>   For the good that I can do."

God richly bless, I pray, the organization that has so true, so noble, so divine
a mission as that of the Young People's Society of Christian Endeavor. [*Loud
and prolonged applause.*]

After a number of notices and telegrams had been read, the doxology
was sung, and the session adjourned with the Mizpah benediction.

THE TENT.

The exercises began with a song service, led by Mr. Lindsay and
the Park Sisters, cornetists. Rev. Dr. M. Rhodes, of St. Louis, the
presiding officer, began the program with giving out the 100th Psalm,
which was read responsively. After this service, Rev. Dr. Chapman,
of St. Louis, led in prayer, followed by the hymn, "Holy Spirit,
Teacher Thou."

DR. RHODES: All the questions discussed by this convention are important.
There is no time here for the discussion of anything that is not important. It
would be very difficult, by contrast, to discover what is the most important, but
I am very certain that there are not a few here who realize that the subject
which is to be brought before us this morning in open meeting is of very great
importance. Whether there is any special significance in its being on the program will be determined by the response you make at this time. I am very
certain that the name of Dr. Rondthaler is not strange among Christian Endeavorers. He is to conduct this part of the service, and he comes to you this morning when the tide is up. I shall mistake very much if he does not carry you
along with him. I am pleased to introduce to you Rev. Dr. J. A. Rondthaler,
of Indianapolis. [*Applause.*]

The Sunday Evening Service.

Open Meeting. Conducted by Rev. J. A. Rundthaler, D.D.

DR. RONDTHALER: Eighty speeches in forty minutes — we can do it! I
want to see whether we cannot give half-minute addresses on this important
subject of how to conduct the Sunday evening service so that it will be a success.
There is no use of having anything in the church that does not succeed, because
you can have the blessing of the Spirit on everything that you have in the
church, if it is according to the Word of God. I am sure Sunday evening
services are according to the Word of God; therefore they ought to be
successful.

Now, we have this subject divided into two parts: first, what have you done?
secondly, what can you do? I understand very well that the Endeavorers here
do not want to give an answer until they have heard from the ministers, because
for Christian Endeavorers to give advice and counsel to ministers is not accord-

ing to our pledge or our constitution. Now we will have a few responses, first of all, from the ministers on this subject. What have you done for the evening service?

RESPONSES: "I give one Sunday evening of each month to my Christian Endeavorers, and they conduct it themselves. On the other Sunday evenings they come and bring their neighbors and friends." - "Every Sunday night my Christian Endeavor society takes care of the evening service, thus allowing the pastor Sunday afternoons to go out and preach at school-houses in the region." "My Endeavor society run the church during the summer on Sunday evenings." "My society contributes a good deal of variety to the music on Sunday evenings." "The Christian Endeavor society has helped the attendance and the attention, especially the attention." "Our Christian Endeavor society holds a service immediately preceding the evening service, and the members stay and labor to have others stay and attend the service. They work to this end during the week preceding. Then we have special services about once a quarter, where we all join in under a Christian Endeavor leader." "We have special services Sunday evening. If a subject is prominent before the minds of the community, I take it up and discuss it in the spirit of Christ and the Gospel. The Christian Endeavor society helps in advertising the meetings and bringing in an audience." "Our Christian Endeavor society conducts an open-air mission every Sunday night after the evening service." "We do not have Sunday evening concerts. Our minister preaches the Gospel every Sunday night." "Members of my society in Washington meet every stranger at the Sunday morning service and invite them to the evening service, and then hold them to the end of the service in the prayer room." "The minister never fails to go to the Christian Endeavor prayer meeting himself."

DR. RONDTHALER: Ah, there is reciprocity! [*Applause.*] The minister never fails to go to the Christian Endeavor prayer-meeting himself, and then the Christian Endeavorers are ashamed to slide out and not go to his service, don't you see? [*Laughter and applause.*] Does the pastor come early before the meeting, or does he come late?

DELEGATE: He is always on time. [*Applause.*]

"We follow up our preaching service in the evening with an inquiry meeting, and we expect the young people of the Christian Endeavor society to take a prominent part in it and look for spiritual results. Our society sends out a circular letter to any one who absents himself regularly from the Christian Endeavor society or from the evening service, if he or she is a member of the church."

DR. RONDTHALER: That's first-rate! I tell you, it makes an old fellow feel bad when he gets a letter from some one younger than he asking him why he doesn't go to church on Sunday evening.

"Every Sunday evening we have a season of five or ten minutes of prayer for the blessing of the Holy Spirit on the Sunday evening service."

DR. RONDTHALER: Good! I tell you if we would rely on the Spirit to give the power to the evening service, instead of relying upon ourselves, we would have the crowd coming. [*Applause.*] One minister always makes the topic of his Sunday evening service a review of the Sunday-school lesson, and the consequence is that the teachers are there and those Christian Endeavorers interested in Sunday-school work are there.

"Our Christian Endeavor society holds an open-air meeting about three or four blocks from the church, and gathers the people into a crowd, and then they have runners going back and forth directing the people to the church. Our society unites with the pastor in shaking hands with the people as they leave the church and asking them to come again."

DR. RONDTHALER: Here is a Christian Endeavor society that stands at the door with the pastor and shakes hands with the people as they go out and invites them to come again; and they look so beautiful and so sweet, so far as the young ladies are concerned, and so cordial and warm-hearted, so far as the young men are concerned, that the people come back and endure the sermon just to be greeted again. [*Laughter.*]

"Our society distributes circular letters at the hotels to strangers who stay over Sunday, inviting them to attend the evening service."

DR. RONDTHALER [repeating]: Here is a society, that, in the first place, consults with the pastor about church work; in the second place they consult with the leader of their own meeting, that he may give special emphasis to the evening service; in the third place, they all take the front seats at the evening service. [*Applause.*] Oh, blessed be the congregation that takes the front seats! What a benediction that congregation is to the minister!

DELEGATE: What would you think about preaching the Gospel on Sunday night?

DR. RONDTHALER: We all agree to that. [*Applause.*]

"We follow up the evening service with a good, wide-awake Christian Endeavor prayer meeting, and gather in the sheaves." "A Christian Endeavor society in New York City holds meetings at the homes of people Sunday afternoons, and gets them interested in attending the evening service." "Our society takes the back seats at the evening service, in order to compel those who need the Gospel to sit up front. Then we give them a personal invitation to come to Christ before they go out."

Dr. RONDTHALER: Now we have had the Christian Endeavor society at the top, at the bottom, and at the rear of the church; what about Christian Endeavor on the side of the church? Anything being done there?

DELEGATE: Christian Endeavor is always on the right side of the church. [*Applause.*] Christian Endeavor is always on the inside of the church, and that makes the Sunday evening service successful.

DR. RONDTHALER: How about the outside of the church during the week?

DELEGATE: They throw their influence outside.

Dr. RONDTHALER [repeating]: Here is a society which holds a special Christian Endeavor meeting before the evening service; then the Endeavorers are scattered through the congregation and invite the people to stay to the after-meeting; then they are scattered again amongst the congregation, inside and outside, and upside and downside, and give the people a personal invitation to come to the Lord.

"Our society marches into the evening service singing 'Army of Endeavorers' as a body."

Dr. RONDTHALER: Now, how do you conduct the evening service?

A MINISTER: I use the Brookfield services. [Published by the Hartford Press, Hartford, Conn.]

Dr. RONDTHALER: You all know what the Brookfield services are. The fact of having the service printed, with hymns and responses, advertises the meeting and makes it fresh and new, and the people come in crowds.

"Do not do all your work on Sunday, but do some during the week, that you may see the results on Sunday evening." "I used to help the evening service by staying away. Now I help by going and giving earnest attention to what is said." "We have the 'People's Services' [Published by the Golden Rule Co., Boston], and a ten-minute sermon." "We have an orchestra to assist in the music, and people we have never seen going to church are drawn in by the music."

A MINISTER: We have Miss Park, the cornetist, to play at our service, there is no difficulty in getting a crowd. [*Applause.*]

Dr. RONDTHALER: That gets them into the church, but the question is, Does it get them into the kingdom?

MINISTER: "Yes, sir."

DR. RONDTHALER: He thinks it does. You can *blow* a man into the kingdom — certainly you can.

"I believe that if the minister of today has a message direct from God, and if he will unfold the Bible as a common-sense living book, he can hold an evening service for sixty minutes and he will draw the crowd. The people today want the Bible opened; the Bible is not opened as it should be. [*Loud applause.*] Our minister preaches Christ and him crucified every Sunday night, except that one night in the year when the gentlemen of the Christian

Endeavor society take charge of the service, and another night the ladies take charge."

Dr. RONDTHALER : I have got two minutes left, and I will tell you what I do. I don't have any evening service. I go out to the missions in connection with my church, and preach there. The Christian Endeavorers go with me in this work, and I get two crowds: one out in the suburbs of the city, and one right in the center of the city. [*Loud applause.*]

This closed the open meeting. Various announcements were then made, after which the Misses Park, by request, gave an illustration of how they are wont to "blow the gospel." They played "Nearer, My God, to Thee " as a cornet duet, with great expression, repeating it a second time with muted instruments. The effect was very beautiful, and was loudly applauded. Dr. Rhodes then introduced the next speaker.

Dr. RHODES : It is in the memory of a great many of us when that event which is now about to take place was not possible in this Dominion nor in broad America. That time, thank God, has passed, and this morning India reaches out her hands to us in Christian fellowship and comes herself, in one of her own sons, to bear testimony to the Gospel of the grace of God. I have the greatest pleasure in introducing to you this morning a brother who has a name in more ways than one, — the Rev. Sumantrao Vishnu Karmarkar, of Bombay, India. [*Loud applause.*]

Mr. Karmarkar came forward, wearing a white silk sash, the token of his Brahman rank, and was given a cordial greeting by the audience. After explaining that his presence in this country was due to an accident which prevented him from returning to his native land as a missionary some time ago, he spoke as follows : —

A Voice from India.

Address of Rev. S. V. Karmarkar.

It was with great pleasure I accepted the invitation to represent again, with my wife, the wonderful country of the Aryans. We expect to sail for India on the 29th of this month. We are, therefore, very glad to be present on this occasion and carry the inspiration of this meeting and the greetings of young people to our country. I want you to bear in mind that it was India which led to the discovery of America. The people of the United States and Canada, therefore, owe a great debt to her ; which can only be remitted by disseminating the religion of Christ among her people.

The voice of India is like the sound of many waters ; nay, I would say of many countries. For the population of India equals the population of Russia, Germany, France, Turkey, Great Britain, United States and Canada. According to the last census, there are 287,000,000 of people ; out of which 200,000,000 are Hindus ; 60,000,000, Mohammedans ; 7,000,000, Buddhists ; 2,050,000 native and foreign Christians and the rest belong to different nationalities and religions. Again, it is a babel of voices, for over 100 distinct languages are spoken there. Would these voices of many countries and people be a feeble one ? The message of India to you in the words of the prophet is, " Prepare ye the way of the people, cast up, cast up the highway, gather out the stones, lift up an ensign for the people." India needs a highway for its loving Prince Jesus Christ. To prepare it many rocks must be removed and many gaps must be filled.

Our special efforts are needed to level down the huge rock of Idolatry. Pantheism, which causes the decline to Buddhism, gave a great impetus to image worship. The 33 deities of the Vedas evolved into 330,000,000, with a mass of legends surrounding each. I could not bring all these deities in my valise here, but I have brought a few domestic idols which the Brahmans daily worship in their homes. Here is the idol of the Trinity, which has three faces, six hands, and two legs. The three deities, Brahma, Vishnu, and Shiva, represent the three properties in the godhead,—the creative, the preservative, and the destructive. The Hindus also believe that the second person of the Trinity has been incarnated nine times, and he is to appear once more to usher in the reign of righteousness. Here is one of the incarnations whose name is Krishna. This image represents him as a creeping child with a piece of candy in his hand. It is said that he often stole candy, and when he grew to manhood he married 16,000 wives; but the Hindus inculcate that the divine essence in Krishna did not participate in the actions of his human nature. Could such an incarnation elevate their morals and save them from sin?

Here is another idol, the incarnation of Shiva; he is called Ganesh, the elephant-headed god of wisdom. Every child in India on entering a Hindu school must first learn to read and write the prayer of this god; which is as follows: Shri Ganashai namaha, or, I invoke the blessing of god Ganesh. After which the teacher gives instructions in the letters of the alphabet. Think of these idolatrous impressions continually being made upon the Hindu child. At home, in the school, at the temple where there are large, hideous-looking idols, the child comes in contact with idolatry. These imprints become so firm upon his mind that no earthly power can eradicate them. Idol worship, in fact, becomes a second nature with him. The power of the Holy Ghost which we believe in can alone transform such minds. To counteract these idolatrous influences and to impart the true concept of God and sin missionary schools and colleges are needed all over India.

The fourth idol is the goddess of food to all mankind. When worshiping these idols, the Brahman washes them in a brass cup and drinks that sacred water to sanctify his soul. He then burns incense and with the aid of a rosary repeats his prayers. Some of their prayers have excellent sentiments. " Papoham papkarmaham papatma papsambhavaha," etc. The prayer I have just repeated means "I am a sinner, my actions are sinful, my soul is sinful, I am born in sin; O thou lotus-eyed Hari (Saviour) protect this sinner." These sentiments are found in the 51st Psalm of David. Fancy a Hindu offering such a beautiful prayer to these idols. The worshipper, after offering flowers and food, rings the bell as a good-bye to the gods for the day.

There is a remarkable correspondence between Romish worship and Hindu worship Romanism is but a new label on the old bottles of paganism containing the deadly poison of idolatry. Often the Hindus ask us, when seeing the Romish worship, "What is the difference between Christianity and Hinduism?" In India we have not only to contend with the hydra-headed monster of idolatry but also the octupus of Romanism.

Another great evil which we need to extirpate is the baneful caste system. For lack of time I shall proceed to consider the colossal obstacle of the Hindu women, which interferes with the progress of the King's Highway.

Woman is the trustee of the Hindu religion. She makes the man to worship idols. If he should not worship and offer food to the idols no high-caste woman would give him his meals; nor could other members of the family partake of it. This compulsory worship of images is the great reason why idolatry reigns supreme in India. Our women need education; but they cannot be well educated as long as the custom of child-marriage is in vogue among us. Every girl under twelve must be married. After marriage she is under the control of the mother-in-law, who being ignorant, does not permit her daughter-in-law to continue her studies. This obnoxious custom was universally adopted by the

Hindus on account of the loose morality of the Mohammedans. When the Moslems were in power they instituted a law by which any Mohammedan could claim an unmarried Hindu woman as his wife, and thus save her and her offspring from the evil consequences of a false religion. When the Hindus found out that they were losing many of their grown-up unmarried daughters they resorted to the early marriage system and thus protected their daughters from the despotic Moslem.

Although there is no need of such a practice under the benign English rule, yet the custom has become so strong that the people are reluctant to abandon it. Connected with the early marriage system there is another evil. No widow among high castes is allowed to marry. She must eat but one meal a day; no one should see her face the first thing in the morning; she must do the menial work in the house; she must also perform extra penance for her husband, whose death, as is supposed, was caused on account of her sins. There are 79,000 of these widows under nine years; 669,000 under eighteen years of age, and 24,000,000 of widows in all. What misery is this? When I look into the beaming faces of the young ladies in this audience my heart aches for my poor suffering widowed sisters in India.

These rocks of idolatry, cast system, early marriage and widowhood must be levelled down; but who is able to do this gigantic work. We are but a handful of workers among so many. Our societies do not number very large. Still each member is striving earnestly to do his best in laying down this highway for his Lord. "For who hath despised the day of small things?" These prophetic words cheer us in our arduous task. We believe that, like the small cloud of Elijah, we shall within a short time cover the whole horizon of India. For this work is not ours; it is to be accomplished, "not by might, nor by power, but by my spirit, saith the Lord of hosts." However, God has made us co-workers with him. What a grand privilege he has given to each one of us! Will you not hear the voice of the millions of Hindus who long to hear the Gospel message?

My father, who was a Brahman, left his beloved parents under great persecution and accepted Christ. His parents thereupon performed the cremation ceremony, to show to the world that their son was dead and burnt. Amidst all such sufferings he came out victorious. After further instructions in the faith, he became the pastor of the Congregational church at Bombay, and when departing from the world he uttered these words, "Hallelujah, amen; hallelujah, amen;" and the Spirit took him away to continue that refrain in the other world. Such was the triumphant death of that Brahman. My friends, you want us to leave our homes, our beloved parents and kindred; and yet you do not wish to leave your country and your homes to preach Christ to your neighbors across the sea. Please consider that there is but one missionary to every 350,000 people in India, while in the states you have one minister to every 800. Again, there is one Christian worker among 40,000 in India, while here you have one in 48. We need many consecrated young women, especially lady physicians, to evangelize the 143,000,000 of women in India. Think how our loving Saviour left his Father's magnificent and blissful throne to save us sinners!

Dear Endeavorers, It is the young people that are going to win the world for Christ. Do come over to India and aid us "to cast up the highway, gather out the stones, and lift up an ensign before the people." [*Loud applause.*]

The audience then joined in singing "Speed Away."

Question Box.

Conducted by Mr. William Shaw.

DR. RHODES: The man that cannot answer questions has no business to be an officer in a Christian Endeavor society. The questions at this time will be answered by Mr. William Shaw, treasurer of the United Society of Christian Endeavor.

MR. SHAW: The people that cannot ask questions have no business to be members of a Christian Endeavor society. [*Laughter.*] First of all, there is a very important work that Christian Endeavor is now doing and in which many are interested. We are often asked, What do you mean by the life-saving work? Who are the life-savers? Where are they located, and what is their work, and what is Christian Endeavor doing for them? I am going to ask an expert to answer these questions for you, and I want to introduce Rev. E. R. Young, of Asbury Park, N. J., who has charge of the life-saving work, and who will tell you what we mean by Christian Endeavor work among the life-savers. [*Applause.*]

REV. MR. YOUNG: In the last twenty-five years the life-savers of the world have saved 1,000,000 human lives. Is it not right, therefore, that we, as Christian Endeavorers, should offer in Jesus' name eternal life to life-savers? [*Applause.*] In the United States and Canada they guard 20,000 miles of lake and ocean front. They are shut out through nearly all the year, year after year, from hearing the Gospel of Jesus Christ. When last year the International Committee announced that they would try to arrange services for all the life-saving stations, one great expression of gratefulness came from all the stations in the land. We have held this year 1,000 services. A great number have been led to Christ. In many cases a church has sprung up where service was first held in a life-saving station. Every life-saving station has a room just large enough to hold 40 or 50 people, and into that room the Christian Endeavorers from the nearest Christian Endeavor society go and hold religious services.

At Sandy Hook, a little over a year ago, it was the privilege of the chairman of this committee to preach the first Protestant sermon ever preached in Sandy Hook, and last September he went and dedicated the new Protestant church of Sandy Hook, which was the result of the religious services held there in the life-saving station. [*Applause.*] This year we have undertaken to arrange religious services in the lighthouses; and this, combined with providing religious services in 1,000 life-saving stations, is a very large work. We want somebody here from Great Britain to come forward and help carry on the work in the 304 life-saving stations in Great Britain. We want somebody in every other land where there is a life-saving station to assist in carrying on the work there; and, God willing, we want somebody to help carry on the work in every country where there is a lighthouse. This is a field which was absolutely untouched until the Christian Endeavor Society took hold of it. This a field, when we include the lighthouses, where 2,000 little chapels are already provided, with a nucleus of population around them, where we may preach the Gospel of Jesus Christ. Who will come and help us? Let me say that this work has received the express interest of the Prime Minister of England, Wm. E. Gladstone [*applause*], of Her Majesty, the Queen of England [*applause*], and of the President of the United States. [*Applause.*] I have asked the Secretary of the International Committee, Rev. J. Lester Wells, of Jersey City, to take two minutes in presenting this subject.

REV. MR. WELLS: In addition to what the President has said with reference to this great international work for the life-savers, I would add this. It may be that there are thousands of young people represented here today who would like to know what they can personally do to help on this great and philanthropic work. I have in my desk hundreds of letters today which would give you, if I could read some of them to you, some idea of the grandeur and the needs of the work. I have received personal letters from nearly every life-saving station in the United States, asking for our co-operation and help. You remember that these brave men are exposed to great danger along the coasts of our country; and as they are thus exposed, it is necessary that we should help them in the protection of their physical bodies as well as that we should give to them the blessings of the Gospel. They need good literature; they need comfort bags, such as are being sent to the sailors. These comfort bags are made of strong material, with a string around the top, and in them these good young people may put a comb and brush, buttons, needles and thread, a Testament, and also a nice little written letter to these men. Such a bag is a comfort to them, and they will send back a letter of thanks to you. They also need woollen mitts, comforters, socks, and other things that will make them comfortable in time of storm. I called on Capt. Abbey, the U. S. Inspector, only a few weeks ago, and he said that in one district along the New Jersey coast the life-saving men walked 1,500 miles during an awful storm when vessels were being wrecked along the coast. Now will you Christian Endeavors give us your thoughts, your prayers, and your help?

At this point, while the questions were being taken up by the usher, and handed in at the desk, the audience sang two verses of a familiar hymn, after which Mr. Shaw read the questions one by one and answered them as follows : —

QUES. What would you advise a young lady to do who believes she is called of God to be a missionary, and whose parents object to her going abroad ?

MR. SHAW : I cannot answer that question any farther than to say that that is a matter the young lady must decide with her own conscience, with her God, and with her parents; but I think it is a grand sign in these days that the Spirit of God is moving in this way upon the hearts of our young people. Certainly if this young lady is held back by others, the blame will not be at her door. Let us pray that the door may be opened that she may be able to consecrate her life to the service of Christ in foreign lands.

QUES. There is a feeling in our society that the Lookout Committee should meet with the candidates for membership and conduct a personal examination. Is this practicable? Is it done elsewhere ?

ANS. I think that every candidate for membership in the Christian Endeavor Society should have the personal acquaintance of every member of the Lookout Committee. I do not know how they are going to get it, unless the committee meets with them. I do not mean by that that you are to examine them, as the Church Committee examines a candidate for church membership, but you ought to know who they are, and whether they know what the object of the society is, and whether they are willing, trusting in the Lord Jesus Christ, to try and keep the pledge that they take. And then I think it would be a very good thing for the committee to kneel down with these candidates for membership and have a few moments of earnest prayer with them before their names are proposed for membership in the society. It will do the committee and the new members also an immense amount of good. I would advise it in every case.

QUES. How can we get our pastor to preach a sermon in place of a prayer meeting on Sunday evening?

ANS. I guess the best way is to give him an audience and have him understand that the people would like to hear him preach, and then if he thinks he can do more good by preaching than by conducting a prayer meeting, he will do it, but you cannot tell him how he ought to run his business. You may suggest this, and he will decide what is best.

QUES. To whom should Christian Endeavor societies apply for information, when they wish to support a Bible reader in India?

ANS. To the secretary of your denominational foreign missionary board. He will give you all the information that you desire. If you do not know who he is, then you need a little instruction on the subject of missions in your denomination, and I would advise that you ask your pastor to preach you a sermon on it and have him give you the names of the men who are spending the money and doing the missionary work of your denomination. I tell you, friends, I am more and more convinced that the reason we do not do more for missions is that we do not know enough about them. [*Applause.*] How many dollars would you give to a man out here on the street who should come and ask you for money, if you did not know his name or how he was going to spend it? That is the way a great many are giving to the missionary boards. Scores of us in this audience today could not name the treasurer of our denominational missionary board. That ought not so to be. It would not do these treasurers any harm if you would write them a letter once in a while. They might not get time to read it, but their stenographer would tell them that there was a great package of letters received from young people interested in missionary work.

QUES. Do you not think there is very great danger, in the effort to make a special service attractive, of overlooking the nobility of the Gospel and dishonoring the Spirit?

ANS. Not if we have the right idea of making it attractive. I do not think we honor the Spirit by preaching to empty pews. I think we honor the Spirit when we use every legitimate means to bring the people under the influence of the Spirit. That is what we mean by making the service attractive. Not that we simply have the people there to be amused, but we bring them there that the Spirit may get possession of their hearts and may transform their lives. People look at these things from two standpoints. Some people think when you talk about making the service attractive that you are just going to have a lot of fun. That is not it. The most attractive services are those in which there is most of the Spirit of God.

QUES. Should Christian Endeavor societies contribute their missionary funds to the woman's boards of missions?

ANS. Why, yes, part of them. I do not think that the woman's boards want to monopolize the Christian Endeavor contributions, nor do I think that the men's boards want to; but I think they all want to feel that we are with them and that our contributions are divided up among them, and so cover the whole field.

QUES. What would you say to a pastor who does not believe in the temperance cause?

ANS. Why, I would say to him that I was sorry for him. I would say that I hoped he might see his way clear to take a definite stand on the temperance question, and I should hope that the stand would be in favor of " God, and home, and native land," and not in favor of the saloon, which is death and destruction to the family and the nation and the kingdom of God. [*Loud applause.*]

QUES. Can I belong to the Odd Fellows and Masons, and be a good Christian? [*Laughter.*]

ANS. Well, I know lots of good Christians that do. I do not, and I am not going to tell you whether you can or not; but if you get into a Free Mason's lodge or an Odd Fellow's lodge where you cannot be a good Christian, I would advise you to get out. [*Applause.*]

QUES. How can we reach the young men in a country town?

ANS. I like that question. I was one of a company of young men that were reached in a country town, so of course I am interested. I want to tell you that it is no harder to reach a young man in a country town than it is in a city. If you do not reach the young men in the country towns, by and by your city churches will be lacking some of the best workers they ought to have in them. [*Applause.*] Who are the people that are filling up our cities to-day? Young people from the country towns. If the city churches were wise, then never would allow one of their members to go into a country town for two months in the summer without having them use every influence in order to win those young people for Christ and the church. They do not know but what from that country town there may go into their city church some of the best workers they will ever have upon their list. You want to win the young men, both in the country towns and in the city churches. Show them the manliness of Christianity. Don't be ashamed of the Gospel of Jesus Christ. Don't think that you must be any the less a man, in order to win souls for Christ. Young men in the country and young men in the city admire manliness and true Christianity. We make a mistake in supposing that we have to come down to their level. The trouble is, our level has been too low, and so we have not lifted them up. Do everything that you can, as a man and as a Christian, to win these young men, and they will respond to it.

QUES. What is the most helpful method of Bible study?

ANS. The one that you'like the best and get the most profit out of.

QUES. Whom should we send to our conventions — active or associate members?

ANS. Both of them, — the active members that they may be more active; the associate members that they may become active members. I have known of associate members whose lives have been transformed and who have been converted in our conventions. These instances ought to be multiplied a hundred-fold. Send the associate members with the active members to the conventions.

QUES. Is a Young People's Alliance of the Evangelical Church that has accepted the Christian Endeavor pledge and topics but will not adopt the Christian Endeavor name with their own, eligible for membership in a local union?

ANS. Our local unions are Christian Endeavor unions. Why should any society that believes in our methods and our plans and our system of work, and takes everything that we have that is distinctive, not take the name, also, in connection with any other name that they prefer? I do not see why they should care to come into our union, if they are ashamed of the name we bear. [*Applause.*]

QUES. How can a person who can give thirty dollars a year for the work in India give it so that it will be most effective in saving the women?

ANS. Your denominational foreign missionary board can give you that information. I wish five hundred of you would ask that question when you get home from this convention.

QUES. How can we make our young people more earnest?

ANS. By being more earnest yourself.

QUES. How can we get into our Christian Endeavor meeting those of other denominations who stand on our church steps and smoke and talk?

ANS. Well, I don't know why you should want to get those of other denominations into your society. I should say that you ought to get them into their own society. There is where they belong. [*Applause.*] I would not like to send them over there to smoke and talk on the church steps, but to work. I think a good plan would be to send a committee over and invite the Christian Endeavor society in their church to come over and hold a meeting with them on the steps, and see if they could not take them back home where they belong. [*Laughter.*]

QUES. What shall the Lookout Committee do when the pastor and Sunday-school superintendent are both members of the Christian Endeavor society, claiming to be interested in the work, and yet do not keep the pledge or attend the consecration meeting?

ANS. I think the Lookout Committee ought to interview them and just ask them how they would like to have every member of the church not attend the Lord's Supper or the preaching service, or every member of the Sunday school not attend the Sunday school. Then I would leave it with their conscience to answer, and I would say, "Go thou and do likewise."

QUES. How can we get our associate members to become active members?

ANS. By praying for them, and working with them, and everlastingly keeping at it until you have won them for Christ.

QUES. Do you think it is advisable to invite only members of the society to the social meetings?

ANS. Why, no. If I was in town where there was a Christian Endeavor society that thought its social meetings were too good for me, you would not see me in their prayer meetings. [*Applause.*] If you are not interested enough in these young people to want to meet them socially, then they will not be interested enough in you to want to meet you spiritually.

QUES. Is there any Christian Endeavor work being done among the firemen of our cities?

ANS. Yes; they are holding prayer meetings wherever they can get an opportunity for the firemen in some of our cities, but I do not know that they have any organized societies of Christian Endeavor among the firemen. In Boston meetings are held in the horse-car stables for the conductors and drivers when they are off duty, and 1 think such meetings are held in other places.

QUES. Should people over forty years be made to feel unwelcome in Christian Endeavor meetings?

ANS. No. 1 expect to be forty years old some time, and I should hate to be made to feel unwelcome, if 1 should come into a Christian Endeavor meeting. I am glad that Christian Endeavor has adopted these words as a text: "Whosoever will, let him come."

QUES. What kind of a member would you call your pastor who does not attend the Christian Endeavor meeting?

ANS. I would call him an absent member, and then 1 would call on him and ask him to be a present member.

QUES. How can we reach the middle-aged business men?

ANS. Do all you can to reach them — anything that commends itself to your own common-sense. Why, suppose you were keeping a store, and you should ask me how to get customers. 1 would tell you to advertise; to make your goods so attractive and your prices so reasonable that the people would come, and then they would come again and bring their friends. Now, just apply the same principle to your Christian work. Do everything that your sanctified common-sense suggests to reach these men; but do not forget that in every boy to-day you have a future middle-aged business man, and if you want to reach the business men, get hold of the boys today. [*Applause.*]

QUES. When members do not come to the business meeting, how can they be made to come

ANS. Make your business meeting attractive. They wont come unless they are interested. If you haven't any business that is of interest, they will not come. Some societies hold their business meeting in connection with their socials, and so after they have disposed of the business they have a general good time together. I think that plan has worked very well in many places.

QUES. Please give some points on temperance work for the Christian Endeavor Society.

ANS. I cannot stop here to give them. Write to the temperance organizations for suggestions. Read the temperance papers; keep a scrap book; have your Temperance Committee keep their eyes and ears open and gather information, and then put into practice that which seems most desirable in your particular place. Get your members to sign the pledge. I remember that when I was a boy, so young that I could not write my own name, my Sunday-school teacher took hold of my hand and helped me to sign a temperance pledge, and that pledge, I believe, kept me in the early days of my boyhood from drinking sweet cider and the other stuff that leads our boys into strong drink. [*Applause.*] Get your members, no matter how young, to sign the pledge.

QUES. How can a roll-call at the consecration meeting be carried out successfully in a society of 175 members?

ANS. I have seen it carried out successfully in a large society by having every one brief, every one prompt. In some places they divide the society for the consecration meeting and have two sections, meeting in different places. They say it works well. I do not know why it should not. If you cannot call the roll successfully in one meeting, then have two meetings for your consecration service.

QUES. Should the corresponding secretaries be members of the local union?

ANS. Yes, I think they should, because they are the only permanent officers that we have in our local societies.

QUES. Is the president of a local society a member of all the committees?

ANS. Yes, in a sense; he is an *ex-officio* member. He ought to be interested in the work of all the committees. It is his duty to see that they are faithful in their work. The president ought to be notified of every meeting of every committee, and he ought to be gladly welcomed to those meetings, and any suggestions that he has to offer ought to be gladly received and carefully considered by the committee. · Furthermore, the pastor ought to be notified of every meeting of every committee, and then, if he has the time and the opportunity, let him come and meet with them. You ought not to make it a duty for him to go, but you ought to give him the privilege of meeting with you, if he can.

QUES. Do any of the societies that refuse to take the pledge live long or bring forth reasonable fruit?

ANS. I have yet to hear of societies whose work has been permanently successful without the pledge. From our correspondence and our personal acquaintance we find that sooner or later they have to introduce the element of obligation as outlined in the pledge in order to sustain their work and keep it up to the highest spiritual level.

QUES. How can we get the young men to pray more willingly?

ANS. Let the young ladies set a good example, and let the young men who pray offer their prayers earnestly and as if they felt it was a privilege to pray. Then personally ask the other young men to offer prayer in the meeting. Tell them how much it will help you to hear their voice in prayer. Personal work along all these lines is the solution of many of these questions.

QUES. What is to be done with members of the Christian Endeavor society who stay away from the consecration meeting and send no excuse?

ANS. The Lookout Committee ought to see them and find out if they were absolutely prevented from sending an excuse, and if they were not, suggest to them that they have given their pledged word that they would send an excuse if unable to be present. If they absolutely refuse to send an excuse, or to give any reason to the Lookout Committee, then, at the end of three consecutive meetings, they should be dropped from the list of active members. You do not drop them ; they drop themselves. Do not ever let them say that you were not faithful on your part, for after every absence you ought to call upon them and show that you missed them from the meeting.

QUES. When a society holds its meetings Sunday evening from 6.30 to 7.30, and the active members think they are justified in not remaining to the regular service, what can be done?

ANS. Well, they ought to remain, unless they have a reason for leaving that they can conscientiously give to their Master. Now, I know active members in Christian Endeavor societies who attend the early morning prayer meeting, the morning preaching service, the Sunday school after church, the mission school in the afternoon, the Christian Endeavor prayer meeting, and then some of them think they ought to get acquainted with their families at home. They think they have a reasonable excuse for staying home Sunday night, and I think some of them have. But, do you know, the people to whom this question refers are not of that kind. Some of them are people who would not go to any service, but they are attracted by the young people's service, and they go in there. We ought to do everything in our power to hold them for the other service, but, perhaps we cannot do it. Then there is another class who are indifferent and careless and who are unfaithful to their obligation. We ought to pray for them and personally set them an example and have them understand that the pastor is under no more obligation to be in the pulpit than the church member to be in the pew. Let that be the standard and work up to it. I want to tell you that during the last year our members have been raising the standard and that we heard from 1,000 societies where an average of more than 60 percent of the active members were present at the evening service, while in those same churches only 20 percent of the church members were present at that service. Now I think that speaks well for the influence of our pledge and for our standard. If we can get 60 percent of our young people to attend the evening service against 20 percent of the older ones, we are working on the right line; and by and by, when these young people become the old folks, we hope to have 100 percent present at the services of the church. [*Applause.*]

QUES. How shall we induce the committees to give monthly written reports

ANS. Require it of them. Lay it upon their conscience, and tell them that if they have n't anything to report, to say so, and then be ashamed of themselves and go to work the next month. [*Applause.*]

QUES. What can be done where one-half the members of a Christian Endeavor society give and attend card parties?

ANS. I think they need a revival of religion in that society and in that church. [*Applause.*] I do not believe that I want to appear at the gate of heaven with a pack of cards in my hand as my admission ticket. [*Applause.*] Personally, while I cannot speak for you, I do not want and I will not have anything to do with that which, two or three years ago, put a young man into the penitentiary. In the home of members of the church he had learned to play cards, and the gambling passion that was in him got possession of him and he forged checks, and he is today in a penitentiary in this dominion of Canada. Anything that will put one of my boys into the penitentiary shall never have any quarter at my hands. [*Loud applause.*]

QUES. Should persons first become members of the church before becoming active members of the Christian Endeavor society?

ANS. That is for your pastor to decide. In some churches they prefer to have it that way; in others they prefer to take these young people into the society immediately on conversion, and then at the earliest possible moment receive them into the membership of the church. There are some people — I think they are mistaken, many of them — who want to test their children before they allow them to enter the church. If your church decides that that is the best way, that is the best way for you.

QUES. How shall we conduct the Christian Endeavor Bible class?

ANS. Get the best possible teacher you can, and then work along his lines.

I have a great many questions about amusements, — theatre-going, card-playing, and all these other things. I want to say that if there is any person here who is so undecided on these points as to feel obliged to ask a question about them, *let them alone.* If you are on the fence, if you are undecided as to what you ought to do, then let those things alone and be on the safe side. [*Applause.*]

QUES. Should church members ever be received as associate members?

ANS. No. They are facing the wrong way.

QUES. What kind of a pastor would you call one who does not trouble himself to look after one of the church members who is drinking himself to death?

ANS. Does your pastor know about it? Your pastor is not omniscient and he is not omnipresent. I tell you, we blame our pastors for many things for which they are not responsible. [*Applause.*] Tell your pastor about it, and then perhaps he can ask you what you are doing about it. You are just as much responsible for the use of your influence with that man as your pastor is, and don't you forget it and try to put it off on to his shoulders. Go and talk it over with him, and not say, "Pastor, what ought you to do?" but say, "Pastor, what can *we* do for that man?" [*Applause.*]

QUES. What would you do where the pastor and old people persist in managing the young people's society?

ANS. Ask them what is going to be done when they have gone home to their reward. [*Laughter.*] Ask them also if they do not think it is the better plan to leave some workers here who are disciplined and ready to take up the work. These good people do this out of love for you; they are afraid you will break down. Tell them your shoulders are strong, and that you want to learn how to do the work.

QUES. Ought a pastor to be president of the Christian Endeavor society?

ANS. Sometimes: but I think it is a great deal better to put a young man in that place; and so increase the pastor's efficiency and his corps of workers. That is the rule; there are exceptions.

QUES. How old ought a person to be to join as an active member?

ANS. Just old enough to know what he is doing and to be earnest enough to try and do it.

QUES. Is it not best to keep your roll clean of members who persist in non-attendance?

ANS. Why, yes. What good does it do them; what good does it do you, to have young people who deliberately make up their minds that they won't do the thing that you require of them? Let them out.

QUES. How do you do this?

ANS. If they are absent from three consecutive consecration meetings, they do it themselves. You do not have to do it. If they have lost their interest, that is the way they usually express it.

QUES. Cannot the Social Committee induce young men to join the society and the church?

ANS. Why, yes; of course they can. We are social people. We love to meet people in whom we are interested. The Social Committee ought to do everything in its power to win people for Christ and the church. The Lord Jesus Christ will ask you to render your account for the use that you have made of your social talents just as much as he will of any talent that God has given you. "Consecrate Everything" is the meaning of "C. E."

QUES. What must a Christian Endeavor society do when the pastor of the church thinks they are doing more harm than good?

ANS. I think there is something the matter with that Christian Endeavor society, and I would advise them to consider their ways and find out what they are doing and how they are doing it. I do not believe that a society, in very many cases at least, can do the right kind of work without having the pastor's co-operation.

QUES. Is the pastor a member of the Christian Endeavor society, if he has never signed the pledge?

ANS. Yes; *ex officio*, as pastor of the church, he is a member, and a member of the Executive Committee, and a member of the Nominating Committee.

QUES. What would you do if you were a member of a church where the pastor does not believe in Christian Endeavor?

ANS. I would work and pray and try to show him that it is just what the church needs.

QUES. What would you advise where a pastor insists on changing the Christian Endeavor society into an Epworth League?

ANS. Ask him if an Epworth League of Christian Endeavor would not do. If he absolutely refuses to compromise on that, then it is your business to do what your church and pastor want you to do.

QUES. What can be done for young people in rural districts where no Christian Endeavor society exists?

ANS. Why, form one if you can. I knew of a vigorous society of Christian Endeavor with only six active members, and they were active, a blessing to the church and a blessing to the pastor. They were all on committees.

QUES. How shall we reach the boys from seven to fourteen years of age?

ANS. Why, reach them, reach them! They are right in your hands. Don't let them go. Just reach them. [*Bell rings.*] They have rung the bell on me and our time is up. I see you are loyal members of Christian Endeavor societies because you know how to ask questions. I am sorry I do not know how to answer them better; but I am glad that in our question-box, as in everything else, we have latent power that will be developed in the service of the Church of Jesus Christ. [*Applause.*] Use your consecrated common-sense, — all your brain, all your power, — and do not forget to be generous with your money. All these questions will be answered aright, if you look to God for wisdom, and to the Holy Spirit for his guidance. [*Prolonged applause.*]

This closed the "question box," which was exceedingly profitable to all present. Several announcements were then made, after which Mr. and Mrs. Karmarkar sang a hymn in their native tongue, accompanying the same with a pair of curiously carved castanets. The audience were delighted with the song, which was a decided novelty, and applauded heartily.

One verse of "Coronation" was then sung, followed by the benediction by Rev. Dr. A. D. Day of Liberia, Africa.

FRIDAY AFTERNOON.

No session of the convention was held in either the Drill Hall or Tent this afternoon. Instead, the time was given up to various committee conferences which were held in some ten different places. These conferences were largely attended, aud proved very interesting and profitable. Reports were given at a later session of the convention.

FRIDAY EVENING.

DRILL HALL.

A very pretty incident took place just previous to the opening of the meeting, while the usual praise service was in progress. The Ohio delegates gathered in the rear of the hall and stretched a long white banner bearing the legend "Welcome to Cleveland, '94," clear across the centre section of seats. Bearing this aloft they marched down the two main aisles singing their famous song of a year ago, —

> "Cleveland, '94! Cleveland, '94!
> Pass along the watchword, Cleveland, '94!"

The audience caught up the song and made the hall ring with their enthusiasm and applause. Arrived at the front of the hall, the delegates found seats and the banner was fastened to the gallery railing, where it remained during the rest of the convention.

At 7.30 Secretary Baer called the meeting to order and announced that President W. R. Harper, of Chicago, who had been announced to preside at this session, was unable to be present and that Rev. Dr. James L. Hill, one of the trustees, would preside in his stead.

After the singing of the hymn "There's a Wideness in God's Mercy," Mr. Baer read a long list of notices. Included in these was the following question, sent up to the platform, in response to which the audience expressed its mind by a vigorous burst of applause : —

"Why do not delegates speak to each other when they pass each other on the street, even if they only say, 'How do you do?'"

Mr. Baer also made the following announcement : —

MR. BAER : It will interest you, as it will certain gentlemen in Chicago, to know that this afternoon the Board of Trustees adopted the following sentiment, which I am quite sure you will wish to ratify.

MONTREAL July 7, 1893,
HON. T. W. PALMER,
President World's Columbian Exposition, Chicago, Ill., U. S. A.,—

The trustees of the United Society of Christian Endeavor, in annual convention assembled in Montreal, representing more than a million and a half of the young people of America, in view of the newspaper report this morning that you have declared that the gates of the World's Fair should be closed on Sunday, have requested me on their behalf and on behalf of the vast convention here assembled to send you by telegraph our hearty approval of your reported position and words, and our earnest hope that your views may prevail, and that the gates of the Fair be henceforth closed on Sunday.   [Signed]   FRANCIS E. CLARK, *President.*

The reading of this telegram was received with tremendous and long-continued applause, cheering, and waving of handkerchiefs. Mr. Baer finally had to stop the enthusiasm with several smart raps of the gavel, after which he asked the delegates if the action of the trustees met with their approval, to rise. Instantly the whole audience rose as one man, and more cheering followed.

The hall at this time seemed pretty well filled, but Dr. Hill stated that there were a thousand more people outside who wished to get in, and gave out a hymn to be sung while the doors were opened. The hymn was sung splendidly, under the lead of director Coates, but one hymn was not enough, and two more had to be sung while the new-comers were getting seated. The program was then taken up as follows : —

DR. HILL: We gave out the notices according to the proper ministerial form. Following in the same order I would like to bear my word of testimony. I have attended every national convention except one, and that was when I chanced to be out of the country on a Christian Endeavor errand ; and I am here to say that, looking down into this ocean of faces, this is the largest convention — with the exception of New York, which was phenomenal and exceptional in every particular,— that the United Society has ever held, and the best. [*Loud applause.*]

I wonder if my friends have realized the exquisite appropriateness of the legend upon the outside wall of this great building. This is the "Salle d' Exercice," the hall for exercise. Did you ever chance to think that the Roman army was called the *exercitus?* They meant by that that the troops drilled. The Roman legions were drilled soldiers. The Y. P. S. C. E. is a drilled army, and this is the hall for drilled people — for the young people that are drilled in Christian work. Just before reaching this place I chanced to be in the great Lexington of the West. They were exhibiting their horses there, and a man who had developed some of the swiftest of them said, " Never believe anybody who tells you to wait until a horse is fully matured. That is all a fraud, a delusion and a snare. Horses are now taken when they are very young, and are disciplined and trained. The fully developed horse never seems to materialize. If horses are not developed and matured and exercised when they are young, they are likely never to be well developed at all." We proceed upon that principle. We think of all of you as simply colts, but we propose to have you drilled and disciplined, and we think we are the persons to do it. [*Laughter.*]

I remember very distinctly a gentleman who said that he would not take the risk of carrying his building without insurance against fire. The building burned down one night, and the insurance agent came around and asked him if it would be satisfactory to him if the company should make good the loss by constructing a new building for him. He assented, and the thing was done. The new building was not only satisfactory, but the man was very grateful, and much pleased with the results of insurance. Then there came around a life insurance agent, saying, "We want to insure you; we want to insure your wife and children." "None of that kind of insurance for me," said the man, "for in case of the death of my wife you would want to make the loss good, and you would bring around one of those foolish virgins, one of those who, according to Milton, only stand and wait. You would say you had made the loss good, but that would not be my wife." [*Laughter.*] It is exactly so in the case of the presiding officer tonight. You expected President Harper; we do not want any of you to think that the loss is made good.

We have before us a rare program, and it is a great pleasure to introduce the first speaker, Rev. J. Q. A. Henry, D.D., pastor of the First Baptist church of San Francisco. [*Applause.*]

The Bible in our Work.

Address of Rev. J. Q. A. Henry, D.D.

Mr. Chairman and Fellow Endeavorers: The three great factors in the redemption of the world are the Holy Spirit, the Holy Bible, and the Holy Man. The Holy Spirit is the agent, the Holy Bible is the instrument, and the Holy Man is to mediate between God and man, that the world may be brought to the feet of Jesus. It will be seen, therefore, that the place of the Bible is at once fundamental and vital; for the Holy Spirit, from the regeneration of the soul, through its development in doctrine and the discharge of its duty to its final consummation in glory, uses the truth as it is revealed to us in the sacred Scriptures.

There are many reasons why we should search the Scriptures. The Bible is the believer's book. It was written for his profit, his correction, his instruction in righteousness, that he might be thoroughly furnished unto all good works. It is the Christian's Magna Charta; it is the source of his rejoicing; it is his inspiration in the presence of difficulty, and gives to him the guarantee of the glory which he is to share with the Saviour which he had from the foundation of the world. We are to search the Bible, because it is the best book in the world. It contains the winnowed wisdom of all ages. When Dean Stanley visited the great scholar, Ewald, at his home in Dresden, the critic, grasping a copy of the New Testament Scriptures, said: "In this little book is contained all the wisdom of the world. In it are hidden all the treasures of wisdom and of truth. Its morality is authoritative and unadulterated. Its spirit is strong and serene. Its precepts are pure and practical, and its service is sacred and sublime. The Bible has been the inspiration of that which is purest in literature, noblest in art, greatest in government, most heroic in life, most blessed in its influence upon the mind of man."

An additional reason for our careful and faithful study of the word of God is to be found in the example of Him whom we delight to call our Master and Lord. Jesus was a faithful student of the Scriptures, and the significant fact is that in all probability he searched the oracles of God in three languages. He evidently read the Scriptures in the Aramaic, the Greek and the Hebrew. There is something marvelously pathetic and suggestive in the thought that Jesus, the carpenter of Nazareth, while yet a young man, during the little leisure that came to him from his unceasing toil, conquered a dead tongue to the end that he might read the record of the patriarchs and the prophets in the language in which they had given their deliverances from God. We are to remember, again, that Jesus the Christ had no Bible of his own. Copies of the Scriptures might not be purchased in the days of the Son of Man for a dime, and the New Testament for a nickel. The copies of the transcribed record of the revelation of God up to that date were few and bulky and extravagant in their price; so that, out of his poverty as the Son of Man, Jesus of Nazareth could not and did not possess a copy of the Old Testament Scriptures. He must needs, therefore, avail himself of the instruction that he obtained at his mother's knee, and that which came to him from the public declaration of divine truth in the synagogue and the privileges granted unto him as an aspiring student of the Word of God at the synagogue. In this way the Son of Man became most familiar with the Old Testament Scriptures. We know of his familiarity with the Word of God from the simple fact that he not only gave his testimony to the writings of Moses and of the Psalmist and of the prophets, but be quoted in the Gospels from 22 different books of the Bible, making in all 140 quotations that are to be found in the 89 chapters of Matthew, Mark, Luke and John. We find Jesus quoting the Old Testament Scriptures 89 times in Matthew, 15 times in Mark, 25 times in Luke and 11 times in the Gospel of John. We find him referring to the conspicuous events that had occurred, and the great personages that had lived under the reign and the rule of God. We find him, likewise, referring to obscure characters and obscure and commonplace events, showing that he was saturated with the Biblical spirit and perfectly familiar with the book from cover to cover. So we know that Jesus was thus familiar with the Word of God. We know, also, that certain portions of the Bible were dearer to him than others. How often does he quote from Deuteronomy, from the prophecy of Isaiah and from the Psalms! And when you remember that the chief thought of Deuteronomy is consecration, that that of the Psalms is life hid with God, and that Isaiah is the most Gospel-like and evangelical of all the prophets, how significant it is, in view of the infinite sacrifice which the Son of God was to perform in the world, that he should be familiar with those portions of the divine oracles which should gird him with invincible strength and prepare him for the onward march in that peculiar mission which he came to fulfil! [*Applause.*]

We find inspiration in the study of the Word of God when we remember the purpose for which the Son of Man thus became familiar with the revealed will of his heavenly Father. We find, from the study of the life of Jesus, that he familiarized himself with the Word of God for a threefold purpose: in the first instance, that he might be able to defend himself against the enemies with which he had to contend in his pilgrimage from the manger to the cross. How deftly and skilfully he uses that Word to put to flight the adversary of his soul in the Mount of Temptation! Read the twenty-second chapter of the Gospel according to Matthew and see how Jesus quoted Scripture for the purpose of silencing the Sadducees and the Pharisees and the doctors, until his human enemies quailed in the presence of the Son of God and his familiarity with the Word of Truth. Then, when we come to that tragical scene of the cross, when the Son of God is to lay down his life as a ransom for many, hear him as he quotes the twenty-second Psalm and pillows himself upon the inabrogable Word of God as he makes his descent into the grave and into hell, to the end that he might perform a complete redemption for you and for me. So that Jesus studied the Scriptures to the end that he might use them for his own defence against the wiles of the wicked one.

Again, he became familiar with the Bible to the end that it might afford him inspiration and encouragement amidst the discouragements by which he was surrounded in this world. There were none who could sympathize with the Son of Man. He was misinterpreted, misjudged, and condemned continually by the populace. There were none who could understand his knowledge, who could appreciate his love and his sacrifice, as there were none who could cheer him in the midst of those discouraging influences which inhered in his sinful environment. The Son of God must have companionship, and he found his comradeship in the experiences of Abraham, and Isaac and Moses and Joshua and Isaiah and David and Daniel. These were the worthies with whom he walked the way of life from the manger to the cross. We find that in our pilgrimage in life we need such enthusiasm and inspiration and impulse as alone can come from the triumphs of God's purpose and God's plan and God's thought, assured that in his time and by his grace we shall come off more than conquerors. [*Applause.*]

We need again to remember that Jesus searched the Scriptures to the end that he might be divinely guided in his path to the cross and into the grave and out of the grave into glory again. His mission was unique; no man had gone that way before; he trod the wine-press alone. And yet he could say of himself, "I delight to do thy will, O God.". And we find that, just as Jesus needed guidance to the end that he might mark out a way across this sin-stained earth that would be worthy for an immortal spirit to tread, he required familiarity with the sacred Scriptures. Such inspiration, such defense, and such guidance will not come from familiarity with a few precious texts of God's word, however important or significant they may be. It requires an apprehension and a comprehension of the whole truth as it is in God to the end that we may drop into the rhythm of his infinite purpose and be borne upon its resistless current, conscious that we are doing what God wants us to do until he shall say, "It is enough; come up higher." [*Applause.*]

I note in this connection, as another reason why we should familiarize ourselves with the Scriptures, the prevalnt ignorance concerning the Word of God on the part even of the leaders of the life and the thought in our churches and in our communities. The fact is, that with most people the ignorance of the Scriptures when viewed in their totality,—when viewed with reference to the grasp of doctrine, the relationship of dispensation to dispensation, of truth to truth, of personality to personality,— is all but impenetrable and inconceivable, and it is most humiliating in view of the cheapness of the Word of God. Not long since there was published in the *London Graphic* an account of an examination on the part of the children in the schools of London who were supposed to have made a systematic study of certain portions of the Word of God, and these are some of the replies that were given to questions asked:—

"Who was Moses?" "He was an Egyptian. He lived in an ark made of bulrushes and he kept a golden calf and worshipped brazen snakes, and he had nothing but whales and manna for forty years. [*Laughter.*] He was caught by the hair of his head while riding under the bough of a tree and he was killed by his son Absalom while he was hanging from the bough, and his end was peace." [*Laughter.*]

"What do you know of the patriarch, Abraham?" "He was the father of Lot and had two wives. One was called Hishmael and the tother Hagar. He kept one at home and the tother he drove into the desert where she became a pillar of salt by daytime and a pillar of fire by night." [*Laughter.*]

"Write an account of the Good Samaritan." "A certain man went from Jerusalem to Jericho and he fell among thorns, and the thorns sprang up and choked him [*laughter*], whereupon he gave tuppence to his host and said, 'Take care on him and put him on his own ass,' and he passed by on the other side." [*Laughter.*]

But, you say, we are Americans; we have had the International Sunday-school Series for a great many years, and our children are more intelligent concerning the Scriptures than these English children were. Only a few months since in the *Sunday-school Times* were published some replies on the part of Christian children, reared in Christian homes, brought into the Sunday school almost in their infancy and who had now reached the intermediate department, which reveal an ignorance almost if not quite as great— and perhaps greater, considering the nature of the questions — as that which was displayed by the children of London.

The first question was this: "Who was Jesus the Christ?" Answer: "Jesus was the father of Christ and he was born in Jerusalem in the year 1."

Another answer: "He was the son of David and Israel and his mother's name was Mary Magdalene."

Another answer: "He was the son of Moses and Mary. He had many sons and his mother's name was Mary, and he drove Adam and Eve out of the Garden of Eden. Most of his life was spent in Jerusalem, preaching the gospel to the heathen." "He had very few advantages," says another, "on account of the Jews being down on the Christians. It is said that after his death he rose from the dead and lived on the earth for forty years."

You remember the story of the United States senator who wagered $10 that another senator could not·repeat the Lord's Prayer, whereupon this man who had boasted of his familiarity with the Word of God began:

" Now I lay me down to sleep,
I pray the Lord my soul to keep."

"Oh," said the senator who had wagered the ten dollars, "you know more than I supposed you did ; you can have the money." [*Laughter.*]

I think it is Dr. Pierson who tells the story of a minister who had faithfully preached the gospel to a parishioner for forty years. This man was one day taken with a fatal illness and was approached by the man of.God who had been so faithful in his declaration of divine truth and asked if it was well with his soul. "Oh, yes," said the man, "it is well with my soul." "Well," said the preacher, "brother, do you know, what your soul is?" "Yes," said he, "it is a bone back here by my spine that lives on after the rest of the body is dead." [*Laughter.*]

These are illustrations which portray an ignorance which is far more common and prevalent than we are accustomed to think.

A word over against this. The record of the race is radiant with the lives and sacrifices and services of men who have cultivated a close familiarity with God and his Son, Jesus Christ, through the record of his wonderful love as he has preserved it to us in the sacred Scriptures. Dr. Henry G. Weston, president of one of the theological seminaries of this country, said in a public address more than ten years ago that for fifty years and more he had read the New Testament Scriptures through every month. The Word of God gives back to us what we bring to it. If we bring to it a grain of knowledge we will get a grain in return ; if we bring a basketful, we will get a basketful in return ; if we bring a granary, full of the truth as it is in Jesus, we shall receive a like blessing at the hands of Him who is the giver of all good gifts. The difference between men's Bibles lies largely in that fact. On the one hand, the Bible is searched and studied and prayed over and meditated upon, and on the other hand it is dull and tiresome and wearisome to the individual. As Dr. Carroll said when teaching a Bible class and one of the members, taking exception to something he had said, remarked, "Doctor, your Bible must be different from mine." "Yes," said he, "it is ; it differs in this respect, that my Bible is studied and yours is not." That is the great difference. It is said that George, prince of Transylvania, read the Bible through 27 times. Alphonsus, king of Aragon, read the Scriptures over, together with a large commentary, fourteen times during his life. Lady Francis Hooper read the Psalms over twelve times a year, the New Testament three times and the other parts of the Old Testament Scriptures once. Susanna, countess of Suffolk, for the last seven years of her life read the entire Scriptures through twice every year. Dr. Gouge used to read fifteen chapters a day, five in the morning, five at noon and five at night. Joshua Barnes had a small pocket Bible which he carried with him and which he ·read through 120 times. It is said that the Rev. William Romaine studied absolutely nothing but the Bible for the last forty years of his life. Bishop Foss makes this comment: he has noticed two things, that the best Christians are those who are most saturated with the spirit of the Scriptures, and those who read the Bible most live it best. He tells the story of an old man, Father Knapp, whom he visited upon his death-bed and found him faithfully reading the book of Psalms, and he said, "Do you never tire of reading the Scriptures?" He replied, "Tire? Why I have read the Bible through 67 times and I am as far as the Psalms in the 68th reading, and I tell you the truth, pastor, that I never found so much that was new and fresh and comforting and inspiring in it as the last time that I read it." Oh, how these faithful students of God's Word rebuke our indifferentism and our unfamiliarity and our want of acquaintance with God and with his will as he has given it to us in the Bible!

I desire now briefly to call your attention to some of the preliminary considerations in connection with the method of study of the Bible; and my first point is this: you must have your Bible. A copy of the entire Scriptures is the indispensable possession of every man and woman and child of God who expects to be a good Christian, to get the most out of his life, to be of the greatest service to Jesus Christ and win most men to the Son of God. There are other things that are desirable — fine pictures and horses and books and houses and landed estates and bank accounts, but none of these are comparable in value to your life, your personal life, your personal success, your personal victory as a believer and a Christian — with a simple copy of the Word of God. So that in the study of the Scriptures the very first condition reminds us of the recipe that was given for the cooking of a hare : " First, catch the hare. " So, if you would study the Bible, first obtain a copy of the Scriptures for your own, a copy that is clear in type, well bound, with a wide margin so that upon it you may place the comment and reflection and meditation as a result of your study of the Word of the living God. A few years ago a Roman Catholic clog dancer was converted, and he beheld for the first time an entire copy of the Scriptures. So profoundly was he impressed with the message of Jesus' love and sacrifice, that before he left the mission hall on the night of his conversion, on bended knee he dedicated himself to God and to the study of God's Word independently of everything else for the first five years of his Christian experience. Need I say that that young man is one of the foremost Bible students in this country today? It was a thought and a purpose and a spirit and a consecration that is worthy of you and worthy of me and worthy of every man who would be a skilled workman in the vineyard of God, — " a workman that needeth not to be ashamed."

Again, in the study of the Scriptures, it is vastly important that you read the Bible as God's revelation to you. Martin Luther used to say that the value of the Bible lay chiefly in its use of the personal pronoun ; and until you can read the Bible and say, " It is my Father's letter of love to me ; I need it all from cover to cover for the discipline of my soul and my equipment for service and for victory," you will never learn to read the Bible with a relish. You need to read it as a wounded soldier read the story of the prodigal son, crying out, as he read verse after verse, " That 's me, that 's me."

Then there is this thought : that our relationship to Jesus Christ implies all that. The story is told of a young woman into whose hands was placed a volume with the request of a friend that she read it. It was a book very different in its contents from what she had been accustomed to read, but she said, " For your sake I will read it." She read it, but confessed it dry and dull. Afterwards she was introduced to the author, and the introduction resulted in acquaintanceship and acquaintanceship in love and love in marriage. As she came to know the author better and better and stood in new relationship to him, every word that fell from his lips and every word that came from his pen was near and dear to her. When we remember our relation to the Son of God, our knowledge of the Scriptures ought to intensify, as the days pass by and the years recede.

I note again that we are to mark our Bibles. I have already referred to this. I do not believe that the average man or woman can get the best results out of Bible study without a free use of pen or pencil, marking upon the margin of your Bible the result of your study and meditation. Your Bible in that way becomes a record of your Christian experience, a memorial of God's mercy, and a triumph of his redeeming grace. The fact is, that that Bible is worth more to me than all the Bibles in this hall and all the Bibles in Montreal tonight, because it has been my daily companion for thirteen years, and on its margin are recorded the experiences and many of the thoughts and the results of my Christian life, both of failure and of victory. [*Applause.*] Many of us come to the Word of God from time to time, not knowing where to turn, what portion of the Scripture to read; but when once we open the Bible to a given page, and find the marks upon its margin, immediately questions arise, " When was that mark made? Under what circumstances? Through what experience was I passing? Does it mean more to me or less today ? " You thus have a memento, and in that way you have the foundation laid for a continual relish in the reading of the Word of God. In London, a few weeks since, Dr. Pierson held aloft, in the presence of a great congregation, the Bible which has been his companion for ten years, and said, " That book contains more than 5,500 distinct markings which have been made with my own hand within the last ten years." You may scorn the thought, you may neglect it, but I am persuaded that 99 out of every 100 who refuse such a procedure and such a method of study of the sacred Scriptures will find, at the end of a decade or a score of years, that they have lost incomparably in their efforts to become familiar with the Word of God. Why, it is an inspiration to pick up the Bible of Moody, or of Whittle, or of many other men who might be named, and look upon its margin. I shall never forget the first glimpse I had of the inside of D. L. Moody's Bible one Thanksgiving Day, thirteen years ago. As I saw its pages marked with red and blue and green and yellow and black, there was created within me a desire, by the evidence of his thorough searching of the Word of God, an emphatic personal determination, which has stayed by me in all these years, to make the study of the Scriptures supreme in my life as a Christian and in my career as a minister of Jesus Christ. [*Applause.*]

Read the Bible regularly; read it systematically; read it prayerfully, remembering that the Spirit which inspired the book is absolutely essential in your heart and in your life to interpret that book to your thought and to your life. I may not dwell upon that thought, further than to answer the question which is frequently asked: Why was it that Richard Baxter had such a profound knowledge of the sacred Scriptures? The answer is found in the patent fact that day after day, through a series of years, he was accustomed to put his finger on a given passage of God's Word and on bended knee say, "Father, what does this verse mean, what does this word mean?" And God, who giveth wisdom liberally to all men and upbraideth not, made Baxter the mighty, eloquent man in the Word of God that he was.

I notice another thought, and that is that we are to read the Bible copiously and profusely. George Mueller for sixty years has adopted this method of Bible study: beginning with Genesis and reading straight through to Revelation. But whether you begin with Genesis and read to the last cover of the book or not, it is important that you read the Bible copiously, to the end that you may have a perspective of divine truth. It is not enough to use the microscope in dealing with texts; you want to use the telescope that you may see the relationship to relationship. There are mountain heights of divine truth; there is mountain gloom and there is mountain glory; and until a man climbs the rugged sides of these mountains by faithful and diligent study, he never will be able to get a glimpse of the entire outspread canvas of divine revelation.

Suppose you take the Bible and read in it about the three great tragedies — the Fall, the Flood and the Cross. If you have never read it from that point of view it will help you amazingly to try it. Or take four great events — the Exodus, the Monarchy, the Restoration and the Cross, and group the 66 books with their incomparable contents about those four mountain peaks that lift their heads high up into the vault of heaven, and never rest until you press your feet upon those mountain heights, and you will breathe the unsullied and the invigorating air that God breathes, and you will come down refreshed to work mightily for God. [*Applause.*] Read Genesis and Revelation together; read parts of Isaiah and parts of Revelation; read parts of Daniel and Revelation, because the imagery is much the same. Read Joel and Nahum; read Hebrews and Leviticus; read Joshua and Ephesians; read the sixteenth of Exodus with the sixth of John — the great "bread" chapters of the Bible. And then we need also to read Kings and Chronicles side by side, — the Kings representing the disintegration, decay, downfall and destruction of the kingdom of God, until you think that all is gone; and then read Chronicles and see how that out of the chaos God begins with one man and keeps that man heart-true and so saves himself before the people and saves his revelation by the development and the ascent of life and of hope and of blessing. Read the Decalogue and the Sermon on the Mount always together. We need these mountain heights; we need this breadth of vision, to the end that we may appreciate what God has done for us. It is the man who climbs that sees; and it is the man who is content with the microscope. or with the twenty-third Psalm on Sunday or a part of the fourteenth of John on Sunday or a few verses from the eighth of Romans,

whose faith is eclipsed and who became disheartened and useless in the kingdom
of the Son of God.

I note again that we are to read the Bible with reference to its development
and the historic evolution which it contains. We are to begin at the beginning
and follow the ascent of life and of doctrine, of truth and of duty and of redemption, as God adds to it from time to time. There is history, there is
poetry and there is prophecy, and the difficulty with many people in finding a
relish in the study of God's Word is that they do not begin at the beginning.
They wonder why they do not understand the eighth and the ninth of Romans.
It is because they have not read the gospels and the Acts and the first seven
chapters of Romans. The man who understands the Bible up to the eighth
chapter of Romans will understand the eighth and the ninth and so on, *ad in-
finitum*. Dr. Monro Gibson once said that a young man came to him at one
time and said, " Doctor, I want you to tell me all about the devil and God and
Jesus Christ." " No," said the doctor, " you don't want to know about the
devil and God and Jesus Christ. You have got hold of the wrong end of the
string. What you want to know is about Jesus Christ and God, and then, if
you still desire it, I will tell you what I know about the devil." [*Applause.*]
There are a good many people who are more anxious to understand about the
devil than they are to understand about Jesus Christ and the revelation of the
Father in his heart.

I must very briefly notice another thought : that we are to read the Bible in
the light of the very best helps, of the truest science, of the best philosophy,
of the latest ethnological and archæological and geological discoveries, assured
that the God of the Bible is the God of nature. I cannot dwell upon that
thought, save to illustrate it by a single question. We have four gospels: why
are there four? Why not three, or five, or seven? The answer is an ethnological one as well as a spiritual one. How many great races were there on
the earth when Jesus came? The Jewish, the Roman, the Greek. Jesus war
neither Jew nor Roman nor Greek. His mission in the world was to save s
company that no man can number out of the Jews and the Romans and tha
Greeks. So you have Matthew written to prove that Jesus was the Messiahe
you have Mark written for the benefit of the Roman, whose thought was wa;
and kingdom and conquest, and Jesus is represented as the tireless worker and
as the servant of God. The key-word of Mark is "straightway." The Greeks
loved culture and beauty; they strove for ideal manhood; and so we have the
gospel of Luke, written to the Greeks, presenting Jesus as the man of Nazareth, the complete and the perfect man. And then we have the gospel of John,
written for the Christians who are to be gathered out of the Roman and the
Greek and the Jewish and the barbarian world. There are many things that
might be said but time will not allow.

Mr. Henry's address was interrupted at this point by the entrance of
a large crowd from the tent, the services there having ended, so he
simply closed his remarks by thanking the audience for their kind
attention.

After the singing of a hymn and the reading of more notices, including a telegram from Rev. Thomas Spurgeon, expressing his regret at
not being able to be present, and conveying his heartfelt greetings to
the convention, Dr. Hill introduced the next speaker as follows : —

Dr. Hill: On my recent visit to the West a gentleman was exhibiting to a
would-be purchaser some horses. He referred to certain ones and said, " There
are some horses that have an excellent pedigree," and he would name the speed
that had been attained by such a horse's sire, and what had been done along the
line of the pedigree, and show the record that the horses had themselves made
in other years. " Now I want to show you," he said, " some other horses that

have great promise, horses that certainly will do well on the track in the days to come. I am sure they have a great future." But the purchaser didn't seem to be satisfied, and finally the owner of the horses asked him, "What is it you want?" "Why," said he, "in showing me these horses you have shown me the have-beens and you have shown me the are-to-bes, but the horse that I want is an is-er." [*Laughter.*] I am going to introduce to you now, not one of the "have-beens," not one of the "are-to-bes," but I am going to introduce to you an "is-er." [*Applause.*] I expect to have you all, if there is time, come and take me by the hand and thank me that the Hon. Breckenridge is not present tonight. He has sent a telegram saying that he could not be here, imperative engagements preventing. But I am glad to introduce to you an orator after my own heart, — Rev. Nehemiah Boynton, pastor of the Union Congregational church, Boston. [*Loud applause and the Chautauqua salute.*]

Our Relationship to the Sunday School.

Address of Rev. N. Boynton.

I thank you very heartily, my good friends, for this kind token of the expression of your sympathy to me at just this moment. I take it to be a marvelous and a practical illustration of the age and its possibilities. [*Laughter.*] I regret that you are in this cave of Adullam by necessity; and still your kindness to me impels me to do alone, if I can, what it took three mighty men of old to do; namely, at any hazard and at any peril, to find my way to the laughing water of the bubbling springs at the well of Bethlehem, and bring to you at least one drop in my little dipper, which if it be ill-suited to slake the peculiar thirst which is yours at this moment, may, by some of you at least, I hope, be deemed appropriate to be poured upon the altar of your memory, if not of your affection.

Is there anybody in this hall now who wants to leave? [*Laughter.*] I am very much like the dear old lady who sailed, let us say, from the beautiful port of Montreal, upon one of your magnificent Allen liners; and when she found herself in the midst of the deep blue sea, having had enough of the aquatic experiences which are plentiful for those who journey over the deep, she found the captain and said to him, "Sir, be you the captain of this ship?" "Yes'm," said he, "I am." "Well," said the old lady, "I want to get out!" [*Laughter and applause.*] But, my friends, however much I may want to get out, I can't. [*Laughter.*] There were two ministers riding side by side in the cars, so one of my good friends has said to me, and evidently their experiences in life had been cast at almost opposite poles. One of them was dressed in broadcloth and the other wore plain homespun. One of them had hands as delicate as a woman's; the other's hands were bruised by the stirring toils of life. One of them had a brow of marble, and the other a brow which the sun had kissed with every hour of the summer's day. They talked for a little while together, and then he of the broadcloth said to the stranger, " Really, you have the advantage of me. Who are you?" And the plain, simple, homely man looked up into his face and said, "I am a mighty poor preacher of a Glorious Gospel. Now who are you?" [*Laughter.*] It has occurred to me that whatever might have been brought to you from the lips of him who should have addressed to you this evening words of eloquence, quick thoughts and beautiful rhetorical sentiments, he would have been false to the true idea of Christian Endeavor save as his words and his thoughts and his beautiful rhetoric had found their centre and their heart in the glorious Gospel of Jesus Christ. And as I have come to know that that Gospel is not the monopoly simply of those who are favored in the earth, but that it belongs to every noble soul, I considered it to be not only my duty but my privilege, when the command came from President Clark, to stand and recite to you in feeble accents, some of those things which are blessed in the experience of us all with relation to this glorious Gospel of the Son of God.

And so tonight, for a little while, I am to speak to you upon the theme which should have been mine next Sabbath afternoon: Our Relationship to the Sabbath School.

Mr. Bushnell once remarked that this was the era of great beginnings, that the world was like an unhatched egg—that all was possibility, that all was probability. We are living in the morning and not beneath the blaze of the noonday sun; and it is in the morning that we may specially look for those specific and marked providences of God by virtue of which the world has felt her deepest impulses and her most marvelous propulsion. Take, for example, the Sunday school. Born a little more than a hundred years ago, out of the loins of the church, it was a special providence. Take, for example, our Young People's Society of Christian Endeavor. Born, as one of my friends reminded me today, just a century after the Sunday school, it was one of the direct and specific providences of God. Now, God's providences do not clash, they cog, they coalesce, they coincide. And therefore there cannot be between these two great specific providences of God anything but the closest fellowship, the largest unity and the deepest sympathy. We need to remind ourselves, in these days of segregation and isolation, I think, not only that we have some relationship to the Sabbath school but that we *are* the Sabbath school — bone of its bone, flesh of its flesh, blood of its blood, and that the blessed bond of union which binds us to the Sabbath school is a bond which is to be made more and more close and firm, — that there is to be absolutely no power and no influence which can separate our Young People's Society of Christian Endeavor from its place, its privilege and its work in the Sunday school, which has been a blessing to so many in the days that are past and which is still one of God's choicest agencies for the redeeming of a lost world. [*Applause.*]

There was a deacon once, — or rather an elder, for he was a Presbyterian, — who was also the president of a horse-railroad company. As the Lord's Day dawned, at one time, he had some tracks laid which were absolutely unnecessary. After a while the justice of the city called the president of the horse-railroad company before him for trial, and when he was placed upon the stand one of the lawyers said to him, " I believe, sir, you are one of the elders in such and such a church." "I am," said he, "but I want the Court to distinctly understand that I laid those tracks as president of the railroad company and not as elder of the Presbyterian church." [*Laughter.*] But the Court could not see the point, and fined him. He was elder although he was president. He could not, in his one capacity, divorce himself from the relationships which were his in another capacity. No more can we, as members of the Y. P. S. C. E., divorce ourselves in any way or in any sense from the Sunday school in which we were trained, where most of us received our first and perhaps our most lasting impressions with relation to the truth of God and to the peace of God. Mr. Gilman, who has given us recently a most marvelous book upon the socialistic spirit in America, declares that we shall not realize the socialism that we seek, which is nothing more or less than the renaissance of Christianity, by the literal interpretation and application of the New Testament letter, but only as we are able to breathe into the heart of our body politic — our national, our universal life — that which is the spiritual core and center of the Gospel of Jesus Christ, that one magic, all-enswathing word, "together." I want to lay specific emphasis upon this point, that we, as the Y. P. S. C. E., labor not simply in connection with, but absolutely together with and as part of the Sabbath school, which is of God's own planting and which is doing God's own work.

I should suggest to you, under this general proposition, as my first declaration, this: that we are in relation and in accord with the Sabbath school concerning an intelligent knowledge of the Word of God; but the eloquent and remarkable address which my brother has but just now made leaves it for me simply to remark, "A word spoken in due season, how good is it? It is like apples of gold in pictures of silver." [*Applause.*] Let his speech be my first point, and I pass on to the second; namely, that, having a special and a practical knowledge of the Word of God, we seek, in common with the Sabbath school, to apply that Word of God to the lives we have to lead and to the communities in the heart of which we dwell.

Somebody has said that the Sabbath school is the nursery of the church. If that is true, the Y. P. S. C. E. is the laboratory of the church. Somebody has said that the Sabbath school is the church studying the Bible. If that is true, Christian Endeavor is the church studying human life and applying the principles of the Gospel of Jesus Christ to the life which she is continually studying. To take the Word of God and practise it, making it tell for power in the world, this is the mission of the Christian Endeavor Society.

That must have been a very marked experience of Nicholas Nickleby, when he looked for the first time upon that little company of half-a-dozen scarecrows in Mr. Squeers's institution, known as Dotheboys Hall. You remember how Mr. Squeers mounted the platform and said, "First boy, stand up!" "Please, sir," said another little fellow, "he is out washing the windows of the back parlor." "Certainly," said Mr. Squeers, "we have a very practical application of our teaching here. C-l-e-a-n, verb, to wash, to scour, to make white. W-i-n, win, d-e-r, der, winder, noun substantive. Now, when we have taught a boy that out of the book," said Squeers, "we send him out to do the thing which we have taught him. Second boy, stand up!" "Please, sir, the second boy is weeding the garden." "Certainly," said Mr. Squeers, "b-o-t, bot, t-i-n, tin, n-e-y, ney, bottiney, the science of vegetable life. When a boy understands that we send him to work out the thing which we have told him. Third boy, stand up!" "Please, sir, the third boy is grooming the horse." "Certainly," said Mr. Squeers, "h-o-r-s-e, horse. What is a horse, my boy?" "A horse is a beast." "Certainly," said Mr. Squeers, "a beast, a quadruped. Quadruped is the Latin for beast, as anybody knows who has had the advantage of a liberal education. [*Laughter.*] Now, my boy, you go and rub down that horse, and if you don't rub him down well, I will rub you down. Mr. Nickleby, we have a very practical kind of education at Dotheboys Hall."

I know there is sarcasm underneath it all, but even the sarcasm rests upon the pillars of a mighty and a majestic truth. Your theories may be formed with all the beauty and all the symmetry of a circle; still, if you are unable to work them out in practical life, they are absolutely of no use. You may have read your Bible 165 times from Genesis to Revelation, but if there has not been generated in your soul through that reading and studying of God's Word something which so burns in your spirit that you cannot rest until you have practically laid the thing down by the side of another life, it will come to pass that your life shall be useless, misspent and unfruitful.

You remember the story they tell about poor old Wang, that Chinaman who became a disciple of the Master. He had everything against him. To look upon his face was simply a horror. His character before he came to God was absolutely reprehensible and low and vile and mean. Nobody, not even the missionaries, had any confidence in poor Wang. Still, a drop of the Gospel blood of life found its way into Wang's soul, and he went out into the world just to live among his degraded brother men the little bit of an end of the Gospel that he had seen and known. After he died they put this simple legend on his tombstone, as the testimony of the missionary and the heathen alike: There was no difference between Wang and the Word." I claim, my dear young friends, that you and I have a practical mission in connection with the Sunday school — so to put the principles of the Gospel down by the side of the needy life that is all around us that when the world looks into our souls and estimates our actions it shall say, as was said of poor old Wang: "There is no difference between them and the Word." [*Applause.*]

I want to say a single word about the Y. P. S. C. E. in its re-enforcing capacity; and to that end I wish to test this audience. if I may, simply asking that all of you who are here tonight, who are either officers or teachers or students in the Sabbath school will just stand up for a moment. [*Nearly the entire audience rose.*] The thing I want to say is this : that absolutely, beyond all question, the Y. P. S. C. E. is a re-enforcing power in our Sabbath schools, the strength and the potency of which can only be realized in some such council as this We have had a show of hands, and with that simple remark about re-enforcement I leave you to work out the application yourself.

I pass to the last point which is in my mind which I wish to suggest to you, namely, that our relationship with the Sabbath school is identical in this respect: we strive for symmetry of personal character through the redeeming and the cleansing blood of Jesus Christ our Lord. There was a young Buddhist who was once speaking with his friend about the Gospel which is so precious to you and to me, and he said, " There are very many things that I find in my own religion which are upon a par with the things that I find in the religion of Jesus Christ, but there is one thing in your religion which I cannot find in mine or in any other." "What is that?" said his friend. "A Saviour," was the reply of the Buddhist. My friends, the most precious thing that you and I have in connection with our personal lives is our personal relationship with Jesus Christ. If your character is taking on proportions which are noble and true and good, it is because Jesus Christ is enshrined in your heart. A symmetrical character for ourselves, a symmetrical character for the unsaved all around us, and the character for the one and for the other obtained through, and achieved by the cleansing blood of Jesus Christ our Lord. There are multitudes of young lives who need to hear from your lips and from mine the glorious invitation of the Gospel which for more than eighteen centuries has been ringing up and down the corridors of time.

You remember when they laid that first transatlantic cable, that marvelous specimen of human ingenuity and invention and skill, that after they had proceeded upon their journey, something like 90 miles, they found in the testing-room that the cable did not respond; the electricity was dead. By other testings they also found that the fault was twelve miles astern. What was to be done? With 500 men on board, it took two whole days just simply to coil that twelve miles of wire back again into the bosom of that great ship; and when they found the fault, it was just simply this: a bit of wire, the size of a needle, had pierced the covering, had come in contact with the live wire at the heart, and therefore was permitting all the electricity to scatter itself in the midst of the water—a very, very little thing, but bringing untold mischief and failure and ill success to those who had staked their all upon the enterprise which was being undertaken. You can look out into the life that is about you and find many a young man or young woman whose life, to all surface appearance, seems to be lived upon an even tenor. Go into the testing-room of the soul of that life and you find that somewhere there is a fault in the cable which binds every soul to God, that the wire is not alive. Search for the cause, and you will find that some little needle of sin and of iniquity has pierced the outer covering and has touched the heart, and by its corroding it is permitting that life to take its way toward those things which are vile and base and toward the place where it is always dark and never light, always sorrowful and never joyous. I want to say to you that if we have any mission in connection with our Sunday schools and with all the religious development of our church life, it is this: to hold up high above the heads of the people the glorious Gospel of Jesus Christ and to declare that only can symmetry and proportion of character come into the life as we are hidden with Christ in God.

I want to say one thing more before I sit down by way of illustration of this thought. I read the other day of a man who had charge of a wonderful revolving light which worked by machinery, casting its rays out upon the dark waters of the night to the relief and guidance of whoever might be passing by. It happened one day that the old man fell sick and the machinery gave out at the same time. There was nobody there but a lad of about thirteen summers, and so the brave little fellow climbed into the lighthouse and began the wearying task of turning that light all night with his own hands so that it would continually shed the proper ray upon the troubled bosom of the deep. The storm was high, the night was dark, but when the morning dawned it was found that two vessels with 500 souls on board had been saved from disaster and shipwreck and death simply because that little fellow was willing to stand in the lighthouse and, at the expense of the very last ounce of energy and strength he had, turn the light. The comment which was made by a friend who

gave the illustration was this: "The stars do not shout: they only shine."
[*Applause.*]

I say to you, my friends, that it is not only within the province of those of us who are in the morning of life, it is the most imperative duty and obligation we have, to perfect the light within us, and though our hands be weary and our courage fail, to shine out upon the troubled waters of life. "Some poor ship-wrecked sailor you — *you* may save." One has said that eternal life is to be eternally re-won. You must win it for yourself first that you may win it, with the help of Christ, for your brethren and your sisters afterwards.

And now, sharing with you the bitter disappointment which has been the portion of us all in that we have been unable to listen to the words of the silver-tongued orator from the South, I thank you for the patience and for the in-dulgence with which you have received these few simple words which, in Christ's name and for Christ's sake, I have in this way thrust upon your atten-tion. [*Long and prolonged applause.*]

DR. HILL: There may be some here tonight who have not been in ore of our international conventions before. In dismissing the audience we shall first have the benediction, and then we will start a familiar hymn, and I am going to ask you to see how far you can carry that hymn out upon the streets. [*Applause.*] Nothing in this convention has moved me more than to hear you sing your songs as the electric cars go bowling along the streets.

The benediction was then pronounced by Principal Barbour, of the Congregational College, Montreal, and the hymn "Throw Out the Life-line" was given out. The delegates sang the hymn spiritedly as they left the hall, and Dr. Hill's suggestion was carried out as the various lines of street cars bore their crowded loads of delegates to different portions of the city.

THE TENT.

One of the largest audiences of the convention gathered in the tent on Friday evening. The song service was conducted by Mr. L. F. Lindsay and the Park Sisters. Dr. Clark presided. The devotional services of the evening were led by Rev. Asher Anderson, of Connect-icut, who read for the Scripture lesson the twenty-third Psalm, after which Rev. Dr. Hoyt led in prayer. Then the hymn "O worship the King, all glorious above" was sung, and Dr. Rondthaler offered a brief prayer.

After several announcements, made by Mr. Shaw, the telegram which was sent to the Hon. T. W. Palmer, president World's Colum-bian Exposition, was read and unanimously adopted with great ap-plause and cheers.

The Endeavor hymn, "Blessed Assurance," was sung.

DR. CLARK: Two of the greatest subjects which have come before our convention, — two of the greatest subjects which can come before any conven-tion, are those which are to be considered tonight, and in this consideration we know no North and no South. [*Loud applause.*] We are to hear from those who can teach us in regard to these great subjects of the evening. First, in regard to Christian Stewardship, we shall hear from Bishop B. W. Arnett, of Mississippi. [*Loud applause.*]

Christian Stewardship.

Address of Bishop B. W. Arnett.

Brothers and Sisters of the Christian Endeavor: We have met to-night under favorable auspices. We have invaded the Dominions of Her Majesty the Queen of England, the Empress of India and a faithful servant of Jesus Christ. The authorities of this magnificent and historic city have thrown open her gates and have given us the keys to their homes, to their churches and to their hearts; and to their full and generous hospitality which is cordial and as boundless as the wants of the guests. [*Loud applause.*] Never before were there so many Christians assembled in this city, never so many kings and priests, never so many heirs to the throne, so many members of the royal family of heaven as meet here tonight.

We have come, not in our own name, but in the name of the King of kings and Lord of lords, but at the same time we recognize human government and human affairs; we recognize the fact that the British lion is the king of beasts; that the American eagle is the king of birds, but the cross of Calvary is the ensign of power and victory. [*Applause.*] The army that has the British lion on one side and the American eagle on the other side, and that follows the cross, is assured of victory over the world, the flesh and the devil. [*Applause.*] Let every heart, let every tongue of this vast audience join in singing the Coronation, so long and so loud that the sound wave of the music shall encircle the globe, cheering the inhabitants of the islands of the sea and giving joy to the Christians of all continents.

My fellow-Christians, I greet you as soldiers of the cross, and congratulate you as the heroes in the moral and religious conflict, the Loyal Legion of the Church of God, the burden bearers of society, the heart-binders and emancipators of the races. Allow me to greet you, and say that we be brethren and fellow-laborers in the vineyard of the Master. Let every denomination and every division of this vast army realize as never before that " United we stand, divided we fall." Let us in the presence of God and before the world consecrate ourselves anew to the cause of Christ and the Church, declaring ourselves an eternal foe of sin, crime, rum, tobacco, dancing, and human oppression, and announce to all mankind our faith in the Holy Bible, our belief in a Christian Sabbath, and our loyalty to the principles of the fatherhood of God and the brotherhood of man. [*Loud applause*]

The subject assigned me by the honorable committee is the " Christian Endeavor and Christian Stewardship." Either branch of this subject is so intimately connected with man and with the church that to analyze either of them would require more time than is at my disposal. The subject of Christian Endeavor would embrace the efforts, the struggles of Christians in all churches, in all ages, to perform their duties, to spread the Gospel of the living God. While Christian stewardship would require the explanation of the extent of human duty, of human obligation, as understood to apply to those who have been interested, and are now interested in the affairs of the Church of the living God. Christian stewardship finds its place in the interdependence of man upon man, and forms the basis of our civil and political government, our social and civil rights, political and ecclesiastical privileges. All are based upon the interdependence of man upon man, of family upon family, of nation upon nation.

Early in the history of man God interrogated Cain and said: " Where is thy brother Abel?" Cain answered and said: " I do not know," and then said to God, "Am I my brother's keeper?" He received no answer or explanation. I will not discuss the question whether it was a voice spoken by God from between the cherubims and heard by Cain as we hear the voice of father or mother, or whether it was the voice of conscience whispering it in his breast. It nevertheless was the Divine voice, and it went direct to the murderer's heart. He felt that justice was on his track, and showed that he was not only a murderer but a liar, speaking as though he could hide his sins from God by denying any knowledge of his brother's whereabouts. He tried to throw the responsibility on God when he said:—"Am I my brother's keeper?" He was wicked and profane, obstinate and desperate. The omniscient Judge spoke to the guilty fratricide and said: "What hast thou done?" A shudder seized the guilty culprit, a shriek of horror ascended from the multitude, and the house of Abel rent the air with their cries. The murderer could not speak, the God of heaven heard the cry of the martyr's blood, the Judge was the witness of the guilt. In silence he heard his sentence, which exceeded the sentence of death itself; for his ears were filled with the wailings of his brother's household, and the bitter curses of his tribe. For hundreds of years he was doomed to toil and banishment, and he was cursed of the earth which had opened her mouth to receive his brother's blood. The ground refused to yield her strength, and he became a vagabond and a fugitive from his own kindred and his own children, and that he should not be killed, God set a mark upon him, and his punishment became an answer to his own question, "Am I my brother's keeper?" And from that day until now the question has been asked by each successive generation. " Am I my brother's keeper?" The consensus of at least 180 generations of men is that every man is his brother's keeper. [*Applause.*]

But one of the perplexing questions through all the centuries has been "Who is my brother, or who is my neighbor?" But the true interpretation of the question is found in the Gospel of our Lord Jesus Christ and in the marvelous address of St. Paul on Mar's Hill as he stood in the presence of the highest court of ancient civilization and proclaimed in the face of the intelligence of forty centuries the new and true conception of God, his nature, his attributes, and his relation to the physical and spiritual worlds; the new and true conception of the origin of matter; the origin of the world; the origin of vegetation and animal life; the origin of spiritual and eternal life, and the origin of man as never before; that God hath made of one blood, all nations of men to dwell on the face of the earth, and hath determined the time before appointed and the bounds of their habitations. In this address one of the principles of the Christian Endeavor was proclaimed; viz., the unity and spirituality of God; the fatherhood of God, and the brotherhood of man, thereby laying the foundation that if we belong to one family, having a common father, all that belong to the obligations of brothers and sisters belong to all men and women, to all families, to all races, and to all nations, and that is expressed in the word solidarity, a consolidation of interests, personal and social, in church and state; a consolidation of responsibilities and fellowship, one in honor and dishonor, one in loss and gain, one in peace, one in war, one in poverty, one in prosperity. Louis Kossuth, the Hungarian patriot, was the apostle of the doctrine of the solidarity of nations as the French were of the doctrine of the solidarity of communities. The doctrine of the French was that each community was the other's keeper, that each community stood in the relation of brothers; but Jesus Christ, the great moral and religious teacher, taught the solidarity of man and said:—"This is my commandment, that ye love one another as I have loved you. Greater love hath no man than this, that a man lay down his life for his friends. Ye are my friends, if ye do whatsoever I command you." And again he said, "Bear ye one another's burdens and so fulfil the law of Christ." And again he saith, "By this shall all men know that ye are my disciples, that ye love one another;" and his last prayer was that all his children might be one as he and his Father were one, that the world might believe on him. Thus we have the solidarity of nations taught by Kossuth, the solidarity or communism taught by the French, the solidarity of the individual or the brotherhood of man as taught by Jesus Christ, the greatest of teachers. And if I understand the purpose of the Christian Endeavor Association it is to carry out the thought of the latter. [*Applause.*]

What is implied in being your brother's keeper? It means to preserve, to protect, to guard, to sustain, to support, to defend, to maintain, to provide for, as one has power and opportunity to provide food, raiment and shelter for the body, to provide an education for the mind, to provide moral instruction and spiritual advice to every man, woman and child in our neighborhood, or to the remotest part of the earth as our means and influence will warrant. This is a personal duty and is not transferable. It is a duty that we owe to all the sons and daughters of Adam, because we are one in origin, equal in responsibility, and one in final destiny.

We are all heirs to the effects of evil upon the body, mind and soul. We feel the physicial effects of evil upon our own bodies and we see it in the hospitals. We realize the effect upon our minds by the limitation of our own sense, knowledge and self-knowledge, or objective and subjective knowledge, as well as in the lunatic asylums where reason is dethroned. When we think that all of this is the effect of the disobedience of our father, the general experience is expressed in the following :—

> " How careful, then, ought we to live, —
> With what religious fear, —
> Who such a strict account must give
> For our behavior here."

Realizing the work to be accomplished and feeling the responsibility resting upon the individual, men have through all ages united together to accomplish that which they could not as an individual. They have formed organizations for religious, charitable and beneficial objects; they have met around a common altar, bound themselves together by the sacred tie of personal obligation, pledging each to the other their honor, their talent, their time, their money, and, if need be, their lives, to carry out the sacred obligations of Christian brotherhood.

These organizations for the moral, religious, educational interests of mankind have their foundation in the interdependence of man. It is the foundation of all social organizations. It is the glory of the Church of the living God, " that God so loved the world that he gave his only begotten Son, that whosoever believeth on him should not perish, but should have everlasting life." It is the rock on which the hymenial altar is builded, and forms the chains of connubial and filial affections, and furnishes the foundation of state and the columns on which rests the dome of the temple of justice and liberty, while man's dependence upon God furnishes the plan of salvation through the merits of Christ our Redeemer and faith in his blood.

All men and things are subjects of law, to physical law, to material law, to spiritual law, and to moral law.

There is no independence in nature. Everything in the mineral, vegetable, and animal kingdom is governed by law. Every particle of matter, whether crawling, creeping, swimming, flying or running, bird, beast or fish, are all subjects of law.

The only wilful and constant violator of the law of God is man. Yet he is the only creature in nature that violates law and lives. In the natural world it is the same as it was in the days of Eden. " The day thou eatest thereof thou shalt surely die." But man, as then, violates the law, and dies and yet lives in his death. We find the following facts true: that every man is dependent upon the fellow-man, every community dependent upon some other community, and neighborhood upon neighborhood, county upon county, nation upon nation, finally all nations, all kindreds of every race and clime are dependent absolutely on the one true and living God. The interdependence of man makes him a religious and social being. The very construction of his mind and soul necessitates a God, a law-giver on whom he depends for his being, support and protection. The source of the true, beautiful and the good in the physical, intellectual and moral worlds is traced to the throne of absolute power, law and goodness, the source of all light and the embodiment of wisdom and origin of all life.

That man is a dependent being no one will question, for when he enters the world he is perfectly helpless. He knows nothing, not even his own mother upon whom he has to depend for his food, for care. He is more dependent than the beasts of the field, for he has to depend upon his mother to carry him from place to place. He depends upon some to teach him how to talk, and how to walk. He is the subject of maternal dependence till he reaches the age of ten years, and frequently till the end of his life. He is dependent upon his father for food, shelter and raiment. He. is dependent upon filial affections, he depends on brother and sister. He is dependent upon fraternal affections, upon playmates in youth, and associates in manhood. This chain of dependence produces family government and family obedience, which became the basis of all patriarchal governments of the past, out of which have grown the chief among the Indians, the heads of tribes, and minor divisions throughout the world.

The interdependence of families led to the establishment of civil government, which is divided into municipal, county, state and national governments.

The end of civilized government is to protect life, liberty, property, home and reputation; in fact, it is to protect the weak against the strong, to protect the rich and the poor, the ignorant and the intelligent, the well and the sick, the blind man and his guide, the producer and consumer, capital and honest labor, the waiter and the landlord, the country and the city; all are alike under the beneficial influences of civil government.

The principal systems of government are patriarchal, monarchial, limited and absolute.

All well regulated governments have three general departments: The Executive department, the Legislative department, and the Judicial department. All three are based upon the interdependence of man and the necessity of governmental stewardship.

The executors and protectors of civil society have recognized in all governments the sheriff, the constable, and the policeman for personal and domestic protection, the militia for internal protection, while the army and navy guard the frontier and coast, and stand ready to put down insurrections at home and invasions from abroad.

If any one doubts the assertion that we are our brother's keeper, I invite such an one to examine the general and special divisions of human government and then to ask himself what is meant by nation and state, country and city, town and village, townships, ward and precinct, all organized, maintained and utilized for the happiness of the inhabitants, and to insure domestic tranquillity, to preserve the rights, privileges and immunities of all, from the humblest to the most influential.

The interdependence of man upon man may be seen by visiting the eleemosynary institutions of the country. In 1890 there were, in the deaf and dumb asylums, 33,602 males, 24,845 females, and the people expended more than $14,000,000 in maintaining institutions for the deaf and dumb, because it was acknowledged by all that we were our brother's keeper.

In the many blind asylums, from 1880 to 1889. there were 23,981 patients, whose care, instruction and support cost $6,620,265. In 1890 the poor-houses of the land contained 40,741 males, and 32,304 females, or a total of 73,045. who were fed, clothed and sheltered by the genius of our Christian civilization. In 1890 the total number of persons treated in the insane asylums was 97,535, while the total number treated from 1881 to 1889 was 226,063. In 1889 the expenses on buildings alone were $18,582,647, and for expenses $77,480,759, or a grand total for caring for our sick brothers in the insane asylums for one year of $96,063,406. If Cain himself could read these figures and see the houses provided for the insane of every race for men of all conditions, he would not ask, "Am I my brother's keeper?" The states also recognize the interdependence of men and governments by the manner in which they treat the heroes of the war. The soldiers' and orphans' homes established by the state and national governments show the appreciation in which the defenders are held.

During the year 1892 there were 14,193 soldiers cared for by the national government, while the states cared for 5,375 others. Thus we see the thought that we are our brother's keeper pervades every fabric of our national institutions.

The interdependence of the nation and the citizen soldiers is seen by examining the pension roll to see the amount of money contributed for the support of those who were disabled during the war.

The interdependence of nation upon nation is demonstrated in the intercommunication by sea and land, by the lists of goods imported and exported, by the interchange of commodity for commodity, of product for product. The dependence of nation upon nation is one of the strongest ties known among men; in fact, intercommunication is essential to the peace and happiness of each nation. God has so distributed his bounties that no one nation can produce them all.

Japan and China are essential for their tea; each of the nations have some product peculiar to their country. Thus we are taught by observation and experience that we are each the steward of the other, and that the provisions for rich and poor grow in the same field, are garnered in the same barn and ground in the same mill. Water for king and subject gushes from the same fountain. The same is true of the moral and religious teachers and leaders. Provisions for the soul are as ample as provisions for the body.

The balm of Gilead will cure master and slave, the rich or poor, the black or white.

Organizations among men should be as broad as the want of humanity. There should be no distinction between class and class, rich and poor, and every individual should be eligible to its benefits and protection. [*Applause.*] Human society is so constituted that it is divided by "natural selection" into professions and trades, each becoming the steward of his brother's needs and wants, and by supplying the wants and needs of his brother he supplies his own needs and those of his family. Some become burden-bearers for their fellows; the physician, the school master, and the minister of the Gospel study their profession that they may comfort and protect their brothers; thus proclaiming by every act, "I am my brother's keeper," to the extent of my ability and the opportunity afforded me to relieve him in sickness, to enlighten his understanding, and to teach him his duty to himself, his family and to his God.

The seamstress, the cook, and the washerwoman are the domestic burden-bearers for the housewife. The lawyer is the burden-bearer for the criminal, the protector of the innocent.

If what I have said be true of the interdependence of man upon man, and the dependence of man upon God, what is our duty as members of the Church of the living God? What ought we to do, and what can we do towards rescuing our young men and women from the influence of the world and the wickedness? What can we do to make them better men and women, and assist them in doing more and better work for the Master in the coming years of their lives?

First. All men and women, old and young, who have passed from death unto life should consecrate themselves to the work of saving men and women, and should become more loyal to Christ and the church.

Second. Every man and woman should feel and act as a Christian steward, in the church and community, feeling it to be a part of his religious duty to visit the sick, to relieve the distressed, to bury the Christian dead in the honors of war, to care for the widow in distress and to educate the orphan, thus fulfilling the law of love, which is to "bear one another's burdens."

Third. Every man and woman should become messengers of peace and good will between man and man, family and family, nation and nation, and God and man, thus laying the broad basis of the Christian Endeavor Association which cultivates the feeling of good will between denomination and denomination.

Fourth. Every member of the Christian Endeavor Association should become one of God's stewards and hold in trust his time and his talents for the benefit of his brother, recognizing the fact that all of his possessions, intellectual, moral, or spiritual, were given as a trust to make others happy, and by making others happy to produce happiness for himself. God gives to every one personal health for riches, which is to become a part of his own being and is not transferable to another. Then he gives to every one riches, that are to be given away and which, by holding, one becomes poor; but, by giving away, one becomes richer.

· The Gospel stewardship does not teach communism nor modern socialism; but it teaches the doctrine of " Reward and Punishment " of sowing, cultivating, and reaping ; of seed time, harvesting, and rejoicing. " For whatsoever a man soweth that shall he also reap, and he who sows sparingly shall also reap sparingly." Every Christian should be a Christian steward, for God has committed the propagation of his Gospel to the hands of men and women. They are to teach his doctrines, to live his life, believe his truth, obey his commandments and enjoy the reward of a faithful steward. [*Applause.*]

The ministers of the Lord Jesus Christ are the principal stewards of the Gospel dispensation. The lay workers form another important class ; the Sunday-school teachers are another set of Christian stewards, making provisions for the lambs of the fold. The pastor is the shepherd of the sheep. The officers and members of the Church of God form another important class of Christian workers ; they are to make provision for sheltering the flock of Christ.

The qualifications of a true Christian steward are first, a converted heart, one who knows from experience that he has passed from death unto life, and that he is a new creature, for old things have passed away.

The second qualification is an intelligent head, a cultivated mind, and a consecrated heart. These form the foundation for a successful Christian steward. God does not place all Christian stewards in charge of the same work. He makes some preachers, some teachers, some to lead prayer meetings, some to visit the sick, some to counsel the children of God in time of distress. Some are warriors, cavalrymen, infantrymen, artillerymen and sharpshooters; some belong to the land forces and some to the navy ; but all belong to the army of the living God, and follow the King of kings and Lord of lords.

In discussing the subject of Christian stewardship it is well for us to define the word "steward" as we understand it, and as is generally understood. My first recollection of a steward was one Teuton Plummer who had charge of the house of Jas. T. Rogers, in Brownsville, Pa., and one Samuel D. Honesty, who purchased the provisions for Jas. L. and Nelson Bowman. Their position was that of domestic steward, which was applied to one "employed in large family " according to Webster, " or on a large estate to manage the domestic concerns, to superintend other servants, to collect rents or income and to keep accounts and the like." This was my first impression of a steward. My first experience with a steward was in 1853, when I was employed on a steamboat on the Monongahela River. This is what is termed a nautical steward, or a steamboat steward. His business was to employ waiters, to assign them work, regulate their wages, and superintend the internal arrangement of the cook-house, pantry and storeroom.

A part of his business was to regulate the distribution of food and drink, to wait upon the officers and passengers, to see that everybody was provided with breakfast, dinner, and supper, from the deck hand to the captain.

My third idea of a steward is of one who acts as a fiscal agent for an institution, as the steward of the blind asylum, or of the insane asylum, or of the penitentiary. They are the agents of the state and country, and make provisions for the inmates of the institution of which they have charge.

My fourth idea of a steward came to me from the position my father occupied in his church. He was the steward of a Methodist church, which is one of the most important offices in that branch of the Christian church. The discipline says that to be qualified for the office they must be men of solid piety, who both know and love the Methodist doctrine and discipline. They must be of good natural, and acquired ability to transact the temporal business of the church. Their duty is defined to be to take charge of all moneys and other provisions collected for the preacher, church, sick or poor, and to account for the same ; to seek out the needy and distressed, to relieve and comfort them; to report any who walk disorderly, and will not be reproved. These are the duties of the Methodist steward, and they correspond to the duty and obligation of a Christian steward. The duties, as laid down here, if followed out to the letter and spirit, will give to the church and to the world the idea of an ideal Christian steward from a human standpoint but the divine ideal of a Christain steward is to be found in the 6oth chapter of Isaiah, where the mission of the Lord Jesus Christ is described and His work laid out. Here we find the divine standard of a Christian stewardship. Some Christian stewards have committed to them wealth, money, houses, lands, cattle, bonds and railway stock, which they hold in trust for the minor children of the family of God. They have been appointed administrators through the will of God and have been commissioned by the court of heaven to carry out the principles of the Gospel, and the teachings of the beloved disciple.

Christianity has produced some noble examples of Christian stewardship, men who have executed their own wills and have administered their own estates. Among the many worthy examples is George Peabody, who founded scholarships for the poor student, who built libraries for communities, endowed colleges for Christian education, and set an example worthy of imitation.

William E. Dodge, who took delight in assisting indigent students of all races in obtaining an education. John Stater, who laid a million dollars upon the altar of Christian education. Daniel Hand, who gave a million dollars for the education of the freedmen of the South, and provided for them for a hundred generations.

What we want today is to teach, and practise that which we preach others, such as giving to the cause of Christian education, Christian missions and Christian temperance. These are living questions, subjects that affect every man, woman, and child. There are none so low, none so high, but what are made better or worse by their relation to this trinity effort. There are very many Christians who fail to support the causes named; they are too frugal to give to the cause of humanity, they are spiritual bankrupts and financial paupers.

Dr. A. T. Pearson speaks of seven ways of giving, viz.:

1. The careless way: To give something to every cause that is presented without inquiring into its merits.

2. The impulsive way: To give from impulse, as much and as often as love and piety and sensibility prompt.

3. The lazy way: To make a special effort to earn money for benevolent objects by fairs, festivals, etc.

4. The self-denying way: To save the costs of luxuries and apply them to purposes of religion and charity. This may lead to asceticism and self-complacence.

5. The systematic way: To lay aside as an offering to God a definite portion of one's gains, — one-tenth, one-fifth, one-third, or one-half. This is adapted to all, whether rich or poor, and gifts would be largely increased if it were generally practised.

6. The equal way: To give God and the needy just as much as we expend upon ourselves, balancing all our personal expenditures by our gifts.

7. The heroic way: To limit our own expenditures to a certain sum, and give away all the rest of our income. This was John Wesley's way.

The mission of the Christian Endeavor is to unite the Christian forces into one grand army of consecrated men, women, and children, who have sworn allegiance to the Son of God, and who belong to the empire of religion, morality, and knowledge, and who have determined, through the favor of God, to give no quarter to the world, the flesh, and the devil; but who purpose to spend the balance of their lives in casting up a highway, and in lifting up the standard among the people.

The most important work that the Christian Endeavor Association can do today is to break down the lines in Christian effort and Christian labor, to break down denominational barriers and allow the army of the living God to become interdenominational, as well as interdependent. [*Loud applause.*] My prayer is that the Christian Endeavor Association will be true to her motto, true to her history, true to the spirit of the age in which we live, true to the best interests of the Church of the living God, and true to the principle of the fatherhood of God, and the brotherhood of man. That it may break down the color line, east, west, north, and south, so that we may have one faith, one baptism, one banner, and that the banner of the cross; and that beneath its folds the invitation shall go forth inviting every nation, kindred and tongue, regardless of race, color, or previous condition of servitude, to join in the combat of right against wrong, of justice against injustice, of liberty against oppression, of freedom against slavery, of Christianity against infidelity, of the church against the world, and of God against the devil; being assured that every true and tried soldier in the army of the living God shall conquer, though he die, and that for every cross there is a crown, for every wound an immortal balm, and for death, eternal life! [*Loud applause.*]

My brothers and sisters, the conclusion of the whole matter is that the golden cord of interdependence is like chemical affinity and gravitation in the material world.

It pervades every genus and species of animal life, and is coexistent and co-extensive with the vegetable, animal, spiritual and angelic existence.

The mineral kingdom is the basis of the vegetable kingdom; the animal kingdom is interdependent upon both mineral and vegetable; man stands at the head of the animal kingdom, yet he is dependent upon both animal and vegetable kingdoms.

From the mineral kingdom he receives his water, from the vegetable his bread, and from the animal kingdom his meat. Having satisfied the appetites of his body, he is confronted with the necessity of satisfying his appetite for knowledge, which comes through sense; perception, and self-knowledge, which is satisfied by observation, thought, reading books and nature, conversing with intelligent people, studying good books, and communing with God. Thus the interdependence of man with man, family with family, race with race, and nation with nation, is clearly taught by history, tradition, observation and experience.

It is common with every genus, species, variety, and race of men, for it requires the aggregate sum of the intelligence, industry, virtue, skill, and wealth of all the races to make up the civilization of the age.

No race can say to another: "I have no need of thee." No nation can say to another nation: "I have no need of thee or of thy products," for foreign commerce and internal trade, lists of imported and exported goods, as well as the free lists and tariff schedules, unquestionably teach the interdependence between nations.

This law is as universal as gravitation; it binds nations together with a cord stronger than steel; it produces a fraternal sentiment as pure as gold, and it forms a friendship as lasting as the centuries. [*Loud and prolonged applause.*]

After Bishop Arnett's address, Miss Park favored the audience with a cornet solo, "Under the Palms." Being encored, she played as a duet with her sister "Nearer, my God, to Thee," in which the audience, rising, joined in singing.

Dr. Clark then introduced, as one whom Endeavorers always like to hear, Rev. Dr. David J. Burrell, of New York City, who spoke on "Christian Citizenship."

Christian Citizenship.

Address of Rev. David J. Burrell, D.D.

The man who could not speak to an audience like this, as the great dramatist said, "Is fit for treasons, stratagems, and spoils." I had rather look upon your faces tonight and speak to you, with your warm hearts and flashing eyes, than to speak to any other audience on earth. [*Loud applause.*] It is said that when Cæsar first saw Brutus it was in the Forum, and he asked some one who the young man was, and being answered "I don't know," he said, "I tell you that young man will make his life tell, for I know by the firing of his eyes that he intends strongly." It is a joy to look into the faces of young men and young women who intend strongly, and who mean to have their lives tell for the welfare of their fellows and the glory of their God.

I cannot go further without giving you a hearty hand-clasp, and all the warm blood that is in me is in my hand, when I say to all this goodly fellowship in the bond of Christian Endeavor, The Lord be with you, and the Lord bless you. On the night before John Huss was led away to his death he was being taken from the place of judgment to his prison cell, and the crowd pressed upon him on every side, and there was no friendly face or kindly word. He wore a fool's cap on his head all covered with black devils, and on every side were voices of derision; but in the midst of the press he felt a hand thrust through and seizing his and holding fast. He looked, and presently he saw a familiar face. The next day, just before he died and went to heaven in his chariot of fire, he wrote these last words: "God be praised for that warm hand of Jerome of Prague." God be praised for that warm hand which you and I, who for the most part have never seen each other's faces before, can hold out to one another in the name of our common Lord and Master, and that one God who is the Father of us all!

Ours is a great Gospel. No circumscribed bailiwick is that of its glorious minister. And you and I, if we love the Master, are all ministers of Jesus Christ. Ours is a great, high, deep, broad Gospel, and it touches human life at every point of its circumference. Theology and ethics, science and philosophy, physics and metaphysics, all fall under its sway. The Gospel of our Lord and Saviour is like the air around us, which presses upon us at this moment, we are told, with a pressure equal to fifteen pounds to the square inch, so that our Brother Clark, who is sitting here so innocent looking, is holding up under a pressure at this moment of about 30,000 pounds. It is a great, mighty, irrepressible, far-reaching, glorious Gospel of our Lord Jesus Christ. It is like the sun that "goeth forth out of his chamber, rejoicing as a strong man to run a race, for there is nothing hid from the heat thereof."

I know that men who are without would be glad if we would have nothing to do with civil life. They are all the while saying to us, "Content you with monopolizing heaven, and let this little rolling ball alone." But your function as followers of the Lord Jesus Christ is particularly to have to do with the affairs of this little rolling ball which is the vestibule of the everlasting life. Our Lord and Saviour himself, when he stood between the pillars of the Temple porch, preached science and philosophy, physics and metaphysics, politics and theology, the science of this life and the science of the life to come. "Go tell that fox," said he, — and if he had been in the city of New York today, he would have said, "Go tell that tiger." [*Laughter and applause.*] Our Lord did not hesitate to touch with a mighty hand any point of human life that needed it. He called for a penny and said, "Whose image and superscription is this?" and they said, "It is Cæsar's." His word was then, "Render unto Cæsar the things which are Cæsar's." And that injunction is as imperative as its complement, "Render also unto God the things which are God's." I say to you, young men, and I hope the time will come when it can be said to you, young women, also, Have to do with political life. [*Applause.*] Make your power as true Endeavorers felt in all the affairs of civil life. I am sorry that I cannot speak directly to the dear girls and women who are here, and say to them, "Go attend also to the functions of your civil life;" but I remember the saying that, "The hand that rocks the cradle rules the world," and I remember also how the wives and mothers fought during the Civil War, sitting in the chimney corners knitting stockings for the boys who were far away at the front of the battle. So that when I speak to the young men, I may almost venture to say that I use the term generically as including the women too.

The word Endeavor is a gloriously significant one. It comes from two French words, which mean on guard or on duty. I dare not venture to pronounce those two French words here in the city of Montreal. [*Laughter.*] It recalls the worn legend of the Roman knight at Pompeii, who stood in his place without flinching while the multitudes were flying from the molten stream of death which the great mountain belched forth, faithful among the fearful, on duty to the last. That is what it means to be a true Endeavorer. First of all, it devolves upon us to guard the rights of citizenship and the purity of the franchise; that is, to be on guard at the polls.

> " There is a weapon better yet,
>   And stronger than the bayonet,
>   A weapon that comes down as still
>   As snowflakes fall upon the sod,
>   And executes a freeman's will
>   As lightning does the will of God." [*Applause.*]

This fluttering bit of paper in the citizen's hand is eloquent of the progress of freedom and equality. It means that Paul's manifesto on Mar's Hill is being realized, "God hath made of one blood all nations of men for to dwell upon the face of the earth." It means that, within bounds, every one is a king in his own might. But there is no privilege without a corresponding responsibility. The ballot suggests not merely that a man may exercise his franchise, but that he must do so. This bit of paper is the token of a freeman's sovereignty, and he has no more right to ignore or decline its responsibilities than Queen Victoria would have to cast down her sceptre in a pettish freak and refuse to govern her realm. [*Applause.*] In ancient Sparta it was the custom on election day for officers of the law to draw a vermillion cart through the streets. To bear the red mark was counted a misdemeanor. If you, young man, are an enfranchised citizen of the states or of the colonies, go as a true Endeavorer, and stand guard over your citizenship at the polls on election day. [*Applause.*] One of the grave evils of our time is the withdrawal of a considerable class from the exercise of citizenship. The right to vote involves a corresponding duty, which no true Endeavorer will regard with indifference. It is our business to look to the education of the masses; that is, to stand on guard at the school-house door. [*Applause.*] In the freedom of the suffrage which prevails in all constitutional governments are involved not a few serious possibilities of danger. An ignorant citizen is like a reckless miner with an uncovered light on his visor. The fire-damp is all about him. John Milton wrote in the days of the English Commonwealth :

> " There is a poor blind Samson in this land,
>   Shorn of his strength and bound with bands of steel,
>   Who may in some grim revel raise his hand
>   And shake the pillars of the commonweal."

This blind Samson is ignorance. Wherefore our fathers wisely established the common school, insisting that as the people are princes they should be taught to rule. This institution is fundamental to our welfare. Withered be the hand that shall be raised to destroy it! The result of committing the elective franchise to the ignorant and unworthy was seen in the city of Chicago, a few years ago, when a body of anarchists, foiled in their efforts to possess themselves of the control of municipal affairs, gathered in the Haymarket and assailed the officers of the law with dynamite. Seven of them justly suffered the penalty of death; but that the infamous cause survives them is manifest in the recent pardon of their confreres by Governor Altgeld of Illinois. The prime remedy for such abuse is in the education of the masses. This is our strong buttress against anarchy and kindred political heresies. It therefore behooves the thoughtful youth who gather in millions within the charmed circle of Christian Endeavor to stand unitedly in defence of the public school. [*Loud applause.*]

A true Endeavorer should be on duty close by the dram-shop. There is no more portentous menace to our liberties than this. In the city of New York there are 9,000 saloons. That fact alone is portentous, when we reflect that every one of them is an open doorway into the realm of darkness. But there are other considerations which give it a still broader and deeper significance. Five thousand, or more than half, of these saloons are under chattel mortgages, and these mortgages are, with scarcely an exception, held by a syndicate of twenty men — brewers, distillers and wholesale liquor dealers. The full meaning of that statement is not grasped until we go on to consider that each saloon, at a moderate estimate, controls twenty votes, which gives to the rum-sellers of New York City the balance of political power. But it is a proverb that the vote of New York City determines the political complexion of the commonwealth, and, furthermore, as goes the commonwealth of New York so goes the nation! What then is the conclusion of the matter? The destinies of the American people are practically in the grasp of a group of less than twenty liquor dealers! Were it not for certain moral restraints put upon this formidable power by public sentiment the outlook would be as black as midnight. As it is, it behooves every lover of law and order and national prosperity to use his utmost influence against the dram shop. [*Applause.*] It is not for us at this point either to call in question or to concede the right of the individual to take a social or even a convivial glass. We are not talking about rights but about Christian duties and privileges. There is a right which in the Christian life towers above all others; it is the right to surrender all rights for the sake of one's fellowmen. This is the mind that was in Christ Jesus, who, possessing all the inalienable rights of Godhead, emptied himself and became of no reputation for us. This is the mind that was in the Apostle Paul also when he said, " If meat make my brother to offend, I will eat no meat while the world standeth! " Never was a grander manifesto of human rights — never a sublimer declaration of independence than that! O young men, to whom the welfare of the nation is presently to be committed, be " on duty " just there.

It should be the part of every loyal Endeavorer to be on guard respecting the sanctity of the Sabbath. Our minds revert in the instant to the opening of the gates of the Columbian Fair on the Lord's day? All praise to the noble army of American Endeavorers for the heroic stand they have taken in this matter. They have said with a voice like the sound of many waters, " If the gates of the exposition are open on the Sabbath we cannot attend it." Let others call it a " boycott " if they choose ; a rose by any other name would smell as sweet. It was just such a boycott as was instituted by the Jewish youths in Babylon when they said " Because the king's meat has been laid on idol altars we cannot partake of it." Such boycotts are in line with duty and principle. The Gospel of Jesus Christ pronounces in behalf of the universal church a boycott on every existing form of evil. The Sabbath has always and everywhere been the citadel of national piety and by the same token, of national prosperity. No kingdom or commonwealth has ever persistently violated it and lived. We would therefore not be worthy of our Christian names, certainly not of the name of Christian Endeavor, did we not resent the opening of the Columbian Fair on God's holy day. [*Applause.*] The matter has a pivotal importance as being a new departure. For four hundred years America has regarded the Sabbath. It is now proposed to reverse all precedents and make a new Sabbath policy for the nation. If this fair is a financial success it is safe to say that all similar expositions hereafter will pursue a similar course. If this one is a failure, the experiment of Sabbath desecration will scarcely be tried again. It is respectfully submitted that thoughtful Christian people will not lend their influence to a movement which promises so calamitous a result. In any event if there is a question as between duty and pleasure in this matter conscience should have the benefit of the doubt. " He that doubteth is condemned if he eat." Our young Endeavorers have taken the right position. They feel that their principles are being put to the test, and they are willing that the world shall take note whether they have the courage of their convictions or not. God help them — clad in the full panoply of their profession — to withstand in the evil day and having done all, to stand. [*Great applause.*]

The young men of the Christian churches are presently to bear the full responsibility of the welfare of the state. If they flinch or waver in the hour of trial the generations of the future must suffer for it. If they quit themselves like men, upholding with stalwart steadfastness the institutions of truth and

IN THE DRILL HALL AS THE AUDIENCE WAS GATHERING.

From a photograph.

righteousness, the waste places of the earth shall be glad because of them and the coming of the Lord shall be hastened in his time. They are already being put to crucial tests. God is asking with respect to current questions of political ethics, whether they will be true or not.

> " He hath sounded forth the trumpet that shall never call retreat,
> He is sifting out the hearts of men before his judgment seat ;
> Oh, be swift, my soul, to answer him, be jubilant, my feet,
> For God is marching on." [*Loud and prolonged applause.*]

The meeting closed with singing " My Country, 't is of Thee " and " God Save the Queen."

SATURDAY MORNING.

The morning opened with the prospect for a beautiful day. The early morning prayer meetings were held in the usual places and were attended by large numbers. As giving some idea of the way these meetings were carried on, the following notes of the meeting at the American Presbyterian church may be of interest.

Mr. D. S. Bennett, of Richmond, Va., led the meeting. Nearly 500 people were present. The meeting opened with the hymn " At the Cross." The leader then read the twelfth chapter of Romans, after which the beatitudes were recited in unison. Several brief prayers followed, invoking the presence of the Holy Spirit. Hymn, "Showers of Blessing ; " large number of brief prayers ; " What a Friend we have in Jesus," sung without announcement ; renewed prayers, especially for Montreal ; one verse of " Nearer, my God, to Thee ; " prayers offered especially in behalf of associate members ; " Sowing in the morning ; " renewed prayers ; " Blessed Assurance ; " more sentence prayers ; " Just as I am." Dr. Clark, being recognized in the audience by the leader, was called upon for a word. He said : " I have simply come in for worship and to join my prayers with yours for God's special blessing this day. I am sure these prayers will be heard and answered and this and the following day will grow in interest and spiritual power, if we pray earnestly for the descent of the Spirit and the opening of the hearts of all who have come to this convention. May we take a great blessing with us as we go, and also leave a great blessing behind us." The sentence prayers were renewed ; " Come, Holy Spirit " was sung ; more prayers followed, and then, the hour for closing having come, the leader gave out the hymn " God Be with You," after which the audience joined fervently in the Lord's Prayer and the Mizpah benediction. The spirit of the meeting was deeply devotional, and many were heard to speak of the delightfulness of the hour thus spent at the beginning of the day.

DRILL HALL.

Missions formed the subject of the program at the Drill Hall this morning, and a large audience assembled to enjoy the good things provided. After the preliminary song service, Rev. J. K. Fowler, of Cedar Rapids, Iowa, conducted the devotional exercises. The audience recited together the twenty-fourth Psalm, and prayer was offered especially in behalf of God's blessing to follow the results of Dr. Clark's journey around the world. " Hear us, O Saviour " was then sung.

DR. CLARK: This is our missionary morning, always a session of enthusiasm in the Christian Endeavor convention. One who has contributed not a little to this enthusiasm throughout the past years is Mr. S. L. Mershon, of Evanston, Ill., who will treat of a subject near to his heart, — " Missionary Literature: Why Used and How to Use it." [*Applause*].

Missionary Literature.

Address of Mr. S. L. Mershon.

First, last, all the time, that Book (the Bible) is the missionary classic of all ages. [*Loud applause.*] Thy word is a lamp unto the feet and a light unto the path of all missionary heralds. The Alpha and Omega, the beginning and the end, the first and the last. From it the missionary soldier receives his commission, in it is found the plan of campaign, by it comes the crown now pendant from the Master's hand. Open its covers and let the redemption light gleam out. Under its revelation you must face the awful problem involving you, a lost world and a crucified Lord somewhere between Montreal and the Great White Throne. Hark! Listen! A church member is passing into eternity! The click of a key, the flapping of a wing, the gleam of a light and that soul stands celestially resplendent in the Divine presence. But at that same instant one hundred other souls who have never heard of the Christ, appear at the Christian's side from the heathen world. Endeavorer, are we looking at the time of thine appearing in the King's palace? A voice is speaking from the throne. Does it say, " I was an hungered and ye gave me no meat, I was athirst and ye gave me no drink, I was sick and in prison, and ye visited me not." " But when saw we thee thus?" " As ye did it not unto the least of these my brethren ye did it not unto me," or does it say, "She hath done what she could; " if so then wave back another door of heavenly light that righteous ones move on into life eternal. Hold up that Book and then lift up thy brain and thy heart to its plane and then with that intensity of soul wherewith thou didst seek thy Saviour, seek, seek, seek to find from that Book a message for a lost world. Seek its revelation as thou wilt wish thou hadst sought it when thou and one hundred souls from the heathen world will render up an account together in the presence of thy God. Thou standing with the message of life, they with it not — God acquainted with thy life and reading thy heart. The Scripture, what saith it? Hover with me over that Book. Let out thine imagination, yea, give wings to thy thought — it does not yet appear what we shall be. Dost not thou in thy prophetic vision read thy name in the Divine Encyclopædia of Missions? It's there! For the Book of Life is the completed edition of the book of the Acts of the Apostles. We will need no book of Genesis over there. The worlds of a universe will be flashing at our feet. We will need no book of Exodus over there, for there will be no going out any more forever. We will need no book of Deuteronomy over there, for the word of God is the law of heaven. We will need no book of Psalms over there, for the heavenly choir will let thee into the sublime chorus, singing the songs of the redeemed. Memory will hold the impress of this book for all eternity, but one written book, penned by the fingers of God. Every entry eternal, is the continuance of the book of the Acts of the Apostles. It is the story of the world won to Christ.

In the missionary literature of heaven

> " Is thy name written there,
> On that page bright and fair?
> In the book of that kingdom
> Is thy name written there?"

as faithful to thy pledge?   "Whatsoever he would have me do," is our response under oath in answer to his command to "discipline all nations." All agree that the Word of God is for fallen man.   For God's sake then give it to fallen man.   Turn the heresy hunter into the heathen hunter! [*Applause.*]   What cares that poor soul in Darkest Africa, whether some secluded monk failed to dot an "I" or cross a "t," so long as that Book will bring to him the raft of life over the waves of death!   We are through with the fads and after the lads lost on the mountain sides, wandering from the Father heart of God! God is now writing an everlasting story of the faithful and unfaithful stewards. Thou art a character in that book! Which character is it?   Eternal destinies play upon its pages, and the crown of immortality awaits its true heroes. O Endeavorer! step into thy closet with thy God and study that Book—God's thoughts about missions! [*Applause.*]

With this preparation for safe thinking let us look down the stream of Christian literature which is flowing in ever increasing volume, from this well of water springing up into a world's everlasting life.

It is the war news of the army of God moving to the winning of the world to the Prince of Peace. A campaign inaugurated when in Eden the angel of the flashing swords breathed hope into broken hearts. The narrative runs along the rough crags of time to Calvary where our leader caught victory from a cleft in the rock. Antioch becomes the first missionary headquarters, while foreign missionary Paul makes the Roman Forum ring with his eloquence, and brands the soil of Italy with Christ for his blood. Then the forests of Germany, the plains of Northumberland, and the wilds of Wales, witness the emblem of the cross; while on Scotia's hills the Messiah's banner is kissed by the breezes of heaven. Tramp, tramp, tramp, the sweeping soldiery move over America.

China, India and Japan resound with the songs of Christian triumph, while the sentry fires commence to illumine Darkest Africa.   No other such stories in the annals of the globe.   Behold the stately steppings of the King in missionary history.

Like a mighty army moves the Church of God.   Heroes and heroines have moved across the stage of missionary history like stars of the first magnitude in heaven's galaxy.   The great treasure house of missionary history is crowded full of historic facts so thrilling in character and with such momentous bearing on a world's destiny as to astound the mind of historic investigations.   Within the Church of Jesus Christ exists the brightest minds and ablest pens that bless the realms of thought—able to mould these facts into the most brilliant narratives the world has ever read. Yet a strange vision presents itself.   A press crowded night and day to overflowing with works of fiction, and the youth of our churches devoting time and sentiment to a literature devoid of truth.   Fiction has usurped the throne of fact, simply because the stories of our missionary heroes have been buried amidst the musty archives of the church, while Christian genius has been endeavoring to make imagination create ideal characters which superabound already on a planet pulsating with a billion hearts. [*Applause.*]   The Endeavor movement is a missionary movement just as certainly as the student's volunteer movement is a missionary one.   The world for Christ and Christ for the world.   We will stand by that gun until he whose right it is to reign shall reign from the rivers to the ends of the earth.   We stand the greatest missionary reading circle in the world, two million strong, in front of our boards of missions and great denominational publishing houses, and cry with tremendous earnestness, Give us the literature adapted to youth with its cravings for that which absorbs the imagination, stirs the emotions and stimulates to deeds of devotion and courage.   We like the geography of missions — some. We like the arithmetic of missions — some, but we like the love stories of missions a great deal more. I am glad of it, for it is a God-endowed taste. God so loved that he gave his only begotten Son. The apostle of love, John, said, Hereby we know, because we love the brethren. Then flashes forth the divine challenge from the Throne of God, Greater love hath no man than this, that a man will lay down his life for his friend. God is love! Love — Love — Love! Let every page of the books from the missionary press gleam of love light, glow with enthusiasm, be replete with the marvels of missions, and clothed with literary genius, and we will show the publishing houses an ocean of commercial opportunity for the sale of such literature that will stagger their vision.

We have some rare illustrations and some rich sources of missionary information: the library, the review, the leaflet.

The missionary library.—Every society of Christian Endeavor should have a missionary library. Let your motto be, Quality, not quantity. Better a big shelf with one thrilling missionary book in great demand, than a great accumulation of volumes that will not be read. The day is past when the church is to be satisfied with a heavy, lifeless publication. A dull missionary book is a libel upon the church militant. Already the printing presses commence to teem with wonderful books along this line.

Missionary biography.—The highest type of life, the grandest characters are the soldiers of the Cross of Christ, who lay all upon the altar of fealty to our King.

Missionary history.—The past comes rushing in upon today and from today move out the waves that are to be billows of light or the floods of black despair, to rock with joy or engulf in the darkest woe, the countless throngs on this revolving planet. Armies moving, thrones falling, empires upheaving, continents being torn asunder, voices speaking across continents and thoughts flashing under seas, all mean that a divine plan in history tends to the ushering in of the day of universal kingdom.

Missionary romance.—Consecration to missions freezes not the fountain of love in human hearts. I know something about the bridal vow that took the light of that refined and beautiful home to share the privations and hardships of that missionary hovel in darkest Africa. Many an English and American girl has soothed the fever-stricken brow of a noble Christian husband in the wilds of heathendom, when cruel and naked savages taunted her devotion and wild beasts watched with blazing eyes for the chance to seize her as their prey—all for the Christ's sake and the love of a godly husband. No such romances anywhere else. [*Applause.*]

Missionary poetry.—A department almost untouched, a continent yet unexplored, a well from which might burst the gushing streams that would make the heart to sing. When will the Christian missionary muses wake? Why sleep they so long? O Endeavorers, endowed with mystic powers from on high, wave the wands of thought before this enchanting door and see the sweet messengers come forth.

In undertaking to guide our youth up to the mountain heights of missionary knowledge, be patient while they climb first along the foothills. Don't expect to call down from thy height and see them instantly fly to the summit where thou art. The higher the mountain the greater the necessity for a wise guide. It is as natural for a youth to love stories as it was for Christ to use them for illustrations. It 's as characteristic for a young man and a young woman to make their appeal to the heroic element in human life, as it was for Paul to talk of the arena and the gladiator. Youth is stirred by admiration for the one who, making his appeal to eternity, is impelled by the affections to a bodily death that he may let in the sunlight in the place of shadow, where sorrow has reigned. He knows that joy but watcheth his efforts that she may enter in with her sceptre of light. Youth takes to history with keenness of appetite whetted by the knowledge and ambition that he is to help make history. Play upon these chords with skilful fingers. A troop of young folks are at my door; they come into my library; they have been at school all the week and are tired mentally and nervously. They want something interesting to read. For one, "The Chinese Slave Girl" comes down; a brother by his side with base ball and bat in his hands also wants a book, and I give him the "Life of Paton," in one volume by his brother. Now you give him "Robinson Crusoe" and he will read my book first and love the work in the South Seas. [*Applause.*] Do I want to interest another in missions, I hand her the "Cruise of the Mystery" and the "McAll Mission in France" flashes before the mind. Africa is illumined in the story of "Rivers of Water," and "Moffat Lives Again." To another I lend the "Martyr Church of Madagascar," which stirs the heart to its fountain depths. The "Child of the Ganges" is a good story on India. Has the boy seen an American Indian or is he thinking of the red man of the plains? He then gets "Onoqua" and he companions with the hunter and lives with the Sioux, while he listens to the red man as he learns of the Great Spirit and the Messiah already come. Do I want to catch his thought for Japan? Then I take down "Kesa" and "Sajiaro" and all the exquisite beauty of the polite people comes to mind with an indelible stamp. I may at the same time tuck under his arm the Life of Jerry McAuley and he will read every word of it, and so I interest him in city missions. [*Applause.*] I am waiting to let him have "The Bar Sinister," that he may be stirred with righteous wrath over the Mormon monster. Then I look to the loved sunny land of the South, where that colored problem looms up in such tremendous proportions, and I read "Iola Le Roy," which tells of a Christ love that dwelleth in true hearts and giveth peace. Do I want to fire a musket that will scatter shot in all directions? Then I give out "Our Heroes and Heroines of the Mission Field."

For retrospect, "Heroes of the Mission Field." For additional enthusiasm, "Modern Heroes of the Mission Field," and "American Heroes of the Mission Field." A splendid story on wonderful Alaska is "Kin-de-shon's Wife."

Get these young folks to read these stories and they will read everything worth reading that comes to their hands. These story books are but the foothills; but standing thereon they will see the mountain peaks beckoning them on, on, up, up — into the philosophy of missions.

Philosophy of missions not interesting? Let the world stand up while I simply ask it to believe the fatherhood of God, the brotherhood of man and the pledge of the divine sympathy in Jesus Christ. Then I challenge all the sciences to produce or the arts to bring forth, a line of books more fascinating in interest, more readable to intelligent youth than the procession of works that we are now to suggest: "Modern Cities," "In Darkest England," "Our Country," "Life of Jerry McAuley," "Rotting at the Top," "How the Other Half Lives," "The Children of the Poor." Do you want to be pressed hard as to your fidelity to thy trust, then read: "Gesta Christi," "Heroes of the Mission Field," "The First Three Centuries of Christian Missions." Dost thou want thy heart to leap with joy over the sublime opportunity before thee, then read, "The Miracle of Missions," "The Greatest Thing in the World," "The Holy Spirit and Missions," "The Great Value and Success of Foreign Missions," "The Divine Enterprise of Missions." Watch the stereopticon! See the lamp of dazzling splendor. The light blazes forth. There is the screen. God's word is the lamp. The light of his promises streams forth while those books have caught some wonderful pictures of the fulfilment of his promises. "Medical Missions," "The Women of the Orient," "Our Eastern Sisters," brother, dost thou believe in mother, wife, sister, daughter? Then thy soul will stand back aghast if thou wilt read these three books.

Womanhood, believest thou in God? Then read these three books and in the place or standing in the Divine presence robed in silks, bedecked with flashing jewels, thou wilt wrap thy soul with sackcloth and cry out in agony of spirit to thy God for thy lost sisters. For a complete list of standard books on the mission fields send to the Student Volunteer Movement, Chicago, or New York. It is the best list extant.

Missionary biography — Oh, how God's noblemen loom up like majestic mountain peaks above the almost level of the great sea of human life, earth rooted, heaven panoplied. They sift down upon us the pure atmosphere of their lofty existence while from them flow the sparkling streams of influences that made glad the hearts of the reapers.

Mountains not snow-capped, but heaven crowned! Wouldst thou bedeck the sacred walls of memory's shrine with portraits that would speak to thee as living companions, then read the lives of Moffat, Livingston, Carey, Judson, Martyn, Mackay, Patterson, Paton, Williams.

Wouldst thou have many friends companion with thee in thy loftiest emotions, then lend them a peep at thy catalogue, that they, too, may array upon the walls of their memories (that most sublime of all picture galleries) these portraits made ineffable by the master touch of the Divine Artist.

Thus far I have not pressed the claims of denominational literature. God has not kept the denominational lines clear. I think the files in heaven have become mixed. Adoniram Judson, borne aloft by Baptist prayers, has illuminated that denomination, but overflowed until he has become a common heritage of all churches. God's blessing upon the work of the Methodist church in India has been the divine way of inspiring all hearts in the church universal. The miracles of missions have lost their tags and are delivered indiscriminately to all who pray and labor for a lost world. [*Applause.*] The command is common to all. The awful responsibility of an unconverted world rests upon all alike. The terrible issues of life and death to the human race stare us all in the face. A common faith in a common Christ moves a common church, while over the battlements of heaven come pouring down common blessings upon all hearts consecrated under the cross and the commission. Are you surprised that I cannot keep this literature clear along denominational lines? It is the fault of the denominations! The Presbyterians don't pray any more, "Give Japan to Presbyterianism,"—the Methodists do not pray that India "may be converted to Methodism," nor does the church of England pray for the dark continent to be "won to ritualism;" but all cry, Lord Jesus, conquer for thyself; and they all receive a common answer and the coming of the kingdom draweth nigh. [*Applause.*]

Bending the knees snaps sectarian cords. Do not misunderstand me. While we never pray as denominations, I thank God that we fight in denominational columns but under one banner, against common foes. In this respect the war bulletins are from denominational fields, sent to denominational headquarters. Is it possible that any one here permits our Christian brothers and sisters to go to the front of battle while that one at home does not watch with eagle eye the reports that come back from the field. How can you get these reports? At your denominational headquarters! Is there anything under the sun that you want to know about missions? Write to your missionary secretary; but be interested enough in the subject to pay a dollar or so for your denominational missionary magazine, and as half of the Endeavor Society is composed of ladies, remember also the splendid magazine issued by our women's board of missions. You owe those subscriptions to your conscience; you owe them to your church; you owe them to your denomination; you owe them to a lost world; you owe them to your God.

The leaflet.—All missionary boards publish leaflets in large quantities. They are like rifle balls on the field of battle midst the heavy artillery. Like rifle balls, they are wasted in large quantities. They are good to drop into a Bible or into a volume. Put them where they will stick. The vast majority of leaflets are lost almost as soon as issued, because not discriminately selected and judiciously distributed. There are cracks and crevices where they can be used as entering wedges, but the aim should be to invest your money in a cloth covered book that is almost imperishable.

The booklet.—Some splendid booklets are being issued in England and America. Notably a series of missionary outlines published by Snow & Company, of London, and another by the Rev. J. T. Gracey, D.D., of Rochester and Buffalo. These booklets are short, terse, sensible outlines of the work in various mission fields, with clear-cut descriptions of the people and their history. They are compound extracts of luscious missionary fruitage.

The denominational missionary magazine.—We do not claim that it is always ideal, but that it is entitled to your subscription there can be no doubt. The limited subscription to many of our missionary publications is a glaring indictment against the missionary interest in the church at large. You must overlook the fact that sometimes the editor forgets that young folks are to try and read this magazine. You must also overlook the use of technical terms that no one knows the interpretation of except himself, and a few other enthusiasts with the missionary writer over the sea. Should the articles lack snap and vigor, remember that you are starving the subscription list, thereby curtailing to the advertising editor the circulation, and probably keeping the missionary writer on short pay by lack of financial support in gifts to your denominational board. In all charity overlook the fact that some missionary magazine may be overloaded with unimportant geographical descriptions or details of method of travel and an unimportant and irrelevant generalization on the part of some one who seems forgetful of the vital elements and fierce issues in this conflict for a world's redemption. The Endeavor Society should give this year half a million new subscribers to the denominational missionary magazines. The effect on the quality of this journalism would be as magical as upon the tremendous sentiment it would create. I wish I might ask how many Endeavorers do not take into their homes their own denominational missionary publication.

The general denominational religious press.—You will find in some of our denominational papers a missionary department. In others "a hit and miss" firing along these lines. Missionary flash lights run out at odd times, though these same papers protest against uneven financial support to the work of the church, and would also cry out against unsteady work on the part of the church missionary—when they flash out, oh, how they do flash! but when they don't, how dark it seems. Use their flashes! So many boats are making for "that other shore." The channel is so dark and man's star of hope is eclipsed by sin. The storm is at its height! Oh, Mr. Editor, hang out all the lights! Lend us room at your masthead for the full-orbed Gospel search-light, and keep it there until the full light of the golden day is ushered in and the Lamb becomes the light thereof. To think of a great paper with enormous circulation among the young people of one of our denominations not only crowding out from its columns interdenominational fellowship, but also international redemption.

Throw up the light of temperance and missions, brother Christian Editors, that the life crews in thy wake may steer according to the divine rules of navigation. A Christian nation asserting the right to eminent domain upon a coast line assumes the moral responsibility of a life-saving service for the mariners of other nations as certainly as for the welfare of its own subjects on the shore. Up with the lights! for the sake of your denomination and its glorious missionary enterprises, and for the sake of the young workers in the church. [*Applause.*]

Missionary committees. — Now let us catch up the strings:

1. See to it that your Sunday-school library has a well-assorted line of carefully selected missionary books intensely interesting in character.

2. Make a separate list of these books and hang it on the walls of your Sunday-school rooms, with a notice that "the following interesting missionary books are to be found in the Sunday-school library."

3. On the cards announcing the missionary meeting put on a reference note calling attention to the library books that relate to the subjects chosen for the missionary meetings.

4. It is immensely important that you secure a subscription for your denominational missionary magazine in every home. Your missionary meeting lasts one hour, but that magazine, by its very presence, testifies for missions 365 days in the year. It is a grand work to get a new subscriber to the mission magazine of your church.

5. Occasionally withdraw a copy of an interesting missionary book from the library and offer to lend it to some one whom you desire to interest.

6. All the denominational boards issue leaflets on all phases of missionary

work. These are handy little baits, use them to drop into Bibles and other places where they will stay.

7. It is a conceded fact that every worker must have the Missionary Review, the London Conference Report, and the Encyclopedia of Missions. Why not make your pastor a present of them?

"As thou hast sent me into the world, even so have I sent them into the world." To the hungry of the desert, the dews of the night, the storms of the lake, the refuge of the mountains, the rock-strewn road, the persecutions of men, the blood sweat of Gethsemane, the cross-crowned Calvary, Easter morn, and a world redeemed! He that taketh not up his cross and followeth not after me cannot be my disciple.

His book was the Scriptures, his illustrations were a life, his magazine was the hearts of the people on which he stamped the impress of his divine calling. His joy is sitting upon the throne, while before him they come, a multitude which no man can number, out of all nations and kindreds and people and tongues; cry with a loud voice and saying: "Blessings and glory and wisdom and thanksgiving and honor and power and might be unto our God forever and forever, Amen." [*Loud applause.*]

One verse of "Onward, Christian Soldiers" was then sung, after which Dr. Clark introduced Miss Ella B. McLaurin, another Chicago Endeavorer, who was received with loud applause. Miss McLaurin spoke in a clear and evenly sustained voice as follows : —

Missionary Meetings : How Conducted.

Address of Miss Ella B. McLaurin.

A missionary meeting is the place where you introduce Joseph to his brethren, and the 500,000,000 down-trodden, helpless, hopeless, prayerless women of heathen lands to their more favored sisters. These missionary meetings are the reservoirs from which our boards must draw in order to water the heathen world. At these meetings we become acquainted with those of our brothers and sisters who have not counted their lives dear that they might extend the boundaries of the Saviour's kingdom, whose blood has consecrated the soil of every land, and whose names are written in letters of light in the blue heavens of every Christian denomination. Here we learn to love those who first scaled the almost inaccessible fastness of paganism and toiled on in the midst of discouragements and untold suffering until today that gigantic and hoary superstition is tottering to its fall. And here we come in deeper sympathy with those who through self denial and heroic purpose and sacrifice have sought to do His will and have carried His Gospel to the nations that sat in darkness. Familiarity with these noble men and royal women will make us inheritors of their sublime faith and devotion. The contemplation of what God has wrought through them will kindle in our hearts a glowing gratitude, and a larger desire for the redemption of a lost race. The thought of what remains to be done will increase our dependence on the Divine Spirit. And it is here we learn the nature of their work, that it has to do, not with the relief of physical need and suffering alone, not with the diffusion of knowledge, not with the material progress of society, but rather with the peace, enlightenment, redemption of immortal souls and their restoration to the image of God,— that their work is more than charity, and more than philanthropy and more than education; it is salvation, the very impartation of a new nature and a new and eternal life, the Christ life incarnate in the human soul. [*Applause.*]

We esteem it a privilege to follow Christ anywhere he leads, cheered and encouraged with his gracious assurance, "Lo, I am with you alway." We know he has been and will be with all who are obedient to his gracious command. Soon, dear Endeavorers, we shall be far apart, never to meet again, but he will be with you, and he will be with me,—with us in the days of joy and with us in the days of sorrow, with us in the days of discouragement and with us in days of rejoicing and gratitude. Oh, dear missionary committee, especially will he be with you; and under the touch of his Almighty Spirit plans and methods shall spring forth, whose lapping waves of missionary revival and spiritual consecration shall not fail to reach every nook and corner of the heathen world. And you, my sister, who are soon to bid farewell to friends and native land, and under tropical suns go from hut to hut with a message of salvation, travel in village and jungle, when you cross some threshold of sin and vice and want, suffering and pain, try and see His sweet and kindly face as he steps across with you. And you, my brothers, when you stand to preach in a strange language so far from the home you love, so far from those loved ones you would so like to see, just think that He who sent you is with you all the days. And it is in these meetings we are brought face to face with the fact that at this instant two-thirds of the human family are yet in absolute ignorance of both the Bible and Christ, and that 2,000,000 of souls for whom Christ shed his blood have each month gone into a dark and dread eternity without ever having heard of Him whom we profess to love. Oh, it is here we are brought face to face with the responsibility of proving either that God has called us to stay at home, or of giving ourselves, our all, in glad surrender to God for this work.

Then where can we find a service so important, so helpful, so uplifting, so divine as in this missionary meeting. The preparation of the program should be most thorough and complete. Let the leader of the meeting with another member of the committee arrange and be responsible for the program. Have a new committee for each meeting. These two may call in every member of the society to aid in its execution. I do believe in giving every member something to do. [*Applause.*] Suppose you have twelve or more three-minute guns. This will ensure increased activity, and this is the secret in all the sucess in any undertaking, for responsibility awakens interest. Bishop Hall once said, "I have known a man to come to a funeral in high spirits because he had the management of it." [*Laughter.*] Besides the diversity of gifts and variety of exercises at the missionary meeting, the new treatment of familiar subjects, the old facts in new dress, cannot fail to give a vigor and life to the meeting.

The Scripture lesson or Bible reading should be short and right to the point. The prayer should nor be long, sentence prayers are more desirable. For though I believe in the efficacy of prayer, yet I think that to be of the greatest value here, it should be found with Christ in the closet or with Jacob under the stars. [*Applause.*] We do not make enough of the God-given gift of song. We need the inspiration that comes from God's battle songs. The soldiers of Gustavus Adolphus were accustomed to kneel in the midst of an engagement and singing Luther's hymn, "A mighty Fortress is our God," then charge the enemy and win the victory. We workers are in the midst of a conflict, we need brave hearts, therefore let us sing those hymns which will so strengthen our faith as to lift visibly above us the sign through which we are to conquer. For example:

> " Crowns and thrones may perish,
>   Kingdoms rise and wane,
> But the Church of Jesus
>   Constant shall remain.
> Gates of hell can never
>   'Gainst that Church prevail,—
> We have Christ's own promise,
>   And that cannot fail."

To give definiteness and reality for our study a map must be used. Everytime the lesson is about China, there should be a map of that country on the wall where every person can see it. Make your own maps if you cannot buy them.

Get from a newspaper office some blank sheets, if you want a large map, and place several sheets together; then get some one to draw the map. In this way you can have a full set of home-made maps of all the mission fields at very little cost.

Let two members of the society issue invitations with a copy of the program to every member of the congregation the week previous to the meeting.

Two others should have charge of the music after the leader has selected what is to be sung. Never sing more that two verses at one time and please do away with all preludes and interludes, and postludes, and worship God in song, singing and making melody in your hearts unto the Lord. [*Applause.*]

Ushers.—Appoint two others to act as ushers. They can see that the room is well ventilated and everything tastefully arranged. I have attended two missionary meetings when I have been compelled to hunt the church over to find the room, which was in some out-of-the way place that reminded one of being more fitted for a resting-place for bats than a meeting of the children of light. I do believe the physical discomfort and mental depression that follow on our sitting on an uncomfortable, distasteful room is one reason why our meetings are shunned. Therefore arrange your room as you would your home when you are expecting to entertain most honorable guests, for have you not from your closet sent an invitation to the King of Glory, and do you not hold in your hand His most gracious answer? "Surely I will be with you."

Endeavor to have each one take a pocketbook interest in the treasury. Let your giving be systematically regular, and as the Lord has prospered you. Let this be an act of worship. Let each one place his gift in an envelope, and drop it in the basket as it is passed by the ushers. Some one has said, "We are not sending dollars and cents, but we are sending human hearts thrilled through and through with love for Jesus, and human hands and brains consecrated to his service," and that means love. The most interesting feature of the missionary meeting is the question-box, which arouses deep thoughts and earnest search on the part of those who proffer and those who answer these questions.

Obtain, if possible, photos of your missionaries, and also let one of your number write to some one missionary each month, asking about the field, its needs, and how you can assist. Strive to have each member take special interest in your workers abroad. Be sure and have hanging near your desk a "missionary calendar of prayer," and spend a short time at each meeting in prayer for the workers in the field. See that every person who takes part is heard. The conduct of the meeting must be carefully attended to. Let the program be carried out, giving to each one the allotted time, and no more. Always close your program with some practical application.

But I hear some one say "This means work." It does. When divided among so many, however, it will cost very little work. Besides, when the heavenly vision shines upon you and the heavenly voice thrills your soul, you will have received your reward. When Garibaldi appealed for troops to set Italy free, the young men asked, "What shall be our reward?" Garibaldi replied, "Privation, wounds, scars, and liberty for Italy." We workers in this warfare for the evangelization of a lost world must meet with wounds and privations, work and sacrifice; but at length, under the great leadership of our Captain, ours too shall be the glorious victory, for "the knowledge of the Lord shall cover the earth as the waters cover the sea."

Miss McLaurin's address was a remarkably effective one, and the audience tendered her a genuine ovation at the close. The Illinois delegation stood up and sang, amid the applause of the audience, their state Christian Endeavor song, in token of their appreciation of the eloquent efforts of their state representatives.

Some announcements were then made by Mr. Baer, in the course of which he referred to the courtesy and attention received from the press at this convention as exceeding anything hitherto in the history of the Christian Endeavor conventions.

DR. CLARK : I told you I had one or two surprises for you this morning. This is our missionary morning — home missionary as well as foreign missionary. There is one with us at this time unexpectedly to me, who has done more than any man that I know of to solve the home missionary problem,— the Hon. T. J. Morgan, former United States Indian Commissioner, whom I wish to introduce to you.

Mr. Morgan was given a genuine Christian Endeavor welcome, as he came forward to address the audience. He spoke very briefly as follows : —

Remarks of Hon. T. J. Morgan.

Fellow Endeavorers : — I have no speech to make, but I have a word of most hearty congratulation. I congratulate you upon the history of your organization, that within twelve years has spread from a single church in Maine until it encircles the globe. I congratulate you upon your membership, that within that time has increased from a handful in a pastor's study, until to-day it numbers an active army of a million and a half, with many times that of interested observers and co-workers. I congratulate you on your enthusiam, and on your zeal in the cause that binds you together. What the sunlight is to vegetation that makes the earth to bring fourth its harvests, enthusiasm is to great characters and magnificent achievements in human history. I congratulate you on your spirit, characterized by a love for truth, enthusiasm for humanity, obedience to Christ, love for the Bible, pity for the erring, and charity for all. [*Applause.*] I congratulate you on the success of this convention. You will carry from this beautiful city on the borders of this magnificent river, the pleasantest memories of great gatherings rich in Christian experiences, sweet communions with each other, and you will long remember the striking and cordial welcome that His Honor the Mayor has offered you, the assistance of the press and the unstinted courtesy and hospitality of the citizens of Montreal. May I express for you the wish that the past twelve years, so rich already in achievement, may be but the prologue of that far greater history that is unrolling for you in the future, and that your Christian Endeavor Society may be for many decades of years crowned with Christian success. [*Loud applause.*]

The familiar missionary hymn, " From Greenland's Icy Mountains," was then sung.

DR. CLARK : We have all read in the papers that it was very difficult for Chinamen to get to this country in these days,— that they had to pay a large tax, and even then it is difficult for them to get in. But we have with us this morning a Chinaman — a gentleman from China, at least — who has come without paying any tax, I believe. I am very glad to introduce to you now the Rev. Gilbert Reid, of China.

Mr. Reid came forward, dressed in full Chinese costume, including queue, wooden shoes, and all, and was warmly greeted by the audience. His part in the program was to conduct an open parliament on the subject, "What Is Your Society Doing for Missions ? " He proceeded at once to his work.

What Is Your Society Doing for Missions ?

Open Meeting. Conducted by Rev. Gilbert Reid.

MR. REID: When I met Dr. Clark in Shanghai, he saw me in my fur garments, and he requested that I should wear them at this time [*laughter*]; but knowing that we would have a warm reception in Montreal, I decided to leave my fur garments at home. [*Applause.*] Assimilation is the best way to settle the Chinese question.

John Chinaman gives, through me, his salutations to John Bull [*laughter*], and the Chinese dragon opens its mouth as it watches the British lion and the American eagle. [*Applause.*] The whole Orient sends its cry to the whole Occident; heathendom cries out to Christendom. And now, Christian Endeavorers, what is your response to the call of God that comes to us from around the globe? What are your societies doing for missions? We have but twenty minutes for answers. Let each one respond quickly, in not more than two or three sentences.

Responses came very promptly from the audience, and at times there were ten or a dozen delegates trying to get the attention of the leader. Following are some of the statements made : —

" We are educating an Indian in Pierre' University, South Dakota. He will soon go and preach among his countrymen."

" We have a missionary library of 200 volumes, give two cents a week per member to foreign missions, and have six young people ready for mission work in Africa." [*Applause.*]

" Our society is supporting a missionary in Japan."

" Our society last year sent four of its members to the foreign field, raised $500, and supported three native helpers. On the home field we have three men laboring in a gospel carriage, going from town to town preaching the unsearchable riches of Christ." [*Applause.*]

" Our society supports three children in a missionary field near Smyrna."

" Our society supports a missionary in China."

" We support a native preacher in India."

MR. REID: How much do you give?

DELEGATE: $60 a year.

MR. REID: Well, make it 600. [*Applause.*]

" Another society supports a lady missionary in China."

" Another contributes $500 toward the Fresh Air fund."

" A society composed of two young men and twenty-four young ladies of about the age of seventeen support a native worker in India. Money all raised by freewill offerings."

" Another increased its missionary funds three times what they were before by setting aside a tenth part of their income to that purpose."

" Illinois has a Christian Endeavor missionary interest that is running a Christian Endeavor missionary extension course throughout the state. We hope to carry it through all the states and Canada."

" Another society has four student volunteers and supports two students in mission fields."

" An Indianapolis society helps to defray the expenses of a missionary to the Sioux Indians in Nebraska."

" A Nebraska society sends a good many of its workers every Sunday and during the week to hold evangelistic services on the Indian reservation."

" A society is supporting a missionary in China, the Sunday school support a home missionary in New Mexico, and the mission band support a Bible reader in China."

" We support a student in Bulgaria and a Bohemian missionary in America."
" Our church has three student volunteers; it supports two city missionaries, and I am the first to go to Africa." [*Applause.*]
" Another gives $50 a year to a Southern institution educating colored people."
" Our society support a colored boy and girl, also a boy in China, also helped to erect a missionary church."
" Another society gives $100 a year for a native preacher in Japan."
" A society in Ohio has sent out two missionaries in the last two years, and has two scholarships in the college at Shanghai."
" A lady reports that eleven of their members have gone into the foreign mission field. [*Applause.*] They support three in the foreign fields, and two in the Dominion."
" Another gives $150 toward the support of a missionary in Japan and another in China."

MR. REID: There are many others who wish to respond to this question, but I want to say a word in conclusion. All those who are members of societies that are doing anything for missions, please rise. [*Nearly the entire congregation rose.*] That is the way I thought it would be. Everybody has been doing something. I have heard about your two-cents-a-week plan that was proposed by my brother Fulton in China. Well, I don't think two cents a week will hurt anybody, although it well help to send the Gospel to the heathen. In China I give two cents every hour, out of my own salary, to help the cause of missions, and I think some of the good friends here can give a great deal more than two cents a week. Select your own plan, but don't rest content with two cents a week. [*Applause.*] I have one other thought : remember the great motive of the missionary cause. Whatever you do, link it with the idea born in the bosom of God of world-wide evangelization, and don't separate your methods and your endeavors from that grand purpose. Remember also to pray for the missionaries. Know who they are and pray from the heart, and God will hear your prayer when you raise the money and when you do something for the work. [*Applause*]. May we all hear God's command and give ourselves. [*Loud applause.*]

SECRETARY BAER: In this connection let me say that I have received statements from the different treasurers of the denominational missionary boards which are of great interest. Let me refer to a few. The treasurer of the Presbyterian foreign board says that the gifts of Christian Endeavor societies to their work the past year were $16,446, and to the Woman's Board, over $3,500. The American Missionary Association have received a total of $3,400. The Congregational Church Building Society received $2,100; the American Board, $13,579; the A. H. M. S., $3,300; the Presbyterian Woman's Board and Home Mission, $5,600; the Christian (disciples) $3,400; Foreign, $2,100; Lutheran, foreign, $2,100, and many others. [*Applause*].

Dr. Clark asked all in the audience who had not been able to make their statement, on account of the necessity of closing the open meeting, if they had anything fresh or helpful in the way of missionary methods, to write the same on a slip of paper and hand it in at the platform. The audience then joined heartily in singing " The Morning Light is Breaking."

DR. CLARK: After all, we must have the " sinews of war." We want more than two cents a week; that is only the beginning; we are going on to something larger and better. How to get these larger missionary contributions will be told us by my successor in the pastorate of the Phillips church, Boston, Rev. W. H. G. Temple. [*Applause*].

Missionary Money: How To Raise It.

Address of Rev. W. H. G. Temple.

Mr. President and Christian Endeavorers:—You ask me how to raise money for the Lord's work; I answer in two words, GIVE IT! [*Applause.*]

My address this morning shall be an amplification of that advice. When God gets ready to sell salvation, it will be time for him to purchase man's aid for the great purposes of his love. If I read my Bible aright, the All-Father has been sitting upon the circle of the universe from all eternity and doing nothing but give, *give*, GIVE. And if I have read the history of the race aright, man, ever since he had a being, has been doing little else than get, *get*, GET. God has put to shame every well-to-do and niggardly giver, the world over, by his magnificent benevolence, for he began his existence with nothing. That only goes to show that the disposition to give produces the power to give, until zero becomes infinity.

First, he gave matter in chaos; then he gave order in creation; then he gave the lord of creation,—a lifeless piece of clay. Then he simply breathed upon this supreme sovereign of earth, and man became a living, regal soul,—God's grandest production. Then God gave himself in his Spirit, and, more wonderfully still, himself in his Son as a sacrifice for sin, the soul of which was selfishness, because man would be always getting and never giving. Here, then, is the gospel in one sentence: God gave himself in his infinity to man, that man might give himself in his entirety to God. Hence, when a man says to me, "How can I do this work for God?" I answer: "Give yourself to him. You do not have to do the work. He will do it through you." When a church asks, "How shall we raise money for the extension of the Lord's Kingdom?" I answer: "Raise it in the Lord's way. Give it by giving yourself, body and soul, time and talents, person and pocketbook." [*Applause.*]

I have reduced the gospel to a single sentence. Let me further contract it to a single word, a word so infinite that it is larger than any sentence, any volume, any literature,—LOVE! Its four letters are four eternities. Hear the sublime declaration: God so loved that he gave! Love is that attribute of both God and man which bankrupts itself in giving. He who loves must give, and he who gives must love, else his benevolence becomes malevolence. Thus love manifests itself in *generosity*. If it does not do this, it forfeits its right to its name. This is but its primary work. Failing here, it will never be prepared for its real mission; for it must yet bleed in sacrifice and die in atonement. You cannot be generous with your love without being loving in your generosity.

Now I do not call that man generous who has to be tantalized into a contribution for a worthy cause. We have too much of that sort already. When you put a subscription-paper under a man's eyes, and ask him to give liberally, and he puts down two hundred dollars because his rival in business has previously put down one hundred and fifty, when without that knowledge he would have subscribed only twenty-five, I do not call that act generosity. I do not think you do. You may not have a name for it. I call it a business advertisement. It means one and only one thing, and that is trade. I do not think the Church of God has waked up to a thorough understanding of what true generosity is. I hereby advocate presenting every incoming member of the churches of all denominations, not only a manual of his particular church, with a statement of its distinctive doctrinal belief and the formula of its peculiar covenant, but also an authoritative pocket-dictionary, of the latest edition, with a red line underscoring the word GENEROSITY! I open mine, and although it is not of recent date, and the name of its compiler may be known to but few of you, I find there a definition that will defy improvement,—*A disposition to give liberally.*

For my part, I cannot understand why people want to join churches at all when they intend to deafen their ears, and plaster their mouths, and padlock their pockets.

" He that hath an ear, let him hear what the Spirit saith unto the churches."
" Whosoever therefore shall confess me before men, him will I confess also."
" Freely ye have received; freely give."
These ringing sentences are from God's Word. They read much as they
did when the Spirit put them in the first sacred documents, barring the translation. They mean exactly what they did when the hand of apostle or evangelist
first wrote them with quivering emotion. Thank God, the crying need of the
world's — not of the parish's, nor of the nation's, but of the world's — evangelization is finding its way, not only to the drum of men's ears, but into the deepest
recesses of men's souls. The Christian Endeavor Society is breaking in all
directions the cement that has glued together Christian lips. And now it
considers that it is intrusted with another mission, — that of smashing the
padlocks that have heretofore fastened youthful pockets. A disposition to
give; that is the meaning of the word "generosity," — a disposition so
strong that it will not be crossed in its purpose; a disposition so faithful that
it will not lose a single opportunity; a disposition so aggressive that it will go
and hunt up cases upon which it may lavish its munificence. And I mean
by munificence, not large benefactions necessarily. I mean, if need be, only
five cents, yes, even two mites, which make a farthing, if they bear a large
proportion to all the donor has.

Do you suppose, if the Church of God were in right condition, it would be
necessary to tickle the palates of the saints with savory suppers, and to go to
the very verge of propriety in getting up entertainments, and to aid and abet
the speculative spirit of the age by introducing the Louisiana lottery into church
fairs, themselves unnecessary, only giving it a different name, so as to avoid the
disgrace, in order to induce the people to support the Gospel? [*Applause*].
These things would be as universally let alone as many of the contrivances
often adopted by desperate pastors to secure and hold an evening audience.
I have no objection to church suppers. I rather like them. I like them of
high quality and moderate frequency. I have no objection to church entertainments. At the proper time, of the proper type, and in the proper place,
they improve our social and artistic, as well as our æsthetic faculties, and give
our young, and some of our older people, a taste for something more elevated
than the average amusement the world offers. They must be worth going to
see, however, else the world will laugh in its sleeve, and the church will suffer
by comparison.

I have no objection to church fairs properly conducted, because I think they
bring into requisition talents which ought to be utilized, and which might
otherwise run to waste, and bring together various classes of workers in
harmony for the promotion of some worthy cause dear to them all. I want
them conducted on proper business principles, and not scandalize the whole
Christian community by their manifest unfairness and chicanery. But, while
I admit all this, I do affirm that when a church-member says, in effect, " I
will not give liberally of my substance for philanthropic and missionary purposes unless I can see dollar for dollar in some sort of return," he had better
go to his dictionary and find out anew the meaning of the word "generosity."
If he says in effect, " Here are one hundred dollars; but I want a pew for my
money, and a pew fully up to the price, too; in fact, I would like a hundred-and-
fifty-dollar pew for that sum if I could get it; here is a ten-dollar bill, but I
want a worked afghan, or an embroidered sofa-pillow, or a lace what-you-may-
call-it for my contribution [*laughter*]; here is a quarter, but I want a fifty-cent
supper or a dollar entertainment before I will let it pass through my fingers,"
well, that man needs to be re-educated in the significance of the word we are
discussing. That is buying, not giving. That is barter, not benevolence.
[*Applause.*]

When all our churches get their pocket-dictionaries in such general circulation that this and other test-words of our glorious Christianity shall be illuminated and interpreted according to the spirit of love that brings out of everything
the very best that is in it, there will be a financial revolution that will astonish
the most optimistic prophet. In that day the churches will all be free, and pew-

rents will be looked back upon as curious reminders of a barbaric age. The subscription-paper will be framed and carefully preserved in some museum of antiquities. The supper or entertainment, for other than mere social or artistic purposes, will be an imputation of parsimony scrupulously avoided. Men will give from love. Men will love to give.

To send the gospel to the heathen abroad or to the somewhat more civilized, but less hopeful, heathen at home, it will not be necessary to appeal to the mercenary tendencies or the slumbering appetites of phlegmatic disciples. The church will see her duty and perform it, her privilege and live up to it, by giving according to her ability, and doing it promptly and cheerfully.

No one will ever know who gives the most, and none will be so poor but they will feel able to give something. And the traveller in that golden time will go from church to church, and from Christian to Christian; and wherever he shall find the outward expression of Christianity, he shall find it synonymous with that other word "generosity." This can only be when God's love shall so fill men's hearts that it shall overflow at their pockets.

I believe most emphatically in *individual giving.* Let every unit in the society and church be represented. A father can no more do the giving for the family than he can do the praying for the family. Every soul must be saved by its own faith, be nurtured through its own prayers, and be blessed through its own giving. I know it is the custom for heads of households both to pay the family bills and to manage the family benevolences. "I don't want the plate passed beyond me," said a bumptious parent to an aggressive deacon who persisted in going the whole length of the pew, though he collected all the money from the first member and mostly negative nods and ironical stares from the remainder of the family. "I don't want the plate passed beyond me; I want you to understand, sir, that I have charge of the finances of this pew." [*Laughter.*] He was a foolish father. He had better have taught his children to manage for themselves by allowing them stated sums, at first small amounts, and as they showed aptness, larger amounts, with enlarged responsibility, until they could pay all their own bills and accumulate their own savings. It would be a far wiser policy to let each member of the family do his own giving.

Take a common case. Here sit in the pew father, mother and three children. There is to be taken up a collection for missions. The father concludes to give ten dollars to the cause presented. That is to represent the family benevolence. Suppose we divide it among them. Father and mother give seven dollars. We will not make an individual apportionment in this case, for I have long ago learned that a prudent person will be above meddling in a family between man and wife. Call it seven dollars for the two. That leaves one dollar apiece for the children. Now I say it would be better far for that parent to give each of his children a weekly stipend for his own exclusive use, and teach them to give out of that income for missionary and benevolent purposes, than to give for them a much larger sum than they would give themselves. It would be better for these three children named to give twenty-five cents apiece toward the missionary contribution than for their father to give for them each a dollar! The cause would lose seventy-five cents apiece on that Sunday; but in after years there would grow up three trained givers instead of three successful sponges, that always absorb, but never give until they are squeezed, and think that all they get out of the old folks is so much clear gain. [*Applause.*] I give my children weekly allowances for spending-money. They give ten per cent to benevolence, and, though the system has been in vogue but four years, two of them have one hundred dollars each drawing interest. Let everybody give. [*Applause.*]

I believe also in giving *to individuals.* Somebody has said that consecration in general is a good thing, but consecration in particular is much better; that is, of specific talents, time and means. So I think giving to particular causes, localities, individuals, is better than broadcast benevolence. I would not advocate either one of these methods exclusively. I would combine them. It is well for every society or church to be specially interested in a single mission, while giving more or less to all. It is a splendid idea to support a special missionary, and thus link money and manhood together. The cause then takes on a personality. The letters and prayers that pass to and fro make the mission station, though it be in Turkey or Africa, an outpost of the parish. If your society supports one or more missions in either the foreign or the home field, you will be more likely to gather information, to intensify interest, and to increase contributions for the whole work.

This individual giving I have mentioned is an ideal. There has got to be a very much larger appropriation of divine grace before it becomes a fact. In the meantime, a great deal of *vicarious giving* must be done. It is a simple sum in arithmetic to take the amount requisite to carry on the Lord's work at home and abroad in an efficient manner, and divide it among professing Christians, assigning to each his proportion; but it is a much more difficult task to collect it after you have assigned the amount.

Many are unable to pay their part. Some are unwilling. Somebody else must contribute their proportion, or it will be lost to the cause. Hence, as long as there is sin in the world, there must be vicarious giving as well as vicarious suffering. It is a divine law, and finds its highest illustration in the atonement. All life was under condemnation. All life must be redeemed. But no life was able to help. The life to be given in ransom must therefore have been an infinite life. Tell me Christ was but a man? Then abandon altogether the thought of redemption. He who could give his life to redeem a world must have had dwelling in him all the fulness of the godhead bodily. [*Applause.*] He gave what sinful flesh could not give. The cross always means to me substitution. Now the evangelization for which the cross stands is committed to the church. Give vicariously. Give not only your proportion, though it be your proportion according to your circumstances. Give more still, that they who cannot give, or will not give, may not retard the coming of the kingdom of God to all the earth.

Finally there is such a thing as the grace of giving. It ought to be put in the list as the tenth fruit of the Spirit. I have very little hope of the permanence of youthful piety until I see marked evidences of this estimable virtue. But like all other Christian virtues, it must be *enthusiastically* entered into and enjoyed to produce the best results. Prayer thus emphasized becomes communion. Service thus rendered becomes holy zeal. Giving in this spirit doubly blesses. It leaves its benediction alike upon both donor and receiver. It droppeth it like the gentle dew from heaven, blessing both him who gives and him who takes.

This is the way God intended his kingdom to be built upon the earth. When the church has fully learned this divine principle, and has put it faithfully into operation, depend upon it, there will not be room enough to contain the divine blessing that shall be hers. Give, then, generously, individually, vicariously, enthusiastically. Mark the initials of these, g-i-v-e! I close, then, as I began. How shall we raise money for the Lord's work? GIVE IT! [*Prolonged applause.*]

At the conclusion of Mr. Temple's able and stirring address, the favorite hymn " Speed Away " was sung with impressive effect.

DR. CLARK.—There are two people whom I want to introduce to you. They will not speak at this time, but I want you to see their faces. One of them is a friend from China,— did you ever see him before? [*Laughter and applause as Rev. Gilbert Reid came forward dressed in ordinary American clothes.*] The other is Rev. J. H. Krikorian, of Turkey, more largely than any other man the leader and promoter of Christian Endeavor in the land of the Sultan. Christian Endeavor is persecuted and almost wiped out there, but our brother has done noble work for the young people of that land whom he loves, and for this organization. Will you not rise and give him the Chautauqua salute? [*The audience responded heartily.*] Now for the last address of the morning. We have heard of the direct influence of missions. The reflex influence is quite as important a factor, and this subject will be treated, I am glad to say, by the Rev. J. T. McCrory, D. D., of Pittsburg, Pa. [*Applause.*]

The Reflex Influence of Missionary Effort.

Address of Rev. J. T. McCrory, D.D.

1. Character is the final outcome of Christianity in the case of every individual believer. To grow into the image of the Son of God — to attain to the "measure of the stature of the fulness of Christ," is the thrilling hope, and the solemn behoof of every one born into the kingdom. This glorious attainment, however, is not made without effort. Jesus Christ is worthy to be crowned the head of a new creation, because of his perfect human character. But His perfection of character is the highest outcome of active love-benevolence. That benevolence was put forth in a missionary life. Jesus was the first great missionary. Every element that enters into true missionary enterprise was found in the life of the Nazarene. He was sent. He left his Father; came out of the bosom of eternal love; left behind him the companionship of the angels; descended to the lost and godless world; stooped to the lowest condition of humiliation and sacrificed life itself in his mission to lost men. To grow into his image we must follow in his footsteps. We must be moved by the same spirit and perform the same kind of ministry. The first reflex result of missionary effort, therefore, that I mention is the development of Christly character. Missions are not only the divinely appointed means for the evangelization of the world, but also, for the sanctification of the church.

After conversion, progress in the Christian life depends decidedly on doing. Effort on behalf of the souls of others is essential to spiritual development. The more fully these efforts are inspired by the spirit that brought Jesus down to the world for the salvation of -his enemies, the more they will tend to the development of Christly character. Nothing short of world-wide missions will give full scope to the exercise of that spirit. And this influence is felt by those even but little interested in the mission work of the church. Millions of Christians, who, personally, have slight interest in missionary enterprises, are indedted to this glorious movement for the progress they are making in spiritual attainments, while those whose hearts are in the working are developing an all-round Christian character which, without effort, would not be possible.

2. Another important effect of the reflex influence of missionary effort is the confirmation of the faith of believers in the Bible as the Word of God, and the all-sufficient instrument in the hand of the Spirit for the regeneration of the world. The critics of the century have weakened the confidence of not a few true Christians in the Scriptures, so that they assert with stammering tongue if at all, Paul's great challenge, " For I am not ashamed of the Gospel of Christ' for it is the power of God unto salvation to every one that believeth." But thank God, the era of hurtful criticism has, also, been the era of the most glorious triumphs of missions by means of the simple proclamation of the Word of God. As the word from the lips of Jesus cast out the legion from the Gaderene and restored him to reason and to society, so the simple message of Christ and Him crucified has lifted whole tribes and races from the depths of degradation and barbarism into Christian civilization. The Sandwich Islands is our sufficient answer to those who assert that the Bible is not inspired nor its message divine. And we have ten thousand just such arguments as the result of missions. Without the reflex influence exerted on believers by these stupendous and glorious results among the heathen, unbelief, I am persuaded, would have atrophied ere this the Christian church. But this was God's way to answer the critics and establish the faith of his people. Listen! A score of men sat near a magazine of dynamite. One of them was a philosopher. The others were workmen looking for a job where the work was light and the wages heavy. The philosopher pointed out to the men the misapprehensions that had been entertained in regard to this tremendous dynamite agent. Dynamite has been called an explosive. That was all a mistake. It contained an explosive, that was all.

Much of the compound was nothing but dirt; and some of it was a very poor quality of dirt at that. Certainly it was still better than nothing, but too much must not be expected of it. This wonderful discovery had been made by means of certain marks on the cans, and some strange hierogliphics on the labels and some shrewd reading between the lines of the recipe for its manufacture. The workmen were almost persuaded that they had been wofully imposed upon by dynamite. During all this argument, however, other workmen, who were not philosophers and were willing to work for a fair wage, were busily engaged in stowing away tons of the condemned stuff in a subterranean cavity, when, all at once, just as the philosopher had reached the climax of his splendid argument that was to knock all the energy out of the dynamite, there was a frightful crash as though the heavens had fallen; the earth trembled; the ocean heaved; great masses of adamant were hurled out of the water high into the air; the mountain of granite that had obstructed the channel was seamed and riven and slivered through as though touched by the hand of Omnipotence and "hell gate" was blown to atoms. The philosopher readjusted his spectacles and went on with his argument. That philosopher was a fool.

3. One of the most cheering signs of the times is the drawing together of the people of God of various evangelistic denominations of this continent, and indeed, of the whole Christian world. [*Applause.*] This is another of the blessed results of the reflex influence of missionary effort. The reproach of the Protestant church has been its divided condition. This has been the rejoicing of our enemies. The alienations, jealousies, and cross purposes of God's people have been the glory of infidelity and the argument of Rome. We have seen it and lamented it deeply. We have sought to heal divisions. But it was never seen clearly nor felt deeply until we set about for the salvation of the world; so that the very knowledge of the need of unity is the result of missions. Then movements were set on foot for bringing the churches together in a visible union. But there are more distinct denominations today than ever before. And is the case worse than it has ever been in the past? Thank the Lord it is not. For while we have been appointing our committees and proposing impossible plans for a visible union, the great Head of the church has been consummating and cementing an invisible union; a union a thousand times better and stronger than any oneness secured as the result of compromises which would not carry with them the convictions of the most godly of the people. Precisely as the spirit of missions takes possession of the church, are believers of different divisions of the Lord's army drawn together. I appeal to this great convention. Who are the ones of any congregation or denomination who are most cordial in their relations with their fellows of the other fold? They are the ones most deeply interested in missions. Nor does this enlarging spirit of fraternal regard for other Christians weaken one's loyalty to his own denomination. The grand organization of Christian Endeavorers is both argument and illustration. Here are hundreds of thousands of men and women joined together from all denominations in the closest and realest Christly fellowship. They are not the invertebrates of their denominations. We say it, not as a boast, but as the simple fact, that these, and those joined with them, are among the most devoted in all denominations to the mission work of the church at home and abroad. And why should it not be so? As an increasing interest in missions brings one more into the likeness of the Lord, the ideal missionary, it will, inevitably, bring him nearer those who are making progress in the same direction; and thus true, earnest disciples will draw closer together until the great high priestly prayer of the "upper room" will have its answer in the union of all believers as the reflex result of missionary effort.

4. The assured and realized presence of the Lord, and the help of heaven is the first essential of efficient effort in the kingdom. Jesus meant more than a dull faith finds in the concluding promise of the great commission, "Lo, I am with you alway, even unto the end of the ages." He meant something extraordinary. He meant heavenly leadership projected down into a human organization. He meant power — omnipotent power sustaining and seconding human effort. He meant, in short, that all heaven, under the leadership of the Son of

God, would be joined to humble human agency for the evangelization of the world. Now, what we need to make us aggressive and hopeful, is to realize that help — to have it and know that we have it. Not to read it in the book, merely, but to know it. And has not the Almighty always found some way to make it real to those whom he called to do extraordinary work? Look at the Hebrews. They are ordered to go down into the Red Sea, or out into that great and terrible wilderness. They must realize the Divine presence. But with the pillar of cloud and of fire moving on before them they do not hesitate to attempt the impossible. They are commanded to cross the Jordan when it is sweeping by, a turbulent stream out over all its banks. But when the priests, bearing the ark, the symbol of the Divine presence, go forward, the people press down into the tempestuous flood, as though the waters were adamant. Joshua is about to lead his army against the impregnable fortress, Jericho. As he reconnoitres he is confronted with the captain of the lord's Host, who assures him of victory, and the marvel of the ages is wrought as the walls of a great city fall under the blasts of a few rams' horns. And how are we to realize the Lord's presence and help in our enterprises? Look at this promise, "Lo, I am with you alway." To whom is that promise made? To those whom he has ordered to go into all the world and preach the Gospel to every creature. The church, therefore, that is not missionary cannot claim that promise, nor realize the Lord's presence. But the aggressive church — the church that is obeying the Lord, and engaged in sending the Gospel to the unsaved and unevangelized masses, is not left to do its work alone. Why, you can put that commission into the form of a syllogism — you can forge a chain of irresistible logic that must bring conviction to the dullest mind. Look at it: Jesus said to the missionary church, " Lo, 1 am with you alway," which is the major promise of an argument. Our church is a missionary church — that is the minor promise. The logical conclusion is Jesus is with us. Hallelujah! [*Applause.*] And this thrilling and triumphant assurance is another of the blessed réflex results of missionary effort.

5. To do great things for God one must feel the force of those passions that stir in the higher ranges of being. Deeds of heroism get their impulse up there. The great things of the world have been wrought by men who have felt the sweep of the tides of a mighty passion, and have been carried over obstacles thereby that otherwise might have been insurmountable. But this passion is not felt by mean souls, souls absorbed with selfish considerations, or set on little and selfish enterprises. Take the greatest man, but self-centred with the circle of his operations, circumscribed by merely personal interests, and he cannot do really great things, while the average soul, if absorbed with world-wide enterprises and moved by exalted impulses, can accomplish wonders. Another reflex result of the missionary efforts of this century has been to set in motion these mighty tides of resistless passion. The humblest Christian may be moved by the sublimest aspirations. By means of mission work we have been lifted to the top of an Eiffel tower that enables us to see clear around the world, and down into the coming millennium. And oh, how the heart swells and the divine passion of love for the Lord and for the lost surge through the soul. We see the whole earth stretched out before our eyes. We see its wretchedness, and destitution, and despair. We hear the sobbing wail of a billion dying immortals crying, "Come over and help us!" But we also hear a mighty response from an innumerable company of the godly saying, "We come, in Jesus' name we come." We see these rescuers sailing over every sea; setting foot on every shore; hurrying with swift and eager stride into the heart of every continent; taking possession of every island; and bearing the saving message to myriads of anxious souls. But we see more — we see Jesus and the angel hosts, panoplied with the might and majesty of heaven, forcing back the dark and deadly powers that have so long held these millions of the heathen world in the grip of a blinding, soul-enslaving superstition. And over all this wide field we see the dawn of a brighter day — a day of peace, and prosperity, such as this poor, sin-cursed world has never known. And each one of us engaged in this mission work is a part of this mighty, this sublime and glorious, enterprise.

And now I close with a single other consideration. It is true as the poet

> " We are living, we are dwelling in a grand and awful time ;
> In an age on ages telling. To be living is sublime."

And it must not be overlooked that the type of Christian which the times demand is precisely such as a deep and intelligent interest in missions will produce. Sometimes we hear criticisms of missions from those who are profoundly concerned for the moral and social welfare of our own country, as though the attention given to that subject was just so much subtracted from our pressing and all-important home duties. This is a grave misapprehension. The maintenance of our institutions and the perfecting of our civilization depends on the reflex influence of missionary effort. It is the person intelligently interested in missions, at home and abroad, who appreciates the degradation that ungodliness produces and fosters. Who but the true missionary knows, aside from those who directly suffer, the shuddering, withering, damning curse of the liquor traffic? He is the man who will lift his hand to heaven and swear eternal enmity against the overshadowing curse. So it is with all social and moral evils. He is the man, too, who appreciates the difference between the civil and political institutions of our own and those of heathen countries, and finds the reason for the difference in the religions of the people. And he feels the need and possesses the moral fibre for maintaining these institutions. The great battle for the preservation of the civil and religious institution, known across the line as the American Sabbath, which is being contested with such heroic persistence is being fought with Christian men and women who are most interested in missions. You may count on this—the man who is not concerned to have the will of God made supreme in China will not be an enthusiastic friend of righteousness in his own land. It is the man who will send the Gospel to the Chinaman in his own country, who will defend him against the unrighteousness of "sandlot politicians" in our own country. It is the man who would strike to the heart that "monstrum horrendum" of modern civilization, the saloon, in old England, and New England, who makes sacrifices to send the Water of Life to Africa, and the New Hebrides, but execrates the shipment of "double-distilled damnation" to those helpless millions. It is the man who is giving time, and thought, and means, to have the will of God done on earth as it is done in heaven who believes in the "higher law" for his own country and hesitates not to use his influence for the suppression of anarchy of every kind, and the maintenance of liberty under the forms of law at any cost. Brethren, the great "conflict of the ages" is upon us. The enemies of King Jesus are gathering their forces for one last desperate struggle. Our Revelation; our Christian institutions; our social customs; our civil liberties; all the attainments, in short, of these eighteen Christian centuries, are to be assailed by the forces of diabolism. The only force that can successfully contest the field with these mighty foes of mankind is that consciously led by the Omnipotent Lord, and re-enforced by the angels and inspired by the assurance of glorious victory such as those only who are directly, and heartily, engaged in the mission work of the church can entertain. "And who knoweth," O missionary church, "whether thou art come to the kingdom for such a time as this." Amen and amen. [*Loud applause.*]

The session closed with the usual notices, the singing of the Doxology, and the Mizpah benediction.

THE TENT.

Rain fell previous to the opening of the meeting, making the tent rather damp. The audience, though small, was appreciative.

The prayer and praise service was conducted by the Rev. Dr. John T. Beckley, of Philadelphia, Pa., who presided throughout the session.

Dr. BECKLEY: I think one of the beautiful things about Christian Endeavorers is that they always keep sweet and good-natured, especially in conventions. [*Applause.*] In passing through the Valley of Baca they make it a well. This morning when we first met here under the drippings of the sanctuary, the outlook was rather discouraging, but instead of grumbling we began to sing, and we have sung away our disappointment. Some of us have been kept out all night by the railroad companies, without sleepers. I was on my way until the bright daylight. But, instead of grumbling we sang and we laughed, and our hearts were filled with joy.

Our general subject this morning is WORK. I remember what Thomas Carlyle said once, "Know thyself? Thou wilt never know thyself. Know thy work, and do it with all thy might." That is a good motto for Christian Endeavorers. They seek to know their work; they leave themselves with Christ, but they seek to know their work. "Lord, what wilt thou have me to do?" is their prayer, and then they do it through their power and through the power of the Holy Spirit.

I want to present this morning one who has been a noble worker in the vineyard of the Lord, Mr. H. A. Moulton, secretary of the Province, and a resident of Montreal, who will conduct the reports from the simultaneous committee conferences, held yesterday afternoon.

Reports from Committee Conferences.

MR. MOULTON: In looking over the list of committees on our program this morning, I discovered an omission. There is a committee that you call the sunshine committee, and it would be very useful this morning, no doubt; yet in the face of every Christian Endeavorer here today I see sunshine.

Now, as the chairman has so well said, our general subject this morning is work. Among the various definitions that have been given to those mystic letters, " C. E." "consecrated energy " will apply to our exercises this morning. There was a time when Christian Endeavor was severely criticised, and harped at as a useless thing. We were called a "cheeky young beggar," and all such things. But I wish to say that if there is today one of those croakers left, I wish that he could have gone with me yesterday and made the rounds of every one of these nine committee conferences. I think, Mr. Chairman, perhaps I did something that no one else here did yesterday, — I attended all of the nine conferences [*applause*], and I didn't begin until three o'clock either. And if that croaker, if he exists today, had been with me, I think he would have been convinced that Christian Endeavor means something more than having a good time, or than sitting and singing ourselves away to everlasting bliss, and that a Christian Endeavor convention means something more than a delightful excursion, and sight-seeing, and enjoying each other's company. If he could have been in those meetings, he would have seen a large number of enthusiastic, earnest Christian workers, each one anxious to learn something from another, and each one anxious to help another in this great and glorious work for Christ and the church.

So Christian Endeavor means work, work, work, all day long, — work for every one. There cannot be in a Christian Endeavor society loyalty to Jesus Christ without work being the result. Our pledge is of no effect unless it means earnest service for Jesus Christ, as well as fervent prayer and fervent singing.

Then in our Christian Endeavor societies, in connection with this committee work, we have means of using the energy and the enthusiasm and the buoyancy of the youthful members of our churches. If there is any activity in connection with church work that may not be covered by our committees, there may be some committees not yet named, not yet organized, that will cover this work; but if they are found out, it won't take our Christian Endeavor societies long to organize them, I am sure. All the work that may be accomplished by young Christians may be done through the methods of the Christian Endeavor society.

There is, therefore, I think, no need in a church of any other separate organization for the work of the young people.

Now, I am not going to take up the time. You shall hear from all these nine conferences through the chairmen who conducted them. I don't know why the name of the good-literature committee appears at the top of the list, but I think you will agree with me after you have heard the report, that it is entitled to a foremost place. We shall now hear what this committee does, and how it does it, from Mr. Geo. B. Graff of Boston, Mass.

GOOD-LITERATURE COMMITTEE.

MR. GRAFF: I am very glad to see that, although it is rather damp on the inside as well as on the outside of this tent, the rain cannot dampen the ardor or enthusiasm of Christian Endeavorers. I have but a few minutes to speak, and I shall not take any of your time by telling you of the large, interesting, and enthusiastic conference of the good-literature committee which was held yesterday, but shall go at once to the subject which will interest you most, " The Method of Introducing Good Literature."

Immoral and sensational reading matter abounds on every hand. To counteract its influence is the work of every Christian. How shall we begin?

First, with yourself. Are you reading, you yourself, wholesome literature? Are you taking your own denominational paper? You should do so. Christian Endeavor, above all things else, is for Christ and the church. Your loyalty is, first of all, to your own church. Next, you should support your own denominational paper. Next, are the members of your own family receiving good reading matter? Are your brothers and sisters forming a desire for good reading? See to it that a thirst and a habit of reading good literature is born in their youth. Then go to the members of your own church, to your Christian friends, and then to the unconverted.

The good-literature committee, like many others, should be composed of earnest, consecrated, enthusiastic young Christian people. Besides this, if they have tact, a love for good reading, an acquaintance with books and papers, so much the better.

Now, having formed your committee, how shall you go to work? First, by securing the co-operation of your pastor and officers of the church. Second, by selecting a suitable visiting committee, and commissioning them to call upon all the families. Third, by dividing the congregation into sections of so many families to facilitate visitation. Fourth, have suitable religious and wholesome literature. Fifth, introduce such literature into each family of the congregation, and those outside of its religious influence.

Here are some of the methods of work: You have often heard of a " Vestibule Table," a table in the vestibule of the church, on which are placed different religious papers by the congregation. These are taken care of by the good-literature committee, and distributed to those in the church who do not have the benefit of this reading matter.

There is another good suggestion, and that is to see that your secular papers are given religious news. This perhaps appeals more to the press committee, but where there is no press committee, the good-literature committee can do this to advantage. Secure in every city or country paper, whichever it may be, a weekly Christian Endeavor column, and see that it is kept full of the brightest and most interesting matters relating to Christian Endeavor thought.

In securing subscriptions for religious papers, where the family is too poor, or for any reason cannot subscribe, see if you cannot get two families to subscribe. One family may receive the paper first, and then they can pass it to the next.

Let every Christian Endeavor society have a small Christian Endeavor library, and keep a few of the best devotional books, such as Drummond's Addresses, Miss Havergal's books, and other good, religious, devotional books, so that they may be passed from one to another.

Tracts are helpful. They help the young Christians who do not have the strength and courage. But remember a tract must be as neatly fitted to the man as a glove to the finger, and that man must be made to feel a personal interest. Carefully select your tracts.

Here is another good suggestion that was brought out. Your pastor is turning out many good sermons. Secure one of these sermons and have it printed in leaflet form. Present it to the congregation. Your neighbor does not go to church; he has heard that your pastor is "poky." Show him that he is not.

Arrange scrap-books for each committee in the society, and place in that scrap-book all kinds of helpful hints clipped from *The Golden Rule*, or other Christian Endeavor papers. Also clippings on special religious subjects, such as "Soul Winning," "Doubtful Amusements." If desired, one scrap-book may be used for all subjects.

In some societies large envelopes are used which are indexed, and in those envelopes are placed the clippings, which refer to each subject. These can be used to advantage.

Secure the names of both givers and receivers of papers. There are three ways of doing this: First, let the giver pay the postage and send to a receiver; second, let the committee furnish to the giver the address, upon a stamped wrapper, of the party to whom he wishes a paper sent; third, if the giver will assent to neither of these ways, let the committee secure the papers themselves and see that they are sent.

Interest the Sunday-school pupils to buy especial books, which is a good way of securing a Christian Endeavor library. Last month twenty-one books were added to a Christian Endeavor library in this way.

MR. MOULTON : — The next committee is the lookout committee. This committee used sometimes to be called the outlook committee. That is wrong. It is to lookout: it is to search out: it is to go out. We will now hear from Mrs. Geo. W. Coleman, of Somerville, Mass.

LOOKOUT COMMITTEE.

MRS. COLEMAN: At the conference of lookout committees, the work of this committee was recognized to be of prime importance, because to it in an especial manner is committed the spiritual, watch-care of the individual members of the society. To this committee also there is afforded the opportunity for fostering spiritual growth in the members of the society. Upon the prime importance of the work of this committee, discussion was had along three lines: —

First, new departments of work are being taken up by different lookout committees from the country; and along this line I would like to give you one illustration which was recognized to be of pre-eminent value. One society provides a special committee of the lookout committee, numbering two persons. Their names are known only to the lookout committee. Their names are unknown to the society as a whole, and even to the officers. It is the especial duty of these "watchers" to discover any sign of lack of religious interest on the part of the persons interested in the meeting, and report the name of that person to the members of the lookout committee. You will see that this is a very important and a very delicate, and at the same time a very fruitful work.

Discussion was also had along a second line, that of the special encouragement attending the work of the lookout committee ; and here there was brought out in a very emphatic manner by the pastors present, the value of the lookout committee to the pastor individually, by the closest contact, which may be and should be established between it and the pastor. It was expressed in this way by one pastor: That the lookout committee may be, and has been to him, his right hand, his right foot, his right ear, and his right eye, thus extending all his powers and bringing them into the closest contact with the members of the society, and with the young people of the church. Another pastor gave a most interesting testimony to the effect that through the work of the lookout committee the problem of the Sunday evening service had been practically solved by him. He stated that 90 percent of the members of his Christian Endeavor society attended his Sunday evening service, and gave their practical co-operation and help, and rendered the service a success and inspiration to those who

AN ATTENTIVE AUDIENCE IN THE TENT.

From a photograph

attended it. Another pastor said that the attendance on his midweek prayer meetings was in the proportion of 60 percent of Christian Endeavorers to 40 percent of the older members of the church. The encouragement that is afforded to the pastors, and the close contact that is established between the pastor and the committee on the one hand, and the committee and the pastor on the other, cannot but be a fruitful source of encouragement to the society as a whole, as well as to the lookout committee; and if any one impression was made along this line above another, it was this: The more intimate the relation between pastor and committee, the better for the [work of the society and the spiritual growth of the individual member. You will readily see, I think, how wide a field is suggested along this line, and we trust it may be fruitful as the members of these committees return to their homes; that hereafter there may be a closer contact between the pastor and members of the lookout committee.

The third line concerns the reflex action of the work of the lookout committee upon the members of that committee themselves. It was very fittingly brought out in the statement of one of the members of the lookout committee, who expressed it in this way: The necessity for work is necessity for growth; those who are placed on the lookout committees, if they realize in any degree their responsibilities and their opportunity and privilege, cannot but feel the necessity of close contact with the Master, the Lord Jesus Christ, and close and intimate communion with him in order that they may so grow in him as to be fitted to carry out the responsibilities attending their office. Necessity for work then is a necessity for growth, and this brings spiritual blessings to the members of the committee themselves. Interesting discussions were given by members of the lookout committees as to results along this line in their own experience. Many testified that they had been helped in growth in the Christian life; that they had known members of lookout committees who were diffident and retiring, and who found it a difficult matter to keep the pledge, yet whose spiritual life was deep and earnest, and through the work of the lookout committee had overcome all this. It was also suggested that service upon the lookout committee developed tact and experience in the Christian service, which is so necessary a part of our equipment in the service of the Lord. We trust that the conference was a fruitful one, and that harvests will be reaped from our discussions.

Mr. MOULTON: Miss Ida Bradshaw, of Milwaukee, Wis., will report for the prayer-meeting committee.

PRAYER-MEETING COMMITTEE.

MISS IDA BRADSHAW: We felt that our conference yesterday afternoon was so very rich that it was hard to bring the cream of that conference to you this morning when it was all cream. 'I began to wonder if we did n't have the very best workers of the Christian Endeavor societies on the prayer-meeting committees.

In the first place, we considered new methods for appointing leaders. We found the good old way of appointing leaders for six months ahead was customary in about half of the states which were represented there. Other societies announce topics and leaders for three months ahead. We found only a few who announced leaders one week ahead. One society reported a prayer-meeting committee that believed thoroughly in pledging, and their prayer-meeting committee took a pledge upon themselves besides the active membership pledge. I cannot give you all of that pledge this morning, but it was that they pledge themselves to constant attendance upon the meetings, to make the most possible out of them, to do what they could for them, and to help in any special way which might come to them, the leaders of the meetings.

Another society reported that its committee made one of the prayer-meeting committee responsible for the meetings each month. Another society made a member responsible for one meeting, and that member of the prayer-meeting committee was to see to it that no pauses occurred, and that the music was all provided for, and that everything was done to make the meeting a successful one.

We had considerable discussion as to who was the best person to lead the consecration service. Some societies thought their president, others that their pastor ought always to do this. But we came to the conclusion that it was not wise to confine the leadership of the consecration meeting to any one special member, but that the leader of this meeting ought always to be one of the most spiritual leaders in the Christian Endeavor society. We also considered how best we might bring out the timid members of the society, those who were not accustomed to leading. One society reported that they always had a preliminary prayer meeting, and one of the new-comers in the society who was especially timid about appearing in public always led that meeting, and after leading this preliminary meeting it was an easy thing for them to lead the regular prayer meeting.

Other societies reported that sometimes they appointed two leaders for a meeting, one who was accustomed to leading and the other a timid leader. These timid leaders announced the hymns, read the Scripture lesson, and made the announcements which usually fall to the lot of the leader to announce. It was the more experienced leader who gave the talk concerning the subject and opened the way for the meeting.

We also considered the means of advertising these meetings. Many of them thought that it was a very excellent plan to have the leader and the subject of the meeting announced on Sunday morning from the pulpit by the pastor. One pastor has what is called a Christian Endeavor bulletin board, and upon this bulletin board are placed the names of the leaders and topics for one month ahead.

Another prayer-meeting committee believe especially in consecrated printer's ink. They were not afraid to advertise their meetings. That is, I believe, done by one of our irrepressible Chicago prayer-meeting committees. They hand out invitations on the street.

Another subject that we discussed was variety in our meetings. One committee reported that they had every Saturday night programs printed. The programs were printed for the first and the last of the meeting, leaving a space in the middle for anything that might come up. Somebody suggested that there was too much rope and not enough of elastic, but we came to the conclusion that the rope was all there, and that it was left to the young people themselves to supply the elastic. In another society every single member of the prayer-meeting committee came prepared to lead the meeting in case the leader of the meeting should not be present.

In another prayer-meeting committee each member is given some section of the meeting to look after. For instance, certain members are asked to lead the prayer service, others to see that suitable hymns are selected, and so on.

Another committee takes pains to have ways and means provided for new-comers who find it hard to speak in the meeting; they either handed them some question that they would like answered, or they gave them some suitable selection upon the topic to read, or they asked them to offer up that night a one sentence prayer, and if they could not do that, they supplied the prayer for them.

Another excellent suggestion was that the prayer-meeting committee should always provide for the Wednesday night service immediately following the communion service. They carried their work not only into the Sunday night prayer meeting of the Christian Endeavor society, but out into the week as well. Another prayer-meeting committee always took pains to suit the topic to the leader. They met, looked over topics, and then found the very best person possible in the society to lead the meeting. We laid special emphasis upon the subject of Bible study. There ought to be more earnest Bible study. We ought to have personal training classes in our Young People's societies, and these ought to be provided by the prayer-meeting committee, and then the prayer-meeting committee ought to meet every week for a season of prayer. Prayer was said to be one of the essential characteristics of our Christian Endeavor work; but we came to the conclusion that it was not prayer alone, but that works must go with the prayer, and with good works and earnest, heartfelt prayer, we cannot fail to have a good Christian Endeavor society. [*Loud applause.*]

MR. MOULTON: The Christian Endeavor Society is not very old, but its members are thirteen years older than when the first society was organized, and so we have to supply their places as they get old, and the hope of the Christian Endeavor movement for the future is in the Junior Society. Now we will hear something about it from Mr. Thos. Wainwright, that consecrated and very successful worker in Chicago.

THE JUNIOR SOCIETY.

MR. WAINWRIGHT: At the Junior conference yesterday afternoon a large list of questions was printed on paper and hung from the platform, and two minutes was allowed to each question. Now, I am going to give you just a few of those questions and a few of the answers. What we want, Christian friends, in this Junior work is something practical. We know that it is necessary, we know that we should have it, but we want to know how to work it, so I will give you a few of the questions and answers that were suggested.

How to choose a superintendent; should he be appointed or elected? Never elect superintendents; have them appointed. I find that those that appoint themselves make the best workers every time. The superintendent should be approved by the pastor and deacons.

What should be the term of office of the superintendent? As long as the society flourishes, never allow that one to give up the work.

What to emphasize in meetings? Christ first, last, and all the time. Brotherly love, obedience, soul winning, and make the boys and girls feel that they are at home in the church.

What is the age limit? From six to fourteen, four to sixteen, or when their mothers say they can come. Come in a baby carriage and go out when old enough to lead a meeting.

Music. Do not fail to teach some of the good old-fashioned hymns of our grandparents. [*Applause.*] Occasionally march while singing, and at times read the verse so that the children can get into the spirit and the meaning of what they are going to sing.

Pledge. Find out from the Juniors themselves whether they are faithful to their obligations.

Time of meeting. At the convenience of the superintendent, and when the most children can attend. Sunday is too full a day; if possible, hold them on Tuesdays or Fridays, and never on Saturday; that is the children's play-day and let them have it.

How to teach Juniors to pray. Always kneel. Pray for missions; pray just as they feel. God knows what is best. An acceptable prayer is one which is, " Not my will, O Lord, but thine be done."

Methods of conducting meetings. Open with praise service; never tell a child anything he can tell you; study the catechism; emphasize the thought of prayer; teach them to pray; give them a text at the close of each meeting.

Method of conducting consecration meeting. By the active members and superintendent alone. It should be the last meeting in each month. All should read the pledge together, then let each one tell how far short he has come to it during the month. Will that do for you seniors? Try it.

Business meeting. Once in three months, conducted by the children ; once a month, conducted by the social committee. Never hold a business meeting on Sunday. It should be held on Thursday preceding the consecration meeting. Have them just as near like a senior business meeting as possible.

Home and foreign missionary work. Write to your home missionary board and get the name and address of some of your missionaries; write to them and have the missionaries answer your letter. You will thus create an interest in the Junior Society for mission work, and when they get interested in it the ways and means will come to help spread that Gospel of the Lord Jesus Christ. Let there be a birthday box and in it let them put odd pennies. Then, time can profitably be used in making scrap-books and dolls and sending them to children in hospitals. In Nebraska forty-five members of a Junior society went out into the field and husked corn and made $45.00 and gave it all to home missions. [*Loud applause*].

MR. MOULTON: Miss Caroline H. Brookfield of Belvidere, N. J., will report for the temperance committee.

TEMPERANCE COMMITTEE,

MISS BROOKFIELD: How can I tell you in eight minutes the proceedings of a conference which lasted an hour and three-quarters? I shall not attempt to quote many of the earnest words of the speakers. It is a difficult, if not an impossible thing, to repeat another's words, and to put into them the power, the thought, the feeling with which the speaker invested them.

First. Mrs. Scudder talked to us about Junior temperance work, reminding us that childhood is the impressionable time, the time when strict temperance principles can be best inculcated. She advised that temperance songs be taught the children; that they study in regard to the adulterations of liquor; that they learn by a kind of temperance arithmetic the amount of money expended in liquor; for instance, if a man drinks six glasses of beer a day for six months, at five cents a glass, how many loaves of bread at the same price per loaf could be bought for that money?

Miss Antoinette P. Jones, of Massachusetts, superintendent of Floating Societies, told us about temperance work in these societies. The sailor boys have a temperance clause in the Christian Endeavor pledge. Miss Jones suggested the establishment of reading-rooms for sailors on the shore and neat temperance boarding-houses; this would be practical and telling temperance work.

Mrs. Dr. Williams, president of the Montreal W. C. T. U., made a strong and womanly appeal that home influence be kept pure. I must quote one sentence of Mrs. Williams's: "We Canadians envy you your Frances Willard."

Dr. Burrell began by saying, "There is no use at this time of talking about the evils of intemperance; it is like grinding the wheat with the waters that have run by. My dear fellow-fanatics, what are we going to do about it?" Then he urged in burning words that by all possible means we drive out the dram shop and the entire traffic of strong drink; that we look after our own personal lives, following the example of our Lord Jesus Christ who emptied himself of his glory for the sake of fallen humanity.

We spent a few moments in discussing the advantages of a temperance department in connection with state, county, and local unions. But three of our state unions report temperance departments, although there is an active interest in temperance work in many states.

Mr. E. D. Wheelock, superintendent of the temperance department of the Illinois state union, gave us a few practical suggestions. The work of the temperance department is in part to establish a temperance committee in every society, to carry temperance educational work throughout the state, to circulate temperance literature and to arrange for public meetings and good lectures.

Now a few suggestions that came from delegates present. We had delegates there from twenty provinces, states, and territories, and one representative from Australia. Ask your pastor to preach on the subject of temperance occasionally; establish royal temperance leagues; let each temperance committee see that the state laws in regard to hygienic instructions in public schools are carried out.

Montreal Methodist Christian Endeavor society supports the old Rescue Mission for victims of drink.

Some societies in Virginia are active in bringing illegal bars to light and having them punished by law; others keep a close watch for the violation of the Sunday law, which requires the closing of bars. Oregon state union contributed over $300 to Rest Island Mission, established by Mr. John G. Woolley.

Plymouth Junior, of Seattle, Washington, erected a drinking fountain in front of the church.

At a local Union meeting in a country district in Washington, those waiting for the train-went to the only saloon in town and held a prayer meeting. In a few days the man closed up and left.

A society in New Jersey obtained over seventy signers to the pledge at one prayer meeting.

Permit me to make one or two more suggestions to our temperance committee. We hear a good deal about the desirability of having our temperance literature read, but not so much about the importance of reading it ourselves before we pass it to others.

A wall temperance pledge is an excellent thing. A Sunday school in Pennsylvania has adopted the plan of fixing a small red star opposite the name of any one who is known to have broken the pledge. I am told that the plan works wonderfully well as a preventive. Let the temperance committee prepare themselves for work by collecting facts in regard to locality, the number of boys who drink, the number of children kept from school by drunken parents, etc.

In the last place, let us ask God to qualify us for our work. Methods are important, but personal qualifications are more so. Let the worker be qualified; let him possess common-sense, judgment, a realization of the need, a sense of personal responsibility, and entire consecration, and he is a master of methods — heart and soul in the work, he creates his plans as the work unfolds. It is said of John Wesley that his genius consisted in creating his methods, and I believe that every worker having the qualifications has more or less of the same genius.

One verse of "Throw Out the Life-line" was then sung. Miss Snyder, of Montreal, next favored the audience with a very beautiful solo, "The Good Shepherd."

Mr. Moulton: Mr. F. P. Haskell, Jr., of Tacoma, Wash., will report the Sunday-school committee conference.

SUNDAY-SCHOOL COMMITTEE.

Mr. Haskell: The topic, "How can the Sunday-school Committee best help the Superintendent and Teachers?" having been given, the conference for discussion, was first spoken upon, and many helpful thoughts were brought out.

One superintendent told of various little things that the committee could do to assist him, such as passing hymn books. This brought out the old thought of doing the little things faithfully, that we may be better prepared to master the great ones.

Our attention was then turned to substitute teachers. The question was brought up, "Can the superintendent depend upon the Sunday-school committee for substitute teachers?" Listen to what one delegate says: "The superintendent has been given the names of our Sunday-school committee who have agreed to act as substitute teachers, and when he wants a teacher he simply refers to his list, and there he is sure to find one."

One gentleman said he did not believe in the Sunday-school committee going about calling, for it would surely take the work entirely out of the hands of the superintendent and teachers. Such talk as this must be without any foundation, for even in the rush and bustle of the busy West, the ladies make, on an average, twenty calls in an afternoon and still do not keep up the calling work.

Another excellent thought brought out was the organizing of mission Sunday schools in the parts of our cities and country where they are needed.

A Vermont man said that their Sunday-school committee was organizing Sunday schools in every direction, and that they were not going to quit until their whole state was a Sunday school.

· The normal class idea was then discussed, the idea being to form a class for the purpose of having instruction given in the methods of teaching. One lady told of a class connected with her Sunday school which was very successful. They hold their meetings for study on Monday evening, that they may be ready for duty on Sunday.

We were told that one Sunday-school committee found a silver collection to be very successful. With this money the committee provided flowers and other needful things for the sick.

Helpful thoughts were brought out on the recruiting work of the committee. A society in Chicago appoints their Sunday-school committee; this committee appoints a recruiting sergeant in each class, whose duty it is to gather all the absentees' names and give them to the Sunday school committee to look after. Another Sunday-school committee has found that a Sunday-school social for the children was very good.

The following plan for gathering the children into the church as well as the Sunday school was given. The teachers of each class have text books. In order for the children to get these books they must come to church. Those that are not absent during the year (unless sick) are given a pretty book for a reward. This is a good idea, for if the child goes to church while a child, the chances are that he will go when he has put away childish things and become a man.

I admire the work of one Chicago Sunday-school committee, who furnish Bibles to the scholars who can not get them. This is one of the first things a child needs. Let the Sunday-school committee go on in the work of distributing the Bibles, and their work will be well done, for by this Book we find light, through it we find Christ, and in it we find eternal life.

We had the good fortune of having with us Rev. A. P. Foster, New England secretary of the American Sunday-school union, who said : —

I have recently been taking a tour in the West for the purpose of studying Sunday-school work, and have made what to me was a great discovery. It is that God in his providence is calling the Christian Endeavor Society to a most important work in serving as a connecting link between the Sunday school, when an independent organization, and the church. There are a great many Sunday schools existing independent of churches, and more and more of these schools are springing up all over the country. The American Sunday-school Union alone is planting them at the rate of over 1,500 a year, and other organizations are doing important work in a similar line. It is found that the only way to kindle a Gospel fire in innumerable little communities is to organize a Sunday school. A church cannot go there. There is not money enough to be had to build a church edifice and provide a salaried minister, but a Sunday school is possible. This requires little money. no church edifice and no minister. A dozen families within a mile of each other may get a school. But such schools are sure always in some way to lead up to a church of God. If there are enough in the community to warrant it, the school is likely to grow into a church. If not, the school will at least prove a feeder to the nearest churches, leading many who never went to church before to do so and causing many young converts to join the distant churches. But in both these cases the influence of the Christian Endeavor society is invaluable. It is a more spiritual organization than the Sunday school and it should exist in every Sunday school not connected with the church, that it may open its arms to the young converts, aid them to confess Christ, bind them together in a common life, develop their spirituality, and train them up to Christian service. Where a church does not exist to do this work, a Christian Endeavor society is almost essential. And where the school is a union school, because the community is so broken up into denominational fragments that a denominational school is impossible, the Christian Endeavor society is always possible.

Now in view of these facts we ought to do everything we can to promote the organization of these Christian Endeavor societies in Sunday schools. If anywhere near it there is a Sunday school existing independently of a church, and especially a Sunday school on a union basis, the lookout committee of the nearest Christian Endeavor society might well feel called upon to visit that school and try to organize an Endeavor society there.

Above all would it be desirable that every Christian Endeavor union should have a lookout committee of its own, the province of which should be, among other things, to seek the extension of Christian Endeavor societies, and which should especially charge itself with seeking the organization of such societies in schools not yet connected with churches.

I see no reason why under judicious influences there might not be an increase of Christian Endeavor societies from union Sunday schools, or at least independent schools of from 500 to 700 yearly.

With such excellent lines as these to work out, shall we not determine a Sunday-school committee, if we have none, when we return to our labors?

May the dear Lord grant that we may ever be found at our post, doing our duty to advance his kingdom through the Sunday-school work.

MR. MOULTON: Mr. H. C. Lincoln, of Philadelphia, will now report for the music committee conference.

MUSIC COMMITTEE.

MR. LINCOLN: At our conference yesterday afternoon we had a lot of good things said by a lot of good people. I will just show them to you as points, and let you take them home and build up on them.

In the first place, we found that the music committee could render valuable assistance to the calling committee, some societies sending one or more of their number from the music committee out with the calling committee, so that they may sing as well as pray. This also applies to the hospital work. We found that they could help the missionary committee by furnishing special music for missionary meetings, and the social committee, by preparing music for their socials; also the prayer-meeting committee, by making the singing at the meetings spiritual, furnishing an organist and leaders.

Some societies reported that they had a Christian Endeavor choir or quartette, and even one a male quartette to lead in song once in a while.

One society reported that it had arranged for once a month a grand chorus of 50 voices for the Sunday night service, and it helped to solve the problem of attractive Sunday evening service.

The conference approved of a fifteen minutes' song service at the commencement of the meetings, and also impromptu singing during the meetings, provided the person who did it did n't get too high or too low. [*Laughter.*]

These are simple points; carry them home and build on them, and come prepared next year to tell us how they work.

MR. MOULTON: Now we will hear from the social committee, by Miss Carrie A. Holbrook, of St. Paul, Minn.

SOCIAL COMMITTEE.

MISS HOLBROOK: The keynote of the conference of the social committee was sociality to the van. Very briefly was developed the thought that Christ when here upon earth, was pre-eminently social in his nature, and that to be Christians we must be Christlike, and to be Christlike we must follow in his footsteps. To you and to me, as Christian Endeavorers, is given the privilege of preaching the Gospel of the Lord Jesus Christ — preaching it and teaching it by living it.

A full and free discussion of methods and plans for social work followed, from which I find great difficulty in gleaning the most original, the most helpful, and the best paying suggestions.

First. Organize your committee; put upon that committee a few earnest, consecrated young people; add to this list a few of your associate members; map out the work definitely.

One society suggests that the social committee be composed of the chairmen of all the other committees, and says that this plan works admirably.

Neglect not the diffident, the youthful ones, the new members; see that each one has something to do. Hold a business social at the beginning of your term of office, where, in the most sociable way, you may map out the work for that quarter or year, as it may be. Give a social in honor of the officers of your church; give one in honor of your Juniors; give an occasional thank-offering social. As a rule, don't charge admission or take up a collection; have a short informal program; delicate refreshments served upon delicate china. Decorate your reception room, but not with wall flowers. Be sociable; introduce strangers; break up cliques; have a word of prayer; close with a hymn of praise. Hold a union social, inviting one or two other societies, exchange autographs, introducing back and forth from one society to another. Become acquainted with your neighbors, your church neighbors, your Christian neighbors.

Give an occasional missionary social. One very good suggestion was to give to each attendant a card, upon which was written or printed from twelve to twenty missionary questions, and on the other side a blank space, so that they can answer those questions; if they cannot answer them themselves, they go around and ask others. In that way they will become extremely sociable. You may use the blackboard for the same purpose, if you do not care to have the cards.

You may have a stereopticon social. This you will find very delightful. It was advocated by a pastor who said that in that way he found he could take his young people all over the globe.

The secret of success in social work is the very same secret that is the secret of all Christian work, and that is personal work; give each one something to do. And let each member of your society be a committee of one to be extremely sociable upon all those social occasions. And above all, make the pastor of your society the lion of the evening.

Be social at the beginning of your prayer meetings; greet the strangers when they come in; introduce them to your pastor and friends. At the close of the meeting be very, very social; linger for a short time. It has been suggested that we devote the fifteen minutes before the service to sociability. Do not let any stranger go out the door because he or she was not invited to take a seat in the auditorium. Hold your Christian Endeavor meetings through the week; you will have time to have a social chat at the close of the meeting.

A delegate from Sioux City, Iowa, says, "Be social every day in the week, not only in the church but in the home, not only in the home but upon the street, not only upon the street but in the office, wherever you meet one of your friends, be social, and wherever you meet the stranger, above all things, do be social and cordial."

Let the young men call on the strangers and bring them to the socials and prayer meetings. Let the young women do the same.

A very good suggestion is, If you have not a calling committee, have the chairman of your social committee keep a book in which is a list of all the names of your members. If a stranger comes into your society or church, appoint a few different people to call upon that one person that week, until a large number of the church have called upon this person; in about two months put this stranger on your first list, go to her with a new name, and say, "Awhile ago you were a stranger, now don't you want to go call on a stranger that has come in the past few days?" She is no longer a stranger, but you have made her one of you.

MR. MOULTON: A report of the missionary committee conference will be given by Mr. W. Henry Grant, of Philadelphia, Pa.

MISSIONARY COMMITTEE.

MR. GRANT: The missionary committee is the last fruit on the Christian Endeavor tree, but it is to be by no means the least fruit of the Christian Endeavor work.

First of all, we want to clearly understand what the missionary committee is for. Sometimes we find we give it a larger field in one sense than it is; we try to make it do the work of other committees. The primary object of this committee is to keep the marching orders of the church prominently before the society.

Again, it is to be the missionary stove to warm up our Christian Endeavor societies with missionary information and enthusiasm, and there must be at least one member on this committee who is on fire. You can no more light up a stove full of dead coals than you can light up a missionary committee with enthusiasm without some one in it who is already on fire. So, if your chairman is not that one, let some one of the committee be enthused. Even an ordinary member of the committee may fire a whole committee.

This committee is to be the tuning fork of the society; it is to raise the pitch of the society and give the keynote of Christian Endeavor. The social committee will assist our missionary committee in its missionary sociables, the music committee will assist it, the prayer-meeting and lookout committees will assist in getting the members to take part in missionary work. Our distinctive field of work is not local, but of that kind which we must do by proxy; not microscopic enlarging the field at home and around us, but it must be telescopic, bringing the far near, and magnifying our opportunities in fields more remote.

The missionary committee should be a bureau of information on missionary work and mission fields. An efficient committee must have at least one member who is in earnest. Too much raw material is a hindrance instead of a help; committees must grow by experience.

The committee should meet as often as necessary in order to make the regular missionary meeting of the society a success.

An effective committee will parcel out the work among the members; in other words, will have sub-committees, one on meetings, one on literature, one on the library, one on the collection for the society, one on correspondence, another on assigning the work to the active members of the society, and a still further sub-committee on special meetings.

The meetings of the committee should have a regular order of business, with reports from sub-committees.

In order to make the regular missionary meeting a success the committee must study. It should be a class in geography and missionary history; it should collect and prepare material previous to giving it to the members of the society.

We should have a regular missionary meeting of the society as often as we can have a good one, and not allow our meetings to lack in preparation.

The aim of the meeting must be to promote an intelligent enthusiasm on the subject of missions. It must be for permanent results and growth and not for mere soda water effect.

A good program is a work of art. Many programs are arranged in a scrap-basket fashion. One can scarcely get any idea of what was heard from such a program.

Our field of study is vast and intricate. We cannot swallow the world, as we do pills, without danger of indigestion. Master one great field, like India, China, or Africa, at a time, giving it several meetings.

The pledge covers the missionary meeting. All members should be encouraged to bring at least general items of news on the field of study.

The sub-committee should stimulate the members by giving them information. The committee on systematic giving should report the amount received and the amount pledged.

Every committee should see to it that a lending missionary library is started at once, and that its members know what is in it. Periodical literature and tracts can be circulated through the good-literature committee.

Correspond with your boards for special information; correspond with your missionaries in order to bring them in touch with you and to show them your interest. Exchange ideas with other committees.

Give systematically on the first day of the week; give proportionately as the Lord hath prospered you; give intelligently.

Special meetings, illustrated lectures, receptions, these we will have to leave, but we must not forget that we have now in our midst more than six or seven thousand volunteers for the foreign mission field, and we should utilize these in our society.

I have not time to touch upon the work of our general local union and denominational missionary committees which are doing a great deal of work.

MR. MOULTON: Now, dear friends, what are you going to do with these very valuable and helpful suggestions? Will you take them home and enthuse your societies upon the subject? Do not be satisfied with reporting these things, but see to it that by continuous drumming on the subject, these methods are carried out.

We are sometimes met with the objection that there is too much machinery in connection with our committee work. I do not think that there is too much machinery. If there is any fault along this line, it is because the machinery is not lubricated enough. We want more of the oil of the Spirit, and we want more of the dynamic power of prayer; we want more of the baptism of fire, that this committee work may be on fire and effective for God's work. So, let each committee try during the coming year to make the committee work the means of great and widespread and everlasting fruit for the Master.

The audience then sang one verse of "Work, for the Night Is Coming."

DR. BECKLEY: Some of you remember the day of small things in Christian Endeavor, the times that tried men's souls, the time of difficulty and doubt. And in those days there was a gentleman who held the office of General Secretary of the United Society, and who bore the heavy burdens; he is with us today. I am exceedingly glad to present him to you, and you will be glad to hear him, — Mr. George M. Ward, of Lowell, Mass. [*Loud applause.*]

The Committee of One.

Address of Mr. George M. Ward.

You doubtless remember Rip Van Winkle and his wondrous sleep of twenty years in the mountains. You remember, too, with what confused feelings, and with what puzzled sensations he came down from the mountain and found that thriving city in the place he had left but the night before a little village hamlet. Since I have reached your city and have attended this convention, I have realized just exactly how Rip Van Winkle must have felt, and I have looked with a wonder equal to his upon the vast multitudes that are thronging the city of Montreal.

Is this the little band that sat in the front pews of Portland, Maine? Is this the little band who met at Old Orchard, and then and there organized the United Society of Christian Endeavor? Is this the little band for whom, the following year, with hesitation I engaged the Methodist church in Saratoga, fearing that it was too large? Is this the same society on account of which the hotel keepers of that city demanded a guarantee, fearing they would not have delegates enough to fill their hotels? Is this the same which even Father Endeavor Clark himself and some of these dear trustees thought did not have sufficient western constituency to hold a convention as far west as Chicago? I wish, you could realize how they talked to me about the convention. They thought I was carried away with the enthusiasm of youth. Is this the same little cause of Christian Endeavor for which with fear and trembling I engaged a little desk-room in Boston and without any furniture, save a table a yard square, started in as secretary and trusted to Providence to pay the bills then incurred? Is this the same cause of Christian Endeavor for which the ministers prophesied possibly a year or two of life? Is this the same cause of Christian Endeavor for which the religious press even would scarcely grant us a hearing, and of which the secular press had never heard? Is this the same cause of Christian Endeavor for which I became for three or four years a sort of religious tramp, and wandered up and down all over the United States begging a hearing, ofttimes speaking to most diminutive audiences, and sometimes refused a hearing altogether, because, they said, I was only another added to the already long list of useless secretaries for useless causes?

Do you wonder, then, that today, standing in your midst, standing here on what is to me foreign soil, I cannot fail to recognize the progress made? I recognize the same old principal and the same old tune. I thank God they have not changed.

When your committee gave me that topic of " Committee Work," I said " What is there left for us as individuals to do?" There seems nothing left but admiration for the work of others. But is that true? Is that all God asks of us? No, he has asked more than that, and he has given each one of us, I am sure, a definite, personal duty. It is our duty to seek out and find and complete our own mission. It is that duty, the duty of each individual, which is the same as the duty which God has given all his followers since the time when he first sent his disciples from his presence, simply to do the will of the Father, and to uphold his cause throughout the world. We are to look for our instructions as to what we are to do in the Bible, and before we can do successful works as committees we must be filled with faith in our Lord and Saviour. If we are equipped with faith, equipped with knowledge, equipped with unselfishness, filled with inspiration at the thought of Him whom we are serving, what can we not as individuals do? Columbus, filled with his idea of another continent, stuck to it until he had the means to prove his theory, and gave to the world America. It was as a committee of one that that first society met in Portland, Maine, twelve years ago, and now look at it. It was as a committee of one that Father Endeavor Clark gave his life to the young people, and it has taken him around the world. It is as a committee of one that missionaries go to their field of labor. It was as a committee of one that Queen Esther saved her nation from destruction. It was as a committee of one that Jesus Christ left his home on high and came down here on earth to be a lonely wanderer and to be crucified, that he might give to us the opportunity of everlasting life.

We will equip ourselves as young people, as committees of one, as individual workers. We will fit ourselves, we will strain every muscle, we will strive to use every ability that God has given us, when the opportunity comes to us, that we may push onward and upward the cause of Christ.

MR. BECKLEY: As you go away with your heads and hearts full of these suggestions for work, let me give you a motto. The old philosopher said, " Give me a place to stand, and I will move the world." Stand where you are and move the world, in your big church in the city, in your little place in the village. God has put you just where he wants you. Stand where you are and move the world.

The session closed with the Mizpah benediction.

SATURDAY AFTERNOON.

No session was held at either the Drill Hall or Tent. The program called for a Junior Rally at the American Presbyterian church and denominational rallies at various churches in the city.

JUNIOR RALLY.

At the American Presbyterian church, which was crowded with a large audience, a Junior Rally was held, presided over by Rev. John L. Sewall, of St. Louis. The body of the house was reserved for the children, the older people occupying the gallery. A praise service of fifteen minutes was conducted by Mr. Lindsay, assisted by a chorus choir.

The program proper commenced with singing the hymn "There Is Sunshine in my Soul," and there was no better singing during the convention.

MR. SEWALL: Dear children, one and all, I greet you this afternoon with great gladness. We are all of us children here this afternoon. Do you remember what Jesus did and said when one day the disciples were disputing among themselves about who was to be great in his kingdom? Do you remember how he called a little child to him and set him in the midst and then said to those grown-up men, "Unless you are converted and become like this little child, you cannot enter into the kingdom of heaven?" Some people seem to think that boys and girls must become like old folks before they can become Christians; but Jesus says that it is the other way. So this afternoon we must all of us be like little children, willing to learn and ready to trust.

This is a Junior rally; that is to say, it is a children's rally, and if we are all to be young here this afternoon, of course we are all to be children. Perhaps you think that some of these children look very large, that some of these boys and girls are grown up; but, children, this is our rally and we are not going to have anybody here this afternoon who is not really a child at heart. We are going to talk about the Junior Endeavor Society. Some of you, I think, are members of Junior societies. Now listen. I want to ask every member of a Junior society and every superintendent and helper here in this church to rise. [*A large number rose.*] We have quite a number of Juniors here, and I see there are some who are not Juniors; but I know you will all want to be Juniors before we finish this service.

I want to say that this is a very important meeting. Do you know I think it is the most important meeting of all this great convention, and I will tell you why. When this great convention comes back to Montreal,—we will say in twenty years from now, after it has been in San Francisco, and in Japan, and in London, and all around the world,—these good Juniors who are here before me in these seats are going to be the chairmen of the committees. You are going to wear the white caps; you are going to direct friends to their places of entertainment; you are going to stand on the platform and make speeches and do a great deal of hard work. So I think this is a very important meeting, because we are going to do something this afternoon toward training the committee, we will say, of 1910, for the convention in Montreal.

Now, because this is so important, I think we all of us ought to ask God's blessing on our meeting, and I think we may do this as one society does which I love very dearly in my own church—a society which I love so much that I cannot let any one else superintend it. We sometimes pray in this way: I offer a petition, and then all those present repeat it after me. Let us pray in that way now. I will offer a petition, and then let every one in this church repeat it after me.

Mr. Sewall then offered a brief prayer, the congregation repeating it sentence by sentence. An address of welcome was then given by Mr. Arthur F. Bell, of Montreal.

Address of Welcome.

By Mr. Arthur F. Bell.

Mr. Chairman and Fellow Endeavorers:—We bid you welcome this afternoon to Montreal. Many are the legends and numerous the historical facts that might be told to you of daring deeds and times of trial in connection with our city, and we trust that these will feed the flame of your patriotism, that you may be able to sing with even more spirit and in greater truth than ever before. " My Country, 't is of Thee," also that our Canadian boys and girls may sing with greater spirit that God may save and bless our beloved Queen. [*Applause.*]

Girls and boys, as I look upon you this afternoon. I think that all things are possible to you if you enter the line of action that you shall be called to. Among the many human trumpet calls that you will hear there is one which comes from your country which is not one to be least considered. Who can tell but that a future president of the United States may be sitting here this afternoon as a boy? Who knows but that here, with us this afternoon, is one who shall be a premier of the Dominion of Canada? He who continues to love his God, his creator, above all, and his country through all the temptations of public life, may enter the service of that country and do as grand a work for God as any. We bid you welcome to this convention.

Now I would like to ask who can measure the inspiration that you will receive in this gathering? This afternoon you will learn something about our pledge that you did not know before. You will listen to one who will make you realize that our consecration has not been complete in the past. You will hear the strange tongues that are spoken by children across the sea, and you will see one who has visited those countries and who is going to tell us of their need of our help in their endeavor to be Christians. Some of you today may resolve — and in the future keep that resolution — to go to those who are in foreign lands. Then I would ask you to remember that to him that overcometh, a white raiment shall be given, and before the angels his name shall be confessed in heaven.

> " Then onward from the hills of light,
> Our hearts with love aflame,
> We 'll vanquish all the hosts of night,
> In Jesus' conquering name."

We bid you of all lands welcome. Many are the countries doubtless represented here today, all with one accord. Shall we not pray for that day when we shall all be united, not under one government, but under one God and for one purpose? " If God be for us who can be against us." God's power is felt but it is not always seen. If the visible power of the nations be united and God be for us, who shall dare to be against us?

Then we bid you of all denominations welcome. I was born a Methodist, of Methodist parents, and I am proud of it. I was born again of the spirit through Methodist preaching, and am glad of that. And I hope to be carried on through the valley of the shadow of death in a Methodist chariot of fire. I am also glad that throughout all the ages of eternity I am going to be a Christian Endeavorer. [*Applause.*] We are glad that the Christian Endeavor principles are saturating not alone the Methodist church, but all the churches.

Among the many bright things sent to the *Junior Golden Rule* I remember this story. A certain old Roman soldier watched one of the many processions that the Romans were so fond of having, and as the older soldiers passed by he heard them shout, " We have been brave." " Alas," said he, "these are old; when they are gone what shall become of my country?" Then came the younger men and he heard from them the shout, "We are brave." " Alas, said the old man, "these too will soon be gone and then what shall become of my country?" As he looked he saw the children coming and he listened eagerly for their cry, and it was, "We will be brave." Now this afternoon I am reminded that we have been hearing from the veterans of God's army, and their cry has been, " We have been Christ's," and the younger have followed them with the cry, " We are Christ's." This afternoon we listen for the cry of the children and we are eager to catch it, and that cry we want to be, " We will be Christ's." Now listen. Down from that heavenly home that Jesus Christ once left to come to earth and remain for awhile with us here and went back again to, there comes this afternoon a voice. It is the voice of that Saviour who spoke those tender words about the children, and he says this afternoon as we listen,— we can almost hear him speak, — "Hold the fort, for I am coming." The question I throw out to you this afternoon is, Will you "Wave the answer back to heaven, By thy grace we will?" If you do so, then we bid you welcome to the kingdom of our Lord and Saviour Jesus Christ. [*Applause.*]

Mr Sewall then introduced to the audience Mr. W. H. Pennell as the first signer of the Christian Endeavor Constitution, who was heartily greeted by the audience. He then introduced the first signer of the Junior Endeavor pledge, Mr. Raymond C. Brooks, of Tabor, Iowa, to respond to the address of welcome.

Response.

By Mr. Raymond C. Brooks.

The members of the Junior Society of Christian Endeavor, coming as we do from all parts of our fair land across the border, from almost every state, I presume,—from the Golden Gate to Plymouth Rock, and from the Great Lakes which we share with you a common heritage to the Gulf of Mexico,—and coming too, I suppose, from every quarter of your own fair Canada, respond most gratefully to these noble words of welcome. [*Applause.*]

Many others who, while their age no longer permits them to be enrolled as Juniors, have still their hearts as fresh and interest as keen in the work the Juniors are doing as if they themselves were Juniors, and who have shown their sympathetic interest by their attendance here today, rejoice with us in the welcome you have given us.

We have already proved your words. We shall long cherish in our memory those splendid words because of the solid foundation of thoughtful, kindly deeds which we have already experienced in your homes and from your hearts during our short stay here in your wonderful city. For it has been a wonderful city to us. Imagine, if you can, what anticipation filled our young hearts as we looked forward to this journey across the border into a new land, and into your great city, stories about which we have heard from our earliest days; and imagine with what delighted surprise we have visited the haunts of your fairyland.

We, the children of the United States, have already learned to love the children of Canada,—with brotherly and sisterly love, please understand,—and we shall always remember our stay here as one of the happiest events in our lives. More than ever we shall be inclined to urge our Uncle Sam to win, if possible, the affection of your Fair Canada. [*Applause.*]

Fellow-Endeavorers, you understand, I trust, that I am called upon to respond to the eloquent address and warm-hearted greeting which we have heard for historical rather than oratorical reasons. I count it a fortunate privilege to have been the first signer of the first Junior constitution, although I did not know it until a few weeks ago. It is another illustration of the tireless energy of our General Secretary, Mr. Baer, for it was through his efforts we of Tabor were discovered to be the first Junior society, although others had for some time laid claim to precedence. With this fact in mind you will not expect an address from me in the ten minutes given for response, and you will not therefore be disappointed.

Nevertheless I am glad to bear for you your heartfelt thanks for the greeting we have received. It has been a remarkable convention for us,—perhaps in nothing more remarkable than in the prominent place given to our Junior work. The first afternoon of the convention was very appropriately given up to the discussion of "Junior Work; Its Growth and its Possibilities." We shall go to our homes realizing more than ever the importance of this branch of Christian Endeavor.

If, to any of you who have long been acquainted with our older sister and have joined in the universal praise which is given her, but have not been acquainted with the youngest member of the family until you have met her at this convention — if it has seemed to you that the place this child has assumed in this great convention is out of all proportion to its size and age, we beg of you to put it down as a piece of youthful indiscretion on its part and not on that account to underestimate its real importance as a factor in the church life. For we assure you, with all modesty and with all earnestness, that the Junior Endeavor Society is of the very greatest importance. [*Applause.*]

The world has always belonged to young people, you know. The conquerors of the world have always been young men. Alexander was scarcely twenty-one when the foundation was laid for the conquest of the world by overthrowing the Persian power. Cæsar was a young man when he gathered the reins of Rome into his hand. Napoleon at twenty-seven was recognized as the " man of destiny." Yea, the world in every age has belonged and still belongs to the young. Ruskin says the noblest works of art have been conceived and executed by artists while they were young. So, too, the freshest, grand :st conceptions have come from the young life of our poets.

The same is true in education and in religion. As a rule the best work done by the men whose names we cherish belongs to their young life. Newton was twenty-five when he made his greatest discoveries. Calvin was twenty-five when he gave to the world his " Institutes." When one of our great colleges not long ago in the United States would find a man to stand at the head and direct its great work, it found such a person in a young man only twenty-seven. When the Trustees of our Endeavor Society would find a man capable of directing its tremendous business as General Secretary, after long, careful and prayerful searching it found such a man in our young Secretary, Mr. Baer, who has so magnificently borne the responsibilities laid upon him. Do you say all this has nothing to do with the Junior Society? The Y. P. S. C. E. is the training school for the statesmen and the preachers and the home builders of our nation. I answer you, God always works through instruments. If the Y. P. S. C. E. is to be in the future the means of giving to the world the best manhood and womanhood, then that manhood and womanhood must be first trained in boyhood and girlhood. Why do we not have a better quality of manhood today, even in our church life? Why do we find so many young people in our older society who cannot efficiently undertake any work outside of the regular routine? The answer is plain ; the training did not commence early enough. As Dr. Wayland Hoyt once said: " If we accept any truth or any system of truth, we must adapt ourselves to the structural idea of that truth or system of truth."

If then we believe that the Christian Endeavor idea is a means ordained of God to do great things for the manhood and womanhood of the world, we must adapt ourselves to its structural idea. The structural idea of the tree is the leaf. The tree is the leaf cut on a large pattern. The structural idea of the Y. P. S. C. E., Senior Christian Endeavor, Veteran Christian Endeavor, or any other Christian Endeavor, is the Junior society. The manhood and womanhood of the next generation is the boyhood and girlhood of our present Juniors grown large.

Within the Junior Society today are the future presidents and statesmen, the earnest preacher of the Gospel message, the consecrated missionaries of the cross, and those who shall make the homes that shall determine in great measure the character of the next generation.

.Within this company you have welcomed today are those who represent in good measure the best of the manhood and womanhood of the next generation. Some will follow the cross of Christ into the uttermost parts of the earth and will live themselves the Christlike life before those who have not heard of Christ. Many more, it may be, will tell the story of Jesus the Saviour of men once again to those who are perishing in our own lands. But perhaps the greatest company of us, unnoticed by the world, in the humblest stations to which God may call us, will live that life of earnest consecration and true Christian Endeavor which alone can prepare us for the greater privilege, the larger responsibilities, which God will call us to by and by.

All of us, I am sure, will go forth from this convention full of the inspiration which has come to us, with a larger outlook upon life, with a more earnest desire to realize in our own lives the ideal which has been set before us; and with hearts beating loyal to our one Master, even Christ, we will go on and on into a more abundant life in Christ.

Let that inspired and inspiring faith in God and that consecrated courage which we have learned in this convention is so characteristic of the young life never forsake us.

We will go back to our homes and our societies and to the duties that once seemed so discouraging to us, better and more loyal Christians and will thank God as long as we live for the convention at Montreal in 1893. [*Applause.*]

After the singing of another hymn, Mr. Sewall introduced Mr. C. J. Atkinson, of Toronto, to speak on the Junior Endeavor Pledge. **Mr.** Atkinson spoke as follows : —

The Pledge.

Address of Mr. C. J. Atkinson.

Mr. Chairman and Fellow Juniors: After this very cordial introduction that we have had, I think we may consider ourselves acquainted and shake hands generally all around. Although I do not know your names, I know that we all bear the one name, Junior Endeavor, and that we are all in one army and fighting under one Master, Jesus Christ, whose banner over us is love. What an army it is? You have seen on the streets during the past days thousands of Christian Endeavorers from all parts of the world, with their badges fluttering in the breeze, and you know that they represent hundreds of thousands at home. These are all soldiers, fighting under this one Master, and they are all pledged soldiers. They have all taken the pledge to be true to their Master, and it is about this pledge I am going to speak this afternoon.

The question often arises and is asked of those engaged in the Junior work, "Do the children keep the pledge? Is it wise for them to sign a pledge of this kind?" In speaking to you, children, I do not need to answer that question; but it does seem as if the Juniors were trying much harder to keep their pledge than some of the young people are to keep theirs. I know a Junior society of boys in a very large school where there are nearly two hundred boys living together, and where to take that pledge means that they have to stand a good many jeers and taunts, and yet those boys have their pledges tacked up over their chairs in the reading-room, and are living just as true to that pledge as they can, trusting in the Lord Jesus Christ for strength. Of course they sometimes make mistakes and say things they are sorry for afterwards, but when they do, they go and ask forgiveness of those to whom they have said such things. I knew of a little girl at the consecration meeting of a Junior Endeavor society who began to sob bitterly while the superintendent was speaking about the pledge. At the close of the meeting the superintendent asked her why she was crying. She said she wanted her name taken from the roll; she had not been able to keep the pledge and could not keep it. On inquiry it was found that she had not had an opportunity of reading her Bible every day. That was all, yet she felt badly about it. Provision was made whereby she could read the Bible every day, and she is now an active Junior.

Some years ago I heard William Reynolds, the great Sunday-school man, say that when he first entered the Sunday school he did not believe in taking the pledge; but one day there was a railway accident to the train on which he was travelling, and many were injured. He was not injured himself, and be helped to carry the injured to homes near at hand. Among others was a little boy about thirteen years of age who was badly injured, and the doctor said that one of his legs would have to be cut off, in order to save his life. This would cause the boy so much pain that the doctor poured out some liquid into a glass to give to the boy to allay the pain. The boy asked what it was, and he was told that it was liquor. He said he could not drink it. They wanted to know why, and he said he had signed the temperance pledge, and had promised his mother never to touch it. "But," said the doctor, "you may not be able to stand this; you may die when your leg has been taken off. Won't you take it?" "No," said the boy, "I can die, but I cannot break my pledge." That is just the spirit we want among our Junior Endeavorers. We know they are willing to suffer to keep their pledge.

Every one should take the pledge because it enables them to stand. In Paul's letter to the Ephesians you know that he tells them, "Having done all, stand." To enable them to stand he recommended a Christian armor which they were to wear. You remember what that armor was, I dare say. I think that Christian armor represents our pledge, and represents it beautifully, and I wish this afternoon to illustrate the pledge by this Christian armor.

You remember that Paul said, first and foremost, that we are to take the shield of faith. Now if some boy will come up here, I will give him a shield.

A small boy came up to the platform and Mr. Atkinson placed upon him, one after another, the various portions of the armor which he was describing. The several pieces were made of bright tin, appropriately lettered, and the whole made a very impressive illustration.

You will see on the shield the words, "Trusting in the Lord Jesus Christ for strength." That is the first part of our pledge, — faith, trusting in Christ for everything, and not in self. A child's definition of faith was, "Doing whatever God wants me to do and asking no questions." Could you wish for a better definition? It is one of the most difficult things we have to do, to trust in the Lord Jesus for everything and keep self in the background. How we do want to put ourselves in the front! What letter is it that you have the greatest difficulty with in the alphabet? The letter "I." It seems to be right in the centre of everything that is bad. If we had a blackboard here and I should write upon it the word "Sin," you would find that letter "I" right in the centre of it. Self, it seems to me, is at the heart of nearly all sin, so that we want to trust in Christ for strength.

Another piece of the armor is the breast-plate — the breast-plate of righteousness. You will notice that we have on the breast-plate the words following those on the shield, "I promise him that I will strive to do whatever he would like to have me do." This means right living, righteousness, doing right under all circumstances, and amid great difficulties standing true.

Then another part of the armor is the Sword of the Spirit, the Word of God. This bears the words "I will pray and read the Bible every day."

Then, fourthly, there is the helmet — the helmet of salvation. This bears the words, "So far as I know how I will try to lead a Christian life." No boy or girl can take this pledge or should take it, unless they are true Christians and can wear this helmet of salvation. [*Applause.*]

Mr. Atkinson then asked the congregation to unite in singing "Onward, Christian Soldiers," which was done with great enthusiasm.

MR. SEWALL : The next speaker is one who has come all the way across the continent to speak to us this afternoon. I am sure we will give a very hearty welcome to Miss Belle P. Nason, the state superintendent of Junior work in the great commonwealth of California, as she tells us about the consecration meeting. [*Applause.*]

The Consecration Meeting.

Address of Miss Belle P. Nason.

Boys and girls, I bring you greeting from the Juniors of California, so many thousands of miles from here. Many of them are now praying for the Junior rally. We feel, we know, God's spirit has been and is present here with us. May each of you be filled with the fulness of his spirit; then indeed wil you accomplish great things the coming year.

How grateful I am that this great international convention has given us, the Juniors, so large a part in their program. Does it not prove that we are becoming a power and that the seniors are in deep sympathy with the work? A few years ago they did not realize that mere boys and girls could exert the influence and do the work they are now accomplishing for Christ. And boys and girls, there is no outlook so great for any other organization. Great possibilities stretch before us. In the near future the Juniors will represent the working forces in our churches, the trained active members of the senior Christian Endeavor, and the Christian leaders in this world's work. Yes, Juniors, *you* are to bring the world to Christ. Every boy, every girl, with the right influence thrown around them can be won for Christ, and the great potent influence is and will be the Junior Christian Endeavor. "Behold, I have set before thee an open door, and no man can shut it." I believe that the Junior Christian Endeavor is a great door that Christ has opened.

I am to speak to you on the consecration meeting. Stop but a moment and think what the word "consecration" means? Setting oneself apart, devoting one's life, giving up self entirely, unreservedly. Our consecration meeting is not simply a roll-call meeting. The consecration meeting is a meeting between ourselves and our God, for it is to him alone that we consecrate ourselves, and how can we do so without speaking directly to him. In the truest sense it should be a prayer meeting. This definition of prayer was given in a Junior rally in Brooklyn: "We speak, God listens; God speaks, we listen." This is the key of the true consecration meeting.

This part of the pledge, however, should be present with us: "I will strive to do whatever he would have me to do;" and the thought comes to us, What can I give him this month? What service can I render to him? "Lord, what wilt thou have me to do?" "I have not kept my pledge this month, but I hope to keep it better next month," are words often spoken in our consecration meeting by seniors and Juniors. I wonder as he listens what he thinks of such words used as a consecration to him. If used insincerely, they must indeed deeply grieve that great loving heart. We do want to keep all form out of our consecration meetings, so I think it wiser and better, not to have the regular roll-call every consecration meeting. Vary it by asking the officers of the society to first consecrate themselves to Christ. Then request the prayer-meeting committee — how much there is for them to consecrate to him in their work! — to rise and separately consecrate themselves; then the lookout committee, and so on through all the committees. Another time, ask all on one side of the room who wish to consecrate themselves to rise, one following the other in prayer or sentence; then call for those in the different parts of the room. Another way is to ask those first to consecrate themselves who are His professed followers, having united with his church. Then here it would be well to ask if there are not others who are ready and want to join the church at the next communion. Always ask at the close of the consecration meeting, if there are not associate members or strangers who will for the first time make the consecration of their lives to Him and his service. And, boys and girls, if all have truly taken part and earnest prayers have been raised to Him to send his Spirit in our meeting to help, to strengthen us, we will rarely hold a consecration meeting without new consecrations from those we have been praying for. Yes, prayer is the stronghold of our meeting — of our lives.

This badge or medal represents a society, organized two years ago in the most southwestern city in the United States, with a membership now of 181 Juniors who gave me this token of their love as I was leaving for the East. In looking back over our work I realize what the consecration meeting has been to us. One hundred and forty-five boys and girls have consecrated themselves to Him. Last year over 40 united with our church, so many have stepped over the line from associate to active membership.

We know Christian Endeavor could not mean what it now does to us without this consecration meeting. One young man who greatly assisted me in my work, but who had never before done any active Christian work, was deeply moved by the consecrations of our boys and girls, and he felt with me that his usefulness was greatly hindered with the boys and girls by being such an inveterate smoker. He had tried many times to give it up, but to no avail; but after listening to B. Fay Mills's sermon, "They rolled the stone away," he realized what a stumbing-block his smoking was to himself, and many he would help. The following Sunday he came to our consecration meeting, and publicly before our Junior society gave himself in deeper consecration to Him, and said with God's help he would never smoke again. His few earnest, determined words stirred many, and many of our boys made the same resolve. A few days after I met his mother, who told me that on going to his room the next day, she saw three cigars hanging by a string on the wall, and these words written under them: "I've rolled the stone away." Since then he has thrown himself into our Christian work, and is a power.

Boys and girls, let us make our consecration practical. "Ye are my witnesses," means you Juniors who are serving Him; and as our conditions are different from others, so should our consecrations be. Be true to yourselves. You cannot be true to Christ, unless you are. Do not try to use the words of others for your consecration. Let us give our love, our service to him as naturally, as sincerely, as we pledge certain things to our parents. A boy rising among his fellow-companions with the prayer, "Help me this month to lead such a consistent life that I may bring my friend to feel that he will also determine to serve Thee" will become a power among his boy friends. They admire him for his sincerity, and God's spirit blesses him, because he asks for and wants the help. We need praying boys. With a prayer you can resist any temptation. "Quench not the holy Spirit;" and if a feeling or thought comes to you in your service for Christ, give expression of it to him. How sad we would feel if our bodies were dwarfed, deformed! What intense mortification it would cause! But our bodies only last for a short time, our souls for an eternity of time, and how much more terrible for us to willingly dwarf our souls! God's Holy Spirit is near to help us to grow, to feed us, but if we quench this spirit in our hearts, then indeed we become dwarfed and deformed.

One of our celebrated ministers has said our judgment day is every day, for God is a living God, knowing and seeing each daily act of our lives. So daily meeting his approval or displeasure, do let us realize this in our consecration meeting. Each meeting we should feel and know that we have more and more of his spirit. Knowing this, there will be then no fear of a judgment day, and we shall feel assured of his welcome when we go to live with him, for we are his children. We know of one dear Junior Endeavorer, who knew he was soon to go home and be with his Saviour, to whom he had consecrated his life. He took his tiny Christian Endeavor pin and put it in his father's coat as a reminder of his love to his earthly father; and children, if you look upon Mr. Baer's coat, you will see that bright, shining little Christian Endeavor pin that he always wears, feeling that his boy's presence comes to him in such bright, loving, Christian helpfulness. Do you wonder that he has such a deep, tender love and sympathy for the Junior Endeavorers, and that he longs to see the boys and girls consecrated to Christ's service.

Let this coming year be a year marked by the consecration of the boys and girls. Let our consecration meetings be meetings of direct prayer to God, realizing that our own Saviour, the King of kings, is near us to help, strengthen, guide, and receive us, and to fill us with his spirit. [*Applause.*]

MR. SEWALL: We are now to hear some voices from across the sea, in a service which is to be led by one whom all the Juniors and all the Junior workers of our broad land know and love, one who has done so much for Junior work, who presided over the first rally of the Juniors last year in New York,— Mrs. Alice May Scudder, of Jersey City. [*Applause.*]

Mrs. Scudder then ascended the platform and read the following original poem. Seated in chairs in front of the pulpit platform were a dozen girls, each one clad in the costume of some foreign country. These costumes had been brought to the convention by Mrs. Clark, who secured them during her tour around the world. As Mrs. Scudder mentioned the name of a certain country, the girl representing that country arose in her place and repeated in foreign accents the verse of Scripture or the hymn which Mrs. Scudder announced. The whole effect was very beautiful, and the participants were loudly applauded.

Voices from Across the Sea.

Dialogue. Conducted by Mrs. Alice May Scudder.

Old Father Time has turned his glass,
   Another year has flown ;
We come to greet each other here
   In old familiar tone.

Our Junior work shall be our theme,
   The children still our song ;
For if the youth grow up aright,
   Our nations will be strong.

These little hands must do good deeds ;
   These hearts must loyal be
To the blessed God who reigns above,
   To church and unity.

Our Master gave a broad command,—
   "Go and all nations teach,"
That Father, Son, and Holy Ghost
   Hereafter men may preach.

So show by ministries of love
   The brotherhood of man ;
Unselfish action can best prove
   The noble Gospel plan.

To forge a chain of Christian love
   To reach around the earth,
Our loving leaders went abroad
   To give " Endeavor " birth.

In vast Australia's far-off land
   The noble truths they plant ;
Which friends, inspired by Christian love,
   With wondrous beauty chant.

On Japan's island shores they halt,
   And, though the days are few,
They strive by thoughts of Christ and Church
   To wake a purpose new.

And other lands they visited,
   Saw people strange and new.

And while they gave them helpful thoughts,
    Their love for missions grew.

The boys and girls of these far climes
    They sought to form in bands,
That pledge and pin may soon appear
    In all our heathen lands.

And children, too, are here today,
    In foreign garments clad,
To hear them speak in language strange
    Will surely make you glad.

Samoa comes in native dress, —
    Let not a sound be heard,
But listen, one and all so still,
    To drink in every word.

Response. — God so loved the world that he gave his only begotten Son, that whosoever believeth in him should not perish, but have everlasting life. — *John 3: 16.*

A Chinese song is rare to hear,
    The words to you unknown,
They sing of " bringing in the sheaves"
    After the seed is sown.

Response. — " Sowing in the morning, sowing seeds of kindness,
    Sowing in the noontide and the dewy eve,
Waiting for the harvest and the time of reaping,
    We shall come rejoicing, bringing in the sheaves."

And Japan, too, may come and speak,
    In queer and foreign way.
Attentive still we all must be,
    To hear what she will say.

Response. — " Let the people praise thee, O God, let all the people praise thee."

The India girls, in rich attire,
    May now come forth to view,
And they will speak in native tongue
    Their Bible verses, too.

We first shall hear the Telugu,
    Which in the South they speak ;
Her verse sets forth the Master's praise
    For those who help the weak.

Response. — And the King shall answer and say unto them, Verily, I say unto you, Inasmuch as ye have done it unto one of the least of these my brethren, ye have done it unto me. — *Matt. 25: 40.*

In India North the people speak
    The language called Urdu,
And we shall have a Scripture verse
    Much loved by each of you.

Response. — For God so loved the world that he gave his only begotten Son, that whosoever believeth in him should not perish, but have everlasting life. — *John 3: 16.*

Bengalee in Calcutta heard,
    A language strange in sound,
Yet Bible message is the same
    The whole wide world around.

Response. — He that believeth on him is not condemned, but he that believeth not is condemned already, because he hath not believed in the name of the only begotten Son of God. — *John 3: 18.*

And now Armenia's child will come,
    Dressed as in days of old,
When Christ abroad in all the land
    The Gospel story told.

Response. — " Will you go, will you go, to the promised land ?
    Will you go, will you go, to the promised land ?
    My Father calls me, I must go
    To meet Him in the promised land."

Poor Turkey, sad and oft oppressed,
    You have a welcome, too,
Speak up right loud, so all can hear
    The Golden Rule from you.

Response. — " Do unto others as ye would that others should do unto you."

In Turkey, too, they speak the Greek,
    The language that was used
For writing the New Testament,
    Which oft should be perused.

Response. — I will arise and go to my father, and I will say unto him, Father, I have sinned against heaven and before thee. — *Luke 15: 18.*

Through length and breadth of sunny France
    Is heard the Gospel truth,
And in Endeavor's ranks now shine
    Her sunny-hearted youth.

Response. — " Tell me the old, old story."

" Racontez moi l' histoire,
    De l'ami du pecheur,
Parlez-moi de la gloire
    De Jesus, mon Sauveur.
C'est une simple histoire,
    Qui rejouit le coeur,
Je veux dans ma memoire,
    L' inscrire avec bon-heur."

To Spain we look with gratitude,
    On this Columbian year ;
And may the people of that land
    The Gospel message hear.

Response. — " He that believeth on him is not condemned, but he that believeth not is condemned already, because he hath not believed in the name of the only begotten Son of God."

The aim of all our hearts should be
    These lands for Christ to win,
And caring for the children first,
    We shall aright begin.

These little ones of every land,
    Committed to our care,
Shall shine with beams of heavenly light,
    As jewels rich and rare.

[*Turning to Mrs. Clark :*]

And you went forth, beloved friends,
    On mission grand and brave,
To introduce our Junior work
    Across the ocean wave.

You had a welcome large and wide,
    You wore their garlands gay,
And after absence most a year
    We meet again today.

And gratitude is written deep
    In each devoted heart,
For God his watch between us kept,
    Though we were far apart.

A double welcome waits you here,
    For two great countries meet
To sit in loving harmony,
    And hold communion sweet.

[*Enter child dressed in English costume.*]

And Canada will greet you first,
  In blest "Endeavor's" name;
And for the Juniors of the land
  A welcome home proclaim.

We are but new in Junior work,
  Yet wiser we shall be
After this great convention here
  In eighteen ninety-three.

The helpful words heard here today
  Shall hope and courage give,
And memories of this pleasant time
  Stay by us while we live.

[*American costume.*]

America I represent,
  And all her children dear
Now bring their tribute to lay down
  With other nations here.

We are the last, but not the least,
  In fond affection's chain,
We, too, would say the loving words
  Of "Welcome home" again.

We greet you in the Master's name,
  And sing of union sweet,
When all the nations of the world
  Around God's throne shall meet.   [*Great applause.*]

The two children representing Canada and America each presented a beautiful bouquet, one containing an English flag and the other an American flag, to Dr. and Mrs. Clark. The organ started the hymn "Blest Be the Tie That Binds," and Dr. and Mrs. Clark ascended the pulpit platform amid the enthusiastic waving of handkerchiefs while the singing continued.

MR. SEWALL: I am sure that it is not necessary for me to give a formal introduction to the next speaker. I want to introduce her with a single word — I mean literally one word, — and that word is "*Mother* Endeavor" Clark. [*Applause.*]

How Some Boys and Girls Are Endeavoring.

Address of Mrs. F. E. Clark.

It is a very pleasant thing to be here in this beautiful church, and to see all these happy faces, but it is still pleasanter to think of the reason why we are all here this afternoon. We are Christian Endeavorers here today and we have come here, I hope, because we want to make our Endeavor a better one. We have heard this afternoon some very earnest, helpful words that have made us all feel that we want to do more work for Jesus than we have ever done before. I am sure it would help you all, as it has helped me, if you could see, as I have seen, how some boys and girls in other lands are working for Jesus. I am going to tell you about a few of them this afternoon, and when we think of what they are doing, I hope we shall want to do more.

I remember when I was a little girl in school and studied geography, I learned that the world was round like a ball or an orange. I have been studying geography in a different way lately, and I know that the world is round because I have travelled all the way around it to see for myself. I have seen funny little Chinamen with their long queues and queer Chinese costumes, and bright little Japanese boys and girls carrying their baby brothers and sisters on their backs, and pretty little brown children in India, and all kinds of children in many different countries; and, best of all, I have seen, in all of these countries, boys and girls who are trying, as you are trying, to do whatever Jesus would like to have them do. I have not time today to tell you much about them, but I want to tell you where some of them are, and what some of them are doing. If you could look right through the earth to a point in the southern hemisphere, nearly opposite to Montreal, you would see the boys and girls in Australia, and you would find some very earnest enthusiastic little workers over there. It would take me all the afternoon to tell you all the things those Juniors are trying to do for Jesus, so I am not going to attempt it, but I am going to tell you one thing about one society.

They have a birthday committee, and they collect birthday offerings from all their members and from any one else who will give it. Sometimes it is as many pennies as they are years old, and sometimes when the fathers and mothers want to give an offering, too, they make it as many shillings as they are years old, and then their missionary box fills up very fast, and these children, with their pennies and their pounds, are helping Junior Endeavorers in many other lands as well as in their own. I think their contributions to missions last year was larger than that from the older society. If we should follow their example and give generously to the missionary boards to help the children in other lands, would it not be doing something " Jesus would like to have us do "? [*Applause.*]

But we must hurry on if we are going around the world in fifteen minutes; that is faster than even Nellie Bly could do it. If you could go into one of the mission schools in Canton you would hear some Christian Endeavor girls singing

" Cha cha ko ie ho' chung,
Kek chu fu lkeng kleng sing,"

very much as these girls have just sung it, only their pronunciation might be a little more correct.

If you could look into the Southgate church in Shanghai, you would see a boys' Junior Endeavor society. The missionaries told me that every one noticed what good boys these little Chinamen were, and that there was a great improvement in their behavior, at home, and at school, and everywhere, since they joined the Junior Endeavor society, and that the Christian Endeavor boys were known from other boys because they behaved better. If we in Christian America should follow the example these Chinese boys have set us, and show our Christian Endeavor by our daily lives, would it not be one of the things that " Jesus would like to have us do "? [*Applause.*]

If I could bring in a little Japanese boy this afternoon, he would probably be very much surprised to see so many children here, and he would not want to speak to us, but if we told him he must speak for the sake of Christian Endeavor, he would probably say, " Shkataganai," " It can't be helped," and then he would tell us about those Japanese boys in Nagoya, who have formed a Junior society there and who have already raised some missionary money and brought a good many heathen boys into their meetings, who mean to do some earnest Christian work for Japan one of these days. [*Applause.*]

And we must have just a word from that little American society in Kioto. There are about a dozen little missionary children there who meet every week; and I wish you could have heard how earnestly they prayed for the children across the water in the dear homeland. As I listened to those prayers, some of them offered by children only seven or eight years old, I wondered if the children over here remembered to pray for their brothers and sisters in Japan. I think when we pray for Japan we generally pray for the missionaries and for the Japanese, and we do not always remember to include the missionary children in our prayers. We do not realize that they have their own little privations and hardships to bear as well as their fathers and mothers. I have been very much pleased to see how cheerily these children bear their share of the burden, and how earnest they are in their Christian life. I think some of the best Christian Endeavor societies I have ever seen have been those formed by missionary

A CHINESE JUNIOR SOCIETY.

Picture from a photograph of the Chinese Junior Society of Christian Endeavor in the South Gate Presbyterian Mission of Shanghai, showing Dr. and Mrs. Clark and their son Eugene.

children in different lands. I suppose the missionary children in Japan could, if they chose, tell you of a good many little trials that they have to bear, but they very seldom do choose to speak of them, for they like to make the best of things. Because I want you to know how to sympathize with them, I am going to tell you of just two of their trials; one is a big one and the other is a very little one. The first and hardest one is loneliness. They have very few little friends or playmates. Usually, only two or three missionary families live in one town, and as the older boys and girls have to be sent home to England or America to study, the younger children who are left are lonesome. How would you like to be the only white boy in the town in which you live? How would you girls like it, if your only playmates were Japanese girls, and, perhaps, you could not speak their language very well? Don't you feel sorry for these boys and girls who must do without all the fun and jollity and good fellowship that you have in the schoolroom and on the playground?

And now for the little trial, though perhaps some of you might not call it a very little one. They can never have any candy unless some one from across the water sends them some; for the Japanese candy is usually made mostly of rice flour, with a very little sugar, which is not very tempting. Perhaps this trial is only a blessing in disguise, for it does not probably injure their health to do without the candy, still I think some of you would consider it a hardship never to taste any candy from one year's end to another, not even at Christmas time. I think if I were a boy or girl in America I should once in a while find a way to send some candy to the missionary children in Japan, and I should occasionly send some toys and pretty books too.

But we must hurry on and have a short visit with the little brown-faced Juniors in India and Ceylon. I know some brown-faced boys in Bombay who pleased me very much, because they were always so bright and cheery, and so ready to do any Christian work that was appointed to them. They did not ask to do the kind of work that they liked best, and they did not say they were too busy, but they did cheerily and quickly just the work that was given them to do. Would not theirs be a good example for us to follow?

I know some black-eyed maidens in Madura who were so anxious to help their little sisters in China that for a good many weeks they gave up their cocoanuts, having only rice and curry for their dinner, so that they might give money the cocoanuts would have cost to help the children in China. [*Applause.*] And this meant giving the best part of their dinner every day for the sake of children whom they had never seen. Have any of us made as great a sacrifice as this for the missionary cause? If we could sail from Bombay across the Arabian Sea, and then up through the Red Sea and the Suez Canal, and across the Mediterranean, we should come to Turkey.

There are seven little missionary children in Talas who have a Junior society of their own. The eldest one is twelve years old and the youngest four. The little four-year-old boy is the "sunshine committee," and in one of their last meetings he prayed that Jesus would help him not to be a "thunder-cloud" committee, but to make sunshine all the time. The little six-year-old boy prayed, "Please help us when we want to be naughty to put up our hands quickly and feel for our badges, and to remember what those letters mean, and then not do the naughty things." It might be well for some of us who are older to offer the same prayer.

In another part of Turkey there is a Junior society which has only two members, a missionary boy and an Armenian boy. They hold their meetings regularly, and they sing and pray and take up a collection, and are just as much in earnest about it as if they had a hundred members.

The missionary boy has no other playmate than this Armenian boy, and one of the trials that he has to bear is that he must go to a girls' school and be the only boy in the school. I think some of you boys would call that a pretty big trial. He wrote a composition in school a little while ago on "The boy I would like for my friend."

It is touching to think of this lonely boy in a foreign land, longing for boy friendships and boyish plays, and consoling himself with a composition, and making an imaginary friend for himself on paper. ·

He wanted "A boy that is not afraid of anything, a boy that knows how to get along on a desert island, a boy that likes to play, a boy that knows how to fish, a boy that carries a string and a knife in his pocket." He wanted an American boy but he thought perhaps an English boy would answer the purpose. If you read the "*Junior Golden Rule*" for July you will find out all about the friend he wants, and if there is any such boy over here, I hope he will write to that boy in Broosa, and tell him that he has a string and a knife in his pocket, and if the string is not long enough to reach way over to Broosa, perhaps they can stretch an imaginary line across that will bind their friendship together.

There is not time this afternoon to tell you all I would like to tell about the children across the waters, but I hope you will find out the rest for yourselves. I want you to read your missionary papers, and learn all you can about the children in other lands, and to follow everything that is good in their example; and then I want you to do everything you can to help the children who have not your opportunities and privileges, and I hope you sow many little Christian Endeavor seeds in other lands all the world around.

> " Ever so little the seed may be,
> Ever so little the hand,
> But when it is sown, it must grow, you see,
> And develop its nature, fruit, flower, or tree,
> The sunshine, the dew, and the air are all free
> At His command." [*Loud applause.*]

MR. SEWALL : We have now come to the closing consecration service, which is to be lead by Miss Gertrude W. Wood, of Brooklyn, N. Y.

Consecration Service.

Led by Miss Gertrude W. Wood.

Miss Wood was given a most generous welcome as she came to the platform. One stanza of the hymn " Just as I am, Thine Own to be " was then sung.

MISS WOOD : Christian Endeavor, if it means anything, means loving service. Consecration, if it means anything to us, means that we are willing to be used for Jesus. This is a consecration service — a loving service it may be to all of us. I would ask you for a few moments to think about being used for Jesus.

We were made to be used, you and I, — not meant to live idle, selfish, useless lives, to receive without giving, to be served without serving ; but we were made to be used for somebody and for something. Men are making all the time hundreds of things, many of them simply for ornament, but the large majority for some practical use. God creates hundreds of thousands of people, but he never made one simply for ornament. Every one is for use. We are made to be used, first of all and most of all, for God and for Jesus Christ. Do you remember the words of Jesus in that last prayer of his recorded in the seventeenth chapter of John, where he says, " Thine they were and thou gavest them me "? Boys and girls, God has given you to Jesus Christ to be a little instrument in his hand for the bringing about of his kingdom in the world. That is our work in the world, to do what we can to establish the kingdom of Christ upon this earth. God asks that a part of this work be done by you.

Do you ask me what can you do? Let me tell you. You know what the boys and girls do in the household, — not the large things, not the great tasks, not the cooking for the family, or the planning or providing ; but there is one thing we are so glad to have them take charge of — the errands. How much the boys and girls help us in this way! How many steps they save father and mother and dear, old feeble grandmother! What should we do, boys and girls, without your ready and willing feet, and your quick and careful hands? I wonder if you are glad to serve in this way? I hope you are, because this is your way, and it is not a little insignificant work, but it is a great work, and you can do it so well, if you will.

Now we belong to God's great family. Do you know what you can do? Errands for God. A gentleman came home one afternoon, and going up the steps of his house he met his little daughter with a basket. "Where are you going?" he said. "Just on a little errand." "An errand for mother?" "No," she said, "I am going on a little errand for God." In that little basket she had some fruit and jellies which she was going to take to a poor sick woman not far away. Perhaps you will have an opportunity to do a similar errand for God some day. Do you think that the angels do all of God's errands for him? I know that the angels are busy every moment doing God's will; but he has not given them all the work to do, he has saved plenty of it for us boys and girls. Ah, there is a little boy crying over there! Something is the matter. Not an angel is wanted to come to that little boy's assistance, but some bright Junior boy or girl, some Sunday-school boy or girl with a kind heart and willing hands, who will sympathize with that little fellow and help him. That is a little errand to do for God. Here is a letter that wants to be mailed right away, carrying good news to some one over the sea. Not an angel is wanted to post that letter, but some bright, ready boy, some quick, willing girl. That is an errand for God. God has just as many errands for us to do for him as there are things in the world to do. There is a little sick girl living down the street. Perhaps you do not like to give up all the afternoon and go and see her and cheer her up, but that is a little errand for God. Perhaps in your society there is something to be done that is not very pleasant, something that no one else wants to do. Make that a little errand for God, and go and do that work just as quickly and gladly as you can. Perhaps in your society there is a stranger. Ah, there is a little errand for you! Go and seek out that stranger; give to him a cordial welcome and invite him to your meeting again and again. There are just so many ways in which we are provided with errands to do for God — just as many things as we can possibly do to help any one else we can do as little errands for God.

I wonder if here in Canada you are like our boys and girls in the Brooklyn schools. The boy or girl who can sit up in the front seat and wait on the teacher and carry her messages considers that a great honor. I wonder if the Canada boys and girls like to wait on the teacher. Are you not as ready and as glad to wait on our King in that way? When Lady Somerset was once introduced to speak before an audience, she was introduced with all the numerous titles which belong to her, but she said, "It almost frightens me to be introduced in this way. All that I desire to be is just the Lord's little hand-maiden." I wonder if the girls here have that for their chief desire, to be the Lord's little handmaidens. I wonder if you boys want to be pages, standing ready to do the King's bidding, going swiftly on his errands. I want you to be glad to go on the King's errands, ready to serve him in this way.

May God help you boys and girls who are Junior Christian Endeavorers, and those who are not members of the society, but who soon will be, I trust, so to go upon his errands and to be so faithful to him that when you are men and women he will give you the larger and the greater things to do, because "He that is faithful in that which is least is faithful also in much."

Now I would like to ask all the boys and girls here, whether Juniors or not, to rise and let us read the Junior pledge together.

The children all rose in obedience to this request and repeated together the Junior pledge, after which the service was closed with singing the last verse of "Just as I Am,"—

> " Just as I am, young, strong, and free,
>   To be the best that I can be
>   For truth and righteousness and Thee,
>   Lord of my life, I come, I come."

Dr. Clark then called upon all to join in the Mizpah benediction, and thus closed one of the most impressive meetings in connection with the convention.

DENOMINATIONAL RALLIES.

These all met simultaneously at the hour of half-past two. Most of them were large and enthusiastic gatherings. The following reports, which were mainly furnished by eminent representatives, of the several denominations are copied from *The Golden Rule* of July 27 and August 3.

Methodist Protestant.

About fifty delegates assembled. Rev. H. L. Elderdice, president of the Denominational Union, took charge in the absence of Secretary Reynolds. Rev. A. D. Melvin, of Westminster, Md., led in prayer. President Elderdice spoke of what Christian Endeavor had done for the denomination, — made its members acquainted with each other and with other denominations; and of what the denomination had done for Christian Endeavor, — officially indorsed it and organized over 700 societies.

Rev. J. F. Cowan gave a retrospect of the work. Rev. W. D. Stultz spoke for New Jersey; Rev. George R. Brown, for Alabama; Rev. S. J. Smith, for the District of Columbia. The meeting was then thrown open for all.

Representatives were present from West Virginia, Ohio, Connecticut, Indiana, Pittsburg, Maryland, Alabama, Japan, etc. Dr. Lewis, of the Western Maryland College, and Miss Jennie White, denominational vice-president, also spoke.

United Presbyterian.

Representatives of fourteen presbyteries and several states — as far west as Kansas and east to Vermont — came together at the United Presbyterian rally. Several earnest addresses were made, all deprecating the fact that not all the societies in the United Presbyterian church are in connection with the Christian Endeavor general movement, the speakers pledging each other to do all in their power to promote Christian Endeavor interests. Testimony from several pastors to the effect that affiliation with Christian Endeavor does not decrease, but rather strengthens, the loyalty of the young people to the distinctive principles of their denomination was given, and appeared to be unanimously concurred in.

Lutheran.

This meeting was quite well attended, and was full of intense interest, being led by that enthusiastic Endeavorer, Dr. Mosheim Rhodes, of St. Louis, Mo. The conference was especially happy in having present the Rev. Dr. David A. Day, superintendent of the Muhlenberg Lutheran Mission in Liberia, Africa, who reported an excellent Christian Endeavor society in the mission. There is one young chief, now in this country, who used to walk twelve miles on Sunday to attend the prayer meeting. The first young lady Endeavor missionary sent to the Africa mission died only three days after touching the shore of the Dark Continent.

There were also present Rev. George Scholl, D.D., secretary of the Home Mission Board, Rev. Leander S. Keyser, Rev. A. J. Turkle, Rev. L. P. Ludden, and Rev. D. W. Lawrence, all of whom expressed intense satisfaction in the fact that their church has part and lot in the great Endeavor movement.

A representative from California reported that all the General Synod Lutheran churches of that state had Young People's societies of Christian Endeavor, and most of them also Junior societies. Many ringing words, pledging loyalty, both to Lutheran and Christian Endeavor principles, were spoken, and the determination was expressed that the Lutheran church should have a still larger part in the great convention of 1894.

Baptist.

The Baptists met in the Olivet Baptist church, Rev. W. H. Geistweit, of Minneapolis, presiding. The opening address of the chairman emphasized three needed characteristics of young Christians: conviction as regards truth, concentration of effort, and consecration of soul and body to God.

Dr. Wilkins, the general secretary of the Baptist Young People's Union of America, was the first speaker, following the opening words of the chairman. In a pleasing manner he defined the relation of the Baptist Union to Christian Endeavor. There was no need of changing names or organization in order to affiliate with the Baptist Young People's Union. The whole matter of inter-denominational fellowship was left to the local organization; all that the Union asked was that all societies of every name in Baptist churches affiliate with the B. Y. P. U. A.

General Morgan presented the work of the American Baptist Home Missionary Society, and Mr. Boston W. Smith, of Minnesota, spoke of the Sunday-school colportage and chapel-car work of the American Baptist Publication Society.

Mr. A. A. Ayer and Rev. Walter B. Hinson dwelt on the work of the Grand Ligne Mission in Canada; Miss Ella B. MacLaurin spoke of the work in foreign lands.

The Rev. Dr. Wayland Hoyt closed the meeting with an address, in which he urged increased loyalty to the Christian Endeavor Society, and at the same time urged all societies to affiliate with the Baptist Young People's Union.

Reformed Episcopal.

In the absence of Dr. Tracy, Bishop Samuel Fallows presided at the Reformed Episcopal rally in St. Bartholomew's church. Bishop Fallows organized the first society in the reformed Episcopal church. He spoke of its magnificent growth, alluded to the inspiration arising from these conventions, and urged forming societies.

Mr. John Ridgeway gave a helpful address on the helpfulness of the convention. Mr. W. Sloan spoke on the need of prayer, and especially for the Holy Spirit. Mr. M. G. Garrigues, of Philadelphia, spoke of the blessings of the convention to him. Among other speakers were Mr. Hubert Baker; Miss Hayne, of Chicago; Miss Vail, of Germantown, Penn.; Mrs. Baker, who spoke of the work among the policemen; Miss Price; Miss Bella Scott; Mr. Golf Ridgeway; Mr Frank Reynolds, and Rev. W. D. Stevens.

An informal tea was then served, and a delightful time had with happy, Christian talk. Bishop Fallows says that, though not so large in numbers, this in interest was far ahead of the New York rally.

United Brethren.

The United Brethren met in the Sunday-school room of the Crescent Presbyterian church. A number of states were represented, and a very pleasant meeting was had. Dr. R. L. Swain presided, and, after a brief devotional service, a number of interesting talks were given by persons present. All were glad to note the presence of Dr. M. R. Drury, associate editor of *The Religious Telescope*, who was an interested delegate. Rev. Mr. Kephart and Rev. Mr. Mundon, of Pennsylvania, were also present, and added much interest to the meeting. The burden of the meeting was, "How can we advance Christian Endeavor in the United Brethren church?" The meeting also furnished a splendid opportunity for handshaking, which was improved.

Christian.

The denominational rally of the representatives of the Christian church was held in the vestries of the Emmanuel Congregational church, Rev. Thomas S. Weeks, of Wolfborough, N. H., presiding. Gratulatory addresses were in order, and words of greeting were uttered by many of the Canadian brethren. The relation of the Christian Endeavor movement to church unity was the principal topic of several speakers, and all were agreed that the movement was doing much toward the chief purpose of the Christians. Denominational and interdenominational co-operation were considered, and further action provided for. The possibilities of the Christian Endeavor society in the pastorless church were presented by Rev. M. Summerbell, D.D., of Lewiston, Me.

Reports of work done by various societies occupied a large part of the time. Special interest in mission work was a marked feature of all reports. Representatives were present from eastern Maine, and from Oregon, and from many places between. The service closed with singing, " Blest be the tie that binds." During the shower which came up just as the meeting was closed, the friends were all appointed a social committee, to make everybody acquainted with everybody else.

Cumberland Presbyterian.

The denominational rally was held at the St. Gabriel Presbyterian church, Rev. H. Clay Yates, of Vincennes, Ind., presiding. As this church is confined, in its denominational operations, to the middle, western, and southern states of the United States, its delegation was principally from Texas, Georgia, Arkansas, Tennessee, Kentucky, Indiana, Illinois, and the states and territories of the great West; yet its delegation was large at the rally, and the exercises were very interesting, enthusiastic, and spiritual. The general topic was, "Cumberland Presbyterians as an Integral Part of the Y. P. S. C. E. Movement." This was discussed by Rev. H. Clay Yates in a pithy, pointed, and forcible manner. He showed that the Cumberland Presbyterian church had entered into this movement formally and officially, as a whole, by making the Y. P. S. C. E. the official young people's society of the church, and that there rested a great responsibility upon the pastors and sessions of the Cumberland Presbyterian church to conserve the benefits of this movement of God, in the interest of the church, by seeing to it that a Y. P. S. C. E. be organized in every congregation. The indications of the Divine hand in the Endeavor work, and the great blessings dispensed thereby, were vividly presented.

The following are the subordinate divisions of the general topic, viz.: 1. " How To Awaken Greater Interest, and Better Train the Workers in Our Own Denomination." Discussion opened by M. D. Crakle, Evansville, Ind. 2. " A Distinctive Literature for Our Young People." Discussion opened by Rev. T. Ashburn, Tennessee. 3. " How To Utilize the Endeavor Movement in Conserving Denominational Interests." Discussion opened by Rev. G. H. Silvins, Tennessee. 4. " What Christian Endeavor Has Done and Should Do for Cumberland Presbyterians." Discussion opened by Rev. C. Francis, Arkansas. 5. " The Young People of Our Land for Christ." Discussion opened by Rev. J. L. Hudgins, Indiana.

All these phases of the general topic were excellently presented by the speakers who opened the discussion, and in the free parliament which followed the presentation of each of the above themes, many brief and happy talks were made, and valuable points set forth. At the close of the rally the pastor of the St. Gabriel Presbyterian church delivered an impressive and sensible talk, in which he warmly welcomed the delegates and commended the service, which was appropriately responded to by the chairman of the rally, Rev. H. Clay Yates.

Evangelical Association.

The representatives of the Evangelical Association met in the Directors' Room of the Y. M. C. A. building. Rev. W. F. Heil, of Allentown, Penn., was elected president, and Rev. U. F. Swengel, of York, secretary. A free parliament on Christian Endeavor work in the denomination was conducted by the president.

Rev. L. S. Richard of Baltimore, Md., addressed the meeting on the Keystone League of Christian Endeavor as a denominational organization. Rev. J. D. Woodring, of Allentown, Penn., spoke of the brighter outlook for the church because of the Christian Endeavor movement. Rev. J. C. Crouse, of Pennsylvania, spoke of the adaptation of Christian Endeavor work to the needs of the church. Rev. D. M. Metzger, of Writhsville, Penn., advocated strongly the organization of Junior societies of Christian Endeavor, and spoke of the good done in the way of conversion among children in a society with which he was connected in Baltimore, Md.

Rev. B. D. Albright spoke of the development of the young people through the instrumentality of these organizations, and of the need of personal effort. Mr. J. B. Suiter, of Bucknell University, Lewisburg, Penn., spoke of what the Christian Endeavor Society has done for him personally in the way of work and Christian development. Mr. Charles A. Shaffer, of Harrisburg, Penn., spoke of the privileges of visitors in societies of other churches when away from home. Rev. W. F. Heil spoke with enthusiasm of the inspiration he had received from the great convention then in session, and of the strong position maintained by the officers, speakers and members of the convention, on public morals, and especially in reference to the Sunday closing of the Exposition in Chicago, and the temperance question.

Rev. U. F. Swengel, secretary of the managing board of the Keystone League of Christian Endeavor, pressed the importance of organization both along denominational lines and for interdenominational inspiration and fellowship. Some steps were taken in the way of providing for a grand denominational rally at Cleveland, in 1894.

Reformed Church.

The Endeavorers of the Reformed (Dutch) church filled the auditorium of the Dominion Square Methodist church with numbers and enthusiasm. No fewer than twenty-three pastors, from various sections of the church, were present, thus conclusively showing the interest of the ministry of the Reformed church in Christian Endeavor.

Rev. A. DeW. Mason, of Boonton, N. J., presided, and, in his opening remarks, dwelt on the significance of these conferences as showing the desire of the leaders of our Society to emphasize the denomination as well as the interdenominational character of our fellowship and labor. He called attention to the large percentage of Endeavor societies in the Reformed church, there being 306 societies on record as organized among the 603 congregations of the church. In missionary work the Reformed church societies have taken a high stand, especially since the formation of the " Christian Endeavor Missionary League of the Reformed church." In the five months ending June 1, 1893, they gave $2,500 to the denominational missionary board, and have built two " Christian Endeavor churches," one at Edgerton, Minn., and the other at Wakonda, S. D., besides helping to sustain the Chittoor station in the Arcot Mission of India.

Rev. Prof. James F. Riggs then spoke on " Missions and the Bible," and his thought was, " These two words are the two poles of the Christian idea, — what God speaks and what we are to speak for him. As in science the problem of the age is to generate light without heat, so in Christian work our duty is to enlighten the world without generating the heats and jealousies and rivalries. To do this it is essential that we have knowledge of the right kind, — both knowledge of the Bible and knowledge of the work, and knowledge of the relation between them."

Rev. H. D'B. Mulford, of Syracuse, N. Y., speaking of " Missions and the Church." said, " It is a satisfaction to know that, of the three great divisions of the church, the Greek, the Roman, and the Reformed, it is the latter which is best fitted, by doctrine and polity, to be a working church and a leader in all modern reforms. It is, therefore, to be regretted that we fall so far below the measure of our possibilities in this regard, and turn aside so easily from the fulfilment of Christ's command to evangelize the nations."

In the necessary absence of Dr. D. J. Burrell, of New York, the Rev. Daniel H. Martin, of Newark, N. J., spoke briefly on "Missions and Christian Endeavor." He said that many are tempted to rest satisfied with the wonderful numerical growth of the Endeavor movement, but to do this is wrong and foolish. We are here to work for Christ, and the key-note of success is to be found in the three words, Consecration, Co-operation, Concentration. Beware of size or enthusiasm without corresponding results.

Rev. George W. Furbeck, of Stuyvesant, N. Y., was the last speaker, and in his remarks upon the topic, "The Missionary Work of Our Societies: What It Is," said, "Our *name*, Christian Endeavor, signifies exertion along the line of highest duty, — that to Christ. Our *work* is to bring Christ to the world, and to win the world for Christ. This work of ours is (1) to *know;* (2) to *pray;* (3) to *give;* (4) to *go.*"

The final feature of the rally was an open conference on the methods and results of mission work in the Reformed church societies. This was led by Rev. Dr. I. P. Brokaw, of Freehold, N. J., and was enthusiastically entered into by those present, some twenty-five or thirty societies speaking through their representatives. When this was concluded, the service closed with the "Mizpah benediction," and the remark of one speaker, "This is the pleasantest service, to me, of all the convention," was generally echoed.

Disciples of Christ.

The Disciples held their rally in the First Baptist church. Rev. J. H. Wright, president of the Iowa State Union, presided. Brief and spiritual addresses were made by Rev. F. D. Power, of Washington City; Rev. H. A. Northcutt, of Illinois; Rev. H. T. Morrison, of Iowa; Rev. J. L. Darsie, of Kentucky; Rev. A. B. Philputt, of Philadelphia; Rev. J. H. O. Smith, of Indiana; Rev. H. O. Breeden, of Des Moines; Mr. W. H. McClain, of Missouri; Rev. J. Z. Tyler, of Cleveland, O.; and Rev. J. H. Hardin, corresponding secretary of the General Christian Missionary Convention.

Half-minute speeches from the floor were necessary to give some vent to the pent-up enthusiasm of the Endeavorers who filled the body of the house. The purpose to plant a church in Montreal met with hearty favor. The work inaugurated one year ago to build a memorial church in Salt Lake City was reported as making favorable progress, and the mission there will probably be housed before the winter. It was also made known that about $2,500 more would be needed, by the first of next October, to meet obligations incurred in building. A resolution was adopted to prosecute this enterprise to completion, and for this purpose about $500 were pledged by those present.

The suggestion that a session of the next meeting of the General Christian Missionary Convention be devoted to the work of Christian Endeavor among the Disciples was greeted with applause, and Rev. J. H. Hardin, the corresponding secretary, promised to give that matter his personal attention in the preparation of the next program. The rally was a season of delightful social and spiritual fellowship. The Disciples are coming to the front in Christian Endeavor.

Presbyterian.

It was a thoroughly loyal gathering of Young Presbyterians that assembled in the Crescent Presbyterian church. The speakers — all of them true blue to the core — faced a goodly audience, whose enthusiasm found frequent and pronounced expression. No time was wasted in idle words. A few snappy practical sentences from Rev. J. Clement French, the president of the conference, opened the meeting and outlined its purpose.

As Presbyterians, all were anxious to learn of the progress of the work in the denominations. Mr. W. Henry Grant, Rev. Thornton B. Penfield, and Miss Wishard, secretaries of the young people's work in the foreign, home, and woman's missionary board, were heard with great interest. The addresses were inspiring and filled with information — too much of it to be more than barely touched upon in this brief space.

Although Presbyterian Christian Endeavor has done wonderful things for foreign missions, yet, according to Mr. Grant, only fifteen out of every hundred societies are enrolled on the books of the board for contributions.

Endeavorers have doubled their offerings to the home field during the past year, and with the great opportunities for doing effective work, the course of which can be followed up by the givers, recited by Mr. Penfield, there certainly ought to be a still larger rate of increase during the ensuing twelve months. Miss Wishard told of the interesting field of labor now occupied by Presbyterian women, of the wonderful work being done, and of the opportunities on every hand for still greater successes.

"Are Presbyterian pastors, as a rule, wide awake to the work of the Christian Endeavor Society?" was the question propounded to Dr. Rondthaler; and he discussed it in cyclonic fashion. The principal fault found by the speaker with his brethren of the cloth was that "they don't know how to take collections." Miss Caroline H. Brookfield, of Belvidere, N. J., proved conclusively, in a discussion of the subject, that the attendance of pastors on Christian Endeavor meetings was both wise and desirable. "They there hear confessions of faith that create no questions of revision," was one of her bright remarks. Dr. French said he attended every meeting of the society, "and never talked more than two minutes."

Philadelphia's popular Endeavorer, J. Howard Breed, had for a subject, "Intenser Loyalty of Christian Endeavorers to the Sabbath and Midweek Services." Rev. Arthur W. Spooner, who spoke of the Holy Spirit in the Society's work, delivered a thoughtful and helpful address. A general discussion of the foregoing topics closed the conference.

Reformed Church in the United States.

The denominational rally of the Reformed church in the United States, held in the vestry room of the Dominion Square Methodist church, although not announced or planned for beforehand, proved to be quite successful. Sixteen societies, having a membership of 725, were represented; these are located in Pennsylvania and Ohio.

Rev. Rufus W. Miller, Hummelstown, Penn., was elected chairman, and Rev. R. Keller, West Alexandria, O., secretary.

Reports were given from each society present, and plans were discussed for the extension of the work throughout the Reformed church.

After a hearty discussion, the following committee were appointed systematically to plan for a representation of Reformed church societies at the Cleveland convention of 1894: Rev. J. H. Bomberger, Columbiana, O., chairman; Rev. Messrs. R. Keller, I. A. Sites, C. B. Alspach, of Ohio; and Messrs. C. E. Miller, Dayton, O.; W. R. Stearley, Cleveland, O.; and J. C. Crume, Dayton, O. This committee is also to prepare a program for the denominational rally at that convention.

Methodist.

The beautiful St. James Methodist church, the pride of Canadian Protestantism, held a highly enthusiastic audience when Rev. A. M. Phillips, of Toronto, opened the Methodist rally. Prayer was offered by Rev. Charles Roads, president of the Pennsylvania State Union. Rev. George T. Lemmon was elected secretary. Several awakening songs prepared the way for the feast of good things arranged. Rev. S. P. Rose, D. D., president of the Montreal Union, and Rev. E. K. Young. D. D., of New Britain, Conn., gave spicy addresses on "The Compatability of Denominational Organization and Interdenominational Fellowship."

Rev. George T. Lemmon presented the report of the Methodist Episcopal Christian Endeavor Advisory Board, and gave an address on the subject, "Affiliation with the Epworth League." Rev. Wallace MacMullen, of Philadelphia, spoke on "The future of Christian Endeavor in the Methodist Episcopal church."

Among the other speakers were the Rev. George Douglas, D. D., LL. D., the noble patriarch of Canadian Methodism; Bishop B. W. Arnett, of the African Methodist Episcopal church, and Rev. J. F. Cowan, editor of *Our Young People*, of the Methodist Protestant church.

The following resolutions were adopted, and the committee called for was appointed:—

We, the representatives of Christian Endeavor societies in the various Methodist churches of this continent, assembled together in denominational conference, desire to express our heartfelt thanks to Almighty God for the blessings of his Spirit vouchsafed to our churches during the past year. We rejoice together in our common Methodism, which we love so dearly, and desire here and now to reaffirm our unswerving loyalty to her doctrines, her polity, and her connectional interests. While we heartily cherish, and shall cheerfully cultivate, our fellowship with the Christian Endeavor movement, we shall also strive to inculcate and develop in our young people the spirit of truest denominational loyalty.

Resolved, That we are in full accord with that principle of our Christian Endeavor movement which inculcates most active support and fidelity to our own church. We, therefore, joyfully, for love of our Methodism, earnestly advise all our societies in those branches in which the Epworth League is the official young people's society to affiliate with it, maintaining in such affiliation, conscientiously and unswervingly, our Christian Endeavor pledge, methods of work and name. We earnestly covet for all our Methodist young people the blessed interdenominational fellowship and spiritual uplifting which has so greatly helped us.

Resolved, That, since it is manifestly desirable, and in accord with the providential leading of our time, that Methodist young people's societies, in all branches of Methodism, should be more closely united in fellowship and Christian effort; therefore,

Resolved, That we appoint a committee, consisting of one from each denomination here represented, to consult with such other organizations as may become likewise represented, as to the best means of accomplishing this result.

COMMITTEE.

Methodist Episcopal church, Rev. Wallace MacMullen.
Methodist Episcopal church, South, Rev. J. W. Lee, D.D.
Canada Methodist church, Rev. A. M. Phillips, B.D.
Methodist Protestant church, Rev. J. F. Cowan.
African Methodist Episcopal church, Bishop B. W. Arnett.
African Methodist Episcopal Zion, Rev. A. Haywood Stitt.

Congregational.

"The attendance at the Congregational rally of the Young People's Society of Christian Endeavor at Montreal," says Dr. Dunning, in an editorial note in *The Congregationalist*, "was as large as that of the Home Missionary Anniversary at Saratoga, in June." And its numbers were no more significant than its spirit. The presiding officer, Rev. James L. Hill, D.D., turned upon the speakers and enjoined them to be modest. They could not. One speaker was cataloguing the colleges founded by Congregationalists: Harvard, Yale, Amherst, Dartmouth, Williams, Bowdoin, Olivet, Beloit, Yankton, Iowa, Illinois, Middlebury, and the others, and was called down by a generous brother for unduly inflaming the denominational spirit. Reminiscences of Puritan and pilgrim history had to be largely eschewed for the same sufficient reason.

Congregationalists were shown by their unapproached authorship to be not lacking in intelligence; nor, secondly, were they wanting in the sinews of war, as their endowed institutions would prove; nor yet in years, dating as they do from the earliest days of the apostles; nor have they any fault of creed, as each brotherhood of believers writes its own; nor yet any want of respectability, as the audience then present so palpably proved. The whole history of Congregationalism is full of warnings against despair. In view of all these facts, unless something was said, the stone would cry out of the wall, and the beam out of the timber would answer it.

To prove that they do not lack in eloquence, some twenty-two speakers were introduced in quick succession. To speak successfully in the open air one must conform to a rule that obliges him to say something every three minutes, but here, with such a theme, it was insisted that each speaker should say something every half minute and stop, having, at that rate, said two things. Thus the speaking did not descend to a wordy drizzle. Having raised the temperature, it was kept up high until the end. The speakers were exhorted not to travel far to get a theme, but to take Congregationalism and begin anywhere, and they could not fail to be eloquent.

The speakers were Dr. Dunning, General Secretary H. L. Gale of Worcester, William H. Pennell, Rev. E. M. Hill, of Montreal; Principal Barbour, Rev. Messrs. Cowan, Temple, Mills, Northrup, Boynton, Rev. Gilbert Reid from China, who wore a Chinese costume and a queue, two ladies of graceful speech, Miss Jeanette Prince and Miss.Carrie W. Hunt, Mr. William Shaw, Rev. Mr. Brokaw, Rev. Messrs. Day, Birnie, Dyer, Silcox, Prentiss, Collins of California, Dickinson, and others.

Protestant Episcopal.

Rev. Canon J. B. Richardson, of London, Ont., presided at this meeting, and made the opening address. He was very glad to see those who were interested in organizing Christian Endeavor societies composed of Church of England members. It was not long since that there was not a single Christian Endeavor society in connection with the Church of England in either Canada or the United States. He was glad to state that now the movement was progressing well, especially in Ontario, where, as a result of a convention held in London, Ont., last year, the number of Church of England societies in the province had trebled. In London, alone, there were no less than five good societies, strong, vigorous, and flourishing, and all doing the best of work. He appealed to all to extend the movement, as it could not fail to prove beneficial to the Church of England in Canada and the United States. The church must be a part of the movement, for it was one of the greatest Christian movements extant. There were many features that stamped Christian Endeavor as being appropriate in connection with the Anglican church. For instance, the Christian Endeavor motto itself, "For Christ and the Church," was coined by the Church of England. The Christian Endeavor pledge was similar in all points to the confirmation and baptismal vows of the church.

Rev. C. J. Palmer, of Lanesboro', Mass., dealt with the progress of the movement in the United States. He had started the first society in connection with the Anglican church in the United States. At the Minneapolis convention he was elected corresponding secretary for all Anglican societies. Since then he has been engaged in a world-wide correspondence with most successful results. He was of the opinion that the movement, considered in one light, belongs more particularly to the Church of England than any other church, especially as regards the regeneration of children to a normal Christian life.

The Rev. H. Gomery, of Montreal, remarked that, had Christian Endeavor been in vogue in his last parish at Huntingdon, P. Q., some 25 years ago, there would have been six churches in the parish where one stands now. Christian Endeavor helps to build up the Church of Christ.

The following resolution was moved by Mr. J. Thompson, of Quebec, and seconded by Mr. Hinchliffe, of Montreal: "That this meeting do strongly and very respectfully urge upon the Bishop of Montreal and the clergy of the Church of England of this city and the vicinity the great importance of sanctioning the organization of societies of Christian Endeavor as a means of utilizing the latent undeveloped energies of the young, and preventing the loss of large numbers of church members."

The resolution having been adopted, after a few parting words from Canon Richardson, the proceedings of the conference terminated.

Canadian Presbyterian.

Rev. Dr. MacVicar, president of the Presbyterian College, occupied the chair at this rally, instead of Rev. William Patterson, of Toronto, who was prevented from attending. An interesting address upon the subject of "Home Missions" was delivered by Rev. Alexander Urquhart, of Brandon, Manitoba. Dr. Urquhart was well qualified to speak on this topic, having had over ten years' experience in the mission fields of the Northwest. He was · pleased at having an opportunity of bearing testimony to the great impetus which the United Society of Christian Endeavor had given to home-mission work. There was no possibility of the organization ever drifting from the church and the congregation. He spoke of the manner in which the Society had operated in developing the gifts of the young Christian. Over and over again his heart had been gladdened as he had heard the somewhat lisping, stammering tongue of the beginner seeking to breathe out the heart in prayer to God.

Rev. J. Robbins, of Truro, N. S., spoke of mission work in the Maritime Provinces. There missionaries preached among the fishermen of the coast and in the lumber and mining camps. The Presbyterian church had proved its title to its reputation as the friend of all and the enemy of none. Its work was not done to antagonize. The young men sent to the mission fields left behind them there a blessed influence. The speaker had never known a band of young men who had preached the gospel in its purity and simplicity more forcibly than the young men occupying the mission fields in- the Maritime Provinces. Of many of them it could be said, as of John Geddes, "When he went there, there were no Christians; when he died, there were no heathen."

Addresses were also delivered by Rev. R. P. McKay, secretary of the Board of Foreign Missions, western section, and Dr. McTavish, of Toronto.

Friends.

The denominational meeting was held in the Calvary Congregational church, with Rev. M. M. Binford, of Carthage, Indiana, as chairman. Every delegate of the Friends' church in attendance at the convention was present, except two or three. The devotional exercises were conducted by the chairman, a number of persons offering brief prayers.

Delegates were present from twelve states and provinces, and reports were received from twenty-two, including all the Friends' Endeavor societies of America, Jamaica, and Mexico. Three reports show a total of 312 societies, including 44 Junior societies; and an aggregate of 12,000 members. This shows an increase of 100 percent over last year's report, and an average of one Endeavorer for every six and two-thirds members of the church.

During the past year the Christian Endeavor movement and the formation of the Friends' International Christian Endeavor Union have been endorsed by all the higher official bodies of the Friends, where there are Endeavor societies, and by the General Conference at Indianapolis, last October.

The denominational Fellowship Unions have been turned into Christian Endeavor societies, and united with the International Union.

Rev. M. M. Binford was chosen as president of the union for the coming year, and Miss Stella F. Jenkins of Kansas City, Mo., was chosen secretary.

The Christian Endeavor department of the *Christian Worker* was accepted as the official organ of the Friends' Endeavor work, and Miss Jenkins was chosen as editor of the same.

Suitable resolutions of respect in memory of Rev. A. C. Hathaway, whose death took place the past year, were adopted.

Revs. Levi Rees, E. O. Ellis and Esther Cooke, of Indiana, Edward Mott, of Michigan, H. F. Keats, of Canada, B. F. Farquhar and Seneca Stevens, of New York, and others took part in the discussions.

SATURDAY EVENING.

DRILL HALL.

The evening services were looked forward to with some little appre-hension on the part of the officers of the convention. At the close of the session on the preceding evening a large crowd of French students were noticed to be parading some of the streets, singing "La Marseil-laise," and making something of a demonstration. Afterwards a crowd of roughs on the Champs de Mars succeeded in cutting some of the ropes of the tent, but were soon dispersed by the police. The occa-sion of this was a bitter editorial in *La Presse,* a French Catholic paper of Montreal, which took up a paragraph in Mr. Karmarkar's address of Friday morning referring to Romanism in India, and made this the basis of a severe arraignment of the convention itself, and called upon all true Catholics to resent the insult. This editorial was deprecated by the other papers of the city the next day and the fact pointed out that the convention should not be held responsible for the utterance of a single individual. Still, it was manifest that there was an element in the city quite ready to take advantage of any opportunity to make a hostile demonstration, and various rumors were heard as to what was going to be attempted in connection with the Saturday evening ser-vices. The mayor stationed an extra force of policemen on the street in front of the hall, and anybody who attempted a disturbance was vig-orously hustled out of the way. The French students again paraded the streets, carrying tricolor flags, but as they neared the hall they were charged by the police and dispersed, their flags being captured.

A heavy shower came up just as the audience was assembling, a cir-cumstance which, while it caused inconvenience to some, doubtless proved an advantage to the convention as a whole. It prevented the use of the tent, but it effectually dampened "La Marseillaise." Whatever demonstration had been contemplated by the outside crowd received a complete set-back by the tempest of rain. It was announced that the program for the tent meeting would be given at the St. James M. E. church, but by far the greater portion of the audience remained in the Drill Hall. The roof of the building did not prove to be perfectly water-tight, and during the heaviest part of the shower it was necessary to raise umbrellas in several portions of the hall.

The preliminary song service was carried out with the accustomed enthusiasm, Mr. Lindsay and the Park Sisters leading. Rev. C. A. Dickinson, pastor of Berkeley Temple church, Boston, one of the trus-tees of the United Society, presided.

The program opened with the hymn "Sun of My Soul," the audience rising. All then united in repeating the twenty-third Psalm. Prayer was offered by Rev. Dr. Rhodes, of St. Louis, after which another hymn was sung. The committee on nominations then reported as follows:—

Honorary Vice-Presidents.

ALABAMA	Rev. George R. Brown.
ALASKA TERRITORY	Mr. Edward Marsden.
ARIZONA TERRITORY	Lieut. H. R. Lee, U.S.A.
ARKANSAS	Mr. A. H. Thomas.
CALIFORNIA	Mr. W. G. Alexander.
COLORADO	Mr. E. B. Clark.
CONNECTICUT	Rev. Henry H. Kelsey.
DELAWARE	Mr. William E. Rothwell
DISTRICT OF COLUMBIA	Mr. W. H. Lewis.
FLORIDA	Mr. G. W. Van Sickle.
GEORGIA	Rev. C. P. Williamson.
IDAHO	Miss Bertha L. Hess.
ILLINOIS	Rev. L. A. Crandall, D.D.
INDIANA	Rev. J. H. O. Smith.
INDIAN TERRITORY	Rev. M. J. Williams.
IOWA	Rev. E. R. Burkhalter, D.D.
KANSAS	Prof. D. S. Kelly.
KENTUCKY	Rev. J. L. Darsie.
LOUISIANA	Rev. F. S. Parker.
MAINE	Mr. James W. Stevenson.
MARYLAND	Rev. T. H. Lewis, D.D.
MASSACHUSETTS	Rev. Henry M. Hinckley.
MICHIGAN	Mr. C. L. Stevens.
MINNESOTA	Rev. W. H. Geistweit.
MISSISSIPPI	Bishop B. W. Arnett, D.D.
MISSOURI	Mr. O. E. Rumer.
MONTANA	Mr. C. C. Fuller.
NEBRASKA	Mr. Frank F. Cook.
NEVADA	Rev. F. L. Nash.
NEW HAMPSHIRE	Rev. O. J. White.
NEW JERSEY	Rev. J. Judson Pierson.
NEW MEXICO TERRITORY	Rev. Norman N. Skinner.
NEW YORK	Rev. Henry T. McEwen.
NORTH CAROLINA	Mr. B. K. Proctor.
NORTH DAKOTA	Mr. William J. Lane.
OHIO	Rev. H. C. Applegarth, D.D.
OKLAHOMA	Miss Nellie Whitfield.
OREGON	Rev. Charles H. Curtis.
PENNSYLVANIA	Rev. Charles Roads.
RHODE ISLAND	Rev. Francis A. Horton, D.D.
SOUTH CAROLINA	Rev. C. A. B. Jennings.
SOUTH DAKOTA	Mr. Wilbur Lawrence.
TENNESSEE	Mr. W. L. Noell.
TEXAS	Rev. W. Scott.
UTAH TERRITORY	Mr. Robert J. Caskey.
VERMONT	Rev. T. H. Thompson, D.D.
VIRGINIA	Rev. E. T. Dadmun.
WASHINGTON	Mr. John P. Hartman, Jr.
WEST VIRGINIA	Rev. C. M. Alford.
WISCONSIN	Rev. David Spencer, D.D.
WYOMING TERRITORY	Mr. Robert Lawson.

CANADA.

BRITISH COLUMBIA	Mrs. J. J. Banfield.
MANITOBA	Mr. James R. Greig.
QUEBEC	Mr. A. A. Ayer.
NORTHWEST TERRITORIES	Rev. Charles McKillop.

ONTARIO	Mr. Thomas Morris, Jr.
MARITIME UNION	Rev. George O. Gates.

FOREIGN.

AFRICA	Rev. Charles N. Ransom.
SOUTH AUSTRALIA	Rev. Silas Mead.
NEW SOUTH WALES	Rev. W. J. L. Closs.
NEW ZEALAND	Rev. William Blaikie.
TASMANIA	Mr. W. M. Williams.
QUEENSLAND	Mr. George H. Scott.
VICTORIA	Mr. W. H. McCutcheon.
BRAZIL	Miss Carrie E. Hough.
CHILI	Mr. Charles R. James.
CHINA	Rev. O. Wisner.
ENGLAND	Rev. A. E. Hutton, M.P.
INDIA	Rev. W. I. Chamberlain.
IRELAND	Mr. J. Newman Hall.
JAPAN	Rev. T. Harada.
MADAGASCAR	Rev. W. E. Cousin.
MEXICO	Rev. James D. Eaton.
FRANCE	Rev. E. C. Greig.
PERSIA	Rev. Lewis F. Esselstyn.
SAMOA ISLANDS	Rev. J. E. Newell.
SANDWICH ISLANDS	Miss W. Wing.
SCOTLAND	Rev. John R. Fleming.
SPAIN	Mrs. W. O. Gulick.
TURKEY	Rev. G. H. Krikorian.
WEST INDIES	Rev. George E. Henderson.
SYRIA	Rev. H. H. Jessop, D.D.
REPUBLIC OF COLUMBIA	Rev. Clifford N. Clark.
NORWAY	Mr. Edward Ellefsen.
HOLLAND	Rev. J. Irving Brown.
FLOATING SOCIETIES	Miss A. P. Jones.

The report was accepted and adopted. Several announcements were then made, after which a trio of hymns was sung successively, — "My Country, 't is of Thee," "God Save the Queen," and "Blest Be the Tie That Binds."

Before calling the roll, Mr. Baer read the following resolutions : —

At a meeting of the Press representatives held on the platform immediately on adjournment this morning, the Rev. T. B. Penfield of the *New York Tribune* presiding, the following resolution was read and adopted:

"Appreciating the most admirable, generous and complete arrangements that have been made for the accommodation of the representatives of the secular and religious press of the land by the Press Committee of the Montreal Christian Endeavor convention of which Mr. Herbert B. Ames is chairman,

"We, the reporters and correspondents of the Press, desire to express our most hearty and sincere thanks to Chairman Ames and to his able corps of assistants for their faithful and untiring efforts.

"We congratulate him upon the promptness and efficiency of the service he has caused to be placed at the disposal of the newspaper representatives and upon the unprecedented success that has attended the efforts of the committee on our behalf."

Signed by the representatives of over fifty papers.

The roll call of states, territories, and provinces was then conducted by Secretary Baer.

Roll Call.

MR. BAER: Those who are to respond to this roll call are supposed to be on the platform. They will each have sixty seconds, and I think you will say when we have finished that we have had more in each sixty seconds than we have ever had in the same time before.

ALABAMA, REV. GEO. R. BROWN: Alabama sends greeting to this convention. We are increasing numerically and spiritually.. We find that Christian Endeavor introduced into our churches insures better and more faithful work among the young people for Christ and the church. [*Applause.*]

CALIFORNIA, MR. W. G. ALEXANDER: California is awake to the importance of the Christian Endeavor movement. Our growth during the last year was from 19,000 to 31,000. We promise you 50,000 in 1895. The golden gate stands wide open to receive you and we shall welcome you in 1895 from the lakes to the gulf, and from the rivers to the sea. [*Loud applause.*]

COLORADO, MR. E. B. CLARK: California sings the sunshine song. Colorado has the sunshine all the year. We want you for 1896. Colorado reports progress all along the line. We have 141 societies, 3,800 active members, 1,054 associate members, an increase of 1,046, and about 400 conversions. Junior societies have increased 30 percent. The strongest society is the Methodist society in Colorado Springs, with 198 active members. [*Applause.*]

DELAWARE, MR. JOHN H. COLE: Little Delaware is confronted with many difficulties, and has a small population to work among; but Christian Endeavor is strongly implanted there, and great energy and enthusiasm are being displayed. A goodly number of new societies have been formed, though the greatest interest has been spiritual activity. The New York convention, coupled with the three weeks' crusade of Moody and Sankey, has caused the Christian Endeavorers of Delaware to be up and doing, thus making the year from July, 1892, to July, 1893, the best in the Christian Endeavor history of the state. The Christian Endeavorers of the Diamond state are looking eagerly forward to the annual state convention to be held at Dover, October 26 and 27. We love our little state, and are determined, with the help of God, to win Delaware for Christ.

DISTRICT OF COLUMBIA, MR. P. S. FOSTER: We report 98 societies with over 5,000 members, an increase of 63 percent during the past year. We are doing a flourishing work all along the line, especially in the Junior movement, as was manifested in our carrying away the banner the other evening. We have not been successful — although I hope we will be — in closing the gates of the World's Fair on Sunday; but I will tell you what he did on the last 4th of March. After an order had been given that we should have a Sunday concert in one of the government buildings, the Christian Endeavore s of Washington, together with other Christian workers, were instrumental in having that order rescinded, and the concert did not come off. [*Loud applause.*]

FLORIDA, MRS. M. L. SELDEN: Florida reports 119 societies, with 3,500 members, seven district organizations, and a superintendent of Junior work. [*Applause.*]

GEORGIA, MR. A. B. CARRIER: Georgia is holding her own in commendable shape. But Georgia needs the help of the Christian Endeavorers throughout the South and throughout the United States. We need the great convention, and I can only say tonight that we must have Atlanta as the place of holding our convention in 1896. [*Applause.*]

IDAHO, MISS BERTHA L. HESS: Idaho, the gem of the mountains, has 500 Endeavorers, each representing a priceless gem won for Christ. Of this number about 150 are on the Nez Perces Indian Reservation. We propose to labor on faithfully until from every peak shall float the banner, " For Christ and the Church."

INDIANA, REV. J. H. O. SMITH: Indiana, the home of the Hoosier school-master, James Whitcomb Riley, the author of Ben Hur, and Christian Endeav-orer Benjamin Harrison [*loud applause*], has furnished during the past year its state secretary as president of the Presbyterian Women's Board of Missions. We have more than doubled our Junior societies. Our interdenominational fellowship is unbroken. We believe that Y. P. S. C. E. means Young People Shall Christianize the Earth. [*Applause.*]   Our state song is

> "Y. P. S. C. E. forever!
> Magic sign of victory!
> In the strife we take a stand
> 'Gainst sin on every hand,
> And for Christ we take the state
> Of Indiana."

ILLINOIS, MR. C. B. HOLDREGE: Our motto is "Forward." We are glad to take home the banner for the second time in missionary effort. But there is one point yet to be gained. Illinois delegates are going home to Chicago to do their utmost to have the World's Fair gates closed on Sunday. [*Loud applause.*]

IOWA, REV. J. H. WRIGHT: Iowa, the birthplace of the Junior Endeavor movement, the first state to appoint a Junior superintendent, the ground on which the prohibition battle is now raging [*applause*], Iowa is gazing Montreal-ward.   By courtesy of the press committee a Star has dawned upon my horizon, and a Witness from Montreal has said that Canada is inspecting our prohibi-tion system, and finds that it is partially enforced but not entirely. I wish to say that from the western side of the the state, where our Martyr Haddock laid down his life, to our eastern side, where dynamite has recently destroyed homes, our Endeavor young people are being trained to brave citizenship that they may defeat this fearful monster, the liquor traffic. [*Applause.*]

KANSAS, MR. L. L. ROBY: To a man from Kansas there is but one thing on earth larger than Kansas, and that is this convention. [*Laughter.*] That is the reason why we no . ask you to come to Kansas in 1896. Kansas is growing, and the two biggest things in Kansas are Christian Endeavor and prohibition. [*Applause.*]

MR. BAER: I wish to cease calling the roll for a moment, just to introduce to you who belong to the other side of the line a gentleman through whose efforts, largely, Christian Endeavor first crossed the line and came into Canada, — Rev. E. M. Hill, of this city. [*Loud applause.*]

REV. MR. HILL: I have only to say that I became an Endeavorer when I was born in the state of Vermont [*applause*], but I became a Christian Endeavorer in the state of Wisconsin [*applause*], that I became a member of the Society of Christian Endeavor in the Province of Quebec [*loud applause*], and that I shall carry Christian Endeavor with me wherever I go. I expect to carry it into heaven, if I do not find a society already started when I get there. I expect there will be a society of Christian Endeavor among the angels, and a Junior society among the cherubim. [*Laughter and applause.*]

KENTUCKY, REV. J. L. DARSIE: Kentucky sends a delegation of 150 members to this convention [*applause*], and greets you with 5,000 members, an increase of 40 percent during the year; besides 1,000 Juniors, an increase of 100 percent. We say to New York, and Pennsylvania, and Illinois, and Iowa, and the British Provinces: Go on in your mad career and get your banners and sing your songs of victory. We glory in your success and bid you Godspeed: but

> "If you get there before we do,
> Look out for Kentucky; we 're coming too."   [*Laughter and applause.*]

MAINE, MR. V. RICHARD FOSS: A short time since I stood on the historic ground of the bloodless Aroostook war, the result of which doubtless was the boundary line between Canada and Maine. But neither the St. John nor the St. Croix divides us tonight. Blood is thicker than water, as has been said, and the blessed ties of Christian Endeavor break down every fence and leap over every boundary line. [*Applause.*] In behalf of Portland, — the Canadian winter port, and the Canadian's summer resort, nearly as much Canadian as American because of our close relation, — in behalf of Portland, the home of Christian Endeavor, I greet you, friends of Montreal, and I congratulate you upon this magnificent convention which will have glorious results, not only for you but for us who must return from this mount of blessing to our homes. We have 20,000 "true-hearted, whole-hearted" Christian Endeavorers down in the old Pine Tree state. Our motto is "Maine for Christ." [*Applause.*]

CONNECTICUT, REV. ASHER ANDERSON: You know what a nutmeg is. [*Laughter.*] When Henry Ward Beecher was once asked what he thought of Dr. Talmage, he said that the good doctor reminded him of a chestnut,— he had a great many points, but when you got to the heart of the man, there was plenty of meat. You never know a nutmeg to good advantage until you have grated it. When you grate a nutmeg you get the flavor, and as we grate this nutmeg tonight, I am satisfied that you will find flavor for the first things for which we are to have credit. We started in 1883 with eight societies and 320 members. In 1893 we have 481 societies and 32,754 members. [*Applause.*] We have 23 local unions. Our Junior societies number 106, beginning in the year 1887 with three, and our membership in Junior societies is 5,360. Ours is the state that first had local unions and quarterly meetings and the first state banner. We were the state that inaugurated the Sunday closing movement; and, more than that, our state stands first today in evangelistic work, and we are intending to push it along that line if it takes a whole century. [*Applause.*]

MARYLAND, DR. H. E. KNIPP: Maryland reports a growth in societies during the year, of from 182 to 241, with a membership of about 12,000. Junior work is receiving merited attention from our people, and preaching services, Sabbath schools, prayer meetings, and other organized efforts are stimulating us to new consecration. Our growth in the country districts has been especially noticeable. Several counties have been organized into unions, with others white already to the harvest, and several hundred of our associate members have been won for Christ.

MASSACHUSETTS, MR. GEO. W. COLEMAN: Massachusetts is right glad to be here to enjoy the earnest, sincere and thorough hospitality of the City of Montreal. [*Applause.*] Although one of the smallest states in the Union we are proud to say that we have nearly 1,200 societies, and we have here in this city 850 registered delegates, so that, with many more who are not registered, we have on the average at least one representative from every society in the state. We rejoice in the practical and spiritual results of the year. Surely goodness and mercy have followed us all the days of our life and we shall dwell in the house of the Lord forever. [*Applause.*]

MR. BAER: Now we are to hear from two friends who have come from some distance and at some inconvenience, giving their services freely, as have many others who are taking a helpful part in this convention,— the Park Sisters, who will favor us with a cornet duet.

Long-continued applause and the Chautauqua salute followed this announcement. The young ladies played very beautifully, and at the close of their selection the enthusiasm was so great that an encore was given. This only awoke still greater applause, and for several moments Mr. Baer tried in vain to cause it to cease. At last he found an opportunity to say that it was necessary to proceed with the program.

MICHIGAN, MR. C. L. STEVENS: Michigan has 27,489 members in 576 societies, besides 65 Junior societies with 2,250 members; 500 associate members were converted the last year and $3,000.22 were given to missions. [*Applause.*]

MINNESOTA, MISS CARRIE A. HOLBROOK: Minnesota, which gave to the United Society its honored secretary, has for her neighbors on the north the most genial and whole-souled and hospitable people on the face of the globe— the Canadians [*applause*]; upon the south and west the prohibition states of Iowa and the Dakotas; on the east the great chain of lakes and the beautiful St. Lawrence which forms the natural highway to her most beautiful suburb, Montreal. Situated in such a respectable neighborhood, she naturally has a high idea of life, but this does not make her exclusive. She welcomes to her borders all good people from everywhere, and if they are not good she uses the appliances of Christian Endeavor to make them so. To this end she has divided her 80 counties into 24 districts, well officered and well worked. It has been my privilege to attend a large number of these district conventions and they are pre-eminently spiritual in tone. As was said at the Twin City convention two years ago, if Minnesota could add one word to her motto it would be the word "souls,"—"Souls for Christ and the Church."

At this point a disturbance was heard at the rear entrance of the hall, and many of the delegates were made somewhat nervous by the entrance of a large number of roughly dressed men who proceeded up the gallery stairs and along the gallery to some rooms on the side of the building. Mr. Baer announced, however, that these were some of the Royal Scots just returned from camp, and in response to his request the audience joined in singing, for the benefit of the returned soldiers, the hymn, "Onward, Christian Soldiers." After this the roll call proceeded without interruption.

NEBRASKA, REV. L. P. LUDDEN: Nebraska, the gateway state between the old East and the new West, brings her greeting to this convention tonight with over 12,000 Christian Endeavorers. The great watchword in our state in temporal affairs is, "Stand up for Nebraska," and the Christian Endeavorers have paraphrased that into, "Stand up for Christ and the Church." [*Applause*.]

NEW HAMPSHIRE, MR. H. A. MCKNIGHT: The old Granite state is as solid for Christian Endeavor as the eternal hills. Much progress has been made in Junior work, and our financial condition has been improved. Many local societies have been organized and the state work has advanced. The motto inscribed on our banner is "New Hampshire for Christ and the Church."

NEW JERSEY, REV. J. JUDSON PIERSON: New Jersey is busy enlisting and disciplining soldiers for Christ and the church. We have 708 societies with 3,500 members. We are laying siege to the State House, which was captured last winter by the gamblers, and we propose to turn them out. [*Applause*.] In this we have the co-operation of the Christian and moral sentiment of the state. We are paying special attention to Junior work at this time, also the life-saving work along the coast.

NEW MEXICO, MISS ABBY F. HULL: New Mexico, where the sun shines every day in the year and Christian Endeavor stars multiply, greets you. Last year we had seven societies, or seven stars,—the spiritual Pleiades of New Mexico. Now we have a great constellation, and soon we hope to have a shining galaxy. Then New Mexico will be ready for state work. One word about our beautiful banner down at the Custom House. We would like to see it, but we can wait for it; for we have a more glorious banner, even the banner of our Lord Jesus Christ, and we shall never, never trust it beyond our lines, but there it shall float forever. [*Applause*.]

NEW YORK, REV. H. W. SHERWOOD: The Christian Endeavor organization spreads in New York like the banyan tree, taking root in every part of the state. Last year's history in Christian Endeavor was the best we have had. Organization was made more perfect, workers more consecrated and persevering, and conversions were more frequent. We formed our state organization in 1885 with 1,400 members in the state. We expect to celebrate our eighth anniversary next October with a round 175,000. [*Applause*.] After you have basked in the sunshine of California in 1895, we will welcome you back with open arms to the Empire state, to the magnificent hotels and the thirst-quenching springs of Saratoga for 1896. Come. [*Applause.*]

SCOTLAND, REV. JOHN R. FLEMING [*loud applause*]: You have heard from a great many states; now you are to hear from the good old country of Scotland. I am proud to stand here, although I stand alone, but I am glad to tell you that although we cannot take a very large place as yet in the ranks of Christian Endeavor, we have commenced well. We have at present, I believe, about 30 societies, and we gave a right hearty welcome to Dr. Clark on the 12th of last June in Glasgow. I was glad to be at that meeting, and I believe it marks the beginning of great things for Scotland. May I venture to suggest that before the end of the century you hold one of your great international conventions on the other side of the Atlantic? [*Loud applause.*]

FRANCE, MISS LUCILLE TWYEFFORT: The Fleur-de-lis sends greeting to you all. The Protestants of France are taking a strong hold on Christian Endeavor. We have now nine societies in France, and several others in the Provinces. Dr. and Mrs. Clark's visit to Paris was hailed with much joy, and an address from Dr. Clark at the French Christian Endeavor mass meeting was received with as much enthusiasm as it could have been in Boston. The meeting-room of the American church is small and we cannot accommodate you all, but we shall be most happy to have many of you who happen to be in Paris during the next few years join us in our services. One of the young men who attended the convention of last year is now the best worker in our society. We want the prayers of every Endeavorer to help us in our work in the most wicked city in the world. [*Loud applause.*]

FLOATING SOCIETIES, MISS ANTOINETTE P. JONES: There are 900 floating Christian Endeavorers, — none of whom are with us tonight, save in spirit, — on 200 vessels. They are heroes for Christ every one.

NORTH DAKOTA, MR. JAMES AUSTIN: North Dakota, the home of the rustler, the bread basket of the world. We bring greetings from our state in the north, where we have a glorious prohibitory law. Though we are but a comparatively young state, we have secured this law for at least three years more, and we ask your prayers that the United States may adopt national prohibition. A large advance has been made in our Junior work during the year.

OHIO, REV. W. F. MCCAULEY: First, there are 24 denominations in our Ohio work, white and colored, ranging from Quaker to Episcopal. Second, many floating Christian Endeavorers are on the bosom of our lake. Third, we still believe in the Ten Commandments, and " We wont go to the World's Fair if open on Sunday or liquor sold there." [*Loud applause.*] Fourth and last, welcome to Cleveland in 1894. [*Applause.*]

AFRICA, REV. D. A. DAY, D.D. [*applause*]: The Christian Endeavor society from the spurs of the Congo Mountains sends greetings to this convention now in session, and thanks God that Christian Endeavor has reached the Dark Continent, believes that it is God-inspired, God-sent, God-given, and asks your prayers that the time may not be far distant when Ethiopia shall stretch out her hands to God. [*Applause.*]

OKLAHOMA, MR. HERBERT J. LEACH: Oklahoma is booming! [*Laughter.*] Four and a half years ago Oklahoma was a vast uninhabited prairie; today it is a magnificent commonwealth of 160,000 of as good people as you will find anywhere. [*Applause.*] Four years ago we had one society in Oklahoma; today we have 53, besides four Junior societies. The enemy is there, but we have jumped his claim [*laughter*], and we are going to win Oklahoma for Christ.

OREGON, MISS CAROLINE STRONG: Oregon Endeavorers, 10,000 strong, greet you by telegram. We have made a gain of 23 societies in the last six months. We have made a great gain also in Junior work. We have a state paper, a rousing state convention, and many earnest workers. The gifts of God to Oregon are very great. That her men and women may be as noble and firm as her snow-capped mountains is our prayer. We want Oregon for Christ. [*Applause.*]

PENNSYLVANIA, MR. WM. S. FERGUSON: Pennsylvania desires to return thanks to the people of Montreal for the kind and courteous manner in which we have been entertained. During the year, so far as we can learn, almost 5,000 associate members have been won for Christ. We have increased our membership by more than 35,455, and the Junior work is being pushed. The Philadelphia Junior Union holds a quarterly meeting, at which the average attendance is more than a thousand boys and girls, and they take part in the meeting just as you and I do. We are going to Cleveland next year and will occupy an entire hotel, and we expect to take with us double the number of delegates we have here.

RHODE ISLAND, MR. FRANK O. BISHOP: Rhode Island is called the land of clams, but there is nothing clammy about the greeting which comes up from "Little Rhody" tonight. We have about 6,000 Endeavorers. Junior work has increased largely in the last year. [*Applause.*]

Mr. Baer here announced that he had received the following cablegrams of greeting : —

MADAGASCAR.
MADANAPALLE, INDIA.
JAPAN.
LUDHIANA, PUNJAB, INDIA.
SANTIAGO, CHILE.
SPAIN.
SOUTH AFRICA.
PARIS, FRANCE.
SIDNEY, N. S. W., AUSTRALIA.
BRISBANE, QUEENSLAND, AUSTRALIA.

THE GERMAN SOCIETIES, MR. HERMAN HARTING: Two years ago in Detroit, in the German Evangelical church, there was a young people's society that was of no use on the face of the earth. You know what kind of a society I mean. We didn't know what to do with it, but we heard of the Christian Endeavor plan and we thought we would try it. So we started our Christian Endeavor society with seven active members. We have today about 80 members, and we have also spread the idea among the other German churches. A year ago we had our first anniversary, and we invited people from Buffalo and Ann Arbor and Sandusky and other cities, and after the meeting they went home and started other societies in their churches. Now we have altogether about 80 German societies with about 2,000 members, and the Christian Endeavor movement is spreading among the Germans something like the measles. [*Laughter and applause.*]

SOUTH CAROLINA, MR. DUNBAR ROBB: The South Carolina delegates went home from New York last year promising to organize a state union. We did so and organized our union last October. We hold our second state convention next October. The young people's society have increased 200 percent, and the Juniors are thriving.

TENNESSEE, MR. W. L. NOELL: Tennessee came to this convention with 125 delegates. We are here tonight, the happiest delegates in Montreal. The Christian Endeavor camp fires are burning all along the line in Tennessee. We have 200 senior societies with 8,000 members, and 64 Junior societies with 2,200 members; 666 of our members have joined the church during the last year.

TEXAS, MR. G. W. ALLEN: Christian Endeavorers of Texas send their state officers and their delegation numbering 97 to this convention. [*Applause.*] We can tell you that we have seen that Christian Endeavor is the same from the Rio Grande to the St. Lawrence, and that the cow-boy on the plain and the planter in the field are serving the same great Captain in the ranks of Christian Endeavor, whom these brave soldiers follow so enthusiastically. We have put into our motto, as loyal Texans, our "lone star," but we have girt It around with the golden legend, "Our Star is the Star of Bethlehem." [*Applause.*]

MARITIME UNION, REV. JOHN ROBBINS: In speaking for the Maritime U ion I practically represent four states along the Atlantic shore, New Brunswick, Nova Scotia, Newfoundland and Prince Edwards Island. The Christian Endeavor movement has taken a firm and fast hold upon the Maritime Provinces. Many of us are of Scottish birth and Scottish blood, and in a great many of our Endeavor societies we have this for our motto, "Like the Scots of Bannockburn who went forth in a solid phalanx to conquer or to die, the Christian Endeavor Union of the Maritime Provinces is to conquer and *live*." [*Applause.*]

UTAH, MR. J. N. HAYDEN: Utah, the home of Mormonism, is a missionary field and one of the hardest on earth. The past year has been a most prosperous one in the history of the Christian Endeavor work. Twenty-two new societies have been organized, ten of which are Juniors, making a net gain of over 30 percent. I am a little surprised that we have not more Junior societies to report, because in a great many families in Utah you will find from five to 150 children. We have upon our roll 1,308 members. Our societies are moving out in missionary work very successfully.

JAPAN, REV. FRED. C. KLEIN: There are Christian Endeavor societies in nearly every large city of the Empire, and they are bound to multiply. The Japanese churches cannot do without them any more than you can in this glorious land. I only wish there was a large delegation of our Japanese Endeavorers here that they may join with me in deadening the cry of the California delegation by shouting our own, which is (giving it in Japanese), "Christian Endeavor Society, Live Ten Thousand Years." [*Applause.*]

VERMONT, MR. M. J. NORRIS: Vermont is noted for maple sugar, beautiful scenery, and loyal Christian Endeavorers. We are solid for Christian Endeavor. We are going home to organize more Junior societies and we hope that before long we shall have a Junior society in every valley and on every hill. [*Applause.*]

PROVINCE OF QUEBEC, MR. H. A. MOULTON: It has been the pleasure of our people, Catholic and Protestant, French and English, to have you enjoy our hospitality. We want you to come again. [*Applause.*] It is an honor, and a privilege, and a joy to our Christian Endeavor societies in this ancient province to welcome this host to our metropolis city. This is the event of our lives, and we hope to profit by it. We are here from the town and country districts of the province 500 delegates strong, exclusive of the Montreal delegates. Many of our societies have sent half of their whole membership, and in the case of one society, 130 miles from Montreal, away back in the woods, the whole society has come. [*Applause.*] Our difficulties are many, but our faith and zeal are strong. We want your prayers. [*Applause.*]

MISSOURI, MR. W. H. McCLAIN: Missouri greets you with 616 senior societies, and 154 Junior societies, with a total enrolment of 30,722 Christian Endeavorers. We come here pledged, with God's help, to organize a Christian Endeavor society in every church in Missouri that is willing to receive the benefits of this organization. We ask your prayers that we may be successful in this undertaking. [*Applause.*]

WASHINGTON, MR. C. L. MEARS: Washington is the state with a *future*. We are just learning what nature has done for us, and are beginning to develop the wonderfully fertile soil and storehouses of wealth that lie beneath our snow-capped peaks. Along with these possibilities there are also great possibilities for labor in Christian work. In some respects our Christian Endeavor work during the past year has been *discouraging*, in others it has been *very encouraging*. While we are not able to give the numerical increase of the year, we can report progress and a bright outlook for the future. Trusting God for help and guidance we will labor until the "Evergreen State" stands "For Christ and the Church."

LOUISIANA, (Letter): The Louisiana Christian Endeavor Union was organized February 2, 1893, with twelve societies enrolled — active membership about 275; associate, 75. The first annual convention was held in New Orleans, May 19-21. It was in every way a grand success. Other societies have been added and more is being done for Christian Endeavor work in Louisiana today than ever before. The members are feeling their strength, the churches are being built up, and all the societies are actively engaged in mission work, both home and foreign.

MR. BAER: We have gone somewhat beyond our time, and I will simply ask the representatives of the remaining states and territories to rise as I call their names: Arkansas, Virginia, West Virginia, Wisconsin, Manitoba, Northwest Territory, Ontario, British Columbia. [*The delegates called upon arose.*] You see they are all here. [*Applause.*]

During a brief intermission, while the doors were opened, two hymns were sung, — "Bringing in the Sheaves," the audience in sections singing the lines of the refrain, and "At the Cross," the chorus repeated softly. These favorite hymns were sung with great enthusiasm.

MR. DICKINSON: About two years ago one of our distinguished Christian Endeavorers ran away from Canada and took refuge in one of the great northwestern cities of the United States. We have succeeded in capturing him and bringing him back to Canada; but to tell you the truth, we have become so deeply attached to him that we do not mean to leave him here. We will simply lend him to you for a little while and we know you will treat him very kindly. It gives me great pleasure to introduce Rev. Dr. Geo. H. Wells of Minneapolis, formerly pastor of the American Presbyterian church of this city. [*Loud applause.*]

International Fellowship.

Address of Rev. Geo. H. Wells, D.D.

Mr. Chairman, Canadians and Americans, Fellow Endeavorers and Christian Friends: — I shall not attempt to express the deep delight and satisfaction that I feel in this occasion and in the services of this hour. It would be in vain for me to do so; that task would far transcend my powers of thought and speech. It must suffice to say that I most keenly feel the honor of standing before this vast assembly and of speaking upon the magnificent theme your kindness has assigned to me tonight. My joy is only tempered by the consciousness of inability to do justice to the situation and also of the enforced lack of preparation to speak as place and time and theme demand.

And yet my deep regret is relieved somewhat by the consoling thought that it is after all in accordance with the eternal fitness of things that I should be called to this platform and this task. Surely, if any man within the four seas that girt us round should speak worthily, or at least sympathetically, upon international fellowship, it must be one who, like myself, has almost equally divided his years of active life between the two countries chiefly represented here tonight [*applause*], — one who has lived with equal contentment and enjoyment on both sides of the line of 45, who began his career upon the southern side, received his training and spent his early years of service in the land of the Stars and Stripes and then for more than twenty years lived and labored in this fair city of the Royal Mount [*applause*], and who, as he stands before you now, hardly knows whether he should most appropriately be called an American or a Canadian. [*Applause.*] One thing is certain: it is with varied and almost evenly balanced feelings that I look into your faces. For those who have come up hither in vast pilgrimage from all portions of the American Union I feel the thrill of brotherhood and national sympathy; for those who live in this fresh northern clime and look out upon the fair scenes of the Canadian Dominion I feel an equal thrill of fellowship, arising from sweet and long-continued acquaintance and sympathy in Christian work. [*Applause.*] No man can tell the feelings that move me as I come back once more; for as my life began in the United States, so in these recent years I have returned again to the old country — as a strain of music, after many variations and wanderings, comes back to die on its initial key. [*Applause.*] But as I come here to the city that was no longer my chosen and my happy home, and as I look into the faces of many who are among my dearest and my truest friends on earth, a rush of memory, a thrill of emotion, sweeps through my soul, and I feel as if I stood again upon my native heath. [*Applause.*] If I forget thee, O Montreal, may my right hand forget her skill and my tongue forevermore be dumb. [*Applause.*]

Now, do not think that I am sitting by the rivers of Babylon and hanging my harp upon the willows and lamenting the happy past. No such thing. I dwell beside the Father of Waters. I am proud to be named a citizen of Minneapolis [*applause*]—a city of intelligence, of enterprise, of magnificent progress and possibilities. I joy to be one of its citizens and engaged with worthy fellow-laborers in the great field that God opens to us there. But I rejoice also in the memories that cluster around my years of service here; and I would tonight, upon this platform, grasp the hands of Canada and of the United States, one in each of my own, and bring them together in one fraternal and indissoluble clasp. [*Loud applause.*]

Where could I find so fitting inspiration for my address, so grand an illustration of my subject, as in this very audience that mingles the people of both these great countries inextricably together? Our Society has been interdenominational from its very inception. It has been international almost from the first. In the early conventions were sprinkled here and there some ardent Canadians who had already caught the infection of Christian Endeavor and gone to see more of it in its headquarters and its home. As the years have passed, those delegations have grown in interest and in enthusiasm continually, until upon this grand, eventful night they have captured the entire convention and brought it over bodily upon Canadian soil. [*Applause.*] O friends, it is, as I have said, a grand and an eventful occasion. Ten years since, in the early years of the Christian Endeavor movement, if some bold prophet had dared to foretell that, in the old Province of Quebec, the oldest settled portion almost of the North American continent, the stronghold of the Roman Catholic church upon this western soil and the chosen home of the French people, translated from the banks of the Seine to those of the St. Lawrence, then would we have said, with mocking and jeering lips, " If there were windows in heaven, then might these things be." Thank God, there are windows in heaven. They have never been closed so tightly that the hand of grace has not been able and ready to open them, and the promise has always been : " Bring ye all the tithes into the store-house and prove me now herewith, and see if I will not open the windows of heaven and pour you out a blessing that there shall not be room enough to receive it." [*Applause.*]

Friends, that time has come. We see the literal and glorious fulfilment of prophecy and promise here tonight. There has not been room to receive the blessing that has been poured upon us in this place. To think that the leading members of the Roman Catholic clergy from their pulpits have noticed this, our international gathering, and have bidden it a hearty Godspeed and welcome [*loud applause and cheers*]; to think that the French Canadian press of this city and this province have re-echoed the words of the ecclesiastical leaders and emphasized the welcome that they have extended to us,— all this is far more than I would have dared to believe was possible upon this earth of ours. And yet we have seen it. " Mine eyes have seen the glory of the coming of the Lord," here in this city that I thought I knew so well, where I have labored so long, but where my fondest hopes have been exceeded so many times over. [*Applause.*] God bless the old city of Montreal; and may this convention be the date from which many of the old differences and alienations that have hindered its progress and kept its people sundered from one another shall be buried out of sight [*voices : "Amen !*"], and a fairer day of Christian sympathy and acquaintance shall dawn, which shall bring all who love the glory of God and the good of man together into one solid phalanx, marching on to victory under the banner of our common Lord. [*Loud applause.*]

Among the peaceful triumphs of this remarkable occasion I note, as not the least, that we are gathered here in the drill hall — a building that was erected and consecrated to the exercise and preparation of war, whose very existence is owed to the purpose to rear and train defenders that may fight for the national honor upon the bloody field of war. We have pitched our tent — the tent of peace and gospel truth — directly opposite, over on the Champs de Mars, — the field of Mars, the god of war, — also dedicated like this building to warlike exercises and pursuits. Here, within these walls that have re-echoed to the clang of arms and to the sound of martial commands and watchwords, we sing the songs of Zion, we unfurl the flag of the Prince of Peace, we re-echo the angels' song: "Glory to God in the highest, and on earth peace, goodwill toward men." [*Loud applause.*] This is emblematic — may it also be prophetic — of the time

> " When the war-drums throb no longer,
> And the battle-flags are furled,
> In the parliament of man,
> The federation of the world." [*Applause.*]

But now tonight, as we stand upon this platform and feel that, as far as Christian Endeavor matters are concerned, the international fellowship between the Dominion of Canada and the Union of America is perfect, — feel as if the old boundary between the two countries was obliterated and buried out of sight in Christian sympathy and labor together for the common cause, — we are not satisfied. We are not inclined to rest upon our laurels and shout " Hosanna " for the victories that we have gained. We turn our faces to the future and we look for a broader and better day of international fellowship that shall unite, not only these two great countries that are contiguous throughout their whole extent for more than 4,000 miles, as they span the continent from the Eastern to the Western seas. Our hearts are kindled with a nobler ambition, and we look not for international fellowship alone, but for intercontinental — for world-embracing and world-surrounding fellowship in this noble Society of Christian Endeavor. [*Applause.*] And here we find the promise — I might almost say the fulfilment — of our aspirations and hopes; for, as that roll call sounded through this hall a little while ago, you noticed that it included not only every province and portion of the Dominion and every state and territory of the Union, but that it crossed the seas and summoned to this platform, either in person or by salutation flashed beneath the sea-waves through the electric cable, the good wishes and sympathies of Christ's people everywhere throughout the earth. During the past year our honored pioneer and president, accompanied by his excellent wife and faithful fellow-laborer in Christian Endeavor, has put a girdle around the globe. He has traveled in the northern and southern, in the eastern and western, hemispheres; he has trodden every habitable continent, and returns to us laden with the greetings and the spoils of all the nations and races upon earth. In every country he has visited he has been welcomed as a leader and a friend. In every tongue that he has heard spoken, the old familiar pledge that he wrote in that little parsonage in Portland has been repeated By men of every nationality he has been hailed as their leader and their teacher in new and improved methods of Christian work. Why, think of it! We have heard tonight from almost every portion of the vast British empire, and we have been told that in every land and country that calls the good Victoria their empress or their queen [*cheers*], in that vast empire whose morning drum-beat heralds the rising, and whose evening gun-shot salutes the setting, sun around the world, in every place where the Union Jack waves as the emblem of patriotism and of courage, there Christian Endeavor is recognized and welcomed as a prominent and potent factor in religious work. [*Applause.*] We have no representative, so far as I am aware, from the celestial country — from China, the oldest and the greatest of the nations. We would have had some Chinese delegates with us if the infamous laws of our civilized and Christian states had not prevented them from coming [*loud applause*], and they would have told us that, foremost among the Christian agencies to which they look for the enlightening and uplifting of their vast race from heathenism and from darkness, and to which also they look with hope for the reformation and improvement of those nations that boast themselves to be already Christian until they shall sweep from their statute books all such disgraceful legislation as I have named and shall accept and acknowledge the brotherhood and equality of nations everywhere around the globe [*applause*] — that among the best of these agencies they look with hopefulness and assurance to Christian Endeavor. [*Renewed applause.*] We have heard brethren from the dark continent, Africa — that land which has been so little known, so greatly wronged by other people hitherto, but whose day of exploration has already fully come, and whose dawn of salvation draweth nigh,— and they have told us that they also love Christian Endeavor and clasp our hands in assurance of their sympathy and love for this great work. Subjects of the unspeakable Turk — that mysterious power that always seems ready of die and to vanish away but which has surprising resurrections and returns to power — tell us that they wait with longing eyes until the day of liberty shall come, when they shall be permitted to form associations like our own and take their place beside us in the Christian Endeavor ranks.

My friends, it is marvelous; it is glorious. "There shall be a handful of corn in the earth upon the top of the mountains; the fruit thereof shall shake like Lebanon " and shall fill the entire earth. It seems as if some of these old prophesies had been written with special foresight and reference to the Christian Endeavor movement in these days in which we live. Nothing so really ecumenical, so nearly universal, in the way of Christian assembly, ever met upon this world of ours before these conventions of Christian Endeavor. [*Applause.*] Already we are circling and embracing the entire globe. To some extent we are already reaching almost the highest ideal of international fellowship, as for the extent to which it reaches.

Now is it not possible for us on this occasion to consult together how we can make this world-wide brotherhood and fellowship something deeper and more practical and beneficial in our daily lives and work? I think we can. I have one or two suggestions to make in this direction.

In the first place, in order that we may reach the best and highest possible international fellowship, I want to urge upon all those who hear me, from whatever country they come, under whatever form of government they live, whatever type of flag they hail, — I want to urge upon them the duty as well as the privilege of intelligent, earnest, devoted, patient patriotism for the land in which they live. [*Applause.*] I know that patriotism is a word that in some quarters has fallen into disrepute. A prominent divine in the United States preached a sermon before one of the national societies not many months ago in which he denounced the sentiment usually called patriotism and stigmatized it as a narrow and selfish prejudice that means, by loving one's country, hating all other countries and seeking for their overthrow or their humiliation. Our beloved friend, Dr. Deems, the silver-tongued orator, who has so often pleaded the cause of Christian Endeavor, not only in the zenith of its popularity and power but in the days of its youth and obscurity as well — may God raise him from his present illness and spare him yet for many years to be our leader and our speaker upon these great occasions [*applause*] — Dr. Deems published an article the other day which caused me a thrill of joy as I read it, and I said, " Thank God, if Dr. Deems cannot preach he can yet write and his pen is better than most men's tongues." In this article he pursued somewhat this same line of thought and deprecated much of the popular patriotism of the day. Well, it is one of the misfortunes of poor human nature that any word, however excellent and noble it may be in its essential meaning, may be brought down from its high estate and devoted to uses utterly unworthy of its parentage and its real significance, and "patriotism" shares the common fate of language to some extent. But patriotism yet remains in the thought of most men as one of the grandest and noblest sentiments that can fill the human mind, and sway the human heart, and nerve the human hand to action. How much of that which is grandest and sublimest in the history of the world, how many of the names that most stir our heart's blood and thrill us through and through are those who stand before mankind as the representatives of that sentiment of patriotism, or love of native land !

Now, my friends, we shall never reach true internationalism except through true nationalism. We get to the performance of no larger duty and the filling of no larger space except as we faithfully perform the duty that is nearest to us and fill the smallest and most intimate sphere in which we are placed. You reach the perfect family only through the perfect individual, and the worthy society only through the noble household. You reach the great nation only through the individuals and the communities of which it is composed. So we shall never get to that fulness and blessedness of international fellowship until we have first well fulfilled our duties and sounded the significance of patriotism, of love and devotion to our own country.

Now I fear that a revival of this old-fashioned and sometimes stigmatized virtue is greatly needed. I have noticed in society so many youths who are growing up with fingers too delicate and tastes too refined to mingle in the muddy stream of politics. I have noticed some men who are altogether too good to associate with surroundings that are so rough, to dabble in affairs that are so displeasing to their sensibilities or their principles as the scenes of the caucus and of the ballot box. May God protect Canada and the United States — these nations still in their gristle, with their history to make — from citizens like these. [*Loud applause.*] Let it be understood that upon the best and the most intelligent, the most thoroughly refined and cultivated inhabitants of the country, rests chiefly and most pressingly the duty and the dignity of government, of interesting themselves in national affairs — an interest that is not too proud to condescend to the humblest details, an intelligence that is informed regarding the history, the interests, the policies, the outlook, the dangers, the possibilities of the country.

> " Love thou thy land, with love
> Far brought from out the storied past."

It is not possible for us on this continent to go back a millennium of years to scenes like those that inspire the youths of Europe and of Asia, but it is possible for young Canadians to read the thrilling history of the glorious adventures and exploits of the French who came to this country from two to three centuries ago and wearied not until their footsteps had traversed every wilderness, until their frail batteaux had navigated every river and reached the ocean upon the eastern and the southern sides of this great continent. [*Applause.*] It is possible for Americans to go back to the oft-told but always worthy-to-be-repeated story of the Pilgrim Fathers and the early settlers of all the original colonies, of that terrific strife that tore the new world from the grasp of the old and gave us freedom to perform the best that was within us on this continent. We have a history, let us be proud of it; let us be instructed in it, and from the wisdom of our fathers as well as from their failures and their mistakes, let us gather the prudence that is needed now for our direction safely in the tortuous and dangerous paths we tread.

To whom shall I appeal for patriotism if not to the young people of our land? And if any one says, " Yes, talk to the young men who are the voters and who will be the rulers," I say, No; in this, as in so many other things, the young men embrace the young ladies. [*Laughter.*] You know not what fair sister or sweetheart sitting beside you will by-and-by sit upon the bench of justice or in the hall of legislation to make the laws, or to determine their administration in these lands of ours. I come to you, then, and plead for a patriotism that shall be intelligent as to your country's needs, that shall thank God for the native land he has given you, and that shall love it and be devoted to it not with the blind and narrow prejudice that conceives that it is the only land on which the sun can shine, the only people that a just providence can favor, but that recognizes it exactly as one recognizes his own mother — not thinking her the handsomest and the wisest woman upon earth, but recognizing that she holds a relationship to him that is dearer and more sacred than any other, and that she is in a peculiar sense the best woman in the land. [*Loud applause.*]

Let us love our country, not with a blind partisanship that shall excuse her errors, that shall magnify her successes, and that shall turn her vices into virtues and defend and uphold them in the teeth of all men. Let us say, indeed, " Our Country, right or wrong," but let it be with this proviso : " If wrong, to make her right; if right, to keep her so." [*Applause.*]

I said only a little while ago that I had lived both in Canada and in the United States. I love both countries and believe that they are among the choicest heritages that God has ever given to people. How great is the privilege and the glory of us who live here upon this western continent, free from the traditions, the oppressions, and the mistakes of the thousand years that lie behind us, unfettered by the precedents of the past, free to do whatever we think right and best to do in the name of God and for our fellow-men! I recognize the glory and the excellence of our heritage ; but O dear friends, I recognize also the dangers of our position. While no nations have perhaps ever been so highly exalted and favored, upon no other nations in the world's history has there been laid so great a burden of responsibility as upon us at the present time. Because we are so free, because we are the heirs of all the generations that have gone before us, therefore it behooves us to act most wisely and faithfully, not for ourselves alone, but for all mankind as well. It is our glory and our duty to do that. Let us love our country, citizens of Canada and of the United States, so well that we shall always form an intelligent and decided opinion upon its interests and its policies, so that we shall always faithfully and fully exercise our franchise as citizens — the real sovereigns who determine the policy and the destiny of our land. Let us do it in such a way that we shall purge our countries from all evil legislation. If we live upon this side of the line, we shall watch our legislators at Ottawa and at Quebec and at the other provincial centres, and demand and secure from them clean hands and a pure administration and a just and fearless according of rights that are inherent in Canada to every citizen within the borders of the country. [*Applause.*] Let us rise above the prejudice of nation, of race, of locality. May I speak freely to my Canadian friends and say that it was to me one of the chief sorrows of my residence here to see how strong was the local and how weak the national feeling in the Dominion of Canada,— how men would plead and pray and work and sometimes plunder and cheat for Quebec or for some other province in the Dominion; but when the interests of the entire country, from sea to sea and from the river to the ends of the earth, were in question, then how few and lukewarm were the defenders and these friends. If we live upon the south side of the line of 45, let us so love our country and watch over its interests and its administration so well as to make impossible such acts of legislation as we have witnessed and have blushed with shame to confess were written upon the statute books of our nation [*applause*], — as shall forever make impossible such unjust and hideous decrees as that infamous act known as the Geary Bill for the exclusion of the Chinese [*applause*], which insults the law of God, the father and creator of us all, and which brands with shame every individual of the greatest nation upon earth irrespective of his character or his conduct, be it what it may, — as shall forever make impossible such tampering and trickery of legislation as we have witnessed in connection with that magnificent Columbian Exposition which the United States fondly planned and thought should be the crown of her glory, the high-tide mark of the progress that she had attained in the 400 years since the keel of Columbus touched the soil of the new world,— as shall make forever impossible in future a legislation which bids defiance to the law of God and breaks the most solemn compact with man, which takes the price and puts it in the pocket and then failed to deliver the goods it had promised in return. [*Loud applause and cheers.*]

Thus shall we be able, as Canadians and Americans, when we come together in these annual assemblies, to look into each other's faces with mutual pride and congratulation, thinking of the course of events in each country during the twelve months that are past, and thanking God for his preserving mercy that has been above us, guiding us in paths of pleasantness and of peace, in ways of righteousness and of judgment, and for bringing upon us in ever-increasing showers the reward that he has promised to that happy people whose God is the Lord. Then we shall come together, not with mean and petty jealousies for one another, not with covetous eyes for self-aggrandizement by the swallowing up or annexation of the other, but we shall come mutually recognizing our privileges and responsibilities, the differences in our government and our administrations, and accepting the great principal announced by the apostle to the Gentiles that we are all of one family, members one of another, and that if one member suffer, all the members suffer with it, and if one member be honored and glorified, then have all cause to rejoice together. Then shall we reach ideal international fellowship. Then shall we be able to discuss together those great principles that refer, not merely to any local interest or to any national or continental reform or progress whatever, but the principles which lie at the foundation of the very welfare,— yea, the very existence, of the human race,— the principles that bind us together in brotherhood and unity forevermore. Then shall these occasions be times of rejoicing undimmed by any blush of shame. Then shall we thank God for the past and take courage for the future, until, in the grand time that is as sure to come as the sun to rise in tomorrow's eastern sky, the sun of that day shall rise that shall be the dawn of righteousness and of redemption for all the peoples of the earth. May God hasten that time, and grant in his goodness some humble but earnest word that I have spoken tonight, some word that pleads for charity and kindness toward our neighbors even when we differ from them in opinion, may increase their charity and moderation which is so magnificently illustrated by these two nationalities. You know there is a dispute concerning certain rights in eastern and western seas, — concerning the catching of the seals on the one side and the fishing for cod upon the other, and this has worked mischief and irritation between the peoples until, like some single nerve that aches or some small spot of the skin that itches, we forget the welfare of the general body in the irritation of the local member or the little spot, and we are all in irritation and in anger toward one another. We have found a better way already; and while we are gathered here in these magnificent assemblies of Christian discussion and communion, over there on the other side of the sea, in that imperial city of Paris, threatened even while I speak by the malice of the communists and the anarchists, there our national representatives and advocates are pleading before able and impartial judges the question in dispute between us. And by and by when the verdict shall be rendered, we will submit to it without a murmur whether it gives all the seals to the United States and all the cods to Canada or not. [*Loud applause.*] This blessing of international moderation and arbitration is worth more than all the cods and seals that ever swam from the time of Adam until now. [*Renewed applause.*]

Now, I say, we have a right for encouragement, for hopefulness, for expectation and assurance; but I say also, that in this very business we have occasion for the deepest earnestness and faithfulness. False and evil theories are abroad, —theories that would be subversive of every interest that is dear to all the nationalities that we represent. There is the labor question, the social question, the money question, the immigration question, the property question, the ballot question, the enforcement of law and obedience to the statute question,—all these are before us. How many problems there are to perplex the earnest man in these days of ours. Go home, then, Americans and Canadians, to love your own country, your own state, your own territory, your own city, so well that you will do your best to free it from all that is shameful and disgraceful in its own administrations and methods, that it may present a pure and inspiring example to all its neighbors.

Brethren, the world is not going to be saved by holding conventions and passing resolutions and making speeches, however earnest and eloquent they may be. It is to be saved by daily earnest work and practice of the principles we here profess to hold and to obey. Go home to vote as you pray, to feel toward your country as you feel when you sing the songs of Zion. Look at those colors there on the national banners, — the red, the white, the blue. What do they represent to us? The blue — the color of the sky above, the hue of the great ocean beneath, the color that has always been appropriated as symbolic and expressive of truth. Let us hold it dear. The red — It represents blood, earnestness and zeal, devotion of the being to life and death, if it be needful, for the cause that we hold dear. The white — the color of the unsullied snow as it falls upon us from the heaven above, the emblem of cleanliness and purity forevermore. In doctrine let us be true blue; in earnestness let us be blood red; in faultlessness and blamelessness let us be pure white, through and through. [*Enthusiastic applause.*] Then shall the kingdoms of this world become the kingdoms of our Lord and of his Christ, and he shall reign forever and ever. [*Prolonged applause.*]

A number of notices were then read, including a telegram from California which announced that the news of the convention for 1895 had been received in San Francisco with the music of brass bands. Miss Hollingshead, whose singing on the previous evening was greeted with so much enthusiasm, then rendered a solo which was again received with prolonged applause. Just at this moment there was considerable noise and shouting outside the hall, and the audience was briefly dismissed with the Doxology and the benediction by Bishop Fallows.

When the delegates left the hall, they found a large crowd on the street, kept in good order by a strong force of policemen. Nothing was done to cause any annoyance or disturbance, and the delegates, though somewhat nervous, proceeded home as usual.

ST. JAMES M. E. CHURCH.

Naturally, the audience which gathered here (the tent, on account of the storm, being unfit to use) was rather small for a Christian Endeavor audience, yet the session proved an interesting one.

Dr. Clark first introduced Rev. Dr. John L. Campbell, of New York City, who not only conducted the "Pastors' Hour," but also relieved Dr. Clark of the duties of presiding officer for the evening. Rev. Dr. Silcox, pastor of the Emanuel Congregational church of Montreal, led in prayer.

DR. CAMPBELL: At first thought there is a feeling of disappointment that comes over us in the comparative smallness of a congregation such as that which we have tonight, but every pastor knows that when a storm arises, and a congregation is small, then we have often our very best meetings.

Last year in New York City there were twenty-four who took part in the "Pastors' Hour," each speaker representing a distinct religious denomination. We are going to have twenty-six who will address us tonight. All those good brethren who are to speak to us are going to tell us of what the Christian Endeavor Society is doing for themselves and for the denominations which they represent. Addresses that might easily occupy several hours are going to be pressed inside of two minutes.

However wide the influence of the Columbian Fair at Chicago may be, the influences that are going forth from these meetings will be far broader and more blessed, circulating from your beautiful city to every shore on our globe, and they will endure.

> " When the sun grows cold and the stars grow old,
> And the leaves of the judgment book unfold."

Last Thursday the marriage of Prince George to Princess May of Teck was celebrated, and the heart of a great nation, on whose domain the sun never sets, and the beating of whose martial drums follow the march of the morning light around our globe, is inspired with enthusiasm and filled with gladness, and, brethren, we are here to rejoice with you. When President Garfield fell, and the nation across the line was bowed in grief, we remember that good sovereign, who, out of her own widowed heart, sent such womanly and queenly messages of sympathy to the stricken wife in our White House. From across the line we bring you a nation's greeting, and with all our hearts we say, God bless your noble, Christian Queen, long may she reign! [*Loud and prolonged applause.*] May our own beautiful star-spangled banner and the flag of old England, that grand old piece of bunting that for a thousand years has braved the battle and the breeze, — may they ever remain entwined in loving wedlock. But, dear brethren, we are celebrating tonight a marriage far more regal than any one of these, the united Church of the Living God, the Bride, the Lamb's Wife, united to Christ her living head.

There are some who talk a great deal about Christian union, discuss it in the newspapers and pass resolutions about it, and hope for it and pray for it as something that is coming sometime in the sweet by-and-by, or off in the indefinite future; but, brethren, on this platform and in this congregation we have Christian union. [*Loud applause.*] I open the hymn book that I use, and I find Christian union there: a Roman Catholic hymn, that grand song of Cardinal Newman's, "Lead, kindly Light;" an Episcopalian hymn, "From Greenland's Icy Mountains;" a Calvinistic hymn, "Rock of Ages;" an Armenian hymn, "Arise, my Soul, Arise;" a Lutheran hymn, "A mighty Refuge is our God;" a Baptist hymn, "O Thou, my soul, forget no more," and so on throughout the whole book. Why, we have Christian unity already in the psalmody of our church; we have it in heart and prayer and sympathy, and we are having it in the line of Christian work. "One is your Master, even Christ, and all ye are brethren." Never did Christianity look up to a bluer sky, or out upon a broader prospect than she does at this very hour. [*Applause.*] This old world of ours is swinging out into the glorious light of God; already I hear the bells of the twentieth century ringing all over the world of a sweeter, simpler, richer, more living faith, and a more consecrated service. Christian Endeavor is one of God's mightiest agencies, bringing near the time of which Tennyson sang :

> " Ring in the valiant man and true,
> The larger heart, the kindlier hand ;
> Ring out the darkness of the land,
> Ring in the Christ that is to be."

I observe on this programme that I am asked to say something in reference to this work in regard to my own denomination, the Baptist. Baptists believe in standing shoulder to shoulder with their brethren of every name in every good word and work; they believe in loyalty to Christ and loyalty to the Church; they believe in denominational work and interdenominational fellowship; they believe in missions, and in their Carey centennial they have just been celebrating the founding of the great foreign missionary enterprise. We nail our banner to the mast and shout first, last, always, now and forever, " Fidelity to this whole Christian Endeavor movement; God bless it!" [*Loud applause.*]

The next speaker represents the Disciples church; a silver-tongued orator who comes from Denver, Colorado, Rev. W. F. Richardson, will now address us.

MR. RICHARDSON : The Church of God in this reformatory age is feeling the mighty impetus of that divine principle which makes man free, and which has been searching for the fountain of perpetual youth, that she might in its living waters renew the early vigor with which she met and conquered the pagan world. She has found this fountain of youth at last, this blessed spring, not upon some far distant and strange shore, but within her own familiar borders, in the consecrated lives of her younger sons and daughters. The progress of Christian Endeavor has been marked by a revival of faith, hope, and love, and of willing service to God and man; it has brought back the glorious springtime to the garden of the Lord ; it is giving to the world a new proof of the divine power of the Gospel of Jesus Christ, and is preparing the church for the advent of her glorified Lord. It is for these reasons that the Disciples of Christ rejoice in the progress of Christian Endeavor, and feel that it is to them a most efficient means of advancing his kingdom in the world. In their behalf, therefore, it is my privilege and my joy to say to you, All hail! and God speed you in your glorious mission for Christ and the church. May his blessing rest upon the Young People's Society of Christian Endeavor. [*Applause.*]

MR. CAMPBELL: Rev. Edward O. Ellis, of Fairmount, Ind., will speak for the Friends.

MR. ELLIS: The Christian Endeavor Society is doing much for the Friend's church. I am glad to say that the Friend's church is recognizing in the Endeavor movement something that is helpful. We are especially thankful that the church is standing by it. The Friend's church in America stands solidly for Christian Endeavor. We now see hope where before we had none, because we see that our young people are being trained as they never have been before. We are enemies to sin, but friends to the sinner; we are friends to God and to his people everywhere, and are glad to recognize in this movement the opportunity to shake hands with our brethren sailing under other names, and so we are friends to them all. [*Applause.*]

MR. CAMPBELL: I have great pleasure in calling upon Rev. C. J. Kephart, of Lebanon, Pa., who will speak in behalf of the United Brethren, and we are all united brethren in Christian Endeavor work.

MR. KEPHART: It affords me unmeasured happiness to bring to you tonight the greetings and the good will of the church of the United Brethren in Christ, and we breathe into the ear of our common Lord an earnest prayer for his continued blessing upon this movement. Her pastors and people feel, as never before, the mighty heart-throbs of her young people, and we are providing in this direction for the lengthening of our cords and the strengthening of our stakes, until by the united effort of young and old, the Gospel of the kingdom shall be preached to all nations, and the heathen shall be given to the Lord for an inheritance. I speak the sentiments of our church when I say, God bless the Young People's Society of Christian Endeavor; may its achievements of the past be but the promise of the future, and may this motto, "For Christ and the Church," be so blest of God, that from year to year it shall be the means of bringing increased multitudes into the kingdom, and increase the glory of God through our Lord Jesus Christ. [*Applause.*]

MR. CAMPBELL: The next speaker represents the Reformed Presbyterian church. We shall now hear from Rev. J. W. F. Carlisle in reference to the work of Christian Endeavor in that denomination.

MR. CARLISLE: The old Covenanter church, while it loves the old, likewise loves the new when the new is found to be good and true. We have found the Christian Endeavor Society to be good and true, and have made it our denominational society, and have found it to be the best Covenanter society that could be devised. We know no other society and have no use for them at all. First of all, I can say that I personally admire the sanctified common-sense of the leaders of Christian Endeavor, that they give us no hobbies to ride, and we pray that God may guide them with divine wisdom. We love Christian Endeavor because it emphasizes absolute loyalty to Jesus Christ as King. We Covenanters believe, in the most practical sense, in the kingship of Jesus Christ, that Jesus Christ is King in politics and in governments. We love Christian Endeavor because it is making a bold protest against the social crimes of the age, like the Louisiana lottery business, like the opening of the World's Fair on the Sabbath. It is breathing new ozone everywhere into the Covenanter boys and girls. It emphasizes three blessed things: daily study of God's Word, daily talking to God at the throne of grace, and daily working out what you are working in. I consider the pledge one of the most blessed features of the Christian Endeavor organization. Our prayer is simply this for all societies, that the society that has given us such wonderful height and breadth may be blessed of God, and may it give us such wonderful depth that we may be rooted and grounded in Jesus Christ to do the work which the age demands. [*Loud applause.*]

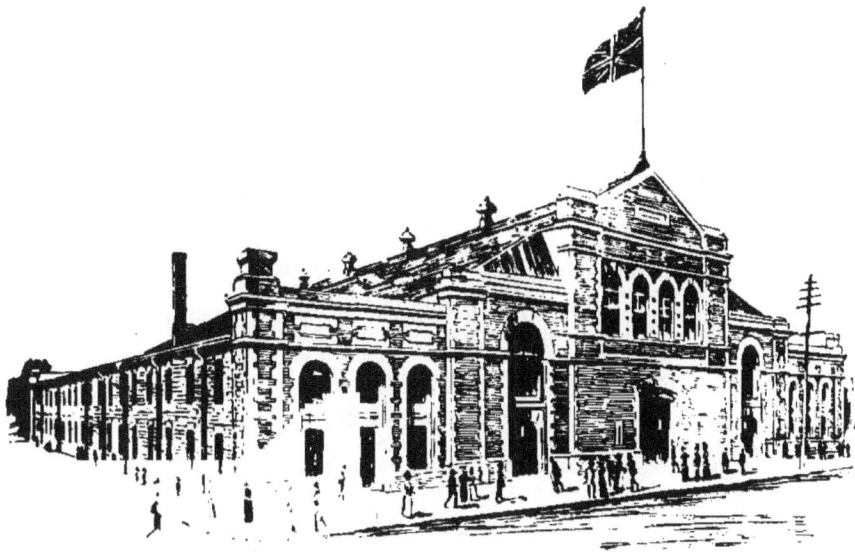

THE DRILL HALL

THE MONTREAL CONVENTION TENT.

Enlarge the place of thy tent and let them stretch forth the curtains of thin-
habitations spare not, lengthen thy cords, and strengthen thy stakes — Isa. 54 2

MR. CAMPBELL: Rev. Chas. Roads, of Philadelphia, will now speak for the Methodist Episcopal church.

MR. ROADS: Fifteen hundred Methodist Episcopal societies still enthusiastically keep step with our army of Christian Endeavorers [*applause*], and the number will no doubt increase. In several states new societies are being organized. We rejoice in this for the sake of Methodism. The fire is kindled in thirty denominations and nothing can extinguish it. Methodist Episcopal Christian Endeavorers are taught to love their own church so much, and they are profoundly sorry that the late General Conference did not adopt the Christian Endeavor society as its young people's society. But we cannot believe that our church, so magnificently liberal to all that love Christ, can long be kept away from the blessed interdenominational fellowship and spiritual power of Christian Endeavor. It is only necessary that a more accurate knowledge of our Young People's Society of Christian Endeavor should come to Methodists to make all her young people join us. [*Applause.*]

MR. CAMPBELL: We shall now hear what Christian Endeavor has done for the Cumberland Presbyterian church. Rev. W. T. Rogers, of Nashville, Tenn., will now address us.

MR. ROGERS: The birthday of the Christian Endeavor Society and that of the Cumberland Presbyterian church comes on the same day of the year. We believe that God hath called them both for a great work in the world. The Cumberland Presbyterian church was born just seventy-one years before the Christian Endeavor Society. In a great revival of religion God called it into existence to meet the infidelity, scepticism, and fatalism that were spreading over our sunny South and the frontier and western states. We believe in the broad commission, "Go ye into all the world and preach the Gospel to every creature; he that believeth and is baptized shall be saved;" in other words, we believe that salvation is possible to all men, and that it is certain to all Christian believers. Our church is a missionary church. Since its organization, more than one-third of its preachers have been missionaries. There are so many young people in the Cumberland Presbyterian church that it is just as natural for it to be Christian Endeavor as it is for water to flow down the hill. We are Christian Endeavor to the very core [*applause*], because we see in this great movement principles and influences tending toward the union of all Christians in one grand movement for the speedy evangelization of the whole world. Our attitude toward all denominations has ever been this: In non-essentials, liberty; in essentials, unity; and in all things, charity. [*Applause.*]

MR. CAMPBELL: I will now introduce Rev. Hugh L. Elderdice of Pocomoke City, Md., who will speak for the Methodist Protestant church.

MR. ELDERDICE: "Though little among the thousands of Judah," the Methodist Protestant church has advanced to the front rank of this modern army, whose triumphant tread is heard upon our own and distant shores. Among the million and a half of youthful soldiers who have volunteered to conquer this world for Christ, there is no troop or company more loyal to the Christian Endeavor banner than are the boys and girls of the Methodist Protestant church. Whether the bugle call against the battlements of sin that have entrenched themselves in our native soil, or against those pagan powers which sway their Christless sceptre over foreign fields, Commander Clark may safely number among his armor-bearers the true and tried of the Methodist Protestant church. Our General Conference has given its official seal to this movement, and about a score of annual conferences have swung into line. We have given to Maryland and Alabama presidents for their state unions; to the literary world, "Jonathan Hayseeds;" and our motto is: "A Christian Endeavor society in every Methodist Protestant church." It has introduced into our church a better system of work, making specialists of our young people. What used to be done by anybody in any way is now done by somebody in the right way. It has placed in our hand the pen to sign the death warrant of denominational rivalry, and pledged us to aid in exorcising that demon which has too long possessed the broken church. It has led us to the threshold of unity, not organic but spiritual. We clasp hands with all believers in Christ, whether they say "Shibboleth" or "Sibboleth." [*Applause.*]

MR. CAMPBELL: The Lutherans will now be heard from in the person of Rev. Leander Keyser, of Springfield, Ohio.

MR. KEYSER: I have been thinking during the last few months, as well as the last few days, that if Martin Luther had lived in the present age instead of several centuries ago, he certainly would have been a Christian Endeavorer, because he had the spirit of Christian Endeavor in him. I have been thinking also that if he had lived in the Christian age of Christian fellowship and fraternity, he would not have refused to give the hand of fellowship to Zwingli, but he would have said, "We may differ in non-essentials, but we agree upon the fundamental doctrine of justification by faith in Jesus Christ." Do you want to know why we of a certain branch of the Lutheran church like Christian Endeavor? It is because it is fundamentally right. That is the chief and the greatest reason. [*Applause.*] Christian Endeavor never puts the cart before the horse; it always puts that first which is first, and that second which is second, and that is precisely Lutheran doctrine. That is the reason that we Lutherans have accepted the Christian Endeavor pledge. [*Applause.*]

MR. CAMPBELL: We heard a little while ago from the Reformed Presbyterians. Now we shall hear from the Canadian Presbyterians. The Rev. John McMillan, of Halifax, Nova Scotia, will speak for them.

MR. MCMILLAN: The Christian Endeavor Society has a strong hold upon the affections of the Presbyterian church in Canada. All who know it love it, and if they do not love it, it is because they do not know it; and those who love it are ready to defend it, commend it, and to extend it. It is a priceless boon to our church, a priceless boon to our young people, and to our ministry. When Lazarus was raised from the dead, the Lord said to the disciples, "Loose him and let him go." He had life, but he had no power of motion. The Christian Endeavor Society has done more than anything else to loosen our young people and let them go and work for Christ and speak for Christ. [*Applause.*] Over a church door was once written these words: "Dying for want of sympathy." This can never be written over a church door where there is a live Christian Endeavor society. [*Applause.*]

MR. CAMPBELL: Rev. Martyn Summerbell of Lewiston, Maine, will speak for the Christian denomination.

MR. SUMMERBELL: We are a very old church, and we love very old things. We love the old Bible with all our hearts; we love the old faith and we love the old Gospel. We are a very conservative people, and it was for that reason that when Christian Endeavor took its start, we had to tarry a little while to find out just what it was and whither it was tending, but just as soon as we discovered that, we fell into line very promptly. I can say that Christian Endeavor is making large strides among our people. Counting up this year and last year, I find among the churches having Endeavor societies reported in those two years a gain of one hundred percent. We come with a fair delegation this year, considering our size, but next year we hope to increase the delegation at least tenfold, and we are going to try to make it an hundred-fold when we go to Cleveland. [*Applause.*]

MR. CAMPBELL: We remember that the first Young People's society of Christian Endeavor was organized in a Congregational church. We will all be glad to hear from this denomination through Rev. Ralph W. Brokaw, of Springfield, Mass.

MR. BROKAW: Yes, the first society of Christian Endeavor was organized in a Congregational church, and Christian Endeavor has blessed the Congregational churches with a truer spirituality, with a broader fellowship, and with a more intelligent and effective Christianity. Our missionary societies "arise and call her blessed." The Congregational churches would as willingly part with the Sunday school as they would with the Y. P. S. C. E.

MR. CAMPBELL: We will now hear what Christian Endeavor is doing for the M. E. church South. Rev. H. G. Scudday, of Longview, Texas, will address us.

MR. SCUDDAY: I come to give expression to the M. E. church South. While her hands are busy pushing her rapidly developing enterprises and reaching out for greater conquests, she is not unappreciative of Christian Endeavor. I tell you she loves it. She is the noble mother of a rapidly increasing family now numbering nearly one million and a half members. She is now nursing a babe which has been christened "Epworth League." I have a secret to tell you. The baby's eyes and heart are being caught by a look of love from a curly-headed boy of twelve summers, whose name is the "Young People's Society of Christian Endeavor." He has been born of the spirit in the fulness of time to preserve denominational loyalty and to foster interdenominational fellowship. Is it any wonder that the Methodist girl should fall in love with such a suitor? Who will dare object to the courtship? Whom God would join together, let no man seek to keep asunder. [*Loud applause.*] Time will demonstrate to the somewhat reluctant mother that the union will preserve and enhance all the virtues of the daughter, and beside, deck her with a bridal wreath of olive leaves which will appropriately express that good will and cordiality toward all believers that has characterized Methodism in all ages of her history. [*Applause.*]

MR. CAMPBELL: We will now hear from another Reformed church, the Reformed Episcopal church, represented by Rev. Wm. D. Stevens, of Montreal, P. Q.

MR. STEVENS: The Reformed Episcopal church sends the Christian Endeavor Society greeting and its love. It loves you because of what you are; it has no suggestions to make to you; it has no corrections; it has no axes to grind; it takes you just as you are and loves you for yourself. We love you for what you are doing for us; you are drilling our young people and teaching them how to pray. Our prayer is, God bless you and increase you and make you a blessing. [*Applause.*]

MR. CAMPBELL: The next speaker will be Rev. Chas. J. Palmer, of Lanesboro, Mass., who will speak for the Episcopalians.

MR. PALMER: The Episcopal church is one that tries in its methods to embrace that which is universally applicable. Its methods are adapted to the humblest cottage and to the most gorgeous cathedral. It is the only church that is both Protestant and Catholic, and therefore we indorse a society whose methods are universally applicable. Inasmuch as our liturgy tries to be the resultant of everything worthy to be given in all the ages, we have the survival of the fittest, and so we indorse a movement which is the cream of all previous experiments in the line of young people's work. We believe not merely in the Holy Ghost who was present in the writings of the Scriptures, but the Holy Ghost who is at work today. We accept the movement that has been born within the last few years, the fruit of the Holy Spirit. We endorse a movement which pledges a daily study of the Scriptures, and then last of all because you have adopted the same motto, which was the motto of the Church of England for two or three centuries: "For Christ and the Church." Having the same motto and the same end, we can work side by side. [*Applause.*]

MR. CAMPBELL: The Rev. N. B. Grubb, of Philadelphia, Pa., will speak for the Mennonites.

MR. GRUBB: I represent the Mennonite church, the immediate, direct descendants of the Waldenses, and hence the oldest Protestant church. There was a time when our young people were satisfied with doing nothing, simply because they were not taught to do anything. Times have changed. The Christian Endeavor movement came along, and we are "right in it" and expect to stay in it for good. The attitude of our church toward the Christian Endeavor Society may perhaps be expressed best by four words. These four words are: Admit, submit, commit, and transmit, — that is to say, we admit the Christian Endeavor Society into our church; we admit into our hearts and minds the truth and power of Jesus Christ. Then we submit our prejudices to the conditions of the pledge, just as we submit our ill-will to the will of Him whose will is always right and perfect. Then we commit ourselves in consecration to the service of the Master, as we commit all things to Him who knows how to keep them for us. Then we endeavor to transmit the truth in its simplicity and purity to all at home and abroad. [*Applause.*]

MR. CAMPBELL: We will now hear from still another Reformed church, the Reformed Dutch church, represented by Rev. Geo. W. Furbeck, of Stuyvesant, New York.

MR. FURBECK: The Reformed church of America, — the old Dutch church,— was one of the first to be established on this continent, and was also one of the first to endorse Christian Endeavor. We love this sturdy child of twelve even more than when an infant in years. We could not do without Christian Endeavor. It gives me pleasure to bring the greetings of this old, tried, and true denomination, and in her name speak words of approval of Christian Endeavor principles and Christian Endeavor workings. There has arisen in our Christian Endeavor societies, during the past year, what I look upon as the beginning of a wonderful missionary movement, — the first denominational Christian Endeavor missionary league has been formed, the first denominational Christian Endeavor missionary conference has been held, and special work is being carried on both in the foreign and in the home field. Christian Endeavor has been found to mean all that its name implies, endeavoring to be like Christ and to do Christ's work. We bid Godspeed to this divinely directed and divinely blessed movement. [*Applause.*]

MR. CAMPBELL: The Presbyterian church will be represented by Rev. Dr. J. Clement French, of Newark, New Jersey.

DR. FRENCH: We believe thoroughly that Christian Endeavor was heaven-inspired and heaven-descended. We have confidence in the wisdom and admire the faith and zeal of its distinguished founder and his coadjutors. We put our own heart against the heart of· our young people, and we pledge ourselves to this great army of the living God that is now sending its battle-cry all around the world: " For Christ and the Church." [*Applause.*]

MR. CAMPBELL: The Rev. U. F. Swengle, of York, Pa., will speak for the Evangelical Association.

MR. SWENGLE: The denomination I have the privilege of representing, though smaller in numbers and in the number of her societies than many others, rejoices in the existence within her borders of a union of young people's societies known as the "Keystone League of Christian Endeavor." We rejoice in the precious truth that " One in our Master, even Christ, " and that we are all brethren. We aim at the development of an earnest Christian life, efficiency and faithfulness in work "for Christ and the Church," systematic and thorough Bible reading and study, active efforts in works of philanthropy, and the cultivation of the greater sociability among our members. We keep pre-eminently before us a trio of interests to which we desire to hold our young people; viz., loyalty to Christ, loyalty to the church, and loyalty to Christian Endeavor and its principles. We believe that trained workers are more capable thinkers and more efficient toilers, and that organized Christians are a much greater force than independent laborers in the Master's vineyard. Therefore we seek both to organize and to train our young people who are coming on so speedily to assume the positions of usefulness and responsibility in the Church of Christ. We seek to enlist all the young people within our denominational circle under the Christian Endeavor banner, and to establish them on the firm basis of Christian Endeavor principles. [*Applause.*]

MR. CAMPBELL: I take pleasure in introducing Rev. Jno. S. Moore, of Sherman, Texas, who will represent the Southern Presbyterian church.

MR. MOORE: I am glad to say, dear friends, that I represent a church that has indorsed the principles of Christian Endeavor. We consider it one of the greatest movements of the nineteenth century. [*Applause.*] Edison has taken the electricity that lay dormant in the material world to run these street cars about Montreal, and he has a grand exhibit at Chicago. Father Clark has taken another great thing that lay dormant in the church, and we have had a great exhibit here in Montreal in the last three days. [*Applause.*] Two of my people came up last year to New York and saw that great meeting and told me about it, and I came up to Montreal and brought five others this year, and I say, like the Queen of Sheba, " The half was not told me." [*Applause.*] Now, dear friends, you will excuse me for making two suggestions: one is, I think we ought all to pray that God will raise up another Father Clark to have a Christian Endeavor movement among the older people. [*Applause.*] The other suggestion is, that two years from now, when I trust many of us will go to California, we shall have a special train for the objectors, the pessimists, and the unbelievers, and take them all out there, and if we can't convert them, turn them over to the Pacific Ocean. [*Laughter and applause.*]

Bishop Arnett being absent, another brother spoke for the African M. E. church as follows :—

I bring you this evening greetings from the African Methodist Episcopal church concerning this God-given work. This work has proved a great help to our church. Let us be baptized by the Spirit, moving onward and upward " for Christ and the Church." [*Applause.*]

MR. CAMPBELL : I now introduce a brother who will speak in behalf of the Moravian church, Rev. C. E. Eberman, of Brooklyn, N. Y.

MR. EBERMAN : The Moravian church is old enough to know its mind and heart, and it is dead in love with Christian Endeavor. I am glad to say that I hold in my hand the official endorsement of the Provincial Synod of the Moravian church, endorsing the Christian Endeavor movement and its work. I am also glad to say that the Christian Endeavor societies in the Moravian church are going grandly on; where the vanguard rested last year the rearguard is resting today. It is only a question of time when all the young people will flock into the Christian Endeavor societies, and all the old people will shout, Hallelujah! when they see them tripping in. We bid you Godspeed, and ask God to direct and control, and to give us all the victory. [*Applause.*]

The speakers for the Free Baptists, United Presbyterians, Methodists in Canada, Reformed church in the United States, and the Church of England in Canada were absent. Dr. Clark then thanked the ministers for responding so promptly and for coming out on such a disagreeable evening. A hymn was then sung, after which Dr. Clark introduced Rev. J. W. Lee, whose subject was " The Raw Material of a Great Life."

DR. CLARK: It affords me the greatest pleasure to introduce to this audience one who has come from so great a distance,— and yet whose fame has come on ahead of him,— the author of a book that has attracted so much attention throughout the world, " The Making of a Man," and we have a man to speak to us tonight, the Rev. J. W. Lee, D. D., of Atlanta, Georgia.

The Raw Material of a Great Life.

Address of Rev. J. W. Lee, D.D.

The raw material of life is found in the conditions which environ it. With the grade and quality of life must the raw material correspond, which is to support and nurture it. As we go up from the lowest degree of plant through the different ranges of animal life to the highest plane of human life, we find the raw material which is to furnish each order thereof more and more complicated and refined.

To know what the raw material of a particular grade of life must be, we have only to analyze the contents of the structure of that life. Seeing that the constituent elements of a tree are carbon, oxygen, hydrogen, etc., we are ready to declare what its food must be. For the contents of the food of a tree make an equation with the constituent elements of the structure of a tree. The environment of a tree contains trees in diffusion ; through acorns or other forms of potential life, they are precipitated into oaks or elms.

Knowing the elements which enter into the structure of animal life, we are prepared to say what the raw material must be, which is to sustain it. Finding that oxygen, hydrogen, nitrogen, carbon, lime, phosphorous, soda, iron, etc., go to make up the body of an animal, we know the raw material upon which that animal is to subsist; for the contents of its food make an equation with the structure of its body.

Elements can only become the raw material of life in so far as they constitute the duplicates of it.

In one of the late declarations of Mr. Herbert Spencer on the subject of religion, he expresses himself in the following remarkable language : "Amid the mysteries, which grow the more mysterious the more they are thought about, there will remain the one absolute certainty, that man stands in the presence of an infinite and eternal energy from which all things proceed." Here we have matter, force, life, plant, animal and human, mind and personality, all marshalled on the same plane and keeping step to the same music.

Pope and cardinal and bishop and priest and layman, differences of hierarchy and degree, all on the same line and moving without respect to age, or rank, or merit, because moving without significance or purpose.

General and colonel and captain and lieutenant and private and camp-tramp and dead-beat, all on the same level and marching in accordance with the pulsations of unending dynamics.

It is not at all surprising that Mr. Spencer regarded this procession a mystery, which threatened to become the more mysterious the more it was contemplated.

He would have reduced the mystery well nigh an infinite degree, had he taken the name of the greatest thing he noted in the procession rather than the lowest, with which to label the source of it.

It was my pleasure to observe a procession once go along the street and to count seventeen elephants as making up a part of it. They were enormous manifestations of conserved force. Quotations they were from the wilds of Asia and Africa. But this was not known as the elephants' circus, but as Adam Forepaugh's globe-encircling, world-eclipsing, child-intoxicating, unprecedented and unparalled show. [*Laughter.*] Adam Forepaugh was not to be compared in size to any one of his elephants, but in the quality of his endowment he distanced any elephant in the lot by an infinite degree. Adam Forepaugh stood for and included all the spotted horses, and Shetland ponies, and steam-played pianos, and grinning clowns, and cages of monkeys and bears in the whole rollicking outlay. The whole gay movement proceeded from the brain of the great showman.

With a philosophic fancy for defining the world in terms of energy, and seeing life and mind as part of the outcome, Mr. Spencer determined, rather than raise the grade and heighten the quality of his source, to becloud the whole subject by successive layers of growing mystery.

Has not the last analysis of philosophic indisposition to see been reached, when men reduce the universe to forms of force and then seek to silence the mild plea theologians make for an explanation of life and mind, by declaring the whole thing a mystery, which threatens to become the more mysterious the more it is thought about.

Mystery enough hangs about the problems of existence, even when mind is called in to help solve them. But when force is substituted for mind, and energy for thought, and agnosticism for knowledge, with no other seeming purpose than to envelop the universe in the folds of impenetrable mystery, the movement can be fitly called by nothing less than iridescent imbecility. [*Laughter.*]

Where hides the occult error, and lurks the belated narrowness in saying that we stand in the presence of an infinite and eternal mind from which all things proceed? The source of a thing is entitled to the rank and standing of the highest that proceeds from it.

The effect has no right to assume airs and put on uniform which leads outsiders to suppose it out-generals the cause.

When all things are represented as proceeding from an infinite and eternal energy, mind becomes a mode of matter and matter a form of energy, and the hierarchy of nature and attribute among things is broken down. This is a direct insult to the tuitions of the human race. All organized intelligence rests upon the conviction that there are differences in things, not simply in quantity, but in quality and essence.

In the Troilus and Cressida of Shakespeare, Ulysses is represented as saying: " O, when degree is shaked, which is the ladder to all high designs, then enterprise is sick ! How could communities, degrees in schools and brotherhoods in cities, peaceful commerce from dividable shores, the primogenitive and due of birth, prerogative of age, crowns, sceptres, laurels, but by degree, stand in authentic place ? Take but degree away, untie that string, and hark! what discord follows ! Each thing meets in mere oppugnancy; the bounded waters should lift their bosoms higher than the shores and make a son of all this solid globe; strength should be lord of imbecility, and the rude son should strike his father dead; force should be right, or rather, right and wrong, between whose endless jar justice resides, should lose their names, and so should justice too. Then everything includes itself in power, power into will, will into appetite; and appetite an universal wolf, so doubly seconded with will and power, must make perforce an universal prey, and last eat up himself."

We shall take it then as an incontrovertible proposition, one in accordance with the concensus and intuitions of the human race, that man stands in the presence of an infinite and eternal mind from which all things proceed. Getting round to the absolutely safe and infallible proposition, we are not on new ground, we are where St. John, the beloved disciple, stood when he wrote " In the beginning was the word, the logis, or the eternal mind, and the eternal mind was with God, and the eternal mind was God, and without the eternal mind was not anything made that was made." All things proceeded from the eternal mind. The eternal mind was made flesh. And God's Son, who was the embodiment of the eternal mind, said, " Except ye eat my flesh and drink my blood, ye have no life in you."

In 1892, during the month of February, I stood on the edge of a tropical forest in the state of Vera Cruz in the republic of Mexico.

The Blanco Rio de Agua flowed at the bottom of a deep chasm on the left. Just above, and in full view, the Cascade Rincon Range, made by the perilous plunge of the waters over precipitous rocks, baptized the surrounding winds with abundant spray. Against the watery particles in this, which floated like so many liquid notes, struck the rays of the sinking sun, and the soft and nimble fingers of light played a symphony in color, which hung in a radiant and variegated arch over the yawning abyss.

On the right stood Orizaba, grim and hoary, lifting its crystal peak 17,000 feet into the sky.

Between the river and its singing cascade and the mountain with its silent snow there was to be seen such a luxurious growth of rich vegetation, such a gorgeous outlay of color, such a swing and rush of unfolding life as the eye seldom beholds elsewhere.

There was the banana plant, loaded with ripe and half-ripe fruit, in all its glory, there stood the coffee tree competing for a place in the soil and enough of the sunlight to redden and ripen its berries. The orange tree and lemon sprung side by side from the fertile ground, and yielded without stint their fruit to sweeten and sharpen the taste of the natives. Here and there, alone and apart, were trees which bore no fruit, but seemed to find reason for their existence in holding out the deep scarlet flowers which glowed like fire on the end of their limbs, as if they were so many torches to illuminate the scene. Above this rare assemblage of vegetable wealth and splendor, huge butterflies flitted on wings shot through with golden bars, and splashed with spots of black and white.

Penetrating this glorious labyrinth of tangled leaf and bloom in company with a friend, who, to the function of a missionary, has the added merit of being an accomplished Spanish scholar, we came at length upon a diminutive cabin built of cane and covered with palm leaves. In front of this stood a woman, surrounded by a group of nearly naked children. Opening a conversation with her, we learned the details and incidents of a piteous story. She was besieged by evil spirits. Day and night they were threatening her destruction and were only kept from consummating their hideous purpose by the intervention of the Virgin, who pitied her and sympathized with her. She dwelt in constant terror lest the Virgin, after awhile, might be no longer able to protect her, and lest, after all, she might be overcome by the fiends which she imagined surrounded her. In all that radiant orchestra, uniformed and bedecked in the brightest hues of the light, and playing their pieces between the rainbow and the snow, there was but one discordant note, that came like a wail from the torn and tormented spirit of that poor Aztec woman. Why did it happen that the only discordant note that marred the melody of all that living chorus should have been struck from the heart of a woman?

The sun braided a bunch of fruit in the top of the banana plant sweet enough for the table of a king.

He formed and packed in a bright red hull the berry that sweetens with its essence the heart of the human race.

He moulded the rind and distilled the juice of as sweet oranges as were ever fixed in a setting of green.

He built a bridge of color over the river with no better foundation than the dissolving mist of the falling cascade.

Why did it happen that the sunlight falling in bright spots over the cabin of that poor Indian woman provoked no better response from her heart than the ferment of horror and the cry of fear? Why was there a dirge in the cabin and a song of triumph in the woods? Why did the sunlight pressing upon the nerves of the bird make it sing, and upon the leaves of the orchid make them flame, while it fell across the path of the woman but to disclose her misery? There being a realm where the orange tree finds its leaf of green and its fruit of yellow, and its symmetry of development, are we to conclude that there is no climate from which the human spirit may extract the tincture capable of refreshing and enriching and completing itself? Are we to assume that there is a country from whose light beauty falls on the plumage of the bird, and from whose sky gladness comes to round its songs, but no land where the human spirit may find repose from its tumult and comfort for its sorrow? We look to Kentucky for perfect horses and to the island of Jersey for perfect cows, and to Minnesota for perfect wheat, and to Florida for perfect oranges; but is there no climate in which we are to look for perfect human beings? Who can tell us where high and wide and deep and rich and holy men and women grow? That is the country we need to find. There must be such a realm. It cannot be that human life, susceptible of such high attainments, is doomed in the nature of things to be mean and grovelling and wretched.

We take representatives of the life found in our Mexican forest. First we take an orange seed. It is composed of the same elements found in the domain of unorganized matter. The elements as we find them in the seed differ from such as we find in the chemical domain by the way they are combined. Some strange power has had to do with the arrangement of these particles which make up the contents of the orange seed. The same letters are here that are scattered throughout nature, but they are put into a wondrous formula. They have come together seemingly to make a definite utterance, and in conjunction with life they are to get themselves into the syntax and prosody of the grove. They are to spell themselves out in tree and leaf and flower and fruit. They are to be developed into the literature of the plant world.

Now what takes place as the orange tree passes from its germ in the seed to the full and free and perfect expression of itself in the tropical woods? This, it partakes every moment of the elements which constitute its own structure. It feeds upon the originals and duplicates and fundamentals of itself. Next we have an egg. The albumen in this egg consists of the same elements found in the chemical world. But here they have been lifted and combined after the provisions of a marvelous formula. Here we have the alphabet, which, in conjunction with animal life, is to express itself in the song and plumage and flight of the bird. What happens as the bird passes from its place in the egg to the full realization of itself in the sky? This, the bird partakes every moment of the very food which makes an equation with the contents of its structure. It lives upon the duplicates of itself.

We are in the presence of the Aztec woman. She may be a descendant of Cuatehmoc, who, when hanging on the cypress, addressed to the dying sun, as it sank in the west, the requiem of his race. We find in the case of the woman, as with the tree and the bird, that as far as her physical organization is concerned, it is duplicated in the food she eats. As far as her physical organism is concerned, it is composed of the same elements found in the hydrogen, carbon, nitrogen, lime, soda, iron, etc., and replenishes itself and keeps itself built up by partaking of the same elements as they are found in the bread and meat and fruit and vegetables and milk. But unlike the tree and the bird, there is something in the woman that the material duplicates of her physical frame do not feed. And this seems to be by far the greatest part of herself, for it is intense and strong enough to cloud and make wretched her entire life. The wail from this woman's heart advertises the presence of something that perpetually creates a domain of misery in a surrounding republic of joy. Find the duplicate of that something, and feed her spirit with it, and you have found the secret of making human life as perfect and free and joyous as life among plants and animals. Man's perfect growth and culture is not to be by bread alone, but, as One said before, by every word that proceedeth from the mouth of God. Man, in the high sense, of himself, is made the image of God He is an expression of the eternal mind, and is to find his perfection in partaking of the effluence of intelligence of the heavens.

The permanent vital environment of man then is the eternal mind that was made flesh. The eternal mind was made flesh that we might get an angle of vision from which to contemplate an eternal and omnipresent and vital reality. Christ on the cross discloses what is always true of the nature of God. The electric light advertises the presence of a power universally diffused. Christ on the cross advertises an all-encompassing, all-enswathing, loving Father, who folds us round and loves us always enough to give his only begotten Son to die for us. We often fix our gaze upon the cross, and forget that the God who permitted his Son to die between two thieves because he loved us is nearer to us than breathing, or hands and feet. We live and move and have our being in the very innermost heart of the Father of our spirits. Jesus Christ mediates this love which surrounds us like the air we breathe, directly to our needy and weary souls. We are complete in him.

We are to find the duplicates of our higher and nobler selves in the eternal mind and we are to feed on them in order to get our growth and fill ourselves out.

The elements of mind are thought, affection and will.

We must feed on thought. But how can we get at eternal thought and universal thought? In the most simple and natural way. We begin life as little children. We find ourselves in the room where we first see the light, surrounded by chairs and blocks and cradles, and blue things and green things We hear noises and sounds and see sights from the start. We push out our senses against these things and get a response and commerce between our minds and the expressions in things, which the eternal mind has made of itself. The things that we play with are limited and material. They are symbols and first letters which are placed before us to lead us into the meaning and sweep of an infinite literature. After awhile, when childhood days are over, we wake up to the fact that we have great principles and convictions in our minds that did not come to us from the material objects we found around us in the outside world.

We come to believe that a straight line is the shortest distance between two points, that a thing cannot both be and not be at the same time, that every effect must have a cause. We come to believe in law, order, personality, no one of which ideas was imported into the mind from the outside world. Things on the outside only stimulated us to the discovery of them lying within the illimitable territory or our own being. We come to see roads leading out from ourselves. We find that we can go from mathematics to infinity. That we can begin with one-half plus one-fourth plus one-eighth plus one-sixteenth plus one-thirty-second plus one-sixty-fourth plus one-one-hundred and twenty-eighth, and through plus all the rest reach infinity. We can begin with power, limited and definite, and reach, in thought, power illimitable and infinite. Beginning by feeling after things and learning that things answer back, beginning by a process of action and reaction between the mind of the child in the room and the objects contained in it, finding the outside world striking chords within our souls that render necessary an intellectual interpretation, we find by-and-by that correspondence has been set up between our limited, narrow minds and infinite intelligence.

Now, all God's thoughts are expressed to man through the eternal mind which took living form in Jesus Christ. Through Christ the worlds were mediated, and law was mediated and truth of every realm was mediated. All truth is Christian truth. That we find in the material world has to do with our temporal well-being. That we find in the realm of law has to do with our moral well-being. That we find in the person of Jesus Christ has to do with our redemption and spiritual completion. The lines of all truth of every grade converge about each individual life. These lines of truth lead out every whither to infinity. Man begins to get ready for an everlasting intellectual movement by appropriating the truth nearest to him. . He gets ready to journey toward mathematical infinity by first learning to go from one to ten. Let it be remembered that there is no truth, in atom, in compound, or tree, or bird, or sky, or man, law, or religion, but is God's truth, and has been expressed through the eternal mind. Then, in adjusting ourselves to the true thought nearest to us, and appropriating it, we come to the recognition of the mind within ourselves. We come, also, to the recognition of ourselves as the mental children of God, in no less sense than we recognize ourselves as the children of his heart and will.

We are to feed also upon affection. We are to appropriate the love of God. Thought alone does not suffice. How are we to partake of the love of God? In the most simple and natural way. We find ourselves placed in childhood in families. . We are surrounded by fathers and mothers and brothers and sisters. We project our senses against material facts and get thought. We project our spiritual powers against the personal facts of father, mother, brother and sister, and get love. By coming into relations with those around us in terms of kindness, politeness, truth, sacrifice and service, we find ourselves growing rich in sympathy and tenderness and love. At first we are having to do with persons, but they are infinite, spiritual facts, because persons are the children of God. Persons come from God, who is our home, and they come, "trailing clouds of glory." Serving them, denying ourselves for them, coming into sacred and holy relations with them, we find, when the days of childhood are over, that we have come into the possession of something more than human sympathy and affection. Our hearts have come through this process to be large and wealthy in the possession of infinite love. Serving God's children, we have come into spiritual commerce with the good Father of us all. The universe is a loom God has provided for the purpose of weaving a marvelous fabric, a perfect and holy humanity. Human beings are threads of which this fabric is to be woven. It is only when we are in perfect relation to our fellows that God finds it possible to weave us in as parts of this wondrous texture. When we come into right relations with all human beings, we have come into right relations with the universal man, who was the Son of God, and who was the embodiment of the mind of God, and thus we have connected our hearts with the lines which run, through the human race, through Jesus Christ, straight to the heart of God.

And while we are going about doing good, often weary and heavy-hearted, serving our fellows and relieving their wants and seeking to assuage their sorrows, the divine shuttles are flying and the great loom is in constant motion, but never forgetting to deposit in our lives the very hues and figures which are necessary to make us beautiful and complete.

For every good gift we make to the betterment of our kind, for every good service rendered, there is an equivalent in the heart of God, which every law and force in the universe is under the necessity of helping toward us. When a grain of corn drops from our hand into the open ground, then the rains and the winds and the sea and the sun take it up, and all the machinery of the round heavens begins to move with reference to increasing and repeating it. When a good deed passes from us looking to the health of another, then it ceases to be a little, local, human thing. It is at once caught up by the forces of infinity and passes into the spiritual currency of the stars. And be it remembered that the throne of God itself would as soon dissolve and pass away as that the person from whom the deed proceeded should lose his reward — a reward, too, out of all proportion to the deed, a reward consonant with the nature of God.

When a piece of bread passes from the hand of a kind, Christian woman to satisfy the hunger of a poor little boy on the street, it at once assumes infinite proportions and the spiritual equivalent of it, which, too, is illimitable, will surely come back to enrich the heart of the woman. Isolated and alone, we are fragments, we are nothing. It is when we stand in terms of service and love with humanity that we become great and strong and perfect. Of God we learned through our fellows; to God we are to go through our fellows. Of the depths of ourselves we learn through our fellows; to the heights of ourselves we are to go through our fellows. Christ became perfect man by perfect relation with humanity, and through perfect sacrifice for humanity. He gave us the method and the secret of the Almighty. The refreshing streams, which are to bless and perfect the race, flow from the heart of God, through humanity, the structure of which and the nature of which Christ assumed. Touch humanity perfectly, and you touch God's Son, and you touch God's heart, and you get all that is gracious and tender and sweet and holy God has to give.

We had in Atlanta, Ga., a few years ago an intellectual, noble woman. She was the principal of the Girl's High School. When the duties of the schoolroom were over, it was her daily work to go among the poor and sick and heavy-hearted to comfort and cheer and guide. Forgetting herself and working to bless and lift up God's poor, it happened that God was constantly throwing into her face such an unearthly and ineffable light as advertised the heavenly zeal, from whence it came. So much of the spirit and mind of the Master did she appropriate, while serving the needy, that she felt impelled to go, after awhile, where the need was greater. And today that saint and great-souled woman is in China, a sort of emigration agent sent from the skies to solicit volunteers for the land of unending day. [*Applause.*] A good brother of hers, a wise bishop in a great church, is doing all he can to lift people to God on this side the sea, while his sister is giving her life and the treasures of a great mind on the other. Thus, these two, the consecrated son and daughter of a saintly home, like the Christ they love, carry the globe with all its woe and sorrow in their hearts. God in the meantime sends them the morning and the evening light charged with intimations of a glad, good time, that abides now and always.

> " A sense of an earnest will
> To help the lowly living,
> And a terrible heart thrill,
> If you have no power of giving !
> An arm of aid to the weak,
> A friendly hand to the friendless,
> Kind words, so short to speak,
> But whose echo is endless.
> The world is wide ; these things are small ;
> They may be nothing, but they are all ! "

Another element of mind is will. We call it law. We are to feed upon it. This begins, too, in the home. We obey our parents when they tell us to do this and not to do that. Beginning thus we find when we are grown that the seemingly hard and arbitrary commands of our parents were parts of great, fundamental, universal laws, and that in obeying them we have come to the mastery of ourselves. So, partaking of thought and affection and will, as mediated to us through the eternal mind made flesh, we find the alphabet of a great, infinite literature gradually coming to the surface in our lives. These letters gather themselves into words, these words into sentences, and to utter their meaning becomes the passion and work of our lives. The conviction comes to possess us, that the invisible manuscript, folded in the depths of our lives, is a quotation from the eternities God has placed us in the world to utter. The grapes which the branches bear are drawn from the vine that supports the branches, but unless the branch bears the grapes the vine sends to it, it has no further right to existence. Men are in the world to bear the fruits of the spirit. These are drawn from the true vine. If a man is not good he cumbers the ground and has no high right to live, and does not live in any high sense.

Some one wants to know what of the atonement in all this. Jesus Christ, who is the eternal mind made flesh, is the atonement. Jesus Christ, the embodiment of the mind of God, living, dying, rising from the dead, ascending into heaven, is the atonement. Faith stands for the connection, consciously made, between sinful, perishing human life and the eternal Son of God, who is life. On getting Christ one gets atonement for past sins, and victory over present sins, and a species of life that finds it convenient to get along between the lines of law and faith.

Christ is the duplicate of ourselves. Man is made in the image of God, and Christ is the express image of his person. In Christ God issued a second edition of humanity, but the second edition was upon the same pattern as the first. Finding Christ we find ourselves, our essential, fundamental, real selves. Religion is not what men need to get these days. What the world is dying for and needing most of all is Christ. Religion is not a very good thing to have much of, unless it has been lifted and refined by contact with Christ. Many people have got too much religion; it weakens them and disqualifies them for thorough, honest work. It makes them indolent and conceited and often in the way of people who want to do needed Christian work. Such people should throw away their old, wheezing, self-contained, self-included religion and get the Lord Jesus Christ, the way, the truth, and the life, into their lives. Christ is ethics, Christ is truth, Christ is love, all summed up in the unity of a perfect, holy, divine life.

Much is said these days about how to get people to go to church, and to do Christian work. Get them to partake of Christ. Not of something said about him, but of the Son of God himself. The person who appropriates spiritual and mental food from Christ will be sure to work. He cannot help it. [*Applause.*]

> " First seek thy Saviour out and dwell
> Beneath the shadow of his roof,
> Till thou have scanned his features well
> And know him for the Christ by proof ;
> Such proof as they are sure to find
> Who spend with him their happy days,
> Clean hands and a self-ruling mind,
> Ever in tune for love and praise.
> When potent with the spell of heaven,
> Go, and thine erring brother gain,
> Entice him home to be forgiven,
> Till he, too, see his Saviour plain."

Feeding on Christ we become like him. We come to the full stature of men and women. We cease to be pinched and meagre and small. The royalty within ourselves begins to assert itself and to claim its vast estate. So partaking of the raw material of a great life, which is Jesus Christ, the eternal mind made flesh, human beings find they can fill out the invisible life-plan folded in the depths of their being. Feeding on Christ, people find growing within them a desire to move toward " the imperial palace whence they came."

This celestial food God has provided for his children produces such vigor of hope and spirit that man is enabled through the strength and insight which it gives to contemplate without fear the coming season of calm weather when he shall cross the immortal sea which breaks on the shores of limitless day. [*Loud and prolonged applause.*]

MR. CAMPBELL: So far as the committee on registration can decide from the number of badges that have been given and the number of slips that have been filled, there are at this convention nearly 17,000 delegates [*applause*]; and this is by far the largest Christian Endeavor convention ever held, except the one in New York City last year.

The Doxology was then sung and the Mizpah benediction pronounced.

SUNDAY MORNING.

The last day of the convention opened with clear skies and cool temperature. The morning program called for no session of the convention, either at the Drill Hall or tent. The early morning prayer meetings were well attended, and the hour of church service found the delegates distributed throughout the city at the various places of worship. For the most part, the city pulpits were occupied by visiting clergymen. Among the appointments were the following : —

American Presbyterian. — Rev. Dr. G. H. Wells, of Minneapolis, Minn.
Emmanuel Congregational. — Rev. Dr. J. W. Lee, of Atlanta, Ga.
Taylor Presbyterian. — Rev. J. L. Campbell, New York.
Melville Presbyterian. — Rev. Dr. J. L. Hill, of Medford, Mass.
Mountain St. Methodist. — Rev. W. F. Richardson, of Denver, Col.
East-End Methodist. — Rev. Thomas S. Weeks, of Wolfboro'.
Reformed Episcopal. — Rev. Dr. Tracy, of Philadelphia.
Calvin Presbyterian. — Rev. J. W. Cowan, of Tabor, O.
Erskine and Knox. — Rev. Dr. Burrell, of New York.
Cote St. Louis Presbyterian. — Rev. Dr. J. T. McCrory, of Pittsburg, Pa.
Calvary Congregational. — Rev. N. Boynton, of Boston.
Presbyterian Church, corner Atwater Avenue and St. Antoine Street. — Rev. W. H. McMillan, D.D., of Allegheny City, Pa.
St. Gabriel Presbyterian. — Rev. M. Rhodes, D.D., of St. Louis, Mo.
St. Andrew's (Church of Scotland). — Rev. Howard D. Grose, of Chicago, Ill.
St. Henry Methodist. — Rev. R. W. Miller, of Hummelstown, Pa.
Point St. Charles Congregational. — Rev. J. Z. Tyler, D.D., of Cleveland, Ohio.
Sherbrooke Street Methodist. — Rev. C. J. Kephart, of Lebanon, Pa.
Olivet Baptist Chapel, Point St. Charles. — Rev. Hugh L. Elderdice, Pocomoke, N. Y.
Chalmers Church. — Rev. M. M. Binford, Carthage, Ind.
Presbyterian Church, Point St. Charles. — Rev. Dr. E. K. Young, of New Britain, Conn.
Stanley Street Presbyterian. — Rev. Dr. Swain, of Westerville, Ohio.
Zion Congregational. — Rev. A. L. Reynolds, New Brighton, Pa.
First Baptist Church. — Rev. J. Q. A. Henry, D.D., of San Francisco.
Olivet Baptist Church. — Rev. Wayand Hoyt, D.D., Minneapolis.
St. James Methodist. — Rev. B. Fay Mills, of Pawtuxet, R. I.

Dominion Square Methodist. — Rev. Chas. P. Mills, of Newburyport.
Douglas Methodist. — Rev. Martyn Summerbell, D.D., of Lewiston, Me.
Dorchester Street (corner St. Urbain) Methodist. — Rev. Dr. Grubb, of Philadelphia.
Cote St. Antoine Methodist. — Rev. G. W. Furbeck, of Stuyvesant, N. Y.
Centenary Methodist. — Rev. U. F. Swengel, of York, Pa.
Montreal Junction, Methodist. — Rev. L. S. Keyser, of Springfield, Ohio.
West-End Methodist (Coursol street). — Rev. W. H. Geistweit, of Minneapolis.

SUNDAY AFTERNOON.

DRILL HALL.

An immense audience assembled at the Drill Hall in the afternoon, filling the huge auditorium. Bishop Fallows presided. After the opening praise service, Rev. W. B. Stevens, of Montreal, led in prayer. "Jesus, Lover of my Soul" was then sung heartily, after which came several announcements from Secretary Baer, among which was the following statement and explanation with reference to the evening service : —

MR. BAER: All are familiar with the trouble we have been having. I am very sure, from all that I have learned, that the citizens of Montreal irrespective of creed are sorry for the trouble which we have experienced. Now, then, having had personal witness of the demonstration last night from beginning to end, and wishing to know whether the police would be able to keep back the turbulent element, I called upon the chief of police this morning. Before telling you what he said, let me say this. Last night the chief of police himself, with plenty of assistance, handled that crowd as I never saw a crowd handled before. [*Applause.*] That the crowd were bent on making a disturbance is true. That they did not succeed very well is also true, on account of the fact that the chief himself led the assault upon them and dispersed them, taking their flags. They did, some time during the evening, cut some of the ropes of the tent; but on investigating the tent this morning I found the ropes replaced. On visiting the police headquarters I was shown the flags that were captured. The chief said to me, "Mr. Baer, your people need not have the least uneasiness. This crowd is a lot of hoodlums and roughs; they are cowardly and we can take care of them. That you have had the trouble is true, but you need have no further apprension. You are in no danger whatever; this police force stands back of you and the city is back of the police force." [*Loud applause.*] This is true, however, that ever since we have been here there has been more or less confusion in the streets. There may be tonight; and we have thought, inasmuch as we have reached the Sunday evening service, which is our consecration service, when the environment must be as favorable as possible, and inasmuch as the noise outside is more easily heard in the tent than here, that we had better abandon the tent meeting entirely tonight, doing away with all occasion of trouble, the delegates attending the meeting here and in the several churches which I shall now name. The tent meeting in all its completeness will take place in the St. James M. E. church, where Rev. B. Fay Mills will preach the sermon and lead the consecration service; in the Olivet Baptist church, where Rev. James L. Campbell and the pastor, Rev. W. B. Hinson, will be the speakers; in the First Baptist church, where Rev. Dr. Wayland Hoyt will preach; in the American Presbyterian church, where the speakers will be Rev. Dr. A. N. Carson, of

St. Paul, the pastor, Rev. M. McWilliams and William Shaw; at the Douglas Methodist church, where Rev. Dr. James L. Hill will preach; and at the Erskine Presbyterian church, where Rev. Dr. J. Z. Tyler will be the speaker. Consecration services will be held in connection with every one of these meetings; also the collection for the family of Mr. Rogers, the member of the Montreal reception committee who fell dead upon the street last Tuesday afternoon while conducting some of the delegates to their places of entertainment, will be taken at the same time.

I should have said last night that the banner, presented by the Montreal committee to that delegation which should cover the greatest mileage in coming to this convention, has been won by Pennsylvania. This being Sunday we will have no ceremony of presentation. I simply make the announcement and present the banner to your view. [*Holding up the banner.*] The Pennsylvania delegates travelled 393,000 miles; Massachusetts, 297,500; New York, 270,000; California, 267,500; and Illinois, 261,000. From a careful examination of the registers it is estimated that the total attendance at this convention cannot be less than 16,500. This is the largest attendance, save that in New York, in the history of the movement. When I was asked before coming here if I thought we would have an attendance of 20,000, I said that if we should have 15,000 I should feel that we had had a tremendous convention. We have had 16,500, I feel confident.

At this point in the program the Park Sisters rendered a cornet duet very beautifully.

BISHOP FALLOWS : Three or four weeks ago Mr. Herbert Gladstone was introduced by the chairman of a meeting in Birmingham, England, with this preface : "If it had not been for his father we should not have heard from the son." [*Laughter.*] You remember the younger Pitt, the son of that illustrious Earl of Chatham, both of whom rendered such glorious services to the American cause, and the honor of whose names is as precious among Americans as it is among Englishmen, — when the younger Pitt had made a magnificent address which brought the House of Commons to its feet, one of the leading English statesmen said to another, "Why, he is a chip off the old block." "No," was the response, "he is the old block itself." Now, very possibly the speaker of the afternoon who leads off in these exercises might not have been heard of if it had not been for his illustrious father, Francis E. Murphy, the great apostle of temperance and my beloved friend [*applause*]; but I want to say that Mr. Thomas E. Murphy is not simply "a chip of the old block." — he is "the old block itself." [*Applause.*] I take great pleasure in introducing him to you this afternoon. [*Loud applause and the Chautauqua salute.*]

Gospel Temperance.

Address of Mr. Thomas E. Murphy.

Mr. Chairman and Friends : — I esteem it a great honor to be presented to this magnificent congregation as the son of my father. [*Laughter.*] I believe him to be the best man in the world. [*Applause.*] Some of you may say that that assertion sounds somewhat egotistical. Perhaps it does; and if there be any odium in connection with it, I am willing to bear it, for I believe that a young man who has a good, kind father should think him just a little better than any other man in the world. [*Applause.*] I believe, further, that a young woman who has a good, kind mother should think her just a little better than any other woman in the world. [*Renewed applause.*] In other words, I believe in the divine command : "Honor thy father and thy mother, that thy days may be long in the land which the Lord thy God giveth thee ; " and as young people, as members of this great Christian Endeavor organization, if we desire to do this we will struggle to make the world better because we have lived in it.

I am reminded, however, that I am not to deliver an address on my father,—though with such a subject I certainly ought to be eloquent. There are those present who have heard him, and in addressing you this afternoon, if I should use any argument which you have already heard him advance, you will naturally know where he got it. [*Laughter.*]

I am announced to speak to you on gospel temperance, or gospel temperance reform, and for a few moments I will trace the history of some reforms and point out the analogy between them and the gospel temperance reform. There are two great principles in this world, formation and reformation. When God made this earth he formed something, and great and majestic was the formation. Since then man has fallen, and a work only a little less divine has been going on. Reforms are the life of the world. They have arisen in all ages of the world, and the reformers, though perhaps not recognized in their own day, have since been looked upon as those who have marked out the way humanity should go in its progressive course. I read that in the Grecian period Solon and Clisthenes were great reformers; and coming down to Switzerland, who was it that first laid down the principle that it was a right of the people to govern themselves, and fired the hearts of his countrymen until they arose and threw off the yoke of Austria? It was William Tell, whose name today is the synonym of patriotism. After that there came a time when the horizon of religious life waxed dim, and when the hope and light and love and joy of the Christian's heart had almost faded away; and as he looked out upon the sea of infidelity that greeted him upon either hand, he almost doubted the existtence of a divine creator. But, as Cowper has so beautifully said,

> " God works in a mysterious way
> His wonders to perform ;
> He plants his footsteps on the sea
> And rides upon the storm."

In his own good time, in the fulness of his plans, he raised up a man whom he anointed and sent forth as an apostle, and his preaching and his writings shook the German empire from centre to circumference. On the wings of influence his power was felt in the sunny fields of France, and then it crossed the English channel and made its advent into that grand old country, and the people there realized that the dawn of religious liberty was at hand. There was an epoch in the history of our own beloved land when God in his wisdom caused us to pass through severe and disastrous affliction such as but few nations have ever been called upon to endure ; for of all wars, a war of sections under the same government is the most disastrous and vindictive. But when reform is needed it must either come by peaceful measures or through a resort to more potent means. The curse of slavery rested upon us and for years had been the source of strife and contention, and it was apparent that our government could not much longer retain its stability unless the accursed stumblingblock that stood in the way was forever removed. You remember how peaceful measures and compromises were resorted to in vain. Finally fierce war, with all its sad effects, resulted in striking the shackles from the limbs of 4,000,000 of God's downtrodden children ; and tonight, like the Union Jack, wherever the Stars and Stripes wave they are acknowledged as the standard for physical freedom and religious liberty [*loud applause*], and we, as lovers of truth, as lovers of virtue, as lovers of justice, thank God for it.

Now, then, in pointing out the analogy between these reforms which I have briefly sketched and the gospel temperance reform, I would say, in the first place, that all these reforms were advocated for a long time by a minority of the people. This difficulty the gospel temperance reform has had to contend with ever since the day it was born into existence. Because of this fact a great many good and excellent people treat it with indifference. To be consistent, they should also treat Christianity with indifference, for I hold that the gospel temperance reform is an integral part of Christianity. But alas! Christianity has been and still is represented by a very few of the people who inhabit the nations of the earth. But will Christianity therefore be wrong? Will every precious promise in our old Bible be a delusion? Will every doctrine be a fable? Will every fruit of the Spirit be an apple of Sodom and Gomorrah? Will every act of benevolence be a cruel wrong? Will the sacrifice of Christ be a common fetich? Will the new Jerusalem be without foundations? Will its eternal mansions be without inhabitant? Will its rivers of pleasure become waters of Marah? Will its everlasting throne be without its king? Yea, will God himself be a liar, until we have at least one more in the ranks of virtue than is numbered in the present ranks of her foes? Nay, verily,—

> " Truth forever on the scaffold;
>   Wrong forever on the throne;
> Yet that scaffold sways the future
>   And behind the dim unknown
> Standeth God within the shadow,
>   Keeping watch above his own."

And in the end the right shall conquer everywhere. [*Loud applause*].

The inconsistency of the argument which asserts that because a movement is represented by a few, therefore it is wrong, is well illustrated by an incident concerning a man who was a victim of drink and was led to sign the pledge and give his heart to God. When he did that he was imbued with a desire to get others to do likewise. He had the missionary spirit, and I would that every member of this great organization might be energized by this holy desire. This man as he walked the streets carried pledge cards, and whenever he met a man who had not identified himself with the temperance reform, he asked him to sign the pledge. In doing this missionary work he came in contact with a prominent citizen to whom he said, " You have always been profuse in your expressions of sympathy for temperance reform. A great work is going on here. We would like to have the prestige of your influence and the force of your example. Won't you please sign this pledge?" "No, sir," the man replied. "Why not?" "You temperance people are in such a minority that I do not care to be associated with you." I am not a political temperance man in any sense of the word, but I wish to say this: when I see some man who desires to go to Congress and who has not the courage to give expression to his honest convictions regarding a principle that is so vital to the happiness of the homes of this nation and of every other nation, I say, elect him to stay at home by a large majority every time. [*Loud applause.*] This man said, " You are in the minority." " Well,"said the worker, " are minorities wrong?" " Certainly," was the reply; " this is a country of majorities, and the majority rules. The minority must necessarily be wrong." " Then," said the worker, " if that is the case, I would like to ask you how you would like to have been in the majority at the time of the Flood." [*Laughter and applause.*] If you remember the history of those few people in the olden time, they were right, and eventually they triumphed; and we, as gospel temperance advocates and workers, though we may be in the minority today, can derive consolation from the fact that the principle which we advocate is right, and right shall eventually triumph.

> " Truth, crushed to earth, shall rise again;
>   The eternal years of God are hers;
> But Error, wounded, writhes in pain,
>   And dies amid her worshippers."

Again, all these reforms were in the interest of physical, intellectual, and religious liberty. So is the gospel temperance reform. The man who is so unfortunate as to fall beneath the power of intoxicating liquor and becomes a drunkard, and goes reeling and staggering through the streets of the community in which he resides, has no control over himself while in that condition and he does not therefore enjoy physical liberty. And the man who is a drunkard has no intellectual freedom. Why? Because his mind has lost its vigor. As to religion, it would be needless to argue that a drunkard has not forfeited all religious liberty. Then, if we apply the force of reason to this analysis, we find that the gospel temperance reform, as it stands forth at the present day, is in the interest — directly so — of the fundamental principles that underlie the government under which we exist; for it is the glory of America, as well as of England, that she preserves physical, intellectual and religious liberty to the lowliest of her subjects. This being true, then we, the people, who compose the government, — because the government in these countries is of the people, for the people, and by the people, — those of us who elect the members of Commons and create the legislators and senators, have a duty to perform. What is it? That we shall exert our influence and put forth our energies to hasten on the dawning of that day when the sentiment which now sustains the drink traffic shall be replaced by a total abstinence sentiment. [*Applause.*]

How shall that be best brought about? is the question which naturally suggests itself. Now, I am not here to enter into any intricate analysis regarding the law, but simply to say that public sentiment is the basis of all law, and public sentiment in the aggregate is simply individual sentiment, and where an individual drinks intoxicating liquor, all the force of his example and all the power of his influence goes to perpetuate the drink traffic. Now, while there are many methods and many plans, I believe, by the grace of God, as surely as I stand on this platform this afternoon, that the remedy lies along the line of individual total abstinence. [*Applause.*] If all the people in Great Britain and in the United States who drink liquor even moderately will sign the pledge of total abstinence and keep it faithfully, within twenty-five years the race of drunkards will have died out and prohibition will be established. [*Loud applause.*]

The strength of the drink traffic is not in the legislature; it is not in the gilded saloon; it is not to be found in the distillery; but it is in the appetites and passions and customs of the people. A stream cannot rise higher than its source; and while this traffic is licensed, I want to say that I thank God with all my heart that no man has a license to make me drink. No man has a license to take the cunning out of my hand or the genius out of my brain. If these go, they go of my volition, and I stand on the platform of an individuality that has the right, by the grace of God, to establish and inaugurate prohibition that will close the saloon that is located between my chin and my nose [*laughter and great applause*], and if everybody else will do this we shall have prohibition.

What we need is agitation and education on this question. I am thankful that I have the privilege of addressing so many young people. I am a believer in young people all the way through. I come from the state of Connecticut, where I have been for nine months carrying on a gospel temperance campaign, and where 60,000 people have signed the pledge and put on the blue ribbon. [*Applause.*] I want to say to you that the success of that movement, humanly speaking, is largely due to the Christian Endeavor organization. [*Great applause.*] I see over yonder a member of the Christian Endeavor society of Dr. Munger's church in the city of New Haven. When I went to that city the dogs even would not bark at me in the street [*laughter*], — just as true as you live. People said, " He 's a crank, a fanatic." If I am a fanatic, I thank God for a fanaticism that never broke up a home [*applause*], that never populated a jail, that never dimmed eyes with weeping. If this be fanaticism, in God's name let us focus as much of it into human experience as we possibly can. [*Applause.*] Dr. Munger, through one of his members, sent word to me that it was a good work, and he invited me to come down and address the Christian Endeavor society. I went down there and we had a great meeting and about sixty members of that society put on the blue ribbon. Now that is a tony society [*laughter*]; the members belong to the aristocracy; and when it was noised abroad that Dr. Munger and his Christian Endeavor society had become interested in this work, that became a precedent, and the city followed until 12,000 people in that classic precinct put on the ribbon and identified themselves with the reform. [*Applause.*]

So it is the prerogative of the Christian Endeavor organization to agitate, to instruct, to lay down the principle that Christ, by his Holy Spirit, regenerates and disenthralls. I am a believer in the young people. Some folks say that boys are not like what they used to be. Some old gentleman says [*mimicking*],

"Boys aint what they were when I was a boy." Thank God, they are not. [*Laughter and applause.*] Some people do not understand young people. I once heard of a man who had two lovely boys, and there came a small-pox epidemic into the community. Wishing the boys to be out of danger he sent them to a friend in the country who had a stock farm and told them to remain until the epidemic passed away. The boys were boys,—exuberant, filled with surplus energy,—and they made it lively around the farm. At the expiration of a week the farmer called the boys to him and said, "I want you to go home, and when you get home, hand this letter to your father." They went home and gave the letter to their father. He opened it and it read like this: "Dear Sir: I return you your boys. Please send me the small-pox." [*Great laughter and applause.*] Now that man did not appreciate the primary processes that make humanity great. And so I want to say to this young organization that it is our privilege not only to practise the principle of total abstinence, but by a gracious and winning spirit try to impress others. There are some here who teach school, there are others who teach Sunday-school classes. I wish to say that the rising generation need very much to be instructed in regard to the deleterious effects of alcohol on the system. If we can show how it vitiates the mind, how it shatters the nerve centres and eats out the lining of the stomach, an impression will be made which will work for righteousness.

The young women of this organization can use their influence on the young men. I tell you, it is a marvelous thing—the influence that a young woman has over young men. I speak from experience. My wife sits on this platform—the very best woman in this world,—yes, sir, the very best. [*Loud applause.*] I don't take much stock in a man who does n't think that his wife is a little better than any other woman [*applause*], and he ought to be as chivalric and as courteous and as gentle in her presence, after he has been married for years, as he was when he used to come down to her house with a little rosebud and say, "I have brought you this, dear." [*Laughter and applause.*] What an influence young ladies possess. Why is it that so many young men find it convenient to drop along at the door of the church about the time that the benediction is pronounced? Is it because they want to shake hands with the pastor? I wish it were so. The young ladies attend the evening service and the young men come along about the time the benediction is pronounced, and as the young ladies come out they tip their hats and say [*mimicking*], "How do you do? Delighted to see you. May I have the pleasure of walking home with you?" "I should be delighted to have you." Now I want to say to the young ladies in this great audience that if I were a young lady and a young man did n't have interest enough in my company to go with me and attend church Sabbath evening and listen to the preaching of God's Word, I would have such a sacred regard for my Christianity that he could not meet me at the church door and walk home with me. [*Prolonged applause.*]

So I say, let us work along the lines of truth. Let us try and practise the principles of righteousness in our lives. If I could tell the young people of today of a mother's love, how she sacrifices and how anxious she is for her children to grow up to be useful, I could cure the young men of going to the saloon. I remember my mother; she was called home to heaven when I was a little fellow, but I remember her upon one occasion in my childhood, when a circus came to town and I wanted to go. I asked my father if I could not go, and he said, "You go to school." I started for the North Grammar school, but when I got my hand on the gate I heard the music of the band. That is a very trying position for a boy to be in. I listened and said to myself, "I would like to see the elephant." I left the schoolhouse and followed that circus procession, and I forgot all about school the rest of the day. When I started home that evening I felt just like everybody feels when he has done wrong. Wordsworth says:—

> "The child is father of the man;
> And I could wish my days to be
> Bound each to each by natural piety."

As I walked into the house I met my father. He said, "How did you get along at school today?" I replied, "Pretty well." He said, "You are wanted in the parlor." I went into the parlor and there sat my mother talking with my school-teacher. She had to pass our house in going home and she thought she would drop in and see why Edward was n't at school. That did not increase my happiness any. Presently mother looked at me and said, "Edward, you have n't been a very good boy to-day." I said, "I know that." Just then father walked in and looked at me and said, "You got along pretty well at school today, did you? I will teach you,"—and when he said that I knew I should see the elephant. He started toward me, and I ran over to mother. She put her loving arms about me and said, "Father, don't whip him this time; he will never do it again." Twenty-five years have passed away since that incident occurred, but I remember it this afternoon just as plainly as though it had happened this morning. Oh, this mother love! it is akin to God's love; it is the embodiment of self-abnegation. And it is the prerogative of this great organization to teach every young man to abstain from that which destroys the happiness of his mother. As young people, if we desire to succeed, if we hope to write our names high up on the roll of honor, if we are anxious to make the crooked places straight and to cause the wilderness to blossom as the rose, let us today consecrate and re-consecrate ourselves to the truth and let us become workers for the principle of gospel temperance reform.

The saving power is the Gospel of the Lord Jesus Christ. I know whereof I speak. My father is known to many of you; the distinguished gentleman who presides here today is his personal friend. He was a victim of this drink habit. They said he could not be saved. But a Christian man told him of the Gospel and of Christ's sympathy and love,—and I can remember how he knelt and prayed, and I want to tell you that that prayer was answered,—and my father was redeemed, and for twenty-five years he has proved to the world that the grace of God is stronger than the whole drink traffic. [*Loud applause.*] And so, my friends, I come here, not to sound any discordant note, but to say that the assertion that the church is responsible for the drink traffic is a libel. The church is a unit against this evil and we are to stand together and go forward courageously until the last saloon shall have been closed, until the last fire in the last distillery shall have been put out, never to be lit again. God hasten the day! [*Applause.*]

I am grateful to Mr. Baer for a place on this program. I thank the friends who have been so kind and considerate toward me in my work. I believe I am a servant of God, and I will tell you that it is my impression that what the masses wait for today is the Gospel. Every man would like to be a Christian. The proper definition of Christian is Christlike. Read the story of the Master. Follow him as he went about doing good. Follow him in that experience when he was summoned before the supreme council and sent over to Pontius Pilate, who listened to him and then sent him back again to Herod, and Herod listened to him and sent him back again to Pontius Pilate, and the crowd shouted, "Crucify him, crucify him." Pontius Pilate was a politician; he represented Cæsar; he had to do Cæsar's will and he was afraid to offend the Jews; and when finally he said, "Which shall I release, Barabbas or Christ?" the crowd shouted, "Barabbas!" You remember that according to the Roman custom his back was bared and a whip of thorns was brought down upon him. Then he was told to take up his cross and carry it up yonder to Golgotha. Weak and weary and worn he proceeded on his way, but the burden was too heavy for him and finally he fell by the wayside, and Simon came along and took up the cross and carried it up to Golgotha. There he was crucified, nailed to the cross, and in his great agony he cried, "Father, forgive them; they know not what they do." Finally, when the sun was eclipsed and all was dark, out of his great agony he shouted, "Why, O why, hast thou forsaken me?" Then the angel came and release was given to his spirit. His last declaration was, "It is finished." The platform had been laid for a holy manhood. Redemption had become a fact. I hold up the world's Redeemer as the great liberator and the hope of every man who is cursed by the slavery of drunkenness. [*Prolonged applause.*]

After singing "At the Cross," the next speaker was introduced as follows : —

BISHOP FALLOWS: As many of you know, sixteen or seventeen years ago we of the United States were wrestling with a very great problem — how to resume specie payment. The answer came from the wisest of our legislators, "Resume, resume;" and when that was done every dollar pledged by the United States government was immediately redeemable in 100 cents of ringing gold. How shall we reach the masses? Reach them! We are to be told how the masses have been reached by one whom God has gloriously blessed in this work of reaching and rescuing the people. I have great pleasure in introducing Mr. A. W. Millbury of New York City. [*Applause.*]

How to Reach the Masses.

Address of Mr. A. W. Millbury.

Mr. Chairman, Fellow Endeavorers : — I am very happy today to make my first public address in my native land. It happens that I am a Canadian, born 'way down east, — where they pry up the sun with a crowbar, — down in New Brunswick. But I may well claim to belong to both the United States and to Canada. My ancestry was strictly Puritan from New England, and I am proud to belong to both countries and to both flags; and to both countries and to both flags I believe I am truly loyal. But the banner that I wish to be loyal to here this day is the banner of Him who rescued me, our common Lord and Saviour, Jesus Christ. I have never stood before so inspiring an audience as a Christian Endeavor audience. It has been my good fortune a number of times in the last two years to speak to Christian Endeavorers, and as I look into the faces of these young men and young women I see before me the vision of a new crusade, a modern crusade, not to secure possession of the empty tomb of a risen Lord, but a crusade to secure possession of the earth for his kingdom. Hear me, young warriors of Christ, the future belongs to you The gospel of the future is yours; it is yours to carry the Gospel to the uttermost ends of the earth. It is yours to bring new methods to bear upon the eternal principles of our religion.

Tons of paper and tons of ink have been wasted in the discussion of how to reach the masses, and our chairman this afternoon has used some of the very words that I intended to quote — those words of John Sherman, "The way to resume is to resume;" and the way to reach the masses is to go to the masses with the love with which Jesus Christ came to them. Ah, we do not read about a long discussion in heaven about how to reach the masses: but in the fulness of time the Prince of Glory made himself of no reputation and came to earth to live among the masses, to preach the Gospel of good tidings. We read that the common people heard him gladly, and why should they not? He came to preach the Gospel to the poor; why should they not have heard him gladly? He touched their lives at many points; he healed their sick; he raised their dead children; he opened eyes long shut to the glories of heaven; he opened ears long closed to the merry prattle of children and the fond words of wife; he opened ears to the blessed message of the Gospel of Jesus Christ. He comforted the sorrowing; he feed the hungry; he touched the lives of the poor. He touched the lives of the people at many points. Why should they not have heard him gladly? And think you that human nature has changed? Think you that people are different from what they were in his time? Think you, if the church goes to the people, as Jesus went, touching their lives at all points, making their lives in all things happier and better, that they will not hear the Gospel gladly? I read of Paul, that wonderful scholar, that young man of most brilliant promise, from whom his friends expected such a wonderful career, being converted; and his first question is, "What wilt thou have me to do?" And when he is told, he abandons the brilliant future, humanly speaking, and he goes out to hunger, contumely, shipwrecks, danger, death — and victory!

The Christian religion appeals to the heroic in human nature as nothing has ever appealed before. It calls upon men and women to give their flesh and blood, to give their brains, to give their spirit, and it promises,— what?. Not preferment on earth, but a crown of glory hereafter.

We may discuss the methods of reaching the masses till the sun shall shine no more, and unless we are willing to do as Jesus did, as Paul did, as multitudes are doing today who go forth to bear the Gospel to foreign lands — and to dark places in our own land — unless we are willing to forget self, to lay down all hope of preferment and ease and earthly reward, we will never reach the masses. It is easy to stand in a splendid church, as I have sometimes seen men stand, and deliver beautiful essays upon how to reach the masses. That is easy; but ah, it is a different thing to go as Joseph Avery did a few years ago in New York. He came from England and went down on Oliver Street, right down in the very slums of our great city and took a church there that was almost dead. Men said to him, "You can't do anything down among those people, those Italians and sailors, those poorest of the poor colored people." But he went down there alone, without money and without helpers. No, he was not alone, for One walked with him who once walked in a fiery furnace. He labored there among those people, and a little less than a year ago he laid down his life. Just as truly as Jesus gave his life upon the cross, Joseph Avery gave his life, worn out in the Master's service. And when he was gone people remembered what he was and realized that an angel had gone from among them; and in honor to his memory there has been established there one of the grandest missions in New York City. All honored his life and God honors him still now that he is no longer with us.

The fires of our religion are not kept burning by great convocations like this or by an occasional giant church preached to by a giant preacher; but they are kept burning, thank God, in millions of Christian households, in multitudes of humble churches the world over. God keeps many of his choicest jewels hidden away in remote corners of his vineyard where men may not see their beauty, where he alone shall see the devotion of their lives and he alone shall have the joy of crowning them. Often are they comforted by the words of the Master, "Thy Father which seeth in secret shall reward thee openly."

The masses,—what are they? Do they exist in the little hamlets you come from? Are they to be found in your remote village? When I was a small boy, away down on the St. John River, in a little village of not more than 150 people we had the unreached masses. There were not many of them,—only three or four families that did not go to church. But ah, my little heart used to ache as I dimly recognized the fact that the good people thought they were hardly fit to be asked into church, and I doubt very much if some of those families were ever asked within the walls of the house of God. I doubt very much if any good Christian man or woman ever went to them with words of hope. I remember a man who kept a saloon there and who lived an awfully hard life. There were very few drinking men there, and he and his wife and half a dozen children barely existed. I remember one Christmas eve that I rode by their house with my dear mother, and we could see those little children, literally half naked on that awfully cold night, huddled around a scanty fire. The next morning my mother filled a basket with good things and told me, a little fellow of six or seven, to take it down there. I went into this poor apology for a home and told the woman that my mother had sent me down there with that basket. "Oh," she said, "you don't mean me." "Yes," said I, "she told me to come here with it." "But there must be some mistake," she said, "no one would do that for me," and the poor woman burst into tears and I cried with her. I have often thought, since I became a Christian, that that was "reaching the masses."

I have often thought since that if that little act could have been followed up, that woman and those little children might have been won for Christ.

I knew a young man once who had a Christian father and mother, who had the advantages of Sunday school and church, yet who deliberately wrecked his life through sin. I knew how he walked through the streets of a great city, with his wrecked life and breaking heart, and how often he wished that some one would come to him and help him to the better way. He had many friends, many Christian friends, yet no one ever spoke a word of hope to him. I often thought of it, and then I resolved that I would never allow any man whom I knew or thought was going to the bad, without going to him and telling him of a better way. That is one way of "reaching the masses."

The religion of Christ was designed to fit the lives of men. It was not designed to fit men to die merely, but to live. And so if the church is going to reach the masses it must reach the great problems of life. There must be not less preaching but more practising. Social conditions change and church methods must change. I was very much struck yesterday afternoon, in the Presbyterian denominational rally, with the remark of Miss Wishard, who said that some of the elders of the Presbyterian church proposed to introduce kindergartens into their church work; when one old brother said, " Has the Presbyterian church come at last to be a schoolmaster?" "Worse than that," said Miss Wishard. "It has come to be a schoolmarm." [*Laughter.*] I thank God for it. [*Applause.*]

How shall we reach the masses? A little while ago, in connection with this work in New York of which I have the honor to be secretary, we took a building in which were 60 or 70 Italian families, huddled together in that great building, with no water above the first floor and no conveniences of any kind. Poor, helpless foreigners they were, not speaking the English tongue, the prey of rapacious landlords; yet their children were as beautiful as any I have ever seen, fit to be the models for cherubs. I thought as I saw the condition in which Christian landlords made them live, " I wonder that they are so good, not that they are so bad." No one had taken the church to them. The modern methods of church work must reach the mass of the people in the day nursery, in the kindergarten, in the gymnasium, in the free reading-room, in the free library, in house to house visitation, setting up small stations in the centre of the enemy's domain. In the city of New York last year the Children's Aid Society spent $368,000 reaching the children of the poor. I believe they did more to reach the masses than all the churches down town,—and the sad fact is that it was all church money, the teachers were all Christian men and women, and the church gets no credit for it. I believe that work should be done by the churches and not by outside organizations, and I should be very happy if this great Christian Endeavor organization, which holds the future in its grasp, should take up this idea and prosecute it in our great cities. [*Applause.*]

As an appropriate hymn at this point, " Rescue the Perishing " was sung.

BISHOP FALLOWS : The next topic is a very important one, as every Christian Endeavorer knows,— the Religious Press. I would like to know what Christian Endeavorers would do without the Golden Rule in their hearts and *The Golden Rule* in their hands. Now we are to have an address by one who is himself an expert in this matter of the religious press, who is, I was going to say, the Nestor of any of us in the work of the religious press. — Rev. Dr. A. E. Dunning of Boston, editor of *The Congregationalist.* [*Applause.*]

The Religious Press: Its Part in our Work.

Address of Rev. A. E. Dunning, D.D.

I will take up the subject where the preceding speaker left it. I am glad to be called the Nestor of the religious press. I have been in that work almost four years, but I came from Boston and I suppose that is the reason why he called me the Nestor.

The three great apostles of reform today are the press, the pulpit, and the platform. The press has the most multitudinous voice and reaches the most ears — perhaps I should say eyes, but it gets there just the same. This is a great audience, but the editor of your religious paper addresses an audience ten times as large as this every week — perhaps twenty times as large. And the tonic of reform is in the religious press.

The newspaper mirrors the world's life from day to day. The secular press did not create the Christian Endeavor; did not notice it till it began to be conspicuous as a part of the world's life. Then the newspaper began to reflect it. The religious press mirrors the world's life in perspective from week to week. It told the Christian world what Christian Endeavor might be while, as yet, it existed actually as an experiment only, and existed potentially only in the minds of its founder and the few whom he associated with him. The religious press joined with them in introducing, developing, and guiding this great movement till, in a dozen years, local societies have joined in unions, and unions have enlarged into state bodies, and state bodies have grown into great national organizations; and now, twelve years after the first society was started in Williston church, in Portland, in another country its representatives gather to the number of many thousands to greet its founder on his return from a journey round the globe, planting Christian Endeavor societies in Australia, China, Japan, India, and along the very highways where the great Apostle Paul planted the first Christian churches in Asia and Europe. But a dozen years after the ascension of Christ no accredited messenger of the Gospel had set foot in Europe. No Christian church had yet been formed outside of Palestine.

No wiser or more zealous laborers for Christ have ever lived than those apostles and disciples on whom the Holy Spirit first rested. Could the modern apostles have so outrun them as to girdle the globe with Christian Endeavor societies while their great prototypes had not passed beyond a region of the size of Massachusetts, if the religious press had not multiplied their message a million-fold and itself been an apostle of the new life for young people of every nation and clime? Eighteen years after the first Christian church was planted in Jerusalem, Phebe carried Paul's first editorial to the Christians already to be found in Rome, and three years later he followed it in person. Eleven years after the founding of the first Christian Endeavor society in Portland, this modern Phebe, the religious press, bore the greetings of the founder of that first society to Sydney, Melbourne, Hong Kong, Yokohama, Calcutta, Jerusalem, Constantinople, London, and scores of other cities, and the same year he appeared among the brethren, and the same year he finished his journey. Could that vast work have been accomplished without the religious press, his letter of greeting, of introduction, of instruction, before him, with him, following him in every place, fifty-two times in the year?

You will see that I have given you but a single illustration of the work of the religious press as related to Christian Endeavor work. It is a mirror of the world's life as seen from the Christian point of view. The secular press reflects all things, and the most of you look into that mirror day by day. The religious press is eclectic. It reflects what the Christian needs to see of the world's life in order to know God, and to know his fellow-men, and to know how they are working under his guidance, and to strengthen faith in their possibilities of likeness to God. It studies and interprets the world's life that it may transform it into the kingdom of God. [*Applause.*]

What has the religious press done for the Christian Endeavor movement? It has introduced it to the church. It has been the letter of commendation going before the messengers of that movement, presenting them to associations, conferences, assemblies, and conventions. It has presented the news of the movement, spreading from church to church, from one locality to another, taking on new forms as it came in contact with different sorts of people, correcting its mistakes by experience and learning from reported experiences of others. The press has helped this movement to adapt itself to the city church and the scattered settlement, to old organizations with historic traditions, and to new communities with social customs hardly begun; to soldiers and sailors and students and prisoners. The religious press has corrected misrepresentations about the Society, has explained its character and defended its motives where its own representatives could not get a hearing, has made it, not denominational, but national and cosmopolitan, and it has yet an increasing work to do in this direction.

What can the Christian Endeavor do through the religious press? It can make constant use of the press for the growth of its own members. Christian Endeavor is not philosophical, but practical. It is not speculation, but life. Its members are the young men and women of the churches, whose intensest interest is in the present, who want to use the present to improve the future, and who have the future largely in their power. They want to know, not only about their society, but about the whole life of today; as related to Christian life and Christ's kingdom, and this is what the religious press comes to tell them.

It was born out of a hunger to know these things. The Christian church has a history of almost nineteen centuries, and the religious newspaper is the product of this nineteenth century, and mostly of this last half of it. It is the offspring of the first great aggressive Christian movement of modern times. In the second decade of this century the Protestant church in America began to knock at the doors of distant nations with the message of the Gospel. Those who sent the messengers wanted to know how they fared and what success they were having. News of these missionaries was in demand. New organizations were needed to direct their work and to raise funds for its support. To meet this demand the first religious newspaper, which still lives and flourishes,— the *Boston Recorder*, — was born seventy-eight years ago. It is now the *Congregationalist and Boston Recorder*. In the last century there was little news of the churches to tell, and that little was mainly of local interest. The people depended on their ministers to tell it.

But the new purpose expressed in the motto, " Christ for the world, and the world for Christ," began to create an interest throughout the world which demanded the religious paper, and which would have died without it. The development of modern missions at home and abroad originated it and made it a prominent factor in carrying them on. First of all its purpose is to furnish news to Christian households of the condition and progress of the kingdom of God throughout the world.

The religious papers in which Christian Endeavor can do most for itself and the world are denominational. There are able and powerful papers which find a constituency among all denominations and are of great service. But I place the denominational paper first for opportunity and usefulness, and for reasons easily stated. Its survey of the progress of the kingdom must be as broad as the world, but its audience and its space are limited. It must, therefore, select its field and its constituency — what news it will bring and to what households. The natural limitations of a religious constituency are denominational. Up to this time, at least, the kingdom of God had depended mainly for its avancement on denominational organizations. They have their disadvantages which we are constantly trying to remove. From time to time some leader has arisen to form a new denomination to remove all these disadvantages by absorbing all other bodies; and if the new body is particularly aggressive and antagonistic, it calls itself by some comprehensive name which implies that it claims the whole field, such as American, Christian, Brethren, or Union. But so far the evils of denominationalism have not been overcome by increasing the number of denominations to promote union.

Co-operation among denominations was never so practical and genuine as now. Could we have a more inspiring testimony to the fact than this great assemblage of youth, none of them ashamed of bearing the names of the bodies to which they belong, yet all uniting in a common love and loyalty to Christ, binding them in a brotherhood as close as any denomination has ever created? [*Applause.*] Yet, as I see it, organic church union which will destroy denominations was never farther from being realized than it is today. Denominations are as essential to the kingdom of God as commonwealths to republics, as nations and races to mankind. [*Applause.*] But as the more thoroughly men come to know and honor mankind, nations less and less contend with each other and more and more develop their own life with the aim to exalt humanity, so denominations find new and nobler life as the church broadens to the conquest of the world and becomes comprehensive to touch all social and political movements with Divine life; and as each denomination becomes more thoroughly organized for its own work it becomes more appreciative of that of every other and more closely united with all as they discover how better to minister to the whole kingdom of God, of which they recognize each other as parts. [*Applause.*]

The religious newspaper then fosters in wise ways the denominational spirit, which you want to have strengthened and directed to the best ends. It furnishes to the churches the news in which they are most interested, the inspiration they most need, and aims at the leadership which will insure their broadest sympathies and their highest success. It must have many correspondents, and these cannot be found and instructed without much labor and time. A religious paper, like a college, is a growth, and its value depends much on the extent and variety of the sources from which it draws.

Perhaps I have dwelt too long on this point, for if the paper is only denominational it can never be a safe guide. Is must never forget that its denomination is only one corps among the Lord's hosts, and that it must be kept in touch with the whole army. The things which are of chief importance in all the churches, their meaning and bearing on the movement of the whole kingdom of God — these must be rightly approved and presented by the editors of your religious paper. The religious newspaper must be both Catholic and Christian — like the Mayor of Montreal. [*Loud applause.*]

But you require of it more than this. Your religious paper must also interpret the meaning of current secular events as they are related to the religious world.

The idea of the Christian life has greatly changed in our time. Half a century ago it was regarded as largely apart from secular life. Salvation was believed to be a title to enter a kingdom of God as a future and distant realm; and the Gospel was regarded rather as an aid to fortify men to endure the ills of this present life than as a power to remove them. But today men are coming to be possessed with the conviction that the evils of this life are surmountable, and believers in Christianity are proclaiming that it is able to make sovereigns of the common people and to give them deliverance from oppression, to remove blindness from their eyes, and heal their wounds here and now. This great social evolution has brought the religious newspaper into a new field and given it a new opportunity. It has made present events a means of revealing the Divine will, and given to present life in the whole world a voice calling each Christian to present duty. It puts the religious newspaper next to the Bible as interpreting and applying its eternal principles to world movements and showing how God through these movements is revealing himself. In these days the Christian life is recognized as touching every department of human service and duty. The Christian is a citizen, and cannot serve Christ unless he gives himself to maintain Christian principles in government, local and general. He is also a member of society, which, beginning with the one who lives nearest him, overpasses the bounds of church and neighborhood and nation and race, and makes the world, which is the subject of redemption, a unit, the movements and influences in which act and re-act on each other to hinder or advance the kingdom of God. The great questions which society is striving to answer are moral problems, and in their last analyses are questions of personal duty depending on Divine sanction. The integrity of the family, the relations between employers and employed, the education of the people by schools, platforms, and pulpits, and by literature, their social habits in eating and drinking and amusements, the discoveries, inventions, and methods which affect social and business life in their moral relations, the making of nations by law and policy, and the dealings of nations with each other — all these pass under review in the religious newspaper, and its success depends largely on the editorial instinct which can select from this varied and vast field what things the ordinary reader most craves to know, and which can interpret the meaning of events most truly and simply on a plane which the educated Christian conscience approves.

This, then, as I conceive it, is what the religious newspapers should aim to accomplish in the Christian civilization of today. It stands for a definite constituency, chiefly in its own denomination. It furnishes news of the progress of the kingdom of God — first, of the part which that denomination is taking in it; then in the broad outline what others are doing, the great movements of the church and the directions they are taking. It aims to interpret the religious significance of what is taking place in society and in government, and in the relations of nations with each other. It seems to quicken the individual conscience, to encourage its righteous endeavor, to enlighten and guide it by applying the Word of God to personal and social and political life, as an element in the family, an ally of the church, a friend to good government, a prophet of the Lord. To this end it gathers news, gives the outlines and character of the books of the time, defends the faith once delivered to the saints, and addresses in its various departments, all ages and classes of its constituents.

No paper which represents mainly local interests, no paper whose purpose is to stand for a religious society or single organization, can do this broad service, however admirably conducted in its own sphere. Those who thus confine their religious reading of current life can hardly help being narrow, prejudiced, and of very little influence. All Christian Endeavorers need this broader education, this intelligent sympathy with present life, as the religious press interprets it. They need to hear the Christian voices of the larger society which they are entering, and to recognize the call of the church at large for their services. To use the paper which answers to this description, to help it to be all it should be, and to fill to the full its opportunity — you have no more important work than this, no better instrument with which to build up the kingdom of Christ. Without it how would your protests against the forces which threaten that kingdom be heard? How could you have made clear and effective your denunciation of the adroit dishonesty and deliberate dishonor to this Christian nation of the Sunday opening of the Fair? Did the secular press echo the clear voice of the Christian youth of this land bravely rebuking a great national wrong to manhood? In part it did, but it was the minor part. Did the secular press lead your attack on the infamous Louisiana lottery? Yes, it did, when the pressure grew too strong to resist. But many journals denounced that lottery on their editorial pages while they carried a standing advertisment of the lottery till they were forced by law to take it out. Does the secular press teach the people the evils of gambling in its many and insidious forms? How many secular papers in New York stand firmly against the race track gambling which is ruining armies of young men and carrying its blight into so many homes and business houses? Just one. How long would the secular press speak out at all against all these evils which you have made it your business in Christ's name to overcome, if the religious press were silenced?

Then what voice pleads like that of the religious press for temperance, for social purity, for love, for the virtues which are lifting the ideals of manhood and womanhood, till a great army of youth are growing into the likeness of Christ and becoming inspired in his strength to conquer the world with love? The religious press is your great ally. No other printed page appeals so effectively to the family life, which is the heart of the nation. No other human voice penetrates so often and so far into the closet where man talks with God. No other voice is so patiently and respectfully heard interpreting the principles of the kingdom of God as applied to the social, business, political and religious life of individuals and households. The family that lives without it shuts itself from the most potent silent influence leading all its members through avenues of truth and courtesy and love into the perfect divine society. The pastor who introduces it into the homes of his people finds his own voice multiplied, and most important information, counsel, and inspiration given, which he has neither time nor opportunity to utter.

Choose the best religious newspaper. Take it. Pray for it. Counsel it. Have patience with it and faith in it. Circulate it. Work with it for the perfect day of light and truth. [*Prolonged applause.*]

At the close of Dr. Dunning's address a telegram was read by Mr. C. B. Holdrege, of Illinois, from Commissioner Tousley of the World's Fair, in answer to a request that he should give the convention some assurance in regard to the closing of the Fair on Sunday. The telegram was as follows : —

" Matter to be settled Tuesday, July 11. If commissioners are well represented. the rule for Sunday closing will carry."

The convention received this telegram with great enthusiasm and cheers. Mr. Holdrege requested the prayers of the delegates in behalf of the approaching meeting of the commissioners, and at his suggestion Bishop Fallows led in fervent prayer. "I Love to Tell the Story" was then sung.

BISHOP FALLOWS : Let me say, to the credit of the secular press of Chicago, that when we were fighting the battle for the closing of the race course on the west side of the city—we are now fighting for the closing of the race course on the south side—nearly every secular paper joined heartily in the movement. [*Applause.*] Let me also say, in introducing the eloquent speaker who is to make the last address this afternoon,—a man who is known on both sides of that "imaginary line," whose grand words years ago in an address before the Bible Society upon the claims of this Book of books upon the human heart I feel to this very hour,—that sometime ago, when we were in the thick of that fight in the city of Chicago, Dr. Douglas uttered some ringing words in this city regarding the wickedness which was prevailing in certain quarters ; and this same secular press of Chicago outvied the religious press in publishing *verbatim et literatim et punctuatim* those words of Dr. Douglas, and we felt their influence in that great storm centre in helping us win the fight. [*Applause.*] I now take the greatest pleasure in introducing my honored friend and beloved brother, Dr. G. Douglas, of Montreal, to this audience.

It was an impressive sight as Dr. Douglas, gray-haired, blind, and partially paralytic, came forward to the speaker's stand with the assistance of a friend. He was greeted with prolonged applause by the audience. He stood erect and spoke clearly and eloquently, though with much moderation. The time would permit of his delivering only a portion of his address as it had been prepared, but his words made a deep impression. The address complete was as follows : —

Social Purity.

Address of Rev. G. Douglas, D.D.

In venturing to offer a few observations on the subject of social purity, I frankly admit that it is one from which I shrink, and toward the discussion of which I come with a reluctance unutterable. Most gladly would I relegate it to the realms of shade and silence, but the controlling powers of this great convention have selected the theme, and I bow with loyalty to their dictum, and accept the responsibility in dependence on the Master, whose I am and whom I serve. Whoever enters the ranks and consecrates his endeavor to the work of the White Cross Reform, and I trust thousands among you will so do; whoever enters the ranks of this reform must in lower sense and at an infinite distance walk the via dolorosa of the Man of Calvary. Like him he will meet the buffetings of an insolent populace and know the secret of a lone Gethsemane; like him, he will ascend the altar of sacrifice, and be ready in times of depression to exclaim, "Reproach hath broken my heart;" and like him whose apotheosis of love and self-sacrifice blossomed into the joy and triumph of moral victory — like him, he too shall know the gladness of planting some flowers of home amid the aridities of desolated hearts.

In the accomplishment of this work, you will be antagonized by forces within the church. I have known men who have reviled the pulpit for its fidelity when their own sons were authenticated as the patrons of vice, and the habitués of shades infernal. You will be antagonized by the *laissez-faire* men of club life, of lax morals and indifference to the sanctions of virtue. You will be antagonized by the tainted and the damaged, whose sinister interests are imperilled; they will let slip the dogs of invective, and howl when they are hit.

But on the other hand, I have stood in astonishment at the plentitude of voices that will ring out in your defence. Some years ago we were induced to speak a few words on this theme, and from the banks of the Irrawady in further India; and from the mountains of Switzerland; the sunny vales of France, and the Motherland, and from every province of this Dominion; from every Northern state, with some of the Southern states; from infidels; from men of the world; from the ruined; from the poor actress of Ohio, up to the crowned leaders in Christian Endeavor, words of inspiration came to bear witness against the malign forces that like the foul cancer are devouring the virtue and confidence of existing society. Approval of God, ye young Christian workers, will find approbation coming from sources of which you little dreamed affluent with encouragement.

This audience has listened to the trenchant and thrilling sentiments of our friend, Mr. Murphy, relative to intemperance; that is the crime of a class. On yonder parade, Mr. Anthony Comstock, in the maturity of his knowledge, is uncovering the villanies of gambling; that is the crime of a class. The defiance which is flung in the face of the Divine command, ordaining Sabbatic observance, that is the crime of a class. And right here let me say that the Christianity of this continent will quarantine the Chicago exhibition, or in modern parlance, boycott it, as the Christian answer to the Heaven-daring insolence which would trample the American Sabbath in the dust by the feet of the unprincipled Chicago directorate. But the crime of social vice is all invading. It looks every man, every woman, in the face, and says "Beware!" It touches the palaces of royalty in Europe, and the dwellings of elegance and wealth in America, down to the rusticities of agrarian conditions. It touches the ducal splendors of a Marlborough down to the swags and tramps,— pariahs of society. It touches the great and dishonored statesman, Dilke, whose election has made the Forest of Dean infamous forever, down to the obscurities of student and school-boy perversity. It touches the ultimate of Parisian refinement, down to barbarities aboriginal. The White Cross Mission is a mission for the race. If the Bishop of Peterborough affirms that the sin of England is not intemperance, but impurity, equally does this apply to the conditions of American society; if the Government and Council of Hong Kong have been made infamous before the world by their official recognition of the outcast in that colony; if from Rangoon there comes the sad intelligence that men representing Christian civilization sustain a conventual institution to receive the contraband of their illicit depravity; if in every military cantonment of Continental India, in defiance of the abolition of the discredited Contagious Diseases Act, there is state-protected vice, making Lucknow, aromatic with memories of Havelock and victory, a hissing and a reproach; if from the Barbadoes we learn that corrupt men are laboring to legalize vice, which is the blast and mildew of West India society, and, indeed, of the entire Spanish Main; if, on this continent, the reckless relaxation of civil law and social usage are shaking loose the very foundation of the family institution, striking down from five to ten percent of the family life of 70,000,000 people; if a tide of growing laxity is abroad, shall not the dwellers in the valley of years cry aloud to them upon the mountains to hide them in the sanctities and securities of religion until this cyclone of ruin be o'erpast.

It is forever true that as sure as God planted an angel with flaming sword to guard the gateways to the tree of life, so sure is it that an angel with sword more avenging guards the gateways to life physical, intellectual, and immortal. I say a sword more avenging. Nemesis! goddess of vengeance, lame but colossal of stature; with huge left arm she grasps her victim, while with the other she holds aloft the unsheathed sword to destroy. Nemesis! more terrible than the fabled goddess is the power of social sin to destroy, root and branch, the entirety of our manhood's being. Nemesis, the goddess of vengeance! What is the most regnant attribute of our mental being? I answer, the creative and winged power of imagination. Its ideals always surpass the possible in human achievement. There is never a statue of beauty, never a monument of splendor, but you can picture a finer; there is not a resplendence in nature, not a sun, not a system in God's universe, but this power can enshrine in a regalia that transcends the actual. Minister of sweetest piety, it can set Jesus evidently before the eyes and ascend the empyrean to the very footstool of the Divine.

Yet look at this kingly attribute, which is our nearest approximation to the infinitude of God. Like Lucifer, son of the morning, this winged power can fall from heaven to hell, from realms pure and spiritual to regions foul and pestiferous — regions where every thought of the imagination of the heart is evil, only evil, and that continually. Behold the steps downward! The imaginative thought, the intent, the act, the habit, the character and the destiny. When Felix Adler, the ex-Rabbi, the agnostic and aesthetic sceptic of New York, came to this city, he presented a contrast to the malicious, the insolent, and the despicable Ingersoll, whose name, thank God, is given over to universal contempt. That agnostic Jew, as I heard him, acknowledged that the temple of dogmatic religion had crumbled into ruins about him, but he affirmed that the great Nazarene stood before the ages as the grandest upholder of purity in the imaginative citadel of the soul. Ringing out the words, "He that looketh upon a woman, that sinks into the concupiscence of desire, he is branded as a criminal in the presence of eternal truth and right," ringing out these words, he affirmed that they are the loftiest, the most incisive and authoritative words that ever fell from human lips, since they offer the only law of safety for the integrity of the race. "Keep thy heart," cries the wisdom of Solomon; the wisdom of God, "Keep thy imagination with all diligence, for out of it are the issues of life."

Nemesis of vengeance! I turn to the dark record of solitary vice. This is the crime of innocence that benumbs the conscience and kills with its unkindly blast the flowers of early piety. The crime that blanches the cheek, that shakes the nerve system into ruin, that clouds the intellect, that breaks down the integrity of the will, that launches emasculated ruin into asylums of hopeless insanity, collapsing in premature death. Years ago I counted as my friend a noble Christian man who in early life had been the trusted physician of a great historic family, famed for valor at the opening of the century. That man has told me in tones pathetic that the scion of this noble house presented the most tragic and appalling example of ruin. The gentle youth fell under the seductive power of this vice; it ruined his moral being; it smote his intellect with the paralysis of weakness; it destroyed every power of purpose. All the resources of wealth were in vain, all the kindling excitements of travel were in vain, all the appliances of medical skill were in vain; in vain, as a last resort, was restraint. He crushed the casket that held the living jewel, went shivering out into a hopeless, hapless immortality, and the great heraldic name of Lord X, that had flung out its ensign on many seas, ever as the ensign of victory, was, by this form of vice, consigned to the oblivion of a now forgotten past. On the authority of our leading experts relative to insanity; on the authority of one of Ontario's greatest physicians, I affirm that this unsheathed sword overhangs almost every family where young life abides on this American continent. He that hath ears to hear let him hear, what the ethical teacher of the ages has to say to his son Timothy, " Keep thyself pure."

Nemesis of vengeance! I turn to the consequences of associate vice. In early life it was my lot to matriculate in medical science. From the halls of the post mortem anatomic analysis I have gone to the clinic wards of our hospitals. I have seen the West India fevers in their delirium; I have seen the famine plague, when over almost every couch, in every ward, there fluttered the white-winged angel of death, until some ten thousand entered the temple of silence from whence there is no return. As a pastor I have gone through three visitations of cholera, have stood by one at the midnight hour, in the article of death who heard the voice of the pulpit in the morning, and I have witnessed a home made desolate by a winding-sheet that enfolded the entire household in the grave; but I stand here and solemnly declare that I never knew fear until I witnessed the terrible consequences that follow the violation of God's own law of purity. I have seen a young man who, listening to the voice of the siren, once and only once, passed the boundary of eternal right. I have seen him struck with fangs more terrible than those of the cobra di capello; I saw him when every bone was necrosised and the very cranial covering destroyed; I saw him mourning at last when his flesh and his body were consumed, exclaiming " How have I hated instruction and my heart despised reproof." Over ruined girlhood, found dying in an abandoned house, that eloped from a New England Christian home, enticed by a villain who plucked the summer flowers, and entwined them and enshrined them in the clusters of her hair, only to betray, renounce and ruin — over this dying girl have I grieved and vowed at her side eternal war against the destroying evil. Shades of Lazarettos in Blackwell and Ward's Island in Long Island Sound, ye can tell your tale of horrors tragic and terrible as those of Dante's Inferno. In many a home of elegance and wealth in England, says the Bishop of Oxford, you can find some poor Lazarus, hidden away, victim of his own wickedness, who is moaning out his life without hope of a place in the bosom of Abraham.

In New York harbor on Bedloe's Island, the statue of liberty lifts high its head mid upper air, and holds in her right hand the finest electric light in the world. Every night the birds travelling in the darkness are attracted, dazzled, bewildered, and dash themselves against the glass of that light. In the morning the keeper gathers up the maimed, the dying, the dead, and casts them into the sea. There is never a night in our cities but wanderers go forth from Christian homes of purity and peace; with the word liberty on their lips, they are attracted, dazzled, bewildered, and dash themselves against the seductive chimeras, entailing ruin worse than the grave. I heard a voice calling out of the past: " Whoso is simple, let him turn in hither; but he knoweth not that the dead are there, and her guests are in the depths of hell," and Revelation attests that none return to innocence, to purity, to the paths of life, and to God. None return. None! none! Nemesis of vengeance!

My theme widens from the individual to the community, the nation, the continent itself. I turn to France, where civilization has reached its most exquisite adjustments and æsthetic achievements, but where morality is dying out as the result of licentious and ante-natal destruction. This great race, and indeed the Latin races, are tending to imbecile decrepitude. What is alarming the statesmen of France but the fact that every year is witnessing a decline of forty thousand in its population. I turn to this American continent. As you well know, the most august race that God ever built up came over the seas in the "Mayflower." They planted themselves on the sterile New England coast; they battled with starvation, disease, and death; decimated by Indian war, out of this conflict came the great Puritanic New England race, which held empire in its brain, progress in its eagle eye, morality in its ultimate intent, — a race whose heart beat time to the anthems of justice and liberty. Yes, I say liberty, for it was the conscience, the courage of the men who came out of the loins of the Mathers, the Winthrops, the Phillipses, that amid great tribulation, wiped off the black dishonor of three hundred years and gave this continent forever to justice and liberty. I look at this great race, this civilizing factor of the continent. As surely as the Indians are dying out of the West, the great New England race is dying out of the East. Look at the statistics, — 100 families in Five Points record 600 children; 100 families in Madison and Fifth Avenues record 60 children: 100 families in Worcester, Nashua and Fall River record 750 children; 100 families in West Boston record 55; 100 families in West Montreal, 300 children; 100 families amid the proletaria of the East End, 800 children.

It is thus seen that the outcasts of Europe and the inferior races of this continent are going in two generations to possess the land, and all by reason of the crime that accepts marital relations, but rejects the responsibilities, through devices that I refuse to suggest or name, a crime that strikes in the very heart of the church, as well as in the world, vicious and degraded. Hide your faces, crimsoned with indignation, ye prudential ones; point, if you will, the finger of reproach and scorn at the speaker. Let my name be discounted and dishonored. What care I, with the sobbings of the immortal sea sounding on my ears, expectant that ere long I will launch on its waters, that roll for evermore; what care I, if we can only warn off this great crime of the age, a crime against God, against man, against the future, against the hereditary hopes of the race, a crime before which culture and moral advance go down to the dust, and the very purposes of the infinite, touching the advance and ascent of the race, are seemingly defeated by a dread depravity.

But, tremendous as are the physical and sociological aspects of social vice, still more appalling are its moral results. What are the loftiest products of human achievement? They are not what he has built up in stone or marble. They are not what he has accomplished, but what he is in himself. Character-building, on the line of righteousness, is at once the most thrilling, enduring, out-reaching, and divine possibility in man. Character, righteous character, standing with feet on the earth; its head is in the heavens, holding in one hand the excelsior beatitudes, with the other, like the Master, it scatters benedictions. Character, it shall never die; the tomb is its enfranchisement for wider influence; it shall travel out until it touch the shores of the infinite. The most fundamental crime that man can commit is the sin against his own character, which is sin against God. Some months ago our musical society produced Berlioz's opera, "The Damnation of Faust." There is never a day, in never a month, in never a year, but the damnation of character is going on apace.

What are the foundations on which immortal character is built? I answer, purity and truth. Purity and truth! Time writes no wrinkle on their brow; age smites with no paralysis of weakness. Purity and truth! Hold them by the hand; they shall lead thee by the steeps of time and on to a blissful forever. I am assured by my friend Mr. Budge, who knows young manhood across the continent, I am assured that intellectual scepticism is rare indeed. Your free-thought men, sincere they may be, are but scant in number. As George Eliot asserted, they are without power or organic adhesion, and, as a consequence, but feeble folk who follow an ignis fatuus which is at war with the hunger of the heart and alien to every intuition of the soul. A thousand times more perilous is the infidelity of indifference, which is generated by moral decadence and wreckage. This is the devastation that is abroad amongst young men, alienating from the church and leading them to speak with a thoughtless bravado, in flippant tones of denial, concerning sanctions immortal and retributions eternal; a bravado which I have oft seen vanish before the spectre of an immediate guilty future. It is notable that good men and women who enter upon evil courses generally part company with purity and truth forever. Over every such brow there is stamped by an invisible hand, liar, destroyer, deceiver. The very character is sin-saturated with finesse and deception that ripens into the defaulter, a great army in every American and Canadian city. Reform the man if you will. The mission is godlike and beneficent, but you can never bring back the man into the purity and truth of innocence. The very fibre of the warp and woof of his character is impaired. He carries with him memories, undying memories of a guilty past, of tortuous evasions to hide the wrong, which are fatal to the fundamental idea of purity and truth.

This ruination of character is more melancholy and alarming than any wreck than ever stranded on rock-bound shore. I will illustrate. Think of a great western editor, a political leader, I blush to say it, a prohibition advocate, seeking to corrupt an officer who was set to crush and guard a place of infamy. Think of justice branding him before the face of the country as a villain with character laid in ruin. Think of a great capitalist and leader of fashion, in St. Louis, whose household were in Europe, confiding to a Jezebel his purpose to defraud the customs when the jewels and wardrobe should arrive. Think of that Jezebel transfixing him before the country as a villain. Peerless on this continent stands the city of Toronto for Sabbath observance, for suppression of wrong, for loyalty to church organization, thanks to the noble moral inspectors, Archibald and Reyburn. Think of a man with such civic surroundings decoying a daughter of beauty, despoiling her in a cab, dragging her to a Lombard Street inferno and finding a legal defender. Law, I bow before the imperial majesty of law. Her imprints are the footsteps of God telling that he has passed that way. For the expositor of law, I cherish profound admiration, but for the ghouls and vampires who for a paltry fee will defend wrong against right, pestilential villany against innocence, who will villify a minister of God who is standing for the protection of youth against the liquor curse! Robe such an one as a councillor, ermine him as a judge, chair him as a professor, I care not. Such a one gives his name to infamy, reproach, and disdain as a bankrupt in that character, that priceless jewel of every righteous man.

But social vice has an alarming power to eliminate every noble, merciful instinct from character. Not far from where I speak there exists in a public thoroughfare, an abode, the sad antithesis of the divine, with its purple curtains and garish light, tolerated by that sham and mockery that heads our police, who with repellant audacity, told a delegation of ministers that he was in favor of securing the legality and safety of vice. In that abode there are some fifteen dejected Marianas, who smile out of the withered leaves of broken hearts on the gilded and vile scoundrelism that toy with them as their pastime. Right well do these villains know that this once innocent girlhood will, by their patronage, sink to poverty, want, and woe; sink to the dives of brutal abuse; sink to the street, the prison and the hospital; sink to the morgue and the poena damni — where, ah where! But what care these selfish, brutal men! Thoughtless youths are they, think you? Be not deceived. They are your men political, your men legal, your men banking and commercial, your men that swing the round of pleasure and dissipation in fashionable saloons and clubs, your men that come reeling up from abodes of infamy, look purity in the face, and listen to the sweet prattle of children — children who will yet plough up the memory of their father's name with curses and seed it down with scorn.

Many years ago, when in the pastorate, I was called to visit a dying girl in the Maternity Hospital. To my ever-abiding regret, when I arrived, she was gone. As I stood before that ruined form, majestic in feminine grace as the Venus of Milo, with poise of head and arched brow, with fringed eyelids half closed as if looking into the darkness, with lips parted as if the spirit had just passed their portals, with arms overhanging the couch as if waving a last fare-

well to hope, as I stood there and thought of the hills of Windsor, in the valley
of the St. Francis, thought of a home where the sire would never smile again,
and the mother weep until the hand of death shall wipe away her tears, I declare
the truth, I lie not, before God, if a pistol had been mine, I would have been
tempted to smite the villain to the death who, with relentless and merciless
cruelty had ruined an immortal, and broken hearts that God omnipotent could
never heal in life. Of all rubbish beneath the heaven, I count Universalism the
worst. Where in God Almighty's moral universe can you commit a man with
heart worse than the Malay pirate who, smiling in your face, strikes you to the
death, where but to an eternal hell.

If apology I must offer for my language then must it be that the crime transcends the possibilities of human expression. And tell me, what are the social
forces that are ever aiding and abetting this moral and social ruin of our
humanity. I charge this social ruin on the drink traffic. In the city of Corinth,
side by side stood the temples of Venus and Bacchus. The shrine of the latter
was held to be the support of the former, a relation this which is still perpet-
uated. Behind every bar of stately hotel, every room in club house for wine-
bibing wassail, every drinking restaurant down to your illicit cellars, there is a
league and covenant between such and the house of death and hell. Wipe out
the drink traffic from the land and you would abate and well nigh abolish the
ruin which comes from our social immorality.

I charge this ruin on our theatres and operas. Nothing is more preposterous
than the pretension that you can moralize the stage. For 3,000 years the problem has been studied and its solution is as remote as when Aeschylus sang in
Hellenic times. Moralize the stage! I take the socially dishonored Sarah
Bernhardt, who flings her genius into her fleshly loves and portraitures of sexual passion as expressed in her favorite play of " Camille," the French outcast. I take the " Bohemian Girl, " " Lucrezia Borgia," " Norma," with their
extravaganza librettos of impure passion and vile suggestion set to the passion
music of Donizetti, Balfe, or Verdi. When stewards and elders and church
wardens rush to these sensuous spectacles; when mothers, with their trooping
children hasten to the matinees to witness the ballet with its abbreviated
skirts before which modesty hides its face and decency should retire — specta-
cular exhibits like these once seen are immortal in the memory, and innocence
is lost forever. If Edward Keane confessed that the influence of the theatre was
to destroy the sensibilities and harden the heart; if Macready, the noblest trage-
dian of his day, never allowed a child of his household to enter a theatre, knowing as he did that the trend was to ruin; if the greatest authority on theatrical
management affirms that the exclusion of sexual passion from the stage would
in six months necessitate the closing of every theatre on this continent; what
shall be said of the coquetting with this evil which is abroad amongst the
Christians of our times.

I charge this ruin on the literature of the period. 'From the splendor of
Byronic, salacious innuendos, which, like the whip-snake among the flowers,
stings to the death, down to the brutal and swinish brilliance of a Swinburne;
from the scrofulous French novel down to the innoculating sensuousness of
Ouida, and the surreptitious pamphlets which float into academies and schools;
from the editorial witticisms that garnish vileness, to the abatement of moral
revolt, down to the scandal in pictorial illustration, we have a force that is working to the moral disintegration of society.

I charge this social ruin on the abounding divorce in modern society. Discount Catholicism who will, I applaud that historic church for its fidelity to the
sancity and integrity of the family institution. Applaud Protestantism who
will, I publicly impeach and discount it for its tolerance of indiscriminate divorce, that is shaking loose the very ligatures of social life on this continent.
When I am told by Nathan Willis that out of every twelve Protestant mar-
riages in New England one culminates in divorce; when I learn that within the
last 30 years nearly 500,000 divorces have taken place; when I reflect on the
sin and sorrow that are concomitant as the unhappy sequence of such disrup-
tions; with Protestant ascendancy on this continent that can reach the very

fountains of legislation, I affirm with undaunted front that it is an ignominy and humiliation before the world that the churches of America have stood by and winked at this ever-augmenting tide of woe, that threatens the Divine institution of the family in this land.

And yet once again I charge this ruin on the moral brigands, your leering, your loose, your men redolent with fumes of liquor and tobacco, your covert consorts with the Bohemians of our Canadian cities, the dire Dianas of Chicago, the false Penelopes of New York, the Dulciana derelicts of Washington, the Sultanas of depravity of New Orleans, the Sodom of the Gulf, and San Francisco, the Gomorrah of the Pacific. I charge this ruin on men of this class, the professional corrupter of young men, who, with slimy facility sneer at the honor, the fidelity, the virtue of woman, an act this which authenticates the moral putrescence of men, who have reached the antipodal of all hope for recovery. If there be one thing more than another that inspires me with hope, it is the ever ascendant power of women for good. In the circles of literature, of moral reform, of church life, give her but time, give her the ballot, give her the recognition that is coming on apace, and woman — seventy percent of the churches of America thus loyally and politically enfranchised — will regenerate and cleanse political life and put the impress of her purity, her elevation, on all that pertains to the recovery of this world for God. Indignation knows no bounds when we think of the damnatory endeavors of many to sneer at the honor and ministries of woman.

In the face of these overshadowing forces for evil, I thank my God that he raised up a Clark to originate this revival of Christian Endeavor amongst those who hold in their keeping the gigantic future, that hold in their keeping a power which will yet dominate the earth. Force, stupendous force; I can shut out the light, I can shut out the heat, I can shut out the potencies of matter, but I cannot shut out the omnipotence of love. Love, supernal love, indefinable as the fragrance of the flower, ineffable as the witchery of sweet music heard in dreams, ecstatic as the vision Divine; there is not a type of manhood on this earth that holds within it a beating heart that pants for the immortal, but is amenable to the forces of love. This is our warranty, our guarantee, in seeking to rescue the perishing and the lost.

When the fine and fiery genius of Michael Angelo had broken down the rigidities of mediæval art, when he had carved his rough-hewn Moses, and in the passion of his soul tossed his colorings against the walls of the Romaic chapel, till they glowed in all the wild, the gorgeous and sweet angel forms of the "Last Judgment," how truly did he symbolize the work of the spirit of love, which out of stones can carve sons unto Abraham and fling out its colorings of grace and beauty amid the versatilities of human degradation. See yon girlhood, bleared, bruised and degraded to the last extremity, the consort of an abandoned negro in a Baxter Street cellar, the worst in New York. See you the shivering creature with no covering but a wrapper, dripping in the autumnal rain, finding her way to the Florence Mission. See her kneeling in penitence and breaking out amid streaming tears: —

> " The mistakes of my life have been many,
> The sins of my heart have been more,
> And I scarce can see for weeping,
> The way to the open door."

See her bruised form folded in the arms of Christian charity and her spirit led to the Redeemer; see her slowly recovering her womanly grace and beauty; see her standing on the platform of the Cooper Institute, with the poise and power of the orator, swaying three thousand entranced listeners, who at the magic utterance of the name of Jesus bow in sympathy and prayer as the waving corn bows its head and drops its tears in summer showers; see her suffering the inevitable of her wasted life, declining like the gentle summer day, and then, with the name of Jesus on her lips, ascending to the beatitude of God. See her, ye men and women of the Christian Endeavor, as a trophy, an example of great possibility, which beckons you onward to rescue the perishing and save the lost.

I have heard the splendor of Gladstone, the sagacity of Cobden, the majesty of Sumner in the American Senate, and the statuesque brilliance of Wendell Phillips. I have heard the genius of Beecher, the magnetism of Simpson, the opulent diction of Punshon, but I declare, I have never had my heart so moved, my spirit so thrilled, as by the testimony of some poor Magdalene that Christian charity has pulled out of the fire. I charge you, men and women of the Christian Endeavor, never to degenerate into the *tête-à-tête* dilettante church parlor trifling that endangers such organizations, but strike out for God in hard work to recover the lost. I charge you to endure hardness and become good soldiers of Jesus Christ.

Many years ago, when in Philadelphia, I witnessed the return of some ten thousand men from the war. How came those valiant men to carry victory in their eyes and march to the music of conquerors. Were these American lads made such by their comely uniform and the drill of their parades? How came they to carry victory in their eye? I will tell you. Their manhood's courage was tramped into them by the march through Georgia, was rained into them by the storms of the wilderness, was frozen into them by the wintry watches around Richmond, was starved into them by the famines of Libby Prison, was burned into them by the hospital fevers of New Orleans, was driven into them by the bayonets of Gettysburg; it was the blood-red discipline of war that made them good soldiers and victors. And whence come the good soldiers of the Christian Endeavor? Men and women who take as their models Mrs. Josephine Butler, who sacrificed her social status and amid the serenities of age and the severities of sorrow is still laboring for God to save somebody's daughter; Frances Willard, who turned aside from the affluence and elegancies of scholarship to give the brilliance of her powers to inspire the world and lead to endeavor on behalf of the fallen; Miss Barber, who with her refinement and culture walked the streets of this city at midnight to bring back some poor lost sheep of the sheep-fold who might never come home again. Ye sceptic crowd, ye indolent and luxurious loungers who yawn out the wail, "Is life worth living?" if you would bring the beatitude of heaven to earth and the joy of the Triune into your hearts, then strike out to rescue the perishing.

Christianity, maid of the morning, draped in the white robes of purity, I see her skipping along the hills, stepping upon the mountains, and from her sunlit pinnacle evermore stooping down and lifting up wasted humanity and clasping it to her heart of love. Hide thee, my brother; hide thee, my sister, in the folds of her purity. Advance with her into the twentieth century, and on the hills of time you may see many a white-robed pilgrim, saved by your instrumentality, hasting to the heavens.

"Paint me a picture," said a great master to his favorite pupil, "paint me a picture." Said the student, "I cannot paint a picture worthy of such a master." "But do it for my sake, for my sake," was the response. The student retired. He hid himself for weeks and months. At length, returning to the master he said, "Come and see." When the curtain fell, the greatest picture of the age was before him, "The Last Supper," of Leonardo da Vinci. "Paint me a picture," says the Master Divine to every Christian worker in this vast gathering. Do not say you cannot, for his aid is promised. "Paint me a picture of consecrated service. Do it for my sake." And in the coming time when we walk the corridors of the immortal, perchance we shall see on its jasper walls your pictures of consecrated endeavor, which shall be to the honor of that Name, which is forever blest. [*Prolonged applause.*]

The session closed with singing the Doxology, and the benediction by Bishop Fallows.

THE TENT.

The tent was filled with a large and attentive audience, and outside, thousands of Montreal people stood and listened. During Miss Kearney's addresss, some drunken men created a disturbance, and the police had to disperse the crowd. Dr. Clark presided. The praise service was conducted by Rev. E. P. Chappell, of St. Louis, Mo., who made the opening prayer. The audience then sung the favorite hymn, "Throw out the Life-line."

DR. CLARK: One of the beatitudes speaks of those who are blessed because they are persecuted for righteousness' sake. I do not know of any man in all the world that has been persecuted for righteousness' sake more than the first speaker this afternoon. We love him not only because he is a friend of every righteous cause, but we love him for the enemies he has made. [*Loud applause.*] Mr. Anthony Comstock will speak to us.

Mr. Comstock was greeted by the audience with the Chautauqua salute.

Foes to Society, Church, and State.

Address of Mr. Anthony Comstock.

Verily, verily, this is a business for eternity. We are this afternoon to have presented before us, not the mighty host that is following under the leadership of our Father Endeavorer, but we are to bring before you the boys and girls of Canada and the United States. For the future welfare of these two countries is bound up in the boys and girls, and when you touch them with corruption you have touched the future welfare of society, church, and state. We are brought face to face this afternoon with a work that has extended over more than 21 years: taken up by an insignificant country boy without money, without friends, and without position in society, but, with the blessing of God, that insignificant beginning has reached the position where we claim the promised reward for well doing. I remember when in 1881 I had the honor of spending a night beneath the roof of Brother Clark, in Portland, Maine. I had the honor and the proud distinction of speaking to that first little band of Christian Endeavorers in Williston church, and I remember how earnest Brother Clark then was that the hearts of his boys and girls should be touched, and that I should present to them some of the victories and some of the conquests that had been achieved by faith and prayer to Almighty God, and I have been more than gratified that Brother Clark has seen that his boys and girls were helped by that meeting.

But we sit here this afternoon, earnest men and women, to look the foes of society, church, and state in the face without flinching. I bring you three great crime breeders in America, three great crime breeders in Canada and the United States: intemperance, gambling, and evil reading, and the greatest of these is evil reading. [*Applause.*] There are some here who have the white ribbon upon their breast that will be shocked at that statement. I have been in a position for 21 years to know, and I unhesitatingly declare that I believe of all that which defiles the chamber of imagery in the hearts of our children, evil reading is the most deadly foe with which we have to contend. How many of you have stopped to see the practical working of a child's mind? When we went to school, we learned A, B, C, and today the printed page of God's Book is a blank unless, when your eye rests upon it, you bring up the A, B, C, from memory's storehouse.

Let me picture to you the simple illustration of the workings of your child's heart. The Bible says, "the chamber of imagery;" what is it? Let me take a room with four walls. There is an entrance, and at the threshold of that entrance we read, "Behold, I stand at the door and knock." Then there is an entrance into your child's heart, and there is a messenger stands there pleading;

but there are four walls to be decorated, and those four walls are being decorated whether you will it or not. Everything that the eye of that bright boy or girl rests upon is carried into, the storehouse; it is a picture made and hung up upon the walls of that chamber, — it is a negative, if you please, stored away,— and just as sure as the spirit of evil stands by to brand each new-born soul as its own, just so sure that same spirit of evil will pursue that soul, taking advantage of every inherited appetite and passion, and seeking to turn that child away from the paths of virtue, righteousness, and truth. I ask you if in your own experience it is not true that the things you learned in early youth are constantly intruding themselves on your mind. Have you not recalled stories told you, and have you not attempted to stamp out ugly things that have flashed across your memory? Dealing with the fallen, we too often forget that they have weaknesses that the soul has to struggle with, and in that struggle they are sometimes overthrown. They are brought to the edge of a precipice and in an unguarded moment the foot slips into an abyss of sin, and then shall we brand them as most sinful or reach out the helping hand of God's love to help them back upon their feet? [*Applause.*]

I ask you now, men and brethren, come with me to some mountain top and look with me over on the other side of the beautiful St. Lawrence River and upon some mighty plain and see what your eye catches; not a few thousand faces, such as sit here; but see! with united irresistible tread that makes the very earth quake and tremble beneath it, there are 22,400,000 boys and girls marching, marching, marching on from youth to maturity. What does that mean? It means that the men who occupy positions of trust and responsibility are being crowded out of the plane of active service and these new souls are marching on to take possession. What does it mean? It means that the reins of government shall slip out of the hands that now hold them; it means that the pillars of the churches shall be removed and others brought in to support the institutions of the church. Then what kind of men and women will you send to the future?

Come with me again, and on another mighty plain on this side of the beautiful St. Lawrence, and look again, and as far as the eye can reach, there is another moving procession, and that is the beloved youth of Canada and the Provinces. There they come with steady tread, and they come with firm purpose and resolve to take possession and to rule this nation. The question then is, shall we be upon the defensive for our children, shall we allow our patriotism to reach far into the future, or shall we be content to pass along indifferently and let the evil one have control of the decoration of these chambers of imagery?

Are you, men and brethren, awake to the awful constituency for which the Society for the Suppression of Vice in New York City for these twenty odd years have labored? Think you that it is a small thing to stand between the beasts of prey by night and the birds of prey by day? Think you that it is a small thing to stand between these mighty hosts, the beloved youth of these two nations, and those that seek to devour them, — intemperance, gambling, and evil reading? There are communities that say, "We will go into partnership with crime and allow these evils to exist if they will pay a little something to reduce taxes." [*Applause.*] That is what high license is.

Now, if I were an artist I would place upon the canvas here three pictures. There should be the drunkard's home, the gambler's home, and the home of the libertine. I would paint you this first. From the altar of God's house there should go a couple, rejoicing in the love and affection of matrimony. They should leave the altar of God's house and go up to take possession of a home beautified by the loving touch of father and mother. In a very little time, as the husband yields to the appetite of strong drink, I see a shadow creeping over the loving face of that wife and mother. I see later on the scarcity of food upon the table; but that noble, patient, suffering woman says not a word, but by her love and affection seeks to keep bread in the mouths of her beloved children and the shame of her husband's downfall from the world. We go a little further and we find that home a blank, — aye, the mother and her children have been forced out of it; poverty and want have come in at the door and hope, peace, and happiness have flown out of the window. I seek for that noble, patient, self-denying, godly woman, for that loving, affectionate mother, for those beautiful children, and I find them where? In some hovel. That is the business that high license indorses, and that is the result of that kind of devil's seed sown in a community. [*Applause.*]

I draw another picture on this other panel. It is the gambler's home. Ah, there is that signal of alarm in intemperance that we see in passing along; it is the most honorable of these three crime breeders, because it hangs out a danger signal. The red nose, the bleared eye, the bloated countenance, the tainted breath, foreshadow to the loving ones about him the downfall of this loved man. But not so the gambler. The gambler becomes infatuated. By quicker process often than intemperance, the family are driven out into the presence of squalor and want, and all at once the speedy hand of suicide makes away with the man who has not the courage to meet the defalcations and crimes he has been led to commit because of the allurements of the gambling-table.

In a city on the Hudson but a few months ago there was a man living in an elegant mansion with five motherless children within. One morning his body was found stiff and cold at the hotel; and when kind friends entered that home to minister to those orphan children, it was found that there was not money or means enough in that beautiful house to provide for the wants of those five children. And when the facts of that suicide became known, it was found that that man, in order to preserve a respectable position in society, had been a defaulter for more than $400,000.

A young man came into my office a short time ago, and he said to me, "If you don't close up such and such a place I shall commit suicide. I can't go home to wife and children and know that they are starving and see the misery that my folly has brought upon them." Then he said, "You may say I am a fool, but I cannot go by the door of that place without going in, though I know my family are starving at home, if I have a dollar in my pocket."

I have here a little memoranda, a simple straw that shows which way the wind blows, shows how our young men are being swallowed up in this vortex of vice, are being undermined, reason dethroned, and are being made defaulters and thieves. From my scrap-book I made a synopsis of crimes committed. I find that 128 persons were shot or attacked through gambling. Twenty-eight were stabbed and 55 shot over gambling-tables. Besides those who attempted suicide 24 committed suicide, and 60 persons were murdered in cold blood. Out of these defalcations and forgeries and crimes there was an accumulation of $3,000,000 taken from the honest pursuits of business and turned over to the dishonest gambling fraternity. Here comes our respectable citizen who walks up to the book-maker at the race track. He holds his hand out and the receiver of stolen goods receives the spoils. The respectable man goes away and spends his money freely because it costs him nothing. Is there anything honest about that? It is a violation of the fundamental principles of all good government, that a person shall not be deprived of his property without a just and fair equivalent therefor.

These are themes that are secondary to the last theme upon which I am to speak, — the decoration of the chamber of imagery in the hearts of children. Hark what sound is this that drowns Niagara's? It is the whirl, the united whirl, of the devil's printing-press as it is striking off millions of pages of printed matter to infatuate our boys and girls; to defile their minds; to corrupt their thoughts; to pervert their imaginations; to sear their consciences, harden their hearts and damn their souls. With all this you say that our children are not in any danger. How do you know they are not? I had occasion to take a train to New York one time and on it I saw one boy pass a piece of paper to another and noticed the exulting look on the boy's face as much as to say, "What do you think of that?" I saw a third boy hand a paper and say, "Look at that and see what you think of it" to his companion. I said to them, "Let me see that paper." They hesitated, but I turned down one corner and saw what it was. I said I wanted everything of that kind of literature they had in their pockets. I asked them where they had got it, and I went to the school and found nearly every boy in that school with matter so gross and so deadly that if I had to decide between that and the microbes of the scarlet fever I would prefer these microbes in my home.

I have been a post-office inspector in the United States, and since 1872 have the honor of serving upon the staffs of 22 postmasters-general, and I am in a position to know something of what the devil is doing to destroy the youth of America. I am in almost weekly communication with the commissioner of police at Ottawa, and I know something of what is going on in Canada. At one post-office in the United States 45,000 printed circulars were mailed, asking post-masters or post-masters' wives to send the names and addresses of persons in their locality. You loving father and mother, will you say that your child's name is not in that list that was given back? I am glad to say that it is my duty to hunt out such things as that, and bring the hyenas to justice.

Our society for the Suppression of Vice has had the pleasure of reporting more than 1,800 arrests, and the seizure of 67 tons of matter that may justly be called the devil's goods. I discovered that there were 169 books being printed and sold in the United States of bad literature, and that there was a business systematically carried on through the mails of this country and the United States. They collected names from catalogues of schools and seminaries and sent their missives to them. I said something ought to be done, but I had no money. I could not sleep; I went upon bended knee and asked God that I might be used of him to do his purpose in this work. I knew not what the mighty business was, but I say to you frankly that I did not try to put myself in touch with this horrible evil until I was assured in answer to my prayer that I should he kept by Almighty grace. [*Applause.*]

It was revealed to me in the month of March, 1872, that there was a business of scattering evil books all over the country. Something told me that if I only had some money to work with, I could do something to suppress this business. I did not know where to turn; so, in my closet, I turned unto Him who giveth all things liberally. There was sent to my place of business a princely man, Morris K. Jessup, who invited me to his house. When the facts were laid before him, he gave me a check for $650. I took that and went forth,—and if I had time I could tell you stories that sound like romance—how with that money in hand, in less than two weeks' time we had gathered up more than $40,000 worth of books and papers. Within a short time we gathered in ten tons more. So, little by little, the way has been opened, and the wave of opposition has reared its head. There has been the stroke of the assassin, but it has failed; nerve and artery have been severed, but they have been healed. The scar that marks my face is the token of God's goodness, for by that scar help has been given me. [*Applause.*]

Let me paint a background. Into my house have come smallpox scabs from infected mail; into my office have come diseased packages, and one poor fellow who was my trusted stenographer today cannot straighten his limbs or get his hands to his mouth, because he received one of those diseased packages that was designed for me. Whatever God had in store for that man, he held a defence around about me, and I am here to tell of it today. Then I can tell you of the constant following of this work with opposition, with hardships, with trials, with distrust on the part of good men, but over it all is written, "Fear not, I am with you; be not dismayed." I can thank God that the enemies' own weapons have turned against them. I am glad to say that in spite of all opposition, we have been enabled to carry the work forward in the interests of the 22,400,000 boys and girls in America, and our brothers and sisters on this side of the St. Lawrence.

May God bless you in your work of saving souls for the Master. [*Loud and prolonged applause.*]

DR. CLARK: We never have a Christian Endeavor convention without having upon the program "Gospel Temperance." It is treated both in the tent and in the Drill Hall this afternoon. In this audience room we shall listen to Miss Belle Kearney, of Mississippi, the national organizer of the Young Women's Christian Temperance Union. [*Applause.*]

Gospel Temperance.

Address of Miss Belle Kearney.

I bring you greetings from the 200,000 members of the Women's Christian Temperance Union, and the 40,000 of the Young Women's branch. We are all Christian Endeavorers in spirit, and many of us in fact. We are all striving for the accomplishment of the same grand purpose,— the extension of Christ's kingdom on earth. In the noontide hour of this great day of the onward march of stupendous moral reforms, the far-reaching and splendid results of Christianity, and all things widening and deepening manward and Godward, the word "union" with Christians is not a relative, but a positive term. It is a well of hidden and shadowy depths whose waters are for the healing of the nations. It means that the hearts and minds of Christians are united; that invisible bonds, soft as silk, and fine as faith, have tied their soul together; that the currents of their being move only at the impulse of one divine love. It means that all the petty jealousies and dissensions and criticisms and unholy rivalries, that have often characterized the intercourse of Christian bodies with each other, have been melted in the fiery furnace of a common sorrow and a common hope, and recreated, without one base alloy, into a chain of gold, whose links are oiled with charity, running its easy length through the jewels of human sympathies, and connecting them by the strong lock of comradeship with the great, loving heart of Christ.

The brotherhood of man is fast becoming one of the leading features of earth's grandest philosophy; the fatherhood of God one of its most blessed assurances. The world of men and women are meeting on one platform. The unceasing cry of earth's humanity for greater light and greater freedom has burned away all barriers. The hands of creation are clasped; the feet of creation are winged; the eyes of creation are lifted — all toward

> " One God, one law, one element,
> And one far-off divine event
> To which the whole creation moves."

How inspiring it is to find so many young people in this great international convention! How glorious it is to be allowed the precious privilege of being with you! At the mere suggestion of youth there rises before the imagination visions of strength and freshness and power. All that is lovely and tender and gracious nod and smile at us. Enshrined possibilities, undeveloped energy, irresistible enthusiasm, which means " God in us," here finds its happiest expression and truest translation. Hope and confidence and ambition, like imprisoned eagles, struggle to be free, and spread their sinewy wings in the bracing air of untried endeavor, lifting our whole beings high into the shining light.

It is in youth that great questions move us, and we become disciples of doctrines, and disseminate the contagion of noble thoughts and purposes. It is in youth that whisperings of immortality are most clearly heard in the soul, stirring us on to splendid action; that pulses beat quick and fast; that the life current runs swift and strong; the mind moves like electricity, and the will stands firm and unbroken, all desiring, all encompassing, all subduing!

In this day what would religion and philanthropy do without the young? They fill our Sunday schools, they form our Epworth leagues, our Christian Endeavor Epworth leagues, our Christian Endeavor societies, our Young Men's and Young Women's Christian Associations, our Young Women's Christian Temperance Unions and Loyal Temperance Legions, and are the strength of every movement. Without them the tide would soon turn, and the advancement of the world be stayed. I pray God that in these formative years of the mental and spiritual growth of the youth of this age, such elements of honor and courage and strength may enter into their lives as to form a basework upon which a superstructure of the new civilization will be built, without the wine-cup in society, and the saloon in politics. [*Applause.*] The foundation rock of the temperance reformation is Christianity. From it we draw our inspirations; upon it we establish our authority; toward it we look for salvation; in it we rest and have our being. "All for Christ" is our creed, our watch-word, our war-cry. Ours is a practical Christianity, coming in touch with the multitude —not the Christianity of vaulted roofs and stained-glass windows and kid gloves, and operatic singing, but the Christianity of Jesus of Nazareth, founded upon righteousness, exemplified in purity of heart and life. When one is made to realize the pain and sin and need of the world, the only life that seems worthy to lead is that modelled as closely as possible after that of the Man of Galilee, with its divine pity and strong, sweet helpfulness. Every weak, hungry, tempted soul yearning for a touch of better things; men enslaved by drink, cowed, hopeless, besotted; women struggling with the grinding fiend of poverty, or staggering under a load of sin, outcast, discouraged, with none to pity, none to appeal to; little children, with wan faces, and poor, starved hearts, in which the lovelight has never dawned; the homeless, the friendless, the despised, all who are weary and heavy laden, we reach out to with a yearning cry: "Come unto me, and I will help you."

There has to be a living expression of faith in Christ in our opposition to personal and national sin. The cardinal doctrine of the gospel of temperance, and the leading plank in its platform, is total abstinence for the individual and prohibition for the nation. [*Applause.*] Realizing that intemperance is the shoal upon which the ship of state is stranded; that it is the jagged rock upon which the home is wrecked; that it is the quagmire into which humanity sinks to rise no more, save through the interposition of divine grace, the Great-hearts in the vast army of reformers have left no stone unturned to cause its annihilation. They have pressed into service all the available forces in the material universe to forward their heavenly mission. They have taken the lamp of religion as a guide to their feet. They have called forth the clear, undeniable voice of science to substantiate their declarations. They have brought in the strength of the arm of the law to defend them. Realizing that the monster they were grappling was hydra-headed and dolphin-hued, they have enveloped themselves in a coat of mail of many links, and armed themselves with various weapons of warfare, so as to be prepared on all sides for the defensive, and to carry the fight into the enemy's country unhurt, and to come off ultimately triumphant. By training the children in the principles of total abstinence they are speculating in futures that promise a glorious return; by educating the young women up to the idea of equal standards for men and women, so they will shrink with horror from marrying a man who is not as free from the taint of alcoholic and tobacco poison as themselves [*applause*], they are laying the foundation of a higher civilization, obtaining a new declaration of independence, and shouting the battle cry of freedom! The hearts of our young women are cordially enlisted in the heroic struggle for God and home and every land. They have assisted in campaigns for constitutional amendments, secured signatures to petitions to be presented to our own and other governments for the abolition of the liquor traffic, supported rest cottages, headquarters and tea rooms for working-girls, and established resorts for them on the seashore during the summer months. They have taken charge of mission meetings at night; supplied singers to the hospitals; dispensed substantial charity through the medium of the Flower Mission, in visiting prisons, jails, alms-houses, etc.; studied the subject of physical culture, and formed hygiene clubs; established 100 loan libraries; founded industrial schools; engaged in evangelistic social purity, Sunday school, juvenile, and press work; labored among lumbermen and sailors, foreigners and the colored population; conducted Demorest Medal contests; held gospel temperance meetings, and secured hundreds of signatures to the pledge. The temperance workers, by calling in the aid of the press, have obtained a mighty coadjutor, whose power is incalculable; by having law-givers take the words of their lips and inscribe them in imperishable characters upon the statute book of Christendom, they have built a wall of solid masbary about them that no encroachments from the side of the foe will be able to break down; they have built upon a rock. The waves and billows of opposition may beat against it, but it shall not tremble. They have built upon a rock with the strength of Gibralter and the everlastingness of ages.

In this day of science and revelation, when the trend of all creation is toward the light, how pitiful it is to think that men, in the face of all that has been done to rescue and relieve them, will deliberately undertake to ruin themselves. In this day, when the noblest women on earth have, in fact, laid down their lives, as a ransom for many, have been crucified for truth's sake, the other women will continue to draw their skirts close about them for fear of touching the common herd, although its heart-beats sound like trip-hammers, and its smothered sob of anguish and groans for sympathy cut like a knife and is freighted with prayer. Above all things, it is hard to understand how a man who calls himself a Christian can vote for the continuance of the saloon, and thus give strength to the heaviest curse that ever rested upon any civilization, simply because he prefers the supremacy of one party to the other. [*Applause.*] Friends, there never will be a justification of righteousness, nor a purification of the political world, until the Church of God stands squarely upon a platform of principles as unimpeachable as divine law, and until its individual members live up to the high-sounding resolutions against the liquor traffic that are drawn up with such a flourish of trumpets every year at synods, conferences, and associations. The question of the legalized saloon must be settled in the church. What a speedy and glorious victory for righteousness there would be if every Christian did his duty. Upon the character of the citizen depends the safety of the state. "God give us men, tall, sun-crowned, who live above the fog in public duty, as in private thinking." [*Applause.*] God give us just such men now, in this crucial period. We shall never be a free people while the private citizen prays one way and votes another. [*Applause.*] We shall never be a secure nation while our leading officials are leagued with sin, and enter into a covenant with death. In the United States we boast loudly of our national independence; the Fourth of July has recently been celebrated with great eclat. Meanwhile, the flag of our country floats serenely over the saloon for its protection. The contract of the government of the United States with the Christian people has been grossly violated by opening the gates of the World's Fair on Sunday. Liquor is sold to the teeming millions in Jackson Park, although it is prohibition ground. The Pabst Brewing Company has the assurance to put out on advertising cards that its goods are sold in every great building on the Fair grounds, even in the Government buildings, although the Government, in establishing its buildings, did so with the distinct understanding that no liquors should be sold in them. I am glad to say that the Women's building has no liquor sold in it. [*Applause.*] The civil statutes are impudently trodden under foot and God's law boldly defied. The Christian people must be massed together. They must stand together, hand to hand, heart to heart, shoulder to shoulder. They must be true to themselves, they must be true to God, if they would overcome evil, and capture the world for Christ. [*Applause.*] If they will, they can triumph gloriously. With the Church of God flashing and thundering along the line, awakening and quickening and strengthening the moral sentiment of the millions within its ranks, with this grand army of Christian Endeavorers, hundreds of thousands strong, in the first flush of a splendid young manhood , and an educated and consecrated young womanhood, and scores of benevolent, and philanthropic societies straining every nerve and sinew, working with heart and brain and soul, a time could soon be ushered in that would shine more and more unto the perfect day.

The temperance cause may seem at a standstill to many who have not looked into the seeds of time : but in all these years there has been a leaven at work that has known no defeat, suffered no discouragement, but. with the light of immortality impressed upon it, it has gone from triumph unto triumph, and still goes on, until now, from the battlements of the higher tower of faith it discerns the hand of God at work in the destiny of the nations of the earth. The different governments, rife with an anarchy, quaking with the throes of nihilism, filled with corruption in high places, the hand of labor raised against the vaulted head of capital, the liquor traffic holding high carnival, and sending out its emissaries of fraud and pauperism, murder and annihilation, promise to suffer a fate similar to that of ancient Ephesus. But the temperance reformation, filled with redeeming power, swelled from a pitiful handful of brave hearts, scorned and outcast, to a vast army with banners, comes marching with its conquering legions to tear down the stupendous structure — the liquor traffic, which has been reared over the prosperity of untold lands — and cast out the saloon [*applause*], the mighty god, under the iron wheels of whose car the blood of millions of victims has been crushed, and rear in its stead a governmental policy that shall stand as a veritable temple of justice, where Jesus Christ, the Righteous, shall sit in judgment, and rule in the hearts of men. It is coming, this army with banners, vast, triumphant, shouting in glad acclaim, " Hallelujah ! the Lord God Omnipotent reigneth." [*Loud applause.*]

DR. CLARK : When we wrote to Miss Frances E. Willard, asking who should represent this great cause on this platform, you will be glad to know that she wrote to us that of all the women in the country, she did not know of any one who could present it better than Miss Belle Kearney. [*Applause*]. You are glad you have heard her, I am sure, and are ready to vouch for what Miss Willard told us.

The hymn " Faith Is the Victory " was then sung.

DR. CLARK : You know at conventions we always like to give more than is promised on the program rather than less. There are two gentlemen here, — one who represents the work in Ireland and another in Turkey, — who have done more than any others in their respective countries in Christian Endeavor work. They will speak just one minute each. Rev. Mr. Boynton, who was to speak this afternoon, spoke, as you remember, the other evening, taking the place of Hon. W. C. P. Breckenridge, who was detained at the last moment, and only wrote us on the day he was to speak that he could not be here. Mr. Boynton's place will be filled by Mrs. Von Finkelstein, who is known by many of you as a distinguished lecturer and orator. She will speak for a few moments after Rev. Mr. Mills has given his address on one of the most important subjects of this convention, — " Senior Societies." I will now introduce Mr. J. Newman Hall, a young layman from Belfast, Ireland. [*Applause.*]

MR. HALL : I bring to all my fellow-Endeavorers here the greetings of a small band of Endeavorers in Ireland. The work in Ireland is but three years old; still, we have thirteen societies with nearly 600 active members. We love our beloved president quite as much as you do, and it is our desire that the work in Ireland shall progress even more than the work here. You in this country owe a great deal to Ireland, but you have repaid that debt in sending us the Christian Endeavor Society. [*Applause.*] Therefore, please take from me the good wishes and greetings of all your fellow-Endeavorers in the Emerald Isle.

DR. CLARK : There is a man with us from Turkey whose face you will all want to see. He has accomplished much along the line of Christian Endeavor in that land, — Mr. G. H. Krikorian.

MR. KRIKORIAN : It was in 1889 that we organized our first society. We have our hindrances and difficulties in that country, but we have been able to organize seventeen societies by personal work alone. The work has spread, and Dr. Clark reports that there are 41 societies there, proving that the work is going on there in spite of all its hindrances. Our motto is, "The Turkish Empire for Christ." [*Applause.*]

DR. CLARK : Senior Christian Endeavor I believe is coming, and you will hear about it from one who has tried this plan in his own church, the man who formed the second Christian Endeavor society that was ever formed in all the world, nearly twelve years ago last October, Rev. Chas. Perry Mills, of Newburyport, Mass.

Senior Societies.

Address of Rev. Chas. Perry Mills.

One hundred and eighteen years ago Dr. Samuel Spring, pastor-elect of the church from which I come, stood upon the wharf at Newburyport, and preached a sermon to Benedict Arnold and his command as they were about to embark on an expedition to capture Quebec. Quebec did not capitulate, but in an engagement about its citadel Benedict Arnold was severely wounded. 'T is a thousand pities that he was not killed then and there, long before that fateful hour when he betrayed his country in negotiating with Major Andre. "'T is best to die, our honor at the height." Today a second expedition is before you from that historic wharf; and my proposal is to capture all Canada and this world-gathered convention for the idea of Senior Endeavor. [*Applause.*] Having gone so far with this providential movement it would be treason to train our guns against its glorious advance; it is only logical loyalty to carry our banner another step forward. The note that I now strike at Montreal '93 will be the keynote at Cleveland '94. By a senior society we mean simply a senior department; not graduation from Christian Endeavor, but graduation up from the junior and young people's department with the same principles raised to the third power. Dismiss forever the word and the idea of graduate Christian Endeavor. Adopt this maxim: Once a Christian Endeavorer always a Christian Endeavorer. [*Applause.*] Look at the arguments for this advance as they fall in and march.

1. The argument of analogy. The Sunday school is classified into primary, intermediate, and senior departments. The senior department of the Sunday school insists especially upon this ideal: All the church in the Sunday school and all the Sunday school in the church. Analogy forces us to the conclusion that we must not have graduated but graded Christian Endeavor, and when we have achieved this three-fold classification we too can insist on our ideal: All the church in Christian Endeavor and all Christian Endeavor in the church.

2. The argument of growth. Consider the juniors, how they grow; by the law of life they become the young people. Consider the young people how they toil and spin, until they weave for themselves a garment of experience and training. Consider them as they preserve and carry forward all their discipline and efficiency until they blossom out as seniors, and I tell you that Solomon in all his glory was not arrayed as one of these. What shall be the age-limit in these departments? The juniors correspond to the rootage of our growth, the young people to the foliage, and the seniors to the fruitage. In the growth of our tree, the time of figs is come, and if the Master beholds nothing thereon but leaves only, the whole tree will dry up from the roots. Open your eyes to Jeremiah's vision of figs: "One basket had very good figs, even like the figs that are first ripe ; and the other basket had very naughty figs, which could not be eaten, they were so bad." A few senior societies have already been formed; these are they that are first ripe, and the vision that I declare unto you today, supported by concurrent witnesses, beholds only one kind of figs — "good figs, very good." My plea is for more figs. [*Applause.*]

3. The argument of economy. The problem of invention is how to economize fuel and force; 90 percent of the fuel that goes into the furnace goes out of the chimney, or smoke stack, as waste. It carries latent energy that is not used and produces live steam that does not do its work. Mechanical progress lies along the lines of the mastery of this wasted force and its conversion into utilized power. The first marine steamship could scarcely carry coal enough to make the voyage across the Atlantic; to-day a modern man-of-war from a single coaling can go around the globe. The difference is between the simple engine and the triple-expansion steam-engine. The triple-expansion steam-engine expands its steam in three successive stages in three separate and distinct cylinders, one taking its steam from the boiler and each of the others taking its

steam from the output of the cylinder working at the next higher pressure. If now we wish Christian Endeavor to drive the ship of Zion — a mighty spiritual man-of-war — around the world, we must pattern its motive power after the triple expansion steam-engine. [*Applause.*] Kindle first plenty of fire under the boiler, and then conduct the steam that has been generated into a series of three cylinders. The juniors receive the steam at highest pressure, starting us off with the stir of life and promise of power; the young people then use the steam a second time, pushing the piston to another application of force; and the exhaust steam of the young people the seniors are already to condense and use, conserving energy that otherwise would be wasted. These three cylinders, the juniors, the young people, and the seniors, reciprocating and co-acting, will bring the ship into port. It is in this shape at any rate that Christian Endeavor has come into Newburyport. Moreover, it was the son of a Newburyport captain, sailing in his father's vessel, who carried Christian Endeavor to Australia, which has organized this movement on the triple-expansion plan. Australia, all hail and Godspeed! But give Connecticut her due. She is the banner state, as witness her resolve in state convention in 1887: "That inasmuch as the Y. P. S. C. E. is the new application of an old idea, the church covenant reduced to particulars, we recommend the formation of senior and junior societies." This argument of economy may be set forth in another light. In our churches we must do, not less work, but more; and this work we must do, not with more organizations, but with less. Complete the organization of Christian Endeavor, and then whatever work presents itself do through the Christian Endeavor committee system. The principles of Christian Endeavor are the principles of all Christian life and service; and whatever is desirable to accomplish can be efficiently done in the live hands of Christian Endeavorers, in process of time endeavorizing the whole church, and making the whole of it a working force. This is not the hour to insist on the conviction that the King's Daughters and the King's Sons, the Boys' Brigade and the Brotherhood of Andrew and Philip, with kindred orders, shall become related departments of Christian Endeavor, but experience and forecast certainly do indicate the wisdom of pushing out new lines of service through Christian Endeavor committees, rather than through new organizations, distinct and separate. A great light is about to dawn upon my own denomination in its prosecution of Home Missions. Seven societies, all with their own elaborate organizations, are in the field, one planting Christian schools, another building churches, a third starting Sunday schools, and so on to the end of the list. It is my contention that the consolidation of the seven societies into one central organization, with related departments, is the plea of economy. And then the hour will be ripe for the combination of the foreign board and the home board of the Congregational missions — this central controling, comprehensive board. — using the committee-system to do its whole work, on week day or Sunday, in school or church, at home or abroad. Deliver us from the despair of more organizations, that weaken and conflict with one another; but develop the Christian Endeavor society to its three-fold fulness, and then adapt and enlarge its committee work to meet all necessities, to push all enterprises. [*Applause.*] You Canadians have but one sovereign, the queenliest of queens [*applause*], Victoria; subordinate to her you have a governor-general. whose name it is a pleasure to speak with plaudits, the earl of Aberdeen; obedient to him you have your various provinces centralized and harmonized in the unity of your political system. Akin to this, we have our queen, the church; let the church appoint a Christian Endeavor governor-general, and under this generalship create and control all the provinces of her work, exalting as Lord over all, King Jesus. [*Applause.*]

4. The argument of opportunity. If it becomes youth to reverence age it becomes age to consider youth, to create for it opportunity of expansion. The juniors have demonstrated their right to be; having their own meeting, their own officers and their own committees. Let the young people make way for the juniors, opening for them doors of entrance into the one Christian Endeavor fold. In the light of this demonstration let the seniors make way for the young people, giving to them a fair field of development and laying upon them the

burdens of responsibility. My opinion counts one, only one, I know, and yet I am unanimous in this opinion [*laughter*], that it is a mistake for older Endeavorers to tarry in the young people's department, occupying places and positions to which the young people should be advanced. [*Applause.*] Opportunity means before the port. Here is the general prayer meeting of the church as a port of entry; let the seniors sail in and take possession, carrying with them the application of their pledge and all the pulsating push of their power. The senior Endeavorers too, can form themselves into an advisory board and be the statesmen of the church, shaping its policy and guiding its course in wisdom. How our churches will spring forward with leaps and bounds when they can command the trained and devoted services of the large body of its men and women. The young people are educating just such a body, and this body, it seems to me, will be best held together and made permanently effective by keeping up the Christian Endeavor organization in a senior department. Negatively, experience has already shown that graduates out of the young people's society and out of Christian Endeavor altogether have not continued as voiceful and efficient as when they were still Endeavorers. A link in their devotion has dropped out when they passed from the particular and strenuous obligations of the Christian Endeavor pledge into the more general and loosely held obligations of the church covenant. Positively, I bring you the testimony that when active young people have graduated, not from Christian Endeavor but into senior Christian Endeavor, they kept unbroken their particular and their general efficiency. "These things saith he that openeth and no man shutteth; behold I have set before thee an open door, and no man can shut it." Let the procession of Christian Endeavor move in with colors flying.

5. The argument of spontaneity. Time was in the States, you know, when there were two colors in the field, the blue and the gray; today we can go that one better, for we have three colors, the red, the white, and the blue. The Maryland girls and the Massachusetts boys hug these colors to their patriotic hearts with an equal devotion, our animosities being buried as the Welsh woman wanted to have the devil buried, face downward, so that if he ever tried to rise the harder he would dig, the deeper he would get. [*Laughter.*] Our animosities being thus buried, I may be permitted to make use of a battle where the blue and the gray were opposed to each other. It was on the field of Missionary Ridge that there were three lines of rifle pits opposed to General Grant, one at the base, the other midway, the third at the crest. When the order for battle came Grant directed his command to take the first line of entrenchments. It was done in accordance with the plan of the commander-in-chief. But the soldiers, enforced by the discipline of the trained warfare and thrilled by the enthusiasm of the fight, moved right on and took the second line and then the third. Grant with headquarters in the rear, watching the spontaneous forward movement with amazement, turned to General Thomas and said: "Who ordered those men up the heights; did you?" "No, I did not." To General Granger he said the same thing, and Granger replied: "No, I did not; but I tell you, general, that when those fellows get started all hell can't stop them." [*Laughter.*] After the crest had been gained General Granger rode along the line and said jokingly, "Boys, you have disobeyed orders; I am going to have you all court-martialled." But you can't court-martial a whole army. The characteristic feature of Missionary Ridge was that it was a soldier's battle; the army out-generaled its general. Father Endeavor Clark has led us to the first line of Christian Endeavor organization; but who has swept on the junior advance, and who are now rising to the summit of achievement, lifting the senior banner? The Christian Endeavorers themselves. There may be some in the valley who are saying that this thing cannot be done, but there is too much of the push and power of Providence in this still-rising movement for us to stop; we must go on, with orders or without orders, wherever the Spirit of God leads. The great Commander-in-chief has promised that the gates of hell shall not prevail against his church. We have enlisted under the banner of Christ and the church, and to the end that that banner may move forward and prevail, w

say: Let senior societies rise as rises the tide of victorious battle. [*Loud applause.*]

DR. CLARK : Rev. Dr. Rondthaler, of Indianapolis, Ind., will now introduce the next speaker.

DR. RONDTHALER : We have heard from everything under the sun, and we have heard from all the animals that God has created from the beaver up to the eagle ; we have heard from almost everything in the matter of religious association during the time of this conference, but we have not heard from the Russian bear, and we have not heard of the Russian nation or the Greek church in any way, so Miss Lydia Mamreoff Von Finklestein, now Mrs. Mountford, will speak to us for anything under the sun she has a right to. [*Laughter.*]

Mrs. Mountford was greeted with hearty applause by the audience, as she stepped forward upon the platform.

Address of Mrs. Mountford.

I bring to you this afternoon a message of peace from the land of my birth. I begin with this in order that you may know that I am not quite a bear, although of Russian nationality. I was born and brought up in the city of Jerusalem, the city of the great King. [*Loud applause*]. I am, so to speak, a true daughter of Zion, and with the salutation of Zion, I come to you and say, " *Salaam Alekam,*" i. e., " Peace be unto you," the salutation of our Saviour Jesus Christ to his disciples. The order that he gave them was, " Wherever you go, carry this message with you, ' Peace be unto you. ' " From the north, the south, the east and the west comes the salutation, " Peace be unto you." and the response comes back, " And unto you be peace and the mercy of God and the blessing of God."

I represent to you this afternoon a combination of four nations. By nationality I am a Russian,— there is a Russian bear for you ; by birth I am an Arab, a Turk or a Mohammedan. I was born in a Mohammedan country, and I look upon that land as my native land, the land of Palestine. By adoption, I am an American. [*Loud applause.*] When I first came to this country, a few years ago, I was so enraptured with the system of your government that I declared my intention of becoming a loyal American citizen [*applause*], and I am a full-fledged, naturalized citizen of the United States of America. [*Loud applause.*] Last, yet not least, but the greatest of all, by marriage I am an Englishwoman. [*Laughter and applause.*] That, to my mind, is the greatest tie of all. Here we are assembled from the United States and from Great Britian, and may this assemblage unite you as the tie in the holy bonds of matrimony. [*Loud applause.*]

" Christian Endeavorers." What do I understand by this word ? I understand that with me you are journeying toward the heavenly Jerusalem. I come from the earthly Jerusalem, but I hope to reach that golden shore. We are all journeying toward that great city, endeavoring to come up to the portals in order that we can see that great light, our Saviour Jesus Christ. I am so glad that upon this platform of Christian Endeavor all sects, all creeds are forgotten, all meet together in the name of our Saviour Jesus Christ. [*Loud applause.*]

The question is asked everywhere, " What is this gathering that is here ? " As I walk through the streets of Montreal I hear people inquiring in French, " *Qu'est ce que c'est ?* —"[What is this ?] Do you remember the same question when the children of Israel were in the desert? They were hungry and were asking for bread, and Moses said to them : " Tomorrow you will have bread." The next morning when the Israelites arose they could not see the loaves of bread anywhere, but they saw little round white seeds lying upon the ground, and exclaimed in Hebrew, " What is this ? " So these little seeds, these Junior societies, are the manna all over the world, and here is our Moses [*pointing to Dr. Clark*) who is leading the children of Israel out of the wilderness. Protestants, Roman Catholics, Greeks, all who believe in the religion of Jesus Christ, come to Him according to the light they have in his glorious name.

Yesterday when I visited the Cyclorama of the City of Jerusalem which you have here in your midst, I was absorbed in meditation; and as I glanced upon that picture of the crucifixion of our Saviour Jesus Christ, and as I looked upon the picture of the two thieves, one on either side, I thought, from my oriental experience, How little we appreciate and understand the character of the thief on the cross. We forget him altogether; we simply sometimes sing of him. We forget that the thief on the cross was the first Christian Endeavorer. That thief recognized in the Saviour a glorious King, and nobody else had yet recognized it so largely as he did, because, when the Saviour was on the cross, a thief on one side and a thief on the other side, the thief on the one side reviled him, and said, "If thou be the Son of God, come down and save thyself." The people around were scoffing and mocking him, and suddenly we hear a voice which has been ringing down these nineteen centuries, and the other thief rebukes him, and says, "Dost thou not fear God? We deserve this punishment justly, but this man unjustly." And then he turns to our Saviour, and with a pleading look in his eyes, he says to him: "Lord, remember me when thou comest into thy kingdom." Here was the grand sympathy that this man showed for our Saviour. Jesus had many servants and followers, but here is this thief on the cross testifying that this was the noble One who had been usurped of his rights, and that he was now going to that far country of which Jesus had just spoken to his disciples. And Jesus turned and said to him: "Verily, I say unto thee, this day thou shalt be with me in Paradise."

The question is often asked, "Why did our Saviour take a thief with him into Paradise?" In a few words I shall explain to you. In the nineteenth chapter of St. Luke, seventh verse, you will find where our Saviour speaks about a nobleman who went into a far country and gave so many talents to his servant. In the east today we have similar noblemen that go to the far country. Our political conditions in Palestine today are the same as they were in the days of our Saviour, inasmuch as that in the days of our Saviour the Jews owned the country. They were the inhabitants of the soil, but the Romans were their rulers, and they hated the Roman yoke. Today the Arab is the owner of the soil, and the Turk is his ruler, and he hates his ruler with the same hatred as that with which the Jews hated the Roman ruler. I want to show you that a nobleman when he goes into a far country takes with him his most sympathetic servant in order to cheer him up, and so here this man recognizes the Saviour; therefore, there is no question why Jesus Christ took this servant with Him into Paradise. To Jesus' name be all the glory, for Jesus Christ is the same yesterday, today, and forever. We can still hear the echo of that wondrous song that was sung upon the plains of Palestine, "Glory to God in the highest, and on earth peace, good will to men." [*Loud applause.*]

Dr. Clark offered prayer, after which the benediction was pronounced and the meeting adjourned.

SUNDAY EVENING.

DRILL HALL.

The closing consecration service is always the culminating point of every Christian Endeavor convention. In spite of the general feeling of uncertainty concerning a possible outside disturbance, the delegates gathered early at the hall in great numbers, and soon the auditorium was crowded to its utmost. Placards had been posted at different points among the seats, indicating where the various state and provincial delegations were to sit. Hitherto no particular assignment had been made, but at this service it was thought best that the delegations should sit together as far as possible, in order that their responses in the service should be made most effectively. The different delegations came in singing hymns and greeting each other with an enthusiasm which was very impressive to those who had never attended a similar service before.

The program began with a praise service led by Mr. Lindsay and the Park Sisters, several of the more popular hymns being selected, such as "Showers of Blessing," "Coming," "True-hearted, whole-hearted," "Stand up for Jesus," "Nearer, my God, to Thee," and "Jesus, Lover of my Soul."

Dr. Clark presided. Rev. Mr. Fleming, of Scotland, led in the recitation of the one-hundredth Psalm, after which Rev. Mr. Swengle, of Pennsylvania, offered prayer. The audience then joined in singing the hymn "Hide Me." Rev. H. B. Grose, chairman of the committee on resolutions, then presented the following report : —

Resolutions.

Resolved, That we reaffirm our adherence to the principles which we believe, under God's blessing, have made the Christian Endeavor movement what it is today.

1. Personal devotion to our divine Lord and Saviour Jesus Christ.
2. The covenant obligation embodied in the prayer-meeting pledge, without which there can be no true society of Christian Endeavor.
3. Constant religious training for all kinds of service involved in the various committees, which, so many of them as are needed, are equally with the prayer meeting essential to the Society of Christian Endeavor.
4. Strenuous loyalty to the local church and denomination with which each society is connected.
5. We re-affirm our increasing confidence in the interdenominational spiritual fellowship, through which we hope, not for organic unity, but to fulfil our Lord's prayer for spiritual unity, "that they all may be one." [*Applause.*]
6. We also re-affirm what has been so often declared, that it is not the province of Christian Endeavor to legislate for the individual conscience.

To this platform of principle we renewedly pledge ourselves.

Resolved, That the thanks of this convention be extended to the Montreal Committee of 1893 [*applause*], to the pastors and churches, to the Y. M. C. A., and to all others who have aided the committee in their most efficient and admirable work, which has contributed so much to the splendid success of this Twelfth International Convention. [*Loud applause.*]

Resolved, That we express to the Mayor of Montreal and to the City Council our hearty appreciation of the welcome which the Mayor so graciously tendered in person on behalf of the city authorities and the citizens; and that we most cordially thank the people of this beautiful city for the generous aid given to the committee, and for the manifold courtesies and kindly hospitalities which have made our coming to Montreal possible and contributed to our comfort and pleasure during our stay.

Resolved, That we thank the city press for the excellent reports and kind editorial utterances; and that to the agent of the Associated and United Press, to the official reporter and his staff, and to all those who are engaged in reporting this convention, we extend our appreciation of the valuable service rendered. [*Applause.*]

Resolved, That we commend, as one of many forms of useful and suitable work for Christian Endeavor societies, wherever feasible, the holding of Gospel meetings at the life-saving stations and light-houses where picked men are isolated and deprived of church privileges, and the ministry to these men of good reading and such other cheer and comfort as Christian love may suggest; also the work among the police forces, the charitable and reformatory institutions, the commercial travellers and the railroad employees. [*Applause.*]

Inasmuch as the Y. P. S. C. E. was the pioneer of all similar organizations and existed for eight years before any of the present societies, modelled on the same principle, were formed; inasmuch as it is today the only interdenominational society of the kind; and inasmuch as it demands no uniformity of creed or ritual, but insists only on supreme loyalty to Christ and entire allegiance to the church and denomination with which each society is connected:

Resolved, That, rejoicing in the fact that so many denominational societies have come into our fellowship on the basis of the prayer-meeting pledge and the consecration meeting, we cordially invite all societies on this basis to join our brotherhood by uniting with their own denominational name our own loved interdenominational title, — Christian Endeavor. [*Applause.*]

Resolved, That we emphasize the international feature of Christian Endeavor as illustrated by the world-round journey of the president of the United Society during the year, and now, at its close, by this first international convention held outside of the United States. [*Applause.*]

Resolved, That we recognize in the liquor traffic the chief evil of the times and chief obstacle to the advancement of a Christian civilization; that we condemn intemperance in every form; that we stand for the suppression of the saloons and the abolition of its power in the politics of our land as one of the first duties of American citizenship; and that we heartily commend all righteous agencies whose purpose is the protection of our home and of the true interest of humanity by the extermination of the liquor traffic. [*Applause.*]

Resolved, That we declare our allegiance to the sacred observance of Sunday; that we believe it to be one of the corner-stones of our civil and religious institutions, and that we will, as patriots and as Christians, do all in our power to guard its sanctity and preserve it from desecration. [*Applause.*]

Resolved, That as the representatives of a million and a half members of the Y. P. C. E. of America and the world, in Twelfth International Convention assembled in Montreal, we do hereby, in the name of God, in the interest of humanity, in behalf of integrity and of the rising young manhood and womanhood of the world, solemnly protest against the desecration of Sunday by the opening on that day of the Columbian Exposition, which is national and not local, and should, therefore, reflect the sentiments of the whole people. [*Applause.*]

Resolved, That we deplore the action of the majority of the local directory in this matter as contrary to the will of the people expressed through their representatives in Congress; as repugnant to common honesty, and a flagrant breach of good faith, the moral effects of which cannot fail to be harmful. [*Applause.*]

Resolved, That to such members of the national commission and local directory as have opposed this lamentable action, we tender our cordial approval and hearty thanks. [*Loud applause.*]

Resolved, That the local directory of the World's Fair have brought lasting disgrace upon what ought to be a glory, and against this we make our appeal to the highest of all tribunals, the public conscience. [*Applause.*]

Resolved, That with profound thanksgiving to God we recall the fact that during the past year 158,000 of our associate members have been won for Christ and united to the church, thus making the remarkable total of 430,000 conversions in the last four years. Truly may we say, "What hath God wrought?" and press forward with joy in renewed efforts to win the world for Christ. [*Loud applause.*]

Resolved, That we recognize the deep importance of the three suggestions for enlarged service made by our president in his annual address and would urge upon every society the careful consideration of these great subjects; namely, Christian citizenship, missionary benevolence, and Christian fellowship.

Resolved, That we express our hearty appreciation of the most efficient and more than ordinarily arduous services which Mr. Baer, our secretary, and Mr. Shaw, our treasurer, in the absence of President Clark, have rendered the cause of Christian Endeavor during the past year. [*Applause.*]

Resolved, That we express our gratitude to God for the providence that guided and guarded our loved President and Mrs. Clark, in their missionary Endeavor journey around the world and brought them back in safety and health to family and friends and the great work to which their lives are consecrated; that we rejoice in the vast impulse they have imparted to the missionary cause in the home society of Endeavor, in the good they have been permitted to do abroad in so many lands, in the cheer and hope they carried with them, and in the blessed results achieved in the furtherance of that sublime cause, in the brotherhood of man in Christ Jesus—the tie that shall yet bind a redeemed humanity in

" The parliament of nations, the federation of the world." [*Loud applause.*]

Amid great enthusiasm the resolutions were carried unanimously, while snowy handkerchiefs waved in the air. " Onward, Christian Soldiers " was then sung.

Rev. Dr. T. H. Lewis, of Westminster, Md., was then introduced by Dr. Clark. This was the signal for the Maryland delegation to rise and sing their state song, to the tune of " Maryland, my Maryland."

Every Man's Vocation a Call of God.

Sermon by Rev. T. H. Lewis, D.D., Pres. Western Maryland College, Westminster, Md.

TEXT. — Also I heard the voice of the Lord saying, Whom shall I send, and who will go for us? Then said I, Here am I: send me.—*Isa. 6 : 8.*

This familiar passage is associated in our minds with the sublimest conceptions. We remember it as part of that wonderful description Isaiah gives of his vision of the Lord of hosts when he was called to his life work.

But we must not allow this sublimity of phrase and picture to deprive us of the significance of the lesson this passage has for us. What gives greatest significance to this description of God is not, after all, its royal imagery, nor its majestic eloquence; it is the connection of the interests of humanity with a vision of God. God appeared to Isaiah precisely when Isaiah most needed God, and when Israel most needed Isaiah. And what God had to say to Isaiah he has at some time to say to every man.

Isaiah lived a truly royal life; he wrought out a call of truly royal significance; and whether the tradition that he was of royal seed be true or not, he will live in our memories as he was buried by his countrymen, with the kings.

But the secret of that life and power is no mystery. Here it is written out large for us. He made himself ready to be called of God, and when he was called he went. What he did every man may do and ought to do, and in doing it every man becomes of the seed royal. God had use for Isaiah as a prophet-statesman, and he called him to that office. Whether that office is higher or lower than the particular one He designs for us, I think we have no adequate means of determining. Nor do I think there is any force in the general impression that this call is a call into the ministry, and that God does not call men into all spheres of life as he calls them into the ministry. I am not sure that Isaiah was called into the ministry in our modern sense; but I am very sure that God has use for other men in this world besides ministers, and that when he wants men he calls them. I hope therefore to justify the use of this text to preach that every man's vocation is a call of God.

1. Life is divine: it is the gift of God; when God calls for it, therefore, he calls for his own. And as he has made all, it should occasion no surprise if he calls for all.

2. The choice of a vocation is the most important act of life, so far as that life belongs to this world. I cannot, therefore, believe that God would overlook it.

It is not only the young, who see all possibilities in a wise choice, to whom it is a great matter; but the oldest and the wisest in this audience will testify, as they look back upon life, that success and failure are bound up with this choice. To choose wisely is to secure success with easy effort and unlaborious strife; while no energy or perseverance seems sufficient to conquer the difficulties that spring up about an unwise choice.

But it is more than a question of success in getting rich or in getting famous. It is the tremendous question of living well, of living easily, of living right, rejoicing in life as a strong man to run a race. It is so great a question it seems to me, this question of getting started to live, that no gospel ought to be regarded complete which, after showing a man how to get religion, does not go on to show him how to use his religion while he lives in this world. For is there any vocation in life which any man has a right to be in which can mean any more or less to him than just this: to work out before his fellow-men the principles he holds as his religion? Choosing a vocation, then, is simply answering the question, How can I best use my religion? and therefore God is in that question. And much more; to speak within the limits of sober philosophy, human salvation is in that question. For to say that a man's vocation has nothing to do with his religion, or in other words, with his salvation, is the same thing as saying that a man can be saved without any reference to what he does.

3. It is impossible to choose a vocation outside the sphere of God's jurisdiction.

No fact is pressed upon our attention so often, and perhaps none is attended to so little, as the fact that God is always interposing in all the affairs of this world. God not only reigns, he rules. And he rules, not only in a general sense, "upholding all things by the word of his power," but he is actually present in the things themselves, permeating with his all-controlling will all history, politics, and civilization. He can use nature for this purpose, for "he maketh the clouds his chariot and rideth upon the wings of the wind." But he sends war and peace, he blows the sails of commerce, he guides the fingers of diplomacy, he whispers the secrets of inventions as truly as he sends the rain and the sunshine; and for the same reason, to reach and govern men.

Victor Hugo tells us in his dramatic way that Napoleon was invincible until the Almighty joined the coalition against him. And this was nearer the truth than the irreverent sarcasm of Napoleon himself that God was always on the side of the strongest battalions. Yet God *is* always on the side of some battalion; and not to believe this, not to believe in God directing men and events, sending forth and holding back the influences that shape history and save the world, is not to believe in God at all. "God is not the God of the dead, but of the living."

If we believe in such a God, why then should we not have a real faith also in his sending men into this or that vocation as it pleaseth him, to work out through them the history of the world as he has designed it? This is not fatalism; it is simply believing that if there is any one who has planned the history of this world — and see if you can help believing that? — then he would use the most effective means for realizing his plan. And if men, far more than all other forces combined, are the makers of history, then he would use men. And if history is shaped not by the few, but by all who labor at its mysterious loom, then he would send men into life everywhere and not only into those stations men might agree to call holy or distinguished.

Let us remember those who fell in the Wilderness because "they limited the Holy One of Israel." And let us remember that the omnipresence which the Bible teaches is not the presence of a ghost or an influence, but the presence of an Almighty Person. If I ascend into heaven, if I make my bed in hell, if I take the wings of the morning and dwell in the uttermost parts of the sea, "even there *shall thy hand lead me and thy right hand shall hold me.*" It is this doctrine of an energized omnipresence which men have recognized instinctively in designating their profession or business or manner of working, a vocation, that is, a calling. But who is there to call if God be left out? There is no power or authority in this universe great enough to call man, unless it be God. It is man's personal dignity as well as his longing that enables him to say, "Whom have I in heaven but thee?"

So I say the man who enters a profession or refuses to enter without reference to God and his call may designate himself by what name he will, but he is practically an atheist; for to him in the largest portion of his life, "there is no God."

4. This atheism in business is perhaps the most deadly assault against Christianity in our day, for it establishes selfishness as the supreme motive of work; and selfishness is antichrist.

You will find men belonging to societies holding Jesus Christ as their supreme Lord who practically refuse to allow any interference with them or with their schemes for six days of the week. On the seventh day they enter his house to listen to his instruction and to invoke his blessing, closing every prayer with a petition to "enter heaven at last," without any notion apparently that the way to heaven for every man lies through the work and experience of the coming six days.

No. Christ to them is the king of Sunday. They refer to him all Sunday questions, that is, questions of religious belief, of religious experience, and such conduct as involves principally questions of morals. But how small a part of life do such questions take up for most of us! May we not, without extravagance, say that the ordinary citizen does not know he has a creed unless some heresy gets noised abroad? May we not say that few persons refer to their religious experience in settling practical questions of business? And while I would not intimate that the ordinary citizen ignores moral principles in conduct, it will be granted that the ordinary citizen does not use unmixed moral principles in conduct to any large extent. But put them all together and take the sum out of the aggregate of life, and have you not left vastly more, as men count, than you have taken? Have you not left six days in the week? Have you not left that whole range of activities and interests called the business of life? Have you not, in fact, taken out just what you suppose God can be appeased with, and left everything that you really want until you have to die?

This is what I mean by saying that men are atheists in business, and that they make selfishness the supreme motive of work. So far from being regarded extravagant, it will strike most persons, I fear, as a truism. Men look for this sort of thing in business; and although they might object to calling it selfishness, yet that a man has the right to select what business he pleases and conduct it as he pleases so long as he violates no moral law — this is supposed to be conceded by all. But it is not conceded by Jesus Christ. Consider, I beg you, how grotesque this view of life becomes the moment we hold it up to the cross! In the light of that awful splendor how dare we talk of doing what we please or as we please?

Our theory of the world is that it is lost. As Christians we are associated to regenerate it. To this end we pray and preach and organize societies. But if there is anything true and vital in such a theory, why do we not take the most effective method of realizing it? Is the regeneration of the world so small a matter that we can afford to give six-sevenths of our time to something else? And if we are not here to regenerate the world by our work as well as by our prayers, why do we not stop claiming to be *servants* of Christ and only claim to be what we really are, worshippers at his altar?

God's condemnation of this folly, this crime of selfishness, is written on every page of his Word and in every act of his blessed Son. But in our day he is writing sentence against it in other and unexpected places. Through the bitter cry of the wretched he is voicing an indictment against a selfish social system and religious forms that support such a system. Men are becoming infuriated through a long oppression, and their fury makes them blind and wicked, but He who " maketh the wrath of man to praise him" will not abate the fury nor deliver us from the peril of this wickedness until the wrong is righted,

> " And man to man the world o'er
> Shall brothers be and a' that."

We have in our holy religion the beautiful principle that " the strong ought to bear the infirmities of the weak," and God, through his oppressed, is bringing against us the serious indictment that we conduct our business on the principle of the survival of the fittest, a principle of brutes and savages. We drive the weak to the wall by our superior strength and shrewdness; we do this for six days and then offer them on the seventh some platitudes on resignation. We show them for six days a business with no religion in it and then expect to charm them on the seventh by a religion with no business in it. But God has put the everlasting arms under this "submerged tenth" and it shall not sink down to hell for all the maledictions of selfish men.

What will convert us from our egregious folly? Must God send a moral earthquake to overturn our whole social system before we will learn that we cannot rise by putting men under our feet? Are we so stupid that we cannot see that we shall never regenerate the world nor save our own souls by giving more money or more churches or more missionaries, but only when we follow the noble Macedonians " who first gave their own selves to the Lord"? Until we can believe and act as if we believed that God sends forth every workman as truly as he sends the preacher, and that every man who works right works for God first and for his fellow-men next and for himself last of all; until, in fine, we abandon our atheism in business we will never reach the masses. And God forbid we should! for we would but petrify them into our own indifference and selfishness. " Therefore if thou bring thy gift to the altar and there rememberest that thy brother hath ought against thee: leave there thy gift before the altar and go thy way; first be reconciled to thy brother, and then come and offer thy gift."

5. The theory that every man's vocation is a call of God is the divine theory of life and will therefore teach us the true idea of consecration.

Men used to think they consecrated themselves to God by hiding themselves in the forest or shutting themselves up in a cell. And I fear we still fritter away the meaning of this great word until we have nothing left but an ideal hung in the air or an emotion flowing out at the eyes.

Consecration as frequently used in the Old Testament means literally, " to fill one's hands." And certainly this is what, above all other things, it ought to mean in these New Testament times. These are the times that quiver with flesh-and-blood questions, and we must consecrate ourselves to what is here and not to what we suppose is in heaven. We must " fill our hands " to God in this world if we do it at all; and that is the meaning of his call.

. Do you remember the call of Bezaleel? " See," said God to Moses, " I have called him by name and I have filled him with the spirit of God in wisdom, and in understanding and in knowledge " —Well, what for? —" to devise cunning works, to work in gold and in silver and in brass." Do you say that this was a call to build his tabernacle? But I tell you God is building a far more glorious tabernacle than Moses reared in the Wilderness. " The tabernacle of God is with men." On the bright plains of this nineteenth century he is building it, and "they bring the gold of the nations into it." Its walls are salvation and its gates praise; it is the temple of redeemed humanity, and it is built out of the hopes and prayers and labors of God's faithful servants. And still he is calling, " Whom shall I send and who will go for us?" " Who will build for me these walls? Who will bring his wisdom or his genius or his wealth and consecrate these to rear up this tabernacle of humanity ?" O, that we had the ambition to reach up to this great consecration! A consecration like that of Aaron whom Moses anointed " with the blood upon the tip of his right ear, and upon the thumb of his right hand and upon the great toe of his right foot." A consecration that leaves no organ nor faculty for the service of the devil; a consecration that liberates every power and makes every nerve tingle with the fire taken from off the altar. O, that we would cease the folly of sighing for some one to come to us from afar and bring us a consecration ready made; and look right at our hands which are to work out for us the only consecration we shall ever know in doing for God whatever we do and whatever is to be done for the helpfulness of man.

6. This theory defines the true dignity of labor; it is the divinity of labor.

Why is it that to some men life seems not worth living? Why is it that work seems so hard and the distribution of rewards so unfair and God so altogether unlovely? Why is it that some men cry out so fiercely for the dignity and rights of labor? Do they see more than other men? Nay, rather they see less. They have left out of their creed the key to the whole riddle of life to the workingman. They have been taught the shibboleth of political parties and the mottoes of unions and fraternities; but the one thing yet unlearned is the creed of the man who has been with Jesus and learned of him to say, "I believe in the divinity of labor." It makes all the difference between a curse and a blessing whether we believe labor is from the devil or from God; whether we believe the man who works is a slave or a son, the lawful seed of Him who made the world and the brother of Jesus the carpenter.

I remember well how disappointing was my first view of Italy. I had heard of Italy as the artist's paradise, the land of sunny skies and vine-clad hills. I had heard that they who love the beautiful do there drink in perpetual delights and revel in all the harmonies of nature and art. But when I landed at Brindisi I saw none of these. I saw instead only a straggling town with narrow, crooked streets whose sombre houses shut out all beauty of sky and hill; and I heard only the discord of unfamiliar voices speaking an unknown language. But what then? I had not seen it all. Wandering along those streets I came presently to the open country; I ascended a gentle hill, and there I saw what I shall bless God forever that he opened to my eyes, — an unclouded sunset in an Italian sky. I cannot describe it to you. I never put it into words, but I know as I stood there in the bewildering beauty of that sky, I forgot Brindisi, I forgot all the ugliness I had ever seen and all the discord I had ever heard, and all the hate I had ever felt. The radiant splendors from above fell over the earth, fell over my life, and kissed every visible thing and every remembered thing into transcendent glory.

So, I think I know men who look at their work as I first looked at Italy, they see no sky. They see the curse; they feel the sweat; they hear the stern voice of hunger driving them forth to daily tasks, and their eyes are fastened sternly on the ground and "they groan, being burdened." But O, my brothers, lift up your eyes to see also the sky! There is a glory shining there which will fall on your labors if you will bring them out from the close wall of your covetousness and selfishness; and its splendors will transfigure your despised tasks and make your common life seem a piece of the divine. Have you not heard it — "Whatsoever ye do, do all to the glory of God?" There is the powerful alchemy of the Gospel which sublimates drudgery.

> " A servant with this clause
> Makes drudgery divine.
> Who sweeps a house as for thy laws
> Makes that and the action fine."

It is the privilege therefore of every true believer of the Gospel to say, I believe in the divinity of labor. I believe, that what I do for the love of God is godly, whether I do it on Sunday or Monday. I believe that a life on the cross may be as precious in God's sight as a death on the cross. I believe that the spirit, the motive, of my work consecrates me and glorifies my work

> " Makes that and the action fine."

And so there comes a great liberty. I am no longer the slave to times nor a cringing beggar to circumstances. Up from all sordid things my heart swells with the joy of deliverance and I cry out with the gladness of a new discovery, "O Lord, truly I am thy servant; I am thy servant and the son of thy hand-maid; thou hast loosed my bonds."

My brothers, the time has come for the last word of this great and interesting convention to be spoken. You have done me great honor in putting me in this place, but not to me belongs the supreme honor of the final word. God has spoken many times and in diverse portions since we assembled, but even he does not wish to speak the last word. It is you who must speak it. As you look out over the fields of human endeavor where men are struggling for self, O, that you may hear His voice calling you to go forth to make them all fields of Christian Endeavor and say, as the final, supreme word of the convention, "Here am I, send me."

At the conclusion of the sermon the grand old hymn "All Hail the Power of Jesus' Name" was once more sung, after which Dr. Clark stated the facts in connection with the sad and sudden death of Mr. J. R. Rogers, a member of the reception committee, and announced that for the first time in the history of these conventions a collection would be taken up, — a collection for the benefit of the family of the deceased. Rev. Dr. Beckley, of Philadelphia, first led in prayer, remembering the afflicted and destitute family, after which the collection was taken.

The hymn "Do not Pass me by" was then sung, after which Dr. Clark read telegrams of greeting from New South Wales, Paris, South Africa, Spain, Madagascar, India, Victoria, and Japan.

DR. CLARK: Let me now say one or two things that are on my mind. Amendments to the resolutions have been sent up to the effect that some desire to give most hearty thanks to those who were in a general way mentioned but could not all be specified. Of course, it was understood by all Endeavorers that they were included, and most heartily. To the leaders of our singing, Mr. Lindsay, Mr. Coates, the cornetists, the Park Sisters, and Mr. Burleigh, the choirs, the reception committee, whose white caps greeted us a hundred miles away from Montreal [*applause*], and all those who in any way and every way have contributed so much to the success of this splendid convention we give to you from the bottom of our hearts our earnest thanks.

And now, my friends, we come to this supreme hour to which we have been looking forward through all the days of this convention. We are all in the midst of it; our sermon brought us to it; our consecration offering brought us further into the heart of this hour. As we begin to-night, there are some things that come to me personally. I feel almost as though this soil of Canada, on which we are today met for the first time in international convention, was sacred soil to me: for here, — though my parents were of Massachusetts stock for many generations, — I was born; and here, a hundred miles to the north, rests the body of my dear mother, who died when I was a little boy, and two brothers and sisters lie in the same cemetery with her. Seventy-five miles to the east, on the banks of the mighty St. Lawrence, lies the body of my father, who died when I was but two years old. You cannot wonder when I say that I feel that this is sacred soil to me; and I have seemed to feel a pathos which has not been felt in any other convention. But these are only personal matters; they are scarcely worth taking your time, perhaps. I am sure, however, we have come tonight into the presence of a great cloud of witnesses. Oh, how many there are! The fathers and mothers, the brothers and sisters, the dear ones of this mighty multitude, — are they not all around us, and is not our Father over all, and our Lord Jesus Christ, our elder brother, interested in us and watching over us? We are, indeed, on sacred soil wherever we are in such a meeting as this. Nothing can be so sacred as the place where we renew our consecration vows to God, and that is what we are about to do in no lengthy words, in a very few sentences, but one thing we will remember, that every word that shall be spoken shall be sincere. O brothers and sisters in Christian Endeavor, speak out of your hearts tonight! That is all that God wants — sincere, true consecration; whether it is a verse of a hymn, a Scripture passage, a sentence of your own, speak it out of your hearts and God will hear it.

I particularly request that there be no applause. We have come to such a sacred moment that we can best show our appreciation of what is said by perfect stillness. That will show that we feel that we are in the presence of Almighty God.

And now, my friends, will you all bow your heads in a silent consecration prayer?

The congregation then remained in silent prayer for a moment, and afterwards, with bowed heads, sang, very impressively, "Just as I am, without one plea." Then Mr. W. H. Pennell led in the Lord's Prayer, the congregation repeating. "Nearer, my God, to Thee" was then sung.

In response to Dr. Clark's request, all the pastors in the audience arose and gave as their word of testimony, "Let a man so account of us as of the ministers of Christ and stewards of the mysteries of God." The Sunday-school teachers in the audience arose and repeated these words : "Whoso shall receive one such little child in my name, receiveth me." The lookout committees repeated the following after Dr. Clark : "Looking unto Jesus, the author and finisher of our faith, may he lead us to look out for the souls of others." The prayer-meeting committees repeated after Dr. Clark the following short sentence : "Lord, teach us to pray." The missionary committee followed Dr. Clark with these words : "I must preach the kingdom of God to other cities also, for therefore am I sent." The music committees arose and repeated, at Dr. Clark's suggestion, "I will sing with the spirit, and I will sing with the understanding." Dr. Clark then requested that the members of all other committees stand and repeat with him the following : "With goodwill doing service, as to the Lord and not to men."

The roll call of the states came next. Each delegation, as its name was called, arose and repeated some words of consecration or sang a verse of a hymn. The responses were as follows : —

ALABAMA : "Who shall separate us from the love of Christ? Shall tribulation, or distress, or persecution. or famine, or nakedness, or peril, or sword? Nay in all these things we are more than conquerors through him that loved us." (Rom. 8 : 35, 37.)

ARKANSAS : We are for Christ, God, home, and every land.

CALIFORNIA : Hymn, "My faith looks up to Thee." Prayer ; "O Lord, our Heavenly Father, we pray thy blessing upon those whom we have left behind, who have been deprived of the wonderful blessings of this convention, and we pray thee that thou wilt give us of thy spirit that we may go back to California and pave the way for '95. Hear us for Jesus sake, Amen."

DR. CLARK : We will all re-echo that prayer thousands of times between now and '95, that the way may be ready, and that God's spirit may bless that convention more than any that have preceded.

COLORADO: Hymn, "Just as I am."

CONNECTICUT: Hymn, "Nearer my God to Thee."

DELAWARE: "They that wait upon the Lord shall renew their strength: they shall mount up with wings as eagles; they shall run and not be weary; they shall walk and not faint." (Isa. 40:31.)

DISTRICT OF COLUMBIA: "I am the vine, ye are the branches: he that abideth," etc. (Jno. 15:5.) Hymn, "Am I a Soldier of the Cross."

FLORIDA: "Bless the Lord, O my soul: and all that is within me, bless his holy name." (Ps. 103:1.)

GEORGIA: "This one thing I do; forgetting the things which are behind," etc. (Phil. 3:13.)

IDAHO: "We are troubled on every side, yet not distressed; we are perplexed, but not in dispair." (2 Cor. 4:8.)

ILLINOIS: State hymn, "Glory, glory, hallelujah."

INDIANA: State hymn to the tune, "Tramp, tramp, tramp, the boys are marching."

IOWA: Hymn, "Stand up for Jesus." "God forbid that I should glory save in the cross of Jesus Christ." (Gal. 6:14.)

KANSAS: Hymn, "Nearer, my God, to Thee."

Rev. Dr. French, of New Jersey, then led in a prayer of special thanksgiving to God for the blessings of the great convention with which God had so favored us.

MANITOBA: Lord, wherever we are called in the name of our God, we shall set up our banners.

DR. CLARK: And now from the Province which has so hospitably welcomed us. What does Quebec say to us as its consecration message?

QUEBEC: Quebec for Christ. Hymn, "Alas and did my Saviour bleed."

MARITIME PROVINCES: "Be ye stedfast, unmovable, always abounding in the work of the Lord," etc. (1 Cor. 15:58.) Hymn, "To the work, to the work."

ONTARIO: "Forgetting those things that are behind, and reaching forth into those things that are before, we press," etc. (Phil. 3:13.) Hymn, "Nearer, my God, to Thee."

KENTUCKY: "Therefore, they that were scattered abroad went everywhere preaching the Word." (Acts 8:4.) Hymn, "Speed Away."

LOUISIANA: "Verily, verily, I say unto you the hour is coming," etc. (Jno. 5:25.)

MAINE: Hymn, "Draw me nearer, blessed Lord."

MARYLAND: "Hear my prayer, O Lord, give ear to my supplications; in thy faithfulness," etc. (Ps. 143:1-8-10.) Hymn, "I am trusting thee, Lord Jesus."

MASSACHUSETTS: State Hymn, to the tune of "Onward, Christian Soldiers."

MICHIGAN: "Create in me a clean heart, O God, and renew a right spirit," etc. (Ps. 51:10-13.)

MINNESOTA: "Stand fast therefore in the liberty wherewith Christ hath made us free." (Gal. 5:1.)

MISSOURI: Hymn, "The half has never yet been told."

NEBRASKA: We will count not our lives dear unto ourselves.

NEW HAMPSHIRE: Hymn, "All other ground is sinking sand."

NEW JERSEY: "Trusting in the Lord Jesus Christ for strength, I promise him,—[singing] 'I will do what you want me to do, Lord.'"

NEW MEXICO: "We will serve the Lord with gladness." Thanks be unto God, and may he give us New Mexico for Christ.

DR. CLARK: We are thinking not only of those who are here tonight, but of the tens of thousands who could not be here, the friends who are holding their meetings while we are holding ours, and praying for us. They are as near God as we are, and I think that as our thoughts turn to them our prayers might rise for them most appropriately.

Rev. C. A. Dickinson, of Boston, then led in a very brief prayer for the Christian Endeavorers at home who could not come to the convention.

NEW YORK: "If ye abide in me and my word in you," etc. (Jno. 15:7.) Hymn, "Draw me nearer, blessed Lord."

NORTH DAKOTA: "I beseech you, brethen, by the mercies of God that ye present your bodies," etc. (Rom. 12: 1.)

DR. CLARK: Next year we go to Ohio; this year Ohio comes to us and brings us her message.

OHIO: "Let us not be weary in well-doing," etc. (Gal. 6:9.)

OKLAHOMA: "The harvest truly is great, but the laborers are few." (Luke 10:2.)

OREGON AND WASHINGTON: Behold thy servants are ready to do whatsoever our Lord, the King, shall appoint.

PENNSYLVANIA: Pennsylvania for Christ. Hymn, "Blessed assurance, Jesus is mine."

RHODE ISLAND: "Whatsoever you do in word or in deed, do all in the name of the Lord Jesus." (Col. 3:17.)

SOUTH CAROLINA: "I will lift up my eyes unto the hills from whence cometh my help." (Ps. 121:1.) Hymn to the tune, "True hearted, whole hearted."

SOUTH DAKOTA: A poem of consecration.

TENNESSEE: Our State motto, "At least one soul for Christ." Hymn, "Where he leads us we will follow."

TEXAS: "Wherefore seeing we also are compassed about with so great a cloud of witnesses," etc. (Heb. 12:1.)

UTAH: Utah wants to thank God for the great things that he has been doing for her during the past year, and she would humbly consecrate herself tonight to him who is able to cleanse from all sin.

VERMONT: "This one thing I do: I press forward," etc. (Phil. 3:13, 14.) Hymn, "True hearted, whole hearted."

VIRGINIA: Our motto is, "Christ for the Old Dominion, and the Old Dominion for Christ." "We know in whom we have believed, and are persuaded," etc. (2 Tim. 1:12.)

IRELAND: On the Irish flag are found these words, "God save Ireland." "We know in whom we have believed," etc. (2 Tim. 1:12.) Christ for Ireland, and Ireland for Christ.

SCOTLAND: "God be merciful unto us, and bless us, and cause his face to shine upon us."

FRANCE: "So teach us to number our days that we may apply our hearts unto wisdom." (Ps. 90:12.) Hymn, "Throw out the Life-line."

TURKEY: "Rejoicing in hope, patient in tribulation," etc. (Rom. 12:12.) The representative from Turkey sang "We praise Thee, O God," in his native language, the audience joining in the chorus.

The Endeavorers from Queensland, Australia, sent a cablegram which read as follows:—

"The Queensland Endeavorers send affectionate greetings. 'Peace be to the brethren, and love from God, our Father and the Lord Jesus Christ.' Our confidence in renewing our consecration is, 'The Lord has spoken, and shall He not make it good?' (Num. 23:19.)"

The message sent from India was as follows:—

"'Fear not, little flock, for it is your Father's good pleasure to give you the kingdom.' (Luke 12:32.) Do not forget your boys across the sea; pray for us."

JAPAN: For Christ and Japan we will labor with all our powers. Who will come and help us?

AFRICA: The down-trodden and oppressed of ages has heard the voice, saying, "Come unto me, all ye that labor," etc.
CAPE COLONY: We consecrate ourselves to the blessed God. "The Lord shall increase you more and more, you and your children." (Ps. 115 : 14.)
CHINA: "Behold, ye that have come from afar," etc.

Dr. Clark then called upon Miss Jones, the superintendent of the Floating Societies, for a word.

FLOATING SOCIETIES: "I can do all things through Christ that strengtheneth me," is the favorite verse of our sailor brothers.

The congregation then sang, at her request, "Jesus, Lover of my Soul."

DR. CLARK: There are societies in some of our reformatories and prisons. One message has come from our brothers in the State's prison of Wisconsin, where for some years there has been an active Endeavor Society, and the chaplain of the Massachusetts reformatory will say a word for this work.
REV. MR. BATT: There are noble Christian Endeavorers sometimes in the prisons. I think their wish is tonight to repeat here the verse, "Brethren pray for us; the spirit truly is willing but the flesh is weak." Please sing one verse of "Throw out the Life-line."
DR. CLARK: In a moment of silent prayer, let us remember such brethren, and also the other societies in strange places, in the hospitals, among the traveling men, among the police.

The congregation then bowed their heads in a moment of silent prayer.

WEST VIRGINIA: The Y. P. S. C. E's. in the picturesque mountains and beautiful valleys of West Virginia are consecrated to Christ and the church. Our numbers are not many, but our aim is like our mountains, high; our faith is like our hills and rocks, strong; and as our many streams receive their supply from the hills, so we depend for our supply upon the grace of God. Hymn, "Not to the strong is the battle."
WISCONSIN: Last but not least, Wisconsin's 25,000 Endeavorers speak through us this sentiment, "Blessed are they that keep his testimonies and that seek him with the whole heart." (Ps. 119:2.) Hymn, "Hear us, O Saviour, while we pray."
BRITISH COLUMBIA: "Come, get you down, for the wickedness is great," etc.

This concluded the responses from the delegations. Dr. Clark then called upon all in the audience to recite together after him the following words : —

> "I have not much to give thee, Lord,
>   For that great love that may be mine;
> I have not much to give thee, Lord,
>   But all I have is thine."

The audience rose and joined in this response, and then, with hands uplifted, all pledged themselves that they would endeavor to work still more for their Master during the coming year.

Then came the singing of the parting hymn, "God be with you till we meet again." All joined in repeating, with bowed heads, the Mizpah benediction, "The Lord watch between me and thee when we are absent one from another," and Dr. Clark pronounced the Twelfth International Christian Endeavor Convention adjourned.

During the evening there was considerable noise out in the adjacent streets, and this fact diminished to some extent the spiritual impressiveness of the meeting. Nothing, however, occurred to interfere with the proceedings in the least. The delegates left the hall singing familiar hymns, and when they reached the street they found an immense crowd, to be sure, but a strong force of policemen overawed any who felt inclined to make a disturbance. The delegates also were surprised to find the "White Necktie Brigade" drawn up in file, ready to escort them home. This was an amusing feature of the evening's occurrences. During the afternoon, knowing that the hoodlum element meditated making a disturbance, a large number of young men belonging to various local volunteer regiments got together and arranged a plan to prevent disturbance. Just before the hour for the evening service, they quietly gathered on Notre Dame Street, not far from the hall, to the number of 1,000 or more. Taking for their uniform simply a white handkerchief tied about the neck, they waited until the services had begun, and then they marched in solid ranks right through the crowd, singing "Onward, Christian Soldiers." Their singing was not quite as correct as that of the delegates, but they were sincere in their purpose to overawe the mob. They succeeded perfectly. They marched around the block in which the Drill Hall is situated, singing marching tunes, and although they were alternately cheered and hissed, they continued in their course until the meeting was over. When the stream of delegates began to pour forth, they drew up in line in front of the hall, and then escorted the delegates away from the proximity of the crowd. Then they marched to the Windsor Hotel and greeted the delegates quartered there, Dr. Clark and Mr. Boynton making brief speeches in response. Afterwards they visited the St. James, Queen's, Balmoral, and St. Lawrence hotels, where a similar program was gone through with. At no time during the evening was the situation on the street a serious one, although the excitement at times was great. The statement of the chief of police was verified. The crowd was a cowardly one, and the police easily kept them in order. Not a few of the delegates were astounded to read in the Eastern papers after they left the city the next day that they had been in peril of their lives. There was at no time the least shadow of such a danger. On the other hand, it was the universal impression that the convention had proved to be one of the best and most delightful yet held in the history of the Christian Endeavor movement.

ST. JAMES METHODIST CHURCH.

In many ways the service at this church was the most delightful and the most spiritually impressive of all the closing services. It was known that Mr. Mills, the evangelist, who was to have preached the sermon and had charge of the consecration meeting in the tent, would preach here, and consequently, long before the hour for beginning the service, the audience began to assemble. Soon the building was packed, upstairs and down, every available space being occupied. The aisles, even, were crowded, many of the delegates sitting on the floor. More than 1,000 people were turned away, not being able to squeeze in beyond the outside doors. On the platform were seated, besides Mr. Mills, Secretary Baer, Bishop Arnett, Dr. Rondthaler, Missionary Gilbert Reid, Rev. C. E. Eberman, who led the singing, and many others.

The opening song service was profoundly impressive. Every one sang ; and with such an immense audience, packed so closely together, led by the great organ, Mr. Burleigh's cornet, and the strong voice of Mr. Eberman, it was one of the most striking features of the whole convention. The volume of song on such a chorus as " This is my story, this is my song " was grand beyond description.

First came the Rogers subscription. Mr. Baer stated the circumstances of the case once more and then said : —

We thought that in this case we would do away with all rules and regulations with regard to taking up a collection at these conventions, and at our board of trustees' meeting it was decided that on the night of our consecration service we would make an offering to God for the benefit of this family. That young man, Mr. Rogers, has passed to the better land and I believe is having a part in this service as much as you and I are. I believe, also, there are a multitude of others with him who are interested in us. I believe there is a little boy there who, not more than three or four months ago, passed away from my home out of my arms back to the dear Father who gave him to me; and I always think and delight to believe that he follows me from Boston wherever I go, and tonight it may be that with Mr. Rogers he sees that we here are attempting to carry on God's work while they are doing his bidding there, more highly honored than we could possibly be here.

Mr. Baer then asked for 50 or 75 volunteer ushers to take their hats and collect the offering. This was done at once, while prayer was offered in behalf of the afflicted family by Rev. H. W. Sherwood, and the hymn "Nearer, my God, to Thee " was sung. Then the hats were passed in over the heads of the audience, where they were emptied in a pile on the floor. When all were in, Mr. Baer announced that enough money had been received to almost fill a half-bushel measure.

After singing the hymn " Holy Spirit, Teacher Thou," Mr. Baer introduced Rev. B. Fay Mills, who spoke as follows : —

Sermon by Rev. B. Fay Mills.

There is no need for any apology when I say to you that the text of the sermon this evening is identical with the one which was selected by my friend of early years and brother, Rev. Dr. Chapman, in preaching one of the opening sermons of this convention, which was delivered in this church. In fact, that is one of the reasons why I have chosen this text, because I have felt that it could not be too greatly emphasized and that it suggested to us the great theme of themes which should concern our thought in this age and in the closing hour of this convention.

The text you will find in the nineteenth chapter of Acts and a portion of the second verse : " He said unto them, have ye received the Holy Ghost since ye believed ? "

We read that while Apollos was at Corinth, Paul, having passed through the upper coasts, came to Ephesus, and there he found certain disciples. This man Apollos was one of the converts of John the Baptist, and for a long time after Jesus had come, he went on preaching as John the Baptist had preached, without knowing that the Messiah of whom John had spoken was identical with Jesus of Nazareth. He made some converts who were similar to those that had been made by John the Baptist. After a time, Apollos, being in a certain city, was taken by two people who were well instructed, and caused to see Jesus as the Messiah. From that time his message was changed from one merely of repentence and prophecy. But Paul found at Ephesus some disciples of Apollos, who had not yet learned the full Gospel concerning Jesus Christ and the descent of the Holy Ghost. This descent of the Holy Ghost had been the greatest event that the world had ever known ; and the one question which would be most naturally asked when the disciples met men and found that they had been disciples of John the Baptist, or of Apollos, was the question, " Have you received the Holy Ghost ? " It meant more to them than did the revelation of God through the ancient prophets ; it meant more than did the coming of the Lord Jesus Christ ; it meant that which should make real to them all that had gone before in God's great plan. It was the question of questions in the early days : " Have you received the Holy Ghost ? "

Now we have a very shrewd adversary, and he takes great pains to conceal the greatest doctrines that might bring us into likeness with Jesus Christ, and this is one of them. This is the doctrine of doctrines of the Church of God. This is the surpassing culmination of all that has occurred in God's dealings with men — the giving of the Holy Ghost and the receiving, on the part of the disciples, the Spirit of God. And the adversary has concealed this doctrine. How little we hear of the Holy Spirit in sermons and in testimony, when it is the one great fact of facts and theory of theories and power of powers that the Church of God may, if it will, be filled with the Holy Ghost. The great adversary, when he cannot conceal a doctrine, endeavors to confuse men's minds concerning it in its simplicity ; for God's doctrines are always simple, so far as we need to know them for any present duty or any emergency. I think this doctrine of the Holy Spirit has been confused in the minds of some people in two ways. Sometimes men have thought that the Holy Spirit came into existence after the resurrection of Jesus. I have recently read a treatise which said that the Holy Spirit did not exist until after the ascension of Jesus, and that he could not have been in the world until Jesus had ascended and sent him forth. I do not believe that. I believe that he deserved the title that has been given to him, of the Eternal Spirit of God, and I believe that the Holy Spirit has always been in the world. We read of men in the Old Testament, that they were filled with the Holy Spirit, that they were baptized with the Holy Ghost. Even the Old Testament, itself, stands as a perpetual witness to this truth, for the very men that wrote it were " men who wrote as they were moved by the Holy Ghost."

And then, in the second place, it has sometimes seemed to me that there has been confusion concerning the Holy Spirit in trying to make the doctrines about him simple. There are some people who would not be satisfied unless they could accurately distinguish in every respect concerning what they call the offices of God the Father, God the Son, and of God the Holy Ghost. I do not believe that this Word of God makes any such distinction. I do believe that the Holy Spirit and the Son of God and the Eternal Father are all said to be the creator and redeemer and regenerator and sanctifier of the children of God.

There is nothing in this Word of God that is said of God the Father, or God the Son, in any important sense, that is not also said concerning the Holy Ghost ; and I believe that when we receive the Holy Ghost we are receiving, not one little degree or manifestation of God, but all that there is of God, the Father and the Son, making real to us the eternal truth — God himself in human life.

Now I am not even going to suggest the question, except in this incidental way, whether the reception of the Holy Ghost by a child of God is what some of our friends call a second blessing or not. I do not regard that as an important question. I have never known a person who received the fulness of the Holy Ghost at the time of his conversion, and yet I believe that that might be a possible thing. I think that a man in the very act of believing in Jesus Christ might be baptized by the Holy Ghost as some people think that Cornelius was, while others think that Cornelius was a believer before Peter came to bring him a message concerning the Holy Spirit. I do not care about that; you need not care about that; for the one question is not whether it be the first or second or twentieth blessing,— the one great question is, " Have you received the Holy Ghost? " and is all the fulness of the life of God filling your soul tonight in this mighty manifestation of God's wisdom and power that has been given to transform us all into the likeness of Jesus Christ?

And yet, while I believe that the Holy Spirit has been always in the world and that all of God is contained in him, I do believe that the revelation of God, the Spirit, has been especially made for this dispensation. There was a time when God did seem to deal with those who knew him as a father with his child. He does that today; He has never ceased doing it. But there was added to that revelation the revelation of the eternal Son of God, the Lamb slain from the foundation of the world, and that knowledge has never been taken from us, and we have, in all its fulness today, all that was meant by the coming and the death and the resurrection of our Lord Jesus Christ. But I do believe that we have, in the fulness of the Holy Ghost, what our fathers never had — that which makes the Kingdom of God possible by the manifestation of God in his fulness in the individual life.

This marvelous manifestation of God is called by a multitude of names: The Spirit of Promise, the Spirit of Adoption and Sonship, the Spirit of Knowledge and Prophecy and Revelation and Understanding and Wisdom and Counsel, the Spirit of Truth, the Spirit of the Fear of the Lord, the Spirit of Meekness, the Spirit of Faith, the Spirit of Power, the Spirit of a Sound Mind, the Power of the Highest. He is also called the Spirit of Grace, the Spirit of Love, the Spirit of Might, the Spirit of Burning, the Spirit of Glory and the Spirit of Judgment. It is all summed up in the word that calls him the Spirit of Christ. Nay, more, he has one name for himself, that great name " Paraclete," which literally interpreted means, " The one called upon," the one to be called upon all through life. One of our most eminent theological professors has said, " If we were to try to give in English an accurate translation of that word Paraclete, which is translated Comforter in our ordinary translation, it would take twelve of our greatest and strongest English words to begin to indicate what the Spirit of God was meant to be in that one word Paraclete."

But there is something more than that; for God gives us fair play for the thoughts and the imagination of the heart concerning this manifestation of the Holy Ghost. He not only defines him in such a fashion as I have suggested, but he gives us the greatest emblems that can be conceived of by the human mind and uses these as pictures of the Holy Ghost. The ancients, as you know, divided all things that exist into what they called the four elements: earth, air, water and fire. The Spirit of God is known by these last three names. He is never called the earth, because the earth as it is, is dull, dead, heavy, immovable. The Spirit of God is called the air, — that is the meaning of the word spirit, — air, breath, wind. He is also called water, as you know, being represented under the figure of a well, a river, a flood, or the ocean. And you know also that he is represented in his culminating manifestation as fire.

He is represented as the air because he is universal. "Whither shall I go from thy spirit?" Neither water nor fire is universal, but air is. Air is necessary to our self-preservation,— unfailing, inexhaustible, and free. Men sell the earth. They carve it up in little pieces and sell it to their fellows. They store up the fountains of pure water and sell that to their fellow-men. Men even sell heat and fire in its various forms, applying it for purposes of power. But they never sell the air. All that a man needs, in order to enjoy the air, is to fulfil the conditions — to open his mouth and let it come in. God's air belongs to you as much as to the king upon his throne. It is universal, necessary, preservative, unfailing, inexhaustible, and free to all who will have it. Like this is the Spirit of God.

And then I am glad he is called also water, because water has some characteristics that air has not. It is refreshing, restorative, healing, cleansing, vitalizing. What would the world be without water? I remember, in my recent trip through California, that I was disappointed when I came to Southern California,—if any of my Southern Californian friends are here, whom I dearly love, I hope they will forgive me. One brother who was always praising northern California said: "You will be disappointed when you go down south; there is not much there except the climate." I did find a great deal besides the climate, but when I first came to Southern California I saw only a desert. There was a marvelous climate there indeed, and the sun seemed to shine perpetually, and there were flowers blooming in little cultivated spots, but I wondered where were the great orchards and vineyards about which we hear so much. As we travelled on through this desert I looked at the great barren rock-ribbed mountains and across the plains of sand, and I said to myself, "How can there be any fertility there?" But even as I looked, just as straight as though I was looking along a straight wall, in one second the train passed from what seemed to be the most barren spot on earth into the most fertile gardens that exist on the planet. I looked out and saw all the glory of God's world at its best, producing the most luxurious vegetation and fruits of which it is capable. What made the difference? Only this. One spot received the water which ran down from the mountains where it had been stored up and the other spot did not. And there is all that difference in the lives of men. Here is a man whose life is barren, without seemingly any hope or possibility of being anything or having anything or doing anything until he knows the floods of redeeming grace in the manifest power of the Holy Ghost. There is air for everybody and God's water that the barren desert may be turned into a fruitful plain.

And then I thank God for this emblem of fire, because there are some things represented by fire that are not represented by air or water. Fire warms us, enlivens us, regenerates us. All the life of the budding spring-time and the glow of summer comes from the fire. The winter binds it up and seems to hold all the forces of life in check; and then when the sun comes, the blazing fire of God from heaven reaches down into the plant life, burns out the impurity, quickens it, and awakens it. All regeneration comes by the power of fire— God's holy fire in the manifestation of the Holy Ghost, the purifying fire, the transforming fire. I came across some words of a former resident of this city the other day that stirred me very deeply. Dr. Monro Gibson says: "What is fire? It is the combination of an invisible, impalpable, ethereal element, with some grosser substance. Take, for example, the familiar case of coal, which is dull, heavy, hard, dead, emphatically of the earth earthy, until this wonderful ethereal element combines with it. Then it lives, it glows, it sparkles, it developes latent power in the most wonderful manner. It drives engines, sets factories to work, runs farms, does the work of a thousand men or horses, and then ascends into the unseen, claiming no credit for itself, only remembered by what it has done. So is every one that is touched by the heavenly flame of the Spirit of God, every one who truly and fully receives the baptism of fire."

Now I believe that in every life that has received the Holy Ghost in the Gospel sense, there are five results that will be made manifest. I might say six results, except that one of them would not be appropriate in connection with this text. Before I mention these five results of the receiving of the Holy Ghost by the believer let me ask this preliminary question: Have you been born of the Holy Spirit? "Except a man be born of the Spirit he cannot see the Kingdom of God;" and if there is any thought that we need to emphasize today it is that there is no life created without life and that there is no Christian life without the Holy Ghost. Unless a man can truly say that "old things have passed away and all things are become new," unless he knows that the Holy Spirit has touched him and renewed him and made him a new creature in Jesus Christ; that man has not come where this question might properly be asked him, " Have you received the Holy Ghost?" Are you conscious tonight that you have become a new creature, that you are born, not by the will of man, nor by the will of the flesh, but of God, by the action on your soul, transforming you, of this marvelous Holy Spirit? I am not so much concerned in this presence tonight about that preliminary question as I am about the other, because I realize there are multitudes of people who really begin by the touch of the Spirit of God to lead godly lives; but oh, the criminally fatal mistake is this: beginning in the Spirit, they think they may go on to be made perfect in the flesh. Just as easily as a man may regenerate himself, just so easily may he live after his regeneration without the continual fulness or the presence of the Holy Ghost.

I want to ask you first of all this question: Have you been anointed by the Holy Ghost? I mean by that: Have your eyes been opened? Has he come upon you for spiritual knowledge and perception and for the conscious guidance of God? I know this word " anoint " is used in two other places where it might not be applied in this way; but ordinarily the anointing is for sight, as when Jesus Christ anointed the eyes of the blind men that they might see. If you have been thus anointed, there are three things that you know concerning which no man can shake your confidence.

In the first place, you know the Son of God and your own salvation. You have no more question but that Jesus Christ is the son of God, and that you are a son of God, than you have that you exist today. Nay, more, I believe that if the Holy Spirit is living in you, he is the most real thing in all the universe to you, and that you could better believe that there is not an individual in this edifice, you could better believe that your body does not live, than to believe that Christ does not live in you, if you have received the fulness of the Holy Ghost. One of my friends was a pastor in a certain city, and his Sunday-school superintendent was a man who fulfilled every religious duty faithfully, as it seemed, but he said to the pastor one day, " I never knew whether I was saved or not; I have always been troubled about that. I have gone about my duties as faithfully as I might, but I have never known whether I was a child of God or not." The pastor said, " I can tell you how you may know. Promise me this; that every time that God calls this thought to your heart, you will kneel down and say, ' O God, send the Holy Spirit fully into my heart that I may know that I am a child of God. You will do it for Christ's sake. Amen.' " The next morning he rose up and came down stairs and took his newspaper to read and he thought of his promise about that prayer, and he knelt down and prayed, " O God, send the Holy Spirit in his fulness into my heart, that I may know that I am a child of God. You will do it for Christ's sake. Amen." After a while he went to his office and there came to him again this thought, and he went into a secret place, and there he knelt down and prayed the same prayer. Over and over again that day he prayed this prayer, until there began to dawn into his soul a new confidence. The next morning. before he took up the paper, he knelt down and offered the same prayer, and when he rose up and took his paper again to read it, he could not read it. It seemed to him as though the page was blank, until at last he bowed again before God and God poured into him the fulness of the confidence of a child of God in that marvelous manifestation of the helpful presence of the Holy Ghost. " Blessed art thou Simon bar-Jona," said the Master when Peter had made the confession, " Thou art the Christ, the Son of the living God," — Blessed art thou, Simon bar-Jona, for flesh and blood have not revealed this unto thee, but the spirit of My Father which is in heaven." I believe that was what the Saviour meant when he said, " On this rock will I build my church," and he is still building it on the fact that spiritual knowledge depends on the reception of the Holy Ghost. Paul himself said, " No one can say that Jesus is Lord, but by the Holy Ghost," and Jesus said. " He shall t ke of the things of mine and shall show them unto you." We shall not only be able to see the kingdom of God, but to walk through the length and breadth of it with this wonderful teacher, if we have been anointed by the Holy Ghost.

But he will not only teach us our own salvation and this personal knowledge of the son of God; he will teach us the will of God and what God has revealed unto men that yet seems to have been written in terms of mystery. How plainly Paul talked. He said, " Eye hath not seen nor ear heard, neither have entered into the heart of man the things which God hath prepared for them that love him," and then he adds, " But God hath revealed them unto us by his Spirit, for the Spirit searcheth all things, yea, the deep things of God." O friends, these two thing are true: that the Bible will never mean anything to you except condemnation until you are enlightened by the Holy Ghost and also that God will make it glow with a wonderful light and power for you if you are willing to receive this marvelous and unspeakable gift. "The natural man perceiveth not the things that be of God, neither can he, because they are spiritually discerned." The man that is filled with the Holy Ghost finds the Bible shining, thrilling, and throbbing with the touch of the Lord Jesus Christ himself. This shall lead you into all truth.

Andrew Murray, one of the most spiritual writers of this day, has well pointed out to us that prepared ground is needed as well as the seed. I believe it is not enough for a man to preach a sermon in the Holy Ghost. I believe it is not enough for a man to have the words of inspiration, but that it is needed that there shall be in the hearts of those who hear, the Holy Spirit, if they are to truly and fully and completely receive this Word of God.

But there is a third thing that God will reveal to you if you have been anointed by the Holy Ghost. He will reveal to you his unrevealed will concerning your personal guidance. Oh, that weary procession that passes through the study of every godly pastor in this land, a procession not of people convicted of sin, but of nominal Christians who say, "How may I know the will of God, and how may I be sure of guidance as to personal duty?" I can tell you. there are three ways: First, the revelation of this wonderful Book. God shows us plainly some things here concerning which we need not ask any questions. Second, he shows us some things by his providence, the issues of life and death, the issues or seeming failure in certain directions, hedging up paths here, and opening them there in a way that we know is the hand of God. But there is a third way, and that is by the direct revelation in the soul of the individuality of the Holy Ghost. He speaks to Phillip and says, "Go." He speaks to Paul, and says "Tarry:" and again he says to him " Go." Beloved, listen. If it be that you have questions about duty and you do not see the light shining brighter and brighter unto the perfect day, it is because you have not committed all your way to God and have not been baptized by the Holy Ghost. I would tonight, if there be such an one here, that you might anoint your eyes with eye-salve that you may see.

Here I pass on to the next question. It is this: Have you been purified by the Holy Ghost? That is a remarkable word in the Old Testament about the Spirit of God. It says, " Then will I sprinkle clean water upon you and you shall be clean from all your filthiness and from all your idols will I cleanse you. A new heart I will give you and a new spirit will I put within you, and I will take away the stony heart out of your flesh and I will give you a heart of flesh, and I will put my spirit within you and cause you to walk in my statutes, and ye shall keep my judgments and do them." O, friends, that is the spirit of purification. And here all of these emblems that have been suggested are applicable. Purification is accomplished by the air. Suppose there have been some noisome, foul, death-breeding exhalations throughout your home; an unclosed sewer has been pouring its deadly gases through every room and you have been breathing the atmosphere. What is necessary in order that the house may be cleansed? Simply this, that you shall cover up the place from which the deadly gases come, and then simply open the windows and the doors. You need not offer any prayers for the air to come in. It would have to come in and it would have to keep coming in until it drove out all of the impurity. I am glad also for the other symbol of cleansing, that of water. " Ye are washed by the spirit of God," but I read something better than that in this wonderful Book, and that is that we are cleansed by fire. There is a deeper cleansing than the cleansing by water. It is the cleansing by the penetration of fire. It changes the substance, it melts the iron, it transforms the rock, and makes it something else. This is the gist of the teaching of the law and even of the teaching of John the Baptist, and of the teaching of Jesus. How the Holy Spirit in the Lord Jesus comes down and divides between the very thought and intents and purposes of a man's soul. Friend, you have made a terrible mistake if you think that what this world needs or what your soul needs is a miracle. A miracle never led a man to have his heart cleansed from sin. The raising of Lazarus sent the Pharisees off to hasten the crucifixion of Jesus. The resurrection of Jesus filled them with a malice that was inexpressible; the healing of the impotent man sent Peter into prison, and caused him almost to lose his life. Miracles in themselves have no power for the transforming of the lives of men. More than that, words have not; the Bible has not; sermons have not; but it is only the spirit of God that has the power to take the things of God, and by them purify the hearts of men.

Ah, friend, what we need today is not philosophy; it is not the wisdom of men, for a man might be a very Seneca of wisdom and yet there might be an audience like this assembly in whose heart there would live not one word of his. What do we need? Not theories about the way of escaping from sin, but the desire and the power to get rid of it — something that shall cause us truly to say, "temptations lose their power when thou art nigh." We want the Holy Ghost.

Then I desire to ask you another question. Have you been filled with the Holy Ghost for the development of Christian character, love, joy, peace, long-suffering, gentleness, goodness, faith, meekness, and self-control? Mr. Finney used to say that it was just as wicked for a man to be disobeying the command to be filled with the Spirit as for an impenitent person not to yield the will to the eternal God, and I almost believe it — nay, I do believe it. But that is a great word—"filled with the Spirit of God." There is room for various things in this tumbler, but if it were filled with water there would not even be room for the atmosphere. "Filled with the Spirit of God." "The kingdom of God is righteousness and peace and joy in the Holy Ghost." "The love of God is shed abroad in our hearts by the Spirit which he hath given us," and then Paul says these wonderful words. "In whom ye also trusted after that ye heard the word of truth, the gospel of your salvation, in whom also after that ye believed, ye were sealed with that Holy Spirit of promise which is the earnest of our inheritance until the redemption of the purchased possession to the praise of His glory.' There are two great words there, and one of them refers to the fact that after we have believed we are to have the earnest of the Spirit. We do not have an earnest in these days and in these countries, although they still do in some Oriental countries. In the Eastern way of transacting business, if a man bought a piece of property, when the transfer was made, in order to indicate that it had been completed, the former owner of the property took a bag of dirt, or a handful of it, and handed it over to the next proprietor, and when he received that he owned the whole field. He did not have it all where he could put his hands upon it in a second, but he owned it all, and he did have some of it of the very same character and quality as the rest. And this is what I believe about the fulness of the Holy Ghost. I do not think as yet that my soul has been large enough to appropriate him all, and I still do hunger, waiting for the redemption of the body; but I have some of everything that I am going to have in the eternal world of glory, something for my body, something for my mind and for my soul, and I expect to have nothing differing in quality but only in degree when I shall stand clad in the white robes of the Lord Jesus — no difference between his face and mine, or between his heart and that which shall beat within my breast. Some of it I have. He has given me the earnest of his spirit, if I will only realize it, something of all the life of the infinite glory that is to come.

He has given me this earnest to be as a seal. What does a seal do? Stamp it on the wax and take it up, and there on the wax is exactly the thing that was on the seal. The Holy Spirit has come to me to be to me something of all that is coming unto me, and stamped upon me to make me over again into the likeness of the Lord Jesus Christ. Many and many a time have I shrunk back from the image of the Lord Jesus, looking as though I might into a spotless mirror and seeing deformity and imperfection, and feeling like crying out, "Depart from me, for I am a sinful man, O God." But, oh, marvelous transformation! "Beholding as in a glass the glory of the Lord," I am changed into the same image from glory to glory, as by the Spirit of the Lord, and at last I shall stand full statured and clear-eyed and look into the eyes of the Lord Jesus Christ and I shall see reflected back no longer weakness and littleness and imperfection, but I shall see Jesus, and when I see him I shall be like him, for I shall see him as he is.

And then I desire to ask you this question: Have you received the Holy Ghost so that you may truly say, "I am walking in the Spirit of God?" "If we live in the spirit, let us also walk in the spirit." I have seen certain places where people thought that just as soon as they were converted, they ought to become ministers of the Gospel. I do not believe that. I believe that some people are like the brother who said that he had seen the letters "G. P. C." in the heavens and that they meant "Go preach Christ," when they only meant, "Go pick cotton." I believe that God today, while he has need of baptized ministers of Jesus Christ, has more need of baptized blacksmiths and manufacturers and merchants than he has of apostles endowed with the power of the Holy Ghost; and I believe that the blacksmith ought to be just as truly baptized with the Holy Ghost for his daily life as any man who preaches the Gospel of Jesus Christ. I thought I would see what the Word of God had to say about this, and I began to read it, and I found, over in Exodus, that before a tailor could make a coat for Aaron he had to be filled with the Spirit of God. Before men could do the delicate work on the tabernacle, they needed not to go to some place of fine training in the schools of men, but they needed to be men that were filled with the Holy Ghost. What a word that is about Bezaleel over there in Exodus! God said, "Now go and search me out a man that is filled with the Spirit of God," and they found Bezaleel and Aholiab and God filled them up with his Holy Spirit that they might be jewelers, that they might fashion gold and silver and carve the woodwork of the tabernacle. I believe that God wants to let men be filled with the Holy Ghost in connection with their daily life just as truly as Peter was filled on the day of Pentecost. God said that before Joshua could be a governor he must be filled with the Spirit of God. He said that because Othniel was filled with the Spirit of God he would make him a judge. He said that unto Gideon it should mean martial valor. and he made him a general. He said that David could not sing until he was filled with the Holy Ghost. Ah, we make a mistake, some of us. When we see rain falling down and we look at the shrub and the flower and the grass and the tree, we never say, "The rain ought to make them all alike," but we do say so practically about our lives. We say, "I think if I had the Holy Ghost I should be just like that other person who is filled with the Holy Ghost." But God meant that other person to be a tree, and he meant you to be a shrub, and somebody else to be a blade of grass, and he meant the rain to fall on it all and make it just exactly what he intended it to be.

I came across the other day, a little book, out of which I read a few sentences. I read the title page and it was this, "Hiram Golf, a shoemaker by the grace of God." Then I read the last page, and it was stated that when this man died they put on his tombstone that which he had requested, "Hiram Golf, a shoemaker by the grace of God." I looked to see what was in the middle of the book, and I read this, that a young stripling of a minister who had just come to be pastor in the town, went down to talk with Hiram because he had heard that he was a spiritual man and he said, "Mr. Golf," and Mr. Golf said, "Don't call me Mr. Golf. Call me Hiram." "Well, Hiram," said the minister, "I have come to talk with you about the things of God, and I am very glad that a man can be in an humble occupation and yet be a godly man." The shoemaker stopped and looked up at him and said: "Don't you call this occupation humble." The minister thought he had made a mistake, and he said: "Excuse me, I didn't mean to reflect on what you do for a living." The man replied: "You didn't hurt me, but I was afraid you might have hurt the Lord

Jesus Christ. I believe the making of that shoe is just as holy a thing as your making a sermon. I believe that when I come to stand before the throne of God, he is going to say, 'What kind of shoes did you make on earth?' And he might pick out this very pair in order to let me look at them in the blazing light of the great white throne; and He is going to say to you. 'What kind of sermons did you make?' and you will have to show him one of your sermons. Now if I made better shoes than you made sermons, I will have a better place in the kingdom of God." From the depths of my soul, I believe that.

Do you remember that story about Madam Guyon, that consecrated woman who lived in the darkest of times, and kept alive a spark of God's grace and a manifestation of the Holy Ghost? At one time, when her husband was called into court, this woman spent some time in prayer with God. Then she went into the court-room, and, standing there before the judges she so spoke by the Spirit of God that she revealed what their stupid understanding had not seen about that case and they reversed their rulings and set her husband free. Shortly before his death, her husband had been made an arbitrator in a suit of great importance, in which twenty-two contestants, who knew that if they took their suits into court somebody else would get the money rather than any of the twenty-two contestants. After her husband died, while this complicated case was still pending, these twenty-two contestants came to this godly woman and said, "We believe in you and we will put this case into your hands." Only for this one thing, that she might be the cause of avoidance of strife among her fellows, she said she would consider it. She took one month — never going out of her room save to her meals and to the place of public prayer — of waiting before God, receiving in an especial manner the Holy Spirit for that purpose. When she finally brought in her decision she made the contestants accept it before the sealed papers were opened, and after they were opened every one of the twenty-two contestants expressed satisfaction with the justice of her decision and with the award that she had made.

When I was in the North-west, I heard of a violin maker in Minneapolis, who some years ago used to make violins and sell them for three or four dollars apiece; but about seventeen years ago, there came to him the thought that whatever he did ought to be done for the glory of God, and he would not touch the violin that he was making in his workshop, except when he knew that he was working by the Spirit of God. The result was that while his other violins were worth $3 or $4, he sold this violin for between $300 and $400. You might think that he would have learned the lesson, but he did not, and he kept on making $3 and $4 violins for ten years. Then there came to him the impulse to pray and work by the Spirit of God on one instrument and he made that and sold it for nearly $400. You would think that he would have learned his lesson then, but he had not, and he kept on three or four years more making cheap violins, until at last the thought came to him, "What I did as a spasmodic thing, I ought to do all the time," and he gave the making of violins over to the Holy Ghost, and now he never sells an instrument for less than $300. I have faith to believe that some tone from out one of those instruments made under the power of the Holy Ghost might lead souls into the glory of God, where all the unconsecrated and unbaptized eloquence of the ministers of Christ would utterly fail.

I want to ask you this one further question: Have you been baptized with the Spirit of God for spiritual power? The words "anoint" and "filling" and "cleansing" are sometimes used in other senses than those which I have given them tonight, but the words "baptized by the Holy Ghost," are never used except in connection with the marvelous power of the Spirit of God. "The works that I do," said Christ, "shall ye do also and greater works than these shall ye do, because I go unto my Father." He also said, "I will send you another Comforter, and he shall be in you; and when he is come — come into you — he shall convince the world of sin, of righteousness, and of judgment." We talk about the work of the Holy Ghost in conviction and conversion, but he never convicts and he never converts, except as he does it through a soul that is baptized with the power of God. God has shut himself up to saving the world through human beings that know the baptism of the Holy Ghost. What did Jesus say unto his disciples? "Tarry, tarry." The Gospel was ready but they might not carry it. The sacrifice had been offered, but they might not declare it. The resurrection had happened, but they might not tell of it. The Gospel in one sense was complete, and yet he said, "Tarry, and speak it not until you have received power from on high." Who were these men? Think of their natural qualifications. Think of their companionship with Jesus. Think of his teaching in personal touch with them. Think of their witness of his wonderful works of healing and raising the dead. Think of the sacrifices they had already made. Think of their evident consecration, and then remember that he said, "Wait until you have been baptized with the Holy Ghost." If they needed it, how much more you and I! The promise of Jesus was that they should be fountains. They had been drinking at the eternal fountain, and now he said, "He that believeth in me, out of his belly shall flow rivers of living water, and this spake he of the Spirit." They had been drinking at the fountain, now they were to be fountains. Peter and John were wonderful fountains, sending forth waters for the healing of the nations. Paul, Luther, Cromwell, George Fox, the Wesleys, Whitfield, Judson, Carey, Finney, Spurgeon, Harms, Mueller, the two Taylors, Moody, and may we not say that man who in the fear of God touched that secret spring by the Holy Ghost that has brought us together in the name of Jesus Christ today, — the results achieved by these men could not have been, save as they became, in some measure at least, fountains for the healing of the nations.

Now, let me call your mind back in these last thoughts to those three elements which I mentioned. The air, oh, the power of the air. The vessel stands as inert and motionless as this church tonight until the air touches its sails and then moves it along with mighty power unto its destination. The wind in its fury comes, the cyclone which could take this building and toss it into the air and carry it a mile away if it so pleased. Then there is the power of water. In the earliest days people had windmills; later on they turned their wheels by water. We still use water-power; but here is an important word descriptive of the spirit, — "floods." A flood could strike this great structure of stone and sweep it on and carry it for miles down the channel in its destructive grasp. Add to that the power of vapor, of steam, and we have another emblem of the power of the Holy Ghost, and yet we have but suggested the whole truth, for you know today that we are learning to drive our wheels and light our buildings and transform the world not by the air and not by water, but by fire. Dr. Gibson has suggested that one hundred years ago, people were receiving the Holy Spirit as air. How they studied the Bible. How they absorbed it. Now we are come into the time of the Holy Spirit as water. We are pouring it out unto the ends of the earth; it is flowing around the world. But the power of the Holy Ghost means something more than that. The touch of the electric spark, the baptism of fire; fire for the minister, for the individual, for the church. You can confine the earth without any trouble; you can confine the air with but little more difficulty, and water with still more difficulty, but see if you can shut up the fire. Nay, if you shut it up it will die, but let it be put into the thickest iron or stone and out it comes through the iron and through the stone. You cannot confine the fire. Oh, for the baptism of fire, the baptism of the Holy Spirit of God!

Rev. Dr. Kean, a Methodist minister in the United States, is a man of mighty power, called of God to go from conference to conference and to speak to the ministers of that great body concerning the deep things of God. But when Dr. Kean commenced to preach some thirty years ago, he preached his first sermons without one touch of the Holy Ghost upon his congregation. One day he announced that he would have a special series of meetings, holding them every night, and that he wanted the people to come. The people came and filled the church, and he preached what he thought was an excellent sermon. Then he asked for penitents to come and kneel at the altar, but no one came. The second night he preached again, and again he asked if there were any who wished to kneel at the altar, but no one came. He did the same the third night, and the fourth, and the fifth, and the sixth, and the seventh, and not one person responded to his call to come and kneel at the altar. As he went home he said to his wife, "Wife, there is something wrong with me. If I were right with God I am sure this would not be." His wife said, "Oh, you are getting blue. You had better throw off this feeling. It is just because you are tired and worn out that you feel discouraged." He said, "Wife, it is not so. If I were baptized with the Holy Ghost, I would see people turning to God." That broke her down and she said, "Husband, if you need this, I need it too. Let us together seek the baptism of the Holy Ghost." And so hand in hand they knelt down and said, "Lord, you may go to the depths of our souls to find the difficulty with us, but we will be filled and baptized with the Holy Ghost." He went into the meeting that night and preached again and asked the people to come forward to the altar. One woman rose up and came forward and knelt down at the altar, and her husband in the pulpit went around and knelt by her side, and they both plead with God for the baptism of the Holy Ghost. The next night he preached again and asked the people to come to the altar. And again his own wife arose from her seat and came and knelt there and he went around and knelt by her side. The third, and the fourth, and the fifth and the sixth night those two knelt there before the congregation saying, "O God, O God, we must be filled with the Holy Ghost!" and all this time God was probing them and searching them and emptying them and preparing them for the sound as of a mighty rushing wind. On the seventh day, after prayer together, he was in his room alone with God. And as it was with Finney and Moody, God opened the windows of heaven and poured into his soul flood after flood of those unspeakable things that even Paul could not utter. He went to his wife and said, "Wife, He has come, he has come! I know that I am filled with the Holy Ghost." He went into the service that night and preached the Word of God; and as it was in the days of old — would to God it might be so now — "while he yet spake the Holy Ghost fell upon them" and the people crowded up the aisle and cast themselves down on their faces and were born into the kingdom of God. There has never passed a year, scarcely a month or a week, in our brother's life, during these thirty years, when that same touch in him and through him has not brought souls into the kingdom of God.

Now for us tonight, if we will fulfil the conditions, we may have the results. When I see and hear of such things as this, I feel like crying, "O God, for me! for my brother ministers! for the young men and maidens!" and then I remember the Word that says, "This promise is to you and to your children, to as many as are afar off, whom the Lord your God shall call." Brother, it is to you; sister, it is to you; it is to us who are here tonight! "Ask and ye shall receive; seek and ye shall find; knock and it shall be opened unto you; for every one that asketh receiveth, and he that seeketh findeth, and to him that knocketh it shall be opened. For if ye, being evil, know how to give good gifts unto your children, how much more shall your heavenly Father give the Holy Spirit unto them that ask him."

Consecration Service.

Mr. Mills then announced that the consecration service would begin, and asked that all who felt obliged to leave the room would do so during the singing of the next hymn. "Just as I am" was then sung, but very few of the audience left. Only a seat here and there was vacated.

MR. MILLS: Some one has defined a business letter as being a letter so plain that a man can not only understand it but could not possibly misunderstand it. I believe that the revelation of God concerning the characteristics and the methods of reception of the Holy Ghost is so plain that if we are not thoroughly filled and baptized with the Holy Ghost it is our own fault. When Samuel Randall, the great statesman, was dying, a man who was disassociated with him in politics, and who was a friend of early years, and later life as well, went to see him,— John Wanamaker. He preached Christ to him, and Mr. Randall said, " John, I want you to make this matter so plain that a man who is very sick and weak can understand it. There are just two things I want to know: first, what are the conditions of salvation; secondly, am I eligible?" In the simplest way Mr. Wanamaker stated to him the conditions and showed him that he was eligible, and Mr. Randall said, " I will accept the conditions," and shortly after, he was received into the Church of Christ. Now, friends, before we come to the words of personal testimony, I want to ask you in a definite, personal way: Have you received the Holy Ghost since you believed? And I want to ask you this question: Will you fulfil the conditions and receive him now? What are the conditions? Briefly stated, there are four.

First, the believe that the Holy Spirit is meant to be what God says he is meant to be, and that he is for you. Do you believe it? Is this inestimable blessing only for one man out of thousands in the century, or is it for you? I feel like lifting up my heart and my soul and my hand tonight and saying, " Lord, God, I believe it is for me, I believe it is for me." How many are there here tonight who are definitely convinced that in the main the statements made here are according to the truth of God, and that for you there should be the regeneration and the cleansing and the strengthening and the enlightening and the joy and the power of the Holy Ghost? Do you believe that this is for you? I wish those who do would please raise their right hand. [*Apparently every hand was raised.*]

There is a second condition: we should be willing to forsake every sin,—the sins that we know and also the sins that we do not know, I believe that we have forsaken some sins, all of us. I believe that God means what he says when he calls us to be, as Jesus was, "separate from sinners, holy, harmless, and undefiled." " If we say we have no sin we deceive ourselves, and the truth is not in us ; but if we confess our sins, he is faithful and just to forgive us our sins and to cleanse us from all unrighteousness." But God never forgave a sin and God never took away a sin until men and women were willing that he should. O friend, no matter what it may be, if there is a touch of sin about it, will you not abandon it tonight? As God searches your heart, if he shall show you anything sinful and impure, will you not make this pledge to him, as though you stood in the white light of the judgment, that you will forever give it up? Every one who will do that, please speak out definitely and clearly and resolutely, " I will." [*The response came promptly from the audience, "I will."*]

Now, there is still another condition. I believe that a man may forsake every known sin and pledge himself to give up every unknown sin as well, and still not be qualified for the filling of the Holy Ghost. There are the good things to be given unto God. There are what we call the neutral things—the friends and the ambitions and the money and the time and the talents—all to be turned over unto God. Oh, so many fail here ! When God calls to them to bring out Isaac, there they hesitate. God has brought some of us in these days of gathering to that place where I would that we might bring out the last good thing and lay it on the altar of God. I believe that for six years, so far as I know, I had given up things out of my life that were in themselves sinful before I was willing to consecrate unto God the things that were good. Are you willing to do it tonight? I know of one minister who knelt to pray for the baptism of the Holy Ghost. I cannot tell you how he prayed, but it seemed to those who listened as if they had never heard such words from human lips. The people all about him, ministers of the gospel and others, opened their eyes and looked at him because of that wonderful stream of renunciation of sin and of consecration and of faith that was pouring out of his lips. And then, in what seemed to be the culminating moment of the complete sacrifice, it seemed as though God's search light flashed down upon some one thing that he was not willing to do or be for God, and suddenly he paused and hesitated and faltered and fell and weakly closed his prayer. After the service the people hardly knew how to approach him. He stood there trembling and weeping, and then he said, " Oh, I almost had it, but I let him go !" I believe God had shown him there something such as he showed Abraham when he called him to bring out Isaac. Beloved, let it not be so with you tonight. Are you willing, so far as God shows you, to give everything to him,—never to make a plan again but let him make it for you; to let him think and speak for you; to let him alter all your plans and all your life, if it be his will; to let him have your will and be your will? Are you willing to do it,—to give to him the known things and the unknown? I want to ask those that honestly tonight, in this hour of consecration, do give to God the things that are good—the money and the time, the talents and the friends, the wisdom and the ignorance, the wealth and the poverty, the strength and the weakness, all that you know or may know, all that you have or may have, and turn it all over and say, "Lord, God, it is mine no longer,"—those who have done it and those who will do it, say now, each for yourself, "I do." [*The audience again responded, "I do."*]

Now, beloved, it is a solemn time for some of us, and there is just one more thing. The Lord says, "Ye receive the Spirit through faith." I believe, if we have been honest before God in these acts, that every one of us has a right to rise up and say, "I am going out now as one that is filled with the Holy Spirit." A friend of mine once suggested how Elisha must have felt when he had said "Let a double portion of thy spirit fall on me," and Elijah his master had said to him, "If you are with me when I am taken away, it shall be so." He saw Elijah when he was taken away, but he only had the word of God to assure him that he had the spirit of Elijah. When they had come to the river, Elijah had lifted up his mantle and smitten the river, and they had gone over on dry ground. How was Elisha to repass that river? On the other side were the theological students waiting to see what he would do. My friend said he fancied that when Elisha came down to the river he might have thought, "I would like to go down behind the bushes somewhere and lift up my mantle and try it on the river first before I expose myself before these people;" but no, he marched down to the river, believing simply the word of God, and lifted up his mantle and smote the river, and the power that was upon Elijah was upon him, because he believed God and received it. Now shall we not spend three or four minutes in just bowing our heads or kneeling in the seats, if you please, or in the aisles, and saying, every one that means it, "Lord, I do receive the Holy Ghost." Every one that means tonight to claim the promise of God just kneel right down and claim it.

All over the house people knelt in the seats or bowed their heads in prayer. Mr. Mills then asked for a few moments of silent prayer, after which Rev. Gilbert Reid and Rev. Dr. Rondthaler led in vocal prayer. During the singing of one verse of "I Hear Thy Welcome Voice," the audience resumed their seats.

Mr. Mills then called for personal testimonies from individuals, stating the best thing received during the convention. A large number of responses came from all parts of the house, the most prominent testimony being that of the spiritual good received. Occasionally a hymn would be sung, and the hour was one of great impressiveness. The time would not permit all to testify who so desired, and Mr. Mills at length asked all who wished to testify to rise and sing one verse of "Now to be thine, yea, thine alone." A great number rose, and the hymn was sung fervently. Mr. Mills then asked the audience to join in silent prayer a few moments, while he asked all present who desired prayer for themselves, in bearing some special burden or in efforts to live the Christian life, to rise. A large number rose. He then asked those to rise who desired prayers that they might become followers of the Saviour. One after another, in the hush of the moment and amid much emotion, over 60 persons thus expressed their desire. Mr. Mills then called for sentence prayers, and a large number of brief words of prayer followed, many speaking at once. Mr. Mills then closed this solemn service with an earnest petition, embodying the well-known prayer of Paul for the Ephesian church. Never in the history of our conventions has the tide of spiritual feeling run so high as during this hour.

The time for closing had now come, and Mr. Baer, before giving out the final hymn, asked all in the audience who would join with him in taking the pledge that, during the coming year, they would try to lead at least one soul to Christ, to rise. Immediately the whole audience rose ; there seemed hardly to be an exception. Then the parting hymn was sung with much feeling, " God be with you till we meet again," and all joined in the Mizpah benediction.

SIMULTANEOUS MEETINGS.

First Baptist Church.

Rev. Dr. Wayland Hoyt, of Minneapolis, was in charge of the meeting in this church. The congregation was very large, and with the multitude of badges and the profuse.-decoration of the platform by choice tropical and other plants, the effect was unusually brilliant.

With the leader of the meeting sat Rev. Mr. Grant, pastor of the church, and other Christian Endeavor workers. After an interesting praise service, Dr. Hoyt gave an inspiring and instructive address, based on the twelfth chapter of Romans. After the address came the consecration service, which was participated in by a large number. A generous offering was taken for the family of Mr. Rogers.

Erskine Presbyterian Church.

A large audience gathered here to participate in the closing consecration service. After the usual preliminary singing, Rev. Dr. Fleck offered prayer and Rev. Mr. Corbett read the Scripture lesson. Then followed the sermon by Rev. Dr. J. Z. Tyler, which was an earnest setting forth of the character of Christ as the standard for true manhood. At the close of the sermon the delegates joined in their customary services of consecration. An offering was taken for the family of Mr. Rogers. With the final hymn and the benediction the meeting adjourned.

American Presbyterian Church.

Rev. Dr. A. N. Carson, pastor of the Central Presbyterian church, St. Paul, Minn., was the principal speaker at this service, which was attended by another crowd of people. He took for his text, " He that is faithful in that which is least is faithful also in much." (Luke 16 : 10.) The sermon emphasized and illustrated the many ways in which faithfulness in little things leads on to larger responsibilities, and was a fitting prelude to the service of consecration which followed. This was conducted by Treasurer William Shaw, who first announced the collection for the benefit of the Rogers family. Then followed singing, prayer, and testimony, a large number in the audience taking part. Special prayer was offered in behalf of the city of Montreal and the churches which had done so much for the delegates. The parting hymn "God be with you till we meet again" was then sung and the benediction pronounced by the pastor, Rev. T. S. McWilliams.

Douglas Methodist Church.

At this church there gathered another throng of delegates and their friends, including, of course, many of the regular church attendants. The speakers were Rev. Dr. J. L. Hill, of Medford, Mass., Mr. R. W. Dillon, of Toronto, and the pastor, Rev. Dr. S. P. Rose. After the opening song service, Mr. Dillon spoke on " Personal Service," his main thought being the responsibility resting upon all Christians to rightly interpret the character of Christ in their lives. Dr. Hill spoke on " The Sources of Strength for Service," making an appeal for a deeper faith in Christ as a Saviour, and for more prompt obedience to him. The consecration service which followed was largely participated in and very impressive. A generous offering was taken for the destitute family of Mr. Rogers, the member of the reception committee who died at his post of duty.

NOTES.

Every reference to the Sunday closing of the World's Fair was received with tremendous applause.

No general excursion was held, but many private ones — to Montmorency Falls, Lachine Rapids, Quebec, etc., — were indulged in.

"Exceptions only prove the rule" was the happy "bon mot" of Mayor Desjardins in speaking of the uniform courtesy of the citizens of Montreal.

"God save the Queen," "My country, 't is of thee," and "Blest be the tie that binds," were three hymns frequently conjoined and sung with immense enthusiasm.

The Royal Mount was, of course, the chief point of outside interest to all sight-seers. Thousands of delegates enjoyed the magnificent views from its summit.

The convention was certainly the most unique and in many respects the most profitable — if not at all times the most enjoyable — of the entire series of annual conventions.

Fortunate is the convention that secures the services of Mr. Robert E. Burleigh as cornetist. For several years Mr. Burleigh has freely given his services in our international conventions.

The great fountain in Victoria square, throwing a huge column of water 100 feet into the air, is very rarely played, but in honor of the visitors the city fathers had it turned on three different times. It was very beautiful.

The sessions were specially marked by deep spiritual feeling and practical suggestion. The editor of one of the leading religious papers was heard to remark that he could not keep back the tears during the session devoted to missions.

The local choir was considerably smaller than usual. The deficiency was not noticed, however, for the audience took things into their own hands and sang magnificently. It is a singular fact that at all these conventions the audience leads the choir.

One speaker illustrated the happy influence of Christian Endeavor by stating that before the California state convention the boys in the street were all singing "Ta-ra-ra-boom-de-ay;" after the convention they sang "There is sunshine in my soul."

The total amount received from the collections for the benefit of the destitute family of Mr. Rogers, the member of the reception committee who dropped dead of heart disease while escorting a company of delegates to their boarding-place, was over $1,500.

The cornet playing of the Park Sisters was superb and received enthusiastic applause. The fact that these young ladies gave their services to the convention, cancelling several profitable engagements in order to be present, lent an additional interest to their playing.

The "white caps" were an original feature of the convention which proved so helpful that all future committees of arrangements will make a mistake if they do not adopt it. It was so easy for anybody with a question to ask to locate a white cap in the crowd or on the street.

The delegates were enthusiastic in their praise of the committee of arrangements. The press committee, Mr. H. B. Ames, chairman, received an especial meed of honor. Never before were such complete and abundant facilities furnished for the press representatives. All of the sub-committees, in fact, fulfilled their duties most admirably.

Dr. Henson emphasized one of the points in his address so strongly that in bringing his hand down upon the railing in front of him he knocked off a huge splinter. Later, as if to shame the Doctor's earnestness, the cannon, celebrating the wedding of the Duke of York and Princess May, punctuated (or more properly, punctured) his address at several points.

By far the most delightful side event in connection with the convention to those who were permitted to enjoy it was the reception and excursion tendered by the mayor and aldermen on Monday morning to the officers of the United Society and invited guests. The party to the number of over 100 gathered at the city hall, where they were welcomed by Mayor Desjardins in a very felicitous speech, responded to in an equally happy vein by Dr. Clark; the national anthems were sung, and then all were transported in a long procession of carriages through several of the principal streets of the city and up the beautiful drive to the top of Mount Royal. Stop was made at the " Lookout "—a covered platform commanding a marvelous view of the city, the river, and the distant mountains. Here tables were spread and an elegant lunch served, the mayor and the aldermen being assiduous in waiting upon their guests. At its conclusion Dr. Clark expressed to the mayor the thanks of the company for their delightful entertainment. His honor responded in another witty and graceful speech, first in English and then in French, which was received with three rousing cheers from the delegates. The company then joined in singing, " God save the Queen," followed by " America," and then all clasping hands, " Blest be the tie," concluding with the parting hymn, "God be with you." How the old "lookout" rang! The party then returned to the city, and the excursion closed with a special display of the " great fountain."

H. W. GLEASON, *Scribe.*

NUMBER OF SOCIETIES JULY 1, 1893.

United States.

Alabama	86	Montana	42
Alaska Ter.	2	Nebraska	511
Arizona Ter.	8	Nevada	2
Arkansas	116	New Hampshire	279
California	645	New Jersey	784
Colorado	220	New Mexico Ter.	18
Connecticut	645	New York	2985
Dakota Ter.		North Carolina	69
Delaware	37	North Dakota	70
Dist. of Columbia	91	Ohio	1766
Florida	121	Oklahoma	42
Georgia	123	Oregon	218
Idaho Ter.	25	Pennsylvania	2628
Illinois	1822	Rhode Island	144
Indiana	1113	So. Carolina	37
Indian Ter.	25	So. Dakota	197
Iowa	1186	Tennessee	247
Kansas	966	Texas	221
Kentucky	178	Utah Ter	66
Louisiana	41	Vermont	352
Maine	540	Virginia	98
Maryland	277	Washington	208
Massachusetts	1152	West Virginia	113
Michigan	709	Wisconsin	622
Minnesota	756	Wyoming Ter.	13
Mississippi	26		
Missouri	762		

Canada.

Alberta	8	Newfoundland	5
Assiniaboia	14	Nova Scotia	393
British Columbia	27	Prince Edward I	33
Cape Breton	10	Quebec	135
Manitoba	94	Saskatchewan	2
New Brunswick	90	Ontario	1072

Foreign.

Africa	15	Japan	34
Australia	525	Madagascar	32
Bermuda	3	Mexico	22
Brazil	2	Norway	1
Chili	1	Persia	2
China	14	Samoa Ia.	9
England	600	Sandwich Is.	6
India	71	Scotland	30
Ireland	10	Spain	1
France	9	Turkey	41
Columbia	1	West Indies	19

INDEX.

ADDRESSES OF WELCOME.
    (*a*) For the Churches, Rev. J. MacGillivray   29
    (*b*) For the City, Mayor Desjardins · · . . . . : : . . .   31
    (*c*) For the Y. M. C. A., General Secretary Budge   33
    (*d*) For the Committee of '93, Mr. A. A. Ayer   34
RESPONSE, Rev. P. S. Henson, D. D.   38
ANNUAL ADDRESS, President Francis E. Clark, D.D.   72
ANNUAL REPORT. General Secretary John Willis Baer   78
ADDRESS, Mrs. Mountford   272
BIBLE IN OUR WORK, Address, Rev. J. Q. A. Henry, D.D.   122
CONVENTION COMMITTEES . . . . [Cover third page.]
COMMITTEE CONFERENCES, Reports from   166
CONSECRATION SERVICE, Drill Hall.   273
CONSECRATION SERVICE, St. James Church   286
CHRISTIAN CITIZENSHIP, Address by Rev. David J. Burrell, D.D. . .   141
CHRISTIAN STEWARDSHIP, Address by Bishop B. W. Arnett   134
DENOMINATIONAL RALLIES · ·   196
FOUR ESSENTIALS OF A CHRISTIAN ENDEAVOR SOCIETY.
    Address, The Pledge, Mr. H. B. Gale   89
    Address, Interdenominational Fellowship, Mr. R. W. Dillon . . . ·   96
    Address, A Typical Church Institution, Rev. Kerr B. Tupper, D.D. .   102
    Address, Consecration, Rev. E. K. Young, D.D.   93
FREE PARLIAMENT. Conducted by Mr. E. A. Hardy   92
GOSPEL TEMPERANCE.
    Address, Mr. Thomas E. Murphy   239
    Address, Miss Belle Kearney   265
HOW TO REACH THE MASSES, Mr. A. W. Millbury   245
INTRODUCTION   3
INTERNATIONAL FELLOWSHIP, Address by Rev. Geo. H. Wells, D.D . .   215
JUNIOR SOCIETIES.
    Address, First Society, Rev. J. W. Cowan   43
    Address, Possibilities, Rev. Wayland Hoyt, D.D.   49
    Address, In Foreign Lands, Mrs. F. E. Clark   55
FREE PARLIAMENT. Conducted by Rev. H. N. Kinney   53
ROLL CALL. Conducted by Miss Kate H. Haus   46
JUNIOR RALLY.
    Address of Welcome, Mr. Arthur F. Bell   180
    Response, Mr. Raymond C. Brooks . . . . ·   182
    Address, The Pledge, Mr. C. J. Atkinson   184
    Address, Miss Belle P. Nason   186
    Dialogue, Conducted by Mrs. Alice M. Scudder   188
    Address, Mrs. F. E. Clark   191
    Consecration Service led by Miss Gertrude W. Wood   194

MISSIONS.

Address, Voice from India, Rev. S. V. Karmarkar 109
Address, Missionary Literature, Mr. S. L. Mershon 146
Address, Missionary Meetings, Miss Ella B. McLaurin 152
Address, Missionary Money, Rev. W. H. G. Temple 158
Address, Reflex Influence, Rev. J. T. McCrory, D.D. 162
Opening Meeting. Conducted by Rev. Gilbert Reid 156
NOTES 302
PRELIMINARY SERVICES, Rev. J. W. Chapman, D.D., Rev. T. L. Cuyler,
    D.D., Rev. H. C. Farrar, D.D., Rev. W. H. McMillan, D.D., Rev. J. Z.
    Tyler, D.D. 4
PRESENTATION OF BANNERS, Drill Hall 83
PRESENTATION OF BANNERS, Tent. 86
PASTORS' HOUR. Conducted by Rev. John L. Campbell 222
RAW MATERIAL OF A GREAT LIFE, Address by Rev. J. W. Lee, D.D. . 229
ROLL CALL OF STATES, TERRITORIES, ETC. Conducted by General Sec-
    retary Baer 208
RELIGIOUS PRESS, Rev. A. E. Dunning, D.D. 248
RESOLUTIONS. Presented by Rev. H. B. Grose 274
SOUL WINNING.

Address, Work for Young Men, Rev. Rufus W. Miller 60
Address, Evangelistic Church, Rev. F. D. Power, D.D. 65
Open Meeting. Conducted by Mr. J. Howard Breed 64
Open Meeting. Conducted by Mr. P. S. Foster 69
Open Meeting. Conducted by Rev. J. A. Rondthaler, D.D. 106
Question Box. Conducted by William Shaw 111
SOCIAL PURITY.

Address, Rev. G. Douglass, D.D. 253
Address, Foes to Society, Church, and State, Mr. Anthony Comstock 261
SUNDAY SCHOOL, Address, Rev. N. Boynton. 129
SENIOR ENDEAVOR, Address, Rev. Chas. P. Mills. 269
SERMON, Rev. T. H. Lewis, D.D. 276
SERMON, Rev. B. Fay Mills. 287
SIMULTANEOUS MEETINGS IN CITY CHURCHES 300
STATISTICS 304
VICE-PRESIDENTS 206

www.ingramcontent.com/pod-product-compliance
Lightning Source LLC
LaVergne TN
LVHW011344080426
835511LV00005B/120